BRUTE FORCE

OTHER BOOKS BY JOHN ELLIS

Armies in Revolution
The Social History of the Machine Gun
A Short History of Guerrilla Warfare
Eye-Deep in Hell
Cavalry
The Sharp End of War
Cassino: The Hollow Victory

BRUTE FORCE

ALLIED STRATEGY AND TACTICS
IN THE SECOND WORLD WAR

JOHN ELLIS

VIKING

VIKING
Published by the Penguin Group
Viking Penguin, a division of Penguin Books USA Inc.,
375 Hudson Street, New York, New York 10014, U.S.A.
Penguin Books Ltd, 27 Wrights Lane,
London W8 5TZ, England
Penguin Books Australia Ltd, Ringwood,
Victoria, Australia
Penguin Books Canada Ltd, 2801 John Street,
Markham, Ontario, Canada L3R 1B4
Penguin Books (N.Z.) Ltd, 182–190 Wairau Road,
Auckland 10, New Zealand

Penguin Books Ltd, Registered Offices:
Harmondsworth, Middlesex, England

First American Edition
Published in 1990 by Viking Penguin,
a division of Penguin Books USA Inc.

1   3   5   7   9   10   8   6   4   2

LIBRARY OF CONGRESS CATALOGING IN PUBLICATION DATA
Ellis, John, 1945–
Brute force : allied strategy and tactics in the Second World War
/John Ellis.
p.   cm.
Includes bibliographical references (p.
Includes index.
ISBN 0-670-80773-7
1. World War, 1939–1945—Campaigns.   2. Strategy.   I. Title.
D743.E43   1990
940.54′012—dc20   90–50047

Printed in the United States of America
Set in Times Roman
Maps by Sue Lawes

For all Armenians, Azerbaijanis, Bosnians, Bulgarians, Catholics, Croats, Czechs, Estonians, Hungarians, Letts, Lithuanians, Lutherans, Macedonians, Moldavians, Montenegrins, Muslims, Orthodox, Poles, Prussians, Rumanians, Serbs, Slovaks, Slovenes, Thracians, Ukrainians, Uniates and Wallachians, in the faint hope that another type of Brute Force shall not give way to chaos.

Contents

Contents

Maps

Tables

Statistical Appendix

'The Battle is fought and decided by the Quartermaster before the shooting begins.'

Field Marshal Erwin Rommel

'One principle bearing on leadership might be stated in relation to resources in war: an enemy with superiority in technology and war potential who makes a series of wrong decisions may, to be sure, leave in doubt the outcome of a battle but he never loses the certainty of ultimate victory. On the other hand, his opponent, far inferior to him in these basic factors, will not be able to avert defeat in a long war, even though he avoids every error in command judgement.'

General Adolf Galland

'The race is not to the swift, nor the battle to the strong, but that's the way to bet.'

Ring Lardner

Preface

I began my last book, a study of the Battles of Monte Cassino in the first six months of 1944, intending it to be mainly a worm's-eye view of the struggle, describing the fighting as seen by the ordinary soldiers. I was not long into the research, however, before it became clear that though the battle certainly did entail appalling sufferings by the 'PBI', it was equally notable for the lack of competence shown by most Allied commanders. Their performance began to seem all the less impressive, moreover, as one realised that they were usually endowed with considerably superior material resources to the Germans. Both these latter points were eloquently summed up by a German officer who complained that, though the enemy insisted on charging their Shermans right down the barrels of his battery of 88s, and were picked off one after another, he ran out of ammunition before they ran out of tanks.

This remark became something of a text in my Cassino book and has remained one in this present work. Here, however, the view from the sharp end is largely absent and I have concentrated instead upon trying to give lucid summaries of the major campaigns of the Second World War – Poland and France, the Battle of Britain, the Eastern Front, the Battle of the Atlantic, the Bomber Offensive, the Mediterranean, North-West Europe and the Pacific – which focus upon and elaborate these twin aspects of Allied conduct of the war. My first major theme, therefore, is to stress Allied material preponderance and emphasise the fact that their enormous advantage in guns, tanks, aircraft and ships was an inevitable consequence of their far superior economic potential. In other words, given both Germany's and Japan's shortage of raw materials, inadequate level of conversion to munitions production and utterly haphazard planning procedures, it was absolutely essential for both of them that they win *decisive* early victories that would bring about a speedy negotiated peace. As it was, once the British had weathered Dunkirk and the Battle of Britain, once the U-boat fleet proved too small to sever Britain's Atlantic life-line, once the Russians had shown that even the loss of much of their industry, millions of civilians and soldiers, and territory to the very gates of their capital could still not diminish their capacity for ceaseless and increasingly effective counter-attacks, and once the Americans had demonstrated that the temporary destruction of most of their Pacific Fleet only served to harden their resolve, then the ultimate issue of the war was as good as decided. Years of hard fighting lay ahead but the prosaic arithmetic of natural resources, generating capacity, industrial plant and productivity was to be incontrovertible. So much so that in the last 18 months of the war the Allies put onto the battlefield 80,000 tanks to the German's 20,000, 1,100,000 trucks and lorries to 70,000, and 235,000 combat aircraft to 45,000; in these same months the U-boats sank 630,000 tons of merchant shipping whilst the Allied shipyards turned out another 20,000,000 tons; between 1942 and 1945 the Japanese built 13 aircraft-carriers, the crucial component of modern naval warfare, but the Americans built 137. The Battle of Production was virtually a walk-over.

My second theme concerns the way in which this enormous material preponderance was actually deployed by the Allies. As the title of this book indicates, my contention is that American, Russian and British commanders made considerably less than optimum use of the resources at their disposal and in almost every theatre serious mistakes were made. This is not to say that there was a wilful disregard for human life (except in the Red Army, Allied commanders were quite explicit in their determination to avoid the sort of carnage that had characterised operations in the First World War), but rather that commanders seemed unable to impose their will upon the enemy except by slowly and persistently battering him to death with a blunt instrument. In Africa, Montgomery was incapable of finishing off Rommel even when the latter was numbering his tanks in single figures and his plans were fully known to enemy intelligence. In Italy, the Americans and British proved utterly incapable of adapting their highly motorised formations to the unpropitious climate and terrain and spent two years crawling up Italy like, in Churchill's memorable phrase, 'bugs up a trouser leg'. Moreover, in both North Africa and Italy, there were repeated examples of the Allies' penchant for using their armour like a latter-day Light Brigade, trying to smash through the enemy line with absolutely no regard for his considerable defensive firepower. During the Bomber Offensive, RAF Bomber Command suffered a death rate of 47.5 per cent men and inflicted some 700,000 fatal casualties of its own (many among the populations of occupied Allied countries) in an indiscriminate bombing campaign whose only benchmark of success was houses destroyed rather than significant production halted. In this same campaign the USAAF did at least pay lip service to the notion of 'precision bombing' but in fact ended up using their bombers as clay pigeons to lure the *Luftwaffe* into the swarms of US fighters. In North-West Europe, golden opportunities to surround enormous German pockets were lost, as at Falaise, the Seine and Antwerp, whilst Montgomery's pace of operations showed him to be even more cautious and ponderous than in Africa and Patton's much-vaunted dash across northern France proved to have been made (just like a previous effort in Sicily) against only negligible opposition. Finally, in the Pacific, though Japanese determination to cling to every island to the last man clearly put severe tactical constraints on the Americans, it is nevertheless the case that there would have been no need to invade all these islands, much less to drop the A-bombs, if proper attention had been paid to interdicting Japan's absolutely vital lines of communication with her far-flung reserves of raw materials – whose seizure had been the motive of her going to war in the first place.

This book, then, is highly critical of Allied operations throughout the war, but I would like to make it quite clear that there is absolutely no intention of casting a slur upon the bravery (or competence) of millions of ordinary men and women, in uniform and out, who gave mightily that Western democracy might survive. If it is easy for me, comfortable at my desk, to pontificate about eventual victory being certain, about such and such an Army moving unconscionably slowly, this Fleet being in the wrong place at the wrong time, that aircrew dying in vain, I do not mean to minimise the suffering or in any way demean the memory of those who perished amidst the nightmare of Hürtgen Forest, Cassino, Stalingrad, Okinawa or Imphal, who burnt to death in the skies above Germany, or choked in oil in the freezing Atlantic.

A final point about the book concerns something of a problem of presentation. As will soon become apparent to the reader, I regard the Russian contribution to Allied victory in the Second World War as being absolutely fundamental, and have thus been keen to avoid the Anglo-American bias that still pervades some popular accounts of this conflict. It is with some disappointment, therefore, that in glancing at the Contents page I find that I have devoted 113 pages to the war in the Mediterranean, even though I am firmly of the opinion that this theatre is consistently over-emphasised in most English studies of the war, and in most publishers' lists. Indeed, when one realises that in March 1943 the Germans had 175 combat divisions (including 29 panzer and panzer grenadier) on the Eastern Front and only 7½ (4½) in North Africa, and that even in June 1944 the figures for Russia/Italy were 157 (30)/22 (6), then it might well be thought that the whole campaign barely merits an extended footnote.

But there are, I think, three reasons why this theatre merits more attention than a quick head-count of divisions engaged might indicate. First, the fighting in Africa, Greece and Italy did not tie up land forces alone, and the *Luftwaffe*'s involvement in these battles was considerable. From May 1942 to June 1943 an average of almost 20 per cent of *Luftwaffe* combat strength was deployed in the Mediterranean, and in 1943 as a whole fully one-third of all aircraft losses were sustained there. Second, the German divisions that continued to be tied down in Italy after September 1943 were lost to other theatres, most particularly to Normandy in June and July 1944, where even a small strategic mobile reserve (there were seven panzer and panzer grenadier divisions in Italy on 30 June) might have caused the Allies enormous problems and prolonged the war for some months. Third, it was in the Mediterranean theatre that the British, Commonwealth and American armies learned their trade, and there, it might be argued, that they developed the ponderous tactics and reliance upon overwhelming material superiority, on land and in the air, that was to characterise all their European operations.

Whatever the value of the end-product, the labours involved in producing this book have been considerable, and I owe a special debt of gratitude to my publishers, André Deutsch and Tom Rosenthal, to my editor, Sara Menguç, and to my agent, John Parker, who have never failed in their support, moral and financial, when deadline after deadline faded into the sunset. My thanks also, and happily once again, to that most scrupulous and helpful of copy editors plus, Steve Cox, and finally to two good friends, Hugh Dent and Andy Callan, whose readiness to discuss the intricacies of the historiography of the Second World War must often have exceeded their actual enthusiasm.

Manchester 1989

Abbreviations

AFV	Armoured fighting vehicle
AP	Armour-piercing
ASV	Air–surface vessel (radar)
Cincpac	Commander-in-Chief Pacific Fleet
Cominch	Commander-in-Chief US Fleet
DAF	Desert Air Force
DAK	*Deutsche Afrika Korps*
FLAK	*Fliegerabwehrkanone* – anti-aircraft gun
HF/DF	High-frequency direction-finder
IJN	Imperial Japanese Navy
JCS	Joint Chiefs of Staff
KOSLI	King's Own Shropshire Light Infantry
LR	Long-range
MOMP	Mid-Ocean Meeting Point
MT	Motor transport
OB Süd	*Oberbefehlshaber Süd* – C.-in-C. South, theatre HQ for southern Germany and various Eastern Front army groups
OB West	C.-in-C. West, theatre HQ for France, Belgium and Netherlands
OKH	*Oberkommando des Heeres* – Army supreme command
OKL	*Oberkommando der Luftwaffe* – Air Force supreme command
OKW	*Oberkommando der Wehrmacht* – Armed Forces supreme command
OR	Operational research
PAK	*Panzerabwehrkanone* – anti-tank gun
POL	Petrol, oil and lubricants
RDF	Radio direction-finding

RTR	Royal Tank Regiment
SASO	Senior Air Staff Officer
Sigint	Signal intelligence
SP	Self-propelled
SU	*Samokyana Ustanokova* – Russian self-propelled gun
TO&E	Table of Organisation and Equipment
USSBS	United States Strategic Bombing Survey
VG	*Volksgrenadier*
VLR	Very long range

Prologue

The Last European War: Poland, France and the Battle of Britain
September 1939 – March 1941

'The tempo of the new warfare is indeed fast . . . [based upon] principles of neck or nothing to the *n*th degree.'

British Staff Officer on operations in France, May 1940

[With regard to the sixteen *Luftwaffe* production plans formulated since September 1939.] 'They were never followed and no one even took them seriously any more. They were nothing but a basis for invoices to the *Luftwaffe*.'

Field Marshal Erhard Milch, August 1941

On 1 September 1939 Hitler, emboldened by his bloodless victory in Czechoslovakia in March, decided to dismember another country by carving up Poland into German and Russian 'spheres of interest'. The 'oppression' of German minorities was again a convenient *casus belli*, but for both Hitler and Stalin the real aim now was the ruthless subjugation of a whole people and the appropriation of much of their industrial and agricultural production. The task facing the German armed forces, the *Wehrmacht*, was somewhat more demanding than the bloodless operations in Czechoslovakia the previous year, but was still hardly formidable. Polish history was resonant with her soldiers' achievements, be they winged lancers before Vienna or Pilsudski's legions driving back the Bolsheviks at the very gates of Warsaw, but the increasing mechanisation of armies in the 1920s and 1930s, as well as the growing emphasis upon air forces, had not been properly appreciated by her latter-day commanders. The Germans, on the other hand, thanks partly to serious analysis of weapons performance in the First World War and partly to Hitler's technological fetishism, had built up very well equipped ground and air forces, giving them, at this stage of the war at least, a telling material superiority over their opponents.

On the eve of the attack on Poland, codenamed *Fall Weiss* or Operation White, the Germans possessed some 3,000 tanks, of which 2,100 were to be used in Poland. Of these, 1,300 were armed with cannon, 300 being Pz III and IVs mounting 37mm and 75mm guns respectively.* The Poles, on the other hand, could deploy only 887 tanks all told and only 140 of these were armed with anything better than a machine-gun. Indeed, their most numerous types were actually more thinly armoured than the British Bren Carrier. The Poles, moreover, managed to make the worst use of those few effective tanks they did possess, parcelling most of them out to individual cavalry brigades and infantry divisions and retaining only two companies of 47mm tanks, with barely 20 tanks between them, as the nucleus of two independent mechanised brigades. The possibilities for a concentrated armoured counterstroke against any threatened enemy breakthrough were thus absolutely nil. The Poles were equally badly outnumbered in the air. In September 1939 the *Luftwaffe* possessed over 4,000 aircraft, of which 2,762 were combat types.† For *Fall Weiss* the operational strength of the units involved was 1,107 combat aircraft. Against these the Poles could muster only 313 operational combat aircraft, less than 40 of which could be said to be on anything like a par with their German equivalents.

But the Poles were also short of almost every other component of modern mechanised warfare. The situation with regard to artillery was typical. On the critical western front in Silesia and the Carpathians, where the Germans massed their major strength, 836 Polish field guns were faced by 3,688 German and 418 anti-tank guns by 2,600. There were also acute shortages in signal equipment and this branch of the services was 'one of the most out-dated . . . of the Polish armed forces'. There was 'an acute shortage of radios and telephones' and an army or army group headquarters had only one

---

* Pz is short for Pzkw, itself an abbreviation of *Panzerkampfwagen* or armoured fighting vehicle.

† These figures represent the operational strength, the actual number of aircraft present with the operational squadrons. Other figures that will be found elsewhere in this book are authorised strength, the number of aircraft if *all* units were at full establishment, and serviceable strength, the number of operational aircraft actually fit to fly.

telephone company, a motorised radio company, a signal park and a carrier pigeon team. A German headquarters at this level would normally include a signals *regiment*. Not surprisingly, equipment on such a meagre level 'precluded adequate command and control of tactical units.'[1] The mobility of the Polish forces also compared most unfavourably with that of the Germans. Their troops had hardly been motorised at all whilst their opponents had made much greater progress in this direction than is commonly acknowledged. Given the usual emphasis upon the German Army's dependence upon horse-drawn transportation, it is worth bearing in mind that a German *infantry* division in 1939 included, as well as its 1,133 horse-drawn vehicles, fully 942 motor vehicles. Whilst this did not match the 2,500 plus attached to a panzer division, it was still more than enough to move at least part of the division very quickly to either exploit a breakthrough or respond to untoward enemy pressure. Even more important, it enabled the Germans to keep their divisional artillery mobile, and thus constantly well up with the forward troops, as well as to ensure a steady and plentiful supply of ammunition.

The marked German advantage in amounts of matériel was mirrored in the head-count of the opposing forces, and sheer weight of numbers was to prove almost as important as material superiority. In the initial onslaught, the Germans massed 28 infantry, 7 motorised and 5 panzer divisions against the Poles' 17 infantry divisions, 3 infantry brigades and 6 cavalry brigades.* The Polish formations, moreover, were spread along the whole 1,250 miles of her western frontiers, with the result that each division was responsible for a 70-mile front even though they were reckoned to have only enough manpower and firepower for the defence of at most eight miles.

In these circumstances, particularly given the Germans' ability to mass their own divisions at a few carefully chosen *Schwerpunkts*, it is not too surprising that the overstretched Polish line snapped almost at once or that the high command was hardly ever able to stabilise any part of it again. They proved particularly vulnerable to the large panzer force, whose armoured columns raced around in the vanguard of the German advance, spreading alarm and despondency and constantly bisecting and trisecting Polish formations such that they were never given an opportunity to form a

* A further 13 infantry divisions and 9 reserve divisions were only partially mobilised when the Germans attacked, but the latter, too, had another 12 infantry, 1 motorised and 1 panzer division in Army and Army Group reserve.

viable operational mass.* Equally important in this regard was the *Luftwaffe* which, after an initial offensive against Polish air-fields, concentrated its attention on their rear areas, attacking forming-up areas for new reserves as well as the road and rail links along which they might be brought to the front. But that most traditional arm, the infantry, also had a crucial role to play. Of great importance was their remarkable mobility, not just that of individual units using motor transport, but that of whole divisions who on occasion were able to march up to 30 miles a day. But their decisive contribution was their firepower, notably that of the divisional artillery which moved with the forward troops and brought down constant fire on the Poles, never giving them a chance to regroup or dig in at leisure. As one recent authority has pointed out:

> The Polish infantry fought as well as the German infantry when the odds were even, but it was repeatedly overwhelmed when the Germans brought their superior numbers and superior firepower to bear. Whilst Western accounts of the September campaign have stressed the shock value of the panzers and Stuka attacks, they have tended to underestimate the punishing effect of German artillery on Polish units. Mobile and available in significant quantity, artillery shattered as many units as any other branch of the Wehrmacht.[2]

Clearly, whilst the Polish campaign went quite some way to vindicating the theories of such proponents of mechanisation as Liddell Hart, J. F. C. Fuller and Heinz Guderian, it demonstrated yet more emphatically that God was still on the side of the big battalions and the big batteries.

The next major German offensive, however, the attack on Holland, Belgium and France in May 1940, must always remain one of military history's major anomalies. For in this campaign the Germans managed to rout the armies of four other European powers in less than six weeks. They achieved this despite the fact

---

* Though there is considerable justice in Matthew Cooper's assertion that the panzer divisions were not given the kind of *strategic* mission that was to characterise authentic armoured *blitzkrieg*, and were almost always closely subordinated to the various mass infantry armies. See especially M. Cooper, *The German Army 1933–45: Its Political and Military Failure* (Macdonald and Jane's, 1978), pp. 174–6.

that they had no material or numerical superiority over their opponents – who were allowed nine months in which to prepare their defences – and that they were operating in a theatre large enough to have offered ample opportunity to buy time through a considered strategic withdrawal.

The point about numerical and material parity bears a little elaboration as there still seems to be a widespread belief that *Fall Gelb* or Operation Yellow, the codename for the offensive in the West, was only successful because of overwhelming German superiority. In fact, their armies in the West mustered only $141\frac{2}{3}$ divisions, ten of them armoured and $6\frac{2}{3}$ motorised, of which 28 were held in OKH reserve.* These were faced by 104 French divisions, 22 Belgian, 8 Dutch and 10 British, a total of 144. Of these, three were heavy armoured divisions, three light armoured, five motorised cavalry and seven motorised infantry. All these latter were French, though the British also put into the field two armoured regiments. This mass of French armour, moreover, was no negligible asset, contributing 3,254 tanks deployed on the north-eastern front as opposed to only 2,574 German. Furthermore, all the French tanks, except for 450 *automitrailleuses de combat* and *de reconnaissance*, were armed with 37mm or 47mm guns whilst almost 1,500 of the German total had only machine-guns or feeble 20mm cannon. Most French tanks were also very well protected and the majority were generously plated with 40mm armour. This seriously limited the effectiveness of the German anti-tank guns, which with a calibre of 37mm could only penetrate French armour at extremely short ranges. The German numerical superiority in these weapons, 12,800 to 7,200, was therefore largely illusory as most of the French ones could penetrate most German tanks at most ranges.†

---

* The *Oberkommande des Heeres* or Army Supreme Command.
† Nor will it do to claim that the French armour was hopelessly compromised by being split into penny packets, scattered hither and thither. Many *were* grouped into independent tank battalions attached to the infantry divisions but this still left roughly 2,000 tanks organised into six armoured and motorised divisions. The three heavy armoured divisions, the *divisions cuirassées*, were fully equipped at the start of the campaign, each containing 160 tanks armed with long 37mm or 47mm guns. There were also three 'light mechanised divisions' which were in fact 'neither light nor simply mechanised cavalry organisations. Each division on 10 May 1940 had approximately 240 tanks and can be considered to have been as powerfully equipped as any of the famed German *Panzer* divisions.' (R. H. S. Stolfi, 'Equipment for Victory in France 1940', *History* 55, 1970, p. 11.)

Two other types of weapon whose availability might usefully be compared were field guns, of which the Allies had 14,000 and the Germans 7,400, and military aircraft, with 2,200 Allied present in the theatre and 2,750 German. Many of the French models, it must be admitted, were obsolete, though in May 1940 the *Armée de l'Air* could put up over 500 modern monoplane fighters and by this date, moreover, aircraft production was functioning so well that when the French surrendered the number of these modern fighters had actually increased.

However, even though a campaign which relied so little on brute force is not of central interest in this book, it does behove one to attempt some explanation of the remarkable ease with which the Germans achieved their crushing victory. Part of the reason, of course, was simply good planning, most notably the decision by Hitler to *concentrate* his armour, with seven out of the ten panzer divisions being massed between Dinant and Sedan and five of these debouching out of the Ardennes, a sector the French regarded as impassable to large units. This left the major portion of the French armour stranded too far north, and though they did go into action with commendable speed their efforts were made well away from the major *Schwerpunkt*, with 1 Light Mechanised Division going into battle around Breda and Antwerp, 2 and 3 Light Mechanised between Gembloux and Liège, 1 Armoured at Charleroi and 2 Armoured at Dinant.

But the most important reason for the abject Allied failure must be the utterly outmoded nature of their preconceptions about the fluidity and the tempo of military operations. Seemingly having forgotten anything they might have learnt from the campaigns of Frederick the Great, Napoleon, Jackson, Sherman or Moltke, and even from their experiences in the 'open' warfare of 1918, Allied commanders in 1939 and 1940 remained mentally immured in the trench lines that had characterised the greater part of the Great War. They were thus incapable of envisaging or responding to a mode of operations that eschewed an evenly weighted broad front offensive and was determined to reinforce local success vigorously and speedily with whatever means were available and without any let-up. French contingency plans in the Phoney War show how operationally arthritic their High Command had become. Whilst one cannot really blame them for not foreseeing that the Ardennes would be the *point d'appui*, one can bemoan the almost complete failure to even query whether the Germans would do anything other than stage a re-run of 1914.* Thus, as soon as intelligence of the invasion of Holland and Belgium was confirmed, the French (and British) assumed that this was merely a repeat of the Schlieffen Plan and immediately put into action their own preconceived plan for a broad advance into Belgium to take up positions along the whole line of the River Dyle. Moreover, during the first days of the offensive all Allied units consistently marched straight to the sound of the guns on this front, their commanders never taking the time to sit back and ponder whether this *was* the main German axis of advance or to hold back a mobile, strategic reserve capable of an effective riposte once the actual axis *was* clear. Here in particular lies the truth of the assertion that the Allies were still trapped in First World War modes of thinking. Not so much because of the static defences of the Maginot Line – the French were after all prepared to advance into Belgium, making their main effort well north of the Line – but because this advance itself had an ultimately defensive purpose, to hold the Germans on the Dyle, and because the manner of this defence, shovelling as many units as possible into the forward line, betokened nothing much different from the trench lines of 1914–18. The terrible consequences of this insistence on pinning all their units at the front were highlighted on 16 May, when Churchill went to meet the French Commander-in-Chief, General Maurice Gustave Gamelin.

> The Commander-in-Chief briefly explained what had happened. North and South of Sedan, on a front of fifty or sixty miles, the Germans had broken through. The French army in front of them was destroyed or scattered. A heavy onrush of armoured vehicles was advancing with unheard of speed towards . . . Abbeville . . . Behind the armour . . . [other] German divisions . . . were driving onwards, making flanks for themselves as they advanced against the two disconnected French armies on either side. The General talked perhaps five minutes without anyone

---

* It has to be acknowledged, however, that if certain senior German generals had had their way, *Fall Gelb* would not in fact have differed much from the Schlieffen Plan. In its original Army version *Fall Gelb* foresaw neither the total conquest of France nor the annihilation of her armed forces, but only the establishment of a zone of occupation north of the Aisne and the Somme. It was only Hitler's support for the more radical proposals of officers like General Friedrich Erich von Manstein, then the Chief of Staff of Army Group A, which ensured that the Operation came to be centred upon a strategy of annihilation, or *Vernichtungsgedanke*.

saying a word. When he stopped talking there was a considerable silence. I then asked: 'Where is the strategic reserve?' and, breaking into French . . . '*Où est la masse de manoeuvre?*' General Gamelin turned to me and, with a shake of the head and a shrug said, '*Aucune.*'[3]

But if Allied commanders suffered from operational arthritis, the whole of their armed forces were beset by tactical palsy. From the very first days of the German attack it was clear that they were incapable of even beginning to match the remorseless pace and violence of the enemy onslaught. A recent historian has convincingly cast doubt upon the extent to which these operations properly merited the name *blitzkrieg*. The drive to the Channel ports, between 10 and 20 May, he suggests,

> degenerated from the armoured enthusiast's ideal of a swift, deep thrust, ending only with the defeat of the enemy, into a succession of short, sharp jumps, with a pause between each for regrouping. Swift though this method of war was, compared with that of the enemy, it fell far short of Guderian's theories. The organised velocity of the armoured idea gave way to the initially powerful, but ever-fading punches of the modernised *Vernichtungsgedanke*.[4]

Mr Cooper supports his argument with numerous examples of excessive caution by senior German commanders, a caution that found its most fateful expression in the notorious halt order, approved by both von Rundstedt and Hitler himself, which stopped the panzers short of the Dunkirk perimeter on 24 May.* The order was revoked on the 26th but it was only on the morning of the 27th that they actually got going again, by which time the evacuation was under way and the defensive perimeter had been considerably strengthened. It was only on the morning of 4 June that the Germans were able to announce the complete capture of the port.

Nevertheless, the recognition of a considerable shortfall between *blitzkrieg* theory and the reality of German armoured operations in 1940 should not obscure the fact that, when compared to the pace of Allied operations, even modernised *Vernichtungsgedanke* qualified as lightning warfare. The tempo of operations expected by the Allies can

---

* Other examples of German caution can be found in Cooper, op. cit., pp. 219, 222–30 *passim*, 233, 235, 237, 239.

be gauged from the details of Plan 'D', which specified the advance to the Dyle in the event of a German invasion. It was expected that the Allied move might take up to ten days, and according to one French general:

> This was far from being an attacking manoeuvre. The French army was leaving its frontier position (which it had fortified somewhat during the previous eight months) to take up another on Belgian territory (which it believed equally fortified). The operation was only attempted because the Command hoped to have time to carry it out without being seriously harassed by the enemy.[5]

But the Germans did not allow anything like this sort of time period, nor indeed did they make their major effort in the Allied-nominated sector, and the latter found themselves desperately trying to match their dinosaur-like reflexes to the swaggering agility of the panzer divisions. Basil Liddell Hart hit the nail on the head when he observed that 'the pace of panzer warfare paralysed the French Staff . . . The orders they issued might have been effective but for being, repeatedly, twenty-four hours late for the situation they were intended to meet.'[6] A more recent writer made an equally pithy summary when he observed that once the German 'armoured columns had broken through, they cut across lines of communications and passed by centres of resistance in such a way that the initial surprise at the front was compounded by perpetual surprise in the rear.'[7] This perpetual surprise was all the worse because of the totally inadequate communications system. In the BEF, for example, during the period of the 'Phoney War', there had been

> an absurd order forbidding the use of radio for training the operators. In consequence when . . . the pace of events moved too fast to lay telephone lines there was a communications failure at unit level; most seriously in the artillery. The whole French command system was abysmally bad. Its structure was defective and its communications rudimentary. General Gamelin . . . was without a radio network. He afterwards admitted that any order from his headquarters was unlikely to bear fruit for forty-eight hours.[8]

But the best comments on the total incapacity of the Allied forces to match the pace of German operations come from two men who served in the campaign and who recorded their impressions almost immediately. The first was a British Air Intelligence Liaison Officer, though himself in the Army, attached to the headquarters of the British Air Forces in France. In 1941 he published, anonymously, extracts from a diary he kept during the invasion. The following is a compression of some of the more pertinent extracts written between 14 and 19 May:

> The tempo of the new warfare is indeed fast. [On our side] caution, safety first, and too late, the usual sequence. All the dash and drive is left to the Germans. The whole development of the southern front has been so fast and has been conducted on such unorthodox principles – principles of neck or nothing to the *n*th degree – that it is hard to believe that the situation is so precarious as it is in fact. They would have us believe that the Battle of the Marne will be fought again, but do they believe it themselves? I am afraid there is not the same probability of being able to establish a fixed defensive line today. The pace is too fast and the battle of movement has come into its own again. The *Panzer* divisions seem insatiable. [Late on the 17th] with the bit between their teeth, [they] are going as strong as ever. [On the 19th] news that the Panzers are in Amiens. This is some ridiculous nightmare. The BEF is cut off. Our communications have gone. I have told myself again and again that the German threat could not be sustained. The Germans have taken every risk – criminally foolish risks – and they have got away with it. The French General Staff have been paralysed by this unorthodox war of movement [and] are incapable of functioning in this new and astonishing lay-out.[9]

The second piece was written by a French pilot, Antoine de Saint-Exupéry, and his version of events as seen from a bird's-eye vantage point is markedly more detached than that of the staff officer just cited, who was personally constantly under threat from the advancing panzers. The airman nevertheless gives a splendidly cogent analysis of the nature of the new warfare and of the helplessness of the Allied armies.* The doctrine of the panzers, he perceived, was that a:

---

* My attention was first drawn to this quotation by David Downing in his stimulating *The Devil's Virtuosos: German Generals at War 1940–45* (New English Library, 1978), p. 42.

division should move against the enemy like water. It should bear lightly against the enemy's wall of defence and advance only at the point where it meets no resistance. The tanks operate by this rule, bear against the wall, and never fail to break through. They move as they please . . . and though the damage they do is superficial – capture of unit Staffs, cutting of telephone cables, burning of villages – the consequences of their raids are irreparable. In every region through which they make their lightning sweep, a French army, even though it seems to be virtually intact, has ceased to be an army. It has been transformed into clotted segments. It has, so to say, coagulated . . . Where once an organism existed . . . [the panzers] leave a mere sum of organs whose unity has been destroyed. Between the clots – however combative the clots may have remained – the enemy moves at will. An army, if it is to be effective, must be something other than a numerical sum of soldiers.[10]

Of course this psychological dislocation of the Allied war machine was not the whole reason for its precipitate collapse. More mundane pressures were also at work, not least the effects once again of German firepower. General Erwin Rommel, the commander of 7 Panzer Division, was especially enthusiastic about the effects of prompt and continual fire from his tanks and artillery:

I have found again and again that in encounter actions, the day goes to the side that is the first to plaster its oppponents with fire . . . Experience in this early fighting showed that in tank attacks especially, the action of immediately opening fire into the area which the enemy is believed to be holding, instead of waiting until several of one's own tanks have been hit, usually decides the issue. Even indiscriminate machine-gun fire and 20mm anti-tank fire into a wood in which enemy anti-tank guns have installed themselves is so effective that in most cases the enemy is completely unable to get into action or else gives up his position.[11]

But the most important component of German fire was that from the air. On 18 May the perspicacious staff officer already cited observed that 'it is the cooperation between the dive-bombers and the armoured divisions that is winning this war for Germany.'[12] In fact, the whole of the *Luftwaffe* in the West was being used in a tactical role. The first day or two's operations were aimed at French airfields and thereafter bombers with strong escorts of single and twin-engined fighters sought out bases, troop concentrations, railway marshalling yards and Allied movements by road and rail. Ports on both sides of the Channel were also attacked, to disrupt essential shipping to France, but only two authentic strategic attacks were made, on the aircraft industry in the Paris area and on fuel depots in Marseilles. But it probably was the Stuka dive-bomber that had the most direct impact on ground operations. Our staff officer spoke with a French officer on 16 May and this latter 'described the troops at Sedan and how the German bombing had destroyed what they called "their physical make-up". They could stand no more, they were finished, mentally vanquished, and finally we heard a word constantly repeated. The armies, he said, were *épuisé*. And all this due to the dive-bombers . . .'[13] According to General Charles de Gaulle, commander of a fourth *division cuirassée* formed during the campaign itself, his counter-attack on 19 May was largely thwarted by Stukas which 'were to bomb us till nightfall, deadly to the vehicles that could not leave the roads and to the artillery out in the open.'[14] But by then whole armies had been reduced to a mere agglomeration of units. Ninth Army, which had manned the sector between Dinant and Charleville, was within only three days on the point of collapse. This

> ravaged army scarcely even *looked* like a disciplined force. The Luftwaffe pitched into the command posts; it scoured the roads, bombed the intersections, made it impossible for reinforcements to be brought up, disorganised communications. The withdrawal very soon acquired the appearance of a rout. The infantry shunned open country. The artillery was paralysed; most of the horses had been machine-gunned from the air; the guns were immobilised and could not be trained. Lorries heaped with men of all services scurried from the front.[15]

In fact, the effect of the German ground attack aircraft might have been much lessened if any of the Allied armies had had significant anti-aircraft support. The Germans did and it is revealing to note that though French attacks on ground targets achieved almost nothing, fully 70 per cent of their aircraft losses were during this type of sortie.

Yet even with regard to firepower one is forced to the conclusion that it was not so much the physical effect of German guns and planes that so incapacitated the Allies as its impact on morale. Their troops were not paralysed so much by the actual losses amongst men and equipment as by the fear of what bullets, shells and bombs might do. Men simply panicked and quit perfectly tenable positions, roads became hopelessly blocked as vehicles were abandoned and march discipline evaporated, and communications broke down because line-layers and operators were simply not prepared to set up or maintain a functioning network. A hundred such failures quickly bred a thousand more, and these in turn gave rise to defeatism, despair and a fixed conviction that the enemy was invincible. By the time Gamelin was replaced by General Maxime Weygand, on 19 May, the rot had taken irreversible hold. The latter had some extremely pertinent ideas about how to halt the German advance, stressing particularly the need for instant counter-attacks against enemy bridgeheads that could become jumping-off points for exploitation by the panzers, but his forces were simply not up to it. Too many men had already been killed or captured to permit the creation of the sort of reserves these tactics demanded, whilst the morale of those that remained was not even adequate to allow Weygand's later *quadrillage* tactics, based upon the static defence of interlocking strongpoints echeloned in depth. The French armed forces that surrendered on 24 June, like the Dutch and Belgians before them, and like the British evacuees from the Channel ports, had been so thoroughly deprived of their self-confidence that nothing could induce them to believe that they could put up any effective resistance to the German *blitzkrieg*. Those at Dunkirk and elsewhere did fight on, and often extremely bravely, but only because they were offered the real prospect of returning home. For the continental Allied armies, however, this could only be achieved by wholesale surrender. By 24 June 1940 the Dutch, Belgians and French had all done just that.

At the end of June 1940 Hitler would have been entitled to feel quite smug about the benefits that had accrued from his blatantly aggressive policies. The Rhineland, Austria, Czechoslovakia, Poland, Norway, Denmark, Holland, Belgium and much of France were all under firm German control. Southern France retained nominal independence, but was militarily and politically negligible, whilst Britain had just seen its regular and first-line reserve divisions participate in a complete military débâcle. The evacuation from Dunkirk and elsewhere had been a true prodigy of military improvisation but, as Churchill himself admitted to the House of Commons on 4 June: 'We must be very careful not to assign to this deliverance the attributes of a victory. Wars are not won by evacuations.'[16]

This is especially true when the departing force leaves behind most of its equipment, in this case 100 tanks,* 2,500 guns, 64,000 vehicles, 76,000 tons of ammunition and thousands more tons of other stores. For this meant that the army left in Britain in June 1940 was appallingly ill-armed, its 26 nominal divisions able to muster only 180 or so tanks,† 786 field guns and 167 anti-tank. Even by the end of August the number of first-line tanks had only risen to 348 medium and Cruiser and 514 light, and the number of anti-tank guns to 500. Between May and August, moreover, only an extra 220 field guns had been produced. Little wonder, therefore, that General Sir Alan Brooke, in charge of Southern Command, wrote at the end of June: 'The main impression I had was that the Command had a long way to go to be put on a war-footing.' His spirits had not lifted appreciably on 15 September, two months after taking over as Commander-in-Chief Home Forces. He confided in his diary: '. . . we have only twenty-two divisions of which only about half can be looked upon as in any way fit for any form of mobile operations . . . Responsibility . . . weighs on one like a ton of bricks, and it is hard at times to retain . . . [a] hopeful and confident exterior . . .'[17]

Happily, a comparison of opposing ground forces was not the best indicator of British strength, and indeed, her army was now only her very last resort. Prior to any fighting on the beaches, the fields, the streets or the hills, Germany would have to cross the Channel, and such an amphibious assault would need to be preceded by an aerial offensive against Britain, attempting to gain air superiority and thus provide cover for the invasion fleet. Thus, whatever the exact course of events, it was clear that it was the Royal Air Force and the Royal Navy that were to be the leading players in the next act. And both the junior and the senior service were in much better shape than their sister.

The Royal Navy, for example, though beset by commitments in the Mediterranean, after the Italian declaration of war in June 1940, and the necessity to provide escorts for the transatlantic convoys, was a far from negligible force in its home waters. Table 1 shows the

---

* On 16 May, 1 Armoured Division, badly understrength, had begun arriving in France.

† Almost all of them were light tanks. There were another 800 tanks available in the UK at this time, but these were next to useless, as there were no effective fighting units to man them and 600 were light tanks.

strength of this force, comprising the Home Fleet as well as Nore, Rosyth, Portsmouth and Western Approaches Commands.* The figure in brackets indicates the additional ships of each type which were refitting or under repair. The figure for Western Approaches Command is given separately as it would have been far from easy quickly to reallocate many of these vessels to a battle in the English Channel, most of them being actively engaged in convoy escort.

Table 1: *Ships available to the Royal Navy for use in home waters June–September 1940*

Date		Home Fleet and Home Command				Western Commands	
	B/Ship	B/Cruiser	A/c Carrier	Cr.	Dest.	Cruiser	Destroyer
10 June	4	3	3	9(8)	57(48)	(1)	16(5)
1 July	3	2	-	10	58	1	23
10 Sept.	3()*	2	2	13(5)	51(18)	(5)	27(1)

*There were also 2 monitors.

The German Navy in June 1940 was in comparison downright paltry. Knowing that Great Britain was likely to be an enemy in any future war, Hitler had during the Thirties shown some interest, if rather desultory, in naval matters. A plan was drawn up for considerably expanding the *Kriegsmarine*, but when Hitler actually went to war only limited progress had been made. Thus, whereas the Navy's 'Z' Plan anticipated that by 1944 it would number 10 battleships, 6 pocket battleships and battle cruisers, 2 aircraft carriers, 18 cruisers and 47 destroyers, the actual number of serviceable ships in September 1939 was only 7 battleships of all types, 8 light cruisers and 22 destroyers. By July 1940, after the successful but costly expeditions to Denmark and Norway in April, these figures were much reduced. During this short campaign, 3 cruisers and 10 destroyers were lost and numerous other ships badly damaged, such that the only serviceable vessels left to the *Kriegsmarine* were 1 heavy cruiser, 2 light, 4 destroyers and 19 torpedo boats. This was hardly a fleet to guarantee freedom of passage for the mass of clumsy barges that were being assembled for the invasion of Britain, dubbed Operation Sea Lion.†

* The sources for all tables will be found after the Statistical Appendix, on p. 567.
† The *Wehrmacht* was first ordered to draw up plans for an amphibious assault on 13 July 1940.

It was clear, therefore, that a great deal of heavy spadework would have to be done by the *Luftwaffe* before the invasion could safely be launched, even to the extent of destroying the RAF, wrecking harbours and naval installations and putting a considerable number of warships out of action. The head of the *Wehrmacht* Operations Staff, General Alfred Jodl, made it quite plain early in the planning for Sea Lion that the *Luftwaffe* was expected to accomplish the task virtually single-handed. He 'believed that the *Luftwaffe* would break British willpower. He commented that German strategy would require a landing on the British coast only as the final blow . . . to finish off an England that the *Luftwaffe* and navy had already defeated.'[18] It was far from certain, however, that such a task was realistically within the capabilities of the *Luftwaffe*, which indeed was particularly ill-adapted to a strategic task of this nature.*

It lacked, for example, any real 'strategic' capabilities, as German rearmament programmes had never been able to spare the resources for building the requisite four-engined bombers. The blueprints existed, as, for example, the He 177 first proposed in 1937, but there was little hope of ever building them in significant numbers, particularly during the 1930s when Hitler was keen to limit the extent to which military production cut into that for civilian consumption. Debates as to whether Hitler, the *Wehrmacht* or the *Oberkommando der Luftwaffe* (OKL) had a clear appreciation of the potential of 'strategic' bombers remain, therefore, somewhat academic. As Williamson Murray has pointed out:

> The Germans possessed almost no natural resources and had to import almost every raw material that a modern war economy requires. Concurrently, they had to export finished industrial goods to cover the costs of raw materials needed by rearmament. Thus, the German economy was most vulnerable to a blockade. All of this put the Germans in a considerable bind in the late 1930s. In terms of air rearmament, it meant that in the pre-war

---

* Discussion of the air war between 1939 and 1945 has become hobbled by the use of the word 'strategic' to mean long-range bombing directed at industrial targets and the military infrastructure. In some cases, usage is so loose that the word seems to signify little more than that four-engined bombers were employed. Such bombing does require an epithet but the one chosen obviates its use in other contexts where general military usage would deem it the *mot juste*. I have attempted to get the best of both worlds, and here I to some extent follow Williamson Murray, by employing the word strategic, as above, for normal contexts and 'strategic' for the specific one of industrial bombing.

period Germany was never in a position to build a 'strategic' bombing force on the scale of the British and American bomber fleets that battered Germany in 1943 and 1944.[19]

Worse than the lack of 'strategic' aircraft, however, was the general debility of the *Luftwaffe* as a whole in July 1940. Though impressive air armadas had been assembled for the Polish and French campaigns, both of these had taken their toll, with operational losses representing a worrying percentage of the total front-line strengths of these types at the beginning of the war.* The actual figures are given below:

Single-engined fighters	35.4 per cent
Twin-engined fighters	53.2
Dive-bombers	43.2
Bombers	58.4

Ominously, some of the heaviest of these losses had been sustained during the week of Operation Dynamo, the Dunkirk evacuation, when the *Luftwaffe* was faced almost exclusively by RAF Fighter Command, the enemy it would have to beat if it were to gain air superiority for Sea Lion. Reichsmarschall Hermann Göring, the Commander-in-Chief of the *Luftwaffe*, had promised that the encircled Allies would be pulverised from the air, making Army intervention unnecessary, but in fact over 240 German planes were lost over Dunkirk and the evacuation went on regardless. This was over 25 per cent of total German losses in the campaign up to 4 June. *Fliegerkorps* II reported in its War Diary that it had lost more aircraft (bombers and dive-bombers) on 27 May, attacking the evacuation, than it had lost in the previous ten days of the campaign. A pilot who fought in these battles, Adolf Galland, later to become commander of the fighter arm, quickly realised that 'the Luftwaffe would not have a walk-over against the RAF . . . The British had a fighter arm which was numerically stronger and better controlled . . . With regard to crews and fighting spirit it was absolutely first class.'[20]

---

* These operational losses represent aircraft destroyed or damaged in combat or other reconnaissance and transport sorties. Training flights are the main ones not included. But operational losses are not all caused by enemy aircraft. Accidents whilst landing and taking off were another common cause of casualties. The exact meaning of 'destroyed' and 'damaged' is not clear from the source of these particular figures. Usually, the Germans classified their casualties by the percentage of damage sustained. 100 per cent was obviously a total loss, but in fact the Germans wrote off any aircraft with 60 per cent or more damage, the exact percentage given merely indicating the extent of cannibalisation possible.

This numerical inferiority was an early indicator to the Germans that they must continue their run of *quick* victories. If the war were to become a protracted affair, then this would expose Germany's Achilles' heel, the serious long-term military inadequacies resulting from her cavalier approach to armaments production. The *Luftwaffe* in mid-1940 was a perfect example of the consequences of such an approach. At the root of the problem was the inherent economic weakness already referred to with regard to 'strategic' bombers, and Hitler seems to have made remarkably little attempt to intervene on behalf of war production. In January 1939, for example, he actually cut the *Wehrmacht's* allocation of raw materials, imposing a 30 per cent reduction in steel, 20 per cent in copper, 47 per cent in aluminium and 14 per cent in rubber. Even after the war started, the battle for production was regarded as the least important front. The mobilisation of the industrial work-force was a case in point. General Walter Warlimont, in charge of the *Wehrmacht's* Department of Home Defence, was to write after the war:

> In the face of the successful Polish campaign, Hitler refused to order mobilisation in the full sense of the word; later on, partial mobilisation was ordered, but the economy was specifically exempted . . . None of the carefully thought-out measures designed to protect the armament industry by keeping its skilled workers on the job was put into effect. Not until it was no longer possible to ignore the fact that the West meant business was any attempt made to undo the damage. By then, of course, it was no longer a matter of putting a certain paragraph of the mobilisation plan into effect, but of ordering back every single skilled worker from the front, provided of course, that he was still among the living.[21]

The aircraft industry suffered as much as any other in this period of absurd complacency. Between September 1940 and February 1941, for example, there was an actual decline in aircraft production, amounting to almost 40 per cent. As one American economist wrote after the war: 'This decision to reduce aircraft production to this extent seems almost incredible, considering that in September, the very month the decision was made, the number of aircraft lost in the . . . Battle of Britain was substantially in excess of new production.'[22] This decision appears particularly out of tune with reality when one discovers that in April 1940, just prior to the Battle of Britain, Hitler had quite sensibly called for increased aircraft production. At the very moment he was losing the battle, however, he reduced it. By January 1941, in fact, production was running at little over 50 per cent of the number planned for *before* the war. The problem was aggravated by the inability of the *Luftwaffe* to draw up effective plans for increased production, owing mainly to the lack of liaison between the *Luftwaffe* General Staff and the technical departments responsible for aircraft procurement. Göring himself was distinguished only by his infinite capacity for total indolence, and all this conspired to render the *Luftwaffe* incapable of formulating consistent or relevant production programmes. Even during the first two years of war,

> German aircraft production remained virtually on a peacetime level. In particular no consistent programme was formulated and adhered to; during the first two years of the war no less than 16 programmes were started, none of which was maintained for longer than 6–7 weeks. The result was that the overall increase in output between 1939 and 1941 was meagre, in the region of 5–10 per cent.[23]

Even before the war began many senior *Luftwaffe* commanders were aware of the inadequacies of their own service, though in the last months of peace they seem to have also been mercifully *un*aware of how little time remained to get themselves on a proper war footing. 'As late as 1939 General Felmy concluded in a study based on the contingency of a war against Britain that the *Luftwaffe*'s existing forces were unsuitable . . . Milch . . . realised that the *Luftwaffe* would not be ready for war until at least 1942 and possibly much later.' The unanimity on this point between the State Secretary and the Chief of the *Luftwaffe* General Staff, General Hans Jeschonnek, was especially depressing. In June 1939, in a critique of a *Luftwaffe* exercise, he 'hedged on the important question of whether the Luftwaffe was ready to fight a European war. He knew it could handle Poland easily, but he was relying on the political leaders to steer a course that would avoid a multifront war, which the Luftwaffe was not quite ready to fight.' Others were yet more sceptical. Göring's adjutant, Karl Bodenschatz, claimed at Nuremberg that there had been a general lack of faith in the abilities of the *Luftwaffe* in 1939: 'The German Air Force, at the beginning of the Polish campaign, as regards leadership, planning or material, was not equal to its tasks.'[24]

Most especially, the *Luftwaffe* was not ready to fight the kind of autonomous strategic campaign envisaged in the offensive against the

RAF in July 1940. Three major shortcomings can be discerned. Firstly, because of all the muddle and confusion described above, as well as Germany's less than favourable economic position, her industry was unable to produce aircraft fast enough. The Battle of France had already made it clear that an aerial assault on Britain would be a battle of attrition, in which the ability to keep front-line units up to strength would be crucial. Production rates, in other words, would begin really to make their mark on the war. But this was an area in which the British already had a head start. One vital decision had been made before the war, in 1938, when the government resolved to challenge Stanley Baldwin's gloomy assertion that 'the bomber will always get through' and gave top priority to fighter production. They thus, in one of history's first Strategic Defence Initiatives, took issue with the offensive-minded 'strategic' bombing theorists within Bomber Command and the Air Staff, and advocated an important role for planes that could defend one's own homeland, industry and airfields.

A second vital decision was that made in May 1940 by Air Chief Marshal Sir Hugh Dowding, in charge of Fighter Command, who continued to assert his essentially defensive mission to the pugnacious Churchill and resolutely refused to commit any more fighters to French soil after the successful completion of Operation Dynamo. His letter to Churchill must still rank as one of the most forthright the Prime Minister ever received. The RAF had left its last French base on 22 May, but had ever since been bombarded by requests for its return, to work in close cooperation with the *Armée de l'Air*. Dowding was adamant:

> I believe that, if an adequate fighter force is kept in the country, if the fleet remains in being, and if Home Forces are suitably organised to resist invasion, we should be able to carry on the war single-handed for some time, if not indefinitely. But, if the Home Defence Force is drained away in desperate attempts to remedy the situation in France, defeat in France will involve the final, complete and irremediable defeat of this country.[25]

The third vital decision, taken at almost exactly the same time, 14 May, was that to appoint Lord Beaverbrook as Minister of Aircraft Production and so give real impetus to the decision to maximise fighter production. The production figures he achieved are more than adequate testimony to his contribution to the war effort, compared either with the targets established in January 1940 (in May fighter production was 24.5 per cent over target, in June 52.7 per cent, in July 50.8 per cent, and in August 68.8 per cent), or with German figures. The latter comparison shows that annual military aircraft production to 1941 was as follows:

	Britain	Germany
1939	7,940	8,295
1940	15,049	10,826
1941	20,094	11,776

The figures for fighter production alone show that the British had a 15.5 per cent advantage in 1940 and one of 49.3 per cent in 1941. In single-engined fighter production the respective advantages were 130 and 150 per cent. Table 26 in the Statistical Appendix gives the figures for these latter types, the Bf 109,* the Hurricane and the Spitfire, the aircraft that fought the real battle in the skies over southern England, and shows the monthly totals for the Battle of Britain and the Blitz. Britain's aggregate total is over twice that for Germany with the former, between June 1940 and April 1941, producing 5,249 planes and the latter under 2,500.†

The distinction between single-engined and twin-engined fighters brings us to a second major shortcoming of the *Luftwaffe* at this time: the quality of its planes. For the distinction is not a devious book-keeping device, intended to inflate the British numerical superiority. Many books, indeed, fall into the opposite trap and present comparisons based on the single category 'fighter' which ignore the serious shortcomings of the twin-engined Messerschmitt Bf 110. The *Zerstörer*, as this type of plane was known, had been designed to overcome the major drawback of the Bf 109: its short range. This initial concept, as Galland recognised, was 'operationally correct' but the plane that actually emerged was unfortunately a 'technically inferior solution'. In fact,

---

* Most German planes are referred to by an abbreviation of the maker's name, e.g. Messerschmitt Me 262, Junkers Ju 87 or Heinkel He 111. The Messerschmitt 108, 109, 110 and 161/2, for some arcane reason or other, take the initials Bf, standing for a factory, the *Bayerische Flugzeugwerke*.

† It should also be borne in mind that by August 1940 the British government had placed orders in the United States for 14,000 aircraft and 25,000 aircraft engines. Conversely, the bare statement of German figures conceals the fact that almost all their factories were turning out aircraft, while little attention was paid to spare parts. This soon led to a chronic shortage of components, and aircraft with less than 60 per cent damage increasingly had to be cannibalised rather than themselves being repaired.

the 'destroyer' Me 110 was no solution to the problem. Its performance compared unfavourably with all other modern fighter aircraft – its maximum speed of 288 mph, for example, was 65 mph slower than that of the Spitfire. In addition, it had all the shortcomings for aerial combat typical of a large heavy plane: incapacity for tight turns, bad manoeuvrability, sluggish acceleration, a good target with its great over-all area and easy to recognise from a great distance.[26]

The Bf 110 was manned by a pilot and an observer/gunner and at one stage during the Battle of Britain the Germans grounded the latter to try and reduce weight.* But this simply meant that the pilot was deprived of advice about an enemy on his tail. As soon as there was the slightest indication of an enemy presence, therefore, the Bf 110s would abandon any pretence of protecting the bombers and adopt a mildly ridiculous formation as the planes flew round in a circle, each trying to protect its neighbour's tail.

The diagnosis that prompted the development of the *Zerstörer* was nevertheless correct, for the Bf 109's short range was a severe handicap. It meant, in fact, that even when operating from bases in northern France the *Luftwaffe* was incapable of providing proper fighter support beyond a line Ipswich–Stanmore–Andover–Cheddar. Even when covering targets well to the south of this line, the single-engined fighters had only enough fuel to provide protection for a very limited period. As a cure for this problem, however, the Bf 110 was less than apposite and it is hard to see how an additional aircraft type, even one with a markedly better performance than the Bf 110, was the best solution to the problem. As Galland pointed out: 'Surely it would have been better, during the further development of the fighter arm, if all efforts had been concentrated on the removal of . . . [the 109's] shortcomings rather than on the creation of a new type of aircraft which, within the framework of the limited possibilities of technics and personnel, could only be accomplished at the expense of the fighter arm.'[27] The precise solution was perfectly straightforward, and simply involved equipping the fighters with extra fuel tanks. These were generally known as drop-tanks because they could be jettisoned once empty. Why the Germans made no attempt to pursue this idea remains a mystery, as they had made partially successful

---

* When fully loaded the Bf 110, supposedly just a more robust alternative to the 109, weighed almost 10,000lb more than the single-engined plane.

experiments during the Condor Legion's stint in Spain. Here one is entitled to assume a fatal consequence of the lack of liaison between operational commanders and the technical departments.

It has been claimed that the Allies showed themselves similarly backward in the provision of drop-tanks for their own fighter escorts during the bomber offensive, but they did at least have the initial excuse that the four-engined 'strategic' bombers were supposed to be sufficiently well armed to provide their own protection. There was no way that this could be said of the twin-engined German bombers, the Ju 88, the Do 17, the He 111 and the single-engined Stuka dive-bomber, the Ju 87. The twin-engined planes, armed only with a few 7.9mm machine-guns, were incapable of putting up any real field of fire of their own and, in Galland's opinion, 'all types showed that they were not sufficiently armed for defence. The existing armament was of moral value only.' [28]

But feeble armament was not the only problem. The Ju 88, for example, was slower than the He 111 it was supposed to supersede, take-offs with full tanks were difficult, the plane had an alarming habit of catching fire in mid-air, and the dinghy could not be released in an emergency. In some Ju 88 squadrons morale reached rock-bottom and a report commissioned by Göring drew up a list of 32 justifiable complaints against the plane. The report completely refuted any suggestion that the bomber crews might be malingering, noting: 'It's not the enemy the squadron's frightened of – it's the Junkers 88.'[29] But none of the bombers seem to have been particularly reliable planes. During the whole of the Battle of Britain the following operational loss rates were recorded for various types of aircraft, with the number in brackets indicating the number of non-combat losses, mainly accidents in taking off or landing:

	Bf 109	Bombers and Dive-bombers	Bf 110
Number of planes destroyed	646(86)	964(230)	243(27)
Percentage accidents	13.3	23.9	11.1

The Ju 87 was another distinctly inadequate piece of equipment, and it soon turned out that it could only do its job when there was no opposition. If the Stuka came up against a well equipped enemy, as it did over southern England in 1940, it was found that the plane's horribly low speed – it cruised at less than 200 mph – and its total helplessness as it pulled out of the dive made it extremely vulnerable to British fighters and anti-aircraft guns. Nor was there much that the Bf 109s could do to protect them, particularly during the bombing phase, as these latter were not equipped with air brakes and attempting to dive with the Stukas was likely to prove a terminal experiment.

The Ju 87 also shared the other major fault of all German bomber types: their very small bomb-load. The lack of a 'strategic' German air force has already been noted but it is worth while emphasising just how paltry were the loads that the existing aircraft could carry. The He 111 carried 4,500lb, the Ju 88 4,000lb, the Do 17 just over 2,000lb, and the Ju 87 either one 1,000lb bomb or one 500lb and four 110lb. The British Lancaster and Halifax, for example, carried between 13 and 14,000lb and, moreover, each individual high explosive (h.e.) bomb was usually several times heavier than the German ones, which gave a greatly enhanced destructive power.

The third major weakness affecting the *Luftwaffe* was the remarkably casual way in which its leaders let themselves be drawn into a major air offensive and their failure to give any real thought to the problems involved. Planning, indeed, had been almost non-existent. In the late Thirties it had been realised, quite rightly, that an offensive from Germany was impossible, but neither was much attention paid thereafter to the possibilities of operating from bases in Belgium and France. Right up to the outbreak of war the *Luftwaffe* staged none of the usual map exercises to test the possibilities of air warfare against Britain. When suddenly faced with this task it fell back on vacuous optimism rather than any detailed appraisal of the actual situation. British production figures, for example, were hopelessly underestimated. In July 1940 Göring's Chief of Intelligence, Joseph Schmid, informed him that 'the *Luftwaffe* is clearly superior to the RAF as regards strength, equipment, training, command and location of bases.' With regard to strength it was confidently asserted that British production could only manage perhaps 250 fighters a month. As we saw above, actual British production between July and October was virtually double this estimate, 1,908 planes as opposed to 1,000. The report then went on blithely to claim that British designers, air commanders and pilots were not a patch on their German counterparts and consequently: 'In view of the inferiority of British fighters to German fighters . . . the *Luftwaffe* is in a position to go over to decisive daylight operations owing to the inadequate air defences of the island.'[30]

Finally, of course, this report made no mention of British radar equipment, a network of stations along the coast which gave Fighter Command valuable early warning about the approach of enemy formations and which, most important of all, was backed up by a comprehensive communications system and overseen by a centralised command.* From the very outset of the aerial battle, therefore, the *Luftwaffe* was beset by a whole array of problems, many of them so intractable that recent historians have come to question whether it was ever in the Germans' power to win. Richard Overy, for example, has concluded that 'the technical and organisational advantages enjoyed by the RAF could only have been overcome by massive bomber attacks for which the Germans were ill-prepared or by an overwhelming numerical superiority, which the Luftwaffe lacked.'[31]

The effect of these three major weaknesses largely determined the course of the Battle of Britain. The essential point about the first of these, comparative production rates, has already been made and the figures in table 26 emphasise what a clear advantage the British had. This point does, however, merit a little further examination if only because one of the enduring myths of the Second World War is the supposed paucity of the RAF's resources at this period, and the notion that they were being progressively eroded throughout the battle.

In fact, the strength of Fighter Command, in terms of serviceable aircraft with the front-line squadrons, remained remarkably constant, and whilst it is true that there was some diminution in the fighter reserve in August and September 1940, even this did not reach anything like the crisis proportions claimed by Air Vice-Marshal Keith Park, 11 Group's commander, who told Churchill on 15 September that the reserves were now non-existent. The relevant figures are given in table 27 in the Statistical Appendix, and those for Total Loss/Production, though showing a net loss in September, nevertheless reveal a healthy overall surplus, and one that stands in

---

* At the time 'radar' was known as RDF (Radio Direction Finding). Its contribution to the Battle of Britain was extremely important, but should not be exaggerated. The skill of the operators was crucial and it was only their ability to match observations against previous experience that allowed them to guess at the size of a formation. The personal element was also decisive in determining a formation's height. One should also bear in mind that only 31 per cent of Fighter Command's sorties against enemy aircraft actually made contact with the enemy which, as Alfred Price has noted, indicates that 'the ground control system . . . was still crude and [that] there was considerable room for improvement' (*Blitz on Britain 1939–45* (Ian Allen, Shepperton, 1977), p. 81).

stark contrast to the equivalent German figures. For the four months in question these latter are: 40 single-engined fighters totally lost/164 built in July, 160/173 in August, 310/218 in September and 136/144 in October. The British, on the other hand, produced surpluses of 315, 183 and 293 aircraft in July, August and October (there was a deficit of 9 in September), which meant that they attained a net surplus of 882 aircraft while that of the Germans was only 53. Aerial warfare, as a later chapter on the bomber offensive will emphasise, is largely a matter of attrition, and even during the Battle of Britain this form of struggle was already beyond German capabilities. This is amply confirmed in the following figures, giving the number of serviceable single-engined fighters available to each side on two dates:

	Fighter Command	*Luftwaffe*
1 July 1940	591	725
1 Oct. 1940	734	275

Of course, the availability of aircraft was not the only constraint on the opposing air forces. Pilots were equally indispensable, and it is true that there were times when Fighter Command was very short of new pilots. Ideally, squadrons would contain two dozen or so pilots to keep 12 aircraft operational, but by late August 1940 they had an average of less than 20, only 16 to 18 of whom were deemed fit for operations. Moreover, only 80 new pilots were being trained at that time, as opposed to the 350 or so normally expected to be in the pipeline. So quickly were new pilots being rushed through that some had only 20 hours' solo flying experience before being sent into action. Nevertheless, it would be misleading to present this as a crisis dragging Fighter Command to the brink of defeat. Reference again to table 27 shows quite clearly that even in the worst days of September the actual availability of pilots never dropped particularly alarmingly, one reason being that new recruits were not the only source of fighter pilots. Many were taken from other Commands and so required only a short retraining course rather than having to learn from scratch. In August and September volunteers were taken from Bomber Command's Fairey Battle squadrons, as well as from Army Cooperation, and in the latter month it was also decided to redirect trainees from other Commands. The RAF also had the option of reallocating pilots within Fighter Command itself. Such serious shortages as were felt were largely confined to 11 Group in south-east England, though Dowding insisted on keeping other groups in the south-west and the north up to strength. He remained throughout the Battle extremely reluctant to plunder these to make good shortages elsewhere, but the fact remains that they constituted a considerable reserve of qualified pilots to feed into the battle over the Home Counties should the situation have become truly critical.*

This latter point brings us back to the baleful effects on the *Luftwaffe* of their planes' performance. At issue here is the range of the single-engined fighters, which meant that it was actually impossible for the *Luftwaffe* to defeat Fighter Command *as a whole*. The point has been cogently put by a modern American historian:

> . . . the limited range of German fighter cover allowed the British one option which they never had to exercise: Should the pressure on Fighter Command become too great, they could withdraw their fighters north of London to refit and reorganise; then when the Germans launched 'Sea Lion', they could resume the struggle. Thus in the final analysis, the *Luftwaffe* could do no more than impose on Fighter Command a rate of attrition that its commanders would accept. The Germans were never in a position to attack the RAF over the full length and breadth of its domain.[32]

But the poor capabilities of the German bombers were another factor that seriously vitiated their air effort in the autumn and winter of 1940 and 1941, when Hitler and Göring turned from a direct assault on the RAF to a 'strategic' attack on first London and later the whole of the industrial north of England. The bombers' poor armament remained a major shortcoming and from the very beginning they proved vulnerable to attack by Dowding's Spitfires and Hurricanes, which were specifically directed to concentrate their efforts against the bombers, only engaging the Bf 109s in self-defence. In this they were extremely successful, accounting for 752 bombers and dive-bombers destroyed between July and

---

* On 1 August, in fact, Dowding actually increased the *official* aircraft establishment of a fighter squadron and thus the *theoretical* number of pilots needed. This latter requirement suddenly jumped by about 200, which has led some historians to claim that the pool of pilots suddenly dropped by this amount. It should also be remembered that German pilot losses were even higher than those of Fighter Command. Between July and September 1940 they lost 521 Bf 109 pilots whilst Fighter Command lost 381. The *Luftwaffe* figure represented 57.5 per cent of the number of fighter pilots available for operations at the beginning of the period, the Fighter Command figure 31.7 per cent.

October and 140 damaged. A further 140 were destroyed up to December.*

It was these high losses that eventually forced the *Luftwaffe*, in October 1940, to halt their daylight raids on London, which had begun only a month earlier, and to switch to night bombing. This, it was hoped, could be undertaken without the need for fighter escort, for the bombers' vulnerability in the day, and the hopeless performance of the *Zerstörers*, had necessitated the use of Bf 109s in close escort duties, which had severely curtailed their freedom of manoeuvre. This attachment to the bombers deprived the Messerschmitt pilots of their favourite manoeuvre, a high diving pass out of the sun. Since the Bf 109 could outdive the Hurricane and the Spitfire this was an eminently sensible manoeuvre, but now the RAF fighters as often as not held the height advantage and themselves swooped on the massed bombers and fighters below. It was this surrender of the tactical initiative to Fighter Command that helps explain the latter's remarkable combat record during the Battle of Britain. For not only did they succeed in destroying the 750-odd bombers just cited but they also, between July and October, accounted for 776 German fighters (of which 560 were Bf 109s) for the loss of 787 fighters of their own.

But, if the switch to night raids did something to relieve the attrition of the fighter arm, it did little to slow down bomber losses. Between November and March 1941 almost another 500 bombers were lost. Combat losses were appreciably lower but the hazards of night-flying pushed up the already alarming accident rate. Between October and December 1940, for example, 64 per cent of all bombers destroyed were lost in an accident of one sort or another.

Worse, these losses were largely to no avail, because neither the daylight nor the night Blitz accomplished much in terms of their 'strategic' mission. Even London, the target of the Germans' most sustained and concentrated effort, never came anywhere near to economic or administrative paralysis. Of the attack on the London Docks, the Official Historian remarks:

---

* My figures are considerably higher than those given in other accounts of the Battle of Britain. They, and the figures for fighters given below, are derived from detailed daily tallies given in F. K. Mason's monumental *Battle Over Britain* (McWhirter Twins, 1969), and include all British Category 3 losses from combat and all *Luftwaffe* combat losses of 60 per cent and over.

In the main the basins, quays and gates, and the equipment and railway lines which served them, remained substantially intact; and in the long run the ability of the Port of London to handle the imports and exports needed to keep the capital and the country going was not much impaired. Wise dispersal of food to depots away from the docks reduced the effects of damage to dockland buildings; damage to communications, power stations and the like was seldom lasting.[33]

A major reason for the ineffectiveness of German raids was the low bomb-loads carried, and it is instructive to compare these with the kind of tonnages dropped during the Allied Combined Bombing Offensive. This latter only began to have any real impact in the last months of the war, when a large enough tonnage could be dropped night after night, month after month. Some monthly totals are given in table 28 in the Statistical Appendix and they make it clear that the *Luftwaffe* never even got close to mounting a viable 'strategic' offensive. Thus, whilst the Germans, from September 1940 to February 1941, dropped a little over 30,000 tons of bombs on Britain, the Allies, in the six months from June to November 1944, dropped 600,000 tons, twenty times as much. It is little wonder that the Official Historian's final judgement on the Blitz was that 'it never brought the enemy within sight of inflicting a decisive stroke.'[34]

It is ratios like those in table 28 that hold the fundamental reasons for the failure of the *Luftwaffe* in the Battle of Britain and the Blitz. Certain writers have tended to concentrate upon the Germans' strategic direction of the campaign, asserting that their constant changes over the choice of targets were the main cause of failure. It is true that the *Luftwaffe*'s targeting policy was distinctly erratic, concentrating during successive periods on defeating Fighter Command in the air, on the chain of radar stations, on RAF airfields, on London and on the industrial regions of northern England. It is not true, however, that any of these switches of itself denied the *Luftwaffe* victory. It has been frequently suggested, for example, that the sudden switch from bombing and strafing the airfields to a 'strategic' assault on London was all that saved Fighter Command from extinction. Considering that the whole assault up to 20 September, when the Blitz began, cost Fighter Command only 16 Hurricanes and Spitfires destroyed and no airfields put out of commission for any length of time, this seems a little far-fetched. Certainly, the assault on the airfields did put extra pressure on Fighter Command and the switch to London provided a most welcome breathing-space, but in fact neither phase of operations could do much to change the fundamental strategic realities that determined the outcome of the Battle of Britain. These have been admirably summarised by Richard Overy, who points out:

> . . . even at the most dangerous moments the German air forces were little closer to achieving the aim of air supremacy for long enough to permit a successful invasion than they had been at the beginning of the battle. Moreover the very strategy of overwhelming an air force in a single 'battle' betrayed the Luftwaffe's failure to grasp that air superiority could not be absolute against a well-armed enemy with large economic resources, a fact that had been widely misunderstood among the pre-war air powers. It was impossible under the conditions of the summer of 1940 for the Luftwaffe to eliminate the RAF because it lacked the operational and material means to destroy the British aircraft industry – in fact the attacks spurred on the industrial effort – or to prevent the RAF from regrouping again over the contested area.[35]

Later chapters of this book will show that once Hitler arrayed himself against the material might of both Russia and the USA, his battle, even for mere survival, was hopeless. But it is worth pausing at this early juncture in the narrative to point out that even on a purely European battlefield, with no 'outsiders' involved, the German war effort had got off to a rather shaky start. The *Wehrmacht* had on the whole performed very well and, though the abject incompetence of the Allies might rather have flattered their opponents' abilities, there was still no gainsaying the latter's overall professionalism and the sheer verve and panache of many of their armoured and air commanders. Nevertheless, the war machine as a whole, embracing also the industrial base and the logistical apparatus that was to keep the services supplied with adequate numbers of up-to-date weapons, had *not* shown itself to be on top of the situation. By the middle of 1940 much of Europe lay at Hitler's feet, yet the very extent of his conquests was in danger of blinding him to serious inadequacies in the total war effort.

In fact, as we have already seen, some of these inadequacies had already become apparent during the Battle of Britain when German aircraft production consistently lagged behind the British and when it became increasingly clear that those types that were being produced were not capable of fulfilling the strategic tasks at hand. The *Luftwaffe* might have covered itself with glory in Poland and France, as a tactical arm, undermining enemy morale by its ceaseless attacks on forward positions, but it had done nothing to prove that it could stand up to the attrition of protracted war against the enemy's industrial and logistical base and against his fully mobilised air force. Even the early 'lightning' victories had cost the *Luftwaffe* dear. In Poland 564 planes were lost in the first few days, only the sheer weight of numbers turning the issue Germany's way. These losses represented over 50 per cent of the combat types available for the start of the campaign and over one-third of all combat planes produced in 1939. The losses in France were 1,469 combat aircraft destroyed and damaged, which was over 50 per cent of total combat strength deployed in this theatre and just under 30 per cent of combat aircraft produced in 1940.

The tallies for German ground equipment, notably the tanks, carried a similarly cautionary message. During the invasion of Poland fully one-third of the assembled panzers were Pz Is, armed only with machine-guns, and half were Pz IIs with 20mm cannon. Whilst these were easily a match for the pitifully few, badly armed Polish tanks, there was nevertheless much indigestible food for thought in the fact that, over four years previously, German production plans had confidently anticipated that by 1939 Pz IIIs would form fully three-quarters of their tank force, the Pz Is would be obsolete and the Pz IIs would be used for training only. Things had not improved too much by May 1940. The panzer divisions now included 627 Pz IIIs and IVs as opposed to 309 in September 1939, but this was still only a quarter of the total tank strength. Pz Is and Pz IIs still accounted for 24 and 37 per cent respectively. Moreover, the heavier tanks were now spread amongst ten panzer divisions instead of being concentrated in one élite unit as in Poland. In fact, only half the expected number of companies in these divisions had been re-equipped with Pz IVs and the rest had to make do with rather cumbersome Czech models captured in 1939. Moreover the only way to accommodate Hitler's insistence on expanding the number of panzer divisions had been to reduce the September 1939 total establishment of 328 tanks per division to 240, two-thirds of these still being Pz Is and IIs. A final worrying indicator to the Germans was that, just as with combat aircraft, the loss rates amongst the panzers had been extremely heavy, particularly given the speed with which the opposing forces had collapsed. In Poland 217 were destroyed

BRUTE FORCE

PART ONE

'ONE CAN ONLY OBEY'
The Eastern Front 1941–45

'The tough and spirited German soldier shames the staff which meticulously tots up numbers.'

General Franz Halder, 17 January 1942

'It is a curious thing that although every individual soldier returning from the Eastern Front considers himself personally superior to the Bolshevik soldier, we are still retreating and retreating.'

Joseph Goebbels, 20 September 1943

'Attack! If you have no results today, you will tomorrow; even if you achieve nothing but the pinning of the enemy, the result will be felt elsewhere.'

Joseph Stalin, February 1942

'Comrades, exert yourselves so that we can lay the Hungarian capital at the great Stalin's feet. Fame and rewards await you; if you fail I fear for your health.'

General Rodion Malinovsky, 5 November 1944

1

Blitzkrieg Founders

June 1941 – June 1943

Precipitate and comprehensive as was Britain's defeat on the ground in May 1940, from it there accrued two enormous benefits. One has already been alluded to, namely Dowding's insistence on hoarding all available fighter reserves in England where they remained available for the Battle of Britain. The other was the impact on Hitler of his remarkable victory. Having driven the British off mainland Europe and secured Dutch, Belgian and French surrender within a mere six weeks, he became convinced that German forces were invincible and that there was no political objective that could not be attained through force of arms. One aspect of his analysis of the German victory was very pertinent, in that he correctly perceived that the enemy had been overwhelmed *psychologically*, their command systems completely disrupted by the speed of the German armoured spearheads and by the continual application of firepower, ground-to-ground and air-to-ground, at the critical points along the front. The momentum of German attacks had rarely been relaxed and thus their opponents had been continually denied the expected breathing space to assemble reserves, work out detailed fire plans, or even gain a clear idea of the enemy's own dispositions.

But the very extent of the Allied collapse seduced Hitler and some of his generals into inferring that war was *almost entirely* a psychological contest in which the superior tactics and the more inflexible will to win must always prevail. Such factors are vital, of course, but it was a grave error to assume that they were the *only* important variables in warfare. The biggest omission in the Germans' *ex post facto* analysis was to ignore several of the *specific* factors that helped to explain the speed of their opponents' collapse. For these latter had been fighting in relatively small theatres and, never being given the opportunity to regroup their forces on some potential defensive line, they were soon driven out of their strategic heartlands and left in possession of only a small national rump that offered no real possibility for sustained national resistance. In these circumstances they had felt obliged to throw in the towel long before the fighting became a test of real military muscle that might show up some of the obvious shortcomings of the existing German military machine, notably the logistical inadequacies outlined at the end of the last chapter. In the *blitzkrieg* campaigns, in other words, many Germans were lulled into thinking that the sound and fury of their Stukas would always outweigh their feeble payload and dubious accuracy, that the mere appearance of Pz Is and IIs and ersatz Czech models was more than compensation for their tiny guns and flimsy armour, and that the mobility of the relatively few panzer divisions meant that one need not worry about the continuing reliance of the mass of the infantry on horse-transport and their own feet. A modest proportion of motorised infantry and artillery might have sufficed in Poland and France, where the enemy was hardly motorised at all or bereft of the communications to move such units where they were most needed, but it was unlikely to be adequate in an extensive theatre of war, against large enemy numbers, where the presence of entire divisions was essential for the effective sealing-off of large encirclements.

But after the French surrender Hitler and most of his gener-als seem to have virtually ignored the fact that warfare might have a logistic dimension, usually being fought over time and space and only exceptionally decided in almost instantaneous clashes between the whole mass of the opposing armies. To be sure, when the latter *was* the case an eminently superior tactical sys-tem would usually bring speedy and decisive victory, but rarely would it of itself bring long-term, immutable strategic advantage. At some stage or other, a belligerent who relied exclusively upon superior tactics alone would come upon an enemy, or combina-tion of enemies, that was capable of absorbing repeated setbacks by using its geographical space fatally to dissipate the enemy's forces, and its superior productive resources to recreate ever larger forces of its own. The military careers of Gustavus Adolphus's successors in the Thirty Years' War, of Charles XII of Sweden, of Frederick the Great after 1763, of Napoleon, of Ludendorff after America's entry into the First World War, all testified to the ultimate decisiveness of such factors. Yet Hitler would have none of it. At a time when one of his original enemies in the

West was still unbeaten, and when that enemy was benefiting from the more than benevolent neutrality of the most powerful industrial nation on earth, he actually chose to go to war on a completely different front against an enemy whose own industrial and manpower resources were considerable, whose geographical space allowed almost infinite opportunity for strategic withdrawal and whose climatic rigours had long been a commonplace of military epic.

By the summer of 1940, then, Hitler and the German High Command seem to have been convinced that they had discovered a radically new mode of warfare that could swiftly overcome any opposition and that was somehow independent of orthodox strategic constraints. Despite the fact that the *Wehrmacht*'s successes were already tarnished by the failure of the *Luftwaffe* seriously to damage either the economy or the political fabric of such a small, centralised state as Britain, and by that of the Army and Navy effectively to combine to bridge the 20 or 30 miles of the English Channel, Hitler and his generals managed to convince themselves that the total collapse of the Soviet Union could be brought about in just a few weeks of spirited campaigning. All their planning in 1940 and early 1941* showed that they had largely jettisoned any notion of warfare as an attritional activity and were now placing an almost mystical faith in the results of rapid movement, breakthrough and encirclement. The Marcks Plan of 1 August 1940 stated baldly:

> Because the Russians no longer possess the superiority of numbers they had in the World War [sic], it is more likely that once the long, extended line of their forces has been broken through they will be unable to concentrate or coordinate counter-measures. Fighting in isolated battles, they will soon succumb to the superiority of the German troops and leadership.[1]

The OKH Deployment Directive of 31 January 1941 was equally sanguine about the likely course of operations:

* Hitler first expressed his probable intention of turning eastward in late June 1940. On 21 July the OKH was ordered to outline the problems of a campaign against the Soviet Union, and on the 31st Hitler announced that a pre-emptive strike would definitely be launched in spring 1941. From then on planning went ahead steadily and without interruption.

The first intention of the OKH within the task allotted is by means of swift and deep thrusts by strong mobile forces north and south of the Pripet Marshes to tear open the front of the mass of the Russian Army which it is anticipated will be in West Russia. The enemy groups separated by these penetrations will then be destroyed.[2]

In a conversation with one of his designated Army Group commanders, Field Marshal Fedor von Bock, on 1 February 1941, Hitler expressed just this same blithe optimism. According to the former:

The Führer . . . regards Russia's collapse as a foregone conclusion . . . I remarked that we can defeat the Russians if they stand and fight, but it may be difficult to convince them to talk in terms of peace. The Führer replied that we are militarily and economically in excellent condition and if the Russians continue to resist . . . we will simply advance all the way to Siberia . . . 'Nevertheless,' I told him, 'we should be prepared for reverses.' Hitler replied pointedly, 'I am convinced that they will think a hurricane has hit them.'[3]

Yet it is impossible to find among the German records any hard-headed analysis of just why the Russian Army was supposed to collapse so abjectly. The underlying impression they give is one of simple wishful thinking. An early planning conference in July 1940 does reveal some evidence of concern about Russian recuperative powers and the dangers of German forces being drawn into a protracted war, the conference minutes warning that 'the quicker we smash Russia the better. Operations only make sense if we smash the state heavily in one blow. Winning a certain amount of territory only does not suffice. A standstill during the winter hazardous.'[4] Thereafter, however, the realisation that the war *ought* to be a short one was translated into the blithe assurance that it *would* be so, no matter how unpropitious the actual military facts.

For unpropitious they most certainly were. A glance at the balance of forces at the beginning of Operation Barbarossa, on 22 June 1941 (table 2), shows that it hardly gave the Germans a decisive edge. Now these figures, particularly on the Russian side, are fraught with qualifications. That for manpower is only an informed guess, and even if the suggestion of near parity with the Germans is correct, it should be recognised that the Red Army divisions were nowhere near as well organised as their opponents.* For one thing they were in the midst of a far-reaching redeployment. In mid-May 1941 the High Command ordered the setting up of a Front of Reserve Armies, to be established in the rear of the forces on the frontier to act as a unified counter-attack force. Sixty or so divisions were pulled out of the Far East, the Urals and other areas and were mostly actually on the move when the Germans struck in late June. Even those that had reached their new sectors were largely caught on the hop, as proper command structures had not yet been set up and most were being re-equipped, along with their air support units.

Table 2: *German and Russian strengths*
at the beginning of Operation Barbarossa, 22 June 1941

		German	Russian*
Men:	*German*	3,150,000	3,000,000
	Allies	530,000†	
Tanks		3,332	12,000
Artillery		7,184	5,900
Mil. Aircraft		2,770	10,000

* On Russia's western front.

† 18 Finnish divisions, 14 Romanian divisions, 3 Slovakian divisions, 1 Hungarian division (equiv.), 3 Italian divisions (from 7 August 1941) and 1 Spanish division (from 1 September 1941).

Other factors also contributed to the general state of disorganisation. At the same time as they were bringing their reserve formations forward, the Russians decided to pull many specialist units – light tank, engineer, signals etc. – back from the frontier itself and redeploy them within the Reserve Armies. But prior to May these units had been organically attached to the old-style infantry divisions on the frontier and so the German attack found these latter without any specialist support and the former with little idea of to whom they were actually responsible. Command relationships were

* Though German superiority should not be overstated, as Hitler's insistence on raising as many new divisions as possible had led to a considerable dilution of the general level of experience and expertise. 'As early as September 26, 1940, the chief of the General Staff's organisation branch informed Halder that too many divisions were being created. Even Hitler's closest military advisor, General Alfred Jodl, concluded that the Führer's decision to field 20 half-strength Panzer divisions constituted a waste of support troops and specialists. The Chief of the General Staff began to speak in terms of "good divisions and bad divisions" on August 12, 1940.' (S. J. Lewis, *Forgotten Legions: German Army Infantry Policy 1918–41* (Praeger, New York, 1985), p. 126.)

further vitiated by the fact that since 1937 a large proportion of the professional, long-service officer corps had been eliminated in Stalin's purges. Three out of five marshals, 13 out of 15 army commanders, 55 per cent of divisional and brigade commanders, 80 per cent of colonels and 43 per cent of all other officers had been liquidated or cast into limbo. The thousands of new officers who had been drafted in had had almost no experience of actual warfare and were virtual strangers to the men under their command, if indeed they were sure whom they were actually commanding. As one scholar has written:

> Hitler caught the Red Army at the worst possible time for the Soviet High Command; a year later and it would have been re-equipped and redeployed, and six months earlier there would have been far fewer men, guns and tanks in the frontier salients waiting for their ammunition, fuel and transport and almost inviting encirclement by the German armoured columns.[5]

But many of the Russian tanks would have needed more than just fuel and ammunition, and it was the Red Army's armoured units that displayed the greatest gulf between paper strengths and reality. In theory the Red Army's preponderance in tanks was overwhelming, the 12,000 machines at the front being supplemented by an equal number in the rear areas. In fact, not many of them actually worked; according to Russian sources only 27 per cent were in any sort of running order. Many of these, moreover, were light tanks with puny guns that were no match for the German Pz III and IVs. In fact, only 1,475 of the available Russian tanks at the front (967 T-34s and 508 KV-1s) could be deemed truly battleworthy, having powerful 76mm or 85mm guns, a good turn of speed and excellent cross-country ability. These, however, were not concentrated in a few powerful formations but were scattered throughout the sprawling military districts. One reason for this was that the Russian tank arm was also in the midst of a comprehensive reorganisation, into large mechanised corps each of two tank and one motorised infantry division. These were to be re-equipped with T-34s and KV-1s when sufficient numbers became available, but production figures had thus far been very disappointing and few units had even seen one of the new weapons. So the German invasion found many of the armoured formations equipped with only token numbers of obsolete models until the new ones might appear.

Despite all these qualifications, however, it is still clear that Hitler had set his forces a formidable task. The Russian artillery, for example, was probably their best arm and the German superiority of 1,200 pieces was hardly overwhelming on such an extended front. Similarly, the 20 per cent margin in troops, even granted their much superior organisation and training, was a slender one to carry out a strategy based upon the complete sealing off of large pockets of the enemy along the whole length of the frontier. But the most serious shortfalls were those of tanks and aircraft, the indispensable tools of the *blitzkrieg* victories Hitler was now hoping to repeat. For the Russians were not the only ones fielding obsolete equipment. Though the Germans had amassed over 3,000 tanks for Barbarossa, many of these were the small and undergunned Pz Is (of which there were 410), Pz IIs (746) and Pz 38(t)s (772). Only the 1,404 Panzer IIIs and IVs, in fact, were battle tanks in any real sense of the word. Yet even they were hardly state-of-the-art. The Panzer IIIs, 965 of them, had recently been rearmed on Hitler's orders, having their 37mm guns replaced with 50mm. Hitler had specified that these latter should be the long L60 version, with a high muzzle velocity and penetrative power, but the Ordnance Department, for no logical reason, had opted for the short L42 with a markedly inferior performance.* In February 1941, eight months after his original order, Hitler discovered what had been done. A programme to replace all the L42s was instituted but by June a mere 44 Panzer IIIs had been properly upgunned. The 439 Mark IVs that took part in the invasion were all armed with the short 75mm gun, but this still meant that in tanks of this calibre the Germans were outnumbered almost four to one. They were thus putting an awful lot of faith in the ability of the panzer divisions to triumph solely through superior tactics and organisation.

The Germans were cutting things equally fine in the air, gambling that the expertise of the *Luftwaffe* and the obsolescence of much Soviet equipment would compensate for any numerical inferiority. It was also believed that the Soviet aircraft industry was small and inefficient, unable to produce replacements of either the old types or more modern variants in any significant number. This was a serious miscalculation. The Soviet aircraft industry had already achieved much even before the outbreak of war, not only raising its strength to almost double the German estimate of 5,500 machines but also producing some 3,700 new types, such as the Yak-1,

---

* The respective muzzle velocities for the L42 and L60 were 450 to 685 metres per second and 1,180 metres per second.

MiG-3, LaGG-3 and Il-2, that were well able to stand up to their *Luftwaffe* equivalents. These new models were intended to form the backbone of a rejuvenated Russian air force and thus, though the *Luftwaffe* was to have extraordinary success in the opening weeks of Barbarossa, 'the bulk of the very many aircraft destroyed . . . were already obsolete, the *Luftwaffe* simply completing a job that was already being carried out by the Red Air Force itself.'[6] Clearly Hitler was making fearful demands on his pilots, in expecting them both to eliminate an enemy air force whose original strength was almost four times their own in the east* and to *keep on* knocking out the modern replacements that were already being produced three or four times faster than in Germany.

But the *Wehrmacht*'s problem entailed more than a simple comparison of numbers. Of equal importance was the question of whether the troops and weapons they could deploy were adequate to fulfil their prescribed tasks within the chosen theatre of war. The whole success of Barbarossa depended on swift and annihilating strikes by the armour and aircraft, and both would have to cover vast distances and areas to make such strikes fully effective. On the tanks rested the whole responsibility for the initial rupture of the Russian front, following which they were to press forward and, like assiduous sheepdogs, herd together all the disorganised Russian units they confronted. The actual liquidation of the pockets formed was to be done by the infantry, the plodding shepherds behind, but until such time as they arrived it was up to the armoured spearheads to ensure that only a minimum of Russian troops escaped to be reformed in the rear areas. This was a formidable task, for sheepdogs have to cover remarkable distances to gather in a flock, constantly zigzagging back and forth to head off the recalcitrants. And in this case they were dealing with particularly large flocks, spread over a vast pasture. The problem has been succinctly stated by a recent historian for whom one of the key reasons for the failure of Barbarossa

> . . . undoubtedly was that . . . [Hitler] did not provide his generals with sufficient forces. He probably failed to give them sufficient men; certainly he failed to give them sufficient equipment . . . The Nazis in 1940 had 2,580 tanks at the start of their campaign [in France]; and this works out at approximately one tank per 75 sq.km. In the Soviet Union, by contrast, the

---

* Nor did it help that fully one third of these German planes were in need of service or repair.

Germans' total of 3,702 tanks* only works out at a density of one per 291 sq.km.[7]

Field Marshal Albert Kesselring, then in command of *Luftflotte* 2, responsible for supporting Army Group Centre, felt that the ultimate aim of Barbarossa, the complete destruction of the Red Army, was impossible simply because 'for this task the Panzer Groups were too weak. Our strategic mechanised forces had to be proportionate to the depth and breadth of the area to be conquered and to the enemy, and we had not anywhere near this strength.'[8] Kesselring also emphasised the point about the plodding shepherds, noting that the German infantry who were to seal off the great Russian pockets properly, and whose firepower was essential to their actual destruction, simply could not move swiftly enough to prevent large numbers of the enemy escaping. Indeed, it must always remain something of a puzzle how such a sober body of men as the German General Staff could ever have convinced themselves that a highly mobile war could be conducted by an army whose infantry divisions comprised 78 per cent of the total[†] and which depended heavily for their mobility on the services of 600,000 horses.

The problem of numbers relative to the space to be covered also badly hampered air operations. These were almost entirely to be concerned with ground support. As Kesselring wrote: 'My orders . . . were primarily to gain air superiority, and if possible air supremacy, and to support the Army, especially the Panzer Groups in their battle with the Russian Army. Any further assignments would lead to a further dissipation and must at first be shelved.'[9] Yet this task of supporting the army was itself to lead to the maximum dispersion of resources, with aircraft at the beck and call of the armoured units as they rampaged hither and thither in the forward areas, as well as the infantry well to the rear. Instead of undertaking concentrated strategic attacks on Russian war *potential*, such as her industrial base, administrative centres, rail communications and assembly points for reserve formations, the *Luftwaffe* became entirely involved in *ad hoc* tactical actions up and down the whole front.

The diffusion of effort involved is again emphasised in Vigor's

---

* No two sources agree on the exact number of tanks used at the beginning of Barbarossa. My figure of 3,332 is taken from M. Cooper, *The German Army 1939–45* (Macdonald and Jane's, 1978), p. 276.

† Based on the number of divisions supposed to be in action by 20 July 1941, i.e. 19 panzer divisions, 13 motorised, 1 cavalry and 150 infantry.

figures, showing as they do that 'in the 1940 campaign the *Luftwaffe* had to operate over a battlefield which, in all, amounted to 193,800 sq. km., and this gives a density of aircraft of one plane per 51 sq. km. On the Eastern Front the battle area consisted of 1,076,250 sq. km. This gives a ratio of one plane to every 245 sq. km.'[10] Equally serious was the fact that although the *Luftwaffe* had been assigned a mainly ground-support role during Barbarossa, it had not been supplied with the proper equipment. Of the five Air Corps to be employed on this front, only one had the requisite number of dive-bombers and other ground-support aircraft. All the others were forced to use their twin-engined bombers and single-engined fighters in this role, in which the bombers showed themselves to be extremely vulnerable and the fighters less than effective. Moreover, both types of aircraft lacked the dive-bombers' ability to land almost anywhere with impunity and were thus incapable of providing continuous support during a swift advance by the ground forces.

Yet another serious problem for the Germans was their assumption that the campaign in the east would be so short, and casualties so light, that there was no need to give serious thought to the question of replacing men or machines. That the human replacement system was inadequate became speedily apparent. By 26 August 1941 the German army in Russia had already suffered 440,000 battle casualties, yet replacements in the same period totalled only 217,000. Even as a percentage of total German forces in Russia, 7.1 per cent, this shortfall was not insignificant. But when it is remembered that 80 to 90 per cent of battle casualties were suffered by men in the infantry battalions, who themselves constituted only 30 per cent of total army presence, then it will be appreciated that the loss of *combat* soldiers was much more serious – as much as 20 per cent.

The supply of replacement machines was also inadequate, thanks largely to two remarkable decisions by Hitler. The first, in September 1940, decreed that aircraft production was to be substantially cut back. And so it was, to the extent that by February 1941 it had fallen by as much as 40 per cent. As one scholar has commented: 'The decision to reduce aircraft production to this extent seems almost incredible, considering that in September, the very month the decision was made, the number of aircraft lost in the Air Battle of Britain was substantially in excess of new production.'[11] It seems more incredible still when one recalls that by this time Hitler was already firmly resolved to add Barbarossa to his military commitments.

The second decision was taken towards the end of July 1941, after the campaign in Russia had been going for only a few weeks, and again involved a substantial retrenchment, this time in the production of army equipment. The drops entailed are detailed in table 3.

Table 3: *German army munitions production during 1941*

Weapon	Month in which 1941 maximum was reached	Decline from maximum by December
Light inf. arms	April	-38%
Heavy inf. arms	August	-49%
Army artillery	April	-67%
A/A artillery	November	-29%

The almost 70 per cent drop in army artillery production between April and December 1941 seems little short of military lunacy.

The index of army production as a whole for 1941 tells the same story. Taking the figure for the first three months as the base (100), those for the successive three quarters were 91, 80 and 62 respectively. Only tank production remained exempt from Hitler's decision and so rose throughout the year, from 598 tanks in the first quarter to 988 in the last. The monthly increase was slow, however, an average increment of only ten tanks, and total production for the year compared badly with both German losses and with enemy production. In all 3,790 tanks and assault guns were produced, but losses on the Eastern Front had reached 2,850 by the end of the year. Moreover, only 2,875 of the armoured fighting vehicles produced were medium tanks (i.e. Panzers III and IV) or assault guns,* whilst total Russian production was 6,590, of which 4,135 were T-34s or KV-1s, all with 76mm guns or better.

But if, even before Barbarossa, there were good reasons to doubt the *Wehrmacht*'s ability to put sufficient men and machines into the field, there should have been yet more reservations about its capacity

---

* Tracked armoured fighting vehicles in the Second World War were divided into four basic types: tanks, tank destroyers, assault guns and self-propelled artillery. The basic functional distinctions between them, in theory at least, was that tanks were to be used in a mobile role, *en masse*, to create breaks in the enemy line that infantry following up might exploit; tank destroyers, usually mounting proved anti-tank guns, were to be deployed close behind the front to prevent such breakthroughs; assault guns, usually mounting non-traversable guns, were meant to provide close, direct-fire support for the infantry (the British Infantry Tank, as opposed to the Cruiser, was essentially an assault gun with a turret); self-propelled guns were artillery on tracked carriages to provide mobile but almost always indirect-fire support.

adequately to supply even those that were there. There were three potential areas of difficulty: the limited availability of ammunition and of fuel, and serious shortcomings in the actual functioning of the German supply system. Ammunition stocks were depleted just as much as those of other munitions by the Hitler decision already cited. The value of production for light infantry weapons fell from 12.9 million Reichsmarks in April 1941 to 6.3 million in December and that of artillery ammunition from 69.1 million Reichsmarks in February to 15.7 million in December. Because of this, the final plans for the Russian campaign were vitiated by some highly questionable assumptions about rates of ammunition expenditure. Early planning had reasonably assumed that the campaign might last five months or more, whilst the commander of the Replacement Army, the depot in Germany responsible for making up front-line losses, who was more aware than most of the fallibility of all operational plans, had urged that reserves be established for a 12-month campaign. By June, however, the planners had convinced themselves that expenditure would be very similar to that in France and so the divisions could rely on those stocks they actually carried with them, plus an unspecified reserve for a mere 20 divisions more.

Such thought as was given to fuel consumption was based on equally dubious extrapolations from the French campaign. Thus, though even in a short campaign the mobile units and the air force would have to cover much greater distances than in France, a reserve of no more than three months' consumption (in the case of diesel oil only one month)* was built up. And this was a reserve for three months of 'normal' consumption. In Russia, as surely at least some planners must have been aware, many of the roads hardly merited the name, and would place enormous demands on engines and fuel consumption. The Germans might be excused for not appreciating the full extent to which fuel consumption would be affected but one could surely expect them to have made some allowance.† As it was, the few supply officers who expressed any concern were calmed with vague reassurances about utilising deliveries from the Romanian oil-fields direct to the front or falling back on captured Russian stocks. The feasibility of the latter option was rather limited by the fact that Russian petrol had a very low octane rating and could only be used

---

* Even though diesel oil represented 75 per cent of the Army's normal consumption of all petrol products.

† Events were to show that fuel consumption in Russia was three to four times that consumed under normal conditions in Europe.

by German vehicles if laced with benzol, which could only be done in specially constructed installations in the rear.

The third problem was the serious doubt about the Germans' ability actually to get the ammunition and fuel to the front, their supply apparatus being seriously deficient with regard to both road and rail transport. Ideally, an operation on the scale of Barbarossa needed to rely heavily on rail transport, with its considerable benefits in terms of cost and labour efficiency, and of range, and this the Germans intended to do. Again, however, the planners seem to have been remarkably sanguine, for even a cursory appraisal of the difficulties involved should have revealed that the Russian rail network could only be of limited value, at least in the crucial early weeks of the campaign. The key problem was that it utilised a different gauge to that in Europe and thus all track would have to be converted to accommodate German rolling stock. Some troops were detailed to this task but they were too few in number, poorly trained for this particular operation, and hopelessly short of fuel, motor transport and signals and communications gear. In theory, there remained the option of using captured Russian locomotives and wagons. However, there was no guarantee that many of these would be left intact by Russian demolition teams, and any attempt to combine German gauges and rolling stock with Russian would inevitably create terrible bottlenecks at those points where supplies had to be manhandled from one type of track to the other.

The opening weeks of the campaign soon highlighted the gulf between the planners' vague hopes and the reality of the situation. Whereas 'one railway behind each army was the normal requirement, conditions in the East were such that it was possible to construct only one line behind each army group.'[12] But neither had proper provision been made for an adequate reserve of motor transport to support the efforts of the railway troops. Certain steps had been taken. Units in the rear gave up their trucks and lorries to the motorised divisions, large purchases were made in Switzerland, civilian commercial vehicles were requisitioned and replaced by ones looted from France, and 75 of the Barbarossa divisions were each equipped with 200 Russian one-horse *panje* carts instead of motor transport. Despite all these measures, however, the motorised supply system remained quite inadequate to its task. One authority has made some calculations that summarise its problems. Even the most optimistic German forecasts about the course of the Russian campaign had assumed that the Red Army could not be defeated within less than 300 miles from their western frontier. Much of this distance was to be covered very quickly, which meant that as soon as army and army group supply units were called upon to replenish divisional stocks, their lorries would have to undertake very long round trips. So long, in fact, that the forward divisions could only each expect to receive an average of 70 tons of supplies per day, one-third of which would be rations. The normal requirement of mechanised divisions for mobile operations was 300 tons per day and that of infantry divisions 200. But if the mechanised divisions *were* given their full allotment this 'would mean that, at a distance 300 miles from the starting point, all the army's . . . [rear echelon] transport put together would be barely sufficient to supply them alone, leaving absolutely nothing for the remaining 111 divisions.'[13]

All in all then, as an example of realistic operational analysis, German planning for the Barbarossa campaign left a great deal to be desired. Justifiably worried about getting drawn into a protracted slogging match in Russia, their High Command resolved that the campaign must be short and sweet, the major battles fought relatively close to the Polish and Romanian borders and the whole campaign over before the onset of winter. Unfortunately, their only evidence that this could be done was drawn from quite different campaigns, in Poland and France, where the theatre of war was much more compact, so that movement was quicker and more reliable, units could operate within proper supporting distance of one another, and the major strategic objectives, e.g. the enemy capital, were within reasonable range.* Russia was quite a different proposition, and much larger forces were required to allow any real chance of duplicating the successes of 1939 and 1940. These forces the Germans simply did not possess, neither the manpower nor the machines, and worse still they were in no position to guarantee that even those they had could be kept properly supplied. But this never seems to have made any real impression on the German High Command. Hitler had decreed that Russia would be crushed, and therefore it would be done. Any rational objections to this thesis were repressed beneath blithe assurances about the ineptitude and obsolescence of the Soviet military and increasingly blinkered assertions that everything would be over so quickly that normal military constraints simply did

* The distance from the German frontier to Warsaw had been 160 miles and that from the Belgian frontier to Paris 220 miles. But 550 miles separated Moscow from the new German frontier in Poland.

not apply.* As one commentator has put it, referring to the glaring deficiencies in ammunition, fuel, replacements and logistical back-up:

> It might be expected that these shortages would have induced the German leadership to reconsider the rationale of the whole campaign. Instead of so doing, however, they managed to convince themselves that what they had originally estimated would take five months to achieve could, in fact, be achieved in four, or even in one. The German general staff seems to have abandoned rational thought at this point. Rather than cutting down their goals to suit their limited means, they persuaded themselves that their original calculations were overcautious, and that the goals could be achieved more easily than they first estimated.[14]

Equally reprehensible was the complete failure to face up to the grave consequences of the campaign *not* being won in the specified few weeks. For should this be so, then all the problems discussed above would be magnified tenfold. Low production figures would be felt more and more keenly as losses mounted. If the initial encirclements were not swift and complete, some of the Russians at least would extricate themselves and draw the Germans deeper into the hinterland, lengthening their supply lines yet more and dispersing their forces along an ever-broadening front. On top of this, the weather would ineluctably deteriorate as the short summer gave way first to autumn mud and then to the fearsome

---

* Though there were a few soldiers who took a more realistic line. In an analysis of the French campaign, von Manstein stated that 'in future all nations would mass their tanks, motorise their infantry and use their air force aggressively in ground combat. There would be no more cheap victories.' (Lewis, op. cit., p. 112.) General Friedrich Paulus, an OKH staff officer in charge of a preliminary war game of the Russian campaign, emphasised that the Germans must encircle and destroy the bulk of the Russian armies along the frontiers as well as ensure the speedy capture of Moscow. 'Should this objective not be attained . . . [the planners] foresaw a long drawn-out war beyond the capacity of the German Armed Forces to wage' (W. Goerlitz, *Paulus and Stalingrad* (Methuen, 1963), p. 107). General Johannes von Blaskowitz was in command of the French occupation forces when he first heard of the decision to invade Russia. His Chief-of-Staff witnessed him receive 'the news in silence, finally leaning forward and placing his hands on a globe resting on the desk, softly spinning the orb until confronted with the familiar representation of Europe. Then, in measured tones he at last spoke: "See this tiny spot here – that's us. And all the rest? Now tell me about hubris." ' (Lewis, op. cit., p. 112.)

extremes of winter. Movement would be slowed to a snail's pace and such progress as was made would exact a terrible price on both the internal combustion engines of the motorised forces and the horses of the infantry divisions. The lorries and trucks of the supply echelons would be likewise affected, as well as the German locomotives, most of which did not have boilers, pistons etc. capable of withstanding very low temperatures. Motorised traffic would use yet more fuel as it laboured through the mud and snow – including, of course, the vehicles actually transporting the fuel – and less would be left for the units at the front. And less, too, for the aircraft, though this might not be as much of a problem simply because they would have to spend much of their time on the ground when conditions were totally unsuitable for useful reconnaissance or ground support operations. As the commanders' whistles blew on 22 June 1941 the two von Moltkes, von Schlieffen and Ludendorff must, sedately and simultaneously, have turned in their graves.

The basics of the Barbarossa plan were very straightforward. German forces were divided into three army groups, North, Centre and South, and each was supported by a *Luftflotte*, respectively numbers 1, 2 and 4. Each of the Army Groups (henceforth A Gp) was spearheaded by one Panzer Group (Pz Gp), except for A Gp Centre which had two. These were Pz Gps 2 and 3, whilst Pz Gp 1 was with A Gp South and Pz Gp 4 with A Gp North.* A Gps North and Centre had axes of advance to the north of the Pripet Marshes and A Gp South to the south. A Gp North's primary objectives were the Baltic states and Leningrad. Their assault on the latter city would, it was hoped, be supported by Marshal Mannerheim's Finns, attacking on each side of Lake Lagoda. A Gp Centre's main axis was towards Smolensk and Moscow, whilst that of A Gp South took in Kiev and the bend of the Dnieper. The major battles, however, were to be fought west of a line running through Leningrad, Smolensk, Kiev and the north-west Crimea. The maximum number of Russian

* The three army groups were sub-divided and commanded as follows:

A Gp North (von Leeb):	Pz Gp 4 (Hoepner) 16 Army (Busch)	18 Army (von Küchler) *Luftflotte* 1 (Keller)
A Gp Centre (von Bock):	Pz Gp 2 (Guderian) Pz Gp 3 (Hoth) 4 Army (von Kluge)	9 Army (Strauss) 2 Army (von Weichs) HQ only *Luftflotte* 2 (Kesselring)
A Gp South (von Rundstedt)	Pz Gp 1 (von Kleist) 6 Army (von Stulpnagel)	11 Army (von Schobert) *Luftflotte* 4 (Löhr)

troops were to be trapped in huge pockets between this line and the frontier. The pockets were to be pegged out by armoured pincers that had sliced through the line of Russian defences and then completely destroyed as the slower infantry armies moved up to establish a firm cordon. In these huge killing grounds* the great mass of the Russian Army was to be liquidated and complete victory as good as won. Subsequent operations, including the taking of Moscow, the Crimea, Kharkov and the Caucasus, with an anticipated advance to the line Archangel–Astrakhan–Baku, would be part of the final pursuit, involving little more than the brushing back of a disorganised rabble.

Early German operations enjoyed much success and went some considerable way towards fulfilling the aims of the Barbarossa Directive.† A Gp Centre had the best of it, in seven weeks executing four successive encirclements at Bialystok, Volkovysk, Minsk and Smolensk, capturing over 600,000 men and 5,000 tanks as well as killing and destroying thousands more. The flank army groups, however, did not fare quite as well. A Gp South was seriously delayed around Lwow and later harried on its left by repeated forays from the supposedly impenetrable Pripet Marshes. By early August, therefore, when the Smolensk pocket had been virtually eliminated, it had only managed to pull off one encirclement, locked on Uman, in which some 100,000 Russian prisoners had been taken. A Gp North had no 'cauldrons'‡ to boast of at all. The terrain covered by Pz Gp 4 proved less than helpful to the armour and the Group was only able to push the Russians back, rather than hemming large numbers against the Baltic coast. Moreover, by early August Leningrad had still not fallen, a great disappointment to Hitler and his planners. Yet the fault was largely theirs. Massed armour having served so well in the open country of Poland and France,

> it came to be assumed that tanks were the answer to all tactical situations; terrain was not taken into account. Too much was asked of the panzer arm, and its planning, which consisted of little more than drawing lines across a map and calling them

* See map, page 56.
† These 'Directives for the Conduct of the War' were issued by the OKW and were usually signed by the Supreme Commander (*der Oberste Befehlshaber der Wehrmacht*), Hitler himself. Occasionally, however, they were signed by Keitel, as Hitler's Chief of Staff in this capacity.
‡ From the German word *Kessel*, and denoting a massive encirclement *à la* Cannae.

axes, was done for it by Hitler and the High Command. Military operations had left the realms of the practicable and were based on ill-founded optimism.[15]

But spirited Russian resistance was also a factor, particularly strong positions being encountered behind the River Luga, where von Manstein's LVI Panzer Corps shuttled back and forth for six weeks in July and August, seeking a weak point in the enemy line and on at least one occasion having to repel heavy counter-attacks.*

Even A Gp Centre could not claim unqualified success, again because of heavy Russian resistance. In late June Pz Gp 3 was held back to seal off the Minsk pocket rather than leaving this to the infantry of 9 Army whilst the tanks dashed on to Smolensk. They remained around Minsk for ten days, a delay that allowed the Russians to establish defensive positions along the upper Dvina and behind the Beresina and upper Dnieper. These were further to delay the Smolensk thrust when it did finally begin. It is perhaps arguable that Pz Gp 3 would have become dangerously overextended had it pushed on immediately for Smolensk, but it is equally the case that its failure to do so gave the Russians the opportunity to assemble stragglers and fresh troops who put up stout resistance around Borisov and Mogilev (4–14 July) and Vitebsk (3–11 July). Many of these troops continued to fight bitterly even as the Smolensk nut-cracker was finally being squeezed, so that fully four weeks elapsed between the mopping up of the Minsk and Smolensk 'cauldrons'. And each week had been a terrible drain on German manpower. Total casualties between the opening of Barbarossa and 3 August were 232,000, which total was half as many again as the number lost in France and Belgium in an equivalent period and which had to be set against less decisive progress.

But it was the unsatisfactory progress on the flanks that monopolised Hitler's attention. On 19 July, therefore, just as the Smolensk pocket had been closed, he ordered Pz Gp 2 to forget the anticipated

---

* Though an unusual degree of tactical inflexibility made the German task more difficult than it might have been. On 24 July, for example, XLI Pz Corps was halted to wait for LVI Pz Corps to breach the Luga–Lake Ilmen gap. It was thus denied the opportunity to utilise an open road to Leningrad. On 30 July General Hans Reinhardt, the commander of XLI Panzer Corps, wrote in his diary: 'More delays. It's terrible. The chance that we opened up has been missed for good, and things are getting more difficult all the time.' (Quoted in P. Carell, *Hitler's War on Russia* (Pan Books, 1967), p. 242.) When the advance was resumed, on 8 August, the road was firmly blocked.

Moscow axis and to turn due south to assist A Gp South in the creation of a vast encirclement behind Kiev. Also to assist was 2 Army, which now had under its command 4 Army's infantry divisions. The order was ill-received by the panzer group commander, General Heinz Guderian, who promptly tried to get himself so embroiled in offensive operations around Roslavl that the move south would prove impossible and the Moscow axis would perforce regain priority. General Franz Halder, the OKH Chief of Staff, was also less than pleased, feeling that this insistence on physically eliminating enemy units along the whole front was robbing the army of the opportunity to use its main mobile elements to keep the Russians off-balance. As he wrote on 21 August, after Hitler had tired of Guderian's prevarication and reiterated that Pz Gp 2 and 2 Army must be sent south, this insistence on cleaning out the Kiev area represented

> a shift of our strategy from the operational to the tactical level. If striking at small concentrations becomes our sole objective, the campaign will resolve itself into a series of minor successes which will advance our front only by inches. Pursuing such a policy eliminates all tactical risks and enables us gradually to close the gaps between the fronts of the army groups, but the result will be that we feed all our strength into a front expanding in width at the sacrifice of depth, and end up with position warfare.[16]

In short, it would spell the end of *blitzkrieg*.

But Hitler's orders were sacrosanct and the move went ahead, as did the similar transfer of another of A Gp Centre's panzer corps* to A Gp North to assist in the push on Leningrad. A Gp Centre, in anticipation of these moves, had already been ordered to halt, still around Smolensk, on 15 August. In certain respects, the ensuing operations rather belied Halder's forebodings. The sealing off of the Kiev pocket went ahead with hardly a hitch and when it was finally eliminated, on 26 September, over 600,000 prisoners had been taken, as well as 880 tanks and over 5,000 guns. The panzer corps transferred north, however, had less impact and A Gp North failed to get more than a few advance guards into the suburbs of Leningrad. This in turn persuaded the Finns to decline to participate in a concerted attack, and on 14 September Hitler had to issue a somewhat rhetorical decree that Leningrad was to be starved and bombed into surrender.

---

* XXXIX Pz Corps.

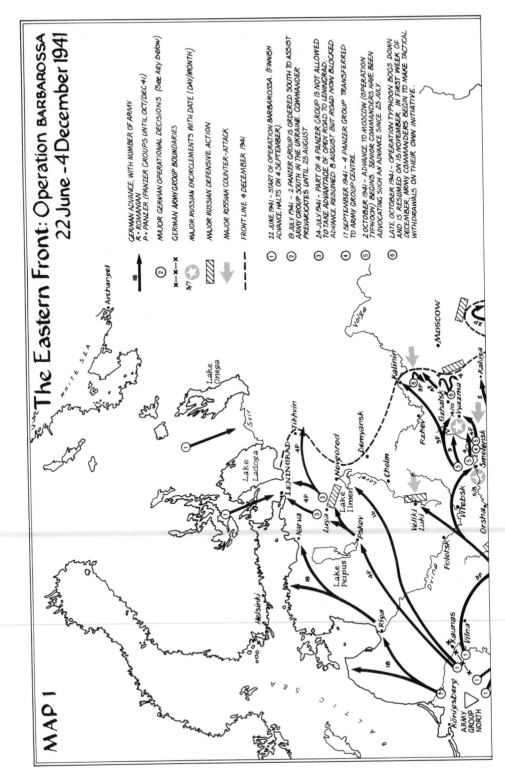

MAP 1

The Eastern Front: Operation BARBAROSSA
22 June –4 December 1941

KEY:

GERMAN ADVANCE, WITH NUMBER OF ARMY
R = ROMANIAN
P = PANZER (PANZER GROUPS UNTIL OCT/DEC 41)

MAJOR GERMAN OPERATIONAL DECISIONS (See key below)

GERMAN ARMY GROUP BOUNDARIES

MAJOR RUSSIAN ENCIRCLEMENTS WITH DATE (DAY/MONTH)

MAJOR RUSSIAN DEFENSIVE ACTION

MAJOR RUSSIAN COUNTER-ATTACK

FRONT LINE 4 DECEMBER 1941

① 22 JUNE 1941 – START OF OPERATION BARBAROSSA. (FINNISH ADVANCE HALTS ON 4 SEPTEMBER).

② 19 JULY 1941 – 2 PANZER GROUP IS ORDERED SOUTH TO ASSIST ARMY GROUP SOUTH IN THE UKRAINE. COMMANDER PREVARICATES UNTIL 25 AUGUST.

③ 24 JULY 1941 – PART OF 4 PANZER GROUP IS NOT ALLOWED TO TAKE ADVANTAGE OF OPEN ROAD TO LENINGRAD. ADVANCE RESUMED 8 AUGUST BUT ROAD NOW BLOCKED.

④ 17 SEPTEMBER 1941 – 4 PANZER GROUP TRANSFERRED TO ARMY GROUP CENTRE.

⑤ 2 OCTOBER 1941 – ADVANCE TO MOSCOW (OPERATION TYPHOON) BEGINS. SENIOR COMMANDERS HAVE BEEN ADVOCATING SUCH AN ADVANCE SINCE 25 JULY.

⑥ LATE OCTOBER 1941 – OPERATION TYPHOON BOGS DOWN AND IS RESUMED ON 15 NOVEMBER. IN FIRST WEEK OF DECEMBER, ARMY COMMANDERS BEGIN TO MAKE TACTICAL WITHDRAWALS ON THEIR OWN INITIATIVE.

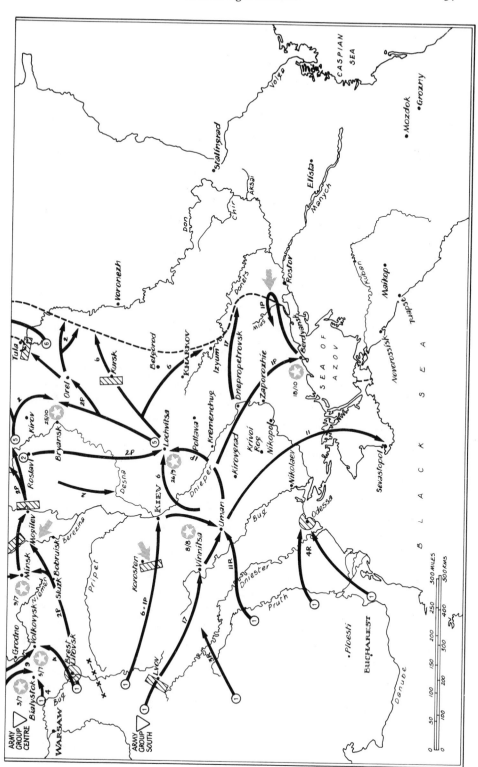

A further reason for giving A Gp North such a static role was that
Hitler was once more turning his thoughts toward Moscow, having
on 6 September already issued a directive that reinstated von Bock's
axis as the focus of operations. The main target, however, was not
Moscow but the *Front*,* under Marshal Semyon Timoshenko, that
blocked the approaches. It was to be destroyed in the tried and
tested manner, in two huge encirclement battles around Vyazma
and Bryansk. To ensure speedy penetration on each side of the
pockets, the bulk of the armour was to be put under von Bock's
command, with Pz Gp 2 retracing its steps northwards and Pz Gp
4 being seconded from A Gp North. A Gp South, however, was to
continue offensive operations of its own, pushing across the Dnieper
at Kremenchug preparatory to a drive towards the Donets, to engulf
the vital industrial concentrations between Kharkov and Rostov.
A drive into the Crimea, ordered in mid-August, was also to be
vigorously pursued.

A Gp Centre's offensive, Operation Typhoon, began on 2 October
and once again the early operations enjoyed considerable success.
Both the Vyazma and the Bryansk pockets were sewn up by the
middle of the month and yielded yet another rich haul of prisoners
and hardware. But Russian resistance had been far from negligible
and by now the weather had started to impose a brake on operations.
The rains had begun in early October and soon turned the roads into
a sea of mud. It began to seem to certain commanders that the
Vyazma–Bryansk operation had represented the army group's last
gasp and that a continuation of the drive towards Moscow was simply
not feasible in the light of the atrocious going, the heavy casualties
and the remarkable ability of the Russian High Command to keep
on bringing up reserves. The coming of the winter snows, however,
persuaded them that simply holding the existing line was an even
worse option and they reluctantly agreed to make one last lunge for
the Soviet capital.

This began on 16 November but was held along all the main axes.
Pz Gp 3, to the north, was actually pushed back by a Russian
counter-offensive at the end of the month, and a few days later both
Pz Gp 2 and 4 Army, on the southern flank, were obliged to call off
their attacks and pull back their forward units. A Gp South had
enjoyed almost exactly similar fortunes. The preliminary armoured

* A Russian *Front* was the equivalent of an army group. When individual *Fronts* are
named later in the narrative, e.g. Kalinin *Front*, the italicisation will be abandoned
as being unnecessarily pedantic.

drive by Pz Gp 1 had progressed confidently to the northern coast of the sea of Azov, cornering yet another mass of Russian prisoners, but the subsequent drive to Rostov, hampered by deteriorating weather and inadequate resources, had completely run out of steam once that city was reached and was fairly easily driven out again by a Russian counter-attack. The *Wehrmacht* had just about shot its bolt.

Since the war, historians have devoted an enormous amount of effort to trying to discover why the Germans found themselves in such a pass in December 1941. Attention has focused on an examination of German options, particularly with regard to the priorities accorded to the three army groups' axes of advance. The decisions taken concerning the advance towards Moscow figure the most prominently, the debate centring on whether more divisions should have been given to A Gp Centre, whether Pz Gp 3 should have gone straight for Smolensk and whether the dispatch south of Pz Gp 2 fatally delayed the start of Operation Typhoon. In many respects, however, much of this debate seems essentially sterile in that it implies real strategic options, 'right' or 'wrong' decisions, when in fact neither the choices made nor their alternatives could have had much bearing on the fundamental cause of German failure – that the *Wehrmacht* was simply not powerful enough to conquer Russia.

The crux of the problem was that, on the one hand, the Germans had neither the men nor the matériel to sustain a balanced broad-front offensive into Russia, and yet, on the other, there existed no realistic alternative to this method of advance. For each of the divergent axes of the three army groups had its own telling strategic justification. Moscow, of course, was a crucial target, representing as it did the Soviets' administrative heart, a large industrial centre and a major hub of rail communications. But Leningrad, too, was not without importance, particularly as a potent psychological symbol to the Russians, people and party alike. The Baltic states, brutally annexed by the Russians only the year before, offered useful potential allies and their occupation, benevolent or otherwise, would deny the Red Navy access to the Baltic where they might seriously interfere with German trade and with U-boat training. The Finns, too, were potentially a considerable military asset, but only if reassured by a significant German presence in the north that could guarantee any territorial seizures they might make.* Finally, it would be

* In the end, Marshal Mannerheim decided *not* to support fully A Gp North, but that was in mid-September, by which time he was far from convinced that the Germans would be the ultimate victors.

extremely dangerous to leave large tracts of northern Russia virtually unmolested and thus allow the assembly of forces that might seriously threaten the *Wehrmacht*'s left flank and the utilisation of airfields that were well within range of Germany. But questions of flank security and airfields were also pertinent in the south and demanded that the Germans allocate at least some of their forces to the Ukraine. Equally pressing was the need to occupy the Donets basin where a substantial proportion of Russian industry was concentrated and which would offer the Germans a useful springboard for a later drive into the Caucasian oil-fields, both to deny them to the Soviets and to supplement Germany's own meagre resources.

All these considerations remained equally valid as the campaign progressed, despite later claims that one axis or another came to acquire an obvious priority. The most common assertion is that after the fall of Smolensk maximum forces should have immediately been committed towards Moscow, whose fall would supposedly have precipitated the end of the war. Hitler instead chose to emphasise the importance of Leningrad and Kiev and sent most of A Gp Centre's armour north and south. But who can really blame Hitler? A Gp North needed all the help it could get to take Leningrad, or merely to tighten the blockade, and on the success of this depended meaningful Finnish participation in future operations, not least a strike to the north-east to cut potential supply routes from Archangel and Murmansk. The case for eliminating the Russian forces around Kiev seems even more clear-cut. Despite Halder's snide remarks about 'small concentrations' and 'minor successes', the Soviet forces in the Ukraine represented a considerable threat that, if given some breathing space and the ferociously energetic leadership that certain Soviet commanders could display even at this early stage, might wreak havoc on the right flank of forces zeroed in on Moscow.

Yet it is equally true, of course, that these redeployments did hamstring A Gp Centre, and for nearly two months it made almost no progress along its own axis. From 18 July to 5 August it was clearing out the Smolensk 'cauldron'. Between 5 and 15 August it was awaiting clarification as to its next tasks, the original order to send Pz Gp 2 south having been temporarily countermanded on 30 July. On 15 August it was ordered to maintain its present positions, and orders for a renewed advance towards Moscow did not arrive until 6 September. Then, however, it had to await the return of Pz Gp 2 from the south and it was not until 2 October that A Gp

Centre's armour was once again properly concentrated for the drive eastward.*

On the face of it, such a pause in operations, especially in view of an imminent breakdown in the weather, would seem to indicate grievously flawed strategic decisions. In reality, all it does is underline the fact that the Germans simply did not have the troops and matériel to undertake all of their equally pressing tasks. Even the oft-criticised delay between 5 and 21 August, when A Gp Centre had completed its mopping up and still retained both its panzer groups,† is at least understandable when one bears in mind the alchemic formula that Hitler was trying to work out, namely how to enable four panzer groups to perform tasks that required at least six, *operating simultaneously*. The formula did not, of course, exist, even for the *Gröfaz*,‡ and he was thus obliged to rob Peter to pay Paul, halting and hobbling each army group in turn and thereby giving the Russians the opportunity to solidify their positions on the temporarily quieter fronts. In short, Hitler was not faced with a sort of military IQ test in which the correct sequence of binary decision-making would lead to the correct answer, but was trapped in a maze in which every option was ultimately meaningless because all the exits had been blocked behind him. His military incompetence in the Barbarossa campaign was revealed not so much by his inability to get out of the maze, as by his ever having allowed himself to be immured there in the first place.

Evidence of the acute shortages that bedevilled the German forces at this time is not limited to the peregrinations of the panzer groups.§ Another major problem, obvious from the map, was that the further the *Wehrmacht* pushed on into Russia the greater the length of the front became and the more the three army groups diverged. The gaps between them, as well as between the component armies, caused innumerable difficulties. That between A Gps North and South began to open up dangerously in mid-July: it necessitated the diversion of

---

* And even then, because of the enormous distances they had covered, only 50 per cent of Pz Gp 2's tanks were fit for action.

† The irrevocable order for Pz Gp 2's transfer was not issued until 21 August.

‡ The most grotesque of Hitler's titles, an elision of *Grösster Feldheer Aller Zeiten* (greatest military commander of all time).

§ A Gps Centre and North were not the only ones affected. Prior to Typhoon, A Gp South was informed that not only must it hand back Pz Gp 2 but it would also have to give up nine of its original divisions, including two panzer and two motorised. It was this as much as anything which accounted for its repulse at Rostov.

part of Pz Gp 3 to secure the line of the Lovat, especially around the town of Velikiye Luki, and thus weakened one prong of the Smolensk pincers. Potentially even more serious was the gap that opened up between A Gps Centre and South. Indeed, it was only negligence on the part of the Russians that saved Pz Gp 2 from being harassed on its eastern flank, both during the march towards Kiev and on the way back. This gap yawned yet wider during October and November, and von Bock persistently complained that 'it was a gross tactical error for Army Group South to veer away into the vastness of the Russian Ukraine and Donets Basin, leaving Russian forces free to concentrate in the Orel–Dimitrovsky–Kursk–Byelogorod areas and thus pose a threat to both his right and Army Group South's northern flanks.'[17] Attempts to fill this gap meant that 2, 6 and 17 Armies were asked to cover quite remarkable frontages. In mid-September, when 11 Army turned towards the Crimea, its left flank was left completely exposed and only by taking units of Pz Gp 1 out of the Kiev encirclement was A Gp South able to fight off a determined Russian counter-attack.

The Army Groups also found that their offensive tasks seemed to be multiplying day by day. On 4 November, von Rundstedt urged that even an advance to the Donets and the lower Don was asking too much of his men, only to be airily informed that his objectives now included Voronezh, Stalingrad and Maikop! The almost complete lack of realism at Hitler's headquarters is further revealed by the fact that only a few days before, the task of taking Voronezh had been allocated to Pz Gp 2, hundreds of miles away to the north. The order was rescinded within a few hours but it was symptomatic of the pressures placed on the panzer groups by the weakness of the infantry on their flanks. In early October, for example, when Guderian should have been concentrating his armour for a decisive thrust towards Tula,

> he was instructed to destroy Eremenko's Bryansk Front, which by then was a hundred miles behind him to his west, seize the city of Kursk, which was a hundred miles to his south, and take Tula which was a hundred miles to the north-east. All orders were to be executed immediately. When Guderian asked for priorities to be assigned to his three separate missions he received no reply.[18]

The commander of Pz Gp 3, General Hermann Hoth, was similarly plagued by demands that he be everywhere at once. Again, in early October, he was ordered to assist Pz Gp 4 in holding tight the Vyazma pocket until the infantry of 4 and 9 Armies arrived, whilst at the same time dispatching units to Kalinin, to begin the encirclement of Moscow from the north, and to Rybinsk, 80 miles further north, where he was to help plug the gap between A Gps Centre and North.

Further questions about the Germans' ability to attain the objectives they had set for themselves arise from the part played by the panzer groups in the encirclement battles themselves. For it soon became apparent that these groups were neither strong enough nor numerous enough both to pin down the trapped Russian divisions and to send other units pressing forward to disrupt Russian attempts to organise fall-back positions. Indeed, it seemed increasingly doubtful whether the German armour could even perform the former task satisfactorily. For the inevitable delay between the closing of the armoured pincers and the arrival of the marching infantry who were actually to reduce the pockets usually meant that for several days the offensive cordon was very thin and thousands of surrounded Russians were able to break out. As one commentator has written:

> In successive encirclement battles, Russian army after Russian army was surrounded and technically destroyed. Again and again, however, the steel cord formed by the panzers was too thin to stop tens of thousands of Russian soldiers from breaking through and filtering east. By any conventional military standard, the Russian forces were out-thought, outmanoeuvred and beaten. But the Russian soldier . . . fought on . . . sucking the scanty German panzers into new whirlpools of battle [and] holding back the German tanks that should have been reinforcing the drive east.[19]

Many German commanders objected to using the armour in this way during the later stages of an encirclement. General Günther von Blumentritt, Chief of Staff in 4 Army, felt the armour should only be used to herd the Russians into a general locality after which it would press forward immediately, not even bothering to turn inwards to form the jaws of the pincers. 'By making the armoured forces turn in each time,' he maintained, 'and forge a ring around the enemy forces they had bypassed, a lot of time was lost.'[20] The commander of A Gp Centre felt much the same way. In early October he complained to one of his subordinates:

> During the battles at Minsk and Smolensk, I urged repeatedly

that the armour be allowed freedom of movement as soon as possible, to prevent the enemy from regrouping his defences. This of necessity places a heavy burden on the infantry, but in this campaign it affords the only chance of defeating an enemy who has traditionally used this vast, primitive terrain to his own advantage . . . At Minsk and Smolensk, because of circumstances beyond my control, I was not able to execute this concept of warfare. As a result, both engagements, though successful, were not decisive.[21]

The 'circumstances beyond his control' were, of course, Hitler, but here again we see an example of the latter's being blamed for making a wrong choice when, in fact, there was none that could have had 'decisive' results. To be sure, the sucking of the panzer groups into the 'cauldrons' fatally weakened the Germans' ability to keep up the pressure on Russian reserve formations, but if they had not fully participated in these battles there would have been no encirclements worthy of the name. Thousands of Russians escaped as it was, but how many hundreds of thousands would have eluded capture if the sealing off of the pockets had been left to the infantry lagging three or four days' march behind? For von Bock to say that his preferred tactic 'would place a heavy burden on the infantry' was something of an understatement. In fact, it would have presented them with an impossible task, since the pockets would largely have ceased to exist by the time they arrived. But the problem went deeper. Experience in most of the major encirclements showed that even when the infantry did reach a pocket still pegged out by the armour, it was rarely strong enough on its own both to take over picket duties and to set about eliminating the surrounded army. Thus the armour was obliged to remain *in situ* even longer, to assist the infantry in its own operations. Such was the case, for example, in the Smolensk pocket where

> . . . the enemy opposition was so fierce . . . that no siphoning off of the mechanised forces eastwards was possible; all their energies were needed to guard the pocket, to attempt to close the pincer, and to ward off strong counter-attacks . . . Not until 27 July were there enough infantry divisions . . . to make the German positions there secure, and even then they had come not to relieve Guderian's force, but to reinforce it . . . Thus from 20 July to 1 August, Army Group Centre was on the defensive. No further advance was possible.[22]

By this time, moreover, the Germans were finding out that not only were their units too thin on the ground but also that each of them was becoming increasingly short of men and equipment. By 26 September total German casualties on the Eastern Front were over half a million men. One official report stated that 14 of their divisions were more than 4,000 men short of establishment, 40 more than 3,000 short and a further 30 more than 2,000 short. These shortfalls mainly affected the rifle component of the divisions, the men who did the actual fighting. By September 98 Infantry Division's rifle companies had only 30 to 40 of their original complement left. One regiment, between 31 July and 10 August alone, had lost 37 officers and 1,200 other ranks. But the first reinforcements did not arrive until late September, when the division was 3,800 men short, and even then battalions received only some 40 replacements each. The commander of 1 ss Panzer Division, whose replacement rate at the end of September was less than 40 per cent of casualties, noted that his losses 'even under the heaviest of Soviet artillery bombardments, were negligible . . . so thin were the troops on the ground.'[23] The infantry component of the panzer divisions was equally hard hit. In late August Halder wrote in his diary: 'The trouble is that our panzer divisions now have such a low combat strength that they just do not have the men to seal off any sizeable areas.'[24]

By November the situation was worse still. By the 4th of that month total casualties were 686,000, and a report submitted two days later showed that the 101 infantry divisions in the east had a fighting strength of only 65 full-strength divisions, the 17 panzer divisions that of a mere 6.* By the end of the month Halder was writing in his diary: '. . . total losses on the Eastern Front (not counting sick) 743,112, i.e. 23.12 per cent of the average total strength of 3.2 million . . . On the Eastern Front the Army is short of 340,000 men, i.e. 50 *per cent* of the fighting strength of the infantry. Companies have a fighting strength of only 50–60 men. At home there are only 33,000 available.'[25] Field Marshal Wilhelm Keitel, the okw Chief of Staff,† was similarly perturbed by the casualty lists and the lack of adequate replacements. Of the position in early November he

---

* At about this time the number of infantry battalions in a division was reduced from nine to six, but it would still have required the disbandment of 20 divisions to bring the rest up to even this reduced strength.

† okw was short for *Oberkommando der Wehrmacht*, the Armed Forces Supreme Command.

later wrote: 'The monthly losses of the land forces alone, in normal conditions and excluding major battles, averaged 150,000 to 160,000 men. Of these only 90,000 to 100,000 could be replaced. Thus the army in the field was reduced in numbers by 60,000 to 70,000 men each month. It was a piece of simple arithmetic to work out when the German front would be exhausted.'[26]

By the time of the renewed Moscow offensive, therefore, the Germans simply did not have the strength to attempt a major encirclement similar to those at Minsk, Smolensk and Kiev. According to von Bock, in conversation with Halder on 11 November:

> The objective that Army High Command has assigned to Army Group Centre can no longer be attained, because of diminishing troop strength . . . In other words it is no longer possible to encircle Moscow . . . I want it understood that it is no longer possible to execute a classical operation here. The time has passed for that, or any other large-scale deployment of troops . . . Also, I cannot suggest how long we will be able to sustain an attack of any proportions. There is a serious decline in morale and confidence among the troops. Losses are very high.[27]

Just as critical as the lack of manpower was the shortage of machines, particularly in the terribly overstretched panzer divisions. Even in the heady days of July the seemingly benign weather was creating serious difficulties. According to General Schaal, commander of 10 Panzer Division, in Pz Gp 2, the actual fighting was much less of a problem than

> the wear and tear on armoured fighting vehicles. The shocking roads, the heat, and the dust were more dangerous enemies than the Red Army. The tanks were enveloped in thick clouds of dust. The dust and grit wore out the engines. The filters were continually clogged up with dirt . . . Engines got overheated and pistons seized up. In this manner the . . . Division lost the bulk of its heavy Mark IV tanks on the way to Yelnya. They were defeated not by the Russians but by the dust.[28]

Regarding the situation throughout Pz Gp 3, in mid-July Hoth told Hitler's aide, General Rudolf Schmundt, that tank casualties in action 'were no greater, comparatively, than they had been in the French campaign; but the wear and tear caused by distances and operating conditions had been far worse than they expected.'[29] At about the same time he informed von Bock: 'The losses of armoured vehicles have now reached 60 to 70 per cent of our nominal strength.'[30] By 25 July all the panzer divisions of A Gp Centre were reduced to 60 per cent of their nominal strengths and those of A Gp South to 40 per cent. The problems of wear and tear were exacerbated by the fact that insufficient provision had been made for an adequate flow of replacements. Not only was planned production less than needed – Halder had estimated that as early as the end of July the OKH panzer reserve would be reduced from 3,350 tanks to a derisory 430 – but Hitler also insisted on using most of the new tanks that were produced to form additional panzer divisions, only some of which would be eventually sent to Russia. Up to the first week of August, in fact, he agreed to release to the Eastern Front only 70 Pz IIIs, 15 Pz IVs and 350 Pz III engines. The subsequent allocation of all the remaining obsolete 38(t)s was not regarded as much of a bonus. Matters did not improve over the following months. By the end of August 1,478 tanks had been written off completely, and on 4 September the four panzer groups had only an average of 47 per cent of their tanks fit for action.*

An effort was made to beef up the armour for Operation Typhoon but it was far from adequate. On the eve of the offensive Pz Gp 2 could still only muster 50 per cent of its establishment fit for action, and by the end of October all the panzer divisions of A Gp Centre were once again sadly depleted. By the middle of November their offensive capabilities were strictly limited, and by the middle of December they were hardly fit for anything. Between 16 November and 10 December, on the Moscow front alone, some 800 tanks were lost, whilst along the whole front, in October, November and December, losses totalled 2,500 tanks and assault guns destroyed or abandoned. Pz Gp 2, for example, could muster only 40 tanks that deserved to be called 'runners'. Not that even these were particularly reliable. At the start of the renewed Moscow offensive fully one-third of A Gp Centre's tanks had been unable to cope with the snow and mud and had broken down completely within a few days, whilst later in the month, in A Gp North's sector, so intense was the cold that only one tank in five was even able to fire its gun.

On top of all this there remained the question of logistics, yet one more critical constraint on German operations in Russia. It could be argued, indeed, that supply problems had an even more malign influence on the conduct of the Barbarossa campaign than

* Ten days later, Pz Gp 2 reported that only a quarter of its tanks were combat-worthy.

did the shortages of men and equipment. Inadequate numbers of troops and tanks, as we have seen, often meant that German commanders were limited to a single military 'option' when the situation demanded that two or three be pursued simultaneously. But shortages of transport, and thus of the fuel,* ammunition and spares that they were supposed to bring up to the front, sometimes meant that nothing at all was possible simply because the divisions lacked the wherewithal to fight or move.

Supply difficulties were apparent from the very beginning. The rate of railway conversion was an early disappointment. By 10 July train movements to the rear of the armies were only 10 per cent of requirements and at some railheads, where supplies had to be transferred from German rolling stock to Russian, the unloading took 12, 24 and even 80 hours instead of the regulation three. Though the minimum requirements of A Gp North, for example, had been set at 34 trains per day, it never received more than 18, even that number being something of an exception. But delivery at the railheads was still no guarantee that the supplies would reach the front proper. Within the first three weeks of Barbarossa, losses amongst the lorries of the *Grosstransportraum*, the transport regiments that bridged the gap between the railheads and the individual armies' forward depots, had already reached 25 per cent, thanks mainly to the appalling roads. A week later the figure for A Gp Centre was one-third, whilst in A Gp South fully half of the lorry companies were out of action. The usefulness of those that remained was also greatly reduced by the appalling roads, which left them without a margin of power to tow a trailer. Carrying capacity was thus reduced by as much as 40 per cent.

Not surprisingly, therefore, shortages at the front became acute, especially that of the POL of which the panzer divisions, on whose mobility rested the Germans' only hope of success, were voracious consumers.† Both of the flank army groups were badly affected. Though A Gp North's spearheads, to 26 June, covered a remarkable 200 miles in five days, it had by then outrun its service of supply and the panzers were immobilised on the Dvina until 4 July and the establishment of a proper forward supply base. Even then further progress

---

* Known in militarese as POL, an acronym for petrol, oil and lubricants.
† Though expenditure of most kinds of military supplies was equally high. The Russians often put up a bitter defence and at Uman, for example, German batteries fired more rounds in four days than they had used in the whole of the French campaign.

was only made possible by allocating almost the whole of the army group's *Grosstransportraum* to Pz Gp 4 and completely immobilising 16 Army. Just the same thing happened a fortnight later as

> . . . Army Group North [had their] best chance for capturing Leningrad . . . when Reinhardt's [XLI] Corps had penetrated to within 80 miles of the city . . . [However], during the second half of July, the supply service was incapable of supporting even the most limited offensive because it was fully occupied in moving its base forward from Dunaburg to the area around Luga, and in this period the start of the attack was postponed no fewer than seven times . . . The offensive was resumed on 8 August but by this time the defences of Leningrad were ready.[31]

A Gp South endured equally frustrating delays. At the end of July progress across the Dnieper was held up by the necessity to establish a forward supply base there, and this was delayed in turn by the lack of progress made in converting the railways, which meant that the army group's *Grosstransportraum* had to drive all the way back to the Polish border to pick up its loads. Only substantial requisitions from 17 Army enabled Pz Gp 1 to make any headway at all during the first half of August. After the liquidation of the Kiev pocket, the drive east was almost completely hamstrung. A Gp South still had only 50 per cent of its trucks operational and the breakdown in the weather brought the movement of supplies completely to a halt on 13 October. Not that the lorries would have had a great deal to carry even had the requisite numbers been available. The railways were still in a parlous state and during the whole month of October only 195 out of 724 trains scheduled actually arrived, 112 of these being left over from the previous month. A railway system running at 11 per cent of expected capacity is scarcely the most secure underpinning for the most ambitious military campaign ever attempted. It is hardly surprising, therefore, that von Rundstedt's subsequent drive to Rostov was mounted on a logistical shoestring or that it was so easily repulsed by the Russians in late November. What is surprising is that it was ever attempted at all in the face of the immense logistical difficulties. Prior to the attack beyond the Kiev pocket, *Aussenstelle Sud** had averred that it simply was not possible to lay track beyond the Dnieper, but there is 'not the slightest hint that its view was taken into account by Hitler, OKH, or indeed Army

---

* The Quartermaster-General's Department within the Army Group.

Group South itself. Even Rundstedt . . . did not intend to suspend operations until *after* the conquest of Rostov. That this objective was itself beyond the reach of his logistic apparatus, not even he seems to have contemplated.'[32]

Equally cavalier behaviour characterised the post-Smolensk operations of A Gp Centre. Of Hitler's baleful influence, one historian has noted: '. . . he allowed logistics to determine his strategy no more than he allowed economics to shape his policies. In his view the problems they both presented could be solved by the exertion of will and determination.'[33] But the generals, too, seem to have colluded in this retreat from reality and when, in August, the Quartermaster-General's staff reached the conclusion that a simultaneous attack by the whole of A Gp Centre towards Moscow was simply not feasible,* no one in authority seems to have paid very much attention. Nor did the swoop south by Pz Gp 2 and 2 Army offer much relief. The enforced delay to the rest of A Gp Centre did allow some stockpiling but ammunition consumption was still heavy and much of the Army Group's fuel had to be diverted to succour Guderian on his round trip. Lorries and trains remained in short supply. On 4 October A Gp Centre had only 50 per cent of its full establishment of motor transport whilst the dearth of locomotives and rolling stock put a decisive brake on operations – much more decisive, in fact, than the terrible weather that featured so heavily in the complaints of the front-line soldiers. As one historian has pointed out: '. . . close scrutiny of the quartermasters' diaries reveals what divisional histories tend to conceal, namely that the difficulties were due as much to the poor performance of the railways as to the ubiquitous mud . . . [and the railway troops] were simply unable to cope with the increased demands of a fresh offensive.'[34]

Not that the weather helped, particularly the onset of the heavy frosts in mid-November. German locomotives, as has already been noted, were not winterised, and within a short time 80 per cent of them had had their main water-pipe freeze up and burst.† Not surprisingly, according to one German general, this 'had almost cata-strophic results for the Army Gp during the entire winter period.'[35] Typical were the experiences of 2 Army, which between 12 November

---

* It was estimated that 25 goods trains per day would be required to meet A Gp Centre's needs. On several days, however, only 7 arrived and the best day produced only 15.

† A locomotive built to operate in low temperatures has the water-pipe running through the boiler itself.

and 2 December received hardly any trains at all, and 9 Army, which between 9 and 23 November received only one solitary fuel train. For Pz Gp 4, from 17 November, there were no deliveries of POL whatsoever. And almost everything else was in short supply, including

all types of ammunition and anti-tank weapons . . . Even the common necessities of life were missing, without which a soldier rapidly became almost totally ineffective. Spades, picks, entrenching tools, saws, vehicle and mechanics' kits, technical equipment and mobile machinery were beyond repair or had been lost. Nothing was being replaced. Guns, radios and vehicles stood derelict awaiting spare parts. The miserable troops were still in their threadbare and dirty summer uniforms which gave no protection from the icy and biting winds. There had of course been no issue of winter equipment, underclothes, boots, gloves or other clothing, nor were there any white camouflage smocks.[36]*

No wonder that von Bock, looking back on the failure to take Moscow, gave one of the principal reasons as

the breakdown of the entire supply system. The primitive highway and railway system in Russia prevented the proper utilisation of our mechanised and motorised forces . . . [resulting from] a shortage of fuel, a shortage of railway cars and locomotives, the inability to change quickly enough to the Russian railway gauge [and] the mechanical failure of thousands of vehicles, which were built to operate on good roads. Added to this was the perennial shortage of qualified personnel to operate the supply system.[37]†

But the problem of logistics was in fact just one of the nails in the *Wehrmacht*'s coffin. Equally deleterious were the grim climate and the acute shortages of combat troops and equipment of all kinds, all of which combined completely to debilitate German offensive capabilities. By November 1941, at the latest, no formation, armoured or otherwise, could think in terms of a genuine war of movement

* It is to be noted, therefore, that even had the German High Command made full provision for the manufacture and stockpiling of winter clothing, which they notoriously had not, it would still have proved impossible actually to get it to the front.
† At the end of November there was only an average of 10 maintenance men per kilometre of track, instead of the prescribed 16, and only 1 of these was a German, specifically trained for this task.

or of the old wide-ranging sweeps into the enemy's rear and around
his flanks. According to one general the panzers had

> lost the ability to manoeuvre. War became one of linear move-
> ment. We did not bother about creating a *Schwerpunkt*. We
> were no longer instructed to surprise, outflank and annihilate
> the enemy. We were told: 'You will hold the front from such a
> point to such and such a point, you will advance to such a line.'
> And it was added: 'Otherwise you will answer for it with your
> command.'[38]

Blitzkrieg, and even *Vernichtungsgedanke*, were now but fond memories. Military operations were reduced to simple attrition, reminiscent
of the crudest set-piece battles of the First World War. On 30
November von Bock told von Brauchitsch: 'My one hope is to
continue the attack frontally. In doing this, however, there exists
the danger of a brutish, chest-to-chest struggle, such as occurred at
Verdun twenty-five years ago. I have no desire to be a participant
in that kind of struggle. I emphasise that Army Group Centre is
at the end of its strength.'[39] On the following day he wrote to
the OKW, reasserting that the heavy losses of the previous months
permitted only 'frontal assaults' and that 'no classical movements of
encirclement' were possible. 'The attack now in progress will gain
some ground, but at bloody cost. It will destroy some of the enemy,
but it will not force a decision . . . Even if the improbable takes place
and my troops enter . . . [Moscow], it is doubtful they can hold it.
The attack therefore appears to be without purpose . . .'[40]

It is indeed difficult to see any real military rationale for the
renewed Moscow offensive. Perhaps the best explanation is that
given by a German historian who sees it as a counsel of despair,
its only merit being that it was 'a better alternative than spending
a desolate winter in the field . . . lying on open ground in snow
and cold only thirty miles from the tempting objectives . . .'[41]
The main objective now was not to capture Moscow because of
its administrative, industrial and strategic significance but simply
because it offered the troops of A Gp Centre roofs over their heads.
Not for nothing was the renewed Typhoon offensive to become
known in Germany as *die Flucht nach vorn*, the flight forward. In
fact desperation was apparent at all levels of the German Army.
The High Command's lack of realistic analysis of the Barbarossa
plans has already been dealt with, but how much more inimical to
the traditions of the General Staff was this admission by Halder, that

he would endorse the renewed Moscow drive and 'reluctantly allow himself to be persuaded by von Bock, even though it was clear to him that the operation could not be adequately prepared . . . not [to] rein in Army Group Centre if it wanted to attempt the attack, for an element of luck belonged to warfare.'[42]

All the evidence given thus combines to demonstrate that Barbarossa was fatally flawed even before it began. Yet it would be grossly unfair to the Russians to concentrate only on negative factors regarding German shortages and unpreparedness. For even in these early months of chronic catastrophe the Red Army and the Soviet leadership gave ample proof of their tenacity and courage, as well as of the ability of even their lumbering economy and hidebound state apparatus to conjure up an effective and extraordinarily resilient war machine. Though whole Russian divisions ceased to exist, armies lost all cohesion, and panic and defeatism were rife, a tight enough grip was maintained at the top to keep the spirit of resistance alive and, above all, to buy time to deploy effectively the enormous reserves of manpower, raw materials and basic industrial expertise that still remained.

It is the performance of the Soviet war machine as a whole that is of most interest in a book of this nature, and this we shall examine in detail, but it would be unthinkable to attempt any survey of the Second World War that did not pay at least passing homage to the Russian soldiers and people and stress their personal contribution to the blunting of the German offensive, even during the darkest days of strategic collapse. A glance at map 1 shows that from the very first days of the invasion the German advance was repeatedly baulked by resolutely manned Russian defences. From 23 to 28 June A Gp South's Pz Gp 1 was held in front of Lwow by 22, 9 and 19 Mechanised Corps. For much of July the same panzers were constantly troubled by 5 Army as it sallied out of its fastnesses in the Pripet Marshes. Referring to this period, one German general wrote:

> The greatest difficulties were encountered by A Gp South . . . A considerable obstacle to the assault of German units came from the enemy's strong counter-attacks . . . which forced a large part of 1st Tank Group to change the direction of its offensive and instead of moving towards Kiev to move northward and engage in battles of local importance.[43]

A Gp North lost a whole month around Luga and Lake Ilmen as the

Russians threw in men to defend the line of the River Luga, and when that was finally pierced found itself incapable of cracking the immediate defences of Leningrad. A Gp Centre was held up time and again. On the Beresina, on 3 July, Pz Gp 2 was stopped at Borisov by 20 Army, and though these positions were outflanked a subsequent attack across the upper Dnieper, against 13 Army at Mogilev, did not gain a secure foothold on the far bank until 10 July. Pz Gp 3, along the Dvina, had more success but it too was involved in hard fighting during the first two weeks of July and did not fully overcome 5 and 7 Mechanised Corps, just south-west of Vitebsk, until 14 July. Yet another river line put to good use by the Russians was the Lovat, and at Velikiye Luki elements of Pz Gp 3, attempting to plug the gap between A Gps North and Centre, were stopped in their tracks by 22 Army which held these positions throughout August 1941.

German sources make it quite clear that the weight of resistance encountered was both unexpected and extremely disruptive to the Barbarossa timetable. Excerpts from Halder's diary show just how quickly Russian tenacity began to have its effect:

22 *June*. After the first shock the enemy has turned to fight . . .

23 *June*. The stubborn resistance of individual Russian units is remarkable.

29 *June*. Reports from all fronts confirm previous indications that the Soviets are fighting to the last man . . . Now, for once, our troops are compelled by the stubborn Russian resistance to fight according to their combat manuals. *In Poland and the West they could take liberties, but here they cannot get away with it . . .*

4 *July*. Very tough fighting . . .

11 *July*. [The enemy] is fighting with fanatical and dogged determination . . .

15 *July*. The Russian troops, now as ever, are fighting with savage determination and with enormous human sacrifice.[44]

Even Hitler began to feel a little unease and justified the dispatch of Pz Gp 2 south to Kiev by lamenting that: 'You cannot beat the Russians with operational successes . . . because they simply do not know when they are defeated . . . It will be necessary to destroy them bit by bit . . .'[45] After the crossing of the Dnieper and Dvina, resistance seemed if anything to become tougher yet. According to von Blumentritt, Pz Gp 4's operations 'assumed a different aspect. The undisturbed tactical advance of the panzer groups [*sic*] was a thing of the past. The engagements became more bitter . . . We encountered resistance everywhere. Where did these masses of troops come from again and again?'[46] Of the fighting for the Mogilev bridgehead one German officer wrote that 'in places masses of Russian artillery carried out bombardments which called to mind the most formidable concentrations of fire ever witnessed during the First World War. Lacking shells, our own batteries had to watch impotently the slaughter of foot soldiers and front-line pioneers.'[47]

Even after the sealing of the Smolensk pocket, the Russians continued to fight fiercely, both those inside and those counter-attacking from outside the German cordon. One German officer wrote:

> The Russians did not confine themselves to opposing the frontal advance of our panzer divisions. They further attempted to find every suitable occasion to operate against the flanks of the wedges driven in by our motorised elements . . . For this purpose they used their tanks, which were as numerous as our own . . . Situations were sometimes so confused and changed with such rapidity that we, on our side, wondered if we were outflanking the enemy or whether he had outflanked us.[48]

But what most depressed the more perceptive German observers was not the undoubted bravery of the individual Russian, but the almost incredible ability of their leaders to keep finding yet more reserves of manpower and matériel, even after the destruction of 'cauldrons' stuffed with prisoners and booty. As early as 11 August, long before the drive on Moscow, Halder confided gloomily in his diary:

> The whole situation makes it increasingly plain that we have underestimated the Russian colossus . . . This applies to organisational and economic resources, as well as to the communications system, and, *most of all*, to the strict military potential. At the outset of the war we reckoned with about 200 enemy divisions. Now we have already counted 360. These divisions indeed are not armed and equipped according to our standards, and their tactical leadership is often poor. But there they are, and if we smash a dozen of them, the Russians simply put up another dozen . . . And so our troops, sprawled over an immense front line, without any depth, are subjected to the

enemy's incessant attacks.[49]

Once Operation Typhoon began, the sheer size of Russia's manpower reserve, and her leaders' continued ability to get these men into the field, became frighteningly apparent. At the beginning of the offensive the Russian position was admittedly a little precarious, the West Front, the main army group defending Moscow, having only 383 combat-worthy tanks in early October. Reinforcements were rushed in, however, and during October and November the Soviets managed to create nine fresh armies, two of which, along with elements from another three, reached the Moscow area by the end of November. Some of these troops were newly inducted but a substantial proportion came from the military districts in Central Russia and Siberia. The Siberians were élite formations, thoroughly trained in winter warfare in the event of a Japanese attack from her mainland positions in Manchuria, and they provided the beleaguered forces in the west with a vital transfusion of some 17 divisions, as well as 1,700 tanks and 1,500 aircraft.* In the opinion of Marshal A. M. Vasilevsky, soon to become Chief of the Russian General Staff, the formation of these nine new armies, particularly those thrown in against A Gp Centre, 'was one of the most important factors in deciding the outcome of the winter war.'[50] It would be difficult to disagree, particularly when one appreciates the full scale of the Soviet reinforcement. The Siberian contribution was only part of the story, and not only were thousands of fresh recruits being inducted but also hundreds of tanks and artillery pieces were rolling off the production lines. Thus in one single fortnight, between 1 and 14 November, the West Front alone received 100,000 new troops, 2,000 artillery pieces and 300 tanks.

The Germans were just as aware as Vasilevsky how important these reinforcements were. General Simon, an ss divisional commander, was convinced that 'the failure [to reach Moscow] cannot have been caused by the terrain or space. Actually this failure was due solely to the resistance offered by the Russian Army . . .'[51] General H. von Greiffenberg, von Bock's Chief of Staff, was just as dismissive of attempts to blame everything on the mud and the snow, asserting: 'It is wrong to put the principal blame for the events on the winter.'

---

* The Russians dared to run down their Far Eastern presence, in all some 25 divisions and 9 mechanised brigades, because of information from a most reliable source, the spy Richard Sorge in Tokyo, that the Japanese leaders were turning all their attention towards an offensive in the Pacific.

The real cause of German defeat, he pointed out, was that 'we had misjudged the combat strength and combat efficiency of the enemy, as well as of our own troops.'[52] Von Bock, too, was adamant that a prime cause of the failure was that 'we underestimated the strength of the enemy, his ability to recuperate after suffering losses that would have toppled almost any other nation, and his great reserves in manpower and material . . .'[53] The truth of the Army Group commander's words was equally apparent to the haggard troops at the sharp end. In late November a young officer of 2 SS Panzer Division wrote this to his mother:

> These Russians seem to have an inexhaustible supply of men. Here they unload fresh troops from Siberia every day; they bring up fresh guns and lay mines all over the place . . . [In] our last attack . . . we managed to take all of the hill and half of the village [Lenino]. But at night we had to give it all up again in order to defend ourselves more effectively against the continuous Russian counter-attacks. We only needed another eight miles to get the capital within gun range – but we just could not make it.[54]

Indeed, if there is one fact more than any other that sums up the German failure to achieve the Barbarossa objectives, it is that between 22 June and 1 December 1941 the Russian armed forces inducted 3,241,000 men whilst German replacements to the Eastern Front cannot have exceeded 100,000 men. The latter figure, it will be recalled, was the number of Russian reinforcements sent to a single army group over a period of only two weeks. In the light of grotesque strength ratios like this the most emphatic tactical superiority was simply not enough. Outflank, encircle and kill Russians as they might, the Germans had no hope at all, given their own heavy casualties, of even beginning to offset such an overwhelming numerical superiority.

Other figures tell the same story. In 1941 the Germans produced 2,875 medium tanks and assault guns, whilst the Russians turned out 6,590, roughly half of which were armed with 76mm guns. Furthermore, only a proportion of the German figure could actually be used in the east, and that this proportion was hardly generous is indicated by the fact that, up to March 1942, the Germans had lost 3,486 tanks in the east and received a mere 873 replacements. The situation with regard to aircraft was no better. From July to December 1941 the Germans produced 1,619 fighters as opposed to the Russians' 5,173.

The former, of course, had to divide their production between the east, the Mediterranean and the home defences, whilst the Russians could concentrate theirs almost exclusively on the one front. The Russian planes, moreover, were all excellent modern types, fresh from the drawing board, and were supplemented by a further 1,293 ground-attack planes, again of first-class design. German ground-attack production was only 507 for the whole year. By the time of the Moscow battles 'the Russians were able to call on largely new types produced at the rate of four aircraft for every one German . . . By December 1941 the serviceable strength of all *Luftwaffe* units in Russia amounted to 500 aircraft. Russia still had over 1,000 aircraft on the Moscow front alone.'[55]

It is no wonder, perhaps, that Hitler simply refused to face up to the implications of such doleful arithmetic and increasingly insisted that it was the German soldier that was at fault rather than his own fantastic underestimation of Russian power. After one visit to the *Gröfaz*'s headquarters, Field Marshal Günther von Kluge, commanding 4 Army, bemoaned the fact that Hitler 'does not . . . permit himself to believe the written reports from Army Group Centre with regard to manpower shortages . . . and the like. He is very disturbed that Moscow has not yet fallen and considers it impossible that we could not have foreseen all of the contingencies.'[56] A few weeks later Halder was still complaining in his diary, this time appalled that Hitler 'cannot be bothered with strength ratios. To him the prisoner of war figures are conclusive proof of our superiority.'[57] Not that these private thoughts seem to have prompted Halder to stand out against the increasing servility that characterised Hitler's headquarters. Shortly afterwards he himself issued an order, to all corps commanders and above, in which he acknowledged that the large number of new Soviet formations identified might be having a depressing effect on morale. Commanders should not, however, fall prey to the psychology of numbers and should sharply remind their intelligence officers of their responsibilities in this regard. 'The tough and spirited German soldier,' he concluded, 'shames the staff which meticulously tots up numbers.'[58]* One suspects, however, that said soldier cursed

---

* For further insight into the air of unreality that pervaded Hitler's headquarters, the reader is referred to the remarkable telephone conversation between von Bock and von Brauchitsch on 30 November. Only full quotation can do it justice and here space does not permit. It is reproduced in A. Turney, *Disaster at Moscow* (Cassell, 1971), pp. 145–8.

those who had *not* meticulously totted up numbers long before the Barbarossa campaign began.

Although the Germans on the Eastern Front were to launch two more major offensives, to Stalingrad and the Caucasus in summer 1942 and against the Kursk salient a year later, the basic pattern of the war in Russia was already set. Having failed to achieve decisive victory in the encirclement campaigns of 1941, the Germans had forfeited their only chance of dealing the Soviets a knock-out blow. The latter's administrative and productive machinery had survived and was henceforth able to raise divisions and arm them at a rate that the *Wehrmacht* could not hope to match. From December 1941 the essential routine of the Eastern Front centred upon the Russians launching or preparing for a major offensive, and even during the lengthy retreats of 1942, along the Don and in the Caucasus, their thoughts were always focused on husbanding reserves for a counter-attack, to be launched at the earliest possible moment.

For the Germans, on the other hand, both their own offensives and the handful of transitorily successful local counter-attacks had an increasingly desperate air about them, large portions of the front being stripped to the marrow to provide a slender local superiority, soon eroded, in pursuance of goals that had less and less real strategic significance. Whilst maps of the 1942 campaigns, in particular, might suggest metaphors like 'see-saw struggle' or 'punch and counter-punch', in fact simple diagrammatic representation is misleading. Certainly the Germans punched, and usually with penetration, but they were a bantamweight facing a heavyweight and their punches soon became frustrated two-handed lunges which were absorbed without too much difficulty and which left them with no guard against the ensuing body blow.

For the blow always came. As early as November 1941 Stalin had made it clear to his generals that he was not interested in mere defensive victories, even when the attritional rate favoured the Russians. His sole aim was to resume the offensive and drive the invaders back to the frontiers. In early November, therefore, planning began for a counter-offensive to push the Germans back from Moscow. In early December, after the offensive had got under way and the weakness of A Gp Centre became readily apparent, this plan was quickly upgraded from a simple frontal attack by West Front to an ambitious double envelopment by four army groups, West, North-West, Kalinin and Bryansk Fronts, jumping off along a 600-mile front between Demyansk and Dankov to slam the door behind A Gp Centre at Smolensk. There was some justification for these grandiose aims. One German general admitted that the timing of the counter-offensive could not have been better and that 'the Russian . . . command has to be given credit for not having lost its nerve [in November], and for keeping back its reserves until they could be massed at the right place, and finally for waiting until the German attack had completely collapsed.'[59] But timing was not everything, and it was surely to be doubted whether the Red Army, composed as it was largely of raw recruits, and having shown so little previous evidence of strategic finesse or tactical acumen, could reasonably be expected to pull off an encirclement on a scale that had eluded even its veteran opponents.

In the event, the Russians fell far short of their aims. Though A Gp Centre was pushed back up to 250 miles, along a broad front, only relatively minor pockets were formed, whilst it proved impossible to pinch the Germans out of a large salient anchored on Rzhev, Gzhatsk and Vyazma. Nevertheless, what the Russians *had* accomplished offered ominous portents for the future. For the drive on Moscow the German High Command had concentrated all the forces it dared and had fought with the utmost skill and courage. Yet the Russians had soaked up the most ferocious punishment and had still been able to bounce back and throw in fresh formations at an alarming rate. Was it possible, as some Germans were beginning to suspect, that experience and superior technique were not to be the arbiters of victory in Russia, but that sheer numbers would decide the issue?

It was not a prognosis that could give much comfort to German commanders. Even Halder, for example, deride the 'totters up' though he might, must have been a little unnerved to discover that during December, whilst A Gp Centre received not one fresh division, the Russian forces opposite it received 33 divisions and 39 brigades. By the end of February 1942 A Gp Centre had received some reinforcements, in all nine divisions. Unfortunately, by the same date the Russians had brought up the equivalent of 117 divisions. Nor could the casualty figures have been a source of comfort. Whilst those of the Russians were undoubtedly heavy, they were able to take shattered divisions out of the line for rebuilding, and replace them from the large number of reserve formations. In A Gp Centre, on the other hand, divisions simply stayed in the line and bled to death, their losses being nowhere near replaced by the drop-by-drop transfusion of replacements. Towards the end of January 35 Infantry Division had lost 2,500 men in a little over six weeks; 23 Division was reduced from nine to three battalions, with only 1,000 infantry instead of 8,000; 106 Division was even worse off, with barely 500 infantry. By the end of February A Gp Centre as a whole had suffered 357,000 battle casualties and received only 130,000 replacements, a deficit of 227,000 men. Even assuming formations at full strength, this latter figure represents the infantry complement of a full 25 divisions.*

Tank losses were also heavy. By January 1942 Pz Gp 4's four divisions included only one with a strength of more than 15 tanks whilst Guderian could count no more than 40 runners in the whole of Pz Gp 2. The artillery was similarly affected. The following was the establishment strength of 4 Army's HQ artillery and the actual strength on 18 January 1942:

	Medium field howitzers	210mm howitzers	100mm guns	150mm guns	Assault guns	Prime movers
Establishment	48	36	48	9	84	252
Actual	5	8	17	2	12	22

In spring 1942 the pressure on A Gp Centre eased somewhat. Stalin, rather than concentrating his burgeoning reserves and feeding them into the Moscow counter-offensive, chose to disperse them all along the front and launch three extra large-scale attacks at Leningrad, Kharkov and Kerch, on the eastern tip of the Crimean peninsula.† This was a serious blunder, for had he concentrated his reserves in just one sector he might well have achieved a decisive breakthrough. Which sector was selected was largely immaterial as the Germans were terribly weak all along the front. In early 1942 the typical German infantry division in each of the Army Groups

> consisted of a reinforced regiment of infantry, usually four or five battalions . . . few if any heavy weapons, a handful of engineers, about twenty light field howitzers, and a rather

---

* The Russian climate was also making serious inroads into German strengths. Up to 20 February 1942, along the whole front, 112,627 cases of frostbite were reported. The front-line infantry were, of course, the most likely victims.

† The bridgehead from which this latter attack was to be launched had been established in late December.

large contingent of support troops. Raw conscripts or recently transferred rear area support troops often replaced the fallen combat veterans in the infantry companies. Many battalions possessed only three companies, and infantry companies consisted of anywhere from 30 to 80 men, rather than the authorised 191 men.[60]

So serious were the personnel shortages that at one stage OKW considered disbanding 15 infantry divisions or else reducing every division from three regiments to two.

Personnel shortages were not the only problem. On 12 February 1942 German operational tank strength along the whole of the Eastern Front was only 142 machines. In fact, the German Army was fast becoming totally unmechanised, because there was also a terrible dearth of motor transport. Even by mid-November 1941, of the roughly 500,000 vehicles in the east, 30 per cent had been abandoned or lost and another 40 per cent required repair. The Army had already been forced to strip the infantry divisions' supply, anti-tank and engineer units of vehicles and the situation improved very little over the next months as German industry could not produce enough vehicles even to replenish the panzer divisions.* This, however, remained somewhat academic as Hitler still insisted on using most of the new vehicles to form new divisions in Germany.

By dispersing his offensive all along the German front, therefore, Stalin let their very weak formations pretty much off the hook, his own forces not being strong enough at any one critical sector of the line to make a decisive breakthrough. None of the three major attacks made much headway. At Kharkov, Kerch and on the Volkhov the offensives were not only stopped in their tracks but were all turned into massive 'cauldrons' in which in all 330,000 men, almost 1,000 tanks and as many guns were lost. The lesson was clear. Strong as Russian recuperative powers might be, they were still not adequate to fuel a concerted push along the whole front. They might, indeed, have been better advised not to take the offensive at all. As had been shown at Moscow, there was much to be said for letting the Germans choose the focal point – for they too were incapable of

---

* Between October 1941 and the following March, 74,000 motor vehicles were lost but only 7,500 new ones received. Similar figures applied to almost every type of equipment. Just before Stalin's offensive, Halder noted that other deficiencies included 1,900 artillery pieces, 7,000 anti-tank guns and 14,000 machine-guns.

launching more than one reasonably well equipped army group at a time – and then concentrating the superior Russian reserves in that one sector.

Nevertheless, these local German victories were bought at a severe price, and by May 1942 all the army groups were suffering similar shortages to those of A Gp Centre. Between 1 November 1941 and 1 April 1942, along the whole front, the Germans had sustained 900,000 casualties but received only 450,000 replacements. By the latter date, according to Halder, personnel shortages amounted to 625,000 men, whilst the firepower of the army groups was put at 33 per cent of establishment for Centre, 50 per cent for North and 33 per cent for South. The Russians, on the other hand, had between December and May brought up 23 newly activated divisions and 18 brigades on A Gp North's front and 40 divisions and 21 brigades opposite A Gp South.

Shortages of equipment were an equal cause for concern. On 31 March the 16 panzer divisions on the Eastern Front had only 140 operational tanks between them. Scales of equipment applying in June 1941 would have called for 2,560. The whole question of resources, and Hitler's casual attitude to munitions production before the war, was a source of some concern in Berlin. On 17 April Goebbels wrote in his diary: 'Our arms and munitions situation is exceptionally strained . . . There is cause for some alarm. Unfortunately there was much neglect in this respect; we took the matter of arms and munitions production far too lightly and now we have to pay for it.'[61] A recent German historian has put it more simply still: 'The figures speak for themselves. Germany's resources were inadequate. She was waging a war beyond her capabilities.'[62]

Hitler, however, remained blind to the basic facts. One member of his headquarters noted that Halder was beginning to moot 'the idea of whether we should not . . . go over to the defensive in the East, since further offensive operations seemed beyond our strength. But it is impossible even to mention this to Hitler.'[63] Von Blumentritt, now the Deputy Chief of the General Staff, soon became aware that 'Hitler did not believe that the Russians could increase their strength and would not listen to evidence on this score. When Halder told him of . . . [Russian tank production figures] Hitler slammed the table and said it was impossible. He would not believe what he did not want to believe.'[64]

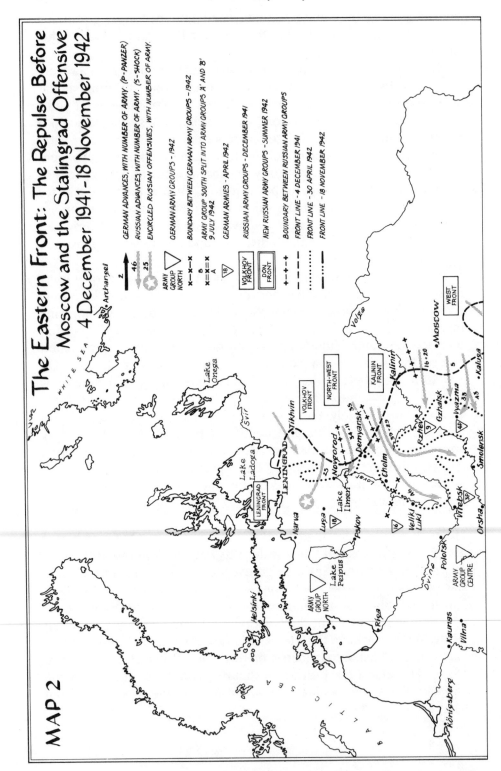

MAP 2

The Eastern Front: The Repulse Before
Moscow and the Stalingrad Offensive
4 December 1941-18 November 1942

GERMAN ADVANCES, WITH NUMBER OF ARMY. (P-PANZER)
RUSSIAN ADVANCES, WITH NUMBER OF ARMY. (S-SHOCK)
ENCIRCLED RUSSIAN OFFENSIVES, WITH NUMBER OF ARMY.

GERMAN ARMY GROUPS - 1942

BOUNDARY BETWEEN GERMAN ARMY GROUPS - 1942

ARMY GROUP SOUTH SPLIT INTO ARMY GROUPS 'A' AND 'B'
9 JULY 1942

GERMAN ARMIES - APRIL 1942

RUSSIAN ARMY GROUPS - DECEMBER 1941

NEW RUSSIAN ARMY GROUPS - SUMMER 1942

BOUNDARY BETWEEN RUSSIAN ARMY GROUPS

FRONT LINE - 4 DECEMBER 1941

FRONT LINE - 30 APRIL 1942

FRONT LINE - 18 NOVEMBER 1942

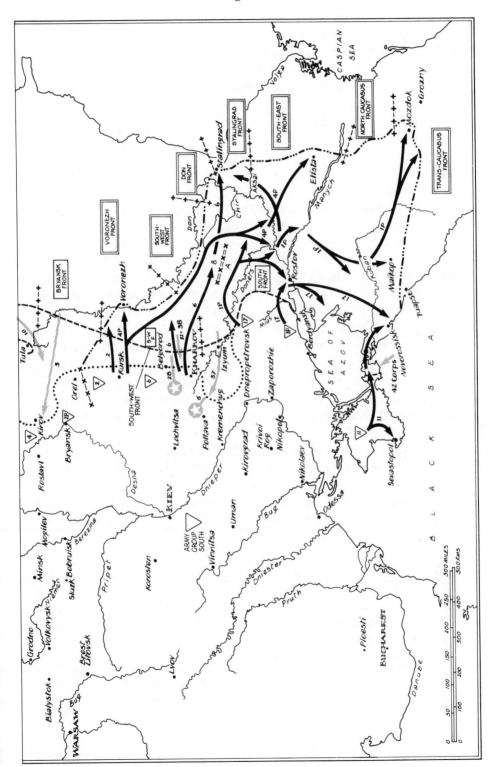

As early as January 1942 he had begun musing on the possibility of a renewed German offensive and no amount of bad news seemed able to deflect him from this purpose. His primary objective was the Caucasus, which contained important oil-fields as well as offering a possible gateway into Iran and Iraq. Later, however, he began to echo the original Barbarossa Directive and stress the need to destroy the maximum Russian forces in the field. The most important of these were the Soviet armies in the bend of the Don, and the German planners not surprisingly rather lost sight of the Caucasus axis and concentrated on creating the conditions for a series of encirclement battles between the Donets and Stalingrad. These were to culminate in the seizure of the latter city, and so sever river communications along the Volga and part of the rail network that connected Moscow with the industries and refineries to the south. Hitler, however, had still not lost sight of the Caucasian oil-fields and the final directive for the projected offensive, issued on 5 April 1942, included *both* objectives, with the occupation of Stalingrad seen only as a prelude to an immediate drive to Maikop, Grozny and Baku.

German preparations for this enormous task soon revealed that there were still serious constraints on their offensive capabilities. Nine panzer and seven motorised divisions were included in the total of 88 allocated to A Gp South and these were only brought up to almost full strength by ruthlessly stripping those left with A Gps North and Centre. The latter's panzer divisions were reduced to only one tank battalion each, their infantry divisions were left with less than 50 per cent of their establishment, and almost all their motor transport was requisitioned.* This latter expedient still did not fully solve A Gp South's problems. Even their spearhead mobile divisions began the offensive with only 85 per cent of their MT requirements, whilst the infantry were still obliged to rely almost entirely on horses.

Despite the ruthless concentration of resources, therefore, the local commanders were still far from convinced that A Gp South had sufficient forces to carry out its prescribed tasks. The original plan envisaged an extremely ambitious encirclement operation in the bend of the Don, during which the armoured

---

* OKW was forced to order that 69 of the 75 infantry divisions with A Gps Centre and North consolidate their existing nine battalions each into only six. This in fact meant that the combat strength of these divisions was only half what it had been in May 1941.

units of 1 and 4 Panzer Armies* would have to cover immense distances and fight their way through possibly a whole series of Russian positions. But the German High Command had drawn certain conclusions from the 1941 campaign, when they had seen their infantry armies lag badly behind the armour and too often come to a halt in front of Russian rearguard positions. For the new offensive, therefore, they allotted several of their mobile divisions to 2, 6 and 17 Armies† and thus seriously weakened the panzer armies' striking power. So seriously, indeed, that local commanders felt obliged to tamper with the original plan. Feeling that 1 Pz Ay, which was supposed to drive head-on through the Russian lines all the way from the Aksai to Stalingrad, was too weak for this task, they moved its line of advance northwards from the north bank of the Don to an axis much closer to the comforting support of 6 Army. The resulting open right flank was to be partially protected by 17 Army and 8 Italian Army, which were to pin down enemy forces encountered around Rostov and the Sea of Azov. But this revised plan substantially reduced the size of the anticipated 'cauldrons' and also offered an excellent avenue of escape, across the lower Donets and lower Don, for any Russian units that evaded 1 Pz Ay's drive or 17 and 8 Italian Armies' mini-encirclement.

There were potential problems, too, for 4 Pz Ay, whose race down the west bank of the Don would leave its left flank completely exposed. Some sort of protection had to be provided and Hitler's Directive airily decreed that 'German forces will provide a strong supporting force between Orel and the Don' and that between Voronezh and Stalingrad 'individual German divisions will also remain available as reserves behind the Don front'.[65] Nowhere was it explained where A Gp South, already concerned about its striking power, was to find the divisions for such an essentially static role. In fact, it was already obvious to the commanders on the ground that this task would have to be undertaken by Germany's allies, the 20 Romanian, Hungarian and Italian divisions that had been pressed into service for the 1942 offensive. That the security of mobile operations depended upon a perimeter pegged out by troops of

---

* Panzer groups had been designated panzer armies (henceforth Pz Ay) on 6 October 1941 (Pz Gps 1 and 2) and 1 January 1942 (Pz Gps 3 and 4). To avoid confusion my narrative has retained the former's original designation longer than is strictly accurate.

† The infantry armies were given three of the nine panzer divisions and three of the seven motorised divisions.

this calibre was not a cheering prospect for the Germans. Of the Romanians, Hoth was to write:

> German commands which have Romanian troops serving under them must reconcile themselves to the fact that moderately heavy fire, even without an enemy attack, will be enough to cause these troops to fall back and that the reports they submit concerning their own situation are worthless since they never know where their own units are and their estimates of the enemy strength are vastly exaggerated.[66]

The drive towards Stalingrad and the Caucasus was launched on 28 June 1942 but after early successes, along the whole front, it fast degenerated into one of the war's more inept campaigns. Its pattern, such as it was, was shaped by the fact that Hitler was striving for yet another *Kesselschlacht* like Smolensk, Kiev and Vyazma/Bryansk, whilst Stalin had determined to deny it to him. The Russians now firmly resisted the temptation to cling to hopeless positions or to pour reserves right into the beckoning German pincers. As soon as positions seemed untenable they were given up and both South-West and South Fronts were permitted to evacuate substantial forces. 'Between 28 June and 24 July . . . [these Fronts] fell back 80 to 120 miles and gave up the important Donets Basin. The retreat severely damaged morale throughout the country, and the forces it saved were severely weakened, but it did deny the Germans a victory of the kind they wanted and needed.'[67] Hitler, however, seemed incapable of grasping the fact that the Russians were not tamely waiting to be rounded up and, when 4 Pz Ay failed to find them as it drove down to the Don bend, he insisted that they must still be concentrated around Rostov and the Don–Donets confluence. On 13 July, therefore, 4 Pz Ay was turned away from Stalingrad and ordered due south to cut across the lower Don and trap the mythical Russians. 1 Pz Ay was also to participate, and it too halted its drive towards Stalingrad, recrossed the Donets and moved westwards along the northern bank of the Don. The advance to Stalingrad was now to be the sole responsibility of 6 Army, though any chance it might have had of seizing that city quickly, before the Russians could bolster its defences, was nullified by the transfer of its only panzer corps to 4 Pz Ay.

These about-turns took time, and with progress further hindered by a spell of wet weather, such Soviet forces as had remained in the Rostov area were able to pull back behind the lower Don and evade the attempted encirclement. With his panzer divisions once again hitting empty air, Hitler plumbed the strategic depths. Rather than admit that the Russians had escaped, and were probably reforming their forces along the middle Don or around Stalingrad, he purported to believe that the lack of prisoners showed that the Russian manpower barrel was dry, that Stalingrad was there for the taking, and that substantial German forces could therefore be spared for an immediate drive into the Caucasus. On 23 July 1942 he issued Directive 45, according to which the *consecutive* tasks listed in the original Directive (No. 41) were now to be performed *simultaneously*. A Gp B* was to take Stalingrad, with 4 Pz Ay turning about once more and heading north-eastwards along the south bank of the Don, after which mobile elements were to push on over the Volga towards Astrakhan, all-in-all a journey of over 400 miles. A Gp A was to conquer the Caucasus, 17 Army clearing the Kuban and the Black Sea coast and 1 Pz Ay driving right through Mozdok and Grozny as far as Baku. The distance from Rostov to Baku was more than 700 miles as the crow flies.

Only flagrant self-deception could have led Hitler to believe that the forces at his disposal were anything like adequate for these twin tasks. Halder wrote in his diary about this time that 'the *Führer*'s underestimate of the enemy's potential was taking on such a grotesque form that serious planning for operations was no longer possible.'[68] The task assigned to A Gp A was particularly ambitious. In Directive 41 it had been assumed that operations in the Caucasus would begin only after Stalingrad had fallen and would thus be able to call upon a large proportion of the divisions deployed by the whole of A Gp South. But the rump of divisions now allocated to the Caucasus offensive were clearly being given a superhuman task. Worse still, even those formations still left to A Gp A were stripped of some of their best men. 11 Army, in the Crimea, should have moved in to help in the clearance of the Kuban, but in the event lost five of its best divisions, all its artillery and its Army HQ to A Gp North which it was to assist in the reduction of Leningrad. This left 17 Army almost alone† to conquer the Kuban

---

* A Gp South had been by now split into two, A Gp B in the north, comprising 2 Army, 6 Army and 4 Pz Ay, and A Gp A, to operate south of the Don and consisting of 17 Army and 1 Pz Ay.
† Only five Romanian divisions remained to assist 17 Army, the Leningrad operation having also bagged 11 Army headquarters and all of its artillery.

and the Black Sea coast, which in turn left 1 Pz Ay out on a limb, this latter formation now being expected simultaneously to protect 17 Army's left flank, drive the 700 miles to Baku and protect a front that would eventually stretch 800 miles across the line of the Caucasus.

With its armoured spearheads concentrated on a south-eastern axis, and with A Gp B being pulled north-east towards Stalingrad, a huge gap would inevitably appear between the two army groups, covering almost the whole of the Kalmyk Steppes between the upper Kuban and the Aksai. The only units that could be spared to cover this gap were a reconnaissance detachment sent out by 4 Pz Ay towards Elitsa. As if to ensure that 1 Pz Ay's task was impossible, Hitler had, early in July, deprived it of two of its élite motorised divisions, 1 ss Panzer and *Grossdeutschland* Motorised Infantry, which had been earmarked for transfer to Western Europe because of rumours of a British landing. Unfounded though the rumours were, the prospect of a two-front war was already beginning to circumscribe German options.

A Gp B was in similar straits. 2 Army was thoroughly involved in protecting the northern flank, between Voronezh and Orel, and thus only two armies, 6 and 4 Pz, were available for an operation that had originally been deemed to require almost the whole of A Gp South. Again Hitler conspired to compound his commanders' problems. Early in July, because he felt that A Gp Centre had been too weakened by the build-up of A Gp South, two panzer divisions were summarily transferred back. A Gp Centre, of course, would have regarded the move as entirely justified, just as A Gp North felt that it could not operate without the reinforcement from 11 Army, OB West* without the two mobile divisions and 4 Pz Ay without 6 Army's panzer corps. But even if this endless *ad hoc* shuffling about of units was justified, this only serves to underline the fact that the Germans simply did not possess the forces to undertake the ambitious operations envisaged. Baku and Stalingrad were just not on as twin missions, a fact that became transparently clear as the latter increasingly monopolised attention and A Gp A found itself giving up more and more units to Paulus† and Hoth, battling their way forward to the Volga.

---

* Short for *Oberbefehlshaber West*, Commander-in-Chief in the West, the German headquarters in France.
† Paulus was the commander of 6 Army. He was made a Field Marshal on 31 January, shortly before the surrender of Stalingrad.

The army group commander, Field Marshal Ewald von Kleist, complained: 'We could still have reached our goal if my forces had not been drawn away bit by bit to help the attack at Stalingrad. Besides part of my motorised forces, I had to give up the whole of my Flak corps and all my air force except the reconnaissance squadrons.'[69]

Whether von Kleist could in fact have reached Baku is doubtful, but what is certain is that he could only have done it by rendering A Gp B completely incapable of fulfilling its own mission. As it was, 6 Army and 1 Pz Ay were operating on a shoestring. Of the advance to Stalingrad in late July and early August one German historian has written: 'In these operations there were two factors, the importance of which cannot be overemphasised: throughout the whole course of the operations, the Army Group was faced with an uninterrupted series of supply crises; and it had no reserves of any kind.'[70] The supply crises were yet another indication that A Gp South had never had the resources for any of the missions entrusted to it by Hitler. Even in early July, according to von Kleist, one of the reasons for the transfer of the two panzer divisions to A Gp Centre had been that 'it seemed impossible to supply petrol for more than a certain amount of the mechanised forces in the southern region.'[71] This became yet more evident when 4 Pz Ay was turned south on 13 July, and 6 Army had to be halted and had to give up almost all of its fuel allocation to Hoth's mobile units. Similarly, after the decisions embodied in Directive 45, it was found that there was not enough motor transport adequately to support both A Gps B and A and Paulus was again called upon to make the sacrifice.

The transfer benefited no one. Paulus, obviously, was seriously handicapped. On 2 August General Wolfgang von Richthofen, in charge of air support for both A Gps B and A, noted in his War Diary: '6 Army's advance on Stalingrad is making no progress, partly as the result of stiff opposition, but mainly because of the lack of supplies.'[72] It was at one stage only able to move at all thanks to convoys of fuel lorries provided by Richthofen's 4 Air Fleet. But A Gp A did not find its own extra trucks an unmixed blessing. The deeper 1 Pz Ay drove into the Caucasus, the more fuel these trucks guzzled, so that by the end of September they themselves were consuming most of the load they carried. Nor did the railways in this part of the world provide a realistic alternative:

The only . . . line, which was a single-track one, linking the 1st Panzer Army to Rostov . . . reached such a degree of saturation that, in order to solve the problem of switching, it was necessary to fall back upon the energetic but costly method of blowing up empty trains. Another proof of how bad the crisis became is shown by the fact that it was necessary to call upon the help of camels to replenish the tanks with fuel.[73]

Slowly but surely, during September and October 1942, both army group offensives lost momentum. On 30 August 1 Pz Ay pushed across the River Terek but more than eight weeks later they still had not succeeded in getting troops into Grozny, and an offensive south-west of that town, on 2 November, soon petered out. This was to represent the furthest east that German troops were ever to reach. Von Paulus almost matched them, but by the time his troops* had reached the outskirts of Stalingrad, in mid-September, they were far too weak to maintain a concerted drive to clear the city completely. Not that they did not continue trying. By 13 November, according to Soviet sources, they had launched three general attacks on the Soviet positions involving up to 10 divisions, 50 attacks with 2 to 3 divisions, 60 with a single division or so, and over 120 with various regimental groups. But the smaller attacks were more and more the norm as shortages of manpower and equipment became yet more acute. For the Russians were keeping up the pressure along the whole front, at all points of which the Germans were badly overstretched. On 8 September OKH Organisational Branch reported that 'all planning must take into account the unalterable fact that the predicted strength of the Army field forces as of 1 November 1942 will be 800,000, or 18 per cent below established strength and that it is no longer possible to reduce . . . [this deficit].'[74] For the army as a whole, therefore, the cupboard was bare and 'with the exception of five engineer battalions, flown out from Germany, all the replacements . . . [Paulus] received for his bled-white regiments had to come from within the . . . [Eastern Front].'[75]

But the other army groups were also sorely pressed, and with fierce Russian attacks pinning down A Gp North on the Volkhov, A Gp Centre's northern wing in the Rzhev area and its central and southern portions around Smolensk, there was no possible chance of their being able to spare reinforcements for 6 Army. The Russians were not so constrained. Though the decision to exert heavy pressure

* Paulus took 4 Pz Ay under command in mid-August.

along the whole front involved lavish expenditure of manpower, the Red Army always managed to maintain some kind of reserve to provide a steady stream of replacements and reinforcements for the Stalingrad garrison. Between 15 September and 1 November, for example, whereas Paulus received not one fresh division, the Russians were able to filter in six fresh and fully equipped divisions, increasing their force from nine to sixteen divisions against Paulus' battle-weary nine.

Nor could Paulus call upon local reinforcements from within A Gp B itself. In the positions on the middle Don and to the south of Stalingrad, shortages were just as acute. In November, for example, the average strength of the army group's panzer divisions was a mere 27 tanks each, whilst its panzer reserve was very much a paper force. There was only one German division, with only 38 tanks in working order, and the other was Romanian, equipped with Czech tanks with 37mm guns and a mere 21 Pz IIIs. Air support was also steadily dwindling. 4 Air Fleet had started off in July with a preponderance over the Russians and did manage for much of the ensuing campaign to fly five sorties for every three of the enemy. But this kind of effort involved heavy losses of men and machines, far too few of which were ever replaced. In June 1942, 4 Air Fleet had numbered 1,600 aircraft. By 20 October it could count only 974, of which 594 were airworthy and 141 first-class fighters. By early November these planes were pitted against 1,200 first-line Russian machines.

Equally serious for A Gp B was the serious imbalance in the deployment of its manpower. For, insufficient though they were, Paulus had sucked towards his own sector the majority of the army group's German divisions and bit by bit the security of the rest of its front had become the responsibility of the less than reliable Romanian, Hungarian and Italian formations.* In early September

* It should be noted that the unreliability of these units was not a function of innate military inferiority. Hoth, cited earlier, and other generals were aware that Romanian weakness stemmed largely from a hopelessly corrupt officer corps whilst their rank-and-file, as well as that of the Allies, could have fought well enough if they had not been equipped with obsolete weaponry. But there was little hope of their obtaining more modern equipment simply because the Germans, as has been repeatedly emphasised, could not even adequately supply their own troops. Paulus himself was clear that it was 'lack of modern weapons, particularly artillery, tanks and anti-tank weapons, that constituted the main weakness of the allied troops, and the promises to supply them with these weapons were fulfilled either to a very inadequate extent, or, in some cases, not at all.' (Quoted in Goerlitz, op. cit., p. 158.)

the Russians began to probe these positions and found that 400 miles of front, from just south of Voronezh to the Don bend west of Stalingrad, were held by 2 Hungarian, 8 Italian and, from October, 3 Romanian Armies. The latter manned 250 miles of front with only 33 battalions. Positions to the south of Stalingrad were even weaker and at the junction of A Gps A and B were virtually non-existent. The gap in the Kalmyk Steppes, already referred to, was by October some 190 miles wide and covered by a single German motorised division. Von Manstein, who was to be recalled to the southern sector in late November, has made it clear what a perfect opportunity this offered to the Russians: '. . . to leave the main body of the army group at Stalingrad for weeks on end, with inadequately protected flanks, was a cardinal error. It amounted to nothing less than presenting the enemy with the initiative we ourselves had resigned over the whole southern wing, and it was a clear invitation for him to surround 6th Army.'[76]

The Russians, moreover, were ready to exploit the opportunity. Despite their having mounted numerous large-scale attacks along the whole of the Eastern Front, and despite the necessity to keep funnelling fresh troops into Stalingrad itself, their vast manpower reserves also allowed them to build up a substantial striking force all along A Gp B's front. For by now the well-timed haymaker had become a deliberate part of Soviet strategy and, having decided as early as September to chop off the 6 Army salient in the bend of the Don, they were content to bide their time, methodically building up their own forces and letting the best German units wear themselves out in the rubble of Stalingrad.

The Russian build-up was entrusted to Marshal Georgi Zhukov, who displayed a fine touch in the way he marshalled his forces, particularly in Stalingrad itself, where he committed just enough fresh troops to baulk the Germans but without ever dipping too deeply into his strategic reserve. By 1 November, as well as having committed six fresh divisions across the Volga, he had activated a further 27 divisions and 19 armoured brigades, all of which he held back except for a brief period of combat in quieter parts of the line. By mid-November the Russians had concentrated half-a-million infantry, 894 T-34 and KV-1 tanks and 230 regiments of field artillery behind the Don. The three Fronts involved, Stalingrad, Don and South-West, could also call upon 1,115 planes, including 600 fighters. In the sector to be attacked, on a 250-mile front between the Aksai and Serafimovich, the Germans could muster only seven

German and fifteen Romanian divisions. These included a little over 300 German tanks* and could call on the support of at most 400 airworthy aircraft.

The counter-offensive, codenamed Uranus, was launched on 19 November and within only four days it had slashed through the Romanian forces holding both flanks of the sector attacked. On 23 November Russian spearheads met at Kalach, to the west of Stalingrad, and 6 Army was surrounded. For anyone but Hitler there could have been only one possible option open to the Germans: to allow 6 Army to try and break out of the encirclement, to pull the dangerously exposed A Gp A out of the Caucasus, and to withdraw the whole southern command behind the Donets or the Dnieper. Such a withdrawal would greatly shorten the front and it could then be reasonably hoped that, as the pursuing Russians halted to regroup and organise their lines of communication, enough time might be granted to the Germans to construct a stable defence line. Behind such a line it might just be possible to inflict such losses on subsequent Russian offensives that even their remarkable recuperative powers would begin to ebb. Hitler, however, never regarded retreat as a viable tactical option. The notion of trading space for time was completely alien to him. Retreat was defeat, pure and simple, and no amount of future benefit could compensate for the loss of face involved. 6 Army and A Gp A must remain exactly where they were and such units of A Gp B as had escaped encirclement were to counter-attack immediately, smash the cordon around 6 Army and fight their way back to the Don.

A new army group, under von Manstein, was created for just this purpose on 21 November. It was dubbed A Gp Don† and comprised 6 Army and surviving units of 3 Romanian and 4 Pz Ays. Over the next three weeks there were added a panzer division from A Gp A (which reduced von Kleist's fuel problems but did little to enhance his offensive capacity), two panzer divisions from A Gp Centre and one from France. Two of these were up to strength but the other two could scrape together only 60 tanks between them, whilst von Manstein's fifth panzer division, a survivor of Uranus,

* In one of the two panzer corps involved, 92 out of the 147 tanks were Czech 38(t)s with 37mm guns.

† An early example of Hitler's penchant for naming army groups after areas which he had just lost. The same was to happen in 1944 and 1945 when A Gps Vistula, North Ukraine and South Ukraine all came into being after the relevant river line or area had been lost.

was so badly mauled that it soon had to be withdrawn as being no longer battleworthy. Nor did von Manstein's infantry component elicit much confidence. Those taken over from A Gp B were little more than remnants, consisting of nine battered Romanian divisions, plus two cavalry, and five woefully understrength German divisions. The only reinforcements were three German infantry divisions, and two of the new *Luftwaffe* Field Divisions. These latter were composed of surplus *Luftwaffe* ground personnel whom Göring had resolutely declined to release to the Army. They had their own officers and training programmes and were generally regarded as being almost worthless as combat troops. What was particularly galling for Army commanders was that Göring used his influence to ensure that these divisions were splendidly equipped at the expense of the ordinary infantry, but could do nothing to prevent them losing most of these precious guns and lorries on their first encounter with the enemy.* All in all, then, von Manstein's new army group was a feeble instrument with which to contemplate stemming the Russian tide. Indeed, 'in spite of its grandiloquent designation, [it] was not an army group since its only offensive element was . . . [two] understrength . . . panzer corps. It could not in fact be compared with a 1941 German army.'[77]

During November and early December von Manstein only managed to hold his scattered positions along the Chir and the Aksai because Zhukov's sure sense of timing rather deserted him when it came to a question of when to halt his offensive. Perhaps because he was unable to believe just how short of men the Germans were, he failed to drive home his tremendous advantage and, rather than pressing forward against the escaping German and Romanian remnants, he satisfied himself with simply strengthening the cordon around 6 Army. A Gp Don, therefore, was given a short breathing-space whilst it absorbed its modest quota of reinforcements and was able, temporarily at least, to hold firm on the Chir–Aksai line. But merely holding firm was not good enough for Hitler, who continued to insist that an attempt be made to break through to 6 Army. Von Manstein pointed out that his existing forces were barely adequate for the defence of existing positions and was only persuaded to attempt the rescue when OKH promised reinforcements that would

---

* In the following year a *Luftwaffe* Field Division attached to 3 Pz Ay lost an acceptable 700 men in one round of fighting. But in the same period it also managed to abandon 2,600 rifles, 1,100 pistols, 550 machine-guns, 30 mortars, 26 anti-tank guns and 40 flak guns.

bring the relief force up to four panzer, three infantry, one mountain and three *Luftwaffe* divisions.

Von Manstein remained less than optimistic, feeling that such a force 'might conceivably suffice to make temporary contact with 6 Army and to restore its freedom of movement. In no event, however, could . . . [it] administer a defeat big enough to enable us, as Hitler had put it . . . to "reoccupy the positions held prior to the attack".'[78] OKH assurances, moreover, were less than cast-iron guarantees and von Manstein received very few of the promised reinforcements. Two divisions had to be sent to shore up 3 Romanian Army's front; half the mountain division was given to A Gp A and the other retained by A Gp Centre; A Gp A refused to release its army artillery; one *Luftwaffe* division was late in forming; two others and a panzer division arrived in such enfeebled condition that they were rated incapable of offensive action. In short, the German army on the Eastern Front was stretched to the limit.

Von Manstein could not now realistically hope to break through to 6 Army, let alone to disperse the cordon around it, and the odds against him increased yet more when a panzer and an infantry division of the already reduced relief force became embroiled in a Russian spoiling attack on the lower Chir and were never able to take part in the counter-offensive. All that was now left were just two panzer divisions, one of which had only 20 tanks, and an assault gun brigade, which were expected to advance 80 miles against extremely heavy opposition. They set off on 12 December and were soon faced by 400 Soviet T-34s and KV-1s. Though they fought with outstanding gallantry, inflicting numerous casualties on the enemy armour, they simply did not have the muscle to effect a significant breakthrough. By 17 December many had run out of fuel and/or ammunition and had to be abandoned, and the eagerly awaited arrival of a fresh panzer division on the same day proved to be something of an anticlimax as it contained only 30 tanks. The Russian reinforcement, on the other hand, comprised a whole Guards Army and by the 18th the attack had completely run out of steam. Von Manstein put it in a nutshell when he wrote: 'The fact that we ultimately failed in our mission was primarily due to the extraordinary preponderance of the enemy's forces and the deficient strength of our own.'[79]

This 'extraordinary preponderance' was amply demonstrated on 16 December, as von Manstein debated the wisdom of transferring another panzer corps from the north of his sector to assist the relief operation. The matter was decided for him by the Russians, who unleashed yet another of their hammer blows. For while von Manstein was wondering whether he could hope to turn the tide of battle by redeploying a battered panzer and infantry division – all that the corps in question contained – along the 200 miles covered by Voronezh and South-West Fronts, facing the northern wing of A Gp Don and the southern wing of A Gp B, the Russians had massed 36 rifle divisions, 425,000 men, 1,030 tanks and almost 5,000 guns and mortars of 81mm and above. They were faced mainly by 8 Italian Army, whose nine divisions contained around 55 tanks and 380 47mm anti-tank guns, all of which were obsolete. Von Manstein's 'reserve' panzer corps immediately became embroiled in the fighting and by 24 December the Germans had lost all hope of clinging on to the Donets–Don corridor, let alone of relieving 6 Army.

The Russians continued to throw in divisions along various parts of the southern front. On Christmas Eve three Soviet armies broke through along the Chir and in the Kalmyk Steppes, in which sector they had massed 19½ divisions, 635 tanks and over 1,500 guns. By early January 1943 their spearheads were only 30 miles from Rostov, the occupation of which would isolate A Gp A from the rest of the front. On 10 January they began in earnest to eliminate the Stalingrad pocket, using seven armies for the task. Paulus' position became increasingly hopeless and, on 30 January, he surrendered, the last flickers of continuing resistance being stamped out on 2 February. The Russians buried 147,000 German and Romanian dead and took 91,000 prisoners. Twenty German divisions, and two Romanian, had been wiped off their order of battle.

Nor was the reduction of Stalingrad the only major Russian effort in January 1943. On the 13th, on the Voronezh Front, two heavily reinforced armies and a rifle corps were launched against what was left of A Gp B, its 2 Hungarian Army. The Russians probably deployed some 900 tanks, against only 100, and at certain points along the front their artillery achieved a density of 180 guns per mile. Breakthrough was almost immediate and by 18 January a substantial pocket had been formed. Some 90,000 prisoners were taken and 2 Army, to 2 Hungarian's left, had to abandon Voronezh hastily to evade encirclement by Russian forces swinging north. As they pulled back, the Russians raced on towards Kursk and Kharkov, whilst other units, from South-West Front, pressed on to the coast of the Sea of Azov, behind Rostov, to cut off A Gps Don and A. On 7 February Kursk fell and a week later Kharkov. The crucial thrusts failed, however, due to a combination of Russian exhaustion, appalling weather and the exceptional tactical ability of von Manstein. Thus, though the withdrawal of 1 Pz Ay through Rostov was not finally sanctioned until 27 January,* the Russians never succeeded either in catching up with these units in the Caucasus itself or in cutting them off by winning the race to Rostov and the lower Don. It had been a close shave, however, with 1 Pz Ay getting its last units through Rostov on 1 February and the Russians crashing into the city on the 6th.

Stalin's final hope of isolating A Gps Don, B and A lay in a strong thrust from Kharkov to the Dnieper crossings at Dnepropetrovsk and Zaporozhie, the seizure of which would cut the southern armies off from the rest of the front as well as from their supply lines to the west. By 17 February Soviet forces were within 30 miles of the Dnieper, but these last few miles proved to be beyond their powers. 'The Red Army troops had already outrun their support and supplies, and they were beyond the range of effective air support since many of the captured airfields were not yet in use. The supply, reinforcement and maintenance system was functioning badly over the extended lines of communication and many formations and units had been reduced by casualties to skeleton form.'[80] In this last bid to duplicate the success at Stalingrad, on a much vaster scale, the Russians had finally outreached themselves. This was not so much because of any strategic shortage – the factories and the induction centres were still working flat-out and producing munitions and men on a prodigious scale – but because their armies as yet lacked a well oiled supply and replacement system that could quickly reinforce the armies at the front in the tactically decisive sectors. Building up for long-planned counter-offensives, behind a semi-static front, was one thing; consistently feeding in men and matériel along ever-lengthening lines of communication had proved to be quite another.

So von Manstein was granted a respite, and he quickly showed himself as adept as Zhukov at launching a well timed counter-attack against an exhausted enemy. More so, in fact, for von Manstein was able to dispense with the kind of laborious preparations undertaken by the Russians at Moscow and behind the Don. Grasping the opportunity offered by the arrival of three fresh ss motorised and panzer divisions, he submitted a plan for a counterstroke on

* 17 Army was ordered to remain in the Kuban in the unlikely event of a renewed offensive towards the Caucasian oil-fields.

17 February. On the 18th it was approved and the operation was launched the next morning. The Russian spearheads were bitten off, around Pavlovgrad, on the 22nd and German forces moved swiftly northwards towards Kharkov. By 12 March the city was engulfed in fierce street-fighting and it fell two days later. Five days after that Belgorod was also in German hands. Realising they had lost the initiative on the eastern side of the Dnieper, the Russians halted and pulled their surviving vanguard units back behind the Donets. With the onset of the spring thaw, the front congealed, though the arrival of Zhukov to oversee the Voronezh Front and the allocation to him of three fresh armies from High Command Reserve indicated that the lull was only to be temporary.

2

The Long Retreat
July 1943 – May 1945

The overall significance of von Manstein's counter-offensive in February and March 1943, which closed the last chapter, should not be exaggerated. Whilst it rightly figures in numerous accounts as an outstanding example of military improvisation and thinking on one's feet, it did little to shift the overall strategic balance on the Eastern Front. Even the assertion that it saved A Gp South* from destruction is not entirely convincing, for one is entitled to wonder whether, even if the Russians had reached the Dnieper crossings, they could have maintained substantial lodgements there. Be that as it may, the positive gains for the Germans were hardly dramatic.

In terms of territory, A Gp South was now occupying very much the same line from which the Stalingrad/Caucasus offensive had been launched nine months previously, though this time the Izyum salient was replaced by one at Kursk.† Most importantly, although the attack had inflicted 40,000 casualties on the Russians and had led to the capture, it was claimed, of 600 tanks and 500 guns, this was hardly a fatal blow to the burgeoning Red Army. As has been rightly pointed out, 'The defeats inflicted on the Red Army were limited . . . temporary and in no way decisive', and the Germans had made such gains as they had only because the opposing forces

---

* On 6 February A Gp B had ceased to exist, whilst A Gps A and Don had both been put under von Manstein's command and renamed A Gp South.

† A Gps Centre and North had not even held their original lines. In February and March Stalin launched supplementary offensives all along the front and forced the Germans to pull out of the Vyazma–Rzhev and Demyansk salients, as well as to surrender a land corridor into Leningrad just to the south of Lake Lagoda. The loss of these salients, however, did not displease many German generals as it shortened the line and led to a greater economy of forces. In the centre, particularly, Stalin might have been better advised simply to hold his ground and draw off a reserve to support the drive to the Dnieper crossings.

'were scattered, poorly supported and ill-supplied troops who had outrun their strength.'[1] The whole Soviet war economy, on the other hand, had far from outrun its strength and over the next two years was able to turn out such a cornucopia of excellent weaponry that the *Wehrmacht* in the east was simply inundated. From now on the Russians were able to marshal huge forces at whatever point of the front they chose and smash through the German lines almost with impunity. Offensive followed offensive, up and down the front, swamping the defenders and inexorably pushing them back, first out of the Soviet Union and then to the gates of Berlin itself.

It might seem a little odd, therefore, that a period characterised as a series of non-stop Russian hammer-blows should begin with a major German offensive, Operation Citadel, in July 1943, aimed at eliminating the Kursk salient. It is important, however, to see Citadel in its proper context, for it in no way represented a significant tilt of the seesaw or indicated that the strategic initiative had passed back to the Germans. The fact is that the Russians positively encouraged Hitler to launch this offensive, having learnt by now that their own strikes were so much more effective when unleashed on an opponent who had already overextended himself. For the Russian High Command the fighting around Kursk, savage as it was, was not a 'backs to the wall' defensive epic as at Leningrad or in the early stages of the Moscow and Stalingrad battles, but a convenient prelude to their own offensive, itself planned long in advance.

Though Stalin himself was not at first entirely convinced by his generals' assurances that it was best to let the Germans make the first move, Hitler soon set about proving them right. By March 1943 German forces in the east had become dangerously overstretched. At that time, according to von Manstein, the ratio of forces against them was 8:1 in the sector covered by A Gp South and 4:1 in those of A Gps Centre and North. The reconstituted A Gp South, for example, had a mere 32 divisions along a 435-mile front, facing 341 Russian formations. Tank strengths were particularly low. On 23 January the Germans had been able to count only 495 battleworthy tanks along the whole of the Eastern Front,* and even when replacement machines began to trickle in, the nominal scale of equipment for the panzer divisions had to be drastically cut back. The number of tank battalions was cut from three to two and the number of tanks per company from 22 to 14. Even in fairly quiet periods, therefore, the

---

* In September 1939 there were 328 tanks in a single panzer division.

strength of the panzer divisions was rarely more than 80 or 90 tanks, and in spells of heavy fighting it could quickly be reduced to almost nothing.

As summer approached, determined efforts were made to remedy this situation and, by the end of June, there were some 2,300 battleworthy tanks along the whole front as well as 1,000 assault guns. But, though this was a great improvement on the situation five months previously, the reinforcement in fact made little difference to the vast majority of the German armies. For most of these new machines were concentrated around the Kursk salient itself – in all 1,850 tanks and 530 assault guns or over 70 per cent of the total armoured strength.* Were Citadel to fail, Hitler would have completely blunted such a cutting edge as the German divisions in Russia still retained and left the whole front extremely vulnerable to Russian counter-offensives.†

Despite this concentration of resources, senior German commanders had remarkably little faith in the operation. Even Hitler confessed: 'Whenever I think of this attack my stomach turns over.'2 For most commanders on the spot a large-scale offensive was simply beyond the army's capability. In A Gp Centre, whose 9 Army under General Walter Model was to attack the northern flank of the salient, the consensus was that it would be much better to let the Russians attack first and then hit them on an exposed flank, rather than become embroiled in 'an operation which included the task of holding the entire length of an overextended front and at the same time required attacking and breaking through a belt of enemy fortifications before the armies could come to grips in open terrain.'3 This opinion was shared in A Gp South, where von Manstein was convinced that

> the German command . . . had very little time left in which to force a draw in the east. It could only do so if it succeeded, within the framework of a – now inevitable – strategic defensive, in dealing the enemy powerful [counter-]blows of a localised character which would sap his strength to a decisive degree – first and foremost through losses of prisoners.4

---

* Indicative of the situation along the rest of the front was the fact that in June, in the adjoining Orel salient, 2Pz Ay did not possess one single tank.

† Nor would he have done much to enhance the security of other fronts. At this time there were 860 tanks and assault guns in France, Belgium and Holland and 570 in Italy, which meant that at Kursk Hitler was committing 46 per cent of Germany's total front-line panzer strength.

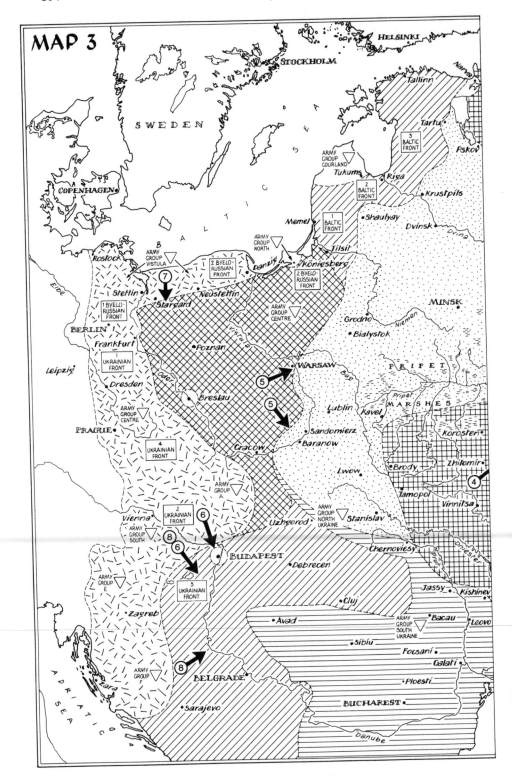

MAP 3

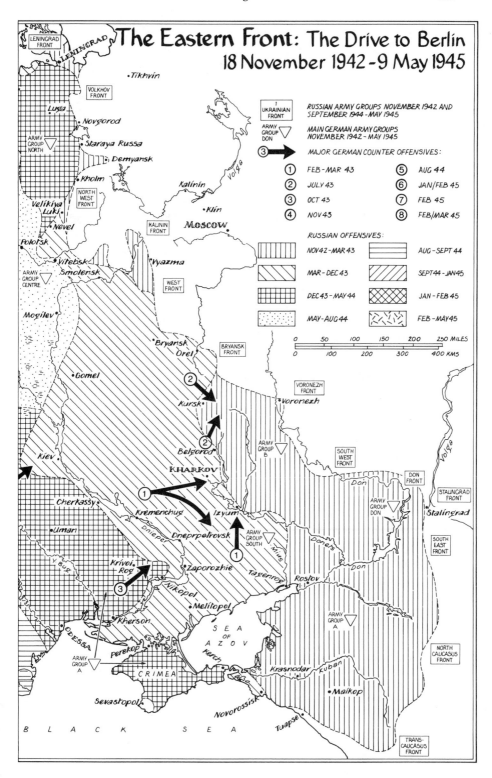

The Eastern Front: The Drive to Berlin
18 November 1942 – 9 May 1945

RUSSIAN ARMY GROUPS NOVEMBER 1942 AND
SEPTEMBER 1944 - MAY 1945

MAIN GERMAN ARMY GROUPS
NOVEMBER 1942 - MAY 1945

MAJOR GERMAN COUNTER OFFENSIVES:

① FEB-MAR 43   ⑤ AUG 44
② JULY 43   ⑥ JAN/FEB 45
③ OCT 43   ⑦ FEB 45
④ NOV 43   ⑧ FEB/MAR 45

RUSSIAN OFFENSIVES:

NOV 42-MAR 43   AUG – SEPT 44
MAR – DEC 43   SEPT 44 - JAN 45
DEC 43 - MAY 44   JAN - FEB 45
MAY - AUG 44   FEB - MAY 45

0   50   100   150   200   250 MILES
0   100   200   300   400 KMS

For it was far from clear exactly what the Kursk offensive was supposed to achieve even if it did succeed in eliminating the salient. Whilst von Kleist claimed after the war that he felt this latter was a possibility, even he went on to admit that 'we no longer had the resources to make . . . [such a success] decisive.'[5] The truth of this was also tacitly admitted by the German High Command, whose orders for Citadel were 'concerned with just a limited objective, the destruction of the considerable Soviet forces within the Kursk salient, and possessed only the vaguest of references to exploitation and to "further operations in quick time".'[6]

In fact, as must have been quite clear to most commanders, exploitation was quite out of the question. The Russians had been aware for several months that Kursk was to be the German *point d'appui** and thus had concentrated enormously strong forces in the salient, in all some 75 infantry divisions and 2,000 tanks and SUS[†] belonging to Central and Voronezh Fronts. Massive allocations of artillery had been made – 14,000 howitzers, field guns and mortars as well as 6,000 anti-tank guns and 920 multiple rocket launchers[‡] – and the efforts of the Soviet engineers had been prodigious, with over 3,000 miles of trenches and 400,000 mines laid on one Front alone. Moreover, because German dispositions and axes of advance were well known to the Russians, they were able to make their most thorough preparations at just the right places. Here guns and mortars were massed as many as 150 to the mile, and the anti-tank weapons were grouped in so-called *Pakfronts*, anti-tank killing grounds at the end of inviting corridors where the going had been made deliberately easier.

The enormous depth of the Russian positions also helped to make them the most formidable in the history of warfare. The main defensive zones were three to four miles deep, consisting of up to five interconnected trench lines, behind which lay similarly constructed secondary and rear defence zones. This pattern was duplicated no less than eight times, which meant that the whole system extended to a depth of between 120 and 180 miles. And manning the rear zones was yet another reserve Front, the Steppe, with a further 1,500 tanks under command as well as four infantry armies.

* Through their agent 'Lucy', who had access to the day-to-day decisions of the OKW. It proved impossible, moreover, for the Germans to conceal the concentration of their élite armoured divisions.
† An SU (*Samokyana Ustanokova*) was a self-propelled gun.
‡ The Germans had only 6,000 guns and mortars.

Against such defences one wonders just what the attackers hoped they could realistically achieve. Though von Manstein* and Model lined their forces up on each side of the salient in the time-honoured manner, seemingly poised to create yet another 'cauldron', their deployment smacks of textbook formalism rather than a genuine appreciation of operational possibilities. For against defences of this kind real strategic penetration was surely out of the question, and even if the two arms of the pincer did link up they would by then be so enfeebled that keeping the pocket closed would be extremely difficult, clearing it would be more so, and mounting subsequent rolling-up attacks to the north or south would be out of the question. Thus the Russians would then be able simply to cauterise the wound and sit tight for a few months, knowing that their own offensives had only been temporarily delayed and that their fecund production lines would soon replace twofold and threefold whatever losses they might have incurred.

In the event the Germans did not even achieve their minimum objective of sealing off the Kursk salient. The offensive began on 4 July 1943 but almost at once began to lose impetus. In the south, penetrations of only five to seven miles had been made by the end of the second day and nowhere had the Russians been prevented from falling back to their second line of defences. By 10 July only the well equipped 2 SS Panzer Corps was making any headway at all, towards Prohorovka, but on this same day 5 Guards Tank Army was transferred from the Steppe Front and on 12 July it clashed with the SS Corps in a huge tank mêlée. Upwards of 850 Soviet and 450 German tanks and assault guns were engaged over the next five days. Losses were enormous on both sides, though exact figures are impossible to verify. But even if Russian losses were double or treble those of the Germans, as seems quite possible, they were in a much better position to absorb them. Progress in the north had been even more limited, with Model's momentum broken within the first 48 hours, almost as soon as he reached the forward Russian defensive line. By the 8th he was defining any future progress in terms of a 'rolling battle of attrition',[7] a sad contrast to the *blitzkrieg* theories of old and a strange prescription for a force that was always heavily outnumbered. On 13 July, using the Allied landings on the coast of Sicily as a convenient pretext, Hitler abruptly called off the offensive.

* A Gp South forces allocated to the attack were 4 Pz Ay and *Gruppe* Kempf.

Absolutely nothing had been accomplished, a conclusion pithily summarised by one German staff officer. The attack, he wrote,

> neither denied the Russians a base of operations at Kursk, nor did it destroy sizeable enemy forces; nor eliminate their intentions for an offensive in 1943, thereby assuring the German command of freedom of action. It had not made possible the establishment of a shorter line, designed to conserve German strengths. On the contrary, the operation had used up almost all reserves on the Eastern Front.[8]

The level of casualties was indeed severe. Most of the assault infantry divisions laboriously brought up to strength for Citadel had been smashed. 106 Division, for example had lost 3,224 officers and men, 320 Division 2,839 and 168 Division 2,671.* The panzer divisions had, if anything, come off even worse. No figures on total German (or Russian) losses have ever been assembled but the state of certain German armoured formations at the end of the battle tells its own story. After only two days the *Grossdeutschland* Division had only 80 of its 300 tanks still fit for combat. The ss Panzer Corps, which had begun with 425 tanks and 110 assault guns, ended with only 183 and 64 respectively. Among the Army panzer divisions, most of which had started the battle with between 70 and 100 tanks, the following strengths were reported between 15 and 17 July:†

3 Panzer Division	30 tanks
19 Panzer Division	17 tanks
8 Panzer Division	8 tanks
2 Panzer Division 12 Panzer Division	20 tanks between them

No wonder that German commanders were thrown into despair after the battle. One staff officer in 4 Pz Ay wrote: 'The German army threw away all its advantages in mobile war, and met the Russians on ground of their own choosing . . . The German command could think of nothing better to do than fling our magnificent panzer divisions

---

* In terms of the combat infantry in each division these were casualty rates of 38, 29 and 27 per cent respectively. Moreover, these losses were incurred within a fortnight. The worst-hit British divisions in North-West Europe, a year later, took six months to match such casualty rates.

† Quite a few of the missing tanks were eventually repairable. Nevertheless, in July 1943 the Germans on the Eastern Front suffered the total loss of 645 tanks and 207 assault guns, over 25 per cent of total battleworthy holdings there.

against the strongest fortress in the world . . .'[9] Guderian, recently appointed by Hitler to oversee the reconstruction of the panzer arm, was appalled at the squandering of his carefully assembled reserve:

By the failure of Citadel we had suffered a decisive defeat. The armoured formations, reformed and re-equipped with so much effort, had lost heavily in men and in equipment and would now be unemployable for a long time to come. It was problematical whether they could be rehabilitated in time to defend the Eastern Front; as for being able to use them in defence of the Western Front against the Allied landings that threatened for next spring, this was even more questionable. Needless to say the Russians exploited their victory to the full. There were to be no periods of quiet on the Eastern Front. From now on the enemy were in undisputed possession of the initiative.[10]

The Russians were all too eager to take full advantage of this initiative. From mid-July 1943 the body blows followed thick and fast. On the 12th the Soviets capitalised upon German exhaustion on the Kursk front and thrust into the adjoining German salient, around Orel. On 1 August the salient had to be abandoned. The Soviet offensive then switched to the other side of the Kursk salient, around Belgorod and Kharkov. These were retaken on 5 and 23 August respectively, and for the rest of the year the offensive rippled up and down the whole line east of the Dnieper. By Christmas this river line had been cleared along almost its whole length, only Orsha and Mogilev holding out in the north, and Cherkassy in the south. In the new year Soviet attacks were pressed home without respite. In January the Germans were swept out of their last toe-holds along the middle Dnieper, and by mid-April they had been driven back over the Dniester and much of the middle and upper Pruth. Striking victories were also achieved at each extremity of the front: the siege of Leningrad was completely lifted on 27 January and German forces in the Crimea largely destroyed in April and early May.

By summer 1944, therefore, the Russians had recreated a giant version of the Kursk and Orel salients, leaving A Gp Centre with its flanks hanging in the air. At this stage of the war there was no possibility of the Germans being able to do any salient-chopping of their own, and they could only wait apprehensively for the next Russian blow to fall. It was delivered just a fortnight after the

Allied landings in Normandy, on 22 June. The battle that followed is generally known as the Destruction of Army Group Centre, a title whose lack of geographical precision amply conveys the extent and scale of the operation. By 10 July, said army group was reduced to battered remnants, and as these were harried into East Prussia the Russians slammed home on each side of the old Pripet/Dvina salient. A Gp North was driven back towards the Baltic coast, almost being cut off by a Soviet thrust towards Riga, and A Gp North Ukraine was driven back across the Vistula, conceding vital bridgeheads just south of Warsaw and around Sandomierz and Baranow.

During August these central and northern thrusts began to lose momentum, but late in that month the Soviet High Command, ever keen on cartographical symmetry, launched an offensive against the southern flank, in Romania. After a crushing encirclement victory against 6 Army, in the north-east of the country, the Romanians renounced their alliance with Germany, enabling the Red Army to sweep forward to the Bulgarian and Hungarian frontiers. In September Bulgaria also defected and was occupied unopposed, though the Russians were able to make little progress into Hungary, where the Carpathians to the north were a particularly formidable barrier.

During winter 1944 operations to the north and south continued to have priority. In September another attempt was made to cut A Gp North off at Riga but substantial German forces managed to slip out into Latvia. In October the attacks in Latvia and Lithuania continued, and this time the Russians succeeded in driving through to the Baltic coast on a broad front, bottling up 27 German divisions in Courland and several more in Memel. These divisions continued to hold out – they were still holding positions in Courland at the end of the war – but their subsequent contribution to the overall war effort was negligible. October also saw large-scale operations in Hungary, where A Gp South was soon obliged to give up all territory east of the River Theiss. For the rest of the year Soviet attention was focused on Budapest. At the end of October their original attempt to rush the city had failed and thereafter they were able to close in only very slowly, not actually isolating it until the end of the year. Though a German counter-attack failed in early January 1945, Budapest itself held out until the middle of February. The Russians could, however, congratulate themselves on having taken Belgrade, in mid-October, and so precipitated a German withdrawal from Greece and southern Yugoslavia.

In the first two months of 1945 the major Russian effort was concentrated on the glittering prize, Berlin, with the enormously powerful 1 Ukrainian and 1 Byelorussian Fronts crashing out of their Vistula bridgeheads on 12 and 14 January respectively. The Russian High Command was now resolved to end the war in one campaign, Konev and Zhukov being expected to slash through A Gp A to the Oder in two weeks, cross it on the run and in the next four weeks take out Berlin and draw up to the Elbe. The northern flank of this drive was to be protected by a supplementary offensive into East Prussia to tie down A Gp Centre. For a while it seemed as though this timetable would roughly be held to, as 1 Ukrainian and 1 Byelorussian Fronts, driving forward on the Breslau and Posen axes, drew up to the Oder by the first week of February. Events on the northern flank, however, did not go as well as hoped and, amidst savage fighting, A Gps Centre and A managed to stake out a defensive line in Pomerania and around Königsberg that denied the Russians anything more than a fingerhold on the southern Baltic coast.

The Russians resolved to overcome this resistance before pushing on to Berlin and in the centre authorised only an advance up to the Neisse until the Baltic coast was cleared. This mopping-up, however, proved a formidable task, the attack still having made little headway by early March. In the meantime, the southern front had also flared into action following a substantial German armoured counter-attack to retake Budapest. The hope of unhinging the whole German front by a single thrust to Berlin had now been given up, and in March and the first half of April the Russians concentrated upon clearing up on both flanks. Pomerania was subdued by the end of March, and Hungary, eastern Austria and eastern Czechoslovakia by mid-April. Then, at last, the Russians felt ready to administer the *coup de grâce* and push on to Berlin. By 26 April the city was surrounded, after Russian and American spearheads had met up on the Elbe, at Torgau. A week later the Berlin garrison surrendered and by 9 May the Russians had also cleared out Mecklenburg, to the north, and taken Prague. On that same day the German High Command formally surrendered to the Russian forces.

Besides its ferocity, one thing increasingly characterised these last two years of fighting on the Eastern Front: the massive numerical superiority of the Russians. Even before the débâcle at Kursk and the pulverisation of their panzer reserves, the Germans' material weakness was becoming apparent to many prominent observers. One such was Goebbels, over whose desk passed numerous reports on all aspects of the German economy and war-machine. In May 1943 he confided in his diary that 'we must get accustomed to the fact that the Soviet Union is still alive and pretty energetically so', and in July, just after Kursk, he acknowledged that Germany had once and for all lost the initiative. 'We must make every effort on the Eastern Front to hold our own even halfway against the advancing Soviets. I suppose we can't possibly change the situation by offensive operations as we have been able to do in the past two summers.'[11] A little earlier Göring had made an increasingly rare effort to interest himself in military matters and had concluded that he felt 'somewhat helpless about Soviet war potential. Again and again he asked in despair where Bolshevism gets its weapons and soldiers.'[12] By early September Goebbels, too, was close to despair. After the fall of Belgorod and Kharkov 'critical reports reached us from the Eastern Front which were anything but pleasing. At this stage of developments we are thrown from one scare into another. We are living in a phase of the war in which strategy – to quote Schlieffen – is nothing but a series of substitutions.'[13]

The commanders of A Gps South and Centre would have been the first to endorse these views. For as the Russian drive to the Dnieper unfolded, the disparities in manpower and matériel became more and more marked. The commander of German 6 Army, on 26 August, in a conference with Hitler, icily presented some pertinent figures:

My XXIX Corps has 8,706 men left. Facing it are 69,000 Russians. My XVII Corps has 9,284 men; facing it are 49,500 Russians. My IV Corps is relatively best off – it has 13,143 men, faced by 18,000 Russians. The relative strength in armour is similar: Tolbukhin [South Front] yesterday had 165 tanks in operation; we had 7 tanks and 38 assault guns.[14]

6 Army's problems were typical of those throughout the Army Groups. In A Gp Centre, 3 Pz Ay's divisions were each defending 25,000 yards of front and combat strengths were so low that in some forward defended localities there was only one man to every 80 yards of front.

Such deficiencies became more and more marked as the Dnieper campaign progressed, for the Germans were never able to replace anything but a small proportion of their losses. In July and August, for example, A Gp South lost 133,000 men yet received only 33,000 replacements. Between the beginning of July and the end of September, along the whole of the Eastern Front, there were

654,000 German casualties and only 279,000 replacements, a shortfall of almost 60 per cent, mainly precious infantrymen.* The Russians, despite even heavier casualties, had nothing like the same problems. Between 17 July and 7 September the three Fronts facing A Gp South were reinforced by 55 infantry divisions, 2 tank corps, 8 tank brigades and 12 tank regiments, giving them by the end of the period an overall superiority of 7:1. In the same period 48 infantry divisions and several tank corps were withdrawn from the line and completely reformed, some of them twice.

By mid-September Hitler himself had to face facts and he reluctantly authorised a withdrawal behind the Dnieper, even, according to Goebbels, also mooting the possibility of giving up Leningrad and pulling back to a line behind Lake Peipus, between Narva and Vitebsk. But the latter move was soon abandoned and the value of the first was greatly diminished by its having been left so late and by the fact that Hitler had consistently refused to permit the creation of strong fall-back positions along the far bank of the Dnieper. Unfortunately, German propaganda claimed that they had been built and Goebbels was forced to acknowledge: 'The troops are naturally indignant that no Eastern Wall has been built along the Dnieper. That is the question officers as well as men keep repeating. No convincing answer can be given.'[15] But even in those few places where good positions had been built, ever more serious shortages of men and equipment robbed them of much of their potential value. As one German commander put it in October, having lost a well fortified town too quickly for Hitler's taste: 'What good are the best positions when you have no troops to hold them?'[16]

The divisions in the east were reduced to yet more parlous states. In October A Gp South reported that 'the average number of soldiers fit for front-line combat duties per division was now about 1,000. [On paper a division's infantry battalions alone should have produced over 6,000 men] . . . Obviously no decisive defence could function on this basis, even from behind the Dnieper.'[17] Divisions had to form their own mobile reserve, which as often as not consisted of a couple of companies mounted in clapped out lorries seized from

* Given that the infantry battalions in Russia at the beginning of July contained approximately 900,000 men, and given that these men absorbed 85 per cent of all casualties, then this meant that by 30 September they were 35 per cent weaker than three months previously. Figures for A Gp Centre certainly bear this out. Between July and September, 6 Infantry Division suffered a net loss of 2,148 men. By the latter date its battalions recorded strengths of between 126 and 216 men as opposed to an establishment figure of 854.

the civil administration. Much heavy equipment had been lost in the endless withdrawals, and for anti-tank guns many divisions had to rely on a few artillery pieces sited in the forward areas, perhaps one per battalion. Ammunition was also in short supply. A report by the commander of 8 Army, in September 1943, stated:

> While we are forced to conduct the most difficult ammunition tactics, the enemy has unlimited artillery and mortar ammunition available to him. With these weapons he creates focal points and thins out our ranks to such an extent that the manning of the main defensive line can no longer be ensured . . . Casualties are exceptionally high. This morning the combat strength of 39th Infantry Division was down to six officers and roughly 300 men.[18]

6 Army was similarly afflicted. On 27 October, 73 Infantry Division reported an effective strength of 170 men and 111 Division one of 200 men. The entire army could muster only 25 operational tanks *and* assault guns. But armour was in short supply everywhere along the front. In the least active sectors hardly any was supplied at all. A Gp North was able to muster only 49 tanks in July, against the opposing Russians' 1,050. By mid-September this whole army group could boast of a ludicrous seven operational tanks. Which was better than 3 Pz Ay directly to the south, protecting the Vitebsk–Smolensk corridor. Its title notwithstanding, the army could not field one single operational tank. By this time official tables of organisation had gone out of the window and of the 24 panzer divisions on the Eastern Front, only two had the designated three tank battalions, eight others had only two and the remaining 14 only one. In early September the 17 panzer and panzer grenadier divisions of A Gp South could between them muster only 477 operational tanks and assault guns (paper strength would have been about 2,800), whilst A Gp Centre had less than half that number with 199. A few weeks later, of the 2,304 tanks and assault guns on the entire Eastern Front, only 700 were serviceable. Tank losses continued to mount throughout the Dnieper campaign, reaching as many as 500 per month,* yet in the last six months of 1943, A Gp South, which was bearing the brunt of the fighting, received only 872 replacements. By the end of the year there were rarely more than 20 battleworthy tanks in any panzer division, and often less.

---

* Not all were total losses, of course.

The general situation on the Eastern Front in late 1943 is well summarised in table 29, in the Statistical Appendix, which shows amongst other things that opposite A Gps Centre and South the Russians had a superiority of over 4:1 in infantry and between 14:1 and 12:1 in tanks. Little wonder, then, that the German military machine at all levels was beginning to have self-doubts. A typical spokesman at the sharp end was a senior staff officer with 31 Infantry Division, who reported:

> We have come to the point where every man counts as to whether the front holds or not . . . What we lack is men. In order to put enough troops in the trenches, we have combined the survivors of each regiment's two battalions into one battalion in the front line, severely reducing support and supply personnel. The disbanded battalions now consist only of a cadre overseeing the remaining horses and vehicles. We 'little people' have entered a struggle of life and death.[19]

Even Hitler himself was subject to occasional attacks of realism. During a conference in December 1943 he actually gave his view that the situation was 'beyond the stage of operations and manoeuvre. I will be quite content if we can hold. I expect no more.'[20]

His gloom was more than justified, for there was every likelihood that the overall disparities just cited would increase yet further as the war progressed. The Russians seemed to have relatively little difficulty in making up their losses and, where necessary, further reinforcing critical Fronts. Between July and December, for example, when A Gp South had received only 872 replacement tanks, the opposing Russian formations had accepted some 2,700. During October and November, as it prepared to press on over the Dnieper and into the Ukraine,

> the Red Army swelled with men and machines: 78 reformed rifle divisions (from what had hitherto been brigades), 126 rifle corps, an array of 5 tank armies, 24 tank corps, 13 mechanised corps, 80 independent tank brigades, 106 tank regiments and 43 regiments of self-propelled guns, 6 artillery corps, 26 artillery divisions, 7 *Katyusha* rocket-launcher divisions, plus a score of artillery brigades.[21]

The Germans, on the other hand, were soon reduced to scouring their rear areas for likely combat troops. According to Basic Order 22, of 5 December 1943, OKW decreed that no men under 30 years of age should remain in rear assignments, all rear and command staffs were immediately to reduce their strengths by 10 to 25 per cent, standards of physical fitness for combat troops were to be drastically reduced, and special press-gangs or *Feldjäger* battalions were to be set up to prowl around the rear areas and dispatch potential recruits forthwith to central collection points.

No wonder that the misgivings at the top became increasingly widespread. Von Kluge, commanding A Gp Centre, wrote to Hitler pointing out that his men 'were beset by a feeling of isolation and neglect, facing as they did the massed numbers of Red Army infantry . . . Recent losses had been so great that the drop in the fighting strength of the formations that had borne the brunt of the attack was frightening.'[22] Two weeks later Goebbels' spirits sunk still lower as he glanced at the latest casualty figures. He noted in his diary:

> We just cannot stand such a drain for long . . . When we consider that our eastern campaign has cost us 3,000,000 casualties . . . nobody can deny that we have paid exceedingly heavily for this campaign. At some point or other we simply must try to get out of this desperate blood-letting. Otherwise we are in danger of slowly bleeding to death in the East.[23]

Unfortunately, Hitler had absolutely no intention of getting out, and the shock of having sanctioned a retreat behind the Dnieper seems to have hardened his resolve that not another foot of ground was to be given up. Shrugging off the earlier realism, he took refuge in complete self-delusion. In February 1944, at the height of the Russian drive into the Ukraine, General Kurt Zeitzler, the OKH Chief of Staff,* told one of Manstein's officers: 'He [Hitler] says the Russians are bound to stop attacking some time. They have been attacking non-stop since last July, and can't go on for ever.'[24]† In the following month, as the Russians continued to roll remorselessly towards the Dniester, Hitler took a leaf out of King Canute's book and tried to stem the tide purely with his own authority and will-power. As Zeitzler's predecessor put it: 'Hitler . . . believed

---

* Zeitzler had replaced Halder in September 1942.

† The concept of giving up ground voluntarily reappeared in early November, in Führer Directive No. 51, which admitted that 'in the East, the vast extent of the territory makes it possible for us to lose ground, even on a large scale, without a fatal blow being dealt to the nervous system of Germany' (H. R. Trevor-Roper (ed.), *Hitler's War Directives* 1939–45 (Pan Books, 1973), p. 218). But this seems to have been a rationalisation for past withdrawals rather than an axiom for the future.

that . . . the unbending will to victory and the relentless pursuit of the goal are everything. Mystical speculation replaced considerations of time and space, and the careful calculation of the strength of one's own forces in relation to the enemy's.'[25]* In this instance he decided, on 8 March, that certain towns, usually those in imminent danger of being overrun, were to be designated 'Fortified Areas' and as such were to hold out to the last man. Amongst the towns so designated in A Gp South's sector were Tarnopol, Proskurov, Kovel, Brody, Vinnitsa and Pervomaysk. Generals on the spot thought the order a military nonsense, the commander of I Pz Ay noting in the war diary: 'One can only obey, even in the deepest anxiety.'[26] During March and early April all these 'Fortified Areas' were lost – so quickly, in fact, that Hitler actually began to doubt his ability to stem the tide. During a supposedly inspirational lecture on the National Socialist *Weltanschauung* and its relevance to military operations, according to one general who was present, 'his summary of the overall situation left nothing to be desired as far as objectivity of presentation was concerned. He described the catastrophic conditions on the Eastern Front where the German troops were suffering one defeat after another . . . The only encouragement . . . was a half-mumbled admonition to overcome all the difficulties through "faith".'[27]

But it was going to take more than faith, for it was now quite apparent that even heavy casualties and material losses were not going to stop the Russians. The vagaries of the Russian climate might bring a brief respite, as they did between April and June 1944, but there was now no possibility that simple attrition, even given the most favourable casualty ratios, could compensate for the enormous disparity between the manpower or reserves and the productive capacities of the two belligerents. First *blitzkrieg* had fizzled out because of inadequate German resources, and now even dour linear defence, with or without a readiness to make timely withdrawals, was doomed to ultimate failure. One has only to glance at the figures detailed in tables 30–32, in the Statistical Appendix, to see that the Germans were facing an increasingly hopeless task. Basic to everything was the relative performance of German and Russian industry, and in every important aspect of munitions production the former was completely outclassed. These tables give details for armoured fighting vehicle, aircraft and artillery production between 1943 and 1945, showing that in the last 18 months of the war the

---

* See also very similar remarks by von Manstein in his *Lost Victories* (Arms and Armour Press, 1982), pp. 276–7.

Russians alone produced 55,000 AFVs (with 75mm guns and above) to the Germans' 22,000; 50,000 combat aircraft to the Germans' 44,000; and 85,000 artillery pieces to the Germans' 51,000.

At first sight it might be thought that ratios of 2.5:1 in armoured fighting vehicles,* 1.1:1 in military aircraft and 1.7:1 in artillery hardly show the Germans as being completely outclassed. Two points should be made. On the one hand, in a war of attrition the production surpluses achieved by the Russians (41,000 AFVs, 20,000 planes and 50,000 guns between 1943 and 1945) are not to be sneered at. On the other, and much more importantly, the comparative figures above represent *total* production for each side, only a portion of which the Germans could bring to bear on the Eastern Front. Whilst it is impossible to determine exactly what this proportion was, one can make a reasonably informed estimate by looking at how the *Wehrmacht* deployed its available weaponry at various stages of the war.

With regard to AFVs and military aircraft, the following proportions of total holdings were the average allocations to the Eastern Front for each year of the war:

	1941	1942	1943	1944	1945
AFVS	65.1	45.9	37.7	44.6	36.5
Aircraft	64.0	60.0	41.2	43.0	34.2

If we apply these figures to the data given in tables 30–32, we arrive at the *approximate* force levels on the Eastern Front set out in table 4.

That the figures in table 4 do give some indication of the real balance of forces on the Eastern Front is confirmed by other types of data.† In January 1943, for example, the Russians had 8,500 tanks and SUs at the front, whilst the Germans could muster only 495 that were fit for action. In April of the same year the respective figures were approximately 7,000 and 600, and in November 5,600 and 700. During 1944 Soviet front-line strengths, with a few fluctuations,

---

* This definition of AFV refers only to tanks, assault guns, tank destroyers and self-propelled artillery and does not include, as it often does, armoured cars, SP anti-aircraft guns or armoured personnel carriers.

† One objection to my inferences from the available data would be that formations in quiet theatres would make much less of a demand on new production than those in the East. From March 1944, however, the armies of OB West were heavily reinforced, and from June were obviously almost as voracious consumers as those in Russia. Prior to this, in 1943 and early 1944, the Tunisian and Italian theatres made some inroads into new production.

Table 4: *German and Russian munitions production deployed on the Eastern Front 1943-5*

		German	Russian	Ratio
AFV	1943	4,279	20,091	
(75mm and	1944	8,285	28,483	
over)	1945	1,436	26,297	
	TOTAL	14,000	74,871*	1:5.1
Combat	1943	7,751	29,841	
aircraft	1944	14,667	33,199	
	1945	2,390	16,418	
	TOTAL	24,808	79,458	1:3.2
Artillery†	1943	10,200	48,400	
(75mm and	1944	18,300	56,100	
over)	1945	3,700	28,600	
	TOTAL	32,200	133,100	1:4.1

*The Russians always kept 2,000 tanks in the Far East to guard against a possible Japanese attack. I have assumed that in all 4,000 AFVs were assigned to this theatre.

†The German figures are a rough estimation in that they assume the same proportions as for AFVs.

were steadily built up from 5,000 to 13,000 AFVs, whilst those of the Germans remained consistently low. In mid-September, for example, the Germans could field 1,437 serviceable tanks and assault guns as against 13,400 Russian.* The individual panzer divisions remained terribly weak. In June each averaged only 40 to 50 fit tanks and in November and December this figure was down to 20. Moreover, even though German production had been substantially stepped up in 1944, as is shown in table 30, the quality of the finished article left much to be desired. In January 1944, on all fronts, no less than 2,260 tanks went through the workshops. By the end of the year 'the panzer divisions were no longer more than a shadow of what they had been. The consequences of an insufficient inspection and test programme at the end of the factory assembly lines were mechanical defects which became more and more frequent in the new machines reaching the front. So the number of tanks available to each division daily was no more than five or six.'[28] By April 1945 the Germans were reduced to only 2,700 AFVs of all types, including armoured cars and the like, whilst the Russians could still field some 13,000 tanks and SUs.

The disparity in front-line aircraft strengths in the last two years of the war was equally marked, as is evidenced in table 33 in the

* The figures for artillery were not much better, with 5,500 German guns of 76mm and over being faced by 31,000 Russian (not self-propelled).

Statistical Appendix, which shows that Russian superiority rose from 1.8:1 in February 1943 to 5.7:1 in June 1944 and 10.7:1 at the end of the war. In many cases, this superiority was even more marked than the ratios just cited might suggest. Throughout the war, German squadrons on the Eastern Front had very poor maintenance back-up. In early 1943, for example, actual availability for operations had fallen below 25 per cent of paper strength. On 22 June 1944, on the eve of the Destruction of Army Group Centre, 6 Air Fleet, with an already puny nominal strength of 275 fighters, 'had according to one account only 40 fighters in working order . . . [and] not enough gas to keep them flying.'[29]* The four Russian Fronts involved could call on the services of 7,000 front-line aircraft.

The Russians made full use of their growing strength, which was felt equally by the German Army and the *Luftwaffe*. In 1944 and 1945 the Red Air Force logged some 1.7 million combat sorties (as opposed too only 334,000 by the *Luftwaffe*, a ratio of 5.2:1), and Soviet sources calculated after the war that fully 46.5 per cent of all sorties were flown in support of ground troops, with even the long-range bomber formations directing 43 per cent of their efforts against enemy troop concentrations. But neither was the *Luftwaffe* spared, and by the beginning of 1945 it had been almost overwhelmed. On 1 January it could deploy 520 day and 47 night fighters in the east, opposing roughly 6,000 Russian. In the middle of that month, the Russian offensive into Poland was backed by 4,800 planes, taking on some 300 German. On 15 January, shortly after the offensive got under way, the Germans managed to put up 42 sorties along the whole of the Eastern Front. The Russians countered with 3,400.

As a final perspective on the massive military preponderance that the Russians were able to bring to bear, table 34 in the Statistical Appendix gives some details about the balance of forces at the beginning of several major offensives in the last eighteen months of the war. On the whole, the figures speak for themselves, with

---

* I have paid little attention to the *Wehrmacht's* fuel problems later in the war simply because shortages of manpower and matériel were of themselves enough to completely cripple the German war effort. It is worth while pointing out, however, that in 1944 the Russian armed forces consumed 4 million tons of motor and aviation fuel. The *entire* production of Greater Germany for that same year (imports included) was only 3.8 million tons. So serious were the shortages towards the very end of the war that around the Baranow bridgehead on the Vistula, in January 1945, over 1,000 AFVs were immobilised for lack of gasoline and overrun.

combat infantry ratios rarely falling below 5:1 and those for tanks and SP guns averaging out at 7:1, and all that needs to be emphasised here is the inability of the Germans adequately to man the vast front at any point along which the Russians could bring such prodigious forces to bear. At times they put up a quite remarkable resistance, but only at the cost of stripping less immediately threatened sectors, which were then in no position at all to counter the haymaker that was sooner or later directed at them.* The 'strategy of substitutions' was no longer even a partial solution.

Model's experiences in 1944 offer a perfect example of this. During the January offensive, south of Leningrad, he took over command of A Gp North when his predecessor was sacked for withdrawing 18 Army to save it from encirclement. Model was never one willingly to give up ground, so he halted 18 Army's withdrawal by reinforcing it from 16 Army. No sooner had he done so than a new offensive broke against the latter and Hitler was obliged to sanction the retreat of both armies. In May the Germans anxiously wondered where the next Soviet blow was to fall and eventually they decided that the sector south of the Pripet was the most likely target. To meet this threat, A Gp Centre was stripped of 15 per cent of its divisions, 88 per cent of its tanks, 23 per cent of its assault guns and 33 per cent of its artillery. The Russians were indeed planning a powerful offensive in the south – towards Lwow and the Vistula in mid-July and into Romania in August – but unfortunately they also had the resources to take out the enfeebled A Gp Centre first. The army group, as we have already seen, was totally crushed and when Model took over command, at the beginning of July, he was only able to re-establish any sort of line at all by stealing divisions back from A Gp North Ukraine, the target of the next offensive.

By then it was apparent to most German generals that they were virtually powerless to put up any significant resistance against the huge forces arrayed all along the front. According to one:

---

* Most formations were weak enough, even without the depredations of their neighbours. The state of the panzer divisions in 1944 has already been alluded to, but the infantry divisions were no better off. The steady decrease in combat strength went on unabated during the last two years of the war. Between July 1943 and July 1944, for example, A Gp South lost 405,000 men and received only 223,000 replacements, whilst between August and October 1944, casualties on the whole of the Eastern Front were 672,000 but only 201,000 replacements were sent forward.

'The overall situation was such that a gap in one sector of the front could only be closed at the sacrifice of another sector.'[30] In Christmas 1944 the commander of A Gp Centre, now General Georg-Hans Reinhardt, was wearying of the endless shuffling of units from one part of the line to another. He knew that when the Russians' New Year offensive came it would be a whole series of mass attacks up and down the line and that 'by the time the last comes . . . we shall be debris.'[31] They soon were, and the survivors who stumbled into Pomerania and behind the Oder could look forward to nothing but total defeat. The following vignette gives a perfect insight into the odds stacked against them. On 26 January 1945, when the Russians deployed something like 14,000 tanks and SUS,

> Hitler . . . ordered . . . the setting up of a tank-destroyer division. The very name of this new formation was remarkable and extraordinarily significant. But that was not the end of it. This division was to consist of bicycle companies, commanded by brave lieutenants; they were to be equipped with anti-tank grenades and were in this fashion to stop the T-34s and the heavier Russian tanks. The division was to be committed company by company. It was too bad about the brave men involved.[32]

As was stated in the Preface, the term 'brute force' implies two things: on the one hand, an overwhelming physical or material superiority and on the other, a marked lack of finesse in applying this superiority. The pertinence of the first meaning to events on the Eastern Front has been demonstrated already, but this theatre also demonstrates, more perhaps than any other, the applicability of the second. A modern scholar has provided us with a neat text for an elaboration of this point:

> . . . the Soviet Union believes it highly desirable to deliver as weighty a blow as possible on each and every occasion, and against any and every enemy. In Soviet thinking the concept of economy of effort has little place. Whereas to an Englishman the taking of a sledgehammer to crack a nut is a wrong decision and a sign of mental immaturity, to a Russian the opposite is the case. In Russian eyes the cracking of nuts is clearly what sledgehammers are designed for.[33]

In one respect, however, this metaphor is not appropriate. In the sledgehammer and nut situation the pulverisation of the latter leaves the former quite unmarked. But where the sledgehammer is an army, the crude reliance on simple material preponderance will inevitably involve considerable casualties. This was most certainly the case with regard to the Red Army. Between June 1941 and the end of the war, the Germans in the east lost 2.3 million men killed and missing. The equivalent figure for the Russian armed forces was, it is generally accepted, about 13.5 million. Even removing the staggering Russian casualties in 1941, upwards of 6.5 million men killed and taken prisoner as against a quarter of a million Germans, this still leaves a casualty ratio for the rest of the war of 3.5:1 in the Germans' favour, or 5 million more Russian dead and missing than German. Considering that the casualty figures for the North-West Europe campaign of 1944–5 were 230,000 Allied dead and missing and 570,000 German,* a ratio of 1:2.5, one is entitled to think that Russian methods demonstrated a certain profligacy with human life. And with matériel: though it is impossible to arrive at any really accurate figures, available sources suggest that between December 1941 and December 1944 the Germans in the east lost roughly 16,000 tanks and self-propelled guns, the Russians something like 60,000. As Russian losses are for combat only and the German include all causes, one can again infer a cavalier attitude to the employment of armour.

German accounts of the war are unanimous in pointing out the Russian commanders' ruthless attitude to their own troops and their predilection for trying to swamp a defender through the use of mass frontal assaults. One report drawn up after the war noted: 'The one feature distinguishing their operations throughout the war was their total disregard for the value of human life that found expression in the employment of mass formations, even for local attacks.'[34] Another stated that 'the characteristic fighting method of the Russians [was] not great achievements by small units with clever leadership, but by sacrifice of masses.'[35] According to a German general:

The most common Russian form of combat was the use of mass ... The Russians repeated the same tactics again and again: employment of masses, and narrow division sectors held by large

---

* The German figure is admittedly swollen by the large number of prisoners taken towards the end of the war. It has been suggested that the ratio of men killed in the fighting in North-West Europe was approximately 1:1.

complements replenished time after time . . . Russian soldiers
. . . seemed to grow out of the earth, and nothing would stop
their advance for a while. Gaps closed automatically, and the
mass surged on until the supply of men was used up and the
wave, substantially thinned, receded again.[36]

What was especially noticeable was the seeming inability of the
Russians to realise when an attack no longer had any hope of success
and should be broken off, or at least switched to another sector.
General Friedrich von Mellenthin summed up his own experiences
on the Eastern Front thus:

> The Russian form of fighting – particularly in the attack – is
> characterised by the employment of masses of men and material,
> often thrown in unintelligently and without variations . . . An
> attack delivered twice will be repeated a third and a fourth time
> irrespective of losses . . . such ruthless methods represent the
> most inhuman and at the same time the most expensive way of
> fighting.[37]

For General Dittmar, who fought on the Finnish front, 'The Russians
were always very bull-headed in their offensive methods, repeating
their attacks again and again . . . without any recognisable change
of procedure. No doubt their great and bloody losses were due
primarily to this method of combat.'[38] General Max Simon, an
ss divisional commander, was continually struck by the 'Russian
officers' lack of flexibility . . . If the Soviets failed in their first
attack, a second, third, fourth, fifth and sometimes even further
attacks were certain to follow at short notice, but in all my years
of experience the repeat-attacks did not depart a single time from
the pattern of the first . . .'[39]

Crude tactics of this sort, and the concomitant heavy casualties,
were observable from the very beginning of the war. On 5 July 1941
Halder wrote in his diary: '[Russian] infantry attacking as much as
twelve ranks deep, without heavy weapons support; the men started
hurrahing from afar. Incredibly high Russian losses.'[40] In the fighting
around the Smolensk pocket, the Russians made intelligent use of
their artillery in defensive operations, but when 'the Russians passed
to counter-attacks, then [our own guns'] action co-ordinated with
that of the machine-guns and anti-tank guns, hastily brought out
of their holes, to execute a frightful slaughter on the dense swarms
of the enemy.'[41] Exactly similar events took place around the Kiev

pocket, in September, and one German infantryman wondered 'how they can find the courage and the men to keep coming on . . . across this carpet of their own dead comrades.'[42] In November, around Rostov, the Russians were still coming forward with this frightening obliviousness to their own losses. When 56 Army counter-attacked across the Don, the German defenders 'were amazed to see Red Army troops, fortified by vodka, coming out of the evening dusk cheering and singing, in some cases even linking arms until fire or minefields forced them to break up. Many of the attackers fell in rows where they were hit by machine-gun fire, while others clambered over the heaps of dead and still went forward.'[43]

It could not even be claimed that such tactics were short-lived aberration, born of the desperate experiences of the first near-collapse. In the following years, as the general comments of German commanders quoted earlier indicate, very little seems to have changed. As long as the Russians had sufficient reserves, they were always ready to seek a decision by sheer weight of numbers. It is this tactical mulishness that helps to explain the differing Russian and German procedures with regard to replacements. Whereas the latter (and the Western Allies) would feed replacements into existing units and try to keep them up to strength, the Russians, knowing what sort of casualties were to be expected, simply let a division or corps* be almost destroyed, pulled it out of the line and rebuilt it almost from scratch.† Another insight into Russian methods is offered by the fact that, even in mid-1943, divisions were expected to manage on their initial allotment of supplies and ammunition. When the Orel counter-offensive was in danger of running down because many divisions had exhausted these supplies and central replenishment dumps had not been established, this 'led to the following admonition – apparently not considered axiomatic to the Soviet commands – "Experience shows that it is necessary to arrange for supplies and ammunition for the infantry as well as the artillery." '[44] In other words, up to then, infantry formations were presumably not expected to last long enough to consume more than the 10-day stocks they jumped off with.

Other examples of the continued Russian reliance on brute force abound. A report from a Spanish ss commander, written

---

* Tank and mechanised corps were approximate equivalents of panzer and panzer grenadier divisions.

† Between June 1941 and June 1943 German intelligence estimated that of the 672 Russian infantry divisions identified thus far, 164 had been completely destroyed and 48 rendered unfit for combat.

in 1942, warned that 'their well-prepared, large-scale mass attacks are undoubtedly very dangerous, since the "Russian streamroller" crushes anything that opposes its progress.'[45] In March of that year Germany's 257 Infantry Division, around Izyum, lost 652 men killed but at the end of the month counted 12,500 Russian dead in front of its lines. In autumn a British war-correspondent visited the Rzhev–Vyazma salient, still held by the Germans after the 1941 Moscow counter-offensive. The visit came 'shortly after the Russians had recaptured a few villages at fearful cost, but had each time been repelled from the outskirts of Rzhev. I was struck by the intense bitterness with which officers and men spoke of their thankless task.'[46] In September, near Stalingrad, a whole series of head-on assaults against XIV Panzer Corps still 'conformed to the accepted Russian principle – once "Ivan" makes up his mind to launch an attack and gain certain objectives, he throws in masses of troops and continues to do so until he has secured his objectives or exhausted his reserves. Consideration for casualties plays no part whatsoever . . .'[47]

There was little change during 1943. Shortly after the Kursk battles, a German soldier wrote home claiming personally to have witnessed 'attacks which were preceded by solid blocks of people marching shoulder to shoulder across the minefields which we had laid. Civilians and army punishment battalions alike advanced like automata, their ranks broken only when a mine exploded, killing or wounding those around it.'[48]* In October, during the slow German withdrawal to the Dnieper, von Mellenthin again had to face 'Russian breakthrough attempts . . . repeated in undiminished strength. Divisions decimated by our fire were withdrawn, and fresh formations were thrown into the battle. Again wave after wave attacked, and wave after wave were thrown back after suffering appalling losses. But the Russians did not desist from their inflexible and rigid methods of attack.'[49] By November these forces faced critical manpower shortages and combed the recently reoccupied territories for potential recruits. They were swiftly fed into the mincing machine. As one historian has noted, in a chilling aside: 'As soldiers they

* In a meeting with Eisenhower, just after the war, Marshal Zhukov admitted: 'When we come to a minefield our infantry attacks exactly as if it were not there. The losses we get . . . we consider only equal to those we would have got from machine guns and artillery if the Germans had chosen to defend that particular area with strong bodies of troops instead of with minefields.' (D. D. Eisenhower *Crusade in Europe* (Heinemann, 1948), p. 510.)

did not amount to much, but their number alone was creating an ammunition shortage on the German side.'[50] Right into 1944 the Russians seemed almost unable to achieve any sort of breakthrough without first attaining an enormous numerical predominance. Even then success was far from assured. According to General Kurt von Tippelskirch:

> At Mogilev, in March 1944, I was commanding the 12th Corps – which consisted of three divisions. In the offensive the Russians then launched, they used ten divisions in the assault on the first day, and by the sixth day had used twenty divisions. Yet they only captured the first line, and were brought to a halt before the second . . . The Russians . . . always lost disproportionately when attacking.[51]

They were also remarkably lavish in their use of armour. Approximate figures for overall losses on the Eastern Front have already been given – a ratio of almost 4:1, even disregarding the stupendous losses of obsolete equipment in 1941. Figures for specific campaigns were sometimes higher, one source giving a ratio of 8:1 for the battles during the retreat to Stalingrad, 6:1 during the drive back to the Dnieper and 4:1 during the Destruction of Army Group Centre and the drive into Poland. In 1942, certainly, the handling of the armoured force was often downright inept. At this stage of the war, according to one German staff officer: 'In tight masses they groped around in the main battle; they moved hesitantly and without any plan. They got in each other's way, they blundered against our anti-tank guns, or, after penetrating our front, they did nothing to exploit their advantage and stood inactive and idle. Those were the days when isolated German anti-tank guns . . . would shoot up and knock out more than thirty tanks an hour.'[52]

In later years, though tank commanders undoubtedly carried out their missions with more conviction and dash, their primary mission still seems simply to have been to crash through the forward German defences, and little attempt was made to effect or exploit strategic penetrations by free-ranging mobile forces. This persistent reliance on mass frontal attacks continued to lead to appallingly high losses. On one corps front, in November 1943 alone, 700 Russian tanks were captured or destroyed, whilst in von Manstein's sector, in January and February 1944, A Gp South claimed the destruction of 3,928 enemy tanks, more than the entire panzer force for Barbarossa. Of Russian armoured tactics right up to the end of the war, one German general remarked: 'They had only a few competent armoured commanders. In the tank force, too, successes were only achieved by the reckless use of masses. However, these tactics failed whenever even relatively adequate defences were available to the Germans.'[53]

This last sentence provides the proper context for an assessment of the much-vaunted Russian drives to the Oder and to the Elbe in 1945. Though Russian tanks clocked up impressive mileages, in very short time, it cannot really be claimed that they had fought a decisive battle of manoeuvre. For by then, as has been amply demonstrated, German defences were anything but adequate and, biased though the German commanders might be, General Lothar Rendulic was surely right to claim that

> the deep thrust of the Russian tank armies under Zhukov . . . in 1945 does not reveal the true picture [about the potential of well-led armoured forces]. In the entire sector . . . there were at best only scattered remnants of the shattered German troops who had been inferior from the beginning, and who were no longer under a coordinated command and were without fuel . . . The Russians . . . were able to march . . . forward as if conducting a *peacetime manoeuvre*. The German armoured units were quickly overrun and disintegrated against 12:1 odds.[54]

The sledgehammer had fallen for the last time.

But let no one think that the lack of sophistication in Russian tactics in any way detracts from the absolutely fundamental importance of their strategic contribution to the Allied war effort. The tremendous scale of the Russian effort has already been made plain, but to underline its overall significance, and to retain a proper perspective on the relative importance of the operations described in the following chapters, it would be as well to keep certain basic statistics in mind. Some of these are set out in tables 35 and 36 in the Statistical Appendix. Table 35 shows the numbers of German divisions tied down on the various fronts to the end of the war. It reveals, for example, that throughout the highly lauded North African campaign, even after the extra commitment demanded by the Allied invasion of French North-West Africa in November 1942, the Russians were consistently facing 70 per cent of the German fighting divisions and usually a higher proportion of their panzer and motorised formations. After the invasion of North-West Europe, in June 1944, the burden on the Russians lightened somewhat, but it is still to be noted that other than in the last weeks of 1944, as the Germans built up forces for the Ardennes counter-offensive, they were still engaging around 70 per cent of the panzer and motorised forces.

In terms of the number of divisions on *combat* fronts, in the period prior to D-Day, the contrast is yet more dramatic. This can be seen in table 36, which details the number of German divisions actually engaged by the Russians and by the Western Allies at various dates. It shows that in June 1941 the Russians were engaging 98.5 per cent of German divisions actually fighting (134 divisions as opposed to 2) and that this figure never fell below 87.1 per cent, the tally for May 1944, when the Russians were facing 156 divisions and the Allies 23.

The scale of the Russian contribution is also brought out most vividly in table 5, which shows the amount of time spent by German divisions on the various combat fronts. The basic unit of measurement is the 'divisional combat month', or one month spent by a division in a combat theatre. Time spent in occupation and security duties are not included. The table really does speak for itself, and all that requires any emphasis is the figure for panzer and panzer grenadier divisions, the cream of the German army and the greatest drain on her industrial effort, which spent over four times as much time fighting the Russians as against all the other Allies put together.

Table 5: *Number of months spent on combat fronts by German ss and army divisions 1939–45*

	E. Front	N.W. Europe	Sicily/ Italy	N. Africa	Total non-E. Front	Other*
Pz Divs	1,029	85	34	65	184	24
Motorised/ PG Divs	493	27	78	0	105	49
Light/ Jäger Divs	277	0	27	13	40	122
Mt Divs	175	6	23	0	29	108
Para Divs	45	66	38	7	111	8
Inf Divs	5,127	453	193	6	652	454
TOTAL	7,146	637	393	91	1,121	665

* Mainly Poland 1939, France 1940 and the Balkans 1941–5.

But it is perhaps the crudest figures that tell the story most directly. Thus, if we look at the statistics for German casualties in the Second World War, we find that between June 1941 and March 1945, a total of 4,900,000 German soldiers were killed or wounded on the Eastern Front as opposed to roughly 580,000 in North-West Europe,

Italy and Africa. The proportion of such casualties accounted for by the Russians, therefore, was almost exactly 90 per cent, and even when figures for the missing and prisoners-of-war are included the Russian share is still some 80 per cent. We shall see in later chapters that American industry was to be a vital component of Allied victory over the Nazis, but there can be no doubt that it was Russian arms and Russian blood, the pitiless, ceaseless haemorrhage of a whole people, that bought the time during which that industry got into top gear. Perhaps even if Russia had been knocked out of the war, the Americans would still eventually have invaded Europe. But in that case they would have come up against 150 more divisions they had to fight and one million extra German soldiers they had to kill.

PART TWO

WAR FROM AFAR
The Battle of the Atlantic and the Bomber Offensive
1939–45

'The build-up of a powerful U-Boat arm, to which all the energy and resources justified by its importance to our war effort should have been devoted, simply failed . . . to take place.'

Admiral Dönitz, after the war

'We should never allow the history of this war to convict us of throwing the strategic bomber at the man in the street.'

General Ira Eaker, January 1945

3

The Battle of the Atlantic
September 1939 – May 1945

If the Battle of Britain was that country's most intimate brush with the possibility of defeat, it was not the only one, nor, indeed, the most serious. From the very outset of the war another grim struggle was being fought, one that really did threaten British survival just as surely as would panzer divisions roaming through the Home Counties. This was the assault on Britain's maritime supply lines, running eastward across the Atlantic and northward from the Cape and the Strait of Gibraltar. These supply lines were basic to Britain's survival, as her economy was self-sufficient in almost nothing of importance. She had to import, for example, two-thirds of her foodstuffs. For vital raw materials she was even more dependent on foreign suppliers, importing 30 per cent of her iron ore, 90 per cent of copper ore, 90 per cent of bauxite, and 100 per cent of molybdenum ore and chromium ore. Other vital imports included 95 per cent of all petroleum products, 100 per cent of raw rubber, 80 per cent of soft timber and 80 per cent of wool.*

These supply lines, moreover, were terribly vulnerable to interdiction, especially by submarines, which had already once decimated British merchant shipping in 1917. But to counter this threat the Royal Navy in September 1939 possessed only 81 destroyers, 39 sloops and 9 corvettes which might be used for escort duties or for aggressive sweeps into threatened waters. Certain of these ships were equipped with Asdic, a device that detected the presence of enemy vessels by picking up echoed sound pulses, but the majority of these – and therefore the most likely to be called away for fleet

---

* Table 63, in the Statistical Appendix, gives a list of the use of major raw materials in the munitions industry.

protection or other duties – were destroyers.* The Royal Navy, moreover, had greatly overestimated the effectiveness of Asdic and ever since its introduction had felt it unnecessary to give much thought to the conventional method of protecting merchant shipping, by grouping them in convoys with an escort of warships. Plans for convoy did exist and the first one in the Second World War sailed on 6 September 1939, but there was no real commitment to this tactic. The body of doctrine evolved in the First World War, which had eventually quelled the U-boat menace, had been largely forgotten, and the number of escorts on hand was grossly inadequate.

Fortunately for the British, however, the state of readiness of the German U-boat arm at the beginning of the war was no better than its opponents'. The whole *Kriegsmarine*, as we have seen, was but a pale reflection of the 'Z' Plan ideal and the number of U-boats available was a particular disappointment. Rear-Admiral Karl Dönitz, commanding the U-boat arm, had stated in August 1939 that 300 submarines would be necessary to carry out an effective campaign against British shipping, but in the following month only 57 were on hand. Despite being a fervent advocate of the submarine arm, which he commanded from 1935, Dönitz had been unable to have much influence on U-boat construction, either in terms of numbers or of types. Not only did the fleet remain far too small,† but Dönitz failed to persuade his superiors to concentrate on building small to medium submarines rather than the much larger types, with a gun as their main armament, that they favoured. Not until the actual outbreak of war did the *U-Bootsamt*, responsible for procurement and construction, abandon this policy and, though Dönitz immediately put in large orders for smaller types, none of these could actually enter commission until December 1940.

In the meantime, he was forced to make do with an extremely low number of boats, and the early history of the German submarine fleet is one of a remarkably hand-to-mouth existence, making it very difficult to keep even a handful of boats at sea. In September 1939 Dönitz was told to expect no more than 17 U-boats to be built in the next 12 months, and though the demands of war did impart a slight sense of

* In all, 180 ships were fitted with Asdic at the beginning of the war, 150 of which were destroyers.
† In September 1939, indeed, it was called a flotilla and Dönitz was only a Commodore. He was promoted in October.

urgency to the construction yards, they were only able to increase the actual number of boats built to 37, only 28 of which entered commission. Losses in the same period totalled 20 boats. During the last quarter of 1940 a further two dozen U-boats were built and only three sunk, though the net result of all this was hardly the powerful submarine fleet envisaged by Dönitz. For the first 16 months of the war, in fact, the number of U-boats actually at sea was extremely low, as is shown by the monthly averages given below:

Sept.–Dec. 1939	Jan.–March 1940	April–June 1940	July–Sept. 1940	Oct.–Dec. 1940
14	13	20	12	11

There were further hindrances to Dönitz during these months. It soon became clear, for example, that Hitler was not wholly committed to the idea of a war against Britain's maritime lines of communication. He often appeared to be very enthusiastic. In late October 1939 he encouraged the setting up of an inter-services staff committee to oversee 'Economic Warfare' against Britain and to direct 'the war against merchant shipping and all other measures for attacking the economic installations, resources and trade of the enemy'.[1] On 17 January 1940 Dönitz was authorised to sink any ships of any nation found in Britain's coastal waters, where it would be possible to lay the blame for the sinking on mines. In July Hitler briefly considered setting aside his plans for Sea Lion and relying simply on interdicting Britain's trade routes, as well as bombing flat west coast ports like Liverpool. On 15 August, though he readopted Sea Lion, he also declared a total blockade of Britain, establishing a War Zone from which all shipping, neutral or otherwise, was excluded. But these measures masked Hitler's continuing uncertainty about the value of trade war, and other decisions, or the lack of them, seriously undercut Dönitz's ability to conduct decisive operations. The inter-service committee, for example, took only three weeks to founder on Army–Navy–*Luftwaffe* rivalries and Hitler made no attempt to reconvene it. In March 1940, oblivious of whether or not the U-boats were having any impact on British shipping, he withdrew them from their hunting grounds south of Ireland and in the Bay of Biscay and ordered that they prepare to cooperate in the invasion of Norway. In February of that year sinkings by U-boats, in all theatres, had totalled 170,000 tons,* but over the next three months they did not even aggregate this figure.

For the rest of the year Hitler remained largely oblivious to appeals for increased production of U-boats. One report pointed out:

> In our present situation the one essential thing is that we should at once set about the task not only of raising the number of our operational U-boats to the highest possible operational total, but also that we should do it as quickly as possible, while the average losses still remain comparatively low and enemy anti-U-boat measures (including the US shipbuilding programme, the effects of which will not be felt before 1942–43), though in process of improvement, are still inadequate. The opportunity we miss today will never occur again, even with increased production . . .[2]

On 24 September Grand Admiral Erich Raeder, the Commander-in-Chief of the *Kriegsmarine*, was closeted with the *Führer* for several hours and expounded fulsomely on the attractions of a largely naval strategy aimed at British shipping both in the Atlantic and the Mediterranean. A key element of such a strategy, he suggested, must be the strengthening of the U-boat arm. But despite verbal assurances at the time, nothing was actually done to increase the quotas of steel or the number of shipyard workers allocated to the U-boat programme. Raeder made another attempt to convince Hitler in December, when he again urged a substantial increase in the monthly production rate, then languishing at only 13 boats per month. But Hitler's sights were now firmly set on quite another theatre and only a few days after this conference, on 18 December, he issued Directive 21, instructing the *Wehrmacht* to prepare for a *blitzkrieg* campaign against the Soviet Union. After the war, Dönitz flatly stated: 'The build-up of a powerful U-boat arm, to which all the energy and resources justified by its importance to

---

* In this chapter, 'tons' denotes gross registered tons, a measurement which takes the total cubic capacity of all 'enclosed spaces' in a ship (i.e. omitting companionways, galleys, open-shelter deck space and superstructures) and converts this to weight on the assumption that every 100 cubic feet equals one long ton. Other measurements applied to merchant ships – dry cargo vessels or tankers – are deadweight tonnage and net registered tonnage. Where necessary, conversions have been made in this chapter according to these ratios:

Net	Gross	Deadweight
0.61	1.0	1.45

our war effort should have been devoted, simply failed . . . to take place.'[3]

The shortage of U-boats had serious effects on their tactical deployment. Ever since 1935 Dönitz had had a clear idea of how he wished to use the submarine most effectively to undermine his opponent's ability to wage war. His doctrine embraced six basic concepts: that submarines should be small, fast and numerous; that they should attack with torpedoes rather than gunfire; that they should attack at night; that they should attack on the surface; that they should attack from close range; and that they should operate in groups. The latter point was the so-called *Rudeltaktik*, derived from the German word for flock or herd, but anathematised by the Allies as 'wolf-pack' tactics. The basic idea was that a group of U-boats should station themselves across the path of an anticipated convoy, sailing towards it during the day, when the sighting was expected to be made, and in its direction at night, to avoid the chance of its slipping through the net in the darkness. The first boat to spot the convoy should report back to Dönitz's headquarters in France,* send out homing signals to the rest of the group, and continue to shadow the convoy until all boats were assembled in close vicinity.

Officially, Dönitz began to implement the *Rudeltaktik* in May 1940, but the paucity of U-boats at his disposal meant that few useful contacts were made. The enormous distances to be covered meant that either the U-boat group's patrol line was so extended that convoys could easily slip through the gaps, or it was so short that only by chance would it find itself in front of a convoy. Of the whole period to April 1941, a leading German historian of the U-boat war has written:

It was therefore largely a matter of luck if a U-boat sighted a convoy early enough for it to summon the other U-boats by sending out shadowing reports and homing signals. The few convoy battles which did come about, and the high tonnage losses sustained by the British in them are quite sufficient to give some idea of what could have been done in these months with effective long-range reconnaissance and more U-boats.[4]

* In January 1943 Dönitz replaced Raeder as Commander-in-Chief of the *Kriegsmarine*. He retained control of the U-boat arm but moved its headquarters to Berlin.

This presents something of a puzzle, as one attempts to reconcile the failure of Dönitz's chosen group tactic and the considerable successes enjoyed by the individual U-boats, which up to the beginning of April 1941 sank almost 3 million tons of shipping in the Atlantic. The solution is to be found in the glaring inadequacies of British countermeasures, which conspired to maximise the opportunities for individual submarines, either by littering the ocean with lone merchant ships or by tolerating convoys so poorly protected that they were not even proof against a single attacker. Not that there was much else that the Royal Navy or the merchantmen could have done. For, fortunately for Dönitz, he was not the only one endeavouring to make a silk purse out of a sow's ear. The British, too, were hamstrung by inadequate resources and neither of the twin defenders of Britain's supply lines, the Navy and Coastal Command,* were in a position to offer much protection against even the retarded offensive mounted by the *Kriegsmarine*.

Coastal Command remained critically short of aircraft in the first years of the war. In particularly short supply were the medium- and long-range aircraft[†] able to carry out the prolonged patrols that were such a vital part of tracking down the U-boats. On 1 September 1939 there were only nine such planes in the whole Command and even by the end of the next year this figure had only risen to 174, all of them medium-range planes. In the early stages of the U-boat war, up to March 1941, when many of the submarines operated within British coastal waters, these planes were usefully supplemented by another 150 or so short-range aircraft, which succeeded in so harassing the U-boats that when they returned from the Norwegian operation, in June 1940, they chose to operate much further out to sea, in the Northern Channel between Ireland and Iceland. This rendered the short-range plane practically useless for anti-submarine warfare and placed an intolerable burden on the limited number of medium-range. Particularly since for most of this early period the Avro Anson,

---

* Coastal Command, set up in 1936 though functionally in existence since 1918, was part of the RAF. From early 1941 it was under the 'operational' control of the Admiralty, though a tradition of cooperation had been established for several months before that, a tradition that continued to be more effective than the Admiralty's ill-defined operational control. The most important joint bodies were the various Area Command Headquarters.

† Long-range (LR) planes could operate between 400 and 600 miles from base and there patrol for several hours, whilst medium-range ones could do likewise between 200 and 400 miles out.

with a 'totally inadequate' range, was the only medium- or long-range plane available. 'The Hudsons that would have stretched . . . [this range] were slow in arriving. Bomber Command absorbed all the British Wellingtons, Whitleys and Manchesters that had a greater reach . . . the Stranraer and Lerwick flying boats . . . had proved to be, operationally, almost useless and were quickly withdrawn from service.'[5]

Equally severe shortages afflicted the Royal Navy. In the inter-war years, as we have seen, excessive faith in the potential of Asdic had led to a general run-down of Britain's escort fleet and a growing feeling that convoy operations were now somewhat *démodé*. The shortage of escorts, particularly destroyers, persisted throughout 1940 and became especially acute after the end of the Phoney War, in May. Operation Dynamo was especially expensive, with six of the 39 destroyers taking part being sunk and a further 19 damaged. An American naval attaché estimated that on 5 June, out of a total of 94 destroyers in home waters after Dunkirk, only 43 remained ready for action. Once the evacuation was over, physical destruction of the destroyers slowed down considerably but the subsequent fear of invasion, between July and October, still meant that a large proportion of these ships were tied down in the English Channel and could not be made available for escort. In this period there were rarely more than 40 escorts available to cover the whole of the Western Approaches, the vital north Atlantic routes that led into Liverpool and other west coast ports.* These few ships were rarely able to provide a convoy with more than two escorts and quite often there was only one.

The shortage of escorts was further aggravated, at least up until March 1940, by the Royal Navy's insistence on forming independent, so-called 'hunter-killer' groups of destroyers which were supposed to maintain an 'offensive' posture and track down submarines wherever they might be. Sadly, wherever they were, the destroyers did not find them and, at the same time, made themselves unavailable for escort duties. And what ships remained were hardly tailor-made for the job. As with most other aspects of defence spending, the Chamberlain government was only panicked into allocating resources for escort

---

* The west coast ports were increasingly used during 1940 because U-boats in the Bay of Biscay, as well as air attacks on the southern ports, made the South-West Approaches (HQ Plymouth) increasingly hazardous. Almost all maritime traffic was shifted to the Western Approaches (HQ Liverpool) in August and September 1940.

vessels at the very last moment. In spring 1939, 56 of them were ordered but there was no time for any in-depth appraisal of the necessary specifications. All that could be done was to look round for an existing design that could be quickly adapted to the new role. A hasty tour of the docks and shipyards led the Admiralty team to a whalecatcher being built at Middlesborough. Though its maximum speed was known to be at least three knots less than the surface speed of the German U-boats, it was still the only *available* ship that was at all suitable. So it was overnight transformed into a warship and a crash programme was initiated for what were now to be known as 'Flower Class' corvettes.

Even these less than ideal escorts might have been able to achieve some advantage over the U-boats if their much-vaunted Asdic had been up to scratch. But its range was only just over one thousand yards, and within that U-boats tended to operate on the surface. A report on one convoy's misfortunes, in September 1940, noted that the U-boats' tactics were to operate 'as surface vessels with the advantage of a minute silhouette, and therefore extremely difficult to see in the dark, and the advantage of being able to dive quickly to avoid collision or make their getaway when sighted by merchant ships. Against this type of attack our Asdic is of little use, whether transmissions are used or not.'[6] So escorts rarely got a bead on a U-boat, and even when they did the resulting attack, usually with depth-charges, seldom had much effect. Well into 1941, when it became possible to fire depth-charges in clusters of ten to fourteen and to prime them for varying depths, the lethality of such attacks was probably never more than 10 per cent. Throughout 1940 it was less than half of this. Usually, though, the U-boats were not even detected. In the battle around convoy HX 72, in late September 1940, only *one* depth-charge attack was made during a seven-hour action in which 11 merchants ships were sunk. The following month, HX 79, unusually well guarded by a destroyer, two sloops, two corvettes and four armed trawlers, lost ten ships in a five-hour running battle in which again no U-boats were sunk and hardly any even sighted.

In these early months, therefore, the convoy system existed more in theory than in actuality. Many groups of ships did cross the Atlantic in some sort of formation, under the nominal control of a Convoy Commodore. But so overstretched were the one or two escorts that no real protection was available, especially to stragglers or in the event, common in these first months, of a convoy scattering after witnessing the first kill. Many ships, moreover, chose to sail independently and thus offered themselves as sitting targets to any enemy that chanced upon them.* Not that the latter had to rely entirely on chance. For British efforts were also severely compromised by the fact that their naval codes had been broken by the Germans in 1936, ever since when they had been reading upwards of 50 per cent of RN signal traffic. A large proportion of this traffic consisted of details about the routings and timings of convoys and independent sailings. In a battlefield as big as the Atlantic Ocean, or even just the Western Approaches, any information that gave even partial or approximate indications of where merchant shipping might be found was of inestimable value.

It is all this that helps to explain the puzzle of how the Germans were able to operate so effectively despite the manifest inadequacies of the wolf-pack system. For effective they most certainly were. During the second half of 1940 the following were the quarterly kill rates for U-boats, expressed also as a percentage of total merchant shipping destroyed in the Atlantic:

July–Sept. 1940			Oct.–Dec. 1940		
Total tonnage sunk	Sunk by U-boat	% by U-boat	Total tonnage sunk	Sunk by U-boat	% by U-boat
1,121,582	756,307	67.4	1,034,930	796,442	76.9

In one week in August the U-boats recorded what was to prove the highest weekly total of the whole war. These sinkings, it should be recalled, were accomplished with a monthly average of only a dozen U-boats actually at sea at any one time, and also represented the highest kill rates – tonnage sunk per U-boat at sea – of any stage of the whole Battle of the Atlantic. Had the *Kriegsmarine* gone to war with anything like an adequate U-boat arm, or even had the correct procurement decisions been made in 1938 and 1939, to bring plenty of boats on stream by 1941, it seems likely that they could have so devastated shipping to Britain that she would have been unable to continue fighting. As Marshal of the Royal Air Force Sir John

* There was also an early lack of official impetus to persuade captains to sail in convoy, partly brought about by a total misreading of the relevant statistics. Churchill's scientific adviser, Professor Frederick Lindemann (later Lord Cherwell), produced figures in early 1940 that showed that convoy had absolutely no effect on the number of sinkings. What he omitted to take into account was that at this stage of the war ships were only escorted part-way into the Atlantic and his figures included a large proportion of ships sunk after their escort had turned back.

Slessor, at one stage in charge of Coastal Command, wrote after the war: 'One shudders to think what would have happened if the Germans before the war had not been so foolish as to build up a third-rate heavy ship force at the expense of their really decisive arm, the U-boat service.' Churchill put the issues more simply still: 'The U-boat attack was our worst evil. It would have been wise for the Germans to stake all on it.'[7]

During the first half of 1941 the Battle of the Atlantic intensified, with both sides indicating that it was now a fundamental part of their war effort. On 6 February Hitler issued Directive 23, which dealt solely with 'operations against the English war economy', and though he emphasised the necessity to hold back considerable resources for the forthcoming attack on Russia, he did stress the value of attacks on the British lines of communication:

> the heaviest effect of our operations against the English war economy has lain in the high losses in merchant shipping inflicted by sea and air warfare . . . The wider employment of submarines . . . can bring about the collapse of English resistance within the foreseeable future . . . It must therefore be the aim of our further operations . . . to concentrate all weapons of air and sea warfare against enemy imports . . . The sinking of merchantmen is more important than attacks on enemy warships.[8]

Exactly a month later, Churchill responded with a directive of his own which gave notice 'that the Battle of the Atlantic has begun . . . We must take the offensive against the U-boat and the Focke-Wulf* wherever we can and whenever we can. The U-boat at sea must be hunted, the U-boat in the building yard or in the dock must be bombed.'[9]

Recognising that the strategic spotlight had at last been turned on his own command, Dönitz made every effort to fulfil Hitler's Directive. His efforts were not unavailing and during the first half of 1941 the U-boats continued to enjoy considerable success. During the second quarter, especially, as the weather began to improve, they were able to score some successes employing the *Rudeltaktik*, though the picking off of ships not in convoy still accounts for a large

---

* The Focke-Wulf mentioned was the Fw 200, or Kondor, a squadron of which had been put under Dönitz's command in January 1941. These four-engined planes had an excellent range (over 2,000 miles) and were employed in reconnaissance duties as well as in making attacks on merchant ships in their own right.

proportion of the tonnage sunk. The actual figures for merchant ship sinkings in the Atlantic during this period were:

	Jan.–March 1941			April–June 1941	
Total tonnage sunk	Sunk by U-boat	% by U-boat	Total tonnage sunk	Sunk by U-boat	% by U-boat
1,196,072	613,691	51.3	1,233,188	979,774	79.5

One reason for this increased success – the April–June kills by U-boats were some 20 per cent better than the previous high record in autumn 1940 – was the growing number of U-boats actually at sea at any one time. The monthly averages for the Atlantic during 1941 were as below:

Jan.–March 1941	April–June 1941	July–Sept. 1941	Oct.–Dec. 1941
11	25	33	33

There were also good reasons for hoping that these numbers would continue to increase as the number of U-boats built rose from 78 in the first six months to 120 in the next. Who knew but that Dönitz might actually reach his 'minimum' total of 300 boats?

In other respects, however, the omens for the Germans in 1941 were less favourable. Despite Hitler's brave words in Directive 23, the demands of the Russian campaign seriously undermined the potential impact of the U-boat offensive. The *Luftwaffe* was just as heavily committed in the east as the Army, and Dönitz was unable to persuade Göring to part with any more Kondors. His original squadron, KG40, had only 12 aircraft, and this presented what Dönitz regarded as

> almost insoluble tasks as far as finding of merchant shipping was concerned . . . The U-boat itself, with its extremely limited range of vision, was the worst possible medium. The most vital and necessary complement to the U-boat, which was our main instrument of battle, was the aircraft. Here the flaw in the conduct of the war at sea was revealed with painful clarity.[10]

That Göring should wish to maintain as many planes as possible for the forthcoming invasion of Russia was at least understandable, which is more than can be said for the decision taken in early 1941 to call up 25,000 skilled dockyard workers to serve on the Eastern Front.

Even granted that Hitler only expected a short campaign, merely the temporary loss of these men seriously affected both the production of new boats and the repair of the existing fleet.

Not all of Dönitz's problems were of the Nazis' own invention. The British by 1941 were beginning to make some progress with convoy management, introducing various devices and techniques that were to prove increasingly effective in the months to come. In March 1941 high-level coordination of the whole convoy effort was introduced with the setting up of the Battle of the Atlantic Committee, comprising ministers, civil servants and senior representatives from the services. The two main military developments this committee helped to encourage were the introduction of radar into escort ships and the use of long-range aircraft to report on U-boat positions and, where possible, to attack them. In this latter role they were assisted by the Leigh Light, a very powerful floodlight that picked up U-boats running on the surface at night.* The first radar supplied to ships was the so-called ASV (Air-Surface Vessel) Mark II, which by mid-summer 1941 was fitted in 97 of the 247 escorts serving in home waters. It was a rather crude device which could only give very rough bearings without swinging the ship. Higher-resolution radar, and longer ranges, demanded that it operate on much higher frequencies than the 1.5 metres of ASV II. In February 1940 the Cavity Magnetron appeared, which for the first time did produce high power at much higher frequencies, within the centimetric range. In March 1941 a prototype centimetric radar, ASV III, operating at 10cm, appeared and this proved able to detect a surfaced U-boat at 5,000 yards. By July 25 ships were equipped with it and in September it was accepted for general service. Soon after this its range was increased to 8,000 yards.

Radar was also fitted in medium-, long- and very long-range (VLR) aircraft, though in 1941 only ASV II sets were allowed as Bomber Command was given priority in the use of centimetric sets, which they knew as H_2S.† Because of this restriction, Coastal Command at this time found aircraft radar not very useful and many more

* Strictly speaking, U-boats were not submarines proper but only submersibles, in that they had periodically, every 90 miles or so, to come to the surface to recharge their batteries. Moreover, only when surfaced could they achieve any reasonable turn of speed (about 17 knots as opposed to only 3 knots submerged) and thus keep up with the merchantmen or make rendezvous with a wolf pack.
† ASV III had many aliases. To Fighter Command it was AI and to Anti-Aircraft Command GL3.

U-boats were sighted visually than were picked up by it. Some of these sightings were made by the first VLR aircraft to be attached to Coastal Command, Liberators serving with 120 Squadron. The squadron was formed in June 1941 and was based in Iceland.* From there the VLR aircraft were able to penetrate deep into the Atlantic, though the normal quota of eight or nine serviceable aircraft severely limited the area they could hope to cover. For few Liberators were made available to Coastal Command. Half of the original 20 Mark Is delivered to Britain were snapped up by Transport Command and BOAC, who used them as transatlantic transports to ferry senior officials between Britain and America. Most of the later Marks went to Bomber Command, which refused to give up any at all for conversion to VLRs, insisting that the Bomber Offensive needed every available aircraft.† In 1941, therefore, there were simply not enough aircraft available to make a decisive contribution to the U-boat war, and their share of the already meagre kill-rate remained low, as the figures below indicate:

	U-boats destroyed by aircraft or by ships and aircraft	U-boats destroyed by other means
1939	–	9
1940	4	20
1941	5	30

Nevertheless, there were distinct improvements in Britain's overall record in the Battle of the Atlantic. The figures just cited show a clear rise in the total number of U-boats destroyed in 1941, a rise mainly attributable to 'a marked improvement in the efficiency of the British Anti-Submarine effort. In the last half of 1941 one out of every three U-boats attacked by surface craft was being badly damaged and one out of every seven sunk.'[11]‡ Even more encouraging were the figures for merchant shipping lost, which in the second half of 1941 fell well below the levels of the previous 18 months. Between April and June, as we have seen, a full 1¼ million tons of shipping were lost in the Atlantic, but in the next six months the figures were as follows:

* Garrisoned by the British in April 1940.
† And this despite the fact that in Bomber Command they were not at all popular, as they had a limited ceiling and produced engine fumes that might identify them to the enemy at night.
‡ In attacks by aircraft, on the other hand, only 2 per cent achieved kills.

July–Sept. 1941			Oct.–Dec. 1941		
Total tonnage sunk	Sunk by U-boat	% by U-boat	Total tonnage sunk	Sunk by U-boat	% by U-boat
471,381	392,118	83.2	395,188	328,690	83.2

One reason for this welcome drop was the improvement in the efficiency of the escorts already noted, as well as an increase in numbers. Thanks to the latter the Navy was able, in May 1941, to mount its first continuous convoy escort, for HX 129, right across the Atlantic. Another reason was the assistance given by the United States. In January 1941 the United States Navy had set up a force of its own to convoy merchantmen and in February an Atlantic Fleet was formed under the command of Admiral Ernest J. King. In March the Lend-Lease Act passed Congress and in April President Roosevelt pushed the limits of the so-called Pan-American Security Zone to a point 30°W, and declared that the US Navy would search for U-boats west of that line, giving merchantmen warning about any that were located. In June this line was moved further east, to 26°W, and in July US troops took over the occupation of Iceland, whose waters were now included in the Security Zone. In August an Atlantic Conference was held where it was agreed that in the following month the US Navy would take over responsibility for convoy escort up to the edge of the Security Zone, now known as the Mid-Ocean Meeting Point or MOMP. On 4 September Roosevelt gave his ships permission to fire on German vessels and later that month Admiral Harold Stark, the US Navy Commander-in-Chief, wrote: 'So far as the Atlantic is concerned, we are all but, if not actually in it.'

But the major reason for the slump in U-boat efficiency in the second half of 1941 was the tremendous breakthrough made in decrypting messages sent to the U-boats by means of Enigma machines. The machines used by the *Kriegsmarine* were somewhat more complex than those used elsewhere in the *Wehrmacht*, having additional rotors, rather like modern 'daisy wheels', to increase greatly the permutations possible in the encoding. The only way the British cryptologists based at Bletchley Park could hope to read German traffic was to lay their hands on an actual Enigma machine. This was achieved in May 1941, and still more progress was made in the following weeks as the British introduced improved shore-based high-frequency direction-finding stations which could pick up signals sent out by the U-boats to indicate their position and bearing. This was not only valuable in its own right, enabling the British to warn convoys in the vicinity of the U-boats, but it also gave them

> great help in cracking the daily settings of the German cypher machines. Because those concerned with traffic analysis knew the normal set-up of a contact signal, and could estimate from their own situation maps the contents of this signal, they could feed the 'bombes'* with a possible clear text and the actual encyphered text . . . [Once] Hut 8 at Bletchley Park got the daily key . . . it was then possible to decypher all intercepted messages of the day, as quickly as the German operator, in a few minutes.[12]

It was then usually possible for the Navy's Submarine Tracking Room to re-route threatened convoys around the patrol-line established by a wolf pack. During the whole period July to December 1941, therefore, 'the Allied convoy routing and rerouting worked so perfectly that *not one* convoy was intercepted as planned on the North Atlantic convoy route. Only some chance meetings led to battles which could never have been avoided by this technique . . . On a very cautious estimate . . . about 1,600,000 gross tons of shipping losses were avoided, one of the decisive successes of Ultra.'[13†]

Dönitz was thus paying the price for Hitler's having gone to war with such a small submarine fleet and with such sketchy plans for increasing it. For, crucial as was the Ultra breakthrough, it would not have had such a marked impact on the wolf packs if they had been present in sufficient numbers to make rerouting almost impossible. Towards the end of 1941, indeed, German weakness was exacerbated as Hitler demanded that the U-boats be transferred from the Atlantic to support operations elsewhere. Throughout the second half of 1941 a proportion of Dönitz's scanty fleet was tied down in subsidiary operations, some being used as weather ships for the *Luftwaffe*, some operating in the Baltic in conjunction with the forces on the Eastern Front, and others in the Arctic, in which areas

---

* These were proto-computers which could test millions of possible permutations very quickly, at least by the standards of the time.

† The Germans, of course, were also reading British signals traffic, even after an improved cypher was introduced in June 1941, but the time it took them to decrypt meant that most of what was learnt about British reroutings came too late to be of any value to the U-boats. One authority has estimated that only 10 per cent of intercepted traffic could be used operationally.

'they found practically no targets and accomplished nothing worth mentioning.'[14] But the biggest drain on Dönitz's resources was the Mediterranean, whither he was ordered to send 25 U-boats at the end of November 1941, at which time his average monthly strength in the Atlantic still numbered only 38 boats. Most of the boats so transferred accomplished little. Many were stationed to the east and west of Gibraltar and, because of the heavy Royal Navy presence thereabouts, were forced to remain almost continually submerged. This hampered their ability to pick up enemy shipping, to the extent that 'during the whole time they were stationed there, they saw no movement of shipping at all in an easterly direction. Reduced as they were to a state of submerged immobility, they could . . . only . . . [attack] targets which happened fortuitously to run straight into their arms.'[15]

These orders remained in force until 2 January 1942 when, largely as a result of the formal entry of the United States into the war, a halt was put to the further transfer of U-boats to the Mediterranean and permission granted to move boats already there towards the Azores if this seemed operationally desirable.* In the meantime, however, as Dönitz noted in his War Diary, 'operations in the Atlantic . . . have been at a partial standstill for at least two months and . . . during the last six weeks have practically ceased altogether.'[16] Nor was it to be hoped that the new concessions presaged an all-out attempt to throttle the British war-effort. In December, after the declaration of war on America and in view of the great disappointments being experienced on the Eastern Front, the OKW suggested that the Russian campaign be run down, with the Army limiting itself to establishing a suitable defensive line to protect the territory already conquered. Priority, they suggested, should be given to 'naval and air attacks against Atlantic communications, as Anglo-Saxon offensive power would depend entirely on transport of American forces and munitions to European theatres of operations.'[17] But this was not to Hitler's taste and, having dismissed the proposal as 'drivelling nonsense', he kept his eyes firmly fixed on the east.

For a while Dönitz was able to endure these constraints. For, in the short term at least, American entry into the war proved a wonderful opportunity for the U-boats. Had Dönitz been required to continue his wolf-pack offensive in the northern Atlantic, he would have

---

* But there were still 39 U-boats in the Mediterranean in March 1942, and they did not quit this area entirely until March 1943.

been unlikely to better the disappointing kill rates of the previous six months, simply because he still had far too few submarines. Thus, in January 1942, U-Boat Command had 91 operational boats available. Of these, 34 were stationed elsewhere than in the Atlantic and of the remaining 57, sixty per cent were under repair. There were thus only 22 at sea in the Atlantic, half of which were sailing to or departing their operational zones. 'Thus . . . after two and a half years of war there were never more than ten or twelve boats actively and simultaneously engaged in our most important task, the war on shipping, or something like a mere 12 per cent of our total U-boat strength.'[18] But fortunately for Dönitz, once Hitler had declared war on the United States, he was able to concentrate on *their* shipping, which was known to be remarkably careless about taking any anti-submarine precautions. Dönitz therefore shifted his few boats to the American east coast where, *operating individually*, they were able to repeat the spectacular successes of 1940. In the first six months of 1942 a total of 3,090,485 tons of shipping was sunk in the Atlantic, and of this 2,138,977 tons, almost 70 per cent, was sunk by U-boats off the American east coast.

The dilatory way in which the Americans reacted to this carnage still seems almost incredible, particularly as they had already had some months' experience of convoying ships out to the MOMP line in the North Atlantic. In sight of their own coastline, on the other hand, the Americans persisted in operating their ships individually. Not until March did Admiral King, now Commander-in-Chief of the US Navy, put in an order for more escorts and not until the end of April did the Americans actually organise coastal convoys. Even then, shipping in the Caribbean remained unprotected and it was into this area that the U-boats moved in June. In July and August they accounted for 841,054 tons of shipping in the Caribbean and Atlantic, 472,178 tons of it, or 56.1 per cent, being lost in the former area.

The British were less than pleased with this considerable bonus being offered to Dönitz, and at one stage offered to lend some escort ships to the US Navy, an offer King refused. The British Trade Division, according to its commander, Captain B. B. Schofield, considered this attitude 'quite incomprehensible' and 'found it extremely difficult to be polite about it'.[19] Mature historical opinion has remained severely critical of King's obduracy. Jürgen Rohwer, a leading German historian, has recently written that the delay in adopting convoy for US coastal shipping 'was without doubt one of the greatest mistakes in the Allied conduct of the Battle of the Atlantic.'[20] What remains especially reprehensible is the fact that such havoc was wreaked by a very small number of boats, operating singly,* a number that would have proved inadequate to mount an effective wolf-pack campaign in the North Atlantic.

During August 1942, however, U-boat operations in these westerly waters became increasingly unproductive and Dönitz decided to bring his submarines back into the Western Approaches. Two factors made him more optimistic about the opportunities for a renewed wolf-pack offensive here. One was that the number of U-boats available for service in the Atlantic was increasing, with 85 boats on average at sea in the third quarter of 1942 and 99 boats in the following quarter. Between January and March 1943 this figure was to peak at just over 100 boats at sea. The second reason was that Dönitz had chosen his battlefield carefully. During 1942 the Allies had made some tentative efforts to improve their air coverage of the Atlantic, and both Coastal Command and the US Army Air Force had increased the number of squadrons of anti-submarine aircraft. In this year, aircraft alone and aircraft acting in concert with ships accounted for 43 of the total 87 U-boats destroyed, almost 50 per cent.

These figures gave Dönitz considerable pause for thought, doubtless causing him to regret a remark made early in the year, when he had airily prophesied that 'the aircraft can no more eliminate the U-boat than a crow can fight a mole.'[21] By August he was much more sensible of the threat posed by aircraft, not just as submarine killers but also as the eyes of Allied naval intelligence as well as a severe constraint on the U-boats' freedom of action. Whenever possible, as we have seen, U-boats preferred to travel on the surface, where they could both recharge their batteries and sail fast enough to maintain contact with a convoy. Also, the quicker they could make the journey to and from the operational areas the more time they could spend on actual patrol. But the sighting of an aircraft obliged the U-boats to submerge, and the more they had to do this the less chance they had of shadowing a convoy long enough for a wolf pack to gather round it. In summer 1942 Dönitz complained in his War Diary:

> U-boat traffic off the north of Scotland and in the Bay of Biscay is gravely endangered . . . by patrolling aircraft. In the Atlantic the enemy's daily reconnaissance . . . forces us

* Even at the end of April only 18 boats were operating in the main killing-ground off Florida and in June, when attention switched to the Gulf of Mexico, no more than six boats were ever present there.

to dispose U-boats far out in the centre of the ocean . . .There are also some aircraft of particularly long range which are used as convoy escorts. They have been met 800 miles from British bases.[22]

Allied air cover did have its blind spots, however, because aircraft patrolling from either side of the Atlantic did not have the range to meet in the middle, and thus there existed an unpatrolled zone, known as the Greenland Air Gap in the north and the Azores Gap further south. It was to exploit this gap, particularly below Greenland, that Dönitz concentrated his wolf packs.

In October 1942 the U-boats' chances of survival in this renewed campaign in the North Atlantic were further enhanced by the introduction of the Metox receiver, a device that picked up emissions from ASV II radar and gave due warning of the approach of a hostile aircraft. By 1943, therefore, the German were operating almost with impunity in the air gaps and, worse, were operating at much increased strength, with four sizeable groups in the Greenland Gap alone. Now, almost for the first time, the *Rudeltaktik* really began to pay dividends, with Dönitz able to deploy up to 20 U-boats against each convoy located and, most important of all, to establish multiple patrol lines around which the Allies were unable to reroute. This advantage of numbers was the decisive factor at this point in the Battle of the Atlantic, and one that threatened to undermine the whole rationale of the convoy system.* In a memorandum of 8 March 1943 the British Air and Naval Staffs commented grimly: 'The North Atlantic convoys must now be considered threatened . . . The numbers of U-boats now at sea have reduced very considerably the chances of evasive routing. In the near future we must expect the majority of our convoys to be sighted and subsequently attacked . . . The scale of the attack will increase progressively as more and more U-boats are concentrated against our convoys . . .'[23] This proved to be the case, and if sinkings did not reach the horrendous levels of

---

* This factor was more important, for example, than Allied difficulties in deciphering German signal traffic, though these became severe between February and December 1942 after the Germans switched to a new cypher known as Triton. In the first part of this period the U-boats, operating individually, were sending few signals anyway, and in the second even exact knowledge of the U-boats' whereabouts would not have made it any easier to route round them. In fact, knowledge about their positions was fairly accurate anyway, thanks to direction-finding equipment and inferences that could be made even from a cryptic signal.

the battles in American coastal waters, they were still a depressingly heavy toll exacted on the mature convoy system. Between August 1942 and March 1943 a total of 3,584,768 tons of Allied shipping was sunk in the Atlantic, 3,552,296 tons, or 99.2 per cent, by U-boats. In March alone 538,695 tons were lost, a figure against convoys only exceeded in March 1941. The Royal Navy came close to despair, particularly as 67 of the 85 ships sunk in the first three weeks of March had been sailing in convoy.

> 'It appeared possible,' wrote the Naval Staff after the crisis had passed, 'that we should not be able to continue [to regard] convoy as an effective system of defence.' It had, during three and half years of war, slowly become the linchpin of our maritime strategy. Where could the Admiralty turn if the convoy system had lost its effectiveness? They did not know; but they must have felt, though no one admitted it, that defeat stared them in the face.[24]

Unfortunately for the Germans, this period of success – except for a few months in early 1941, the only time when the *Rudeltaktik* could be said really to have been working – was destined to be short-lived. For the Allies, though they do not seem to have been fully aware of it at the time, were introducing and perfecting the very weapons and techniques that were necessary to counter this new offensive. Because evasion of the much denser wolf packs was now virtually impossible, the only way the Allies could hope to get their convoys through was by actually *destroying* U-boats. This was something that hitherto they had not been particularly good at, but necessity is a hard taskmaster and from spring 1943 they developed a remarkable proficiency in this sphere of operations. The change is clearly evident from the figures in table 37 in the Statistical Appendix, which presents the relationship between the number of U-boats sunk per quarter and the average number of boats at sea in the same quarter. Up to March 1943 the ratio rarely rose above 1:2 and was often well below that. From April, however, the number of U-boats sunk rose dramatically, so much so that the second quarter of 1943 represented the peak operational strength of the Atlantic U-boats and thereafter the relationship between boats sunk and boats at sea was usually either virtual parity or showed the former exceeding the latter. The effect of this on German capabilities is clearly evident in table 38 in the Statistical Appendix, which gives the Allied merchant shipping tonnage sunk from January 1943 to the end of the war. By the end of

1943 the loss of shipping had already been cut to only one-eighth of the figure in the first three months and, in fact, the Germans never succeeded in bettering this meagre total right through to the end of the war.

Various weapons and techniques contributed towards this new Allied ability actually to destroy U-boats. One was an increase in the number of escort vessels available, which by spring 1943 had risen to an average of seven per convoy. Another was a dramatic improvement in the escorts' efficiency, as more and more commanders and crews went through rigorous training courses organised by Western Approaches and its commander, Rear-Admiral Maxwell Horton. Important scientific advances were also made. Operational Research techniques were applied to convoy management, one important discovery, implemented in early 1943, being that large convoys, contrary to conventional wisdom, were much more cost-effective than smaller ones. A convoy of 48 ships with eight escorts, for example, would offer just the same density of protection as one half the size with six escorts. This discovery released a considerable number of escorts from close convoy protection, such that between March and May 1943 the first five independent support groups were set up, escort ships that were not tied to a convoy across the Atlantic but could be switched from one to another in the most threatened sectors.

Other vital scientific contributions were improvements in available direction-finding and radar equipment, both of which again became available in early 1943. The former capitalised upon the U-boats' having to send frequent radio signals back to U-Boat Command so that it could properly direct an attack upon a convoy. It involved a portable high-frequency direction-finder, HF/DF or 'Huff Duff', which was fitted in the ships of the escort group commanders. This operated by detecting the ground wave emitted by the German radio transmitters, a wave which extended to a distance of about 30 miles. Equally important was ASV III radar, offering much better definition and accuracy. By March it was standard in all escort vessels. In early May 1943, during the battle of convoy SC 128, fought in a fog-bank which considerably hampered the efforts of the wolf pack, the radar-equipped escorts were able to account for five U-boats within a matter of hours.

Centimetric radar was also fitted in many Coastal Command aircraft at about this same time, which enabled them too to make dramatic increases in their kill rates. Over and above its improved performances, this new radar had the advantage of being completely undetectable by the Germans' Metox receivers, which were only able to respond to metric pulses. Like all anti-submarine radar, ASV III in aircraft was particularly useful at night, when the U-boats attempted to run on the surface, and used in conjunction with the Leigh Light it accounted for numerous submarines. During 1943 as a whole, aircraft on their own accounted for 142 U-boats destroyed and aircraft and ships together for a further 13, a total which represented over 65 per cent of the 227 U-boats destroyed that year.

Of course, vital as it was to sink U-boats and begin to prise loose their stranglehold on the Greenland Gap, this was not the only contribution that aircraft could make to the Battle of the Atlantic. It was equally important that they continue to fly patrols over the ocean and force the U-boats to submerge as often as possible, and thus to lose contact with the convoys. From the end of May, Allied aircraft were able to do this all the way across the North Atlantic, the Greenland Gap finally having been closed after the stationing of a Canadian squadron of VLR Liberator Mark Vs in Newfoundland.* These aircraft were supplemented by Fleet Air Arm planes operating from small escort carriers attached to two of the support groups already mentioned.† The latter aircraft were not especially potent submarine killers – the Fleet Air Arm accounted for only 29 U-boats during the whole war – but they played an invaluable role in harrying them and forcing them to submerge when in the vicinity of a convoy. American escort carriers also served in the Atlantic, notably USS *Bogue, Core, Santee, Card, Block Island* and *Guadalcanal*.‡ Again their kill-rate was not particularly impressive – in 1944 they accounted for only 16 of the 242 U-boats destroyed that year – but they were absolutely invaluable in helping to close the Azores Gap, lying across the Central Atlantic route which most American convoys sailed. In December 1943 Dönitz lamented to his U-boat commanders that the constant need to submerge to avoid enemy aircraft meant that 'in the most recent convoy operations it has happened again and

---

* See the Appendix to this chapter for further details of the sorry state of the VLR aircraft in an anti-submarine role.

† The first three escort carriers to be used in the Atlantic (HMS *Audacity* had already proved herself in the run from Gibraltar, with convoying HG 76, in December 1941) were *Biter, Archer* and *Dasher*. By the end of the war there were 43 British escort carriers on active service, many of which were based on Greenock and served with the escort and support groups.

‡ It was USS *Bogue* that provided the first carrier escort for an Atlantic convoy, SC 123, in March 1943.

again that the convoy swept past the U-boats, who were unable to exploit the unique opportunity to attack and found themselves lagging hopelessly astern of the target.'[25]

In fact, Dönitz had all but conceded the Battle of the Atlantic when this signal went out. As early as the end of May 1943, after only two months of unremitting pressure from surface escorts and aircraft, during which 56 U-boats were lost, he had been forced to withdraw from the North Atlantic. Hopes of exploiting the Azores Gap were then quickly dashed by the Americans, as was an attempt to return to the North Atlantic in September. Anti-submarine units now had completely the upper hand and they were to retain it for the rest of the war. The reasons were admirably summarised by Dönitz in his War Diary, as he explained his supposedly temporary withdrawal at the end of May. The reasons he gave were:

a) Enemy radar devices operated both from the air and from surface vessels very greatly hampered the operations of individual U-boats . . . The U-boat is now threatened with the loss of its most important advantage: the difficulty of being located.*

b) The enemy's air force can now provide air-cover for convoys over almost the whole area of the North Atlantic . . . This form of escort operations, when carried out with large numbers of aircraft in a wide area around a convoy, has always resulted in U-boats falling hopelessly astern of convoys and being unable to register any further successes.

c) Operations against submerged U-boats with new methods of location, and attacks with apparently more powerful depth-charges, have also grown more intense.

d) U-boat operations are being made more difficult by the increasing number of escort vessels available to the enemy . . . In conclusion it must be recognised that at the moment U-boat operations are more difficult than ever before.

This left Dönitz with only one option, as he himself explained in his memoirs. 'Wolf-pack operations against convoys in the North Atlantic, the main theatre of operations . . . were no longer possible . . . I accordingly [on 24 May] withdrew the boats . . . to the

---

* Dönitz was, of course, unaware that most of his signal traffic was once again being read at Bletchley Park, the Triton cypher having been pretty much broken by the middle of January 1943. He seems also to have rather discounted the possibility of direction-finders being able to operate on high frequencies.

area south-west of the Azores. We had lost the Battle of the Atlantic.'[26]

It should not be thought, however, that Dönitz simply gave up the ghost. As can be seen in table 37, already referred to, U-boat production remained fairly high throughout the last years of the war* and the number of boats at sea in the Atlantic hardly ever fell below the total achieved in the first quarter of 1942. But this table also shows the heavy casualties suffered in these last two years, 'the intolerable burden of losses' as Dönitz called it, imposed by the ever-burgeoning force of destroyers, escort carriers and long-range anti-submarine aircraft.[27] Table 38 emphasises just how effective this force became in cutting merchant shipping losses and this message is further underlined in table 39 in the Statistical Appendix, which attempts to measure U-boat efficiency by showing the ratio between the average of U-boats at sea in a quarter and the tonnage they sank. The decline in efficiency throughout 1943 and 1944 is plain to see, the average quarterly tonnage sunk per U-boat at sea falling from 70,000 in late 1940 to 2,000 by the end of 1943. So dramatic is this fall, indeed, that one must assume that Allied improvements are not the whole answer. It seems likely that the quality of the U-boat crews also declined, due almost certainly to a foreshortening of their training, as well as to limited opportunities to learn 'on the job' consequent upon the greatly increased attrition rate.[†]

A major theme of this book is that Allied victory in the Second World War rested very largely upon the huge material and

---

* With a sublimely inappropriate sense of timing, Hitler actually acceded to Dönitz's pleas for increased submarine production in May 1943, just when the battle was lost. Had these extra boats been made available in the second half of 1941, when the wolf packs were unable to counter Allied rerouting, the results could have been extremely serious for the Allies.

† This was certainly the case with *Luftwaffe* fighter pilots, as will be seen in the next chapter. But table 39 raises other questions tangential to this book's main theme. It seems clear, for example, that it was not wolf-pack tactics that were the Germans' surest weapon, except perhaps during the single month of March 1943, but rather giving individual commanders their head during periods of weak or non-existent Allied escort. It is interesting to speculate what results Dönitz might have achieved if he had allowed individual commanders more initiative even against the fairly well protected convoys. The spread of the U-boats would have made Allied rerouting more difficult and boats attacking singly might have found it much easier to worm their way into a convoy. Looked at from the Allied point of view, of course, table 39 simply reaffirms how right they were to readopt the convoy system.

manpower reserves that they were eventually able to deploy. At times the argument goes one stage further, suggesting that the deployment of even that overwhelming force was often maladroit and caused battles and campaigns to drag on for longer than they should. It would be difficult, however, to maintain that either of these points is particularly applicable to the Battle of the Atlantic in which, with the sad exception of Bomber Command, every attempt was made to make the most judicious use of fairly limited resources.

Nevertheless, one cannot leave a discussion of this battle without taking proper note of the importance of the sheer numbers in the Allied merchant fleets, both the ships in existence before the war and those built during it. The figures for the latter category in the United Kingdom and the United States are given in table 6, where the annual totals are contrasted with the tonnage of merchant vessels lost – tonnage, it should be noted, belonging

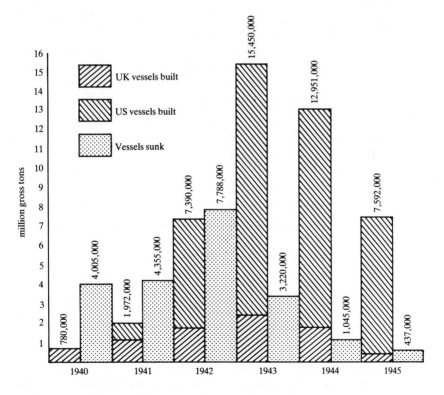

Table 6: *US and UK merchant tonnage built and Allied and neutral merchant tonnage sunk 1940–5*

to all Allied and neutral fleets. Two points stand out. The first concerns the US economy, the potential of which was such that the Americans' ability to build ships far outstripped the Germans' ability to sink them. Even in 1942, the first year of American participation in the war proper, joint US and UK merchant ship building was only just outstripped by the total of sinkings, a total that was far and away the best the U-boats ever managed.* In short, unless the Germans had been able to wipe out the UK merchant fleet within the first two years of war, they stood no chance at all of ever keeping pace with Allied production. Yet these first two years were precisely the ones in which the U-boat arm was allowed to remain relatively weak, both in terms of numbers of submarines and of combat experience. Dönitz himself noted in his memoirs that though his few boats were extraordinarily successful in 1939 and 1940, the victories were bought at heavy cost, with a casualty rate of roughly 15 per cent of the monthly average number of boats at sea.

This leads us to the second point. At first sight it might appear that during 1940 and 1941 the U-boats were at least on the right track in that they were inflicting net losses on the British. What the table does not show, however, is that in this first phase of the war the British were not dependent on new construction for all extra merchant tonnage. Far from it, in fact, and the tanker fleet offers a particularly good example. Between 1939 and 1941 only 320,000 tons of tankers were actually built in British yards, but the gross increase in tanker tonnage under British control was 2,027,000 tons, the vast majority having been time-chartered (almost 1.5 million tons), requisitioned, purchased or having transferred its flag. This meant that between 1939 and 1941 the British-controlled tanker fleet also showed a *net* increase, of roughly three-quarters of a million tons. With this in mind it is interesting to look at the figures for tankers and dry-cargo vessels under British control and those under American flag for the whole of the war, as shown in table 7. In the latter part of the war, as might be expected, the prodigious American ship-building programme sent combined tonnage to ever higher levels. What is perhaps more surprising is that even when one looks at the British fleet in isolation, its size remains remarkably steady *throughout the*

---

* With regard to the American effort, it is still remarkable to consider that in 1938 the US Maritime Commission felt that a building rate of 50 merchant ships per annum should be more than adequate for her needs. In the event, 105 were built in 1941, 760 in 1942 and 1,950 in 1943.

US merchant fleet

UK merchant fleet

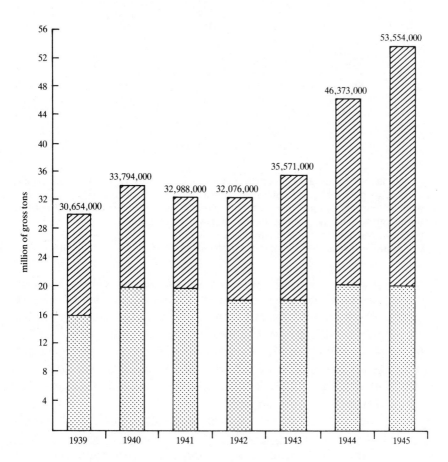

Table 7: *Size of US and UK merchant fleets 1939–45*

whole war, and palpably not as close to extinction as some accounts of the Battle of the Atlantic might lead one to believe.

Another indication that the U-boat offensive cannot really be said to have brought Britain to the very brink of defeat is given in table 8, which attempts to give some impression of the percentage loss of imports into Britain between 1939 and 1945. The loss is in fact overstated, as the tonnage of cargo sunk refers to shipping both entering British ports and leaving, no more detailed breakdown

Table 8: *Cargo lost in the Atlantic as a percentage of cargo docked in the UK 1939–45*

Date	Net tonnage shipping docked UK*	Net tonnage shipping sunk in Atlantic	Net tonnage shipping sunk by U-boat in Atlantic	Total sinkings as % tonnage docked	U-boat sinkings as % tonnage docked
1938	91,880,000	–	–	–	–
1939†	12,125,000	453,000 ⎫		3.7 (2.6)‡ ⎫	
		⎬ 1,506,000		⎬ 2.8 (2.0)	
1940	41,660,000	2,082,000 ⎭		4.9 (3.4) ⎭	
1941	25,496,000	1,979,000	1,390,000	7.8 (5.5)	5.5 (3.9)
1942	24,480,000	3,694,000	3,408,000	15.1 (10.6)	13.9 (9.7)
1943	30,601,000	1,321,000	1,159,000	4.3 (3.0)	3.8 (2.7)
1944	56,937,000	304,000	220,000	0.5 (0.4)	0.4 (0.3)
1945†	18,604,000	220,000	158,000	1.2 (0.8)	0.8 (0.6)

* In this Table tonnage is given as net tonnage as this figure was specifically calculated to give more idea of the cargo-carrying capacity of a ship. Like gross tonnage it was based around the assumption that 100 cubic feet of space represented one ton, but less of the volume of the ship was included.
† September to December and January to May.
‡ The figure in brackets estimates the percentage of *incoming* cargo sunk.

being available.* The percentages given in the table are therefore probably as much as 30 per cent in excess of the actual loss of imports, which simply serves to underline the fact that one should not exaggerate the effect of the Battle of the Atlantic on the British war effort. Certainly the losses suffered were sorely felt, especially as imports for every year of the war were considerably below 1938 levels. But it is nevertheless not really the case that Britain's very survival was seriously threatened.

The 10 per cent of imports lost in 1942 were undoubtedly sorely missed, but it should be remembered that a fair proportion of these were earmarked for building up forces for a projected return to mainland Europe, for which venture Britain served as an advanced base. That munitions and the like for these forces should be lost was unfortunate, but it still only meant that the return across the Channel would be delayed, not that Britain was being completely starved of goods essential to her very survival. Given the feeble

* Dönitz was mainly interested in destroying merchant ships rather than the cargo itself, and for this reason pursued what he dubbed an 'integral' targeting policy, without regard to the type of ship being attacked. Had he attempted to zero in on the more strategically sensitive vessels, tankers or ore-carriers for example, he might have made considerably greater impact on British production.

number of U-boats with which Germany began the war, Hitler's half-hearted support for a proper construction programme, the inadequate number of surface ships and aircraft to supplement the submarine effort, and Britain's, albeit belated, adoption of the convoy system, Dönitz had no real hope of eliminating British merchant shipping early in the war. And once America joined the fray there was nothing that he could do to prevent the U-boat arm becoming strategically marginal.

This is not to deny, of course, that the Battle of the Atlantic was an extremely bitter one, with terrible sufferings on both sides, nor even that Dönitz's last fling, in winter 1943, alarmed the Allies considerably. The historian, cushioned by hindsight, can look back on these months with considerably more sang-froid than was felt at the time, but hindsight also offers valuable perspectives and in this instance can help us to keep in mind just what a formidable industrial base Dönitz was trying to undermine. A comparison with the Japanese experience in the Second World War is particularly revealing. The war in the Pacific is dealt with in detail in Part Five, but a few details are pertinent here. Between 1942 and 1945 the Japanese merchant fleet, whose survival was absolutely basic to Japan's continued ability to wage war, lost 8,616,000 tons of shipping. That was enough to cut this fleet by fully 75 per cent, leaving her at the end of the war with a paltry 1.5 million tons afloat. The Allies, on the other hand, *in this same period*, lost 12,590,000 tons, almost half as much again, yet the size of their own fleet rose from 32 million tons to 54 million. The attritional effort required to make headway against margins like these was quite beyond German (and/or Japanese) capabilities.

Appendix:
VLR *aircraft and anti-submarine warfare*

The story of the struggle to obtain enough VLR aircraft to close the Greenland Gap would fill a book of its own. Suffice it to say that the tremendous delay in getting the requisite number of aircraft actually dispatched to Newfoundland – the squadron in question operated only six VLRs – was symptomatic of bitter and extremely damaging rivalries within the Services, mainly between Bomber and Coastal Command. The former, championed by Churchill, had long opposed the transfer of any bombers for maritime duties and only with great reluctance parted even with Liberators, which were pre-eminently suited to long-range reconnaissance work. In June 1942 the commander of Bomber Command anathematised such works as 'purely defensive' and therefore 'grossly wasteful. The naval employment of aircraft consists of picking at the fringes of enemy power, of waiting for opportunities that may never occur, of looking for needles in a haystack.' Instead he wished to concentrate all resources upon the bombing of Germany, even though, as will be seen in the next chapter, his estimates of the damage this offensive was causing were way over the top and had been shown to be so. That same month, indeed, he went so far as to suggest that the diversion of aircraft to Coastal Command made the latter 'an obstacle to victory'.[28]

The Admiralty and Coastal Command took strong exception to such views, and their vehement protests, though also partisan, must surely be seen with hindsight as indicative of a more balanced assessment of the Allies' strategic priorities. Early in 1942, even before the memoranda just cited, Admiral Sir John Tovey, the Commander-in-Chief of the Home Fleet, actually suggested that reinforcement and re-equipment of Coastal Command and the Fleet Air Arm were so vital that the whole Board of the Admiralty should resign if suitable aircraft were not made available. At around the same time, even the Chief of the Imperial General Staff, General Alan Brooke, was becoming irritated by Bomber Command's attitude, noting in his diary: 'We are now reaping the full disadvantage of an all-out independent air policy directed towards the bombing of Germany. As a result we are short of all the suitable types of aircraft for support of the other two Services. It is an uphill battle to fight . . .'[29] Coastal Command, not surprisingly, was among the severest critics of this reluctance to part with any long-range aircraft. Air Chief Marshal Sir Philip Joubert de la Ferté, at one time the Command's Commander-in-Chief, recalled his struggle to lay his hands on just 27 VLRs to close the Greenland Gap, at a time when double that number of Liberators were soon to be lost in an inconsequential raid on the Ploesti airfields in Romania. 'If not one gallon from this field had ever again reached Germany, the war might have been shortened by a couple of months. Failure to close the "Gap" might well have lost us the war.'[30] An equally forthright comparison was made by Professor P.M.S. Blackett, the Operational Research adviser to Coastal Command, who calculated that a Liberator in VLR role 'saved at least half a dozen merchant ships in its service lifetime of some thirty flying sorties.' The same plane employed by Bomber Command in an area bombing role would in its service life

> drop less than 100 tons of bombs and kill not more than a couple of dozen enemy men, women, and children, and destroy a number of houses. No one would dispute that the saving of six merchant vessels and their crews and cargoes was of incomparably more value to the Allied war effort than the killing of some two dozen enemy civilians, the destruction of a number of houses, and a certain very small effect on production.[31]

A final comment comes from the Official Naval Historian, Captain S.W. Roskill, who at one stage makes a very rare personal comment on the VLR controversy, concluding that 'for what it is worth this writer's view is that in the early spring of 1943 we had a very narrow escape from defeat in the Atlantic; and that, had we suffered such a defeat, history would have judged that the main cause had been the lack of two more squadrons of very long range escort aircraft for convoy escort duties.'[32]

4

The Bomber Offensive
June 1940 – May 1945

After the rout of 1940 the paramount necessity to foil German invasion plans, as well as to keep open the maritime lifeline to the west, meant that Britain's strategic posture had to be largely defensive. Yet this did not imply that her war leaders, notably Churchill, were not eager to make some show of taking the battle to the enemy. Moreover, a force with which this might be done did exist, on paper at least. During much of the previous decade, in fact, successive governments had placed considerable emphasis upon the Royal Air Force, so that between 1935 and 1938 it had enjoyed an increasing share of the Service Estimates, rising from one-fifth to one-third. That such a youthful Service could in this latter year be allocated £73.5 million as opposed to the Navy's £96.1 million was telling evidence of the growing awe with which the air arm was regarded. This was especially true of its bomber component for, despite Britain's last-minute switch to increased fighter production mentioned in chapter 1, it was the bomber that loomed largest in the popular, and much of the official, imagination.*

Ever since the end of the First World War, in fact, bombers had had some spirited publicists, notably General Giulio Douhet in Italy and General 'Billy' Mitchell in the United States. hese men were particular advocates of the bombers' ability to cripple an enemy's industrial base and thus perhaps win the war without the rival land forces having to exchange a shot, and there were many in the RAF who shared, if somewhat more discreetly, very similar views. Lord Trenchard, for example, had been Chief of the Air Staff between

---

* Of the 83 RAF squadrons reformed between June 1934 and August 1939, 14 were equipped with trainers, flying boats, reconnaissance and army cooperation aircraft, 2 with torpedo-bombers, 17 with fighters and fully 50 with bombers (Battles, Hampdens, Wellesleys, Whitleys and Wellingtons).

1919 and 1929 and had told the Salisbury Committee, in 1923: 'It is on the bomber offensive that we must rely for defence. It is on the destruction of enemy industries and, above all, on the lowering of morale of enemy nationals caused by bombing that ultimate victory rests.'[1] This emphasis upon the breaking of enemy morale persisted into the 1930s. In November 1935 an Air Targets Sub-Committee was set up by the Deputy Chiefs of Staff, to try and highlight the economic/strategic component of bomber doctrine, but in the following year Group Captain John Slessor produced a book which better reflected general attitudes in the RAF and which pretty much regurgitated Trenchard's views on the importance of enemy morale:

> In our operations against production the weight of attack will inevitably fall upon a vitally important, and not by nature very amenable, section of the community – the industrial workers, whose morale and sticking power cannot be expected to equal that of the disciplined soldier. And we should remember that if the moral effect of air bombardment was serious seventeen years ago, it will be immensely more so under modern conditions.[2]

However, when war finally came in September 1939, Bomber Command proved to be pretty much of a damp squib. In the first few months it made hardly any effort to live up to its aggressive doctrine and did not even encounter an enemy fighter until 14 December, during a raid on German shipping off Wilhelmshaven. This raid proved so expensive, however, that the Air Ministry was forced to abandon daylight bombing raids entirely.* At first this was not regarded as much of a problem and the then head of Bomber Command, Air Marshal Sir Edgar Ludlow-Hewitt, blithely remarked: 'I see no reason why the major destructive part of our plans cannot take

---

* The other major feature of British bombing theory, in addition to the emphasis upon morale, was the remarkable lack of attention it gave to counter-force operations, the ability of enemy fighters to shoot down one's bombers. A key figure in the development of the bomber force in the 1930s was Group Captain Arthur Harris, the head of the Air Ministry Planning Department, who continued to give 'inadequate attention . . . either to the possible significance of counter-force operations or to the self-defence of the bomber formations. The heavy bombers [of the Second World War], the operational requirements of which Harris played a major part in framing . . ., were to be inherently defective in defensive firepower . . . [By 1939] Bomber Command was fully committed . . . to a policy of ignoring the German Air Force as an obstacle . . .' (M. Smith, 'Harris' Offensive in Historical Perspective', *RUSI Journal* 135, June 1985, pp. 63–4.)

place in the form of precision bombing by night.'[3] In fact, there was every reason. The crews proved incapable of locating targets at night, the weather during the winter of 1939–40 kept the planes grounded for days on end, and the British government's ban on any raids that might conceivably cause unnecessary loss of civilian life limited the RAF to only a few naval targets, where Flak and fighter protection was duly strengthened.* The result was that the bomber 'offensive' had to be discontinued, the squadrons limiting themselves to dropping millions of propaganda leaflets or to mining German waterways.

All this was acutely embarrassing to Bomber Command, of course, but during the Phoney War it was just about possible to get away with such a feeble level of operations. With the resumption of land operations in April and May 1940, however, it was no longer feasible for Ludlow-Hewitt to try and laugh off the grandiose claims that had been made in the 1930s, particularly as the new heavy four-engined Stirlings and two-engined Manchesters were now being tested and were expected to enter service in the late summer and autumn. The 'strategic' bombers they had clamoured for so long were on the way, so there could no longer be any excuse for not initiating a campaign to bring German industry swiftly to its knees. To this end most of the previous strictures about avoiding civilian casualties were abandoned. On 11 April the first attack on mainland Europe took place, on Stavanger, in Norway, and exactly one month later the first attack on mainland Germany. On 15 May Bomber Command launched its first attack on Germany east of the Rhine, indicating that it was not just the industrial concentration in the Ruhr that was to be regarded as a legitimate target.[†] In April, too, the Air Ministry issued the first of its Directives to Bomber Command, specifying the exact industrial and other 'strategic' targets that were to pertain during a particular phase of operations. These continued to be issued right up until the end of the war and for convenience's sake are all summarised in table 40 in the Statistical Appendix.[‡]

The first specific economic target named was oil, the Directive

---

* Flak was German anti-aircraft artillery, the word being an abbreviation for *Fliegerabwehrkanone*.

† Though it was not until May 1942 that attacks on industrial and military targets in occupied countries were permitted.

‡ In table 40 only the Primary Targets are named. Most Directives also included several other targets of secondary and tertiary importance, to be attacked sporadically or when others were impossible. It should also be noted that from January 1943 the Air Ministry was usually only passing on the instructions of the Combined Chiefs of Staff, which applied to both the RAF and the USAAF.

of 13 April 1940 stating that 'the principal weight of attack should be directed against the oil-plants [in the Ruhr] . . . You should be prepared to undertake this operation as a sustained effort . . .' In July 1940, it was 'confirmed that oil is the weakest link in Germany's war economy' and thus its 'destruction remains the basis of the main offensive strategy directed towards the reduction and dislocation of German war potential.'[4]

Unfortunately, it was one thing to write directives full of well intentioned strategic objectives and quite another to pursue them properly, and it was to be many months before the scale of Bomber Command's effort was remotely commensurate with the magnitude of their task. Table 9 makes it clear that for almost three years, from May 1940 to February 1943, the actual tonnage of bombs dropped remained on a consistently low level, rarely more than 6,000 tons per month and usually less than 4,000. The figures for 1940 and 1941 were actually less than the aggregate tonnage dropped on England in these same years, a tonnage which, as we have seen, did not have the slightest hope of bringing British production to a halt or her population to open revolt. When one also considers that British bomb-loads had to be scattered over a much greater land-mass, even when the occupied countries were exempt, it is hardly surprising that their impact on German industry was minimal.

Ludlow-Hewitt's successors at Bomber Command, acting Air Marshal Peter Portal,* who took over in April 1940, and Air Chief Marshal Sir Richard Pierse, who took his turn in October when Portal, now knighted, became Chief of the Air Staff, felt that their crews were expected to achieve results that were little short of pure fancy. On 16 July, Portal pointed out that 'even on the Air Staff's own figures, the operations proposed could not have a decisive effect.'[5] At one stage it seemed that the Air Ministry had concurred, though claiming credit for themselves, and a Directive issued shortly afterwards noted that the Air Staff had come

> to the conclusion that attacks on industrial objectives had hitherto been too dispersed and that, in consequence, few objectives have sustained sufficient damage to put them out of action for any length of time. During this moon phase, therefore, you are requested to direct a greater weight of attack

* Universally known as Peter though in fact christened Charles Frederick Algernon.

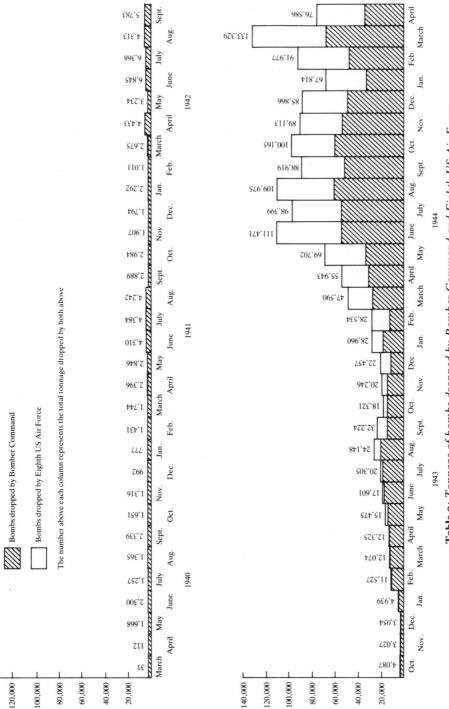

The number above each column represents the total tonnage dropped by both above

Bombs dropped by Bomber Command

Bombs dropped by Eighth US Air Force

Table 9: *Tonnage of bombs dropped by Bomber Command and Eighth US Air Force*
1940–5

on fewer targets with a view to complete destruction rather than harassing effect.[6]

But the Air Staff then seem promptly to have forgotten their own advice, and in late October Pierse was presented with a Directive which 'called for attacks by fifty to a hundred bombers every few nights on a German town selected from a list of twenty to thirty. Pierse replied that he was being asked to achieve the impossible; twelve potential targets would, he argued, be enough. To attempt more would be "to fail all round".'[7]

Another serious limitation on the amount of damage the bombers could be expected to do was the bombs themselves, which until mid-1942 contained an explosive much weaker than that used by the Germans. The casing was also far too thick, using up precious weight, and the fuses were primitive, resulting in an excessive number of 'duds'. But the worst problem was that of accuracy, given that there were severe constraints on both the pilots' ability to find the designated town or city, or recognise it even if they had found it, and the bomb-aimers' chances of getting their loads anywhere near the particular cluster of buildings or whatever that had been singled out for attention. Results had been far from impressive during the brief flirtation with daylight bombing, when precision was supposed to be a natural concomitant of 'good' visibility. When it had to be conceded that only night operations offered any hope of keeping casualties within acceptable bounds, the idea of precision became little more than a bad joke. Not for nothing did the commander of 4 group, Air Vice-Marshal Arthur Coningham, comment in 1940: 'I foresee a never-ending struggle to circumvent the law that we cannot see in the dark.'[8]

Early results indicated that unless the struggle was won, lack of accuracy would almost completely nullify the effect of night bombing. A Bomber Command report on a raid in March 1940 concluded:

> Our general opinion is that under war conditions the average crew of a night bomber could not be relied upon to identify and attack targets at night except under the best conditions of visibility, even when the target is on the coast or on a large river like the Rhine . . . If the target has no conspicuous aids to its location, very few inexperienced crews would be likely to find it under any conditions.[9]

For most of the year, indeed, the Germans remained genuinely unaware of what Bomber Command's targets on a particular night were. What to the Air Staff was a systematic strategic offensive was to the Germans merely a random bestrewal of HE devices most of which, obeying the laws of chance expectation, fell harmlessly into the German countryside.

A raid in December 1940, on Mannheim, brought home the complete ineffectiveness of the bombing effort. The target chosen was the whole city, in revenge for the Coventry raid in mid-November. A Spitfire from the new Photographic Reconnaissance Unit was sent over with the raiders but the pictures it brought back were a sad disappointment. They made it clear that hardly any of the bombers had hit the city at all, though it was almost twice the size of Coventry, and that previous claims about having hit individual factories, oil refineries, marshalling yards and the like could only have been pure moonshine. The Commander of 5 Group, Air Vice-Marshal Norman Bottomley, was obliged to admit that the Mannheim raid provided 'the first . . . real evidence we have had as to the general standard of bombing accuracy which characterises our night operations.'[10] Air Marshal Robert Saundby, who became SASO Bomber Command at about this time, told his staff that when a bomber force claimed to have dropped 300 tons of bombs on a certain target, one could now only be sure that they had 'exported three hundred tons of bombs in its direction.'[11]

Little improvement was made during 1941. In August of that year, a member of the War Cabinet Secretariat, Mr D.M. Butt, was asked to undertake an independent inquiry into bombing performance based on photographs taken of 100 separate raids. He was allowed to regard anything that fell within five miles of the target as constituting a hit, but could still only come up with the gloomiest of conclusions, noting that only one in four aircraft attacking Germany got within five miles of their target, and only one in ten of those attacking over the Ruhr. Moreover, 'all these figures relate only to aircraft recorded as *attacking* the target; the proportion of the *total sorties* which reached within five miles is less by one third. Thus . . . of the total sorties only one in five get within five miles of the target, i.e. within the 75 square miles surrounding the target.'[12]

It was abundantly clear, therefore, that Bomber Command was making a rather less than devastating impact upon the German economy. The relevant figures certainly bear this out, even more damningly than Mr Butt's. Thus, whilst in July the Chiefs of Staff had cheerfully echoed the more extreme Bomber Command zealots and asserted that 'in bombing . . . we find the new weapons [upon] which we must principally depend for the destruction of German economic life and morale,'[13] the reality was that between October and December German arms production had fallen not by the 20 per cent claimed by the Air Ministry but hardly at all, and of the 10,000 HE and 5,900 incendiary bombs dropped during this period, almost half fell on open ground and a further 17 per cent on decoy installations. Professor Blackett, whom we have already seen at work on behalf of Coastal Command, also took considerable interest in bombing statistics. His conclusions were the gloomiest of all, leading him to assert that in 1941

> the average number of bomber sorties per month, then mainly by Wellingtons, was 1,000, and of these some 40 were lost with their crews of five men, giving a loss of airmen, all highly skilled men, at the rate of 200 per month. Comparing this with the estimated number of enemy killed, that is 400 *men, women and children* . . . it was concluded that in the matter of personnel casualties the 1941 bombing offensive had been nearly a dead loss.[14]*

But Bomber Command's confidence in its own abilities was remarkably resilient, and in early 1942 it received a further boost with the introduction of a radio navigational aid, codenamed *Gee*, which enabled an aircraft to fix its position by inferences from the position of blips, transmitted from three ground stations, on a grid displayed in the plane.† The first sets were fitted in February 1942, and by March 30 per cent of the bombers had them. An Air Ministry Directive of 14 February shows what high hopes were now entertained, envisaging virtually a nocturnal equivalent of daylight precision bombing:

> In the opinion of the Air Staff, the introduction of . . . [*Gee*] will confer upon your forces the ability to concentrate their effort to an extent which has not hitherto been possible under

---

* The estimates of civilian deaths were actually twice the real totals.
† It is not my intention to give over much of this narrative to the complex tale of electronic measures and counter-measures during the war in the air. The technological gloss such a detailed account would impart would seriously distort the basic, and very crude, realities of this war. However, an appendix to this chapter lists the more important Allied and German technical developments.

the operational conditions with which you are faced. It is accordingly considered that the introduction of this equipment on operations should be regarded as a revolutionary advance in bombing technique . . . The cardinal principle which should govern your employment of . . . [*Gee*] from the outset, should be the complete concentration on one target until the effort estimated to be required for its destruction has been achieved.[15]

A further boost to the belief that a new era of precision operations had dawned was provided by the Americans. On 22 February 1942 General Ira Eaker arrived in England to take command of 8th US Army Bomber Command, and in May it came under the aegis of Eighth US Air Force, commanded by General Carl Spaatz. In December Eaker himself took command of Eighth Air Force when Spaatz moved to the Mediterranean.* The American bombing formations, largely equipped with B-17 Flying Fortresses, were convinced that these planes, flown in close mass formation, were well enough armed to operate in daylight and might even be able to dispense with a fighter escort. A plan drawn up by the Army War Plan Division in August 1942, AWPD-42, spoke optimistically of a low attrition rate for US bombers and a high one for intercepting fighters due to the former's heavy firepower. It also took it for granted that these daylight bombers would be capable of the most remarkable accuracy and reeled off a whole list of potential precision targets, including submarine yards, power stations, aircraft factories, oil refineries and synthetic rubber plants.

The actual events of 1942, however, provided little evidence of the new era. As can be seen in table 9, operations remained on a very low level throughout the year. American activity was particularly muted, only 1,791 sorties being flown in the whole six months from August 1942 to February 1943 and only 2,452 tons of bombs dropped.†
Moreover, no significant conclusions could be drawn about the

---

* 8th Bomber Command was variously commanded by Generals Longfellow, Anderson and James Doolittle. The latter was in command when it became Eighth Air Force, in February 1944, the original Eighth HQ being upgraded to US Strategic Air Forces in Europe, of which Spaatz once again took command. Eaker took over the Mediterranean Allied Air Forces.

† Spaatz and Eaker had hoped for a more sustained campaign, even at this early stage, but were severely handicapped by the removal of planes and personnel for Operation Torch, an Anglo-American landing in French North Africa in November 1942.

self-defence capabilities of the American bombers, and thus their suitability for mass daylight operations, as they had operated during this period with considerable RAF fighter support.* They had also taken care not to intrude too far into hostile air space, limiting themselves to a relatively narrow area of occupied France and the Low Countries where anti-aircraft defences were nothing like as heavy as in Germany proper.

But if American operations had been indecisive, those of Bomber Command had been downright disappointing, with the *Gee* apparatus failing significantly to improve bombing performance. It had been of some use in allowing bombers to maintain a much tighter formation, the basis of a new tactic known as 'streaming'. This involved putting the whole of a night's operation through one fairly narrow sector in the German defence line, thus swamping the defenders in that sector and rendering redundant all fighters tied to other sectors.† But *Gee* had still made no dramatic improvement to the bombers' accuracy. According to a study made by the Operational Research staff attached to Bomber Command there was some improvement, but so appalling had standards been before the introduction of *Gee* that this was far from enough to bring about the 'revolution' envisaged by the Air Ministry. The OR staff tried to measure the efficiency of pre– and post-*Gee* raids, 'efficiency' being defined as the percentage of the number of aircraft dispatched which actually attacked the target area. The results were as below:

Type of Target	Pre-Gee	Post-Gee
France and Low Countries (poor weather)	6%	11%
German coastal towns	33%	44%
German inland targets	23%	29%

And this, remember, represents the percentage of planes that attacked the target, not those that actually hit it.

This last figure continued to be depressingly low. In May 1942

* Though this support included some 'Eagle' squadrons, manned by US fighter pilots.
† The German defence line, known to the Allies as the Kammhuber Line, was made up of numerous boxes side by side in which one night fighter was directed onto an enemy plane by a ground controller who had in front of him radar blips representing both the friendly plane and a bomber. These blips were generated by two *Würzburg* radars. Early warning of the whole raid was given by a *Freya* radar. While waiting to be vectored in, the night-fighters hovered around a radio beacon in their sector.

analysts concluded that on average less than one-quarter of the bombs dropped on an urban target actually hit and only 30 per cent fell in even partly built-up areas. In the following months various additional aids were introduced. In June the *Shaker* blind-marking technique was used, though so erratic were the results that the Germans did not even divine the location of the main target – Essen. At about the same time *Oboe* was introduced, a system similar to *Gee* except that the position of the aircraft was established on the ground. It was fitted into aircraft of the Pathfinder force, set up in August, which led the bomber stream and dropped marker bombs and flares onto the target. The next major targeting innovation was the device called H_2S (an abbreviation of Home Sweet Home), an airborne ground-scanning radar that presented rough images of the terrain on a screen. It differentiated particularly well between land and water and could thus show up, for example, a river estuary or a lake which enabled the aircraft to establish its position by reference to a map. Yet there was still no significant increase in bombing accuracy and much of the increased tonnage dropped during 1943 – 20,000 tons in August as opposed to only 5,000 tons eight months before – was wasted. Of the Allied effort in autumn 1943, when US daylight attacks were contributing around 15 per cent of total tonnage dropped,* one authority has observed that for daylight attacks the average error in good conditions was 450 yards and in poor visibility 1,200 yards. For night bombers the figure was more like three miles.

From these figures, two points emerge: first, that even under clear daylight conditions, the so-called 'pinpoint' bombing from 20,000 feet or above meant that in reality only half the bombs landed within a quarter of a mile of the aiming point; secondly, that by night or by day under poor conditions, unless the target was approximately circular and had a radius of three miles or greater, at least half the bombs aimed at it would do no more

---

* This percentage might have been more had US heavy bombers, the Flying Fortress and the Liberator, been more efficiently designed. The British 'heavies' could carry between 9,000lb of bombs (the Stirling III) and 14,000lb (the Lancaster I) as against the 4,000 and 5,000lb of the two American planes. All flew at much the same speed, between 180 and 220 mph, though the American planes did have a considerably higher ceiling. It is this discrepancy that explains the fact that, although the number of US sorties between July and December 1943 was 63.7 per cent of the number flown by Bomber Command, the total tonnage of bombs dropped was only 38.9 per cent.

than plough up the surrounding fields ('agricultural bombing', as it was sometimes termed).[16]

Bomber Command's extremely disappointing performance was common knowledge in senior political, military and scientific circles and from quite early in the war its efforts were the subject of serious criticism. Even the Prime Minister, for most of the war a staunch advocate of the bombing offensive, was alarmed by the Butt Report, which he described as 'a very serious paper' that required the Air Staff's 'most urgent attention.'[17] Others questioned the whole rationale of the offensive, suggesting that totally unsatisfactory hit-rates like those just mentioned could not possibly justify the continued diversion of massive resources into the production of bomber aircraft. The objections of Coastal Command have already been dealt with in the previous chapter, but other arms were equally disenchanted. Admiral Sir Algernon Willis, second-in-command of the Eastern Fleet, wrote to Admiral Sir Andrew Cunningham in summer 1942, lamenting: 'If only some of the hundreds of bombers who fly over Germany (and often fail to do anything because of the weather) had been torpedo aircraft and divebombers the Old Empire would be in a better condition than it is now.'[18] The Army, too, had increasing doubts about the 'strategic' air effort. Brooke's objections have already been encountered and in June 1942 his Director of Military Operations, Major-General Sir John Kennedy, wrote in one note:

In my view the only well-founded ground of criticism of our central war direction now lies in the use we are making of our Air Force. . . I should like to take 50 per cent of the bomber effort off Germany even at this late hour, and distribute it in the Atlantic, and in the Middle East and Indian theatres. The price we pay at sea and on land for our present bombing policy is high indeed.[19]

To some extent, of course, rivalry between the Services was endemic and both the Army and Navy would doubtless have questioned the pre-eminence given to Bomber Command operations whether or not they had been effective. But controversy about these operations was not, in fact, confined to the military. An influential civilian voice was that of A.V. Hill, a crucial figure in the early development of radar, who took advantage of his platform in the House of Commons to denounce the exaggeration of the importance of bombing an enemy country . . . The idea of bombing a well-defended enemy into submission or seriously affecting his morale – or even doing substantial damage to him – is an illusion. We know that most of the bombs we drop hit nothing of importance. The disaster of this policy is not only that it is futile, but it is extremely wasteful, and will become increasingly wasteful as time goes on.[20]

Potentially yet more influential was Captain Harold Balfour, the Parliamentary Under-Secretary to the Air Minister, Sir Archibald Sinclair. In one confidential memorandum to his minister, written in January 1942, Balfour wrote: 'As regards [bombing] accuracy, I believe that we calculate that only some 10 per cent of bombs fall in the target area. The public are more and more questioning the effectiveness of bombing policy . . .'[21] Another critic was Sir Henry Tizard, a leading scientific civil servant, though recently displaced by Lindemann as Churchill's main adviser. In a memorandum to the Ministry of Aircraft Production, in December 1941, he flatly stated: 'The war is not going to be won by night bombing.' In the following April he told Lindemann that the latter's claims about Bomber Command's ability speedily to smash the whole fabric of German urban life were 'extremely misleading and may lead to entirely wrong decisions being reached, with a consequent disastrous effect on the war.'[22]

In the last analysis, however, none of these arguments were likely to erode seriously the basic commitment to 'strategic' bombing. The reasons for this had little to do with the military efficacy of such a campaign or with a deeply pondered commitment to the most cost-effective allocation of resources, but simply reflected the fact that there was little else the Allies could do. In 1940 it had been quite clear that it would be a matter of years before Britain could intervene with ground forces on the continent of Europe. It was unthinkable, however, that Hitler be left entirely to his own devices. Not only would this allow him to build up his armed forces at leisure, but it would also have deleterious effects on British morale and do little to persuade American public opinion of British resolve. For Churchill, therefore, a whole-hearted commitment to bombing was a *sine qua non* of any continued British war effort. In the first months after Dunkirk, therefore, he became a fervent advocate of such operations. In July he told Beaverbrook: 'When I look around to see how we can win the war I see that there is only one sure path . . . and that is an Nazi homeland. We must be able to overwhelm them by this means, without which I do not see a way through.' In September he circulated a paper to the War Cabinet which asserted starkly: 'The Navy can lose us this war, but only the Air Force can win it . . . The bombers alone provide the means of victory . . . to pulverise the entire industry and scientific structure on which the war effort and economic life of the enemy depend . . . In no other way at present visible can we hope to overcome the immense military power of Germany.'[23]

As Max Hastings has pointed out, there is more than a hint of desperation in these remarks. Churchill was no unremitting Douhetist and these appeals to bombing as a military panacea derived from the fact that if Churchill 'did not make himself believe . . . that the bomber alone could win the war . . . he could advocate nothing but surrender.'[24] The increasing support from Roosevelt did much to dissipate this sense of despair, and by October 1941 Churchill felt free to tell Portal, now the Chief of the Air Staff, that it was 'very disputable whether bombing by itself will be a decisive factor in the present war . . . Its effects, both physical and moral, are greatly exaggerated . . . The most we can say is that it will be a heavy and, I trust, a seriously increasing annoyance.' In March 1942 he revealed a definite lack of enthusiasm for the whole bomber offensive, grumbling that 'bombing was not decisive, but better than doing nothing.'[25]

Nevertheless, 'attacks by armoured forces' and other more decisive threats to Germany lay far in the future and in another memorandum, penned in October, Churchill was forced to concede that it was 'the most potent method of impairing the enemy's morale *at the present time.*'[26] There were other factors, too, that obliged Churchill to cede precedence to bombing operations. For one thing, it was a strategy that considerably appealed to Roosevelt. Though he himself was desperately keen to afford Britain all help possible, it was not until December 1941, and Hitler's casual decision to join Japan in declaring war on the United States, that he was able to give aid without stint. In the meantime, 'strategic' bombing had offered Roosevelt an option which his commanders could discuss with their British counterparts without seeming to be committing, even theoretically, too many 'American boys' to combat overseas. For this reason as much as any other, the ABC-1 agreement of March 1941, defining Anglo-American measures to be taken if the latter became embroiled in the war against Germany, laid heavy emphasis upon 'achieving as quickly as possible superiority in air strength over the enemy, particularly in long-range strike forces . . . The build-up of the bomber offensive . . . [was to] have a very high priority claim upon our combined resources.'[27]

Another reason for continued stress upon bombing operations was Hitler's invasion of Russia, in June 1941. At first it had seemed certain that Hitler would win another whirlwind victory, but the Russians held. After their victory before Moscow, in December 1941, when the Germans were obliged actually to give up ground, it began to seem possible that the Red Army might be able to maintain a stubborn defence for many months to come. But to do this they would require every possible diversion or destruction of German resources that their Allies could offer, and it was only bombing that could provide even the possibility of making any immediate or significant impact. The fundamental importance of keeping the Russians in the ring was clear to both Roosevelt and Churchill, the latter making repeated reference to the need to offer some sort of tangible support. In February 1942 he fully endorsed a statement by Sinclair that 'the United Nations have two instruments at their disposal for hammering Germany in 1942 – the Red Army and the Royal Air Force.'[28] In 1942 the Air Ministry Directives to Bomber Command also began to make mention of the Russian rationale. In February it was pointed out that it 'would hearten and support the Russians if we were to resume our offensive on a heavy scale . . . The coincidence of our offensive with the Russian successes would further depress the enemy morale, which is known already to have been affected by the German armies' reverses on the Eastern Front.' In May the same year Bomber Command was directed to devote its major attention to the German aircraft factories producing Bf 109 and 110 fighters, because 'the outcome of the critical operations on the Russian Front will depend very largely on the enemy's ability to maintain in operation a certain strength of fighter aircraft.'[29]

Later in 1942 the Eastern Front still loomed large as a justification for bombing operations, though it became yet more apparent that this was largely because the Allies had little else to offer. Stalin's main demand in summer 1942 was for the opening of a second front in mainland Europe, or at least a definite assurance as to when one would be opened. In August Churchill went to Moscow, accompanied by Averell Harriman, Roosevelt's representative, and had the unpalatable task of explaining that neither second front nor even meaningful deadline were in the offing. Desperate to offer some aid to the Russians, Churchill expounded fulsomely on the merits of 'strategic' bombing, promising that the Allies were firmly committed to greatly expanding their offensive. Stalin was considerably mollified, which in turn prompted Churchill to become yet more fulsome about 'the ruthless bombing of Germany . . . [and] striking at the morale of the German population . . . that was one of our leading military objectives.'[30] Whether Churchill was quite as enthusiastic about the benefits that might accrue from such a campaign as he made out is open to question. Nevertheless, on his return to England, he had little option but to allocate yet more resources to this proxy second front and

> a gearing up of the bomber offensive began immediately . . . The British Air Staff reevaluated targeting and proposed a plan of regional 'city-busting' to match Russian operational demands . . . The Air Ministry scoured their lean larder to meet the Prime Minister's demand that fifty bomber squadrons be in action by December . . . Half the bombers for the Middle East were retained in Britain, as industry gave priority to Bomber Command. At the same time, Churchill boosted the RAF's manpower allocation for 1943 by one third above the Secretary of State for Air's request.[31]

It is the two factors discussed thus far – heavy political pressure for a maximum bombing effort coupled with the proven chronic inaccuracy of the weapon itself – that go a long way towards explaining the type of offensive undertaken by Bomber Command. Knowing that their effort must be the major Allied one for some time to come – Eighth US Air Force did not equal the tonnage dropped by Bomber Command until February 1944 – and knowing that technical improvements had so far made only a modest contribution to improving the accuracy of night bombing, those in charge of the British squadrons, notably Air Marshal Arthur Harris, head of Bomber Command from February 1942, opted for the tactic of area bombing, the unloading of high explosives and incendiaries directly over German city centres. Two results were looked for: that the destruction of housing and public amenities would undermine both the ability and the willingness of the industrial workers to maintain their posts at the factories, and that simple chance expectation, within the urban-industrial site, would mean that many bombs fell on the factories themselves. This doctrine was in explicit contrast to that of precision bombing, embraced by the American daylight bombers, who hoped to be able to pinpoint the most important factories, power stations, oil refineries and marshalling yards and at the same time keep to a minimum collateral damage to civilian areas. In mid-1942, however, it has to be admitted that the British position, especially as regarded their own night operations, was the more realistic. Imprecise, crude even, area bombing might have been, but it does seem to have been the only real option given the 'barn door' tolerances applicable to bomb patterns and the Prime Minister's most urgent demand for immediate, large-scale and ever-increasing aerial activity. As Portal confessed in December 1943, it was always known that going for specific 'classes of target' would have been far more effective, might even, indeed, have won the war by then, but 'this was not tactically possible and for this reason we were thrown back upon the general blasting of industry by means of big area attacks in which few bombs are wasted.'[32]

It should not be thought, however, that the decision to target urban areas as a whole was a purely rational response to a particular situation. Throughout the 1930s the Royal Air Force had been imbued with Trenchardian brutalism and some of his most avid acolytes were men who would rise to senior positions during the war. Portal, for example, had long been an enthusiastic advocate of bombing as a direct, if indiscriminate, assault on enemy morale. In 1940 he did acknowledge the need for some sort of restraint. His recommendation in September that a 'hit list' of 19 German cities be drawn up and publicised in Germany itself still meant that one would be attacked only in response to a similar bombing of an English city. That same year he stated in a memorandum that 'we have not yet reached the stage of desiring to burn down a whole town.' Yet he was clearly uneasy with these restraints, and other remarks of his in 1940, during his spell as head of Bomber Command, display a positive eagerness to inflict maximum destruction wherever possible. One note he circulated pointed out that 'in industrial areas there are invariably a very large number of targets . . . In view of the indiscriminate nature of the German attacks, and in order to reduce the number of bombs brought back . . . every effort should be made to bomb these.' The memorandum just quoted also soon dropped all pretence of moderation and went on to spell out the effects of 'city-busting' with the same sort of relish with which Harris was to pore over his photographs of devastated suburbs. It was, he felt, inevitable that at some point the British *would* want to burn down whole towns and 'when this stage is reached we shall do it by dropping a large quantity of incendiaries first and then a sustained attack with high explosive to drive the fire-fighters underground and let the flames get a good hold . . .'[33]

Portal's enthusiasm for unselective urban attacks did not diminish once he took over as Chief of the Air Staff. Objectives of this kind appeared in the Directives to Bomber Command almost as soon as he arrived. That of 30 October brought up the question of enemy morale, usually a prelude to a call for the bombing of civilian targets, and lamented that 'our attacks have not been sufficiently concentrated to achieve that psychological effect which can only derive from . . . closely concentrated attacks.' From now on the 'primary aim' of the bomber offensive was to wreak such havoc that it 'will demonstrate to the enemy the power and severity of air bombardment and the *hardship* and *dislocation* which will result from it.' Some effort was to be made to pinpoint precision targets, such as power stations, irrespective of their location, but 'where primary targets such as the oil and aircraft industry objectives are *suitably placed* in the centres of towns or populated districts, they might also be selected.'[34] The Directive of 9 July 1941 and a supplement of 30 August laid even more stress on the need to attack enemy morale, to undermine the German people's will to fight by making the ordinary city-dweller's lifestyle intolerable. In the former document Air Marshal Pierse was informed that a review of the enemy's overall situation had supposedly revealed that 'the weakest points in his armour lie in the morale of the civil population and in his inland transportation system . . . You will direct the main effort of the bomber force . . . towards dislocating the German transportation system and to destroying the morale of the civil population as a whole and of the industrial workers in particular.' Special attention was to be given to targets that lay 'in congested industrial towns, where the psychological effect will be the greatest.' The supplement issued some weeks later gave Pierse an extended list of urban targets, it being felt that 'from the morale standpoint, by extending our attacks to the smaller towns . . . the more widespread experience of the direct effect of our offensive may have considerable value.'[35]

The arrival of Harris at Bomber Command headquarters, at High Wycombe, clearly did not presage any radical shift of aerial strategy and throughout 1942 there was a happy consensus on the need for a continued assault on the German population as a whole. Much wordage was still devoted to the definition of primary, intermediate and secondary targets, as well as short-term and long-term (the reader is again referred to table 40), but the main objective remained the German people. In August 1942 Portal told the Prime Minister that raids would make an increasing use of incendiaries which would 'have the effect of spreading alarm and despondency over a much larger proportion of the German people.'[36] Towards the end of that year he wrote a paper for the Chiefs of Staff, prior to their forthcoming attendance at the Casablanca Conference, where Churchill and Roosevelt were to meet, in which he laid particular stress upon the general destruction of urban areas and indulged in a gruesome arithmetic. By 1944, he estimated, 'the weight of bombs dropped on major urban areas would result – among other things – in the destruction of 6,000,000 German dwellings, the rendering of 25,000,000 Germans homeless, the incidental deaths of 900,000 civilians and serious injury to 1,000,000 more, and the destruction of one-third of German industry.'[37]

These calculations seemed to impress the Chiefs of Staff, and they in turn convinced the Combined Chiefs of Staff assembled in Casablanca.* For among the instructions issued at the end of the Conference, on 21 January 1943, was a Directive to the RAF and the USAAF calling for the opening of a Combined Bomber Offensive against Germany which was to be an integral part of Allied efforts to end the war. This Directive clearly laid out various precision objectives – in order of preference these were submarine construction yards, the German aircraft industry, transportation and oil plants[†] – but it also put these targets within the 'general concept' of the 'progressive destruction and dislocation of the German military, industrial and economic system, and the undermining of the morale of the German people to a point where their capacity for armed resistance is fatally weakened.'[38] It was this concept, rather than the list of priorities, that caught the

* The Combined Chiefs of Staff were formally set up in April 1942 and consisted of the US Joint Chiefs of Staff and British deputies of their own Chiefs of Staff residing in Washington. These latter were known as the British Joint Staff Mission. In fact, the first informal meeting of the Combined Chiefs was held on 23 January 1942.

† In a more detailed Directive in June 1943, describing what was by then known as Operation Pointblank, this priority was altered somewhat, with the fighter aircraft industry being given first, albeit temporary, priority, followed by submarine yards, the rest of the aircraft industry, ball-bearings and oil.

eye of Harris. From shortly after his arrival at High Wycombe, he had encouraged 'city-busting' operations. One of his earliest efforts, in March 1942, was a raid on Lübeck, on the Baltic coast. The town's significance to Harris lay not in its industrial capacity, which was virtually nil, but in the fact that it was half-timbered. As the Germans had not regarded it as a likely target it was only lightly defended and thus the raid was unusually successful, burning out fully half of the city. Ever since then Harris had been fascinated with the potential of bombing raids on urban areas. Usually he did select targets that included important industrial locations, but only because he believed that their destruction would be an inevitable concomitant to the destruction of the whole city, destruction he believed Bomber Command would be able to lay on at will.

This was Harris's first major contribution to the Bomber Offensive, the fostering of the credo that if only enough bombers were provided they were capable of utterly laying waste the whole of Germany. So sure was he of this that he saw no need for anyone to bother their head choosing the most appropriate precision targets or perfecting the methods with which to find them. It is true, of course, that the Harris strategy did make some sense when political considerations demanded some sort of high-profile Allied activity and bombers, albeit very inaccurate, were all that were available. But Harris then went on to try and make a bogus virtue out of necessity, insisting that area raids were in fact the most effective tactic, and that they must inevitably, *on their own*, lead to Germany's defeat. In August 1943 he wrote to Portal: 'It is my firm belief that we are on the verge of a final showdown in the bombing war . . . I am certain that given average weather and concentration on the main job, we can push Germany over by bombing this year.'[39] In November he minuted the Prime Minister in support of his plan to destroy Berlin from the air. Already he felt that the damage inflicted on German cities meant that 'Germany must collapse before this programme . . . has proceeded much further . . . We can wreck Berlin from end to end, if the USAF will come in on it. It will cost between 400–500 aircraft. It will cost Germany the war.' A month later he was telling the Air Ministry that, to the end of October, 25 per cent of the acreage attacked (acreage, it will be noted, was Harris's yardstick of success) had already been destroyed. By 1 April 1944, he claimed, 40 per cent would have been destroyed.

It is not possible to dogmatise on the degree of destruction necessary to cause the enemy to capitulate but there can be little doubt that the necessary conditions would be brought about by the destruction of between 40 per cent and 50 per cent of the principal German towns . . . Allowing for a loss rate of 5 per cent . . . the Lancaster force alone should be sufficient, but only just sufficient, to produce in Germany by 1 April 1944 a state of devastation in which surrender is inevitable.[40]

But Harris's second major contribution to the Bomber Offensive was yet more pernicious, for it was thanks to him that all Allied attempts to make 'strategic' bombing a weapon of some precision, systematically applied against the vital arteries of the German war economy, were never properly carried through. For, by the middle of 1944, the potential for precision bombing, even at night, had increased enormously, thanks to improvements in both technology and technique. The accuracy of *Oboe*, for example, was greatly improved when it began to operate on centimetric rather than decimetric wavelengths, whilst improvements in technique meant that H_2S operators became much more adept at finding their proper target and the Pathfinder force much better at illuminating it, using low-level marking runs and effective Target Indicator Bombs. By the time Allied ground troops first set foot in North-West Europe, according to one official account, 'Bomber Command had undoubtedly reached a very high standard of accuracy . . . In the attacks on the Ruhr oil refineries 50 per cent of bombs carried fell not more than 500 yards away from the centre of the target . . . [By the end of the year] 50 per cent of [area] bombing [was] arriving within an area just over a mile from the aiming point, or taking the original bombing criterion devised in the early days of the bomber offensive (the number of bombs dropped within three miles of the aiming point), an overall bombing efficiency of 95 per cent was achieved.'[41] Equally importantly, this improved accuracy could be used to good effect because by mid-1944 the Allies were attacking in such strength (35,417 sorties in July as opposed to only 7,923 in June 1943, at the start of the Combined Bomber Offensive) that the *Luftwaffe* could not hope to pick off more than a fraction of the attacking force. Details of the attrition of the *Luftwaffe* follow later in this chapter; at this point a simple comparison of Allied casualties will serve. Thus, in October 1943 Bomber Command and Eighth us Air Force lost 177 planes, and in February 1945 the figure was almost identical,

171 planes. The former total, however, represented 6.3 per cent of all sorties that month, an alarming casualty rate as more than 10 per cent was regarded as unsustainable. The latter total represented a mere 0.7 per cent.*

Many senior RAF officers, notably Portal, were aware of the improved prospects for precision bombing. More importantly, they were also alive to the fact that the increasing number of bombers meant that it should now be possible to inflict really significant damage on those specific 'strategic' targets that had for so long been listed in the Air Staff Directives. Unfortunately, Harris showed absolutely no interest in attacks of this type; indeed, he regarded them with positive hostility, speaking contemptuously of 'panacea' targets whose significance was greatly overrated. It remains something of a puzzle why Harris should have reacted so violently against all calls for precision bombing. For it can hardly be claimed that his own case was rooted in common sense. It certainly was not true, for example, that area bombing was demonstrably being seen to do the job. In fact, very few attempts had been made to test Harris's claims and establish just what effect his indiscriminate raids might actually be having on the German economy. But when such an attempt was made, by Professor Solly Zuckerman's Bombing Survey Unit, in March 1944, it cast grave doubt upon such figures and extrapolations as Harris had produced. When Zuckerman reported back to Air Chief Marshal Arthur Tedder, the Deputy Supreme Commander for the Normandy invasion, he 'was able to tell . . . [him] that whoever it was who had done Harris's sums did not understand what he was doing . . . I said that if Bomber Command were to continue with his existing plans, his Command could not in the available time achieve more than a 7 per cent reduction in Germany's overall output.'[42]

Harris's own pleadings on behalf of area bombing rarely smacked of intellectual rigour. A fundamental precept of this method of attack was that by aiming one's bombs at the centre of a given town or city one could expect to destroy many industrial sites grouped near that centre. Yet when it was suggested to Harris that he might participate in American attacks on the Schweinfurt ball-bearing factories, he claimed that the Americans were being ridiculously over-optimistic: 'I am confident that the Germans have long ago made every possible

---

* Technological improvements also limited the *Luftwaffe*'s effectiveness, notably a whole array of jamming equipment that subverted either enemy radar (*Moonshine, Window, Mandrel* and *Piperack*) or their radio transmissions (*Tinsel, Dartboard, ABC, Drumstick, Carpet* and *Jostle*).

effort to disperse so vital a production. Therefore, even if Schweinfurt is entirely destroyed, I remain confident that we shall hear no more of the disastrous effects on German war production now so confidently prophesied.'[43] A more concise rebuttal of area bombing it would be difficult to imagine. By 1945 Harris's justification for his chosen tactic became still less convincing. In January he attacked the suggestion that Allied bombers should concentrate on German oil production as a way of bringing their entire economy to a halt. He castigated the plan as 'another attempt to seek a quick, clever, easy and cheap way out'. Quite so. He then went on to say that this oil plan, like any other offensive against a single, key product, would be doomed to failure because it was 'no good knocking out 75 per cent of something, if 25 per cent suffices for essentials.'[44] As Ronald Cooke and Roy Nesbit have judiciously pointed out, whatever truth there was in this assertion applied even more to area bombing. But it was far from clear that Harris's men could account even for that 75 per cent. For, whereas the Americans at least knew where the targets they hoped to hit were, Bomber Command was pitching its bombs into the urban void, hoping to hit something worthwhile by local saturation attacks.

Two months later, Harris tried to justify his strategy with what were tantamount to lies. On 13, 14 and 15 February Allied bombers* attacked Dresden, a town almost destitute of Flak or fighter protection. The repeated attacks and the combination of HE and incendiary bombs set up fire-storms which utterly consumed the heart of the city and killed upwards of 100,000 people, many of them refugees fleeing before the advancing Russians. An exact count must always remain impossible, partly because 'many of the victims had been converted by the great heat of the firestorm into heaps of ashes or merged in a fluid which later solidified as a layer of gelatine covering the floor of cellars, so that they could not be counted.'[45] When reports of the appalling devastation began to cause a certain unease among the Western Allies, Harris responded with a mannered loutishness that was typical of the man. In a letter to the Deputy Chief of the Air Staff, on 29 March, he wrote: 'The feeling, such as there is, over Dresden could be easily explained by any psychiatrist. It is connected with

* In February and March 1945 US bombers joined in the area bombing campaign with a depressing gusto. Their earlier, most laudable, insistence on attacking only the German war economy seems, once the skies were largely cleared of German day-fighters, to have given way to a desire for simple revenge, in much the same way as strategic interdiction in the war against Japan degenerated into Le May's horrific fire-raids on major areas of population, notably Tokyo.

German bands and Dresden shepherdesses. Actually Dresden was a mass of munition works, an intact government centre, and a key transportation point to the east. It is now none of those things.'[46]

The claim about munitions works, one of the main reasons given for bombing Dresden at all, was simply not true. Dresden was primarily a cultural centre, built around museums, art galleries and a renowned opera house. Military targets were few and far between, and such as there were – barracks, warehouses, a military airfield and one munitions factory (no longer working) – were *outside the designated target area*, which was centred on the Old Town and the cultural artefacts therein. It is also to be noted that Dresden did *not* cease to be a transportation point because of the Allied raid. The railway station and marshalling yards, although within the target area, were not completely destroyed and in fact rail communication of a sort had been restored within three or four days. This single fact is telling testimony against the whole concept of area bombing, in that it shows that even the most accurate and heavy raid against a 'one-off' target will not put vital installations out of operation for very long. Individual ones, such as railway lines, could be repaired quickly and if the original attack had not been part of a *systematic* offensive, i.e. if there were to be no repeated attacks on this target or on others in the same network, it would soon be operating again reasonably efficiently.

The need for a systematic offensive, based upon precision bombing of certain key industries and installations, had, as we have seen, already become apparent to Portal, whilst the notable improvements in bombing technique had shown that it might well be feasible. As early as January 1944 the Air Staff had intimated that Harris was making far too little effort to undertake at least some attacks against the specific targets listed in their Directives, and he was enjoined to direct at least some of his planes against the same precision targets as in the American daylight raids. At the present time these were

> those industrial centres associated with the German fighter air-frame factories and ball-bearing industry [in particular] the town of Schweinfurt . . . It is realised that tactical difficulties are involved but it is believed that the task is not beyond the present operational capabilities of your Command, with the navigational aids now available, and in any case it is impossible to accept that the successful bombing of any German town within range is impracticable until it has been tried, if necessary several times.[47]

In August of the same year Portal recommended to the Chiefs of

Staff that the whole Allied Bomber Offensive should now be directed against particular targets, in the first instance oil. This suggestion was adopted by the Combined Chiefs and in September two Directives were issued that called for attacks on 'systems of objectives' and insisted that 'our major effort must now be focused directly upon the vital sources of the German war economy' to make 'maximum impact upon the primary objectives.'[48] These objectives were to be oil, transportation (by rail and canal), tank and ordnance factories and motor transport production.

In November Portal entered into direct communication with Harris, which was to last until the following January. His basic aim was to deflect the latter from his fervent endorsement of area bombing and redirect him towards the Oil Plan. A letter of 12 November chided Harris none too gently over a recent suggestion of his that the destruction of 60 leading German cities must bring about the end of the war:

> I know that you have long felt such a plan to be the most effective way of bringing about the collapse of Germany. Knowing this, I have, I must confess, at times wondered whether the magnetism of the remaining German cities has not in the past tended as much to deflect our bombers from their primary objectives as the tactical and weather conditions which you described so fully in your letter of 1st November. I would like you to reassure me that this is not so. If I knew you to be so wholeheartedly in the attack on oil as in the past you have been in the matter of attacking cities, I would have little to worry about.[49]

On the 13th Portal's deputy, Air Marshal Sir Norman Bottomley, also tried to coax Harris away from area attacks, pointing out that American attacks on oil targets were on their own unlikely to bring about the sort of long-term dislocation of this industry that would seriously hinder military operations. On the other hand, 'the weight and density of attack of which your Command has shown itself capable, given adequate marking, far exceeds that normally achieved by the U.S. Air Forces. It is considered that one successful large scale concentrated attack by Bomber Command should, on the basis of past experience, result in the immobilisation of . . . [oil production] which is now required.'[50]

Portal kept up the pressure for the next two months or so. On 6 December he urged that 'our policy is to make the maximum

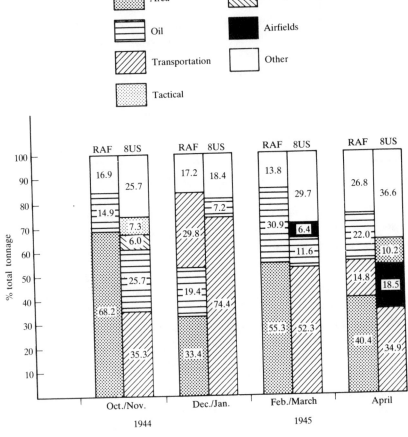

Table 10: *Choice of targets by Bomber Command and Eighth* us *Air Force October 1944–April 1945*

contribution to the battle [in North-West Europe] and to this end priority has been given to the attack of [*sic*] German oil production, wherever it may be, and of the communications system behind the critical part of the front.' Area bombing alone 'would not produce the impact upon the battle that is required.' On 22 December he expressed himself 'profoundly disappointed that you still appear to feel that the oil plan is just another "panacea"' and regretted that Bomber Command was throwing away the chance to 'play as large a part as possible in what is by far the most immediately profitable policy we have yet undertaken in this war.' On 8 January he reiterated the crucial importance of oil to the whole German war effort and said: 'The energy, resource and determination displayed by the enemy in his efforts to maintain his oil production must be more than matched by our own determination to destroy it; and *your* determination matters more than that of all the rest of us put together.'[51]

But Harris could not be shaken from his absolute conviction that the demolition of large tracts of urban Germany must of itself inevitably bring about the total collapse of the Third Reich. The figures on Bomber Command's targeting policy in the last months of the war tell their own story in table 10, where they are compared with those for Eighth US Air Force. This table shows that whilst the Americans, between October 1944 and March 1945, devoted a monthly average of 64.4 per cent of their total effort to attacking those targets stipulated by the Combined Chiefs of Staff, Bomber Command managed on average only 31.6 per cent.* The responsibility for this lay essentially with Harris, who persistently seized upon 'get-out' clauses in Air Staff Directives, allowing area bombing in particularly unpropitious weather conditions, to flout the spirit of these orders. Nevertheless, one has to wonder whether Portal can be entirely absolved from blame. In most respects he acquitted himself extremely well during the Second World War, leading his Service to a rightful equal footing with the Army and Navy. He remained sensitive to the development of aerial technology and technique and was aware at just what point it became feasible to move from indiscriminate area bombing to precision raids. He showed also that he fully understood the wider economic context in which the military now operated, readily grasping the point that attacks on oil refineries and marshalling yards were equally as shrewd blows against the enemy as those against military personnel and hardware. Nor did he ever forget that the RAF was but one part of the total Allied effort, and he cooperated enthusiastically not only with the USAAF but also with the ground forces. As is shown in table 40, between March and August 1944 the Allied bomber forces were under the command of the Supreme Commander Allied Forces in Europe, General Dwight Eisenhower, to assist with preparations for and the early stages of the landings in Normandy. Harris, true to form, had been bitterly opposed to such a 'diversion' of bombing

---

* Over the war as a whole, Eighth and Fifteenth US Air Force bombers (the latter was operating from Italy) dropped only 7.6 per cent of their total tonnage on area targets and 57.1 per cent on oil, transportation and aircraft industry targets. The respective figures for Bomber Command were 52.5 and 28.1 per cent.

effort, but had eventually been prevailed upon by Portal to play his part.*

But once Eisenhower had relinquished control of Bomber Command, Portal failed in one of his major responsibilities – to command. At the end of the day he was Harris's boss and, given his whole-hearted endorsement of the oil and transportation plans as formulated by the Combined Chiefs, he should at some stage have *ordered* Harris to terminate area operations and concentrate on the specific targets so often defined in the Air Staff Directives. If Harris still demurred, he should have been sacked. This would not have been easy. Morale in Bomber Command would have suffered and there would probably have been widespread public resentment, as 'Bomber' Harris had been much touted by the media in the darkest days of the war. But morale can be repaired – if the RAF possessed only one officer capable of welding a Command together then it was in a poor way – and the fear of hostile public opinion should not have been allowed to override decisions that might well have shortened the war and saved tens of thousands of lives. When, in January 1945, Portal abandoned his correspondence with Harris and simply threw in the towel over the question of area bombing, he also condemned to death a large proportion of the 600,000 German civilians who perished in the war.† But, by missing the opportunity of shortening the war even by a few weeks, he also allowed the deaths of several thousand Allied servicemen who fell in Germany and Italy during March and April 1945.

The two main themes of this book are clearly in evidence in the story of the bomber offensive. On the one hand, as we have seen above, it demonstrated a considerable lack of finesse, most notably on the part of its leading director, Air Marshal Harris. On the other hand, as we shall see below, it quite clearly showed that Allied victory in the Second World War depended to a large extent on the

* Which, it should be noted, he loyally did, at least for some of the time. In March and April 37 per cent of Bomber Command tonnage was dropped on marshalling yards, one of the main pre-D-Day targets, whilst in May and June these yards and other tactical targets accounted for 56 per cent. In July and August, however, he rather seemed to lose interest. Area targets then accounted for 56 per cent of tonnage and tactical targets for only 17 per cent.
† The scale of the slaughter Harris was engaged in is highlighted by the fact that total British civilian dead in the war were 6,600,. It may also be noted that Harris's revenge was as indiscriminate as it was disproportionate, in that the Allied air forces also accounted for the deaths of 60,000 French civilians.

enormous material preponderance that they brought to bear as the war progressed. The bare figures tell much of the story, as in tables 41 and 42 in the Statistical Appendix, which give details both of the aircraft production of the major belligerents in the European air war and of their front-line strengths. There it can be seen that over the war as a whole the Allies produced over four times as many combat aircraft as the Germans and five times as many military aircraft of all types. In the last two and a half years, when the major air battles were fought and when both sides were turning out their best aircraft at maximum rates, German production, despite remarkable increases in productivity, was swamped by that of the Allies. In 1943 the latter produced over five times as many combat aircraft as the Germans, in 1944 four times as many and in 1945 getting on for ten times. These ratios were also reflected in combat strengths. In fact, disparities in the latter are yet more pronounced, telling evidence of the Germans' inability to get the aircraft from the assembly lines to the front or to maintain them properly once they arrived. The ratios of combat strengths, therefore, were five to one in June 1943, almost nine to one a year later and over twenty to one by April 1945.

Certain more prescient *Luftwaffe* commanders had long been aware that economic realities would increasingly militate against Germany's chances in a protracted war. In early 1942 Jeschonnek wrote: 'If we have not won the war by December 1942, we have no prospect of doing so.'[52] Throughout the war, in fact, shortages of aircraft hamstrung German attempts to establish any sort of air supremacy. As early as autumn 1941 the less than overwhelming British bomber offensive had so taxed the German night-fighter force that it was forced to abandon its own raids into British air space, even though these were having considerable success in intercepting the bombers as they took off or returned. Instead, the units so employed were concentrated for local defence or dispatched to the Mediterranean to help shore up Hitler's ailing Italian ally.

Nor were the Germans able realistically to consider countering Bomber Command with a 'strategic' offensive of their own. Their bomber arm, inadequate as it had been then, had been destroyed in the Battle of Britain and thenceforward the Germans simply could not spare the resources to rebuild it around more up-to-date aircraft. Such a plane existed, the four-engined He 177, but the first batch produced were sucked into the Stalingrad airlift to operate as transport aircraft, of which the Germans were desperately short. A second 'strategic' Air Corps of sorts was laboriously built up by early 1944 and Russian industry was deemed its most logical target. 'General Korlen tried to carry out the policy . . . by withdrawing . . .[this] Air Corps from the eastern front "in order that it might be prepared for strategic operations against Soviet Russian industrial targets." The suggestion was approved but turned out to be inoperable by 1944. Once again it was a failure of supply. Intention far outstripped Germany's ability to provide adequate weapons.'53*

The Germans also proved incapable of putting up enough bombers simply to repay terror with terror. Hitler attempted this on two occasions, once in April to June 1942, in the so-called Baedeker Raids, directed mainly at British 'cultural' targets which could then be crossed out in his Baedeker guidebook, and again in January 1944. Neither series of raids achieved very much, in terms either of British demoralisation or lost production. The 1944 raids were particularly sorry affairs. Their commander, General Dietrich Peltz, could muster only 550 aircraft all told, many of them fighter-bombers incapable of making any real 'strategic' contribution. Yet even to assemble this motley force, which troubled British air defences hardly at all, and to arrange for its logistical back-up, had taken Peltz all of five months.

Shortages of aircraft bedevilled German efforts to regain air supremacy on all fronts. Losses in Russia in the first 18 months of the campaign were far, far higher than had been anticipated. In autumn 1942 Hitler had told Galland that the Russians were as good as beaten and that in a few weeks he would be able to demobilise 50 Army divisions and transfer them to the Air Force and to the aircraft industry. 'Instead of that,' according to Galland, 'the Eastern Front held Luftwaffe units in its clutches . . . and methodically ground them down. Luftwaffe effectiveness became really nothing more than air support of ground forces on a numerically inadequate scale.'54 Production did increase, but so too did the remorseless tally of losses. In June 1942 the *Luftwaffe* possessed only 60 more aircraft than in June 1941 and by December 500 less. By this latter month, indeed, it was faced with insoluble problems:

> What, the Operational Staff had to ask itself, was the best use of the limited forces available? . . . Could more be spared [for the Mediterranean], or was it better to conserve effort and forces

* Throughout the war only 1,176 He 177s were produced compared with, for example, 8,685 Flying Fortresses, 18,188 Liberators and 7,366 Lancasters.

and concentrate the largest possible force in the East, where it could most effectively be employed? How far could one front be stripped with impunity for the benefit of the others? No answer was found to these questions for the reason that there was no answer.[55]

By 1943 it was clear that it was simply not possible to provide effective air cover on all fronts. In the middle of that year it became necessary to concentrate all single-engined fighters in the Reich, to provide protection against the bombers; Army fronts had to make do with twin-engined planes. And this at a time when the older versions of the main twin-engined fighter, the Bf 110, were proving quite unsuitable to the demands of modern air combat, when its replacement, the Me 210, had proved to be a complete flop, and when the latter's replacement, the Me 410, was not yet in serious production.* No wonder that Hitler showed himself increasingly reluctant to face the facts. At about this time his night-fighter commander, General Josef Kammhuber, suggested a considerable strengthening of this arm, by over 2,000 aircraft, and did manage to persuade Göring that this was necessary. When he put the proposal to Hitler, however, he was not allowed to finish talking. Hitler cut in to state flatly that the OKW's figures on Allied air strength were completely inaccurate and therefore 'a strengthening of the defences was not urgent. The defences were completely in order, and the victory figures of the night-fighter force so high that they would not lose their deterrent effect.'[56]

When economic incapacity was backed up by such a rigid refusal to face facts, or even to make the most rational deployment of the resources that were available, the *Luftwaffe* was clearly fighting a losing battle. This was apparent to the day-fighter force just as much as to the night. In April 1944, as swarms of long-range American escorts were beginning to clear the way for a massive intensification of 'strategic' bombing, General Galland submitted a report of his own to Hitler. In it he wrote:

The ratio in which we fight today is about 1:7. The standard of the Americans is extraordinarily high. The day fighters have lost more than 1,000 aircraft during the last four months, among them our best officers, and these gaps cannot be filled. During

* Only a little over 1,000 Me 410s were ever produced, and few of these actually flew in combat. In comparison, the British produced 6,439 de Havilland Mosquitoes and 5,562 Bristol Beaufighters.

each enemy raid we lose about fifty fighters. Things have gone so far that the danger of a collapse of our arm exists.[57]

But it was American numbers rather than their undeniable skills that turned that battle against the *Luftwaffe*. What was arguably the main reason why the Germans were unable to translate their burgeoning production into increased strength at the sharp end – table 42 shows that front-line strength in December 1944 was only marginally superior to that in June 1943 – was the calculated policy of attrition conducted by the USAAF during 1944.

American aerial tactics in Europe had never been long on subtlety, and though the term 'precision bombing' smacks of the scalpel and neat excision, American methods of actually getting their planes over the target were distinctly less clinical. Their senior airmen had gone into the war so convinced that their new heavy bombers were robust and well armed enough to be self-protecting, even in daylight operations, that far from giving thought to the provision of fighter escorts, they deliberately ignored their value. In the first US raids from England the RAF fighter escorts had helped keep casualties very light, but Ira Eaker chose to disregard their contribution. He claimed instead that the low loss rate from August to October was proof that the German fighters were no match for close formations of American bombers, ignoring the fact that those missions that had gone beyond fighter range had suffered a loss rate of 6.4 per cent. Looking forward to the intensification of an unescorted American effort, Eaker told Spaatz that in the near future Eighth Air Force would be entering a phase of operations which would be 'a demonstration that bombardment in force – a minimum of 300 bombers – can effectively attack any German target and return without excessive or uneconomic losses. This later phase relies upon mass and the great firepower of the large bombardment formations.'[58]*

The results of this policy can be seen in table 43 in the Statistical

---

* Eaker is not entirely to blame for his excessive optimism, for if the claims of some of his air gunners were to be believed, the *Luftwaffe* must soon have ceased to exist. In October 1942 one group of raiders claimed that 56 enemy fighters had been destroyed, 26 probably destroyed and 20 damaged. This was double the size of the German fighter force involved. In the whole of 1942 bomber crews claimed 223 planes destroyed and 88 probables. Eighth Air Force assessors reduced this to 89 to 140. *Luftwaffe* records reveal 7 fighters destroyed in operations against daylight raiders. Claims were still wildly inflated in July 1943, when the US figure was 545 fighters and the actual loss was around 40.

Appendix. In May 1943 Eaker felt that he had enough planes at his disposal to enter the 'mass' phase and he initiated a whole series of operations deep into enemy air space. He did not, in fact, completely dispense with fighter protection, but it was still nowhere near as numerous as it should have been. It rarely escorted the bombers all the way to the target, because of limited range, and it was often provided by inadequate planes, particularly the P-38 Lightning, which was hopelessly ill-adapted to European conditions. In these circumstances losses rose alarmingly and between April and October were as high in percentage terms (an average of 4.4 per cent with two peaks of over 6 per cent) as in any other period in the war. The most disastrous experiences in these months were two raids on the ball-bearing plants at Schweinfurt (the first raid also took in an aircraft factory at Regensburg). In the first, on 17 August, out of 376 bombers dispatched, 60 were destroyed, or almost 16 per cent. In the second raid, on 14 October, out of 291 Flying Fortresses dispatched, another 60 were destroyed, representing this time an utterly unacceptable loss rate of over 20 per cent. According to Joseph Goebbels' diary, on 29 September: 'The reports on interrogations of United States flying officers have been submitted to me . . . They . . . have no real enthusiasm for the war. They also complain of the exceptionally high losses sustained in day raids on the Reich. They describe every flight into Germany as a sort of suicide mission.'[59]

During the following winter, American operations remained at a fairly low ebb, partly because of the terrible losses sustained over Germany and partly because of the appalling weather conditions. The lull, however, was never regarded as being anything but temporary and even during it there emerged several trends that gave American commanders new hope of being able to swamp German defences. For one thing, deliveries of aircraft were increasing apace. The following aside from General Henry H. Arnold, commander of the US Army Air Force, says a great deal about the sheer material might that was being deployed on English airfields: 'By June of . . . [1944], AWPD-I had progressed to the point where we started taking transport planes away from commercial air-lines because we foresaw the necessity of establishing air-lines of our own to bring home the ferry pilots who were delivering planes to Britain.'[60] These planes were not only bombers. Fighters were also arriving in ever-increasing numbers, particularly the redoubtable P-47 Thunderbolt and the peerless P-51 Mustang. Moreover, these aircraft were given longer and longer

range by the addition of external drop-tanks. The range increases
were of the following order, given in miles:

June 1943	July 1943	August 1943	February 1944	April 1944
230 (P-47)	340 (P-47)	375 (P-47)	475 (P-47 and P-51)	850 (P-51)

Göring declared, when interrogated after the war:

> I most firmly believe that the main reason for the failure of the
> Luftwaffe against the Allied air forces was the success of the
> American Air Force in putting out a long-range escort fighter
> airplane, which enabled the bombers to penetrate deep into
> the Reich territory and still have a constant and strong fighter
> cover. Without this escort, the air offensive would never have
> succeeded. Nobody thought such long-range fighter escort was
> possible.[61]

But increasing the range of the Thunderbolts and Mustangs was
only part of the answer. Of equal importance was the tactical decision
taken by Eighth Air Force that the time had now come to carry the
fight to the *Luftwaffe* and wage an explicitly attritional campaign.
Allied industry was now pumping out aircraft at a much faster rate
than in Germany, so the cost of even fairly heavy casualties could
be borne. Moreover, a massive air-battle over the Reich might
well prove to have decisive implications for the war as a whole,
by sucking more and more German fighters into this sector. Even
in 1943 the mounting tempo of operations meant that the percentage
of the total German force involved over the Reich rose from 59 per
cent in January to 67 per cent at the end of the year. A yet more
telling figure emerges when one looks at the overall increase in
German fighter strength in 1943. This totalled 670 aircraft, and
fully 90 per cent of them ended up defending German air space.*
The Americans, therefore, now effected a radical change in the
deployment of their fighters. Up to this point they had stuck close
to the bombers, regarding their mission as being essentially defensive.
As more and more fighters became available, however, tactics were
changed to exploit more fully the characteristics of these aircraft.

---

* By January 1944 the *Luftwaffe* in the West also fielded 70 per cent of Flak
personnel, 75 per cent of heavy AA guns and 55 per cent of light.

Now only a third of the available escorts were needed to stick close
to the bombers and the rest were enjoined to range far out from
these formations and actively to 'pursue and destroy' the enemy to
the limits of their range.

German losses began to rise sharply, and at a rate which could
barely be replaced even by the rising deliveries of new aircraft.
Worried by these unsupportable losses, the *Luftwaffe* High Command ordered its fighters to avoid those of the Americans and to
concentrate on the bombers. 'This command', according to the
commander of one fighter *Gruppe* who fell into Allied hands that
summer, 'led to a vicious spiral of disaster. The German Air Force
concentrated on bombers and were shot down by Allied fighters.
The fighters learned that they were safe from attack and became
bolder and more effective . . . The German Air Force developed an
inferiority complex which got worse each day but the High Command
would not relax the order.' So strictly was it enforced, in fact, that
American fighters were granted virtual immunity from attack. The
same commander commented bitterly that 'the safest flying that was
ever possible was that of an American fighter over Germany'.[62] By
1944 the loss of planes, experienced pilots and morale had brought
the *Luftwaffe* to the edge of disaster. In the three months to the end
of August they lost 9,200 fighters destroyed and damaged, almost
exactly as many as they had lost between September 1939 and June
1942, and over three-quarters of the total losses for 1943. By the
end of the year, American day-fighters had established total air
superiority over Europe.*

It is important to re-emphasise, however, that this victory was an
essentially attritional one. Though equipped with superb aircraft, of
which the highly trained pilots took the most advantage, Eighth Air
Force fighter units did not gain the upper hand over Germany simply

---

* An indication of us supremacy during 1944 itself is that in the second half of
that year the *Luftwaffe* was losing thousands of planes on the ground, to almost
unopposed American intruder operations. One German officer reported on an
inspection trip during which he came across a factory which had lost all but 92
of the 1,000 planes it had produced. Another reckoned that almost all of the
September production of aircraft were destroyed on the ground. There were also
serious losses on combat airfields in 1944 and 1945. This in turn had a multiplier
effect as German night-fighters began to disperse by day on small, camouflaged
emergency airstrips. These were not suitable for landings after night operations,
and many pilots who tried to use them crashed. But those who chose to fly back
to their base airfields in the rear were often pounced upon by enemy intruders,
usually Mosquitoes.

by virtue of their superior morale, technology or tactics. A vital role was also played by the bombers, though as thankless a one as they had played hitherto. Though the Flying Fortresses and Liberators were no longer the sitting ducks of the ball-bearing raids, they were still being used as little more than clay pigeons. For precision bombing began to be used in a rather odd way, not as a direct attempt to disrupt some vital component of the German war machine but as a *threat* of such disruption, to which the Germans would have to respond. In 1944, at least up until the D-Day landings, one of the daylight bombers' main roles was to lure up the German fighters so that the long-range escorts could shoot them down. The task was, to say the least, a singularly dangerous one, and bomber losses were heavy. Table 43 again tells the story and shows that losses of us bombers peaked between January and September 1944. But the Americans were now well able to absorb such casualties. Because they could now put so many planes in the air at any one time, the German home defences simply could not destroy enough of them, allowing American *percentage* casualties to fall to perfectly acceptable levels. In relative terms, therefore, the Germans were becoming increasingly weak, a fact that is amply confirmed by the following statistic. In 1942 the *Luftwaffe* was only destroying 2.3 bombers for every 100 combats with enemy aircraft. By mid-1944, thanks above all to increased armament, this figure had risen to 17.7 destroyed. Nevertheless, this most notable improvement was easily absorbed by the massively increased us production, such that whereas, in mid-1943, 18.2 per cent of attacking us bombers were hit by enemy fire, by the last quarter of that year the figure was down to 6.4 per cent and by mid-1944 to less than 1 per cent. Such are the mathematics of attrition and such the ineluctable logic of brute force.

But it was not simply aircraft production that doomed the *Luftwaffe* to defeat in 1944. Another critically important shortage was that of

* German night-fighter statistics tell the same story. In 1942, 65 per cent of their interceptions resulted in kills whilst the figure for 1943 was 76 per cent. Yet the percentage of British planes shot down did not increase, and if anything slightly declined. In 1944, as the battle of attrition reached its height, the following figures were recorded:

	RAF losses as % sorties	*Luftwaffe* night-fighter losses as % sorties
August 1944	1.6	2.5
October 1944	0.6	6.2
December 1944	0.7	10.6

pilots. From the very beginning of the war, indeed, this aspect of *Luftwaffe* expansion had been given little attention by the High Command, who as usual gave little thought to the possibility of a protracted conflict with high casualties. According to certain *Luftwaffe* officers, problems began as early as December 1938 with 'the establishment of a so-called Führer-program, which called for the expansion of the *Luftwaffe* completely beyond the available means . . . The ultimate consequence was the rapid exhaustion of *Luftwaffe* striking power because of a lack of adequately trained replacement personnel.'[63] Even in August 1939 the *Luftwaffe* had only two-thirds of its authorised crew strength and over 40 per cent of the crews actually on duty were not fully trained. For fighters, bombers, dive-bombers and ground-attack aircraft the percentage of fully trained crews as against authorised strength was, respectively, 57, 27, 27 and 46 per cent.

Nor was there much prospect of speeding up the flow of fully operational crews. For in 1939 there were only three bomber schools, one naval aviation school and, 'fantastic thought though it seems', only one fighter school.[64] The Chief of Training's Chief of Staff, General Paul Deichmann, wrote after the war: 'In early 1939, when the office was first created the Chief of Training prepared a report for the Chiefs of the General Staff and requested authorisation for new pilot training schools. The General Staff refused his request, stating that all technical resources were being wholly utilised in the activation of new front units.'[65] The situation was not helped by the fact that the *Luftwaffe* Chief of Staff, Jeschonnek, according to his associates, 'placed very little value on the development of a close-knit training program . . . [This], by its very nature time-consuming and directed to the future, interested him far less than the employment of already available forces . . .'[66]

The consequences of such short-sightedness were being painfully felt within less than two years. In 1941, the loss rate among pilots had already reached a point where trainees were graduated before their course was completed, so that they could bring front-line squadrons nominally up to strength and hopefully complete their training 'on site'. The squadrons were thus obliged to give these new pilots less hazardous assignments whilst they learned their trade, but this only increased the load on the experienced aircrew, whose losses mounted accordingly. A second consequence was that 'untrained pilots in the dangerous and primitive conditions on front-line airfields had a higher accident rate than normal . . . The combination of a weak flying safety program along with untrained and unskilled pilots was deadly.'[67] In 1941, 2,849 aircraft were completely written off due to enemy action as against 2,153 due to other causes; the respective figures for aircraft too badly damaged for local repair were 475 and 1,193. Combining these figures, one finds that fully 50 per cent of aircraft losses in that year were caused by flying accidents and the like. The ratio of aircrew casualties was clearly much the same. The grim implications of this latter fact were clearly revealed towards the end of the year when 'Jeschonnek declined . . . [the] offer to raise fighter production to 1,000 units per month. The General Staff Chief explained that he had no use for more than 360 per month since he had only 170 air crews to man them.'[68]

Remarkably, however, the *Luftwaffe* actually compounded its serious training problems throughout the first three years of the war. A major source of aircrew were the 'C' Flying Schools which trained bomber and twin-engined fighter pilots.* A basic plane used at these schools was the Ju 52 transport. But a serious weakness of *Wehrmacht* planning before the war, and in the aftermath of the first *blitzkrieg* victories, was that very little attention was paid to the need for a dedicated force of transport aircraft, to fly in reinforcements and supplies along the long and difficult supply lines that must be a feature of any future campaigns. Whenever the need arose for such planes, therefore, there was no option but to pillage the training schools which had to give up not only their Junkers but, more fatally still, the instructors who flew them. In 1940 and 1941 these precious pilots were sucked into the formation of 'special duty bomber groups for employment in the air landing operations in Norway and Holland and later . . . for the conquest of Crete.' A good many of the instructors were well pleased with their more glamorous new assignment and stayed on with the front-line squadrons. 'This source of loss, together with the death suffered by a great many instructors during their employment in air transport duty, represented a depletion in instructional personnel from which the office of the Chief of Training simply could not recover.'[69]

In 1942, far from being given a chance to recover, the 'C' Schools were actually ransacked again and again, the Junkers and the instructors now being employed to mount airlift operations in the east, bringing succour to German garrisons cut off in such

---

* After their disappointing performance in the Battle of Britain the twin-engined *Zerstörers* gained a new lease of life as night-fighters in the battles against Bomber Command.

places as Chelm, Demyansk* and, most notoriously, Stalingrad. In the latter operation 266 Ju 52s were lost and almost as many precious instructional personnel. Those who were left, according to one *Luftwaffe* officer, became 'depressed and discouraged beyond words'.[70] In fact, the instructors were more than discouraged. The 'C' Schools became so overwhelmed with pupils graduating from the elementary schools that they simply could not cope, blocking the flow of trainees into the front-line formations' own reserve training units. In a desperate endeavour to overcome this blockage, the 'C' Schools were disbanded entirely and the responsibility for advanced instruction given over to these reserve units. But these too had neither the personnel nor the planes to cope with the influx of pupils and had to farm them out for training with the operational units, a process which only accelerated the appalling accident rates already referred to.

The training of single-engined fighter pilots also suffered, though this was directly attributable to the very high casualties in the Battle of Britain and the first year of the Russia campaign. By mid-1942 'the reservoir of older, trained pilots was used up and the flow from the schools was no longer sufficient to replace losses.' It became necessary to disband the fourth *Gruppe* of each *Geschwader*,† which had hitherto been used as a training unit for new pilots before they actually served in combat, and the *Geschwader* were forced to take their replacements straight from the area pools. The consequence was 'a curtailment in the period of operational training of fighter pilots at the very time when the increased intake of new and inexperienced aircrew required higher standards.'[71]

In the months that followed, the training situation went from bad to worse as the *Luftwaffe* found itself caught in a vicious circle of inadequately trained pilots being rushed into combat units to replace the mounting casualties, who were then themselves quickly becoming casualties because of their inexperience. The United States Strategic

* The Demyansk operation did succeed in keeping the garrison going until a link-up with the main forces was achieved. It cost, however, another 260 aircraft and as many pilots taken from the training schools and the aircraft factory testing stations. 'And all to save 90,000 German soldiers, 64,000 of whom were either killed, wounded or too sick for service by the end of the air-lift . . .' (R.J. Overy, 'Hitler and Air Strategy', *Journal of Contemporary History* 15, June 1980, p. 414.)
† German aircraft were organised into *Geschwader* (the rough equivalent of a British Group), *Gruppen* (Wings) and *Staffeln* (Squadrons). The respective full complement of aircraft was 94, 30 and 9.

Bombing Survey went so far as to state that 'the deterioration of quality of German pilots appears to be the most important single cause of the defeat of the German Air Force.'[72] By mid-1944 the situation was certainly desperate. The accident rate, for example, had become punitive and in June 1944 accounted for over 3,000 machines destroyed and seriously damaged as against 1,476 lost in action.* Figures for the whole period January 1941 to June 1944 give the following percentages of non-combat plane losses:

Jan.–June 1941	44.5	Jan.–June 1943	45.0
July–Dec. 1941	39.5	July–Dec. 1943	44.6
Jan.–June 1942	45.0	Jan.–June 1944	37.2
July–Dec. 1942	40.9		

Of the lower figure for the first six months of 1944, one historian has noted sardonically: 'The decrease . . . seems to have been the result of the fact that Allied fighters were shooting down German aircraft faster than their pilots could crash them.'[73]†

By November 1944 the *Luftwaffe* was so short of pilots that most night-fighter personnel were assigned to ground-attack operations and only a handful of experienced aces remained to conduct real night-fighter operations against Bomber Command. This obviously reduced their effectiveness against the raiders, whilst it also meant that their own losses to British night-fighters, although not that great, were of much greater proportional significance. The small number of competent pilots also had a serious impact on daylight operations in that the pilots who had been rushed through the training schools joined their units without any experience of bad-weather flying. From

* Pilot error also did much to negate the effects of increased German production. According to well-placed German sources, of the planes that were flown from the factories to front-line units as many as 25 per cent were totally destroyed in accidents.

† During the war as a whole, 11,442 aircraft were completely written off in training accidents and 10,457 in operational accidents. This represented 30.8 per cent of the total number of 70,990 aircraft written off by the *Luftwaffe*. It should be noted that the German experience was not unique. Certainly, their accident rates were much higher because of inexperience, and the heavy attrition of new pilots put insupportable strains on the already inadequate training programmes. But military flying is an extremely hazardous business in any air force. The USAAF, in 1943 and 1944 alone, lost 5,603 pilots and 6,376 other aircrew killed in training accidents in America. Bomber Command, over the whole war, lost 5,327 men killed and 3,113 injured in training accidents. Other accidents, usually during landing or taking off, involving fully trained aircrew, accounted for a further 2,868 aircrew killed. Accidents thus accounted for some 15 per cent of all Bomber Command fatalities.

November, therefore, the Americans 'began to schedule their attacks for bad weather, having noticed that German fighters (due to the lack of adequate pilot training in instrument flying) were completely helpless.'[74]

The training organisation, meanwhile, had all but broken down. A revealing indicator of this are the figures on training hours enjoyed by the pilots of the major air forces. In 1939 the *Luftwaffe* gave its pupils 260 flying hours, of which 100 were in combat types, as against the RAF which allocated 200 and 65 hours respectively. Over the war itself *Luftwaffe* training became shorter and shorter, especially when compared with that provided by the British and American air forces. The relevant figures are given below, showing the number of hours of training:

	Luftwaffe	RAF	USAAF
Oct. 1942 – June 1943	220 (55)	360 (75)	300 (100)
July 1943 – June 1944	175 (30)	360 (75)	340 (140)
July 1944 – May 1954	125 (35)	360 (75)	400 (200)

The lost *Luftwaffe* hours were mainly those that should have been devoted to

> gunnery and tactics. This was revealed in all the fatal mistakes of the inexperienced pilot in combat – absurdly inadequate air-search and preoccupation with formation keeping; an inability to fly the aircraft to its limits; a tendency to forget to jettison the drop tank or arm the weapons when joining combat and, finally, an inability to break off combat and escape when warranted by a tactical situation.[75]

In fact, the last set of *Luftwaffe* training hours figures just cited probably flatters the Germans, at least for 1945. By February of that year, according to one authority, 'the Luftwaffe aircrew training organisation had, to all intents and purposes, ceased to exist.'[76]*

But the decline in the competence of German aircrew was not just a function of the lack of instructors or of the desperate need to rush

---

* Allied training was not only superior in the number of hours allocated. The number of pilots produced was quite prodigious. By January 1945, 105,000 US pilots were being graduated each month. This proved to be far in excess of requirements and by March the figure had been cut to 30,000. The Germans, on the other hand, were reduced to proposing in this same month that pilots be found for the new He 162 jet fighters by taking one year's intake of the Hitler Youth and putting them through a crash course in gliders.

recruits through their training. Equally important was the shortage of aviation fuel, with the training units always being the first to suffer when rationing was introduced. The cut-backs in training hours already mentioned were often as much a consequence of such rationing as it was of the demand for new pilots. The possibility of fuel shortages had always been a serious risk for the *Luftwaffe*, as the high-octane fuel that aircraft required came in large part from Germany's own synthetic fuel industry. But the synthetic fuel industry was also vital to the German economy as a whole, because the recourse to war in 1939 had immediately cost Germany crude and finished oil imports amounting to over 3 million metric tons. These imports could be partly replaced by increased use of Romanian production* and by more vigorous exploitation of Germany's own crude deposits,† but the ability to keep a war economy functioning for more than a few months demanded full recourse to an expanding synthetic production. By 1943, 52 per cent of Germany's total oil production was from synthetic sources, as against only 22.5 per cent in 1939.‡ Only one-third of this capacity could be spared for the manufacture of aviation fuel.

In circumstances such as these, the training effort was very seriously hampered. According to one German source: 'Ever since the middle of 1941, the training programme had been treated like a stepchild by the powers responsible for allocating gasoline, and in 1942 the allocation to the Chief of Training was restricted so tightly that only certain categories of personnel (and these only in limited number) could be trained.'[77] The 1942 restrictions were intensified by the various airlift operations on the Eastern Front, already mentioned, which made considerable demands on fuel supplies. The Stalingrad lifts were a particular drain and in autumn 1942 training hours were cut back still further. For the remainder of the war fuel shortages were a constant pressure on the dwindling training programme, and especially harmful was the constant temp-

---

* In 1939, 974,000 metric tons of Romanian oil were imported into Germany. In 1943, 2,511,000 tons came from this source.
† German crude amounted to 1,883,000 metric tons in 1943 as against only 880,000 tons in 1939. Two-thirds of the former total came from Austria.
‡ Synthetic oil was made from bituminous and brown coal. Two methods were used: Bergius hydrogenation, which split the coal's molecules and forced hydrogen into them under high pressure to produce liquid oil molecules, and the Fischer-Tropsch process, in which the coal was broken up with steam to create molecules of hydrogen and carbon-monoxide which were synthesised into oil molecules.

tation, short-sighted though it was, to maximise the amount of fuel available for combat operations by cutting back still further on training. Certain senior *Luftwaffe* officers did realise what damage was being done, though. Field Marshal Milch once stated baldly: 'The Luftwaffe training program, and with it the Luftwaffe itself, was throttled to death by the gasoline shortage.'[78] The United States Strategic Bombing Survey (USSBS) fully endorsed this conclusion, suggesting that lack of oil, with its detrimental effect on German training, led to 'a deterioration of the quality of personnel which was the principal cause of the defeat of the German Air Force.'[79]

But the fuel famine also had a serious effect on German operational flying, limiting the effort that could be made even when aircraft and pilots were available. The effects were most seriously felt from mid-1944 when oil became a major target of the Combined Bomber Offensive.* The effect on German production is clearly shown in table 44 in the Statistical Appendix, which reveals that between April and September 1944 synthetic fuel production was cut from 348,000 tons to a mere 26,000 and aviation fuel production from 175,000 tons to 17,000.† This latter figure, a drop to only 9.7 per cent of peak production, is closely matched by the figures for one single synthetic fuel plant, that at Leuna, which was the largest plant of its kind. Between May 1944 and the end of the war it was bombed no fewer than 22 times, and its output reduced to only 9 per cent of capacity. The effect of all this on the *Luftwaffe* was immediate and ultimately catastrophic. Between June and September 1944 its consumption of fuel had to be cut down by two-thirds, yet still remained constantly in excess of production. Only by the most stringent economies did the Germans avoid completely using up all their accumulated stocks of fuel, which by December 1944 stood at a paltry 146,000 tons, less than one month's consumption in 1943. By March 1945 these stocks were almost completely gone, down to only 11,000 tons, and production that month could add only another 52,000 tons. The desperate straits to which the squadrons were reduced is well

---

* Though it had had indirect effects on operational flying as early as 1942. During the fuel crisis occasioned by the Stalingrad airlift, the aircraft plants had had their fuel allowances for testing drastically cut back and only one plane in five received a full flight check. The rest were flown for only 20 minutes or so before going straight to the front. The already appalling accident rate was thereby increased yet further.

† The vital products of the synthetic fuel plants, other than aviation fuel, were nitrogen and methanol, both essential ingredients for the manufacture of explosives, i.e. the contents of a shell.

illustrated by the experiences of fighter *Gruppe* II/301. One of its maintenance officers recalled that the getting of fuel

> 'was not so much a logistics operation, more an Intelligence battle'. He would send his tankers on circuitous journeys, picking up 200 gallons in one place, 500 gallons at another; sometimes it might take as long as a week merely to collect the twenty tons of fuel needed for a single operation by the *Gruppe*. The unit made the most stringent efforts to save fuel, using teams of horses or oxen to drag the fighters from their scattered dispersal points to the take-off point.[80]

Every type of operation was grievously afflicted by these shortages. The bomber force, as has been seen, had been severely handled during the Battle of Britain and no serious effort had since been made to develop a powerful strategic air arm. (This was probably for the best, since by summer 1944 it would have been completely out of the question to satisfy the voracious appetite for fuel of such a force.) One *Geschwader* of four-engined bombers, He 177s, was secretly assembled on the Eastern Front in May and June, but by August it regularly had to cancel operations because it had received no fuel at all. The *Geschwader* required about 490 tons of fuel to mount a single operation, but this amount was at this stage of the war equivalent to a day's output of the *entire* aviation fuel industry. The unit was withdrawn back into central Germany where it was disbanded. Strategic bombing was abandoned entirely though, according to Galland, 'bombers continued to be built until no more gasoline was available for their test flights and they had to be reduced to scrap on the very same airfields on which they had been built.'[81]

Fighter operations were also badly hit, most notably the day-fighters. Even in 1943 fuel shortages precipitated a curtailment of air operations. The policy of the German Air Force became one of standing down for considerable periods in order to conserve fuel for mass operations on selected days. In these mass attacks recourse was had to so-called *Sturmgruppen* of heavily armed Fw 190 fighters, and these did have some successes against unprotected bomber formations. In October these formations scored quite a few victories, but only so long as no American fighters were present. Whenever the swarms of long-range escorts were around, however, the heavily armed and armoured Focke-Wulfs, like latter-day knights in armour, proved terribly vulnerable to their more nimble opponents. From January 1944, when German day-fighters were saddled with specific orders to attack only enemy bombers, they could be shot down with ease. By 1945 fighter protection over the Reich in daylight was almost non-existent. In January 'the employment of fighters was . . . rigidly limited to those situations which really promised success' and in February an order from Jodl stated that 'all operations must now be ruthlessly limited owing to the critical aircraft fuel situation, and all operations which did not directly relieve the fighting troops were to be cancelled.' By March, according to *Luftwaffe* commanders questioned after the war, 'the gasoline shortage was so acute that only top-ranking crews were permitted to fly.'[82]

The night-fighters were similarly affected. According to their most recent German historian, by the end of 1944 'only a few leading crews could still fly operationally, while the majority of crews sat around doing nothing for weeks on end.'[83] The level of their inactivity is well illustrated by a few figures. German aircraft production, as has been seen, did succeed in putting on a commendable spurt in 1944 which, though it hardly matched that of the Allies, at least allowed some expansion of the night-fighter force. Thus, in August 1944 it mustered 614 serviceable aircraft, whilst in September the figure had risen to 792 and in December to 982. Nevertheless, the effectiveness of this force sharply declined, the number of Allied planes brought down falling from 164 in August, to 76 in September and only 66 in December.

The same disparity between paper strengths and actual combat records applies to the *Luftwaffe*'s jet fighter force, most particularly the Me 262. Again the fuel crisis was largely responsible. The shortages did not so much affect the ability to fuel the planes, which operated on J2 diesel oil which was in reasonably good supply until the last months of the war, as they did the inability to provide enough pilots trained in conventional machines. The end result was just the same, however. Whilst the Messerschmitt factories performed quite prodigious feats in turning out 1,294 Me 262s in 1944 and 1945, very few of these machines actually saw any combat.* After the war, the chairman of the Messerschmitt Board pointed out that 'late in 1944, at a time when the company had delivered over 650 machines, the Luftwaffe had only 40 operational in combat.'[84] Recent authorities have estimated

---

* Another 500 planes were destroyed before completion in air raids on the Messerschmitt factories.

that only 100 of these planes were used in action throughout
the war. Certainly not many units were equipped with them, and
those that were could put up very few planes. Even in December
1944 one of the four bomber *Geschwader* so equipped was often
only able to put up one sortie at a time. The plane was just as
rare in the fighter role, being used by only two *Gruppen* and a
'Fighter Unit', all of which combined could never put more than
40 planes in the air, a virtual irrelevance when one considers the
thousands of American escorts that were crowding the skies at
this time.

One final point needs to be mentioned regarding the *Luftwaffe*'s
inability to translate rising production into effective combat operations. Again it was Allied bombing that made the significant contribution, and in this case perhaps the most significant of the war.
The target in question was the German transportation system. Rail
transport had been a tactical target between March and September 1944, when the 'strategic' bombers came under Eisenhower's
command and were directed to attempt to seal off the Normandy
battlefield and prevent the arrival of reinforcements or supplies.
Transport remained a target after September, but this time it
was railways and canals in Germany itself and the aim was to
disrupt the entire communications network, not just to interdict
deliveries of finished items but to undermine industrial production
as a whole. This Transportation Plan went a long way towards
achieving its objectives, especially with regard to the synthetic
fuel industry. According to the Strategic Air Targets Committee
in April 1945 such synthetic fuel as was still being produced 'could
not be properly distributed owing to the collapse of the German
transport system.' In fact, the fuel plants were being squeezed at
both ends for, again in the words of the Committee, 'the coal
which the plants transformed into oil . . . had to be brought to
them by rail, in the same way as the oil that was produced had
to be dispatched. The biggest synthetic oil plants were nowhere
near the coalfields.'[85] This increasing stranglehold that the bombers
imposed at both ends of the production process, combined with all the
other constraints on the *Luftwaffe* elaborated above, was sufficient
to snuff the last flicker of life out of this always rather emaciated
Service.

Clearly, then, the Combined Bomber Offensive is to be credited
with having made a substantial contribution towards the defeat of

the *Luftwaffe*. It was the bombers that drew the German fighters into the immediate defence of the Reich, where they could be slaughtered by the ever-increasing numbers of Allied fighters. And it was bombing, most notably American daylight precision bombing, that wreaked such havoc with German synthetic fuel production and transportation, with the deleterious consequences for the *Luftwaffe* already noted. Nor was it only their air force that suffered: towards the end of the war the whole of German industry was being sorely tried by the ceaseless pounding from the skies. The Transportation Plan was particularly effective in this regard and had fatal ramifications throughout the German economy. According to the USSBS, 'the attack on transportation was the decisive blow that completely disorganised the German economy. It reduced war production in all categories and made it difficult to move what was produced to the front.'[86] Senior Germans were in complete agreement. As early as November 1944 Albert Speer, *Reichsminister* for Armaments and Munitions, was informing Hitler that 'constant dislocation of communications made it impossible to maintain a unified programme controlled from Berlin' and that the whole 'situation with regard to German armaments and war production is . . . aggravated by . . . the present catastrophic situation in transport.' In December, in a speech to some *Luftwaffe* specialists, he roundly stated: 'Colleagues, for the next few months our anxieties are governed by the transport situation which has deteriorated to an extraordinary extent . . . Our production is to a great extent dependent on how far it will be possible to put transport back into some sort of order.'[87] According to Field Marshal Albert Kesselring, a *Luftwaffe* commander who rose to become *Oberbefehlshaber Südwest* (OB *Südwest*), the Supreme Commander of all arms in Italy, and later OB *West*, fulfilling the same function in North-West Europe, it was his 'considered opinion that it was your air force that decided the conflict. What was felt very keenly was the effect of raids on . . . [and] the destruction of our transport system.'[88]

By 1945 that system was in such disarray that it could handle little more than essential military traffic and all other types of goods tended to be shoved off into sidings and branch-lines as soon as a military train approached. It soon 'became impossible to trace individual cars of important components or finished armaments. Such material was set aside on all parts of the railway system.' The USSBS goes on:

On the whole it might be said that by the close of 1944 air attacks upon the railroad system . . . had reduced the available capacity for economic traffic to a point which could not hope to sustain, over any period of time, a high level of war production. The loss of transportation facilities completely disorganised the flow of basic raw materials, components, and semi-finished materials, and even the distribution of finished products. Under these conditions orderly production was no longer possible.[89]

It remains somewhat difficult to quantify exactly the impact of this disruption cn the German war economy, largely because, by the last months of the war, 'so great was the disorganisation . . . that no useful statistics were kept by the Germans.'[90] It is known, however, that total railway car loadings on the *Reichsbahn* went into precipitous decline, recording the following sample weekly totals between August 1944 and March 1945:

Week ending

19 August	899,091
28 October	703,580
23 December	547,309
3 March	214,001

It is also known that coal, to which the Germans accorded the highest priority, was severely hit. Speer's memorandum of December 1944, for example, informed Hitler that the bare minimum number of coal wagons required to run in the Ruhr, to supply both that area and other parts of Germany, was 18,000 per day but it had in fact fallen to only 4,000. In that same month, when the minimum demands of German industry were for 590,000 tons of coal per month, only 190,000 tons were actually delivered. In 1945 the situation deteriorated yet further and 'by the end of February stocks had been eliminated and production was reduced to the level supported by occasional fragmentary deliveries . . . The German economy was powered by coal. Except in limited areas, the coal supply had been eliminated.'[91] A final point in this regard is that the campaign against transportation probably had a direct effect on ground operations, although the link can never be proved. It is known, however, that between September and November 1944, 2,199 tanks were manufactured whilst only 1,371 actually reached the troops. Unless the production figures were blatantly padded out (which is possible), it seems likely that the deficit was accounted for by attacks on German railways and the destruction of tanks in transit.*

Despite these manifest achievements, however, many historians have expressed serious reservations about the overall utility of the Combined Bombing Offensive. It has been suggested, for example, that for the Allied bombers to play a part in defeating the German fighter force was an essentially futile achievement in that, had the bomber force not existed in the first place, the Germans would not have needed so many fighters. And building fewer bombers would have freed enormous resources that the Allies could have used more profitably in beefing up Coastal Command and manufacturing more landing craft, tanks, artillery and the like. In fact, this latter point is more applicable to the *Wehrmacht*. By forcing the Germans to devote such a large proportion of *their* industry to the manufacture of fighters to defend the Reich, the Allied bombers, more especially the Americans, were driving them down a strategic blind alley. For fighters were extremely expensive, as well as being the weapon that the Germans were least able to make much use of, because of the dearth of pilots and the terrible shortages of fuel. (It would be interesting to know just how many of the thousands of fighters built in 1944 actually flew in combat and how many of these ever downed an enemy, or even spoilt his aim. Figures already cited suggest that both percentages would be extremely low.) But had these resources used up in producing fighters been employed elsewhere, in turning out large numbers of tanks, assault guns and artillery, personnel carriers, caterpillar tractors and trucks, this must have been a much more cost-effective contribution to the war effort.† It could not, as will become more apparent, have altered the ultimate outcome of the war, but might well have retarded the actual collapse of the Reich by some months.

Having said all that in defence of the Bomber Offensive, it is still

---

* It must also be assumed that the bombing of transportation badly affected aircraft production. In response to the earlier, direct assault on this industry the Germans had dispersed production, splitting the original 27 plants into 729 smaller units. This involved a considerable traffic of components between factories, a traffic that would be vulnerable to aerial interdiction.

† This argument assumes, of course, that factories would have been able to switch from one type of production to another within a reasonable space of time. It should also be borne in mind that Hitler usually insisted on the major proportion of new hardware being used to equip fresh divisions, rather than reinforcing the veterans actually at the front, and this might have dissipated many of the benefits that should have accrued from increased production.

difficult to avoid the overall impression of a very haphazard campaign in which even American 'precision bombing' served as a very crude sort of weapon. One of the saddest features of American raids was that much of the inevitable collateral damage caused, as bombs fell on nearby houses, schools, hospitals and the like, was totally unjustified in that even those bombs that had fallen on the selected target did little long-term damage. There were two reasons for this. One was that US bombers flew in tight box formations, to provide maximum mutual fire protection, and released bombs simultaneously on a signal from the lead aircraft. A raid, therefore, was over in a few minutes, which allowed the emergency services to be on the scene very quickly and to dowse speedily the fires that normally caused most of the damage. The other reason was that US bombs were too small, averaging 388lb each during the whole oil offensive as against 660lb for the RAF. The former could make a considerable mess of buildings, particularly those built for purely civilian purposes, but they were generally unable sufficiently to mangle machine tools and other engineering, construction or transport equipment except by a direct hit.

Another point which Allied commanders failed to realise until late in the war was that industrial targets are remarkably resilient to even the most accurate raids. There were very occasional examples of single attacks putting plants out of the war for the duration, such as the Bottrop-Weltheim hydrogenation plant whose compressor-house was hit by three 4,000lb and eight 1,000lb bombs in October 1944 and never functioned again. Usually, however, factories, refineries and marshalling yards could be brought back into some sort of operation reasonably quickly. The example of the Dresden rail yards, caught in one of the most devastating attacks of the war, has already been mentioned. Equally significant is the fact that, on average, oil refineries, even at the height of the concerted offensive of 1944 and 1945, could be put back into operation within six weeks. Unless, that is, they were *repeatedly* attacked at short intervals, to keep one vital part or another of the refinery out of commission at all times. This lesson was eventually learned, but not until the last few months of the war. Prior to autumn 1944, therefore, it was largely irrelevant whether or not the Americans had isolated the correct type of target, one with a genuinely pivotal role in the overall war economy, or even whether the first attack was delivered with pinpoint accuracy. For unless this same target was attacked again and again it would invariably resume its function quite quickly.

This was indeed the fate of many of the 'strategic' assaults undertaken by the Allies. Before it opted completely for area bombing, Bomber Command had attempted a precision campaign of sorts, against the German oil industry. The targets were well chosen, but so sporadic and weak were the attacks themselves that they had no perceptible effect on German production. The Americans made just the same mistakes. The first potential bottleneck they selected for attack was the ball-bearings industry, correctly adjudged to be a vital component of aircraft production. Moreover, the plant chosen, at Schweinfurt, on its own accounted for a considerable proportion of total output, and thus the two American raids of August and October 1943, despite the fearsome casualties, did deal the Germans a telling blow. But the gap between the raids, and – much worse – the subsequent failure to maintain the assault into 1944, allowed the Germans both to recommence production at Schweinfurt and to increase and disperse other ball-bearing manufacture throughout Germany, thus reducing their reliance upon the single plant. Another target that was not followed up properly was the synthetic rubber industry. One of the most successful raids of the war was against the I. G. Farben synthetic rubber plant at Hüls, on 22 June 1943. Probably only one-fifth of the 183 planes that attacked actually scored hits, but rubber burns very well and such was the damage that the plant was out of action for a whole month, reducing rubber stocks to only six weeks' supply. But the Allied bombers never returned and the damage was repaired. In March 1944 Hüls reached peak production for the war.

Even the renewed campaign against oil was not an immediate success, as reference again to table 44 will show. The early months of the campaign, from June to August 1944, went exactly according to plan with an increased weight of bombs forcing down aviation fuel production at an alarming rate. In September and October, however, there was a pronounced lull* which gave the Germans the opportunity gradually to step up production again, even into November when the Allies resumed their attacks. As one historian has recently pointed out:

---

* Bad weather is sometimes given as the main reason for this failure to deliver a knock-out blow, but the high level of air activity achieved in November makes this excuse less than convincing. Weather certainly limited operations in December and January, but by then it was already too late to take out the refineries 'by storm'. By that stage German repair techniques were so organised that the oil industry could only be slowly stomped into the ground.

Not realising how much Spaatz was accomplishing [from June to August], the other Allied commanders, ground and air . . . failed . . . to offer full support, diversions carried the Fortresses and Liberators elsewhere, and . . . the Reich supply received the respite it needed . . . The Allies had held victory through air power in their grasp but had not persevered to the kill.[92]

Portal and Harris, as was shown earlier, must also bear considerable responsibility for the failure to 'persevere to the kill'. Even though the Americans were at fault in letting their own effort become dissipated, it would still have been possible to destroy the synthetic fuel industry by Christmas if Harris had been prepared to join in a round-the-clock offensive or if Portal, who was keen to do so, had ordered it.* On the whole, then, it comes as no surprise to find that one of Galland's major criticisms of the actual execution of the Bomber Offensive was its dilettante approach to targeting priorities. As he wrote after the war: 'A different selection of targets and priorities, less changing from one target category to another, and adequate repetition of attack would have broken the backbone of the Luftwaffe and of its strategic potential more quickly, with less expenditure of manpower and matériel, and more conclusively.'[93]

Two other major reservations about 'precision' bombing might be raised. One is that the Allies wasted a great deal of effort in attacking multiple sets of targets when concentrating on just one of them would have done the job equally effectively. Such was the case with the Oil and Transport Plans in the closing stages of the war. Thus, by 1945, the latter Plan was having such a devastating effect on the influx of coal to the synthetic oil refineries, as well as on the distribution of the finished product, that it was unnecessary also to launch major raids against the refineries themselves. Moreover, it does not really do to claim that the Allies did not know how effective an assault on transportation could be. As Lord Zuckerman has written, the failure to appreciate this remains 'extraordinary', as both American and British air force commanders

had before their eyes incontrovertible evidence, in the shape of documents and charts left behind by the Germans when they

---

* As further comment on Harris's insane insistence on area bombing it should be noted that in the case of oil there were now absolutely no grounds for suggesting that the refineries were impossibly difficult targets compared with city centres. Not only had bombing techniques improved enormously by 1944, but some refineries, notably Leuna, were immense, covering much the same area as a city centre.

were driven out of Brussels [in September 1944], that the attacks which had already been carried out against French and Belgian railway centres, had had an immediate and devastating effect, not only on all military and civilian traffic, but on all economic activity in the occupied territories of the west.[94]

The question of duplication becomes yet more involved when one takes into account the following testimony of the USSBS, in its assessment of the attack on the German aircraft industry:

The bombing effort expended to achieve reduction in German air power was excessive. In particular, reduction of aircraft output after the early months of 1944 was of little consequence, since beginning in June operations were more and more sharply restricted by shortage of gasoline. The success of the attack on oil production had rendered superfluous any further attack on aircraft output.[95]

In other words, the attack on transportation should have been pursued at the expense of both the oil effort and that devoted to aircraft production, as concentration on the one would of itself have sufficed to nullify completely the existing *Luftwaffe* and the industry which provided its replacements.

The final reservation about 'precision' bombing also involves lapses in targeting policy, though on this occasion it concerns crucial components of the German economy that were hardly attacked at all. Two stand out. The first takes us back once again to aviation fuel and one of its ingredients, ethyl fluid. This was 'an indispensable constituent of high-grade aviation gasoline. The addition of ethyl fluid in very small amounts to gasoline is so beneficial that no modern aircraft is operated without it.'[96] It was made from tetraethyl lead and ethylene dibromide, and production of the former was limited to only five plants in Axis Europe, two in Germany, two in Italy and one in Occupied France. Only the products of their own and one Italian plant were ever available to the Germans, and these were barely adequate to supply the tetraethyl lead for their needs. Plans to construct two new plants in Germany and to expand production of the others never materialised. Ethylene dibromide was supplied by only a single plant in Germany. The USSBS points out that production of aviation fuel was thus ultimately dependent upon four plants, the location and purpose of each of which was known. The Survey crisply concludes: 'These plants were not bombed, although the equipment and the processes used were such as to make them highly vulnerable to air attack . . . A major opportunity in the Allied air offensive against oil was unexploited.'[97]

The other main missed opportunity was the German electricity grid. Even at the beginning of the war there was no surplus electric energy in Germany – indeed, 10 and sometimes 30 per cent reductions in supply were quite common – and efforts during the war to increase supply proved unavailing.* As these efforts grew more and more desperate, greater demands were placed on the grid. This grid was extremely vulnerable – as had been sensed by the Americans very early, when the AWPD-1 Plan made electric power the prime target in Germany – in that only 0.2 tons of bombs per acre of plant area could knock out a generating station for up to three months, whilst 0.4 tons could nullify it for up to a whole year. Moreover, any station knocked out would represent an immediate loss to the system for which it was impossible to compensate, given the simple but crucial fact that electricity cannot be stored. There were in Germany 8,257 generating stations in 1939, but most were of little consequence, with only just over one hundred providing 56.3 per cent of all current generated, and a further 300 bringing that percentage up to 81.9. The location of these plants was known, as was the relative ease with which electric generating (and transmission) equipment can be seriously damaged, much of it being of a fragile nature. If just five of these plants had been put out of action, the German system would have suffered a capacity loss of 8 per cent; if 45 had been destroyed the loss would have been almost 40 per cent; and if 95 had been taken out a more than 50 per cent deficit would have resulted. The very survival of the German war economy would then have been in doubt, for Speer later testified that the loss of around 60 per cent of capacity would have brought German industry to a standstill.[†]

In the event, however, the power grid was almost totally ignored by the bombers; Eighth US Air Force expending only 316 tons

* It was impossible either to build the plants, redistribute or increase coal supplies, or build hydroelectric facilities. (79 per cent of power stations burnt coal and the rest were water-powered.)

† Transformer stations were also extremely vulnerable, since blast alone was sufficient to wreck transformers for good. A German document written in 1944 reckoned that two or three nights' concentrated attacks on only 30 transformer stations could 'paralyse decisively the German power grid' (USSBS, *The Effects of Strategic Bombing on the German Economy*, Government Printing Office, Washington, December 1946, p. 125). An ideal ancillary target would have been the four factories that produced most of the high-tension transformers.

of bombs (0.05 per cent of the total they dropped) and Bomber Command only 532 tons (0.07 per cent). One cannot help but feel that the following remark by a German observer questioned by the USSBS, though it applies to only one city, permits an extrapolation concerning the whole German war economy: 'If the Allied airmen had concentrated on knocking out the two big power stations in the outskirts of Berlin, the city would be just as dead as it is now after months of heavy bombing of the entire city.'[98]

But if precision bombing was not quite the pinpoint instrument, unfailingly applied at the most vital spot, that its proponents claimed,* it was at least an *attempt* to apply military force according to some sort of rational precepts. Harris's insistence on area bombing, on the other hand, must remain one of the most dubious policies, both militarily and morally, of the Second World War. Accepting that in the early months of the war Bomber Command was absolutely incapable of any pretence of accurate bombing, and that it was nevertheless politically essential to demonstrate that the Atlantic Alliance was adopting some sort of aggressive posture, it still seems quite inexplicable that Harris resolutely declined *ever* to abandon the initially *ad hoc* policy of area bombing and, indeed, made it a permanent and central tenet of his doctrine. If 'doctrine' is really the word one is looking for. For, as Max Hastings has tellingly pointed out, one is above all left with a sense of

> extraordinary vagueness on the part of the airmen. The concept of a Trenchardian thunderbolt fascinated them. But as far as it is possible to discover, they never recorded a common assent about the exact nature of what they hoped to achieve by area bombing, beyond the destruction of . . . large areas of German real estate.[99]

It is clear that the Germans were equally bemused. In every one of his interrogation sessions after the war, Speer questioned the purpose of the area attacks, pointing out that the night attacks did not even 'succeed in breaking the will to work of the civilian population'. In another session, described by the interrogator himself, it clearly emerged that 'the purpose of the night attacks directed exclusively against city centers had been "incomprehensible" to Speer; their effects on industry were very slight. Later on, when attacks were

---

* There is an important book to be written examining the use of Ultra intelligence in analysing damage done, and in the selection of the most telling targets.

sometimes directed on industrial areas, damage to plants tended to become more widespread, but Speer considers that area bombing alone would never have been a serious threat.'[100]

The latter point deserves emphasis, even at the risk of seeming unduly callous. Simply killing German civilians, even in the horrific circumstances of a Hamburg or a Dresden, made no especial impact on the German economy, nor even on the industrial infrastructure. Residential areas might be razed to the ground,* railway lines ripped up and factories laid open to the skies, but this did not mean that people or machines completely ceased to perform their normal functions for more than a few days or, occasionally, weeks. The case of the marshalling yards in Dresden merits mention yet again, as does the other victim of a great fire-storm, Hamburg, where it was estimated that total production lost was the equivalent of only 1.8 months. Within five months of this most devastating raid, the city was once again functioning at 80 per cent of capacity.

In other area raids the 'benefits' were yet more ephemeral. In a USSBS analysis of such raids on ten German cities, reckoned to be representative of the 61 with a population of 100,000 or more that had been bombed, it was found that none had suffered a knock-out blow and even where production had fallen off in the aftermath of a raid, 'the local loss of output had had a negligible effect on the annual production of the Reich as a whole . . . Even the devastating raids on Hamburg in July/August 1943 had reduced total production in the Reich by only 1.01 per cent; for the other nine cities, the reductions in national production were all well below one per cent.'[101] Furthermore, this loss was a smaller percentage still if one included only war production – according to the USSBS something like 50 per cent less. Bomber Command's analyses at the time, it went on, 'appear . . . to have been far in excess of the facts.' On top of which there was also no evidence to support Bomber Command claims about the cumulative effects of area bombing. In fact, 'far from being any evidence of a cumulative effect . . . it is evident that, as the offensive progressed, the Germans were able to divert the effects of town area attacks more and more on to the civilian section of industry, so that the effect on war production became progressively smaller.'[102]

For this less than decisive result, Harris had done the lion's share of killing 600,000 Germans, mainly civilians. Nor had he been sparing of

---

* 2,340,000 dwelling places in what is now West Germany alone were destroyed by bombing, and a further three million severely damaged.

his own men. During the war as a whole roughly 125,000 men served as aircrew with Bomber Command. Of these 59,423 were killed or missing presumed killed. This was a casualty rate of 47.5 per cent – *killed*. If men wounded are included the rate rises to 54.3 per cent. For the greater part of the war the casualty rate was probably much higher, as from mid-1944 Bomber Command expanded considerably, inducting quite a high proportion of the total intake of aircrew, and at the same time casualties noticeably declined (see table 43). For the period up to D-Day, therefore, one is probably talking in terms of a *fatality* rate of upwards of 65 per cent. It is not surprising that several writers have compared the slaughter of Bomber Command with the terrible carnage wreaked among the infantry battalions of the First World War. The comparison is perfectly justified, as long as one realises that the 'Tommies' have the best of it. Total casualty rates compare remarkably closely. Thus, between 1914 and 1918, the two battalions of the Scots Guards, both of which spent the whole war on the Western Front, endured a casualty rate of 53.9 per cent. The ratio of men killed, however, was only half that of Bomber Command, at 24.8 per cent. The grim irony of the thing was that Harris himself had first become attached to the idea of strategic bombing because he specifically wanted to avoid a repetition of the bloody stalemates on the Somme and at Passchendaele. He wrote at one stage during the 1930s of his revulsion at the memory of 'morons volunteering to get hung in the wire and shot in the stomach in the mud of Flanders'.[103] The reference to 'morons' and the suggestion that it was somehow their own fault rather tends to vitiate the otherwise laudable aims and, indeed, exemplifies the utter coarseness of soul that permitted, even compelled, Harris to persist with the most brutish offensive of a very brutal war.

Appendix:
Technical measures and counter-measures during the Bomber Offensive

| Date enters service | Device | | Night or day | Function |
	Allied	German		
1940 June		Würzburg		Radar with 25-mile range mainly used to help AA guns find targets. Able to plot altitude of target.
Sept.		Freya		Radar with 75-mile range mainly used for giving early warning of bombers' approach. Could not measure altitude.
Oct.		Würzburg	N	Now used in pairs, one to track enemy bomber, the other to track friendly night-fighter and allow controller to vector it on to bomber.
1941 Sept.		Würzburg Riese	N	'Giant' version with range of over 40 miles.
1942 Feb.		Lichtenstein	N	Airborne radar fitted in night-fighters. Range between 2 miles and 200 yards.
March		Mammut	N	Early warning radar. Improved Freya. Range 200 miles. Still could not measure altitude.
March		Wassermann	N	Early warning radar. Range 150 miles. Could measure altitude. Second World War state-of-the-art.
March	Gee		N	Navigational aid by which aircraft's navigator plots his position with receiver which measures time dif-

Date enters service	Device		Night or day	Function
	Allied	German		
				ference in reception of pulses from three separate ground transmitters. Accurate to within 6 miles at 400 miles distance.
June	Shaker		N	Lead aircraft fitted with Gee drop marker bombs 'blind', as targets for bombers behind.
Aug.	Moonshine	(Freya)*	D	Airborne device that returned Freya pulses, greatly amplified, to give impression of large bomber force. To provoke wasted enemy interceptions. Fitted in Defiants. Used until Oct. 42.
Aug.	(Gee)	Heinrich	N	Transmitters to jam Gee ground transmitters. Gee unusable by Nov. 42.
Nov.	Mandrel	(Freya)	N	Noise jammer fitted in selected aircraft flying ahead of and with the main force.
Nov.	Tinsel		N	Airborne noise jammer to disrupt enemy ground-to-air communications. Amplified bomber's engine noise.
Dec.	Oboe			Twin ground radar transmitters which triggered return pulses from transmitter in bomber. Both worked out bomber's distance from transmitters and when it reached predetermined position triggered release of bombs. 270-mile range. Fitted in lead, target-marking aircraft, the 'Pathfinders'. First used by American day-bombers Oct. 43.
1943 Jan.	H₂S			Centimetric, much more powerful airborne radar transmitter which

* Brackets indicate the enemy device that the device coming into service was to nullify or was parasitic upon.

Date enters service	Device		Night or day	Function
	Allied	German		
				translated pulses bounced back from the ground as a rough representation of the terrain, distinguishing particularly between water, cities and countryside. First used by Americans Nov. 1943. Not fully effective until July 43.
March	Monica			Airborne radar transmitter set in tail to detect approaching aircraft. Range of 1000 yards. Unable to distinguish friend from foe.
March	Boozer	(Würzburg/ Lichtenstein)	N	Radar receiver which gave visual warning if aircraft had been picked up by enemy radar.
June	A1 Mk X			Centimetric airborne radar transmitter for night-fighters. British version of American scr720.
June	Serrate	(Lichtenstein)	N	Radar receiver for night-fighters which picked up Lichtenstein and offered pilot a visual display which allowed him to work out enemy's height and direction.
July	Window	(Würzburg/ Lichtenstein)		Bundles of tinfoil strips dropped from aircraft which when picked up by German radar, completely swamped it.
Aug.	Special Tinsel			Update of Tinsel to jam new German HF transmitters.
Sept.	(H₂S)	Naxburg		Modified Würzburg to pick up H$_2$S transmissions. Could pick up individual aircraft 150 miles away.
Oct.	ABC			'Airborne Cigar'. Airborne transmitter to jam German fighters' VHF radios.
Oct.	Corona		N	'Special Tinsel' transmitters being used to send out false instructions to German fighter pilots.

Date enters service	Device Allied	Device German	Night or day	Function
Oct.		SN-2	N	Airborne night-fighter radar transmitter. Not jammed by Window. Range of 4 miles to 400 yards.
Nov.	(Window)	Würzlaus		Modification to Würzburg which under favourable conditions differentiated the faster-flying aircraft from the almost stationary Window cloud.
Nov.	(Window)	Nürnberg		Modification to Würzburg which allowed skilled operator to aurally distinguish pulse bouncing off aircraft from one off Window cloud.
Nov.	(Monica)	Flensburg		Airborne radar receiver which picked up Monica signals.
Dec.	Dartboard		N	Jamming of Stuttgart radio station which gave musical code instructions to German fighters.
1944 Jan.	Drumstick		N	Ground transmitters sending meaningless Morse signals to jam German efforts to communicate ground to air by Morse.
Jan.	Oboe			Oboe converted to centimetric wavelength.
Jan.	(H$_2$S)	Naxos		Airborne radar receiver which picked up H$_2$S emissions.
April		Jagdschloss		Ground radar transmitter operating on four separate frequencies. Range of 90 miles.
April		Egon		Ground-to-air fighter guidance system. Range of 125 miles.
Aug.	Jostle IV			Improved ABC. Blotted out whole spread of frequencies simultaneously instead of one at a time.
Sept.	Window	(SN-2)		Correct-sized Window strips to blot out SN-2.

| Date enters service | Device | | Night or day | Function |
	Allied	German		
Oct.	Serrate IV	(SN-2)		Modified Serrate which could home in on SN-2 transmissions.
Oct.	Perfectos			Airborne transmitter-receiver which activated German aircraft's identification set and displayed latter's transmissions, thus giving direction and distance of enemy.
Oct.	Piperack	(SN-2)		Airborne transmitter to jam SN-2.
Dec.	Micro-H			American alternative to Gee should latter ever be jammed.

PART THREE

'NO MORE MANOEUVRE'
The Mediterranean 1940–45

'In planning the operation let us avoid as far as we can the slow ponderosity which is apt to characterise British operations . . . I do wish to make certain that if a big opportunity occurs we are prepared morally, mentally and administratively to use it to the fullest.'

General Archibald Wavell, September and November 1940

'. . . the British based their planning on the principle of exact calculation, a principle which can be followed only where there is complete material superiority. They actually undertook no operations but relied simply and solely on the effect of their artillery and air force. Their command was as slow as ever in reacting.'

Field Marshal Erwin Rommel, November 1942

5

The North African See-Saw
June 1940 – January 1943

When Mussolini declared war on Britain and France in June 1940, it seemed that brute force must surely triumph again in Africa just as it had in Ethiopia some four years earlier. In this latter country and in Libya the Italians now mustered 400,000 men, 460 tanks and 2,000 guns as against 84,000 British troops and proportionally smaller allocations of tanks and guns. In the Mediterranean theatre as a whole the Italians could call upon well over 5,000 aircraft and the British less than 400, whilst even naval strengths, after the French surrender, were hardly in the Royal Navy's favour. Battleships were more or less even, and the British had two aircraft carriers to the Italians' none, but there was a deficit of 11 cruisers, 94 destroyers and 90 submarines. So when the Italian advance into Egypt began, in September 1940, it seemed that they must be able simply to rumble over the defenders, just as they had over the tiny garrisons in Sudan and Somaliland in the preceding two months.

In fact, the Italian offensive very soon ground to a halt and its commander-in-chief, General Graziani, simply sat there waiting for a British counter-attack. This duly came in December, and in the ensuing eight weeks General Richard O'Connor's Western Desert Force,* with only 36,000 men, completely smashed the Italians. They were driven right back from the Egyptian frontier to within striking distance of Tripoli, in the process losing 130,000 prisoners-of-war, 380 tanks and 845 guns. Commonwealth casualties were only 500

---

* Western Desert Force became XIII Corps on 1 January 1941, the latter becoming part of a newly created Eighth Army on 26 September 1941.

dead and 1,400 wounded.* By any standards the victory was a remarkable one, and full credit must go to O'Connor.† Indeed, this whole campaign would find no place in an account of the Second World War that stresses the element of brute force were it not for the fact that it does provide a useful cautionary footnote, reminding us that on occasion even a seemingly overwhelming paper strength can be vitiated, in this case by completely inadequate command structure, hopeless administration and obsolete equipment.

In 1939, in fact, Count Ciano, the Italian Foreign Minister, had already written a suitable obituary for the Italian armed forces when he gloomily noted in his diary that there had been 'much bluff in the military sector, and they have fooled even the Duce himself; but it has been a tragic sort of bluff.'[1] Thus, of the 73 army divisions raised by June 1940 only 24 were in any way complete or ready for combat. Even these were badly equipped and the overall commander-in-chief in Libya in early 1940, Air Marshal Balbo, told Mussolini that the units were 'equipped with limited

---

* Despite the unfamiliarity of the term, I have used hereafter the word 'Commonwealth' rather than 'British' to describe Allied forces in the Middle East (although I generally refer to 'British' generalship and 'British' armour). Whilst the latter word might be technically correct, in so far as South African, Australian and New Zealand forces willingly subordinated themselves to supreme British command (the Indians had little option), it grotesquely misrepresents the enormous contribution of the Dominions and the Empire in this theatre. The following table shows the importance of their contingents to Western Desert Force and Eighth Army's front-line strength, measured in divisions. (They were also heavily represented in Ninth and Tenth Armies in Syria and the Levant and supplied other units in Egypt, Palestine, Sudan, Cyprus, Aden and Malta.)

Date	GB	India*	NZ	Austr.	SA	Total non-GB†
Dec. 1940	1	1	-	1	-	2
June 1940	1	1	-	-	-	1
March 1941	1	-	-	1	-	1
Nov. 1941	$2\frac{2}{3}$	1	1	-	$2\frac{1}{3}$	$4\frac{1}{3}$
Jan. 1942	$1\frac{1}{3}$	1	-	-	-	1
May 1942	$3\frac{2}{3}$	$1\frac{2}{3}$	-	-	2	$3\frac{2}{3}$
July 1942	$3\frac{2}{3}$	$1\frac{2}{3}$	1	1	1	$4\frac{2}{3}$
Oct. 1942	$6\frac{2}{3}$	-	1	1	1	3

  * One third of an Indian division's infrantry were British battalions.
  † A polish and a Free French Brigade also figures prominently in Eighth
  Army's orders of battle. They are not, however, included in these totals.

† O'Connor was also ably supported by General Archibald Wavell, the Commander-in-Chief Middle East, and shrewdly advised by General Eric Dorman-Smith, who helped him plan the attack.

and very old pieces of artillery [and were] almost lacking in anti-tank and anti-aircraft weapons . . . It is useless to send thousands more men if we cannot supply them with the indispensable requirements to move and fight.'[2] The tanks were yet another cause for concern, most of them being armed only with a small machine-gun and being so lightly armoured that they could be knocked out by the notorious Boys anti-tank rifle. The few heavier tanks available carried no radio – hardly conducive to orderly manoeuvre and fire control – and their engines dangerously overheated after only fifteen minutes' running. When the Germans arrived in the desert they referred to them as *rollende Särge*, or self-propelled coffins. Italian aircraft were yet another liability, with only a tiny fraction of the massive paper strength of the *Regia Aeronautica* actually being fit for combat. Most of these, moreover, whether because of their slow speed, extreme instability in rough air or engines totally unattuned to desert conditions, were no match for enemy planes. The problems with the engines were compounded by the Italians' scant regard for providing repair facilities or a steady flow of spare parts, and at any one time a high proportion of available aircraft were unserviceable.

The Italian command structure was also a terrible handicap. The problem started right at the top, for Mussolini did much to nullify what should have been Italy's greatest military asset, her Navy. The *Duce* quite clearly went to war convinced that all the military spadework had already been done by the Germans and fully expecting that the British Empire was on the verge of collapse. So from the very beginning of his military adventure he was looking for an imminent peace settlement and was therefore determined that his supremacy in the Mediterranean could be backed up by a strong fleet *in being*, not one decimated in any sacrificial last fling by the British Mediterranean Fleet. Even after the abandonment of Operation Sea Lion, faith in eventual victory persisted. Mussolini, therefore, remained loath to hazard his one really substantial military chip, and throughout the war the Italian Fleet was to be gripped by an almost complete 'paralysis of will' that kept its main units in harbour for months on end and steadily eroded both their technical competence and their self-confidence.[3] The extent of this erosion is amply illustrated by the *Regia Aeronautica*'s contention that 'not a single shot fired from . . . [the] vastly expensive battleships ever hit the enemy vessel during the entire war' and by the incontrovertible fact that the guns of the entire surface

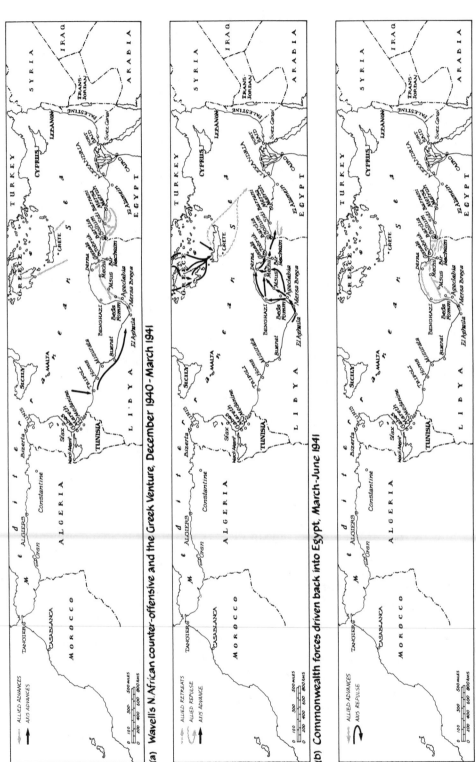

(a) Wavell's N. African counter-offensive and the Greek Venture, December 1940 - March 1941

(b) Commonwealth forces driven back into Egypt, March-June 1941

(c) The Reconquest of Cyrenaica, November 1941- January 1942

(d) Eighth Army pushed back into Egypt, January-September 1942

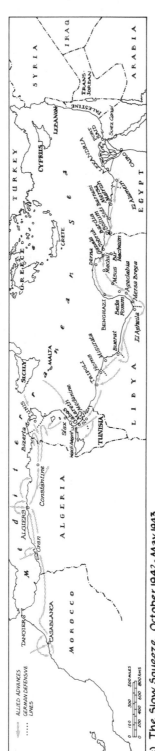

(e) The Slow Squeeze, October 1942-May 1943

MAP 4   The North African Campaign 13 December 1940–12 May 1943

fleet only ever sank three ships, in June 1942, during the Battle of Pantelleria.[4]*

But whether Italian naval commanders would have proved themselves particularly competent remains open to doubt, for it is certainly true that in the army the only glimmer of ability shown by a senior commander was that displayed by General Messe in his dour defensive battles in Tunisia in early 1943. In the army, indeed, the rot went much further down the hierarchy. Brave as many Italian officers might have been, they were not the model of the wartime regimental officer, being particularly averse to mixing with the men during drill or training sessions. Nor could they off-load these duties on to a reliable body of seasoned NCOs. Perhaps one of the most revealing statistics about the Italian Army in the Second World War is that in June 1940 the ratio of NCOs to private soldiers was 1:33, whilst in a more balanced force, in this case the US Army in 1945, the ratio was 1:2. In these circumstances, adequate combat training, even in the most basic principles of fire and movement, was out of the question and a typical level of tactical expertise was that witnessed at Ghirba, in December 1940, by the commander of the 11 Hussars, who 'saw something which beggared description, for the Italians had reverted to the tactics of the past by forming square with their infantry in the open plain, their tanks in the centre and their guns at the corners; tactics designed, in the past, for tribal warfare . . .'[5] The square was duly shot to pieces. Equipped, organised and commanded as they were, Mussolini's new legions were about as effective on the modern battlefield as would have been those of Scipio Africanus himself.

After completing the rout of the Italians in Cyrenaica (eastern Libya) at Beda Fomm, in early February 1941, O'Connor stood poised to press on to Tripoli, thence to effect a possible link-up with French forces in Tunisia and completely eliminate the Italian

---

* It should be borne in mind, however, that the Italian Navy had other weapons in its arsenal, notably mines and torpedoes, and the total number of British ships sunk in the Mediterranean by all naval weapons was not inconsiderable. The actual figure was 132, or 56 per cent of all Royal Navy vessels sunk in this theatre (up to September 1943). However, only occasionally were these losses more than a chronic irritation to the British, and the fact remains that only a much more vigorous deployment of the Italian surface fleet, particularly in the opening months, could have offered the possibility of completely subduing the British naval presence.

presence in North Africa.* But the strategic fruits of O'Connor's splendid victory were to remain unplucked. Wavell was very wary of such a bold stroke as the one proposed by O'Connor and remained reluctant actually to sanction it. Whether he would have eventually accepted the desirability of a renewed advance remains unclear, and is in the end irrelevant, for higher authority had already decreed that he was not to have the means. Ever since October 1940, when Mussolini had made another of his predatory forays, this time into Greece, Churchill had shown a strange enthusiasm for the cause of this distant ally. The Greeks themselves were the more realistic, and persistently refused offers of substantial military aid, realising that a major British presence in the Balkans might well provoke German intervention. The fate of the BEF had not made them sanguine about British ability to parry such a move. But Churchill was no easy suitor to rebuff and, convinced that the Greeks would eventually acquiesce, he formally instructed Wavell, on 10 February 1941, that he was to keep a potential expeditionary force available. Any thoughts of further advances in Libya were thus out of the question. XIII Corps HQ was broken up, and the forces guarding the recent Commonwealth conquests were run down to a dangerous extent. The seasoned divisions that had fought with O'Connor were posted elsewhere and replaced with a hotchpotch of inexperienced Brigades.†

Churchill's *ideé fixe* was to have tragic consequences. On 22 February the Greeks reluctantly agreed to accept a large Commonwealth reinforcement, and the first convoy sailed on 5 March. Barely were they in position when Hitler made the expected response and on 6 April sent his divisions slashing through Yugoslavia and Greece. Belgrade surrendered on 12 April, whilst between the 9th and the 18th the Commonwealth forces were successively bundled out of the Aliakmon and Olympus positions. On the 19th Commonwealth commanders agreed that evacuation was their only option, the first troops actually leaving on the 24th. Many of those lifted off were shipped to Crete, occupied by the Allies since October 1940, and there they were destined to be humiliated once more. On 20 May German airborne forces suddenly descended and within a week a Commonwealth evacuation was once again the order of the day. This

* There were still six Italian divisions intact in Tripolitania (W. Libya) in February 1941.
† Three divisions had fought with O'Connor: 7 Armoured, 4 Indian and 6 Australian. The latter took part in the Greek débâcle.

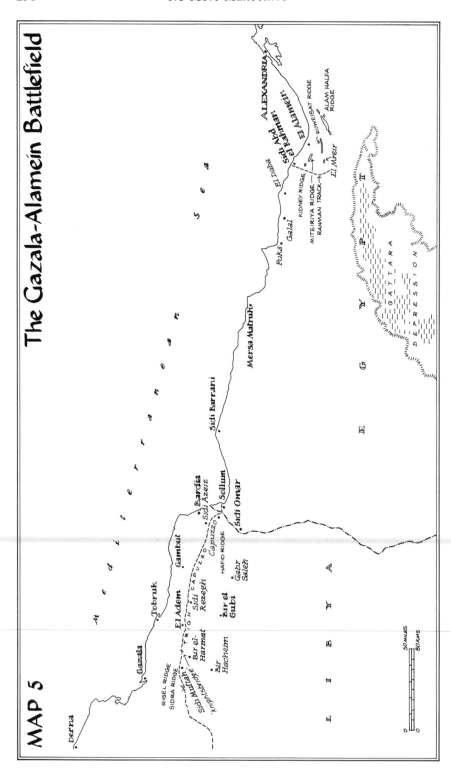

MAP 5

The Gazala-Alamein Battlefield

was completed by 1 June, but in under two months the Germans had exacted a heavy toll on the Allies: 24,000 killed and missing, heavy naval losses including three cruisers and eight destroyers, enormous losses of military equipment, and a massive dent in the self-confidence of the commanders.

But there were other yet more serious consequences of the ill-judged Greek venture. For, in turning his back on any further advance into Tripolitania, Churchill had given the Axis a valuable breathing space. Although the Italians themselves were probably in too much disarray to have benefited from no matter how long a lull in operations, Hitler too was now looking anxiously to the Libyan front, fearful of a hostile presence on the frontiers of Vichy North Africa. But the British concentration in the eastern Mediterranean, he realised, offered an opportunity to ship over a stiffening of German veterans to help Graziani hang on in Tripolitania.* He had considered doing this in mid-January but had been dissuaded when one of his liaison officers gloomily reported that the fall of Tripoli, the only feasible disembarkation point, could not be long delayed. But once it became clear that the British had no intention of advancing this far, Hitler resurrected the idea. On 2 February he offered Mussolini the services of a German division and on the 14th, the offer having been quickly accepted, General Rommel arrived in Tripoli, followed on the next day by leading elements of 5 Light Division. At the end of May he was also to be joined by 15 Panzer Division.†

From the outset Rommel was not prepared to accept a purely defensive brief in Tripolitania, and he soon set about gathering intelligence about enemy dispositions, with a view to launching a speedy offensive of his own if at all possible. Finding the Commonwealth forces spread remarkably thinly, he flew to Berlin on 19 March to seek permission for an attempt to recapture the whole of Cyrenaica. This was refused. Rommel was instructed not to advance beyond El Agheila, and even that was only to be undertaken after 15 Panzer Division had arrived. Berlin's aversion to piecemeal attacks seems

---

* Graziani was soon to be replaced by General Italo Gariboldi.
† 5 Light Division was a rather *ad hoc* formation built around 5 Panzer Regiment, originally part of 3 Panzer Division. It also included two machine-gun battalions, a reconnaissance battalion and two Panzer-Jäger detachments. 15 Panzer Division was a more orthodox formation, though both divisions were to be short of two tank companies right through until the spring of 1942. The two divisions combined were to be known as the *Deutsche Afrika Korps* (DAK).

quite understandable, though in fact Commonwealth forces were even more vulnerable than Rommel had described them. They totalled just four raw infantry and motor brigades and an armoured brigade with only 80 tanks, two-thirds of which were light or captured Italian models. These troops were disposed between Mersa Brega/El Agheila and Tobruk/El Adem.

But it is doubtful whether anything but an absolutely clear-cut Commonwealth superiority could have dented Rommel's boundless self-confidence. The French campaign had convinced him that he and his troops were masters of mobile warfare and the British generals mere dunces,* whilst his flights over his new desert playground had revealed a setting in which his methods could be given the freest rein. Ignoring the strictures of his superiors he moved on El Agheila on 24 March and, encountering no opposition of any consequence, pushed on to Mersa Brega on the 31st. There the difference between O'Connor's seasoned forces and their callow replacements became all too apparent. In the kind of muddle that was to characterise the next 15 months' fighting, the Armoured Brigade failed to intervene against a strong attack on its support group and both formations were compelled to withdraw.

Thenceforth Rommel's progress was a virtual re-run of O'Connor's offensive. The latter's basic method of offsetting his complete numerical inferiority had been neatly summed up in his dictum 'offensive action wherever possible', and it now served as an admirable motto for Rommel's counter-offensive. But this time it was British commanders who were completely overwhelmed by their adversaries' remarkable mobility and their ceaseless attempts to filter men and machines through any weak point along the front. Australian troops along the coast road were given no opportunity to turn and stand and had to give up Benghazi and Derna. The British armour drew back pell-mell towards Mechili, with German columns lapping around both its flanks. The Indian Motor Brigade was sent forward from El Adem to help make a stand at Mechili, but by 6 April the whole force was surrounded and two days later had no option but to surrender.

Soon, the only Commonwealth bastion left in Cyrenaica was Tobruk, though by 12 April it was completely isolated as the DAK swept past and seized El Adem and Bardia. The bemused British commanders could only scrape together weak reinforcements

---

* Rommel seems to have ascribed the Italians' defeat wholly to the deficiencies of their own forces. O'Connor, rightly as it turned out, does not seem to have been regarded as the harbinger of a renaissance in British generalship as a whole.

to make a stand along the Egyptian frontier. Happily for them, however, Tobruk was a potential thorn in Rommel's side, for it possessed a harbour of sorts, which meant that Commonwealth forces could be reinforced by sea. Should Tobruk be bypassed and the main German forces press forward into Egypt, a reinforced garrison might well debouch across Rommel's over-extended supply line from Tripoli. Likewise, to capture Tobruk would give him the opportunity to shorten this same supply line. Rommel thus felt he had to try to storm Tobruk and fight the very kind of dour positional battle, with no opportunity for outflanking, at which his opponents were past masters. Two major attacks in April and May failed. A protracted siege was now the only course open, and any vague notions Rommel might have had of exploiting eastwards from Halfaya Pass, which he seized towards the end of May, were scotched by Halder and the OKH. Unhappy at the way their earlier instructions had been ignored when a limited raid had turned into a full-blooded offensive, they ordered Rommel to concentrate his scattered forces at Sollum and adopt a defensive posture.

But a passive Rommel was a no less formidable opponent, as Wavell was to find out in June, when Churchill chivvied and bullied him into trying to repeat O'Connor's successes. For the new operation, codenamed Battleaxe, the old team of 7 Armoured Division and 4 Indian Division was reassembled* and a convoy of tanks, including 135 heavy Matildas, was dispatched to Alexandria. This armoured reinforcement seemed to give the Commonwealth forces a considerable advantage, as they were able to start the offensive with 180 heavy and medium tanks as against only 95 German mediums.† They had also contrived to deploy adequate air cover, having 105 bombers and 98 fighters serviceable in the desert as against 84 and 130 comparable Axis aircraft. Almost half of the latter were Italian models.

But it was the 2:1 superiority in medium/heavy tanks that should have provided the decisive edge. For there was no particular difference in the quality of weaponry. The German mediums, mainly Panzer III Ausf. Gs and Panzer IV Ausf. Ds, were not very heavily armoured, less in fact than the British Crusader Is and Matildas,

---

* Though without O'Connor, who had been captured on 7 April. He later escaped and commanded VIII Corps in North-West Europe.

† No Italian tanks were present. The Germans also had some 80 light Panzers I and II, but these were as vulnerable as Italian tanks to all British tank and anti-tank weapons.

and were both vulnerable to the fire of the 2pdr tank and anti-tank guns and the 25pdr field guns.* This latter fact had been sharply brought home to Rommel during his second assault on Tobruk, in May, when 17 out of 38 tanks were lost in one attack. Indeed, it was probably this costly rebuff that prompted him to give more thought than had been customary to his own defensive tactics, and in the lull prior to Battleaxe he devoted considerable attention to the siting of his anti-tank guns, having them firmly dug in on any advantageous positions along his front. All in all he disposed of 155 such weapons: 89 37mm PAK 35s, 54 50mm PAK 38s, and 12 88mm FLAK 36s. The PAK 35 was of little use except at very close range, but the PAK 38 was very much the master of the Crusader whilst the FLAK 36, the notorious '88', was superior to any tank, including the hitherto invulnerable Matilda.†

But the mere existence of effective anti-tank guns, even in well sited forward positions, was no cast-iron guarantee of German success. Indeed, the very fact that they were placed well forward made them potentially very vulnerable to counter-fire from Commonwealth guns. Unfortunately, this counter-fire was not available. It could not be provided by the tanks themselves because no provision had been made for supplying them with High Explosive (HE) shells, the only effective ammunition for this kind of work. The shells existed, the QF 2pdr Armour-Piercing Mark I, 'but for reasons never satisfactorily explained, it seems to have seen little use; it was certainly never issued to tanks or anti-tank guns in the desert.'[6] The pernicious effects of this glaring oversight were multiplied by the further failure to provide the armour with any supporting HE fire. O'Connor's successes against the Italians, when the heavy Matildas were employed very aggressively further to undermine shaky Italian morale, had produced a doctrine that the tactical role of tanks was always to go in *before* the infantry when attacking fortified positions. But this also put them out of touch with the supporting field artillery, one of whose main tasks should have been to neutralise enemy gun positions. It had been possible to break this rule during O'Connor's offensive because the Italian guns were powerless against the Matildas, but Rommel's quota of 88s restored

---

* Details on the armour of the major tanks of the Second World War and the performance of their guns and of the anti-tank guns will be found in tables 61–2 in the Statistical Appendix.

† PAK is an abbreviation of *Panzerabwehrkanone* (anti-tank gun) and FLAK of *Fliegerabwehrkanone* (anti-aircraft gun).

the rule, whilst the medium Crusaders were equally vulnerable to the PAK 38s.

This stress upon the vanguard role of the tanks seems to have comprised the sum total of British armoured doctrine, amounting to little more than a series of gung-ho affirmations of the virtues of courage and dash best summed up in General W. H. E. Gott's vacuous advice, whilst commanding 7 Armoured Division: 'No tank commander will go far wrong if he places his gun within killing range of an enemy.'[7] Of the virtues of tactical cohesion within a unit, of the necessity to keep the whole of the armour concentrated, or of the desirability of close cooperation between the different arms, hardly anything at all was said.

The inadequacies of this archaic philosophy, discredited some five hundred years previously at Agincourt, were soon made manifest. The British attack, which opened on 15 June 1941, was made along three separate axes, each directed at the major German strongpoints along their front. On the right, an assault on Halfaya Pass was stopped in its tracks by 88s and minefields. Fifteen out of eighteen Matildas were accounted for. On the left, the Crusaders fared equally badly in front of Hafid Ridge. Attacking 'bald-headed', with absolutely no provision for artillery support, 7 Armoured Brigade was fought to a standstill, having incurred heavy losses.* In the centre, where Matildas faced PAK 35s and 38s only, there was better progress. The first strongpoint was overrun and 4 Armoured Brigade broke through to the German reserve line where a tolerably strong presence was established. Strong enough, in fact, to beat off a vigorous counter-attack next morning by 15 Panzer Division, in which the 2pdrs again acquitted themselves well, helping to account for 50 out of the 80 attacking tanks.

But British losses on the 15th had also been heavy, with only 100 tanks left fit for action by nightfall. Moreover, the failure to concentrate the surviving armour became more and more apparent. Instead of massing their forces for a concerted push out of the hard-won central bridgehead, or for a solid defence within it, British commanders allowed their forces to dissipate themselves along the whole front. The situation worsened on the 16th as 7 Armoured Brigade was itself broken up and pushed away to the south-west by 5 Light Division, which had been brought down from east of Tobruk.

---

* Quite a few of these were due to mechanical breakdown, though one is entitled to wonder how many tanks immobilised in this way were simply spared being shot up further forward.

The gap between the two armoured brigades widened, and into it Rommel threw the depleted 15 Panzer, which suddenly threatened to encircle both the forces in the centre and at Halfaya and pin them against the coast. The danger became yet more acute with the growing disarray of 7 Armoured Brigade, and 5 Light seemed poised to add an outer ring of outflanking armour to close the trap yet more securely. By midday on the 16th, Wavell, who had flown in from Cairo, had sanctioned a withdrawal. Battleaxe had failed, having, in the words of one staff-officer, 'achieved just about as much as that ancient weapon would have done if used in a modern battle.'[8]

The same officer goes on to lay the blame for the defeat on 'obsolete' tanks and the 2pdr 'pop-gun', but it is worth emphasising that the defeat was only prevented from becoming a rout by a sterling rearguard action by 4 Armoured Brigade who, during the afternoon of the 16th, using 'the armour of their Matildas [and] their 2-pounder guns . . . were a match for the superior strength of the two German armoured divisions when unsupported by their 88s.'[9] The real fault had not been inadequate armament but rather a blind faith in its limitless abilities, with no regard to the possible advantages of working closely with other arms, and a complete failure to think through the armoured division's proper role as a compact *masse de manoeuvre*, held in check until the decisive moment, rather than as an unruly mob of latter-day *chevaliers*.

There would, of course, be some justice in the counter-claim that 7 Armoured Division did not really know what to expect from the German anti-tank guns, having hitherto faced only Italian gunners over whom they were able to rumble with impunity. Unfortunately, once they had learned what to expect, the experience provoked hardly any pause for thought, at any level of command. A few commanders were dismissed and a few armoured warfare specialists on Eighth Army staff produced cogent memoranda and pertinent recommendations. But none of these were taken up by officers in authority and 'untrained British tank units continued to career light-heartedly about Cyrenaica in November and December 1941, making gallant charges against anti-tank screens and built-in positions, disdaining the assistance of the artillery, and looking with aristocratic distaste on any intrusion into the tangled affairs of the infantry.'[10]

The events of November and December 1941 alluded to made up Operation Crusader, a second attempt by the British high command to relieve the still-beleaguered Tobruk garrison and if possible drive Rommel out of Cyrenaica. The operation was orchestrated by General Sir Alan Cunningham, commander of the newly formed Eighth Army, and General Sir Claude Auchinleck, who had replaced Wavell as C.-in-C. Middle East. In essence, Cunningham's plan involved a holding attack along the coast, to pin the Axis forces holding the Sidi Omar–Bardia line, and an armoured thrust further inland towards Sidi Rezegh, to bring to battle the DAK which was concentrated between Tobruk and Bardia.* Only after the latter had been destroyed would the siege lines around Tobruk be assaulted, the garrison there staging a break-out attack of their own. The plan had merit, particularly in that it recognised that Rommel always tried to use his armour *en masse* and would therefore have to be engaged by similarly concentrated British formations. To this end Cunningham established a corps headquarters, the XXXth, with special responsibility for coordinating the armour.

Nor was there any stint in the number of tanks provided, comprising five armoured brigades in all. These gave Eighth Army a considerable superiority over Rommel, there being 339 medium tanks and 199 heavies at the front as against 174 German mediums and 146 Italian.† And one must again emphasise that there was not the marked qualitative disparity between British and German armour that certain sources have suggested. For the most part the German mediums were the trusty Panzer III Ausf. G and Panzer IV Ausf. D. The former had a short 50mm gun whose penetration at ranges below 1,000 yards was inferior to that of the 2pdr, whilst the latter's armour-piercing (AP) capabilities were so mediocre that it usually employed HE only. Nor was either particularly well armoured, the IV being, in the words of a contemporary training memorandum, 'completely vulnerable to the British 2pdr'. Tanks of both types had already been knocked out in considerable numbers and 'as usual, the myth of German invincibility of material, when submitted to the cold light of engineering fact, makes a very sorry exhibition.'[11] In other words, Eighth Army was taking on the same types of tank that it had

---

* Since 15 August 1941 the Afrika Korps had become part of a large formation, Panzer Group Afrika, which also included an Italian infantry and a motorised corps. On 27 November 1941 another German division, 90 Light, was attached to the Panzer Group, though not as part of the Afrika Korps. Rommel commanded the Panzer Group and General Ludwig Crüwell the DAK.

† 129 miscellaneous Cruiser tanks, 210 Crusaders, 134 Matildas and 65 of the new Valentine 'Infantry' tanks as against 139 Pz IIIs and 35 Pz Ivs. Eighth Army had in addition 173 Stuart light tanks, which were perfectly capable of taking on the Italian mediums and DAK's additional 70 Pz IIs.

faced during Battleaxe, though this time with considerably increased numerical superiority (538 versus 174 if one concedes that the Italian tanks should be lumped with the light Stuarts and Panzer IIs), and with a laudable intent to fight a concentrated armoured battle.*

In certain other respects, however, the Germans did have an appreciable edge. One was their anti-tank arsenal which, though hardly any larger than during Battleaxe, was now largely rid of the feeble PAK 35s and contained double the number of 88s and three times as many PAK 38s. The artillery had been similarly up-gunned, now including a powerful siege-train, ostensibly for the reduction of Tobruk, made up of nine 210mm, 38 150mm and 12 105mm howitzers. Rommel 'personally controlled its deployment from time to time, and it provided him with a mass of fire-power which the British would not begin to equal until the conflicts of July 1942.'[12] This powerful long-range force was also admirably supplemented at shorter distances by the Panzer IVs which, because of their thin armour and feeble AP ability, were kept out of tank-vs.-tank battles and used to saturate concentrations of enemy guns with HE. As this could be done at ranges up to 3,000 yards, the ability of the 2pdrs and 25pdrs to engage enemy armour was considerably impaired.

But the most serious Allied deficiencies, with regard to the handling of both the artillery and the armour, were their own tactics. The effectiveness of their tanks was especially vitiated, on both the technological and the tactical level. On the former, one regiment found that if the 2pdr tank guns were sighted according to the Tank Gunnery textbook, then a shot fired at a target 1,000 yards away would fall 300 yards short. This crucial piece of information was passed on to higher headquarters but seems to have been disseminated to very few other units. The rest 'were no doubt responsible for the legend that the effective range of the 2-pounder was no more than 600 yards . . .'[13]

The armour's major fault, however, was the lamentable tactical and operational control exercised over it by Eighth Army. On the operational level, despite the explicit commitment in the Crusader plans to maintain a unified armoured corps, the three armoured brigades therein (forming 7 Armoured Division) only once operated in close conjunction, when they crossed the Egyptian frontier south

* The Pz III Ausf. H and Pz IV Ausf. E, up-armoured models of each Mark that figure in some discussions of the Crusader fighting, did not arrive in Africa until 19 December, when the major battle had already been fought. And even then they arrived in very small numbers.

of Sidi Omar on the first day of the battle, 18 November 1941. Thereafter they never functioned as a cohesive force again, and as early as the second day only a single brigade was sent along the main axis of advance, towards Sidi Rezegh and Tobruk. The Germans, on the other hand, almost always kept their armour concentrated and Crüwell's Afrika Korps was able to deal a whole succession of fierce blows against the scattered brigades, and often against their equally dispersed sub-units. 4 Armoured Brigade was hit in this way at Gabr Saleh on 19 November and again on the 20th. By the time another brigade arrived to lend assistance the Germans had already withdrawn. On the 21st, 7 Armoured Brigade was the target, around Sidi Rezegh, and was at one stage reduced to only 11 tanks fit for action. Again, when the other brigades did arrive on the scene they were of little assistance, one never making real contact with the enemy and the other barging straight into an anti-tank screen.

On the 22nd, the Germans rather dropped their guard, when Rommel and Crüwell disagreed about the DAK's next move and compromised by splitting its two divisions. Eighth Army, on the other hand, still had all its brigades in the vicinity of Sidi Rezegh, facing 21 Panzer Division alone. But when the British tanks attacked it was in extraordinarily piecemeal fashion, one attack having run out of momentum before the next was launched. In this way 22 Armoured Brigade lost over 40 tanks before 4 Brigade intervened at all, and when two of the latter's regiments did arrive the Germans simply withdrew. But the third of 4 Armoured Brigade's regiments had been left behind to protect Brigade headquarters, and as evening fell it was hit in the rear by 15 Panzer, moving in from the east to assist its sister division. The lone regiment, 8 Hussars, was completely overrun, surrendering 40 tanks and the whole of Brigade headquarters. The brigade, the only sizeable formation left in 7 Armoured Division, had been decapitated and was completely incapable of intervening in the battle for the next 24 hours.

The fate of XXX Corps was now sealed. On the 23rd, his armour reunited once again, Crüwell swept down into the flank of the South African forces marching up from Bir el Gubi, and completely destroyed 5 South African Infantry Brigade, as well as inflicting more casualties on the remnants of 7 and 22 Armoured Brigades. The latter was now in an even more parlous condition than the former, having no more than ten runners left at the end of the day. The 450 tanks of 7 Armoured Division that had rumbled across the frontier six days ago were now reduced to less than 130, the majority of these without any central coordination.

Clearly, then, the operational handling of this division had hardly been impressive. A German participant in these battles, General Fritz Bayerlein, observed: 'The British obliged us by throwing their armoured brigades into the battle in separate units. This enabled us to gain a series of partial successes, and eventually led to a victory in one of the greatest armoured battles of the campaign.'[14] A recent British historian has been less polite, stating that 'the conduct of the armoured battle, even resisting every temptation to indulge in hindsight and pass judgement from the safety of a desk, can only be described as excruciating.'[15]

But this fatal penchant for dispersion had also been all too evident at the tactical level, and time and again the impact of the armour had been minimised by further fragmenting the brigades themselves and by sending the tanks in alone, unsupported by either infantry or artillery. For Eighth Army's commanders had still not grasped the fact that tanks were not self-sufficient on the battlefield, that they required intimate infantry support to hold any ground captured and even closer artillery support to break up the screens of anti-tank guns that were always to be found in the vanguard of the panzer divisions. As another German participant wrote:

> . . . our high-velocity 50mm anti-tank gun . . . batteries . . . always accompanied our tanks in action. Our field artillery, also, was trained to co-operate with the panzers. In short, a German panzer division was a highly flexible formation *of all arms*, which always relied on artillery in attack and defence. In contrast the British regarded the anti-tank gun as a defensive weapon, and they failed to make adequate use of their powerful field artillery, which should have been taught to eliminate our anti-tank guns.[16]

This lack of all-arms support had been particularly evident in the initial thrust to Sidi Rezegh by 7 Armoured Brigade which was vitiated by its totally inadequate infantry and artillery component, and was thus unable to seize the escarpments to the north and prevent the Germans digging in their powerful siege-train on commanding ground. The lack was equally felt during 22 Armoured Brigade's attack against Bir el Gubi, which ran straight into powerful anti-tank gun positions. The lack of infantry support meant that Italians who gave themselves up found no one to accept their surrender and actually went back to their anti-tank guns when the Brigade withdrew and fired on the departing tanks. 4 Armoured Brigade was just as feebly supported at Gabr Saleh. When they turned to face the attack by 21 Panzer, the latter with all its guns well forward, they could call on only 12 25pdrs and 4 2pdrs – 'a pathetic admission' according to one senior observer.[17] The belief in the absolute autonomy of the armour reached lunatic proportions on the 20th, when the DAK thrust once again against Gabr Saleh. The New Zealand Infantry Division, static to the south-west of Sidi Omar, offered to lend some of its own infantry and heavy Valentine tanks to 4 Armoured Brigade but the offer was politely declined. For 'armoured theory in Egypt was dominated . . . by the doctrine that armour should be left to fight its own battles without calling in the pedestrian assistance of an infantry division.'[18]

The armour persisted in these suicidal tactics throughout the Sidi Rezegh fighting. On the morning of the 21st, 6 RTR charged straight into an emplacement of 88s and suffered heavy losses without gaining any ground. During the afternoon 2 RTR, with no supporting guns whatsoever, was engaged by 15 Panzer and by the evening had only six tanks fit for action. An exactly similar fate befell 22 Armoured Brigade on the next day when, having finally arrived on the Sidi Rezegh battlefield, it was thrown in against the German anti-tank guns and decisively repulsed in the approved manner. According to one participant, when his unit arrived on the battlefield

> nobody seemed to have much idea of what was going on and we milled around for a bit. Just about that time . . . [an officer] came running up in a car, shouted over 'Follow me' and we chased after him for about half a mile . . . and there we were – a long line of Mark IIIs and fifty millimetre anti-tank guns, so we went to town on them. We pulled out to get some ammo . . . and [then] it was decided to give them the good old charge again. Quite frankly, I was not so strong for this charging business . . . but off we went. We went storming in right up to those tanks, firing as we went . . .[19]

Given this abject failure on the part of the British armour, it comes as something of a surprise to learn that within two weeks Rommel had himself admitted defeat in this battle on the frontier and had started a retreat that only ended at El Agheila, some 550 miles to the west. The reasons for this, albeit somewhat prosaic, are of fundamental importance to an understanding of the war in the desert. The key word is logistics.

At the start of Crusader, as we know, Eighth Army had a considerable superiority in tanks – three times as many mediums and heavies – but what should also be realised is that there were a further 216 medium, 129 heavy and 150 light tanks held in reserve, either back in Egypt or in transit to the front, from where they were to be fed into the battle at the rate of 40 a day. Rommel had no equivalent reserve. No tanks at all had arrived in Africa since June 1941, and when the battle began he had at most 50 extra machines behind the front, all of them in the workshops. Unless, therefore, he was able *completely* to destroy 7 Armoured Division, leaving it without even intact cadres to absorb replacement tanks, he faced a virtually impossible task. For Eighth Army would be able to lose medium and heavy tanks at the rate of four to every one German and *still* maintain a four to one superiority in these types. And, of course, even at such a favourable rate of exchange for the Germans, Rommel was much sooner in danger of not having enough tanks left to force a meaningful strategic decision.

By 23 November he was already approaching that point. To date British losses had been dreadful, upwards of 400 in 7 Armoured Division alone, but Rommel, too, had lost 160, leaving the DAK with only 90 runners.* With no immediate replacements in sight, at least not in any number, he was caught in a dilemma. Should he attempt to complete the destruction of 7 Armoured Division, and possibly incur further casualties that might ruin his chances of exploiting his victory,† or should he attempt that exploitation immediately, using his surviving armour to sweep round the flank of XIII Corps and cut off the whole of Eighth Army from its Egyptian communications? He chose the latter course, and over the next few days inflicted heavy losses on the Commonwealth forces as he fought his way to the frontier wire. But his own losses were far from insignificant and the turn-around in his workshops, fast as it was, was not sufficient to prevent a steady erosion of his front-line strength. On 25 November Rommel mustered 67 German tanks of all types but by 2 December his strength had been almost halved, to 34

---

* It is of interest that in the Panzer Regiment for which figures are available, 15 out of the 17 tank casualties on the 22nd were due to enemy artillery. The 2pdr had once again proved itself to be a far from negligible weapon.
† He had every reason to anticipate heavy losses. On the 23rd alone, when he was winning his greatest success, 72 tanks were put out of action.

tanks of all types. Throughout this period Eighth Army contrived to squander its tanks in a most profligate fashion, but it always retained a rump of between 120 and 160 machines, quite enough to offset even Rommel's tactical expertise.

Nor were Rommel's logistical problems simply a matter of the lack of tank replacements. By 2 December he had lost not only 120 Panzer IIIs and IVs but also eight 88mm and fourteen 50mm guns, as well as 60 mortars, 24 field guns, ten heavy guns and 390 lorries. Moreover, there seemed little prospect of these items being replaced, nor even of there being sufficient fuel or ammunition to supply those that remained.* Rommel felt that 'the situation was very grave . . . [His] greatest anxiety was the question of ammunition, the existing stocks of which he considered quite inadequate for a battle . . . The danger of having to surrender for lack of ammunition was very real.'[20]

On the night of 7/8 December, therefore, the DAK began to withdraw from the frontier. The siege of Tobruk was also abandoned, Rommel having determined to pull back to a line running south from Gazala. Many in the German divisions wondered whether the decision had not been taken too late, but in the event the Commonwealth forces showed little enthusiasm for a vigorous pursuit. Thus, in the words of Bayerlein, 'withdrawing a step at a time, fighting isolated and sometimes very troublesome actions as they went, all troops reached the Gazala line by the 12th December, without the enemy having succeeded, during the withdrawal, in cutting off any sizeable detachments of troops or inflicting any serious casualties.'[21] On the 13th the German armour, despite the best efforts of the repair teams, still comprised a mere 33 tanks, whilst Eighth Army had 200 tanks in the field. Convinced that it must attempt to repeat O'Connor's success by thrusting this force through Mechili and cutting him off in the Cyrenaican bulge, and given also, as he reported on the 13th, that 'the supply of arms and ammunition had completely dried up', Rommel decided to pull out of the Gazala line and fall back on Agedabia.[22] Again there were many of his own men who doubted that escape was possible. On 20 December, the commander of 90 Light Division told his staff: 'Nobody can see any escape. The

---

* Eighth Army was fairly untroubled by logistical worries. Its plentiful supply of tanks has already been mentioned, and figures on fuel offer another revealing comparison. During October 1941, when total Axis deliveries of fuel to Libya were 11,950 tons, Commonwealth forces in the Middle East consumed approximately 8,000 tons in simply running their lorries back and forth to establish advanced fuel dumps.

British outnumber us enormously. The puzzle is, why are they following us so slowly? Time and again they have enabled us to dodge encirclement.'[23]

In fact, the real crisis had already passed. On 19 December two convoys of tanks, 45 in all, had reached Benghazi and Tripoli, and once they were at the front Rommel had the wherewithal to consider striking back at his pursuers. The latter obligingly made his task fairly simple. No concerted armoured thrust of their own was ever made and the two attacks they did organise, in late December, broke down with heavy losses. In these attacks, 'British cavalry tradition again overcame common sense' and the armour was once more thrown in piecemeal and completely separated from its support arms.[24] Losses were heavy and the subsequent German counter-attack accounted for a further 70 British tanks for the loss of only 14 of their own. Early in January 1942 Rommel pulled back to El Agheila, confident at last of being able to make a determined stand, and perhaps more.

In Operation Crusader can be discerned most of the major themes of the rest of the desert war: first, that Rommel's options were terribly constrained by logistical difficulties; second, that the Commonwealth forces were much more generously and regularly supplied and could therefore field vastly superior numbers of men and equipment; third, that this superiority was wielded with a remarkable lack of operational and tactical flair, such that Commonwealth victories were largely attritional, gained by stubbornly trading off hardware until Rommel's holdings were virtually non-existent; fourth, that even when Axis forces were reduced to pitiful remnants, British generalship remained unequal to the task of actually finishing them off.

It was Rommel's logistical problems that were the fundamental cause of his defeat. After the war General Ludwig von Thoma, who at one stage commanded the DAK, commented: 'In modern, mobile warfare the tactics are not the main thing. The decisive factor is the organisation of one's resources – to maintain the momentum.' This the Axis was unable to achieve. Yet the reasons for its failure are not those commonly given in accounts of the war in Africa. A particularly misleading statement was that made by von Thoma himself, when he described a mission to Africa, in October 1940, to report on the possibility of sending military assistance to the Italians. After only a few days he had concluded that:

the supply problem was the decisive factor – not only because of the difficulties of the desert, but because of the British Navy's command of the Mediterranean. I said it would not be possible to maintain a large German Army there as well as the Italian Army. My conclusion was that, if a force was sent by us, it should be an armoured force. Nothing less than four armoured divisions would suffice to ensure success – and this, I calculated, was also the maximum that could be effectively maintained with supplies in an advance across the desert to the Nile valley . . . I said it could only be done by replacing the Italian troops with German. Large numbers could not be supplied . . .[25]

In fact, von Thoma was seriously underestimating the capacity of the Italian merchant marine. For despite losing a little over two million tons of merchant shipping to the Allied navy and air force during the war,[*] and despite the fact that an enormous proportion of the surviving tonnage was tied up in other duties,[†] the Italians still managed to keep up a remarkably steady flow of supplies to North Africa. The details are given in table 45 in the Statistical Appendix which shows that throughout the war they provided the forces in Africa with an average of 203,000 tons per quarter, only falling dramatically below this figure at the very beginning of the war, in the early winter of 1941–2, and at the very end of the Tunisian campaign when, as will be seen, Allied air power was utterly overwhelming.

Two hundred thousand tons of supplies per quarter is no mean allocation, being around 11,000 tons per day to be split, for most of the campaign, between something like a dozen divisions.[‡] Even granting that the total tonnage shipped over included most of the

---

[*] Though this represented a net loss of only 750,000 tons, as 1,224,470 tons were added during the war through salvage, construction and capture.

[†] Such as Italian coastal shipping, domestic shipping between the peninsula and Sicily, Sardinia and Corsica (from November 1942), shipping between the peninsula and Vichy North Africa bringing back vital fertilisers, and military traffic between Italy and Greece/Albania. On the latter route alone, between June 1940 and September 1943, 7,055 ships sailed in convoy as opposed to only 4,030 dispatched to Libya and Tunisia.

[‡] In November 1941 Panzer Group Africa consisted of 3 German and 7½ Italian divisions. In January 1942, when it became Panzer Army Africa, the tally was the same. In October 1942 the Panzer Army contained 3 German divisions, plus an anti-aircraft division and a parachute brigade, and 10 Italian divisions. In March 1943 Army Group Africa, combining 5 Panzer Army in Tunisia and 1st Italian Army from Libya, comprised 9 German divisions plus 2 Flak, and 6 Italian.

armoured fighting vehicles and motor transport for the divisions, a combined total of around 200,000 tons, and that such items are not usually included in a division's daily supply requirements, one is still talking of roughly 800 tons of supplies per division per day. Given that even the voracious US armoured divisions in North-West Europe required only 600 tons of supplies per day, including fuel, or that German divisions in Italy, albeit in a more static role, considered themselves well off with less than 300 tons per day, it does not seem that Panzer Group Africa was really scraping the barrel.*

But supplies reaching an African port were not of themselves a solution to Rommel's problems. Indeed, throughout the campaign, he and his subordinates never ceased to complain bitterly about the way the lack of fuel, ammunition, food and medical supplies was hamstringing their operations. Of the campaign as a whole, Rommel once wrote:

> The first essential condition for an army to be able to stand the strain of battle is an adequate stock of weapons, petrol and ammunition. In fact the battle is fought and decided by the Quartermaster before the shooting begins. The bravest men can do nothing without guns, the guns nothing without plenty of ammunition, and neither guns or ammunition are of much use in mobile warfare unless there are vehicles with sufficient petrol to haul them around. Maintenance must also be approximate, both in quantity and quality, to that available to the enemy . . . [One must also have] parity in the air . . . In our case . . . [none of these] conditions . . . were in the slightest degree fulfilled and we had to suffer the consequences.[26]

These sufferings began almost immediately. In May and early June 1941, Rommel had to content himself with laying siege to Tobruk because further pursuit of the Commonwealth forces was simply not possible: 'Unfortunately,' he wrote, 'our petrol stocks were badly depleted, and it was with some anxiety that we contemplated the coming British attack, for we knew that our moves would be decided more by the petrol gauge than by tactical requirements.'[27] Similar considerations were uppermost

---

* The fighting divisions were not, of course, the only Axis troops in North Africa. In summer 1942, for example, only 54,000 of the 146,000 Italian troops there were with the Panzer Army. Nevertheless, it is unlikely that these rear echelon formations placed a particularly heavy demand on ammunition, spare parts and the like. Food they did consume in large quantities, but then there is no record of front-line troops ever having starved to death.

in his mind in the aftermath of the Crusader battles when, as we have already seen, he was obliged to discontinue his offensive because of ammunition shortages. A few days later his subordinates were beginning to wonder whether even retreat was logistically feasible.

Supply problems continued to vitiate his tactical successes. On 21 January 1942 he repeated his offensive of the previous March when he again ripped through a denuded British front line.* The latter, with only one understrength corps forward, succumbed almost immediately and, having given up Benghazi on 29 January, pulled back to the Gazala Line. Fortunately for them Rommel then had to halt, once more for lack of supplies. 'I have never had victory so nearly within my grasp as I have today,' he said. 'Once more they are disorganised. Once more they are wandering about in the desert, ready for the *coup de grâce*.'28

Rommel did not feel strong enough to take the offensive again until 26 May, when he launched the DAK around Eighth Army's inland flank, hoping to encircle and destroy its forward formations. An annihilating *Kesselschlacht* eluded him, however, and he became sucked into a punishing armoured battle in the so-called 'Cauldron', in the very midst of the Commonwealth front line. By 13 June Eighth Army had lost well over 400 tanks, and in an inept attack on the 17th over one-third of its last effective armoured brigade was destroyed. There was now no hope of making an effective stand anywhere west of Tobruk, and Commonwealth troops began pulling back towards Mersa Matruh in considerable confusion. On 21 June Tobruk finally fell, and Mersa Matruh itself had to be given up on the 27th. It proved impossible to establish any sort of defensive line until El Alamein was reached, on the 30th.

Rommel was now deep into Egypt, at the very gates of Alexandria itself. But, in J.F.C. Fuller's vivid phrase, he had 'stretched his elastic' about as far as it would go.29 Kesselring, who had by now left *Luftflotte* 2 in Russia to take over as commander of all German forces in the Mediterranean theatre,† had been against the advance into Egypt all along. In a discussion with his Italian counterparts, on 26 June, he had claimed that:

if the advance is continued, even with a minimum of fighting, the breakdown rate of armoured and motor vehicles must be

---

* So denuded, in fact, that the Axis on this occasion deployed more tanks, 117 German and 79 Italian against 141 British.
† He was named *Oberbefehlshaber Süd* in November 1941.

very high. It has been alarmingly high up to now. Replacements to the requisite amount cannot be expected for a long time . . . [As for the] Luftwaffe, my airmen will land near the Nile completely exhausted. Their aircraft will need overhauling, yet with completely inadequate supplies . . . In view of the decisive importance of air co-operation, from this stand-point alone I must reject the proposal to continue our advance with the objective Cairo.[30]

But Rommel insisted on pressing forward, so sure that the Commonwealth forces were at their last gasp that he blinded himself to the logistical realities of his situation.* His next attack, at Alamein, began on 1 July and was intended to crush his enemy once and for all. Some of his subordinates were not so sanguine. Shortly after the DAK had been committed, the Italian Littorio Division was advised to make ready for a pursuit towards Alexandria in two hours' time. An Italian officer's note pencilled in the margin of this order 'suggests, however, that the Italians still maintained an unromantic grasp of reality: "Littorio," it ran, "has fuel for only 20 km. To Alexandria – 150 km!" '[31]

Two days later Rommel too was finally obliged to make a more objective appraisal of his situation. In his Daily Report he wrote: 'The strength of the enemy, our own decreasing fighting strength, and the most precarious supply situation compelled us to discontinue attacking on a large scale for the time being.' To Kesselring he signalled: 'With the present fighting strength and supply situation an attack on a large scale is not possible for the time being.'[32] As his attacks ground to a halt, Eighth Army began its own counter-offensive, and between 14 and 22 July another dour armoured slogging match took place, with heavy losses on both sides. By the 20th Rommel was complaining of 'extremely grave shortages of munitions and gasoline,'[33] and two days later he broke off the armoured battle, retiring behind extensive minefields to rest and regroup. Looking back on his failure to reach Cairo, he later wrote: 'If success had depended, as in times gone by, on the strength of will

---

* Though he does seem to have been at least aware of his logistical weakness. A German officer who was present at this same conference reported: 'Field Marshal Rommel judges the tactical and operational, but not the supply situation, to be particularly favourable . . . Fuel stocks in the front line are not adequate either for the German or for the Italian side.' (Quoted in W. Heckmann, *Rommel's War in Africa* (Granada, 1981), p. 312.)

of my men and their officers, then we would have overrun Alamein. But our sources of supply had dried up – thanks to the idleness and muddle of the supply authorities on the mainland.'[34]

But at the time Rommel was still not prepared to accept that the army he had sent packing three times before would not once again succumb to a bold armoured thrust and uncover the approaches to Alexandria. On 31 August the panzers of the DAK rolled forward for the last time. Attempting to turn Eighth Army's inland flank, they were directed on to extremely strong Commonwealth positions on Alam Halfa ridge, before which upwards of three dozen tanks were knocked out. By 3 September Rommel was withdrawing once more behind the minefields.

But, heavy though his armoured casualties had been, it was not these that caused him to abandon the field.* Once again it was the shortage of supplies that forced his hand. Throughout August he had been loud in complaints about his inability to build up any sort of reserve. On the 1st he reported to OKW: 'Supplies at the present time are sufficient to cover only the day-to-day requirements of the troops. Stockpiling for large-scale actions or even offensives is impossible.'[35] Fuel was the major problem. As Rommel himself wrote after the battle, one of the major reasons for the failure of the offensive was that 'the petrol, which was an essential condition for the fulfilment of our plan, had not arrived.'[36] The effect this had on operational possibilities was trenchantly described by one of his staff-officers, who recorded that

> on the morning of 1 September Rommel's shortage of petrol was such that he had to limit the attack on Alam Halfa to 15 Panzer Division. It was clear that a frontal attack offered little hope of success, and in other circumstances Rommel would certainly have swung to the east and sought to manoeuvre the British out of position. However, lack of petrol prevented any attempt at manoeuvre . . . The attack of 15 Panzer failed . . . Petrol stocks were almost exhausted, and an armoured division without petrol is little better than a heap of scrap iron.[37]

And if the DAK was unable even to manoeuvre on the battlefield, still less would it have been able fully to exploit any local successes it might yet gain. The 170 kilometres to Alexandria might as well have

---

* The 36 German tanks knocked out still left Rommel with 147 mediums, far more than the number with which he had pressed home earlier attacks.

been 1,700. Rommel had no alternative but to withdraw.*

In the next confrontation, known to the world as the Battle of El Alamein, though technically it was the third such, it was Eighth Army that attacked, now under the command of General Bernard Law Montgomery. The outcome was never much in doubt, because of the tremendous material superiority which the Commonwealth forces were able to bring to bear, but any hopes that Rommel might have had of at least minimising the damage done were dashed once again by acute supply shortages. The lack of fuel was particularly felt. A divisional commander in the Afrika Korps, General Johann Cramer, said after the war: 'El Alamein was lost before it was fought. We had not the petrol . . . Rommel for a long time had known that the campaign in North Africa was hopeless . . . because of petrol shortage.'[38] On the eve of the battle, which began on 23 October 1942, General Georg von Stumme, who had temporarily taken over Rommel's command, lamented: 'We are living from hand to mouth; we fill one gap only to see another one open. We cannot build up the basic supply which would enable us to overcome critical situations through our own resources and which allows operational freedom of movement, which is an absolutely vital necessity for the Army.'[39]

Just as at Alam Halfa, the major constraint was that on the manoeuvrability of the armour. Even before the battle, on 20 October, Rommel signalled that within five days it would be down to three days' battle supply of fuel east of Tobruk and that it 'did not possess the operational freedom of movement which was absolutely essential in consideration of the fact that the British offensive can be expected to start any day.'[40]

Thus Rommel was obliged to split his armour between his northern and southern flanks, for fear that if he concentrated it too far away

---

* The effect of supply difficulties on air operations should also be noted. The build-up of Allied aerial supremacy will be dealt with in more detail below, but the following comments in an official British history of the *Luftwaffe* are pertinent at this juncture: 'Between July and September 1942, ground organisation in Cyrenaica and Egypt was developed on a scale which appeared to allow for the basing of considerably greater [German] air forces in North Africa than had hitherto been possible; but no appreciable increase took place. This, without doubt, was due to the difficulty – in competition with the conflicting demands of the Army – in bringing forward adequate numbers of ground and maintenance personnel, of building and maintaining stocks, and particularly of maintaining the level of fuel supplies.' (Air Ministry, *The Rise and Fall of the German Air Force 1933–45* [1948] (WE Inc., Old Greenwich, Conn. 1969), p. 216.)

from the actual point of attack, there would be not enough fuel left to move it back. Even after the battle had started, and the real *point d'appui* was apparent, Commonwealth attacks during the first three days had only to contend with one half of the enemy armour because no one dared authorise the transfer of the other half, which would use up almost the entire fuel reserves of the DAK. On his return to the front, on 26 October, Rommel did authorise the transfer, but by then whatever remote chance there might have been of catching Montgomery's offensive on the half-volley had been lost. Worse, the movement of the armour was spotted by tactical air reconnaissance and hammered by RAF bombers. From that moment the battle was irrevocably lost.

On 4 November Rommel gave up the hopelessly unequal struggle and began to withdraw from the battlefield. The long retreat that was to end in Tunisia, and eventual capitulation some seven months later, had begun. Despite the fact that the withdrawal daily shortened the Panzer Army's lines of communication, it was continually beset by logistical problems. In December even Goebbels was made to acknowledge unpalatable truths and on the 19th he wrote in his diary: 'The situation of our Panzer Army is terrible. The real trouble is that Rommel has no petrol . . . It's a real catastrophe that we can't supply Rommel with petrol. If he had fuel, he would undoubtedly find ways and means to outwit the English once again.'[41] Nor was fuel the only problem. By the end of December not only were supplies of petrol hopelessly inadequate – 152 tons a day received as against a minimum of 400 tons required – but also ammunition and general supplies – 16 as against 50 tons and 12.5 as against 50 respectively.

But this plentiful evidence of Rommel's crippling supply problems presents us with something of a contradiction, given my earlier assertion that the volume of supplies reaching Africa was quite adequate to maintain the number of Axis divisions deployed there. Happily its resolution is straightforward and lies in the fact that simply getting supplies to Africa was not the same thing as getting them to the front, where they could actually be used. For, just as a panzer division without supplies was simply a heap of scrap iron, so too were supplies without a panzer division just so many old boxes and cans. What fatally hamstrung Rommel, notwithstanding his railings against 'idleness and muddle' at the Italian end of the supply chain, was not the *Commando Supremo*, nor the Italian merchant marine, but the consistent inability of the Panzer Army's own logistics staff to funnel the disembarked supplies to the fighting troops.*

The basic problem was that most of Rommel's supplies had to be shipped in to Tripoli, which offered the shortest route from Naples and western Sicily and thus the least exposure to Allied interdiction attacks. Unfortunately, from April to December 1941 the front line was at Sollum, near the Egyptian frontier, from January 1942 it was at Gazala, and from June to November it was inside Egypt itself, only 106 miles from Alexandria. The distances from Tripoli in these three periods were approximately 1,000 miles, 900 miles and 1,300 miles respectively. Only two ports of any value lay any nearer these fronts, Benghazi and Tobruk. The latter, however, was denied to Rommel for much of the African campaign, not being captured until late June 1942. But by this time the Italian navy and merchant marine were extremely short of fuel themselves and unable to send ships along the much longer sea-route from Brindisi to Tobruk. Thus, though the latter port had been captured intact, very few ships ever docked there. Similar considerations, as well as the greater exposure to attack for convoys using the eastern Mediterranean route, made it very difficult for the Italians to make much use of Benghazi. On top of this, Allied bombing reduced Benghazi's theoretical unloading capacity of 2,700 tons a day to a rarely achieved maximum of only 700–800 tons.

The major proportion of Rommel's supplies, therefore, had to travel east over a distance of 900 miles or more. There were three ways in which this might be done: by sea along the coast, by rail or by

* Happily, a proper epitaph for Italian seamen has come from a British pen, that of Admiral of the Fleet Sir Andrew Cunningham, who served as C.-in-C. Mediterranean Fleet and later as Allied Naval C.-in-C. in the Mediterranean under Eisenhower. Of the performance of enemy sailors in 1942 and 1943 he wrote: 'It was always a surprise to me how the Italian seamen continued to operate their ships in the face of the dangers that beset them. They were liable to surface, submarine and air attacks throughout the whole of their passage from Sicily, and the fact that they stood up to it should be remembered to their credit.' (A Sailor's Odyssey (Hutchinson, 1951), p. 525.)

Rommel's misplaced contempt for the Italians was coupled with a remarkable blindness to the absolute centrality of the supply problem. His cavalier attitude to the latter was amply summed up in an exchange with Halder, in March 1941. According to the latter, 'Rommel explained that he would soon conquer Egypt and the Suez Canal, and then he talked about German East Africa. I couldn't restrain a somewhat impolite smile, and asked what he would be needing for the purpose. He thought he would need another two Panzer corps. I asked him, "Even if we had them, how are you going to supply them and feed them?" To this I received the classic reply, "That's quite immaterial to me. That's your pigeon." ' (Quoted in M. Cooper, The German Army 1933–45 (Macdonald and Jane's, 1978), p. 361.)

road. Neither of the first two was really practicable. On the one hand, there was only enough coastal shipping to carry 15,000 tons, instead of the projected 50,000, and that, of course, was extremely vulnerable to air attack. On the other, there was no adequate railway running eastward from Tripoli. According to General Siegfried Westphal, Rommel's Chief of Staff, even including the railway in Tunisia, the total length of track in North Africa was 'less than 300 kilometres. In the middle of February [1942] the OKW sent an order that work should be begun at once to join up these railways. Constructional progress was to be reported daily. There was no word as to where the rails, sleepers, locomotives etc for 750 kilometres of track were to come from.'42

Rommel had no option, therefore, but to rely on motor transport. This, unfortunately, was quite inadequate for the task demanded of it. An OKH study had determined that one motorised division operating only 300 miles from its supply base would require the services of 1,250 trucks to bring forward the requisite fuel, ammunition, food etc. Yet the Axis forces in Africa, with a nominal strength of around 12 divisions (and even the non-motorised formations required all the items just listed, though less fuel and spare parts), never had more than 10,000 trucks in the whole theatre. Furthermore, 35 per cent of these were under repair at any one time, whilst another 20 per cent at least were required for service within the divisions themselves to move men and supplies that had already arrived. Such was the shortfall in motor transport that in January 1942 Rommel told Berlin that he would require a further 8,000 trucks, a ludicrous demand as 'at the time all four German armoured groups in Russia could muster only 14,000 lorries between them.'43*

But the mere shortage of motor vehicles, acute as it was, was only part of the problem. One of the most vital items they carried was fuel but, as has already been seen on the Eastern Front, the lorries consumed a very high proportion of it themselves. One leading authority has suggested that a reasonable estimate would be that 'thirty to fifty per cent of all the fuel landed in North Africa was wasted between Tripoli and the front.'44 The difficulties involved are brought out in another OKH study, made in late 1941, which tried to estimate the supply requirements of the DAK alone in a

* In May 1942 some units had only 60 of their official allotment of 400 trucks. In contrast, the British, between July and October 1941, sent 34,000 motor vehicles to the Middle East, whilst between January and September 1942 they and the Americans dispatched a further 62,450.

successful drive to Tobruk. Something like 3,500 lorries would be required. The return journey between Tripoli and Tobruk was just over 2,000 miles, to be covered at roughly 150 miles per day. In desert conditions a truck would consume upwards of 75 litres in covering this 150 miles, giving

> a monthly requirement for the whole fleet of . . . 8,250,760 litres, or 5,776 tons. This, mind you, for transport only. This amount would not have allowed one single tank to move an inch; not one tractor would heave a single gun into position; no half-track would have moved any infantry. In the year 1941, the monthly average tonnage of motor fuel arriving for the army in Africa was 4,884 tons.[45]*

Yet another disadvantage inherent in this reliance on motor transport was the vulnerability of the road-bound convoys. Not for nothing are the work-horses of the transport echelons commonly referred to as 'soft-skin' vehicles. Not only were the Axis lines of communication vulnerable to raids by armoured cars and long-range penetration groups, but they were also pounded remorselessly from the air. Disruption reached its height in the second half of 1942, when Rommel was particularly reliant on his battered columns of trucks. On 8 June, with its armour seeking to find a way out of the Cauldron, the DAK reported in its war diary: 'The supply situation, especially with regard to guns and ammunition, is becoming more and more serious . . . In addition to the difficulties connected with the long supply route, daily [air] attacks are being carried out on supply columns even when proceeding with convoy guard.'[46] On 3 July, at the height of the first Alamein battle, Rommel signalled to Kesselring: '. . . an attack on a large scale is not possible for the time being. It is hardly possible to supply the Army by night, as the roads are almost completely denied by enemy air activity.'[47] The Afrika Korps heartily endorsed this appreciation, noting that 'continual air raids by day and night are hindering the troops seriously . . . Continuous bombing raids met with success and the supply columns were blown up.'[48] Allied pressure did not abate, and exactly similar difficulties were encountered during the Battle of Alam Halfa. In his analysis of the battle Rommel lamented:

* An annual total of some 59,000 tons. Granted that this refers only to motor fuel, it is still noteworthy that in the 12 months from August 1941 the Commonwealth ground and air forces in Egypt received 342,000 tons of oil products.

. . . whoever enjoys command of the air is in a position to inflict such heavy damage on the opponent's supply columns that serious shortages must soon make themselves felt. By maintaining a constant watch on the roads leading to the front he can put a complete stop to daylight supply traffic and force his enemy only to drive by night, thus causing him to lose irreplaceable time. But an assured flow of supplies is essential; without it an army becomes immobilised and incapable of action.[49]

Particularly when, as was the case with Panzer Army Africa in 1942, it suffers the loss of 5,250 motor vehicles.

It was this absolute reliance upon a totally over-stretched land supply-line that was the fundamental cause of Rommel's failure in Africa, a fact that was later acknowledged by certain German participants. General Walter Nehring, who commanded the DAK from May to August 1942, complained about the long distances by road between the ports and the troops which meant that 'transport along these routes suffered from delays, fuel shortages and enemy activity in the air.'[50] In another post-war assessment, Admiral Eberhard Weichold, the German liaison officer with the Italian navy, stated firmly:

If insufficient supplies reached the front this was due above all to the deficiencies in the motor transport system of the Afrika Korps, a service which had been the weak point of the Korps' organisation from the very beginning. With the development of land supply routes . . . [that became] extraordinarily long, such a deficiency became graver than ever.[51]*

* A report by Panzer Army Africa to OKW, on 1 August 1942, also emphasised the fact that the volume of shipping across the Mediterranean was not the major determinant of the Axis supply crisis, listing shipping shortages as only one of several reasons, which were: '1) Prevention of coastal shipping from Tobruk to the east by the enemy air force and navy . . . 2) Inadequate shipping space . . . 3) Limited facilities for unloading at Tobruk . . . 4) The establishment of regulated railway traffic . . . is not in sight . . . 5) Lack of transport vehicles . . .' (Quoted in J. Hetherington, *Air War Against Germany and Italy 1939–43* (Australian War Memorial, Canberra, 1954), p. 257.)

Nevertheless, I should point out that it is not my intention in this book to demean the achievements of the Royal Navy and Air Force in the savage war against Axis shipping. Incontestably, had the war in Africa lasted into 1944, or even late 1943, their efforts alone would have reduced the Italian merchant marine to an inconsequential remnant. My contention is only that within the actual time-scale of the desert war, Rommel was hobbled much more by the lack of land transport facilities than by shortages of supplies actually landed in

But what if Rommel's supply echelons had been better equipped to cope with the enormous demands placed upon them? Could they even then have brought forward sufficient equipment and supplies to match the veritable cornucopia that the Allies poured into the Middle East? The comparative figures suggest not. Those for motor vehicles and petroleum have already been cited, but an even more pertinent example is that of tanks, since even though almost all the Axis tanks that were landed in Africa appear to have reached the front, these shipments were dwarfed by the size of British, and later American, deliveries. In the first nine months of 1942, for example, almost 2,500 Allied tanks arrived in the Middle East. Over the same period *total* German production of those models used in Africa was only 2,700, the great majority of which were sent to the Eastern Front or used to form new divisions in Germany.* This relentless build-up of armoured strength gave the Eighth Army a growing numerical superiority, as is shown in table 11, which lists comparative tank strengths at the start of certain battles. (The strengths at the start of Crusader are detailed again for the sake of completeness.)

The figures largely speak for themselves, particularly those for the number of reserves, and if one ignores British light tanks, German Panzer IIs and Italian tanks – throughout the second half of 1942 the latter were, in Rommel's words, 'decrepit and barely fit for action'[52] – the comparisons become even more striking: 800 British versus 280 German at Gazala, 159 versus 50 or so at 1st Alamein, 524 versus 203 at Alam Halfa, and 910 versus 234 at 2nd Alamein. The total dominance afforded by this ever-burgeoning Allied tank strength is brought out in table 12, which details comparative tank strengths during 2nd Alamein and Rommel's subsequent retreat. There it can be seen that despite a most favourable casualty ratio – 500 British tanks as against only 170 German between 23 October and 4 November – the enormous initial British superiority, coupled with

footnote continued

Africa. One could, indeed, speculate that even had there been *no* offensive at all against the shipping lanes, the Panzer Army would still have been in tremendous difficulties. For, unless thousands more vehicles had been sent across (which were sorely needed in Russia), or major items of building equipment to improve port facilities at Benghazi and Tobruk, or thousands of tons of rails and rolling stock (for none of which the shipping space existed even at the start of the war), then Rommel would always have been seriously constrained in the number of divisions he could maintain at the front.

* Four panzer divisions were formed in 1942, as well as six ss Panzer Grenadier divisions which often had a more powerful armoured component.

Table 11: *Axis and British tank strengths at the beginning of certain battles, November 1941 – October 1942*

Date	Battle	German Light	German Medium	German Total	Italian	Axis Total	British Light	British Medium	British Heavy	British Total	Reserves Axis	Reserves British	Ratio of British Front-line Medium and Heavy Tanks to German Medium
18 Nov. 1941	Crusader	70	174	244	146	390	173	339	199	711	50	495	3.1:1
26 May 1942	Gazala	50	280	330	228	558	149	424	276	849	77	450	2.5:1
1 July 1942	Alamein	54		54	30	84	93	106	53	252	?	220	3.1:1
30 Aug. 1942	Alam Halfa	31	234	265	243	508	169	361	163	693	?	250	2.2:1
23 Oct. 1942	2 Alamein	31	211	242	279	521	119	716	194	1,029	22	1,200	4.3:1

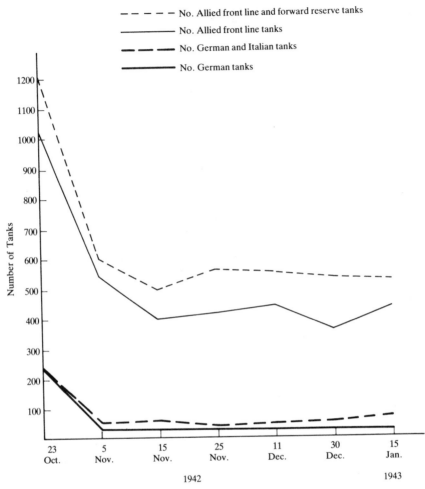

- – – – – No. Allied front line and forward reserve tanks
- ———— No. Allied front line tanks
- – – – No. German and Italian tanks
- ———— No. German tanks

Table 12: *Eighth Army and Axis tank strengths 23 October 1942 – 15 January 1943*

their huge reserves, meant that the balance of forces swung more and more against the Panzer Army. At the start of the battle the ratio of British front-line to Axis tanks was 4:1. By 5 November it was 15:1 and for the rest of the year hovered between 10 and 13:1.

Details on artillery strengths during the desert war are harder to come by but the basic picture remains the same, showing that the vastly superior Allied supply network gradually achieved the upper hand. During Crusader, as has been seen, Rommel actually had an artillery superiority, notably in heavier guns. But the balance thereafter swung ineluctably against him, and by the time of 2nd Alamein Commonwealth superiority was absolute. On 23 October, the Panzer Army contained some 570 German artillery pieces (of which 300 were light) and 370 Italian (150 light). None of the Italian guns were heavy pieces, and those they did have were almost all of First World War vintage and somewhat temperamental. Eighth Army fielded over 900 first-class field and medium guns. The figures for anti-tank guns were 740 Axis versus 1,400 Commonwealth, a 2:1 ratio that also applied to the 'quality' weaponry: pitted against 440 88s, 76.2mm and 50mm guns were 850 of the new British 6pdrs.

Eighth Army had other artillery advantages, notably an outbreak of tactical good sense during 1942. Having been forced on to the defensive ever since Rommel's surprise offensive of January that year, British commanders gradually abandoned the piecemeal dispersion of the field regiments and began to mass them behind the front line for well timed, *concentrated* bombardments on particularly important sectors. The Germans and Italians, on the other hand, having for so long been engaged in *ad hoc* mobile encounters with dispersed enemy formations, were extremely ill-adapted to laying down concerted fire from dug-in positions, as they were required to do at 2nd Alamein.

They were also severely handicapped by chronic ammunition shortages and were unable remotely to match the volume of fire from the Commonwealth lines. At Alam Halfa, according to Rommel, 'the British artillery was very active and fired vast quantities of ammunition – about ten shells were answering every one of ours.'[53] During 2nd Alamein the disparity was even greater. In the first 12 days of the battle the Commonwealth field guns averaged 102 rounds per gun per day (over 1 million all told) and the 4.5 and 5.5 inch mediums over 140 rounds per day. The Panzer Army could not begin to respond. Even by 2 November less than half of its modest daily expenditure was being replaced from the rear (190 tons as opposed to 450). About this time, according to Rommel's (possibly exaggerated) account, 'the British had spent the whole night assaulting our front under cover of their artillery, which in some places had fired as many as five hundred rounds for every one of ours.'[54] By 9 November Eighth Army had established an anti-tank superiority of 30:1 and an artillery superiority of 12:1.

In terms of the war of matériel, the final nail in Rommel's coffin was the rapid expansion of Allied air-power in the Middle East. Not that the RAF's struggle was an easy one. Hitler's decision to station *Luftwaffe* units in the Mediterranean, taken in December 1940, had meant that the air ascendancy gained over the Italians was soon lost, and the establishment of a force based in Libya itself, under the so-called *Fliegerführer Afrika*, in June 1941, meant hard days ahead for the pilots of the Desert Air Force. Many, indeed, regarded the African theatre as the hardest of all, one noting that 'it is certainly tough . . . It all makes the Battle of Britain and fighter sweeps seem like child's play in comparison.'[55]

A major problem was that Commonwealth pilots felt that their equipment was inferior. This applied particularly to the fighters, both the Hurricane II and the Tomahawk being markedly inferior to the Messerschmitt Bf.109. Qualitative parity was not in fact achieved until March 1942, when the first Spitfires began arriving in this theatre. Another serious handicap was the poor serviceability of the Commonwealth aircraft, which meant that often only a small percentage of those present in the theatre were actually fit to fly. By mid-1941, according to the official history of the RAF, the maintenance situation was 'indeed desperate' and unserviceability among the aircraft had reached 'fantastic proportions'.[56]

Happily, in May 1941, there arrived in Africa one of the unsung heroes of the desert war, Air Vice-Marshal G. G. Dawson, who immediately set about rationalising and expanding the repair organisation, laying particular emphasis upon increasing the size and mobility of those in the forward areas and the appointment of an independent Air Officer-in-Charge of Maintenance. Dawson was given the job and the availability of aircraft immediately improved. At the beginning of Crusader, for example, the Desert Air Force was able to field 550 serviceable front-line aircraft as opposed to only 228 equivalent Axis planes. Even more heartening was the number of planes that the DAF was able to keep operational, thanks to its greatly expanded maintenance set-up. As the official history points out: 'Its performance may be judged from a single fact. Between mid-November and mid-March the maintenance units received 1,035 damaged aircraft – aircraft brought in from points scattered over something like 100,000 square miles of desert. During the same period 810 of these machines were delivered back repaired to the battle area.'[57] During 1942 achievements on this scale were pretty much the norm. During the chaotic days of the Gazala battle, with the Army disintegrating around them, the average serviceability of the squadrons actually rose, between 26 May and 15 June, from 67 to 82 per cent.

These were achievements that Rommel simply could not hope to match, for the same supply difficulties that so hog-tied his ground forces also badly undermined his ability to provide adequate air cover. Motor transport was again the key deficiency: it prevented the *Luftwaffe* both from bringing forward sufficient spares and ground-crew and from returning damaged aircraft to the base workshops. Moreover, when the Panzer Army began to advance, Axis squadrons were simply not able to keep up, as there were not enough lorries and low loaders to transport a squadron's administrative base forward to establish new airfields. The severity of Rommel's maintenance problems is well brought out in the following figures. In late 1941, as Auchinleck finally gained the initiative in the Crusader battles, the pursuing Commonwealth forces found 458 Axis aircraft (50 per cent of them German) littering the airfields abandoned by the enemy. In the pursuit after 2nd Alamein the figure was actually in excess of one thousand.*

Nor was the growth of Allied air power simply a function of better serviceability. Once again one has to recognise their tremendous productive and logistical superiority and the sheer number of aircraft that they could pour into this, from the German point of view, peripheral theatre. The relevant statistics reveal, for example, that between November 1941 and September 1942 the Americans dispatched to the Middle East, a theatre in which their ground forces were not yet engaged,† over 1,500 aircraft. The combined Anglo-American effort was more impressive yet, totalling in this same period 2,370 single-engined fighters alone. But total German production of single-engined fighters in these months was only 1,340, and of these not more than 25 per cent, at the very most, could have been sent to the Mediterranean. The ratio of reinforcements, therefore, must have been in the order of over 5:1 in the Allies' favour.

These enormous advantages in logistical support, mobility and reinforcement were slowly but surely translated into a crushing aerial superiority, and this becomes quite evident when one compares the numbers of sorties flown at various periods. At Alam Halfa, for example, the *Luftwaffe* flew some 1,200 sorties as opposed to 2,900 by the DAF. At 2nd Alamein the disparity was yet more marked. On the second day of the battle the DAF flew more than 1,000 sorties as against just over 100 German, whilst during the battle as a whole, up

* The DAF, on the other hand, in the darkest days of the retreat from Gazala, left behind only *five* unserviceable aircraft, and these they burned or otherwise destroyed.
† The first US Army Air Force units arrived in the Middle East in June 1942.

to 4 November, the Allied count was 11,600 and that of the combined Axis air forces only 3,100.*

The effect of such superiority was devastating. Its impact on Rommel's tenuous supply lines has already been discussed, but as time went on the Allies were able to switch substantial numbers of fighters and bombers to direct support of the ground forces. As early as November 1941 their pilots were able to gain at least temporary dominance over the battlefield. So it was on the 25th when one German officer complained: 'Throughout the day the Afrika Korps was subjected to uninterrupted air attacks, which inflicted serious casualties, the more so as the Sollum front was beyond the range of our fighter cover.'[58] In June 1942, as has been indicated, the DAF was able to coordinate its withdrawal with that of the army and thus provide telling support at the most critical moments. The DAK war diary made it clear how troublesome these attacks were, and how the *Luftwaffe's* lack of mobility made it powerless to intervene. On 12 June the diarist wrote: 'Several fighter-bomber attacks are made on the Panzer Divisions this morning. The *Luftwaffe* has carried out no operation as yet.' On the 25th one reads that 'the enemy air force was particularly active . . . Almost continuous bombing attacks were carried out.' On the following day there was little let up: 'Continuous bombing attacks have been in progress since dawn . . . Enemy air activity continues to increase. Bombing attacks are being made every hour, causing considerable losses. There is nothing to be seen of the *Luftwaffe.*'[59]

The air effort during 1st Alamein was a particularly fine achievement, some 5,500 sorties being flown in the first week of July. Enemy reports were quite clear about the serious problems posed by the DAF's relentless attentions. The DAK diarist complained: 'The continuous raids by day and night are hindering the troops seriously.' An Italian officer confided in his personal diary: 'Night and day it seems to go on without interruption, and there is not a moment's peace. We are becoming like potatoes – always underground.' In late July, the tempo continued to mount and on the 21st, according to the DAK, 'continuous heavy bombing attacks are being carried out. Enemy air activity tonight exceeds anything hitherto experienced.

---

* I have said little about the Italian air effort in Libya largely because it hardly figures in any British or German account. The fact that throughout 1942 the Italians managed only to put up 75 sorties per day, with the kind of obsolete aircraft already alluded to, helps to explain why this should be so.

Telephone communications are frequently broken, and there is no contact with the divisions.'[60]

Alam Halfa, in December, saw the DAF at peak efficiency and German accounts of the battle are dominated by references to the enemy's air arm. On 1 September, according to the war diary of Panzer Army Africa: 'Strong enemy aircraft formations in waves made incessant attacks on motorised formations, particularly Afrika Korps. Heavy losses were sustained in the open . . . terrain. German fighters were too weak numerically to divert the enemy formations from their objectives.'[61] General Bayerlein recalled that during this battle 'we were very heavily attacked every hour of the day and night and had very heavy losses, more than from any other cause. Your air superiority was most important, perhaps decisive.'[62] Rommel himself, though he mainly blamed fuel shortages for his failure, acknowledged that the very heavy air attacks 'pinned my arm to the ground and rendered any smooth deployment or any advance by time schedule completely impossible.'[63]

During 2nd Alamein and the Panzer Army's subsequent retreat, Allied air power again dominated the battlefield. German accounts are full of references such as the following, outlining events on 28 October: 'As on previous days, ceaseless bombing attacks hammered down on the German-Italian forces. The *Luftwaffe* tried all it could to help us, but could achieve little or nothing against the tremendous numerical superiority of the enemy.' Eventually the enormous preponderance of Commonwealth firepower broke the Panzer Army on the anvil and obliged Rommel to withdraw. As he himself put it, the battlefield had been 'like a mill. Everything that went into it, regardless of quantity, was ground to dust . . . Anyone who has to fight, even with the most modern weapons, against an enemy in complete command of the air, fights like a savage against modern European troops, under the same handicaps and with the same chances of success.'[64]

It seems clear, then, that throughout 1942 Eighth Army enjoyed a tremendous material advantage over their opponents. Unfortunately, when one turns to examine just how this advantage was utilised by its commanders, a very sorry tale unfolds, one characterised by 'gross military incompetence' and a 'mindless persistence in tactics that proved to be futile, if not suicidal'.[65] The year began particularly badly when the Commonwealth forces, admittedly exhausted after the gruelling Crusader battles, relaxed their vigilance almost to the point of torpor, and ran down their front-line forces to a perilous degree. Rommel, as we have seen, seized his opportunity and hustled his opponents ignominiously back to the Gazala line.

But when he attacked again, in late May, he was faced with immensely stronger forces, the armoured component of which was especially powerful. Nor could British tank commanders claim that their numerical advantage was offset by qualitative inferiority. Certainly, German tanks had been much improved. In late 1941, better armoured versions of the Pz III and IV arrived (Ausf. H and Ausf. E respectively), and by the time of Gazala German armour had been further strengthened by the first appearance of the Pz III and IV 'Specials' (Ausf. J and Ausf. F^2 respectively) with yet more frontal armour and much improved guns. The 'Specials' were certainly formidable weapons, soon becoming the bogeymen of the British armoured divisions, but it is hard to accept the common contention that they wielded any really decisive influence on the Gazala battle. At the beginning of Rommel's attack, on 26 May, only 19 III Specials were with the panzer units, whilst the nine IV Specials were still waiting to be brought forward. Even two weeks later, when the battle was just about lost for Eighth Army, the DAK could count only 27 III and 6 IV Specials. Given that the British armour had started the battle with 700 medium and heavy tanks, and a further 450 in reserve, it seems unlikely that this handful of 'wunderpanzers' could have decided the issue.*

It is true, of course, that even those German mediums that were not 'Specials' were nevertheless much improved tanks (Panzer III Ausf. Hs and Panzer IV Ausf. E and F^1s), all with greatly improved frontal armour, but against this must be set the fact that Eighth Army had also greatly improved its weaponry. Firstly, a brand-new tank had appeared, the Grant Mk. I, which was both well-armoured and possessed of a gun considerably superior to the old 2pdr, and which at longer ranges could engage the Pz III 'Special' with impunity. Admittedly, the Grants had their main gun mounted in a sponson on the side of the tank, which allowed hardly any traverse, but Eighth Army did have 167 of them, with 75 more in close reserve and a further 250 back in Egypt. Secondly, the Commonwealth forces

---

* It is possible, moreover, that intelligence analysts at the time, and subsequent historians, exaggerated even these small numbers of Specials. If their perusal of German shipping lists indicated only that Pz. III Js were on board, this did not necessarily mean that they were up-gunned models. For the first production run of this type (chassis numbers 68001–69100) mounted the old short 50mm gun.

were much better provided with anti-tank guns. Not only had some 2pdrs been provided with high-velocity shot, but a brand-new gun had begun to arrive at the front. This was the 6pdr, of which 112 were available in the Gazala line at the start of the battle. It was a far superior weapon to the PAK 38, and was in fact the master of all German tanks, in any profile, at ranges of well over half a mile.

One might have thought, therefore, that Eighth Army would have been capable of absorbing any Axis offensive with comparative ease. The Grants, in particular, should have been extremely effective in a defensive role, as occupation of a static line would have minimised the inconvenience caused by the fixed sponson, and their long-range ability with both shot and HE should have permitted them to wreak havoc amongst the advancing panzers and the gunners. But it was not to be. For one thing Rommel managed to take Eighth Army almost completely by surprise with the direction of his attack, a sort of Crusader in reverse that swept round the exposed Free French position at Bir Hacheim, at the southern end of the Commonwealth front. For another the British armour was very badly disposed. Though it was all still under the command of XXX Corps, deployed in the southern sector, the individual brigades were badly dispersed. The HQs of the two armoured divisions were ten miles apart, and 7 Armoured, which was to bear the brunt of Rommel's onslaught, was absurdly scattered. The two motor brigades, with many of the precious 6pdrs, were well in front of the tanks of 4 Armoured Brigade and in danger of being overrun before they could combine with the latter in a properly balanced offensive-defensive partnership. Just for good measure, these motor brigades, 7 and 3 Indian, were also widely separated. Though General Neil Ritchie, the new commander of Eighth Army, was just as confident as Cunningham had been before Crusader that the forthcoming battle would enable him to destroy the enemy's armoured forces in a single full-scale confrontation, his actual deployments, again just like Cunningham, were not in the least commensurate with his laudable intent.

By mid-morning on 27 May 7 Armoured Division had ceased to exist as a fighting formation, both motor brigades and the armoured brigade having been overrun without offering any coherent resistance. In his memoirs Rommel noted that 'the dispersal of the British armoured brigades was incomprehensible' and went on to state that 'the sacrifice of 7 Armoured Division . . . served no strategical or tactical purpose whatsoever . . . The principal aim of the British should have been to have brought all they had into action at one and the same time.[66]

Unfortunately, even this swingeing criticism actually exaggerates British competence. For it implies that Ritchie was in command, exercising options about whether to commit 4 Armoured Brigade or whether to have it fall back in front of the advancing DAK. In fact, Ritchie had no idea of what was going on, and it was not until the morning of the 28th that he knew any details at all about these first encounters. But by this time 7 Armoured Division was no more. General Willoughby Norrie, commanding XXX Corps, did have some inkling of these early disasters and, on the morning of the 27th, ordered 22 Armoured Brigade, part of 1 Armoured Division, to move south to lend assistance to its sister division. It dutifully set off, but without the support of its motor brigade, 201 Guards with more 6pdrs, which was locked up in a defensive 'box' performing a static infantry role. The 22nd, thus dangerously 'déshabillé', ran headlong into the whole of the DAK and became badly scattered. Certain units did fight valiant rear-guard actions, but even these were sadly reminiscent of the bravura excesses of Sidi Rezegh. To the Germans the Grants had come as a shock, particularly its immunity to their anti-tank guns at any but short ranges. But British commanders seemed determined to throw away this advantage and 'one wonders . . . why the Grant took the risk of a charge since they had the capability of shelling the 50mm guns out of effective anti-tank range; but the ancient concept of getting blood on the tracks still held the British in thrall.'[67]

On the 28th Rommel pressed on, firm in the belief that, despite considerable casualties of his own, the surest way to keep his opponent on the hop was to threaten him with a bold but concentrated thrust. Eighth Army's response fully endorsed his decision. A German officer present at this battle was quite clear about what *should* have been done. 'On 28 May Ritchie should have concentrated his armoured forces to destroy the Afrika Korps by a concentric counter-attack . . . The main thing . . . was to co-ordinate the armoured brigades, and direct them on a common objective.' In the event, however, the operations on the 28th 'furnish a striking example of the breakdown of command on the British side.'[68] Thus, 22 Armoured Brigade spent the whole day 'observing' 15 Panzer Division, while the survivors of 4 Armoured Brigade confined themselves to harassing 90 Light Division which, though well provided with anti-tank guns, was well to the east of the major battle and could have been left alone. 1 Army Tank Brigade, which was attached to XIII Corps, in the north, and 2 Armoured Brigade operated south of 'Knightsbridge', again well away from the *Schwerpunkt*, whilst the rest of the tanks with XIII Corps, 32 Army Tank Brigade, did nothing at all and remained behind the front.

Casualties were inflicted on the Germans, of course, sometimes quite heavy, but at no stage did the British look like dislodging Rommel or forcing his panzer divisions apart. On the 29th, indeed, he was able further to consolidate his position, in the notorious Cauldron, bringing 90 Light back westwards and re-establishing close contact with Italian units laying siege to Bir Hacheim. At the same time he was able to recover many of his damaged tanks and begin repairs in the mobile workshops. Such attacks as the British did launch over the next days merely produced more of the same, with tanks thrown in piecemeal, and no attempt to coordinate these attacks with the infantry and artillery. To a British tank brigadier captured in one attack, Rommel is reported to have said: 'What difference does it make if you have two tanks to my one, when you spread them out and let me smash them in detail? You presented me with three brigades in succession.'[69]

Having expended the British armour with such spasmodic abandon during these first four days, Ritchie and his subordinates now lapsed into semi-paralysis, dimly realising that only a concerted assault could hope to drive Rommel out of the Cauldron fastness, but seemingly incapable of actually coordinating it. Until 5 June Commonwealth activity was limited to endless inconclusive conferences, with Eighth Army not even intervening when Rommel began mopping up a nearby infantry box, manned by 150 Brigade, an operation which took two full days.

When a Commonwealth counter-attack did come, Operation Aberdeen, launched on 5 June, any thought of concerted action was still conspicuous by its absence. The plan was fairly straightforward. The enemy's forward gun line was to be seized by an Indian infantry brigade, supported by Valentine tanks and masked by a diversionary armoured attack on their left. Once the forward line had been seized, two more armoured brigades were to pass through and dispose of the German armour. The diversionary attack, made against strong positions on Sidra Ridge, was the fiasco that all such isolated forays had hitherto been. An almost apologetic German officer wrote:

For some reason this attack was supported by only twelve guns, and it was brought to a halt with a loss of fifty tanks out of seventy . . . The heavy British tanks lumbered forward in daylight, providing perfect targets for our anti-tank guns, and ending up on a minefield where they were simply shot to pieces. From a tactical point of view this was one of the most ridiculous attacks of the campaign.[70]

The infantry attack achieved nothing, as the preliminary artillery barrage which was supposed to neutralise the enemy gun line was feebly plotted (no preliminary reconnaissance had been made) and thus fell short. Nevertheless, though none of the guns had been destroyed or captured, the exploiting armour sallied forth – or rather one Brigade did because the other had received conflicting orders and took no part in the battle. It was duly immolated. 'Co-ordination with the infantry and artillery was astonishingly bad, even by the standards then prevailing in the Eighth Army. The tanks managed to push the Ariete [Division] back a bit, then ran into a line of eighty-eights and anti-tank guns without any support from other arms. Sixty tanks were lost, and irretrievably at that, since the battlefield remained in Axis hands.'[71] Rommel then sallied forth himself and the surviving infantry, bereft of all armoured support, including its Valentines which had been withdrawn, was swept away.

The final blow fell on 12 June, after Ritchie had pulled back the southern half of his line to form a right-angle pivoting on Sidi Mufta. The British armour pulled back into a Cauldron of its own, between 'Knightsbridge' and El Adem, but then Rommel proceeded to give a demonstration of just how attacks against such positions should be carried out. Both his panzer divisions, supported by Italian infantry, attacked together with one pinning the British armour frontally whilst the other slashed into its rear. As usual, strong artillery and anti-tank forces were well up with the leading tanks, and in just two days' bitter fighting the British lost upwards of 180 medium and 50 heavy tanks.* The whole Gazala position now began to fall apart, and within a week Eighth Army was in full flight. 'The British armour,' in the sombre words of the South African official history, 'had now ceased to have any tactical significance.'[72] On 21 June Tobruk surrendered and on the following day Rommel was up to the Egyptian frontier. On the

---

* British tank losses had been consistently severe. On 27 and 28 May, 150 were lost, and over 100 on 5 and 6 June.

23rd he drove south of Sidi Barrani and by the 25th was investing Mersa Matruh. Auchinleck sacked Ritchie and himself took personal command of Eighth Army. He was unable, however, to save Mersa Matruh, which fell on the 29th.

But he and his Chief of Staff, Dorman-Smith, were possessed of a remarkable sang-froid* and a clear conception of Eighth Army's immediate responsibilities. These were essentially defensive, for which reason Auchinleck devoted much of his attention to the artillery, centralising the greater part of it under Army command and ensuring that the rest, though split into battle groups, was never stationed out on a limb, outside the range of other units. Eighth Army's new artillery doctrine was summarised by a senior officer who told a Commanders' Conference, in July: 'The artillery is being restored to its rightful place on the battlefield. Very large concentrations of artillery fire, including, for example, the co-ordinated fire of the artillery of two corps, are being used with overwhelming effect . . . the lack of effect of small units of artillery used singly is being realised.'[73]

It was this artillery, coupled with the tremendous efforts of the DAF, that ground Rommel's offensive to a halt. He attacked the Alamein positions on 1 July, but by the evening of the 3rd was reduced to only 26 German and 5 Italian tanks fit for action. On 4 July he had no option but to pull his mobile forces back to regroup, and subsequent Commonwealth probing attacks against the Italians who took their place created numerous crises, denying Rommel the opportunity to draw breath before launching another revitalised offensive. By 17 July he had completely lost the initiative. The British defences had held for once and, as Rommel himself wrote: 'The front had now grown static . . . In static warfare, victory goes to the side which can fire the more ammunition.'[74]

Commonwealth success was hardly unalloyed, however. Despite his proper emphasis upon defensive preparation, Auchinleck was a pugnacious commander. With Ultra keeping him well informed about Rommel's pitiful tank strength, he was always eager to switch back to the forehand and try and finish off the Panzer Army once and for all. His armour, naturally, figured prominently in such schemes but remained a constant disappointment. An intended local flank attack on 1 July never got off the ground. On the following day a

* His order of the day on 30 June included the exhortation: 'The enemy is stretching to his limit and thinks we are a broken army . . . He hopes to take Egypt by bluff. Show him where he gets off.'

counter-attack by the whole of XIII Corps, envisaged by Auchinleck as 'a sudden terrible blow coming out of the desert', degenerated into a 'slow and laborious accumulation of pressure', the least effective part of which was an armoured drive into Rommel's rear which only succeeded in charging his anti-tank line head-on.[75] Another attempt was made on 4 July, but again the armoured attack was poorly led and the half-hearted advance became entangled once again in the anti-tank screen. By the 15th the armour seemed to be wearying of its one-sided confrontations with the DAK and an attack by the New Zealand Division, on Ruweisat Ridge, broke down when the tanks of 1 Armoured Division persistently declined to come to their aid.

Perhaps most disappointing of all were the results of Auchinleck's attempt fully to exploit the infantry successes against the Italians, gained between the 5th and the 17th. This began on the 22nd, with an attack along and to the south of Ruweisat Ridge. Two infantry divisions were used, as well as three armoured brigades, one to give direct support to the infantry and the other two to exploit out of the infantry's bridgeheads. In the Battle of El Mreir, as this attack is generally known, the attacking force 'alone was strong enough to send Rommel reeling with a concentrated knock-out blow.' Thus the New Zealand official history, which makes a telling case by pointing out that the three armoured brigades had between them almost 350 tanks, at least 60 of which were Grants. Rommel's *total* tank strength was 38 German and 58 Italian, only six of which were Mark III Specials. The two or three Mark IV Specials had no ammunition. On top of this the three infantry brigades involved were facing only four 'weak, tired and widely dispersed' German battalions and the remains of an Italian division. The Commonwealth forces also had the support of nine artillery field regiments and one medium regiment, as well as supporting fire from XXX Corps along the northern flank. 'Rommel was reduced to counting his guns singly, or at the most, in troops or batteries of three.'[76]

Somehow, the armour still managed to foul things up. When the Indians attacked, before dawn, 22 Armoured Brigade refused to advance with them, their commander asserting that it was impossible for troops to move at night. When the Brigade eventually did set off, after first light, now bereft of immediate infantry and artillery support, it blundered straight into a minefield and a covering screen of anti-tank guns. Thus, although the infantry attack did reach its objective, it was promptly counter-attacked and overrun. The time was hardly ripe, therefore, for armoured exploitation but 23 Armoured Brigade came on anyway, ending up in a large saucer of ground around which were ranged German tanks and anti-tank guns. The result was a massacre, in which 86 of the 97 tanks engaged were knocked out. A little later, XIII Corps threw in good money after bad, dispatching 2 Armoured Brigade to this same killing ground. They were withdrawn after only 40 minutes, having lost another 21 tanks. All in all on that fateful day 1 Armoured Division lost 131 tanks.* DAK lost three. After the failure of another counter-attack, on the 27th, Auchinleck had to give up his hopes of resuming the offensive. This was most definitely not to Churchill's taste and, oblivious to the fundamental importance of Auchinleck's earlier defensive successes, he sacked him. The post of C.-in-C. Middle East was taken over by General Sir Harold Alexander and that of commander Eighth Army by Montgomery.

Both Rommel and Montgomery drew lessons from the disaster at El Mreir. To the former it indicated that, despite his dwindling human and material resources, he might still be able to take advantage of Commonwealth tactical incompetence and break through the Alamein line. To Montgomery it was clear that Eighth Army was for the moment incapable of anything but staunch defence, *à la* Wellington. It must, therefore, allow Rommel to attack first, absorb his punches, and on no account allow itself to be drawn into large-scale counter-attacks.

At Alam Halfa, between 31 August and 6 September 1942, both commanders followed their instincts. That Rommel's proved wrong was, as we have seen, due as much as anything to the tremendous Commonwealth material superiority, but credit must also be given to Montgomery, who resolutely refused to countenance any talk of an exploitative role for the armour should Rommel be checked. According to the commander of 22 Armoured Brigade, Montgomery was adamant that the tanks should not leave the main defended areas as they were 'neither sufficiently well trained nor mechanically sound enough to undertake a mobile battle.'[77] Instead Montgomery pegged much of his armour out in defensive hull-down positions at the western end of Alam Halfa Ridge, with a light screen in front of the ridge which was to fall back and lure Rommel onto this thick

---

* In another smaller attack, well to the north of Ruweisat Ridge, the third regiment of 23 Armoured Brigade contributed a new variety of 'cock-up'. It quickly lost contact with the (Australian) infantry it was supposed to support but contrived to reach the objective well *ahead* of the latter. As it milled around waiting for them to catch up it presented an ideal target and suffered the loss of a further 23 tanks.

defensive screen.* This was Rommel's own recipe, in fact, though without the leaven of subsequent mobile exploitation. Everything turned out exactly as planned. Better, in fact, for Rommel's lunge around the southern flank was beset by fuel shortages and he was forced to turn north sooner than he might have wished. This took him right into the centre of Montgomery's armour-piercing firing-squad. By the evening of 2 September, heavy German losses, upwards of 40 tanks destroyed as well as 50 or more damaged (nearly half his force), left Rommel with no alternative but to retire. British tank casualties had been higher, almost 70 destroyed, but this was less than 10 per cent of their front-line force.

Montgomery's refusal to allow any pursuit has been the subject of considerable controversy. Certainly his opponents were somewhat bewildered, one of Rommel's staff declaring that even on the 2nd, 'the circumstances were extremely propitious for a British counter-attack, but Montgomery made no move . . .'[78] However, though this book as a whole will have little to say in favour of Montgomery as an armoured commander, it seems clear that on this occasion his caution was well justified. Certainly numerous theoretical opportunities were presented,† but the downright shoddiness of the tactical control of the British armour in the preceding months was surely eminent justification for Montgomery's suspicion that there was no opportunity that it could not squander.

He remained content, therefore, to permit Rommel to withdraw behind his own minefields, where he feverishly set about improving his defences against the inevitable Commonwealth offensive. This eventually opened on 23 October, blessed, as has been seen, with a tremendous superiority of matériel.‡ Aware of this overwhelming advantage, Montgomery, like Auchinleck during Crusader, sought to engineer a decisive clash with the panzer divisions, preparatory to mopping up the Italians and the German infantry. To this end

* As well as the tanks, many of them Grants, this screen included infantry liberally supplied with 6pdr anti-tank guns. On 31 August, Eighth Army as a whole had 377 of them.

† The armour might, for example, have tried to cut Rommel's communications to the south of Ruweisat Ridge or the western portion of Alam Halfa. Throughout the battle, moreover, 9 Armoured Brigade remained posted as a back-stop below the eastern end of Alam Halfa. It might have attacked with advantage into Rommel's right flank once he had turned northwards.

‡ To underline this one need only look at the relative strengths for those tanks that might then have been considered 'state-of-the-art'. Of these, Eighth Army contained 170 Grants and 252 M4A1 Shermans up with the front-line forces as against the Panzer Army's 30 Pz IV 'Specials'. Commonwealth workshops contained a further 160 Grants and Shermans, those of the DAK a single Pz III 'Special'.

he grouped the greater part of his armour under a special corps headquarters, Xth, comprising two armoured divisions with three armoured brigades. This Montgomery dubbed his *corps de chasse*, though he was not really looking for the kind of mobile operations that are implicit in some usages of this term. The armoured divisions were seen rather as aggressive sheepdogs who, according to Montgomery, were to corral the enemy 'in his present area and destroy him there. Should small elements escape to the west they will be pursued and dealt with later.'[79] This entrapment was to take place in the northern sector of the front, above Ruweisat Ridge, where XXX Corps, with four infantry divisions and directly supported by two armoured brigades, was to effect a breach in the enemy line, after which X Corps would pass through and force the final armoured confrontation.

Within three weeks of issuing these orders, however, Montgomery began to doubt whether even this rather modest manoeuvre was within the capabilities, or the inclination, of the armoured formations, and on 5 October he revised his plan. Now the attempted entrapment, by a short hook to the north, was abandoned entirely and the tanks were merely to pass through slightly beyond the limits of the infantry bridgehead and there stake out defensive positions similar to those at Alam Halfa in which they would destroy the panzers as they counter-attacked. These latter attacks would be forced on the enemy by XXX Corps' continued 'crumbling' of the Axis infantry in the chosen *Schwerpunkt*, a process which the DAK must surely try and halt. This revised plan makes curious reading when compared with Montgomery's pronouncements on the correct role of armoured formations as expounded in a Training Memorandum of 18 September 1942:

> It is armoured forces and artillery, together with air power, that wins the battles in wide open spaces. But they must have freedom of action and they must not be hampered by calls from the infantry to assist in beating off armoured attack on infantry localities; such localities must be made so strong that they can look after themselves. The armour must be free to choose its own battlefield . . .[80]*

This insistence upon freedom of action also sits oddly with Montgomery's method of introducing the tanks into the battle.

* The Memorandum was actually issued by 10 Armoured Division HQ, but Montgomery's most recent biographer assures us that it perfectly mirrored his own principles and was in fact based upon a Memorandum of his own.

For they were to follow hard on the infantry's heels, the supporting Armoured Brigades passing through the same gaps in the minefields as the infantry, and X Corps through adjacent gaps created by its own engineers. Clearly there was considerable danger of a traffic overload on such congested axes, as for example opposite Meteiyira Ridge, where one of the divisions of the *corps de chasse* was to pass through an infantry division and its supporting armoured brigade. The chances of a serious traffic snarl-up were further increased by Montgomery's insistence that the exploiting armour *must* go at the appointed time and that if the infantry failed to reach its objectives, X Corps was to try and hammer through regardless.

This was surely Montgomery's fundamental blunder in his planning for what was christened Operation Lightfoot. Clodhopper might have been nearer the mark. For it is not mere hindsight which persuades one that the feasibility of this relentless shovelling in of men and equipment was never properly examined. At least not by Montgomery, though his armoured commanders were sceptical from the first about their ability to get forward on such narrow and cluttered axes. Montgomery's latest biographer even speaks in terms of a 'mutiny' by these commanders. Unfortunately their objections did not prompt Montgomery to question his own judgement but actually clouded it yet further. For Montgomery was a very new commander, in a very hot seat, and felt extremely insecure. He simply dared not admit to himself, therefore, that his subordinates, particularly desert veterans like Lumsden of X Corps, Briggs of 1 Armoured Division and Gatehouse of 10th, might actually be right. Thus he closed his mind to all doubts about the plan, forgoing rational analysis, of which he was perfectly capable,* in the name of what he chose to regard as an assertion of his proper authority. Honest doubts regarding the passage of the minefields were dismissed as mere 'bellyaching' and symptoms of a marked aversion to actually getting to grips with the enemy. In one of the arguments with the tankmen, Montgomery produced a terrible motto for his future conduct of operations: 'No more manoeuvre – fight a battle.'[81] At Alam Halfa

---

* The orders to the armoured divisions, *given that they ever found their way forward*, were eminently sound, and showed a shrewd grasp of what had gone wrong during Crusader, at Gazala and at El Mreir. Units were 'on no account to rush blindly on to enemy anti-tank guns or to try to pass through a narrow bottle-neck covered by a concentration of tanks. In such a case a proper co-ordinated plan was to be made, anti-tank guns being engaged by artillery and machine-guns.' (Quoted in M. Carver, *El Alamein* (Batsford, 1962), p. 120.)

this had made good sense and the armour, properly deployed, had won his battle for him. At Alamein, however, the words had a different connotation – no more doubts, no more questions, no more *thought*. 'Manoeuvre' had come to signify to Montgomery pretty much what the word 'culture' is supposed to have meant to Göring.

The first two days of the battle made it perfectly clear that the problem of the minefields had been badly underestimated. Such gaps as XXX Corps did manage to create were not numerous enough for even its own divisions, and when the supporting armour began trying to squeeze through, some regiments could not get forward at all; others ran over mines on each side of the narrow lanes or over others that had been missed, and yet others became entangled in great masses of guns and vehicles milling around in little oases among the minefields. Even X Corps, which was supposed to be creating its own lanes, found its passage obstructed by these same log-jams. Along most of its front 'the congestion was appalling and the confusion considerable. The whole area looked like a badly organised car park at an immense race meeting held in a dust bowl.'[82] Those units that did manage to get through blundered out of narrow exits upon which the Germans were able to concentrate their anti-tank guns. Montgomery's insistence on forcing the armour forward before the infantry had consolidated their own positions, notably for their field artillery which could take on the PAKs and the 88s, meant that the Germans could put their limited arsenal to optimum use by massing them in front of the few exits. By the morning of the 25th, Lightfoot was almost at a standstill.

Over the next few days, Montgomery switched his axis of attack from one point in the line to another, ending up on the night of 1 November with an attack by the New Zealanders and supporting armour along the northern end of Kidney Ridge. The merits or otherwise of this latest plan, known as Operation Supercharge, are somewhat academic, for Rommel was now fast succumbing to the logic of sheer attrition. Eighth Army's tank losses had been very heavy – by 29 October X Corps alone had recovered 213 knocked out tanks* – but so too had those of the Panzer Army. On successive days between 23 and 28 October, the complement of German tanks was 242, 219, 154, 162, 137 and 81, of which an average of 20 or so were the feeble Pz II. Feverish repair work boosted this total to 109 on 1

* Obviously they would not bother bringing in tanks damaged beyond repair, estimated at a further 200 by 4 November.

November, but Eighth Army's own workshops, coupled with copious replacements, enabled it on that same day to field 487 medium tanks, of which 285 were Grants and Shermans. There were also well over 100 heavy Valentines. By dawn on the 29th, indeed, Rommel was already contemplating withdrawing his forces to Fuka, but so critical were the shortages of fuel and vehicles that this would have meant leaving most of the infantry behind. He decided, therefore, to make one more stand, hoping somehow that sheer defensive stubbornness would persuade Eighth Army to call off its attack.

No amount of stubbornness, however, could hold out against Eighth Army's now overwhelming superiority in tanks, guns and aircraft. Nor, for that matter, could the Germans outdo Montgomery in this quality. By the time Supercharge was launched his whole reputation was on the line, and he was determined that it would not be compromised by unnecessary squeamishness. A lead role in the New Zealand attack had been assigned to 9 Armoured Brigade, whose task was to take a ridge to the north-west of Kidney Ridge. At the briefing before the attack General Freyberg, the commander of 2 New Zealand Division, said:

> 'We all realise that for armour to attack a wall of guns sounds like another Balaclava; it is properly an infantry job. But there are no more infantry available, so our armour must do it.' When John Currie, the brigadier of 9 Armoured, observed that this might entail 50% losses Freyberg replied: 'It may well be more than that. The army commander has said that he is prepared to accept 100%.'[83]

The Brigade rolled forward on the morning of 2 November with, it is said, some officers flourishing swords. They availed them little: though the gun line was reached, it was at a cost of 70 out of 94 tanks, and no decisive breach was possible.

The Brigade did, however, succeed in destroying 35 of the enemy guns and, faced with an opponent prepared to make this kind of ruthless trade-off, Rommel realised that he must withdraw or else be totally annihilated.* By the late afternoon of the 2nd, after the

---

* Rommel was also very short of armour with which to counter Supercharge. The attack, it has to be admitted, had taken him rather by surprise and he had allowed most of his tanks to become embroiled in counter-attacks against an earlier Australian assault along the coast. Not only did these keep his tanks away from the most threatened sector but they had also involved heavy losses. It is at least open to question, however, whether Montgomery had explicitly intended to use the moribund Australian attack as a continued diversionary threat.

DAK had launched several costly counter-attacks, it could muster only 35 runners. In the evening Rommel ordered his troops to start withdrawing, and though this was countermanded by Hitler the next morning, he paid little attention, making a partial withdrawal late on the 3rd and beginning to fall back in earnest on the 4th. By now, according to his own account, he had only 12 German tanks fit for action. 'This is the end for us,' he wrote. 'The battle is lost. The enemy hosts are literally flowing over us. We are on the eve of an African Dunkirk.'[84] A report to OKW was less emotional but gave cogent reasons exactly why an 'African Dunkirk' was to be expected:

An ordered withdrawal of the six Italian and two German non-motorised divisions or brigades is not possible in view of the lack of MT vehicles . . . The stocks of ammunition still available are in the front area, while there are no stocks worth mentioning in the rearward area. The slight stocks of fuel do not allow of a movement to the rear over great distances. On the one available road the army will certainly be attacked night and day by the Royal Air Force. In this situation . . . the possibility of the gradual annihilation of the army must be faced.[85]

But Rommel overestimated his opponent. Montgomery's forte was the static slogging match, with a sufficient margin of superiority to allow for the most unfavourable trade-off of matériel. His own notes for a lecture given just before the battle give a terse summary of the kind of battle he had prepared for. Point 7 noted his 'immense superiority in guns, tanks, men. Can fight a prolonged battle and will do so.' Point 8 described the General Conduct of the Battle: 'Methodical progress; destroy enemy part by part, slowly and surely . . . He cannot last a long battle; we can.'[86] Such was 'crumbling'. As one historian has pointed out: 'Haig would have recognised [it] as attrition.'[87]

Having won his ponderous *Materialschlacht*, however, Montgomery proved himself incapable of seizing the fruits of victory, of delivering the final knock-out punch that Rommel felt was inevitable. For here surely was an army for the taking. Its average tank strength through the first half of November was no more than 20, German and Italian. Its petrol and ammunition were in critically short supply. Its artillery was fast disappearing; by 5 November, for example, all its 88s had gone. It was almost totally without air cover. Yet Montgomery never even got close to delivering the *coup de grâce*, either in the immediate aftermath of the battle, or during the long pursuit that followed. On 6 April 1943, having kept several steps ahead of Eighth Army right across Libya and into Tunisia, the remnants of the Panzer Army were still capable of occupying a defensive line, at Wadi Akarit, turning to face their opponents and challenging them to come forward.

Rommel's own verdict on Montgomery gets to the heart of the matter. He was, he later wrote, 'more of a strategist than a tactician. Command of a force in mobile battle was not his strong point.'[88] One who took part in the African campaign, General F.I.S. Tuker, commanding 4 Indian Division, also stressed Montgomery's shortcomings as a mobile or armoured commander, observing that, though he had forced Eighth Army armoured commanders to operate within a proper combination of arms, it was still not an army 'that could snatch an opportunity and it seldom would . . . again. It had assumed its character for the future; it would eschew the battle of manoeuvre and, with the finest equipment, bring the enemy down to its own pace . . .'[89] Unless, of course, the enemy was ahead of it and did not choose to give battle. For Eighth Army was to prove consistently incapable of using manoeuvre or mobility to force him to do so. Under Montgomery it was as deficient in these two attributes 'as a dray horse on a polo field'.[90]

The major problem in the immediate aftermath of Alamein, as Rommel began to give way on the 2nd, was that Montgomery had given no real thought to the exploitation phase. His attention had been almost entirely focused on the slugging matches in his various salients, which had also absorbed most of his mobile units. Attempts to institute an authentic *corps de chasse*, with proper logistical back-up, invariably came to nothing. A scheme to create a force round the headquarters of 8 Armoured Division* and 23 Armoured Brigade was cancelled. A suggestion by General Briggs that part of X Corps should be loaded in advance with the food, fuel and ammunition to sustain it in a sudden pursuit was rejected. But having a *corps de chasse* ready and victualled was only part of the problem. Largely by their own efforts, the New Zealand Division and its supporting armour were in fact so prepared on the 4th, but found that no arrangements had been made for providing them with a clear axis out of the immediate battlefield. Just as the problem of the minefield gaps had been largely ignored during the planning for

---

* The division itself, originally part of X Corps, had been parcelled out among the other formations of Eighth Army.

Lightfoot, so too were the difficulties inherent in speedily releasing a compact pursuit force in the final stages of Supercharge.

When, on the night of the 4th, the New Zealand Division did attempt to break out towards Fuka, to cut Rommel off, they found the traffic situation in the Supercharge salient 'chaotic. There is no other word to describe the incredible confusion . . . Vehicles of every formation were travelling in every direction on every conceivable track, looming up in front of each other from unexpected directions out of the thick stifling pall of dust.'[91] An ancillary thrust by 8 Armoured Brigade, a short hook to Galal, between Fuka and El Daba, also bogged down, though this time largely through an inability to control the brigade's movements in the dark. On the face of it, this was hardly Montgomery's fault, though it might be argued that a more 'balanced' commander, with a 15:1 superiority in tanks, would have had a mobile reserve ready to move somewhat earlier, in daylight. In the event, by the time Galal was reached the main enemy force had gone.

At about this time it also became apparent to Montgomery that the delayed New Zealand drive was similarly unlikely to close the door at Fuka – it had been further held up on a dummy minefield – and so he launched another belated flanking drive, sending 2 Armoured Brigade in a wide sweep towards 'Charing Cross', just to the south of Mersa Matruh. This force actually ran out of fuel, surely an 'unpardonable failure in supply' by a commander who should long ago have made proper logistic provision for just such a drive.[92] On the night of 6 November torrential rain began to fall which put an end to all pursuit for the time being. But it did not explain, as Montgomery later claimed, the fact that the Panzer Army had not been cut off. Before the rains came there had already been several opportunities to close the door on its retreat, at Galal, Fuka and Mersa Matruh, and these had been missed because throughout Supercharge '8 Army was not organised either administratively or morally to cope with the opportunity it had created . . . The truth is that at Alamein there was no properly considered plan for handling a breakthrough effectively.'[93]

In fact, Montgomery seems almost to have welcomed the delay imposed by the atrocious weather. Certainly he never again made much of an attempt to cut Rommel off, seeming content merely to trundle along behind him. As the war diarist of 15 Panzer noted:

The British High Command fell back on their accustomed policy of extreme caution – systematic build-up of the attack until a favourable defensive position was reached – deployment to meet the expected enemy counter-attack – resumption of the attack, always in the same sequence. No effort was made to exploit developments in the situation by the use of mobile forces.[94]

The point about 'expected counter-attack' is particularly pertinent, for Montgomery was continually muttering darkly about not repeating others' mistakes and allowing Rommel the chance for a sudden riposte by thrusting too far forward. For an assessment of just how effective such a riposte might have been, the reader is referred again to table 12, with the additional reminder that Montgomery was constantly informed about Rommel's weakness. As Professor Hinsley points out, Montgomery could never complain about 'the lack of intelligence. Throughout the pursuit . . . [he] was fully apprised by the Enigma, by air reconnaissance and by Army Y [radio interception] of the state of Rommel's forces and, more important, the Enigma gave him advance notice of Rommel's intentions.'[95]

But Montgomery was not to be pushed. On 8 November, when General Gatehouse of 10 Armoured finally entered Mersa Matruh, he suggested that he might press on straight away towards Sollum, as his tanks were all fuelled and his petrol lorries fully laden. Montgomery told him that there was to be 'no mad rush', withdrew his division, except for one brigade, and sacked him for good measure. A drive towards Capuzzo was sanctioned, led by 7 Armoured Division and the New Zealanders, but this failed to cut off the Panzer Army and Montgomery refused to permit any further advance. He remained adamant even when he learnt, on the 11th, that Rommel was pulling out of Bardia and Tobruk, towards Benghazi, and might thus be cut off by a repetition of O'Connor's short-cut across the Cyrenaican bulge during Operation Compass. This evidently smacked too much of 'manoeuvre' to Montgomery, and he unveiled a singularly uninspired plan for letting Rommel retreat back into his old defensive line at El Agheila and attacking him there. Professor Hinsley accurately reflects the exasperation felt at the time when he coldly reports: 'Nor was he deflected from this plan when he learned from the Enigma . . . that 21st Panzer Division was down to 11 serviceable tanks, that 15th Panzer Division had no tanks left and that the Panzer Army had only one quarter of an ammunition issue and fuel for only 4–5 days.'[96]*

---

* At the same time the German artillery strength stood at 25 anti-tank guns, 19 field guns (plus four troops of unspecified strength), and 64 anti-aircraft guns.

On 16 and 17 November Enigma revealed that Rommel had almost no petrol at all and was virtually immobilised in the Benghazi area. Even Montgomery acknowledged that this might limit the Panzer Army's ability to deliver the lightning riposte, and on the 18th he ordered X Corps to execute a strong southern thrust to cut off the enemy. Unfortunately the only force available for such a thrust was 22 Armoured Brigade, almost all of whose tanks were in a lamentable mechanical state. Replacements were only to be had at Sollum, a hundred miles to the rear, and these had to be brought forward on tank-transporters. Hardly a 'balanced' deployment for mobile operations against a defeated enemy. It proved impossible, therefore, to get behind Rommel's forces quickly enough, and he was given time to scrape together a little extra fuel and withdraw unmolested towards El Agheila, which he entered on the 24th. As Rommel wrote of this retreat through Egypt and Cyrenaica: 'The British commander had shown himself to be over-cautious. He risked nothing in any way doubtful and bold solutions were completely foreign to him.'[97]

Montgomery now settled down to organise the set-piece frontal attack that he seems to have been determined to fight all along. A sense of urgency was conspicuously absent. The plan was not completed until 29 November, and this specified that D-Day was to be 16/17 December, over three weeks after Rommel's arrival at El Agheila. In fact, Rommel had no intention of fighting it out and, having already withdrawn some units, decided to pull back the remainder in the face of strong pressure. This intention was revealed by Enigma decrypts on 8 December. It behove Montgomery, therefore, to ensure that his frontal attack was supplemented by a flanking drive suitably positioned to cut off such a withdrawal. This was indeed envisaged in Montgomery's original plan, and was to be undertaken by the New Zealand Division. Sensibly, the outflanking move was timed to begin on 12/13 December so that it might get some way into Rommel's rear before the frontal assault began and thus ensure a successful envelopment. The Enigma revelations of the 8th stirred fears at Eighth Army headquarters that Rommel might not accept battle at all, and they rightly began to think in terms of advancing the date of the attack. But only of the frontal attack. Thus, though this latter was brought forward to the night of 15/16 December, the date of the New Zealand assault remained unchanged, and had in fact slipped back a few hours. They were thus not in a position to cut into Rommel's rear when he began to yield along his front and he was able to withdraw without undue interference. As so often, it was Rommel who provided the most succinct critique of Montgomery's handling of this battle:

> The British commander's planning had shown one mistake. Experience must have told him that there was a good chance that we would not accept battle at . . . [El Agheila]. He should not, therefore, have started bombarding our strongpoints and attacking our line until his outflanking force had completed its move and was in a position to advance along the coast road in timed co-ordination with the frontal attack.[98]

One wonders what Rommel might have said had he known that Montgomery had no need to rely on 'experience' but was in fact reading the enemy's mail.

The Panzer Army now fell back on Buerat, which they reached on 28 December. Montgomery lumbered along behind and as his forces deployed in front of the new line he began preparing for another set-piece assault. Corelli Barnett has commented caustically on his lack of haste: 'Montgomery wanted the port of Tripoli urgently, before the Germans could wreck it as they had Benghazi. He wished to attack before the Germans could anticipate him by withdrawal; and because of the need for speed he only gave himself three weeks to get ready.'[99]

Three weeks in which to prepare an attack with 532 front-line tanks (217 Grants and Shermans) against 37 German and 57 Italian, with 360 artillery pieces against 170 Axis, with 940 anti-tank guns against 119. As an unpublished official account of the campaign concluded, given 'Rommel's supply difficulties and the weakness of his forces . . . the Eighth Army commander's plans for the assault . . . seem . . . most ponderous.'[100] On 31 December Enigma revealed that Rommel intended to employ exactly the same tactics as at El Agheila and strip his line to the bone before gradually yielding to Commonwealth pressure. This altered Montgomery's own time-scale not one jot, not even with regard to the flanking attack that he was again to employ. Once again, therefore, the Eighth Army lashed out against thin air and soon managed to lose contact completely with the retreating enemy, whose only substantial loss was 18 tanks of Centauro Division which had to be destroyed after running out of fuel. By 1 February 1943 the Panzer Army had crossed over into Tunisia. The desert war was over. Against all expectations, however, Rommel's career was not.

6

Tunisia and Italy

November 1942 – May 1945

Probably the major contribution of the Mediterranean campaign to the war as a whole was that it tied down a number of first-class German divisions that could have been deployed to much greater effect in countering the Allied landings in Normandy, in June 1944. Even at the time, at least some Allied planners realised that maintaining a presence in the Mediterranean could have some diversionary value. At the Casablanca Conference, in January 1943, it was agreed by the Americans and the British that one of the prime aims of future operations in this theatre must be the 'diverting [of] German pressure from the Russian front', whilst at the Trident Conference in Washington, in the following May, it was decided that future planning must be predicated upon the need 'to contain the maximum number of German forces'.[1]

This apparent dove-tailing of intention and result is, however, somewhat misleading, and it would be wrong to assume that Mediterranean operations were conducted according to some Allied strategic master plan. No such plan ever existed, and throughout the war operations in this theatre were bedevilled by serious disagreements between the Allies about the proper level of commitment there. To many Americans, indeed, any strategic diversion was synonymous with dispersion and they seriously questioned the value of involving any American forces in the Mediterranean at all. In reality, the conference pronouncements just cited were not statements of fundamental, agreed strategic precepts but anodyne generalisations to mask basic disagreements about the course of future operations, *if any*, in this theatre.

At first there was agreement. As the British had been involved in North Africa long before the Americans entered the war, it was accepted that some assistance should be given to eliminate the Axis forces there, to which end large numbers of American aircraft and tanks were freely shipped out. The Americans also agreed that North Africa offered an excellent base for intensifying the bombing effort against Germany, and were quite happy to establish a substantial USAAF presence there, with the first units arriving in June 1942. Thereafter, however, consensus was hard to find. For the Americans, the prime objective in the land war against Germany must be to get as many divisions as possible into western Europe. This should be achieved, moreover, as quickly as possible and by the shortest possible route. The latter could only be through the British Isles and across the Channel into northern France. Operations in any other theatre would only serve to delay such a cross-Channel invasion and might also weaken its punch by diverting fighting troops, shipping and landing craft. The British, notably Churchill and Brooke,* were less enamoured of this 'bull at a gate' approach. As Britain was already involved in North Africa, as the Mediterranean had for years been a vital corridor linking the British Empire, and as they had an instinctive distaste for squaring up to the enemy where he most expected it, in the very theatre where hundreds of thousands of young men had perished less than 30 years earlier, they favoured approaching Germany via the back door, through North Africa, Sicily/Sardinia, and Italy or the Balkans.

As early as December 1941, therefore, they were trying to elicit American support for a landing in North Africa, from where they could link up with Eighth Army and eliminate Rommel's forces. Roosevelt was not unsympathetic to the idea but other Americans, notably Henry Stimson, the Secretary of War, and General George Marshall, the US Army Chief of Staff, were adamantly opposed. They fought hard against the proposal right through until August 1942, when Roosevelt himself had to intervene, insisting that it was essential that American troops be seen to be doing *something* at this stage of the war and that an invasion of French North Africa offered the only immediate chance of success. But, having been forced to agree to Operation Torch, as it became known, most Americans still refused to view it as a springboard for further Mediterranean operations and Marshall, in particular, looked only to the day when North Africa had been speedily cleared and American forces could reconcentrate in England for the cross-Channel assault.

* Brooke became Chief of the Imperial General Staff in December 1941 and Chairman of the British Chiefs of Staff Committee in the following June.

Unfortunately, as will be seen, soon after the Torch forces had entered Tunisia the campaign bogged down and it became clear that it was going to involve a heavy commitment of men and matériel. By the time of the Casablanca Conference, therefore, the Americans had to face up to the fact that they were saddled with a sizeable Mediterranean commitment and that there was no immediate prospect of their being able to disengage the forces involved. Under relentless hectoring from Churchill and Brooke they conceded that these forces might as well try to gain at least one victory on the cheap and gave their reluctant consent for an invasion of Sicily, hoping that this might prompt the Italians to desert the Axis. It is in this context, of an ill-tempered concession of just one last Mediterranean operation, that one should evaluate the Casablanca gloss about diverting troops from the Eastern Front.

The attention paid to strategic objectives at the Trident Conference was also largely lip-service, and in substantive matters the Americans once again wilted under British pressure. They began the proceedings utterly opposed to any further involvement in the Mediterranean. Summing up their mood, Brooke wrote in his diary: 'The Americans are taking up the attitude that we led them down the garden path by taking them to North Africa. That at Casablanca we again misled them by inducing them to attack Sicily. And now they do not intend to be led astray again.'[2] The ensuing discussions became quite heated, as the Americans attempted firmly to resist all British suggestions about extending operations into mainland Italy. According to one participant, 'the arguments . . . occasionally got so acrimonious that the junior staffs were bidden to leave the principals to continue the battle in secret session.'[3] In the end a 'compromise' was hammered out. Though the Americans refused to commit themselves to anything definite, they seemed in the end to weary of the whole debate and agreed to a vague formulation about mainland Italy that authorised the theatre commander, General Dwight Eisenhower, to plan the whole Sicily campaign and its exploitation in a way best calculated to eliminate Italy from the war. But this exploitation was to be limited: at most an invasion of Calabria or Sardinia, with operations to be terminated as soon as the tottering Fascist state had finally collapsed. Whatever they said in the final communiqué, the Americans had no intention of opening up a full-blooded Italian front with the specific intention of sucking in the maximum number of German divisions.

In the end, because of the leeway allowed to Eisenhower and the other local commanders, an Italian front was opened, though even then it was not really the product of a whole-hearted, preconceived strategic decision. At the Trident Conference it had been decided that seven Mediterranean divisions and most of the landing craft were to be transferred back to England by November 1943, whilst at the Eureka Conference in Tehran, in November 1943, it was agreed that a further six or so divisions would be withdrawn from Italy in July 1944 to stage Operation Anvil, an invasion of southern France to supplement the cross-Channel assault.

Nor did the decisions taken regarding Italian operations themselves encourage a belief that their extension was the fruit of a clear-cut strategic appreciation. Not until 18 July 1943, a week after the invasion of Sicily, did Eisenhower definitely come down in favour of moving on to the mainland, and not until 16 August, when the conquest of Sicily was complete, did he decide how this was to be done. A two-pronged amphibious operation was the method chosen, with Eighth Army invading across the Straits of Messina into Calabria and Fifth US Army landing at Salerno, just south of Naples. The Americans, however, still had no desire to become heavily involved in Italy, and at the Quadrant Conference in Quebec, in August, they named the Foggia airfields as their main target, with a possible exploitation towards Rome if circumstances seemed particularly propitious. But whatever happened, the landing craft used at Salerno were to be returned to England immediately afterwards. On 25 September, three weeks after Salerno, Eisenhower decided that Rome was a feasible objective and gave the appropriate orders. In November, at Tehran, the Americans conceded that the Pisa–Rimini line should be the new objective, but it was not until September 1944, at the Octagon Conference in Quebec, that they gave their consent for an attempt to clear the Po Valley, though only if Eisenhower, by then Supreme Commander in North-West Europe, did not feel that he needed more divisions for his advance into Germany.

In short, though at the end of the day Allied forces in Italy did succeed in pinning down a significant number of German divisions, it would be wrong to see this as a logical consequence of binding decisions taken at Casablanca or Washington. The overall impression, indeed, is of a remarkable lack of direction in Mediterranean planning, with key decisions taken off the cuff, simply because no one, least of all on the American side, could think of anything better to do. It is difficult to disagree with Montgomery's appreciation of overall strategic control in this theatre, and with his complaint at one stage that 'before we embark on major operations in the mainland of Europe we must have a master plan and know how we propose to develop these operations. I have not been told of any master plan and I must therefore assume that there was none.'[4]

The *ad hoc*, opportunistic nature of Allied planning in the Mediterranean had serious tactical repercussions for the conduct of the various campaigns in Tunisia, Sicily and the Italian peninsula. The major problem was always that the final decision for an invasion was only taken because the target was deemed to be a soft option, and thus far too little heed was given to what might happen if the enemy should decide to stand and fight.* This was clearly apparent in French North Africa from the moment the first units of Operation Torch came ashore on 8 November 1942. The *raison d'être* of the invasion was to support Eighth Army's advance in the Western Desert, and the crushing of any resistance in French North Africa itself was seen as a mere formality, to be swiftly completed before beginning the more serious task of closing the vice on Rommel. The planners' assumptions were clearly evident in a telegram from Alexander to Churchill, sent only eight days after the landings:

> I think it is of paramount importance that the campaign in North Africa should this time be driven to a conclusion. Only by finishing off the enemy in Tripolitania can we really release and build up forces for operations elsewhere. Therefore I feel that Eisenhower from the west should afford maximum co-operation in our combined advance on Tripoli as soon as Tunisia is cleared, and before he directs any effort northward.[5]

Thus the Allies landed in French North Africa ill-adapted to tackle anything but the most limited resistance. An initial handicap was that the landings were very dispersed, with three separate task forces arriving almost 700 miles apart at Casablanca, Oran and Algiers. The aim, of course, was to subdue all possible centres of Vichy resistance in Morocco and Algeria simultaneously, but it meant that only one of the three Allied task forces, at Algiers, was within even reasonable striking distance of the main objective, Tunis. And even that force was still some 400 miles away. It was, moreover, very weak, consisting only of two infantry brigades (unmotorised) and

---

* There was, of course, a great deal of contingency planning done even before the decision for an actual invasion was made, but this was largely concerned with the problems of shipping troops to the invasion beaches and not with what they should do once they were ashore.

an armoured regimental group, to be joined later by a Commando and a Parachute Brigade. In other words, though 107,000 troops in all were to be landed in the first few days of Torch, a mere ten battalions of infantry, none of them mobile, four of them without heavy weapons, and a regiment of tanks were expected to carry out the first major strategic mission of the campaign.* First Army, as the Torch forces were soon to be known, had come as an army of occupation rather than a compact fighting force prepared if necessary to contest its preliminary objectives.

The Torch planners had also paid remarkably little attention to the possibility of intervention by German troops, not even allocating aircraft to reconnoitre the relevant sea lanes or to bomb possible landing sites. Unfortunately, Hitler decided straight away that he was not going to give up Tunisia without a fight and, taking advantage of this Allied failure to interdict the sea lanes from Sicily, he began shipping in troops as fast as he could.[†] By the end of November, a total of 15,000 German and 9,000 Italian troops had disembarked in Tunisia, as well as some 130 tanks. This was hardly a fearsome force when compared with the total Allied presence in French North Africa, but its great advantage was that it was concentrated in just the right place and able to strike at the feeble Allied units undertaking the main drive.

Nor did these latter demonstrate any particular sense of urgency, not encountering German blocking groups until 17 November. Moreover, these first small-scale encounters immediately halted the whole advance, with First Army's commander, General Kenneth Anderson, personally vetoing any suggestion of pressing forward whilst the Germans were still relatively weak. As he reported back to London: 'My forces available for the rush on Tunis are woefully weak and before committing them I must be sure of a good start and have a clearer understanding of the odds against them.'[6‡] The advance

---

* The mass of the armour landed in the first waves came ashore near Casablanca, with an American task force. It remains unclear what French armoured threat could justify the placing of most Allied tanks as far away as possible from where they could most usefully be employed.

† During November, not a single Axis merchant ship was sunk along this route.

‡ His understanding might have been clearer had not the Allies compounded their omissions with regard to motor transport, tanks, and aerial and naval interdiction by neglecting 'to make adequate Sigint [Signal Intelligence] arrangements . . . It had the result that field intelligence was virtually non-existent and little operational use could be made of the high-grade Sigint that was made available.' (F.H. Hinsley, *British Intelligence in the Second World War* (3 vols, HMSO, 1979–88)), vol. 2, p. 475.)

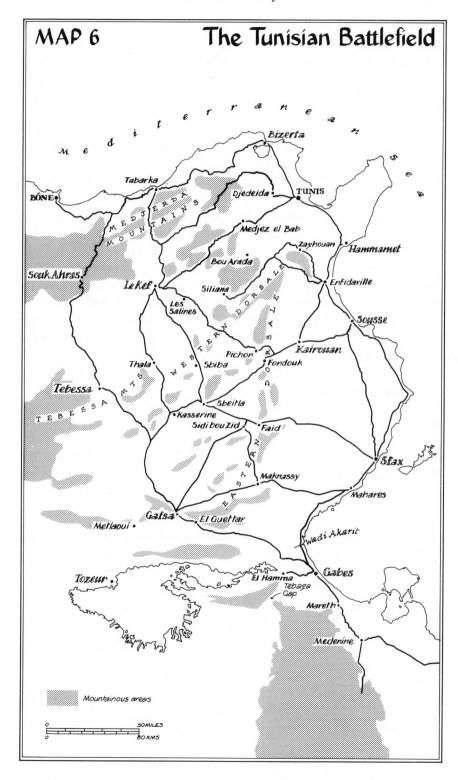

MAP 6

The Tunisian Battlefield

was not renewed until 24 November and German resistance, after a brief instance of panic on the 26th, was daily becoming firmer. On the 29th and 30th, therefore, the advance ground to a halt in front of Djedeida, less than 15 miles from Tunis.

The intensity of German counter-attacks increased and on 4 December the Allies were forced to relinquish Tebourba.* Between the 6th and the 10th several commanding features between Tebourba and Medjez were also given up, some for no good reason, and later Allied attempts to win them back made little impression. On 24 December, with the atrocious weather turning all roads into impassable quagmires, Eisenhower felt he had no option but to call a halt to operations. That day he informed the assembled pressmen: 'Gentlemen, we have lost the race for Tunis.'

The fact of the matter was that the Allies had lost the race to build up forces *in the front line.* For not only had a large proportion of their forces landed many hundreds of miles away from the decisive sector, but even those that were nearest depended as their main source of supply and local reinforcement upon Algiers, which was almost 400 miles from the front and linked by extremely poor roads, made yet worse by the dreadful weather. The Axis forces, on the other hand, had to make only a short crossing from Sicily and could then distribute supplies and reinforcements relatively quickly throughout their constricted bridgehead behind the Eastern Dorsals, Medjez and Djedeida.† The speed of their build-up is illustrated in the figures below, and one stresses again that the vast majority of these men could be thrown into the battle almost as soon as they landed. The totals indicate the number of Axis troops present in Tunisia on the specified dates:

15 December	31,000 (19,500 German)
18 December	42,000 (includes Axis air forces)
31 December	65,000 (47,000 German)

* American armour took part in the fighting around Tebourba, and its tactics were depressingly similar to those employed by Eighth Army in the hell-for-leather attacks of Battleaxe and Crusader. On 2 December, near Djedeida, the favoured tactic 'was still to engage in what were, in essence, cavalry charges . . . isolated and unsupported . . .' (J. Lucas, *Panzer Army Africa* (Macdonald and Jane's, 1977), p. 153.) A battalion of 1 US Armoured Division was duly smashed by a handful of 88s and Panzer IVs sited on its flank.

† The Axis forces were organised first under XC Panzer Corps and then, from 8 December, under Fifth Panzer Army, commanded by General Jürgen von Arnim. The main formations sent over were 10 Panzer Division, part of Hermann Göring Panzer Division, 334 Infantry Division and the Italian Superga Division.

In these circumstances, and aware that there was no prospect of the rains slackening until the following spring, Eisenhower decided that no major offensive towards Tunis was feasible until then. First Army was thereby condemned to three months of unrelieved misery in the cold, rainswept hills.

No commander, however, is content to let his troops remain totally inactive in fixed positions, and there was in the first half of January 'a grumble of activity similar to that which so often marked the aftermath of blunted offensives in the First World War, with Anderson calling for constant pressure on the enemy with . . . forays to seize slices of territory for use later as jumping off places when the main offensive began in the Spring.'[7] But the Germans were in an equally belligerent mood, intent on inflicting maximum damage on the enemy whilst they temporarily held the whip-hand. In the second half of January they made substantial penetrations into the Eastern Dorsale and then began to think in terms of a more ambitious offensive.

Rommel's sights were raised particularly high. Temporarily ignoring Eighth Army plodding along in his rear, he turned his eyes northward, where he perceived an opportunity to drive into the Allied rear, through Gafsa and Tebessa, towards Bône, and thus blunt and even eliminate the threat to his own rear. Von Arnim, however, had more modest ambitions, being mainly concerned with destroying Allied troops and equipment and further strengthening his positions in the Eastern Dorsale. Kesselring regretfully conceded that this latter strategy was more in tune with Axis capabilities and it was decided to launch two limited operations, against Sidi bou Zid and Gafsa. The first was von Arnim's responsibility and the second Rommel's, though neither commander was given the authority to coordinate operations. There was still, therefore, no consensus on whether the essential aim of the attacks was consolidation or exploitation.

Von Arnim jumped off first, on 13 February, and by the 18th had cleared out American positions in his sector of the Eastern Dorsale. He then halted, and it fell to Kesselring to decide what course future operations, if any, should take. For Rommel, who had launched his own attack on the 15th, had taken Gafsa that same evening, swept on through Thélepte virtually unopposed and was now advancing towards the Kasserine Pass. On the 18th Rommel's idea of a deep exploitation into the Allied rear seemed to find favour with Kesselring, for he was given command of all three panzer divisions, hitherto split between himself and von Arnim. Shortly afterwards, however, because the two panzer divisions with von Arnim had become somewhat dispersed, Kesselring changed his mind and decided that only localised attacks into the Western Dorsale, towards Thala and Sbiba, were feasible.

In the event, Rommel's force proved too weak to carry out even this limited assignment.* Though the attack into the Kasserine Pass did eventually break through, the Allies were still able to hold out long enough to rush up reinforcements and stabilise a line not far north of it. Of particular importance was the arrival of most of the artillery of 9 us Infantry Division. On 22 February, Rommel, with Kesselring's concurrence, called off the whole offensive. The essential truth of Tunisian operations, just as elsewhere, had now become apparent. The Axis forces, no matter how high their level of technical expertise, simply could not hope to prevail in the face of their opponents' enormous material reserves. Above all they had no answer to the mighty American production lines, now making their first major contribution to ground operations. Between 13 and 24 February, for example, II us Corps had actually lost more armour (235 tanks and 110 self-propelled guns) than the Germans had deployed at the start of the battle (228 tanks), yet within a week they had assembled sufficient reinforcements and replacements to block the Germans completely on each of their chosen axes.

This material imbalance was to become more and more marked in the last two months of the campaign, as the Allies slowly organised themselves for a full-scale offensive against the Axis bridgehead. It continued, for example, to limit Axis ability to organise spoiling attacks of their own. An assault by von Arnim against Sidi Nsir, between 26 February and 3 March, was easily contained, as too was a counter-attack at Medenine by Panzer Army Africa.† This latter was a particularly forlorn gesture, for though all three panzer divisions were employed they could muster only 142 tanks between them, as against Eighth Army's 400. Montgomery's defences could also deploy 350 field artillery pieces and 470 anti-tank guns. After two futile frontal assaults reminiscent of British efforts in 1941 and

---

* Even on 15 February, 15 Panzer Division, for example, had numbered only 26 German and 23 Italian tanks. On that same date, Rommel's artillery was at only one-sixth of its full establishment and his anti-tank guns one-quarter.
† By then renamed First Italian Army. Later, on 23 February, First Italian Army and Fifth Panzer Army were put under a single HQ, Army Group Africa, commanded by Rommel.

early 1942, the Germans quit the battlefield. They left behind 50 wrecked tanks, having accounted for only one British.

To the Allies, the Medenine attack was little more than an annoying interruption, for they had already come up with a plan to make a decisive break in the German perimeter. Eighth Army was the chosen instrument and was instructed by Alexander to rupture German defences along the Mareth Line, whither Rommel had retreated after quitting Tripoli. First Army's only contribution was to be a drive by II us Corps, now commanded by General George S. Patton, towards Maknassy, with the limited aim of tying down Axis reserves that might otherwise be used to reinforce the Mareth Line. The attack, which began on 16 March, made only limited progress, thanks partly to the atrocious weather, but it did succeed in drawing off 10 Panzer Division which had been in reserve around Sousse. This meant that when Montgomery began his own attack, on the 20th, the 743 tanks available to Eighth Army were faced only by the 73 German tanks belonging to 15 and 21 Panzer Divisions. Eighth Army also mustered a marked superiority in guns, having 692 field and medium artillery pieces as against 447 in the whole of Army Group Africa and 1,033 anti-tank guns as against only 260 German.

But Montgomery's deployment of this overwhelming force showed a remarkable lack of originality or verve. The pace of his operations was as slow as ever. He showed no apparent desire quickly to follow up the victory at Medenine and refused to advance the date of the Mareth attack, fixed for the 20th. The us Official History was of the opinion that 'Eighth Army proceeded to the crucial battle with the majestic deliberation of a pachyderm.'[8] Eisenhower was to write to Marshall a few weeks later suggesting that Montgomery 'is so proud of his successes to date that he will never willingly make a single move until he is absolutely certain of success – in other words, until he has concentrated enough resources so that anyone could practically guarantee the outcome.'[9] His plan for the actual assault relied, in essence, on an old-fashioned frontal attack by the infantry of XXX Corps who were to break into the line near the coast, roll it up and advance on Gabes. The two armoured divisions of X Corps were to be held in reserve for exploitation towards Sfax. One historian has suggested that Montgomery should be compared to Wellington at the storming of Badajoz in that he 'relied on the morale of his troops to reduce the fortifications.'[10] Montgomery's mistrust in manoeuvre was still much in evidence, and though a flanking move through the Tebaga Gap, at the western end of the Mareth Line, was included in the plan, the relative weakness of the force involved and a vagueness and lack of conviction in their orders indicate that this was regarded as little more than a diversionary attack.

It was the weakness of this flanking force that crippled Montgomery's attack. For, though XXX Corps' crude frontal assault made little impression on the German defences, it did at least force their commander, General Giovanni Messe,* to commit 15 Panzer Division in this sector, leaving only a tiny Italian battle group to cover the Tebaga Gap. But the flanking force, conscious of its weakness and discerning no particular sense of urgency in Montgomery's orders, was very slow to move off. By the time it did, it was too late. As soon as Messe became aware of this threat to his flank he brought across 21 Panzer Division from Gabes, and when the attack finally went in British tanks ran straight into a hail of shots from this division's 88mm guns. Of course, Montgomery cannot be held wholly responsible for the dilatoriness of the attack but he should surely from the beginning have accorded this thrust a higher priority. Instead of trying to break through the Mareth Line proper, which in any case would only push the enemy back to a new defensive line, he should have used the frontal attack simply to pin the defenders and draw in their reserves, whilst at the same time reinforcing the Tebaga force and giving it clear orders about the absolute necessity of forcing the Gap as quickly as possible and getting across the Axis line of retreat.

Eventually this was done when, on the 23d, Montgomery called off XXX Corps' breakthrough attempt and transferred his main forces to Tebaga. They attacked on the 26th and, within a few hours, 'a quite irresistible force, its pathway battered clear by an unprecedented weight of air and artillery bombardment, broke straight through the thin [enemy] lines . . .'[11] But the attack had come five days too late, because Messe was now alerted to the danger from this direction and on the 24th had already drawn up plans for a withdrawal from the Mareth Line. The first units began to pull out on the night of the 25th whilst the rearguards fell back on El Hamma, where they were able to establish a defensive screen to cover their withdrawal. By the 29th, First Italian Army was settling into new positions at Wadi Akarit, having yet again evaded all attempts to cut their retreat.

In early April the Allies tried once again, though this time

* Messe had replaced Rommel as commander of First Italian Army when the latter left North Africa for good on 9 March. Von Arnim took over command of Army Group Africa.

Alexander's overall plan looked for a significant contribution from First Army. Hitherto, as has been noted by one historian, 'it really appeared as if Alexander was incapable of conjuring up a really bold and ambitious stroke in the Rommel manner, for never did he do more than hammer away with short hooks and frontal pushes.'[12] The Wadi Akarit attack, however, did at least envisage a genuine Army Group operation,* with Eighth Army forcing Messe out of his defences and First Army's IX Corps driving through the Fondouk Pass to cut off his retreat towards Enfidaville, the next potential bolt-hole. Unfortunately, what looked impressively logical in conception was sadly flawed in execution, and the battles of Wadi Akarit and Fondouk, particularly in their exploitation phases, represent British generalship at its lowest ebb.

Wadi Akarit could have been even more unproductive than it actually was had Montgomery's original plan been adhered to. Axis defences were based on a wadi running three miles inland from the coast, a natural anti-tank obstacle in ground which offered absolutely no cover to an attacker, and below this a series of *djebels*, almost impregnable rocky fastnesses dominating the desert below. Montgomery's plan relied entirely upon a frontal assault by XXX Corps, with X Corps under orders to feed its armour through once a hole had been gouged out. The chosen axes of advance were across the wadi and through a gap between two of the *djebels*, both axes to be subjected to very heavy artillery fire from front and flanks. There seems little question that this projected assault 'highlights another instance of dubious planning by Montgomery in the absence of a personal appraisal of the ground and indicated how, on the crest of success, he reverted more and more to the use of brute force where subtlety might have been more profitable.'[13] Happily there was someone who was prepared to look for a more subtle approach. This was General Francis Tuker, commanding 4 Indian Division, who after feverish personal lobbying managed to persuade his superiors to let him make the first attack, infiltrating by night into two of the *djebels* and thus denying these vantage points to the enemy when the main advance began through the gaps below.

Thus protected, XXX Corps' main attack, on 6 April, made great progress and the situation soon seemed ripe for the armoured breakthrough. Once again, however, this was badly bungled, largely

---

* Anderson's First Army had come under the command of Alexander's new 18 Army Group on 19 February, as had Eighth Army on the following day.

because of an almost total lack of cooperation between the armour and the other arms. The tanks were very slow to arrive at the gap provided by the infantry, and when they did finally attempt to push through they came under anti-tank fire from one of the *djebels* and straightaway halted. It has since been established that this fire was from no more than *two or three* 88mm guns, yet it sufficed to halt the whole assault. Absolutely no attempt was made to subdue this fire because no plans at all had been made for cooperation between the tanks and the artillery. The offending 88s could actually be overlooked from 4 Indian Division's positions on one of the *djebels* seized earlier, and the fire of the whole of XXX Corps' artillery could have been directed onto them. But there was no liaison at all between the Indians and the armour, such that the former's own observers had no idea that there was a hold-up and no one in X Corps was in contact to tell them. In short, according to one account, at this critical stage of the battle 'no-one had the faintest idea of what was happening.'[14]

Slipshod arrangements of this sort must in the last analysis be Montgomery's responsibility. Once again he seems to have given remarkably little thought to the actual mechanics of the armoured breakthrough. Not only were X Corps' operations planned in almost complete isolation but there was again no attempt to imbue the armoured commanders with any sense of urgency.* This lackadaisical attitude persisted throughout the ensuing 'pursuit' to Enfidaville. Though Sfax was taken on 10 April and Sousse on the 12th, the enemy 'were actually allowed to gain distance on X Corps, who gave up the chase on the 11th . . . Again the Axis had escaped much as they chose and again there is a hint of inertia in Montgomery's conduct of the pursuit . . . One is left with the impression of a magnificent opportunity lost.'[15]

Yet another opportunity was lost at Fondouk, during an attack towards Kairouan, to break through into the coastal plain and cut off First Italian Army as it was pinned at Wadi Akarit. This idea had been mooted very much at the last minute, only three days before Montgomery's own attack, and could not be put into force until 8 April. However, the local commander, General Crocker, seems to have regarded the forcing of the Fondouk Pass as something of a formality. His plans for seizing the twin *djebels* at its entrance were consequently cursory and did not allow for a simultaneous attack on both these strongpoints. The two consecutive attacks therefore

* A fact underlined by 8 Armoured Brigade who, when they did finally request a Corps artillery bombardment late on the afternoon of the 6th, were content to wait until *the following day* for it actually to be laid on.

made hardly any progress, as they were in turn subjected to heavy fire from both *djebels*, one of which could select its targets almost at leisure.

The almost complete lack of progress considerably disturbed Alexander, and on the 9th he ordered Crocker to 'bounce' the Pass with 6 Armoured Division, the formation that had originally been intended to exploit the seizure of the twin *djebels*. As at Rhaaman Track, five months earlier, the attack was to be pressed home regardless of casualties. The sacrificial lambs were 17/21 Lancers, who counted Balaclava amongst their battle honours:

> The execution of the charge deteriorated into nothing more nor less than a headlong charge without finesse . . . A few hundred yards beyond the start the tanks of the Lancers struck the first row of mines, and soon the crack of high velocity guns . . . caused tank after tank to burst into flames . . . First . . . [one] squadron then another, rapidly reduced by 80 per cent of their number, tried with incredible persistence to flounder through the mines until hardly a tank could move.[16]

Succeeding squadrons, including those of 16/5 Lancers, did eventually force a way through, but so traumatic had been the impact of the preliminary slaughter that none could be prevailed upon to advance beyond the exit to the Pass. None moved until the following morning, by which time the German rearguard was slipping away through Kairouan to join up with the rearguard of First Italian Army.

The Americans were extremely disappointed with the complete failure to interfere with the retreat from Akarit to Enfidaville. General Omar Bradley, now commanding II US Corps, was convinced that 'Alexander might well have brought the fighting in Tunisia to a swifter conclusion . . . Alexander's IX Corps attack towards Fondouk might have succeeded in splitting the Axis had it been more carefully conceived and launched earlier with far greater strength. On the whole, I concluded, British generalship was too slow and too cautious.'[17] Certainly, 18 Army Group had shown itself incapable of achieving decisive results through a battle of manoeuvre, even of the most elementary kind, and it was almost with a sense of relief that Alexander settled down to exercise his only remaining option, a frontal assault on the small 'fortress' that remained in Axis hands. Brute force was again to be the order of the day, the hopes of success pinned almost entirely on the enormous material preponderance that the Allies could bring to bear.

By now the Axis supply position was parlous, with the Allied offensive against the Mediterranean sea lanes really beginning to have a decisive effect. On 29 March von Arnim signalled OKW: 'Supplies shattering. Ammunition only available for 1–2 days, no more stocks for some weapons such as medium field howitzers. Fuel situation similar, large-scale movements no longer possible . . .'[18] In mid-April, a German officer wrote in his diary: '. . . the task of maintaining the bridgehead is really only a question of time . . . The Luftwaffe cannot supply us and that which comes by sea is a drop in the ocean . . . We are on the defensive because we cannot fight tanks with bodies of men and with shot guns. Yesterday Battle Group Wolff had one 7.5cm pak and a 5cm pak. The latter did not work.'[19]

The Allied build-up, on the other hand, continued apace. Whereas the number of serviceable Axis tanks in Tunisia fell from 130 to 100 between 5 and 22 April, that of the Allies rose from 1,200 to 1,400.* On 15 April Army Group Africa mustered only 475 artillery pieces of all types, many of them virtually without ammunition, whilst 18 Army Group had 1,500 in forward positions. Allied superiority in the air was just as marked. Admittedly their air forces started the campaign in very poor condition, but from January 1943 the relentless Allied reinforcement decisively tipped the scales.† By the time of the Battle of Mareth, Eighth Army was being supported by 535 fighters, fighter-bombers and tank-destroyers, as well as 260 bombers, facing only 170 Axis aircraft of all types. In mid-April, in the whole Mediterranean theatre, the Allies could muster over 2,500 serviceable aircraft as opposed to only 500 German and 450 Italian. In April 1943 the Allies were putting up an average of 1,000 sorties per day whilst the best German performance in 1943 was 100 a day. Between February and April the average daily number of bomber sorties was a mere 37.

The eventual liquidation of the Tunisian fortress was therefore simply a matter of time, and it remained only for Alexander to decide which wall was to bear the brunt of the assault. After the

* The supply of replacement tanks had virtually dried up. The monthly totals delivered between November and March were: November 187; December 191; January 50; February 52; March 20.
† Just as with the ground forces, far too little attention had been paid to the first thrust into Tunisia and forward aircraft had only been available in very small numbers, dependent on supply bases many hundreds of miles in the rear and with a very low allocation of spare parts and maintenance personnel. Allied air units were also seriously handicapped by the fact that their forward airfields soon became muddy quagmires whilst the Germans had already converted theirs into all-weather strips.

failure at Fondouk he tended to favour the approaches to the west of Tunis, on First Army's front, and his orders of 12 April specified that future Eighth Army operations were to be purely subsidiary. This did not please Montgomery, however, and on the 16th he badgered Alexander into giving Eighth Army a breakthrough role of its own. Operation Vulcan, as the whole offensive was known, was thus altered to allow Montgomery to 'bounce' the Enfidaville Line and push through to Hammamet and thence into the Cap Bon peninsula.

Montgomery's plan of attack involved yet another crude frontal assault, this time by X Corps, on the night of 19/20 April. By the 22nd none of the attacking troops had made much progress. A fresh effort on the 24th also failed, as did a particularly futile attempt by a raw British Division on the 29th. The latter ended in something approaching a rout, one eye-witness stating that 'it reminded me of the infantry in open order advancing on the first day of the Somme against predictable machine-guns.'[20] After this Montgomery finally abandoned his plan for bouncing Enfidaville and on the 30th docilely acquiesced to Alexander's request for a further substantial reinforcement from Eighth Army.*

This was needed because Anderson's attacks, which had also begun on the 22nd, had still not yet succeeded in crumbling the Axis perimeter. Again the armour had been handled abominably, the complete lack of attention to a proper combination of arms leading to another failure by X Corps at Bou Arada:

Two armoured divisions were launched side by side and the old idea that tanks did not require any support beyond that of their own batteries firing at targets of opportunity prevailed. There was no coordinated plan, let alone any fire-programme or any arrangement made for the two divisional artilleries to assist each other. What was worse was that the A.G.R.A., the group of Army artillery allotted to the Corps, instead of being used as a source of concentrated fire-power ready to support either division was dismembered and dispersed to subsidiary tasks as soon as the armoured battle began. As a result these two powerful formations were very roughly handled by the usual screen of anti-tank guns well-sited and served devotedly in the usual German way.[21]

Using the divisions taken from Montgomery, 7 Armoured and

* 1 Armoured Division had already been handed over.

4 Indian as well as 201 Guards Brigade, Alexander prepared a
renewed attack, Operation Strike, to begin on 6 May. These formations, along with the rest of IX Corps, were to be massed around
Medjez with the simple aim of crashing through to Tunis. Alexander
'emphasised that the risk of losses had to be accepted. The tanks had
to get through.'[22] It could not be claimed, however, that there was
any real risk of defeat, even for an Army Group as ill-starred as
the 18th. The offensive was conducted with no particular flair, but
given the enormous margins of superiority mentioned above and the
progressive whittling away of the Axis forces – by 3 May the Germans
could field only 60 tanks – one is not surprised to learn that Tunis fell
on 8 May and the last Axis soldiers surrendered on the 13th.

What is surprising, perhaps, are the extravagant claims made
about the significance of the victory, both at the time and since.
Some particularly unperceptive English and American propagandists
sought to compare the victory in Tunisia with that of Stalingrad, and
some fairly meaningless sets of figures were bandied about. The
favourite comparison was between the 290,000 Axis troops killed
or captured in 'Tunisgrad' and the 250,000 or so similarly accounted
for at Stalingrad. A more meaningful comparison, however, is that
between the numbers of *German divisions* destroyed in each battle.
The records show that in North Africa the Germans lost 3⅓ panzer
divisions, 3 light divisions, 1 infantry division and some paratroopers.
In the Stalingrad pocket were lost 3 panzer divisions, 3 motorised
divisions, 1 jäger and *thirteen* infantry.

The *ad hoc* nature of the decisions taken with regard to Mediterranean operations continued to affect Allied operations adversely
during the Sicilian campaign. The major problem was that although
the decision to invade was taken in January, well in advance of D-Day
itself, no agreement was reached as to what should be done *after* Sicily
had been cleared. In particular, the Americans refused to commit
themselves to an invasion of the Italian mainland, thereby robbing
the detailed tactical planning of any wider strategic context and
suppressing vital questions about the ultimate purpose of Operation
Husky, as the Sicilian venture was christened. In consequence, very
little thought was given to preventing the Axis garrison in Sicily from
getting back to the mainland where they could fight again should
the Allies decide to continue Mediterranean operations. The Husky
plans contained no provisions for trying to surround the Germans and
Italians, either by operations on the island itself or by combining with

ancillary landings in the toe of Italy to seal off the Messina–Reggio crossing, the only feasible Axis escape route. Instead the Allies thought only of the physical occupation of territory and ended up fighting a wholly unsatisfactory campaign in which, far from attempting to destroy their adversary, they simply pushed him towards his natural egress. Even though the wheel was rigged in his favour, the Allied croupier proved incapable of raking in the winnings.

For the Allies certainly began Operation Husky with a marked numerical advantage. The Axis garrison on the island had a paper strength of 230,000 but almost 90 per cent of these were Italians, few of whom were in any way combat-worthy. Only 48,000 of their 200,000 personnel were grouped in infantry divisions and only one among these had ever seen any active service. Most of the other troops were in coast-defence divisions or rear echelon formations. The former were scratch formations at best, whose equipment was largely obsolete and in extremely short supply. In 206 Coastal Division, holding a front of 90 miles from Syracuse to Cape Scaramia, there were 56 field guns, 34 mortars and 690 assorted machine-guns. Moreover, in all types of division artillery ammunition was almost non-existent and communications varied from poor to utterly inadequate. No continuous system of coastal defences existed, with very few real obstacles at all having been constructed, many defence posts unmanned, and an almost complete lack of road blocks. Field Marshal Kesselring was utterly appalled when he first inspected the defences. 'On the maps everything was in order. Their plans were cleverly thought out . . . But the only construction work done was mere eyewash. There were no prepared positions on the island, which was inadequately defended, and had unguarded tank obstacles more likely to hamper the defenders than to check the enemy – all so much gingerbread.'23 Overall control on the island was exercised by General Alfredo Guzzoni, commanding Sixth Italian Army, and his only hope of putting up any sort of concerted resistance lay with the two German divisions under his command, 15 Panzer Grenadier and Hermann Göring Panzer Parachute.* Neither was up to strength, however, the latter's two infantry regiments being able to muster only three battalions between them and both divisions combined deploying only 160 tanks and 140 field guns. Moreover, neither division was as mobile as their nomenclature might suggest. Almost all their motor transport was with the supply echelons and thus

---

* The latter's Parachute designation was purely honorary, conferred because the division was part of the *Luftwaffe*.

operational movements demanded shuttle services or the temporary suspension of supply runs.

The Allies, on the other hand, intended to land seven infantry divisions (three British, one Canadian and three American), two airborne divisions (one British and one American), one American armoured division, two British and one Canadian armoured brigades, a battalion of US Rangers and three British Commandos. A further three infantry divisions (two British and one American) were held in reserve. Even discounting these latter, this meant that the Allies, grouped within Eighth Army and Seventh US Army,* were putting ashore, on 10 July 1943, the equivalent of over 80 infantry battalions as well as more than 400 medium tanks, mostly Shermans. The infantry and armoured divisions alone also included 540 artillery pieces. Not for nothing did General Frido von Senger und Etterlin, the German liaison officer with Sixth Army, write: 'Guzzoni was probably right in assessing each German division as possessing only half the fighting power of one Allied division, and he credited one of the four . . . [Italian] divisions with only a quarter of the strength of an Allied division.'[24]

In the air, Allied superiority was yet more marked. On the eve of the invasion they had 3,462 aircraft available for operations over Sicily as opposed to 1,750 Axis aircraft, only half of which were German. Moreover, Allied serviceability rates had once again attained the high standards set by the Desert Air Force, whilst those of the Germans and the Italians were grievously affected by continual attacks on airfields and lines of communication. For most of 1943 the proportion of aircraft actually available for Axis daily operations hovered around the 50 per cent mark, with the result that on any given day they could put only some 900 aircraft (500 German) into the air as opposed to over 2,500 Allied. In Sicily itself, the ceaseless attacks on the airfields meant that even those aircraft that were serviceable were often unable actually to get off the ground. By 10 July, when air power might have been used to maximum advantage against the densely packed invasion armada, a *Luftwaffe* officer reported that 'all the aerodromes, operational airfields and landing grounds in Sicily were so destroyed in continuous attacks by massed forces that it was only possible to get this or that airfield in running order again for a short time, mainly by mobilising all available forces, including those of the German and Italian armies.'[25]

* Eighth Army was still commanded by Montgomery and Seventh US by Patton. The two were combined under 15 Army Group, commanded by Alexander.

The Allies also possessed another enormous advantage in the weight of naval artillery that they could bring to bear against the defenders. The invasion fleet consisted in all of 2,590 ships and boats of all types and amongst these were 6 battleships, 15 cruisers, 3 monitors, 5 gunboats and 128 destroyers. This was an extremely powerful concentration of firepower, whose long range and high manoeuvrability allowed precise concentrations of devastating fire at particularly threatened points. Such concentrations were regularly laid on during the first days of Husky and were of particular importance in breaking up German armoured counter-attacks against the bridgeheads. Post-war accounts of the fighting have tended to underestimate the importance of this kind of fire – not only in Sicily but also at Salerno, Anzio and the Normandy beaches – but contemporary accounts are fulsome in their tribute.

Its greatest achievement was in breaking up the counter-attack by the Hermann Göring Division against the US beaches around Gela, on 11 and 12 July. According to General Bradley, 'it was the US Navy that saved the day.' A colonel of the Hermann Göring Division stated that 'naval gunfire forced us to withdraw', a statement amply supported by his division's losses in this counter-attack.[26] By 12 July its original complement of 99 tanks had been whittled down to only 54, a 50 per cent loss in only a few hours actual fighting. As Eisenhower commented in his dispatch on the Sicilian campaign, naval gunfire had proved itself 'so devastating in its effectiveness as to dispose finally of any doubts that naval guns are suitable for shore bombardment.'[27]

Having crushed the desperate German attempts to halt the invasion on the beaches, the Allies began to move inland. Though soon deprived of naval gunfire support they nevertheless retained a considerable margin of superiority. Most of the Italian divisions had simply melted away, and though the Germans subsequently brought across reinforcements of their own from the mainland they were unable to make much difference to the utterly disproportionate ratio of forces.* The reinforcements consisted of 1 Parachute Division,

---

* Individual Italian units fought on bravely but their usefulness was seriously undermined by the gross lack of training to which we have already referred. On 10 July, for example, 600 infantrymen of the Livorno Division, many of whom had already seen action, 'moved toward Gela in a courageous but nonsensical attack. In almost normal, parade-ground formation, they advanced with precision despite terrifying casualties torn in their ranks by the fire of American rifles, machine guns and mortars. Not a single soldier reached Gela . . .' (M. Blumenson, *Sicily: Whose Victory?* (Macdonald, 1968), p. 60.)

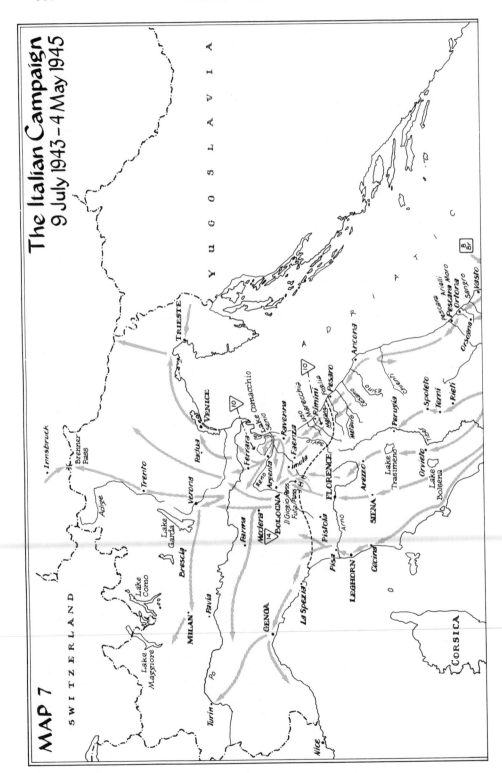

MAP 7

The Italian Campaign
9 July 1943 – 4 May 1945

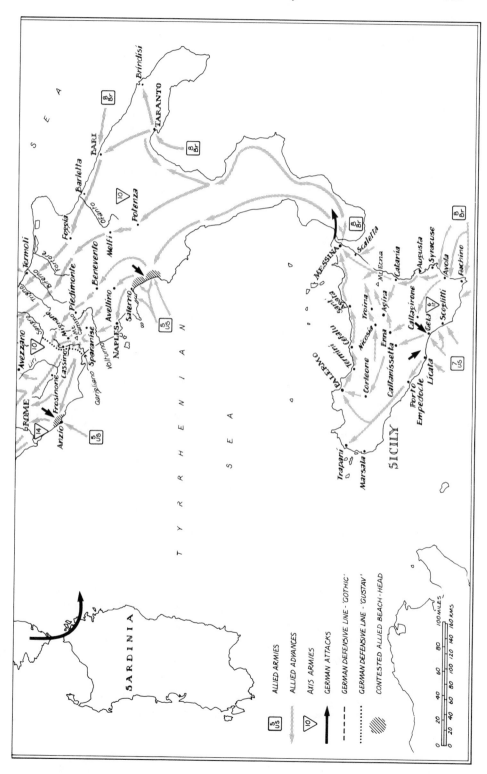

SARDINIA

SEA

TYRRHENIAN

SEA

SICILY

ROME
Avezzano
Termoli
Tagliacozzo
Frosinone
Anzio
Cassino
Piedimonte
Benevento
Avellino
NAPLES
Salerno
Volturno
Garigliano
Sparanise
Foggia
Barletta
BARI
TARANTO
Brindisi
Potenza
Melfi
Otranto

Trapani
Marsala
Palermo
Corleone
Caltanissetta
Nicosia
Enna
Troina
Adrano
Mt. Etna
Catania
Augusta
Syracuse
Avola
Pachino
Scoglitti
Gela
Licata
Porto Empedocle
Caltagirone
Randazzo
Taormina
Scaletta
MESSINA

8 Br
8 Br
8 Br
10
5 US
5 US
7 US
6 Cdn
14
10

ALLIED ARMIES
ALLIED ADVANCES
AXIS ARMIES
GERMAN ATTACKS
GERMAN DEFENSIVE LINE - 'GOTHIC'
GERMAN DEFENSIVE LINE - 'GUSTAV'
CONTESTED ALLIED BEACH-HEAD

5 US
10

0 20 40 60 80 100 MILES
0 20 40 60 100 120 140 160 KMS

which started arriving on the evening of 12 July, and 29 Panzer Grenadier Division, whose first units landed on the 21st. In fact, neither division was transferred in its entirety and the total reinforcement was only seven battalions each of paratroopers and panzer grenadiers. The latter's tank battalion remained in Italy. But the Allies brought in reinforcements of their own, a British and an American infantry division, so that the balance of forces in late July and early August was roughly one hundred Allied battalions *versus* no more than 25 German. In the air, Allied superiority became more and more pronounced. Their 2,500 serviceable aircraft available for operations over Sicily were faced at various dates by the following Axis totals:

	Italian	German
10 July	141	370
13 July	197	164
15 July	76	85
22 July	?	110

Sortie rates were commensurately disproportionate. In the first three days of the campaign, the *Luftwaffe* managed to put up an average of just under 300 sorties per day, and thereafter could manage no more than 150. The Allies, on the other hand, managed 1,700 sorties daily between 10 and 22 July, 1,160 to 29 July, and 1,450 to 17 August.

Faced with such a disparity of resources, having witnessed the destruction of their initial counter-attacks, and aware that the Italian Supreme Command in Rome already felt that the fate of Sicily was sealed, the Germans had little option but to pull back. As early as the 13th, OKW had told General Hans Hube, the local commander, that operations should be conducted with a view to extricating as many German troops as possible, and though there was talk on the 16th of Sixth Army resisting to the last, the consensus between Kesselring, von Senger und Etterlin and Hube was that their forces must withdraw into the north-eastern corner of the island, behind Mount Etna, with a view ultimately to a staged withdrawal across the Strait of Messina. For once Hitler did not condemn such thinking outright, largely because the disasters at Kursk and Orel gave him far weightier matters to ponder, and on the 17th he, too, conceded that such an evacuation was inevitable. On the 25th Kesselring was given explicit orders to that effect.

Unfortunately, the Allies found themselves in no position to take real advantage of these decisions. The Husky planners, as has already been indicated, had never looked in any detail beyond the establishment of the southern beachheads and had thus made little attempt to devise methods of actually trapping the Sicily garrison rather than slowly nudging it northwards. General Bradley was to write after the war: 'Astonishing as it seems in retrospect, there was no master plan for the conquest of Sicily. Nothing had been worked out beyond the limited beachhead objectives.'[28] The possibility of simultaneous landings in Calabria had hardly been considered, simply because mainland Italy was out of bounds as far as the Americans were concerned. Worse still, very little attention had been given to the possibility of staging outflanking moves in Sicily itself, especially along the eastern coast that was to be Eighth Army's main axis of advance. Admiral Cunningham was vehemently to denounce this failure, pointing out that after the first landings

> no use was made by the 8th Army of amphibious opportunities. The small LSIS were kept standing by for the purpose . . . and landing craft were available on call . . . There were doubtless sound military reasons for making no use of this, what to me appeared, priceless asset of seapower and flexibility of manoeuvre: but it is worth consideration for future occasions whether much time and costly fighting could not be saved by even minor flank moves which must necessarily be unsettling to the enemy.[29]

Much of the responsibility for this failure must rest with the local land commander, Montgomery, and indeed his baleful influence is to be discerned in many other tactical failures during the Sicily campaign. As ever, he moved unconscionably slowly. Eisenhower's intelligence officer, General K. W. D. Strong, felt that he could certainly have taken Catania in one or two days if he had been 'less conservative and his forces more mobile' and thereafter 'he could probably have been in Messina during the first week.'[30] In which case, of course, the bulk of the Axis forces in Sicily would have been cut off. But Montgomery seems to have been as myopic as everyone else about the necessity to trap enemy troops rather than simply liberate territory, and never showed himself properly aware of just what benefits might accrue from a vigorous thrust along the Catania–Messina axis.

It is true, of course, that such a push would have come up against strong defences, across a rather constricted route, and would have necessitated just the sort of expensive frontal attacks that this book has condemned at Buerat, Mareth, Wadi Akarit and Enfidaville. But in this instance they should not have been exorbitantly expensive, as they could have been mounted in overwhelming strength, with liberal air and naval gunfire support, and in conjunction with amphibious end-runs in the Axis rear. Moreover, they offered strategic rewards on a scale never realistically attainable during the later stages of the North African trek. Then, frontal attacks merely played into Rommel's hands, allowing him to withdraw at will to link up with von Arnim. In Sicily, on the other hand, even quite heavy casualties might have been justified, as a breakthrough, or even steady forward progress, would have completely unhinged the enemy defences and sealed off his only means of escape. The tactical frontal attack, in other words, would in fact have served as a strategic flanking move.

Perversely, however, Montgomery suddenly became enamoured of the tactical flank attack and on two crucial occasions dissipated whatever chances 15 Army Group might have had of bringing the campaign to a decisive conclusion. The first was on 13 July when one of his corps, XIIIth, ran into firm opposition around Lentini, on the coastal road. Montgomery decided that his other corps, XXXth, rather than attempting to reinforce this drive, should advance through Caltagirone, Enna and Leonforte, around the western side of Mount Etna, and so get behind the enemy troops blocking access to Catania. The road he intended to use, Highway 124, had been allotted to the Americans but Montgomery simply ignored this and took it over for his own transport. General Bradley, whose troops were so rudely shunted aside, described Montgomery's action as 'the most arrogant, egotistical, selfish and dangerous move in the whole of combined operations in World War II.'[31]

Leaving good manners to one side, it was certainly one of the most ill-advised moves of the campaign. For by cutting across the Seventh us Army and forcing it to veer westward, as well as by splitting his own forces along two widely divergent axes, Montgomery did much to relieve the pressure on the hard-pressed Germans. The most easterly us divisions were forced to sidestep some 25 miles to the west, and this took the pressure off Hermann Göring and 15 Panzer Grenadier Divisions which were then able to make a firm link-up and shift eastwards to counter Montgomery. But if the latter had not so peremptorily barged Bradley aside and had let him 'maintain his pressure, the Allies might have driven into a gap covered only by the shattered remnants of the Livorno Division, thus perhaps preventing the two German divisions – the two strongest units in Italy – from erecting a solid defensive wall around Mount Etna.'[32]

The British Official History, not unreasonably, lays the final blame on Alexander, who weakly declined to order Montgomery to adhere to the original axes of advance. Pointing out that XXX Corps had 92 miles to travel between its own beaches and Enna, as opposed to the 42 miles from the American beaches, the authors conclude that the latter would have had every chance of reaching Enna by the 16th, allowing the 'practical possibility' that 15 Panzer Grenadier Division could have been cut off in western Sicily. Moreover, because the Americans would have reached the Enna-Leonforte network of roads before XXX Corps, they would also have had every chance of moving straight on to Randazzo. Once this had been taken, the enemy between Catenanuova and Catania would have been confined to a single, cramped line of withdrawal along Highway 114, between Mount Etna and the sea. On top of this the drive by XXX Corps 'would have remained concentrated, advancing on the axis Ramacca–Sferro–Paterno, and the battle for Paterno, fought by 51st Division in isolation on the 20th–21st July, would have been fought by the whole Corps with the probable result that Paterno would have fallen and the defences of the Catania plain would have been turned before the end of July.'[33]

But none of this came to pass and the campaign fast degenerated into a mishmash of uncoordinated, largely unhelpful prods and pushes. The most spectacular, though probably the most futile, was Patton's dash for Palermo. Having seen Seventh US Army demoted to little more than a flank-guard for the Eighth, Patton not unnaturally began to chafe at the bit. When his subsidiary status was underlined in a new Alexander directive on the 16th, which only called upon him to send a force to the northern coast, well to the west of the German concentrations, he lost his temper and demanded a more newsworthy assignment.* On the 18th, therefore, Alexander

---

* The limited role given to the US forces by Alexander was partly a result of his doubts about their combat ability after the battle at Kasserine Pass, when the original units in the line had fallen back in considerable disorder. It should be noted, however, that he was consistently misled by Montgomery who, not content with grabbing the Americans' axis of advance, repeatedly gave the impression that his forces should be given priority because they were on the verge of important breakthroughs. The relevant volume of the Official History cites five such instances, on 12, 20, and 21 July, when Montgomery's prophecies of imminent captures were later found to be between two days and three weeks ahead of the facts. See C. J. C. Molony, (ed.) *The Mediterranean and the Middle East* (History of the Second World War: United Kingdom Military Series), vol. 5, (HMSO 1973), pp. 88, 110 and 121. See also p. 122 for his 'fanciful' appreciation of the straits to which he claimed to have reduced the enemy.

gave his permission for Patton to move north-east, towards Palermo and Trapani. He began to move with commendable speed and on 22 July Palermo surrendered, Trapani and Marsala being taken on the following day. The offensive had been a model of mobile warfare, save only that it had been conducted against virtually no opposition. Even on the 16th, the only troops in this part of the island were the badly rattled units of XII Italian Corps, and most of these had begun moving eastwards on that day, enabling them to elude Patton's spearheads. The casualty figures tell their own story, Patton having lost only 57 men killed whilst most of the Italian losses were prisoners-of-war. The total seemed impressive, 57,000, but almost all were reservists, militia or policemen. After the war, Bradley was to describe the whole operation as being 'meaningless in a strategic sense'.[34]

But Eighth Army also had its full share of strategically sterile attacks. For, having sent his two corps along such divergent axes, and having given the Germans time to establish strong positions on either side of Mount Etna, Montgomery was now unable to mass sufficient men and matériel to effect a breakthrough at any one point. XXX Corps' drive towards Leonforte ran into difficulties in the mountainous terrain, whilst the drive against Catania was abandoned on 21 July.* Kesselring's opinion on the fighting to that date was hardly flattering, one report noting that 'the enemy has not yet embarked on an offensive of any importance.'[35] It was at this time that Montgomery made another perverse decision to attempt an outflanking move inland, rather than concentrate as large a force as possible against the Catania bottleneck to break through behind the whole Catania–Sant'Agata line. Montgomery decided to switch yet more troops to the west of Mount Etna in a strong thrust towards Aderno and Randazzo, giving as his reason the heavy casualties that must result from a frontal assault. As one historian has said,

---

* The nature of the terrain, and the additional delays caused by ceaseless German demolitions along the narrow roads, was one of the great excuses given by Montgomery for his slow progress. The terrain *was* a terrible handicap, of course, but it should be remembered that it was Montgomery who had chosen to send part of his force inland in the first place. Nor was XXX Corps' mobility much enhanced by the remarkable signal sent by Eighth Army HQ on 17 July, declaring that 'No Pack Transport Units [i.e. mule trains] are required by 8th Army in Sicily.' The troops therefore remained tied to those roads negotiable by motor transport, with the result that 'Allied formations were, in general, tactically slow. Action took a long time to get going and . . . advances sometimes appeared rather like efforts to cram a number of corks into a bottle.' (Molony, op. cit. p. 114.)

his humanity does . . . [him] credit . . . But his change of plan had a vital effect on the entire campaign. It required shifting the pressure from a flat terrain, where he could have used his tanks, to a rugged, tangled interior, perfect for defence; from a seaboard where the Navy could have helped to mountains that naval gunfire could not reach . . . The Royal Navy was ready to give close support to troops on the Catania plain; yet few calls were made on it. With the naval gunfire power available, Montgomery should have been able to blast the tank and infantry counter-attacks against his [River] Simeto bridgehead, as Patton had done on the Gela front . . . In retrospect it would have been worth heavy ground casualties to have pushed the enemy out of Catania. If only he could then have been thrown off balance and pursued to Messina, his mobile forces would have been bottled up and compelled to surrender.[36]

It is conceivable that Montgomery might have made something of his switch of direction if he had moved quickly enough and surprised the Germans by throwing his main weight down the new axis. Typically, however, he took a full ten days to regroup his forces, and by the time Operation Hardgate did begin, on 30 July, even Alexander had begun to weary of the delay. Mistrustful as he still was of the Americans, he had little option but to let them become fully involved in the fray. Patton was ordered to drive east-ward in force, with some units taking the northern coastal road and the rest driving along Highway 120, through Nicosia and Randazzo.* Messina was now up for grabs by whichever Army got there first. Unfortunately, neither push had much chance of cutting off any significant Axis force, whose command was now firmly committed to a policy of staged withdrawal and eventual evacuation. Definite plans were drawn up on 1 August and the withdrawal across the Strait of Messina began in earnest on the 11th. Of the fighting in this period, one historian has written: '[In] military operations in Sicily during August . . . the Allied generals imagined that they were driving the enemy back by a series of brilliant offensives. Actually the Axis was conducting a series of rearguard actions to

---

* In consequence, Montgomery shortened his own axis of advance, the main objective now being Aderno, with Seventh US Army passing in front of them through Randazzo.

cover an orderly evacuation of Sicily, which was carried out with complete success.'[37]

The German evacuation was a particularly noteworthy achievement, and between 11 and 17 August they ferried across to Calabria almost 40,000 troops, 10,000 vehicles, 47 tanks, 94 guns, 2,000 tons of ammunition and fuel and 15,000 tons of other stores. A further 13,500 casualties had been evacuated in the second half of July. In contrast, the Allies had killed 4,300 Germans and taken another 5,500 prisoner, only 20 per cent of the total force.* Most important of all, four seasoned divisions and a corps headquarters had escaped, with their command structures intact and with more than enough experienced cadres to absorb replacements and immediately take up new positions in the firing line.

That this should have been possible was just one more instance of inadequate Allied planning. A most revealing comment was made by Alexander, on 3 August, when it became clear that the enemy was preparing to evacuate. In a signal to Tedder and Cunningham he wrote: 'We must be in a position to take advantage . . . by using full weight of navy and air power [to interdict the evacuation]. You have no doubt coordinated plans to meet this contingency.'[38] That Alexander did not *know* that such plans had been made, plans that should from the very beginning have been a central feature of the post-Husky scheme of operations, casts a poor light on the level of competence at Mediterranean headquarters. In the event hardly any of the German ferries were sunk and Axis sources are unanimous that not a single passenger was lost. For, as the official British naval historian has noted, not only were there no advance plans for dealing with an Axis evacuation, but at no stage during it

> did the three Allied Commanders-in-Chief represent to the Supreme Commander that an emergency, such as would justify the diversion of all available air strength, had arisen . . . The enemy later expressed his astonishment that the Allies had not used their overwhelming air superiority to greater effect . . . Even when the enemy's intention was plain, the action taken suffered from lack of inter-service coordination.[39]

Anyone familiar with the campaign in mainland Italy, and the prominent role therein of 15 and 29 Panzer Grenadier, Hermann Göring

---

* They also captured 78 tanks and armoured cars (mainly the latter) 287 guns and 3,500 vehicles.

and 1 Parachute Divisions, will realise what a golden opportunity was squandered by the Allied commanders.*

The escape of the German divisions in Sicily back to the mainland was to prove particularly unfortunate because during the rest of the Italian campaign the Allies on the ground never possessed the tremendous numerical superiority that had characterised earlier operations. This is made clear in table 13, which shows the number of divisions deployed by both sides each month. (Two German totals are given because a certain number of their troops were always engaged in occupation and counter-insurgency duties.)

Table 13: *Allied and German divisions in Italy*
September 1943–May 1945

	Allies	Germans All	Germans Combat		Allies	Germans All	Germans Combat
1943				July	30	25	22
Sept.	13	18	7	Aug.	22	24	21
Oct.	14	18	9	Sept.	23	25	21
Nov.	17	20	13	Oct.	23	27	23
Dec.	20	17	14	Nov.	23	26	22
				Dec.	22	26	22
1944							
Jan.	21	21	19	**1945**			
Feb.	24	23	19	Jan.	21	24	20
March	28	23	19	Feb.	22	25	21
April	28	23	19	March	19	22	19
May	29	23	21	April	20	22	19
June	28	25	23				

* It was argued at the time, and has been since, that the heavy flak around Messina was 'practically prohibitive for all aircraft except heavy bombers' (Coningham quoted in J. Terraine, *The Right of the Line* (Hodder and Stoughton, 1985), p. 579). Yet on 13 August, when the evacuation was at its height, 106 B-17s, 102 B-26s and 66 B-25s were employed in a huge raid near Rome. They were not concentrated against Messina because, in the words of an air force headquarters report, 'the land battle (on Sicily) was going so well' (Blumenson, op. cit, p. 144). There was no attempt, moreover, to use naval gunfire. Two German 170mm batteries were especially troublesome. 'But could not these guns have been located by air reconnaissance, and knocked out by battleships and monitors firing over the land from waters north and west of Cape Peloro, at ranges between 8,000 and 16,000 yards, or from the southern entrance to the Strait southwest of Reggio? Once these big guns had been silenced, a bold thrust of light cruisers and destroyers up the Strait from the south should have been able to silence most of the 88-mm and 90-mm batteries, and clear the way for MTBs, motor gunboats and even destroyers to operate effectively against the Siebel ferries and other evacuation craft.' (S.E. Morison, *History of United States Naval Operations in World War II* (15 vols, OUP, 1948–62,), vol. 9, pp. 216–17).

The main reason for this unusual parity of forces was once again the continuing disagreements between the Americans and the British about their Mediterranean strategy. The major problem was that the Americans would only concede any expansion of operations in a piecemeal and grudging manner, and this made the British feel less and less confident about pressing them for substantial increases in the number of men and weapons deployed in this theatre. But they still wished to undertake full-scale operations, and increasingly tended to grasp at such concessions about future objectives as the Americans did make without examining in any detail whether they were feasible, in the absence of any commensurate increase in force levels. Two aspects of Italian operations given especially scant attention were climate and terrain. Certain senior observers had perceived their importance. In a letter to Churchill on 3 September 1943 Field Marshal Jan Christian Smuts, the South African Prime Minister and Commander-in-Chief, had deprecated the Allied plan which 'merely proposes . . . to fight our way northward over difficult mountainous terrain in a campaign which may take much time before we reach Northern Italy and the main German defensive position.'[40] Few others, however, seemed prepared to acknowledge just how difficult conditions in Italy could be. Churchill had remarked of the Sicilian campaign, at a meeting of the British Chiefs of Staff: 'It is true, I suppose, that the Americans consider that we have led them up the garden path in the Mediterranean – but what a beautiful path it has proved to be. They have picked peaches here, nectarines there. How grateful they should be!'[41]

They had very little cause to be grateful, however, when they moved off the beaches at Salerno, where Fifth US Army landed on 9 September 1943, and stumbled into the mountainous spine that constitutes the large part of the Italian landscape. There, peaches and nectarines were few, and the invaders faced a country offering nothing but an endless series of obstacles that a resolute defender, even if heavily outnumbered, could turn very much to his advantage. Below the great Italian northern plain lay nothing but one great mountain range, with no low ground except for the narrow coastal strips and the river valleys which fanned out from the central massifs like spindly fish-bones. Each of these river courses offered a superb defensive position, improved yet further when the Germans flooded the attackers' side of the river, built deep dugouts and machine-gun posts on the far bank, and sited their artillery and observers in the mountains behind. Moreover, the attackers' troubles were far from over even when they were not actually going forward under fire. For the climate was just as inimical as the terrain, and a grim surprise to the troops who served there. Wet, cold and raw, it was the very antithesis of the 'sunny' Italy of the tourist handbills. Of the conditions endured by the fighting soldiers in the first winter in the mountains, one correspondent wrote:

> And there were the . . . infantry in their camouflaged water-proof gas-capes, the rain streaming off their steel helmets, their hands gone blue with cold. They climbed numbly, contemplating each step, each few yards in front of them, since no-one there could contemplate the whole battle or the worse discomforts that were to be added. Each man found it enough to contain himself, to keep himself alive and moving . . . [Men slept] for . . . days and nights . . . waist deep in water. In utter weariness they lost all sense of time and place and even perhaps the sense of hope. Only the sense of pain remained.[42]

This was not the country, then, in which to fight with only a limited numerical superiority over the enemy. Still less was it a country in which an attacker so handicapped should attempt to attack that enemy head-on, which brings us to another aspect of Italian operations largely ignored by the British. The most cursory glance at a relief map of Italy makes it clear that any halfway competent defender can block an advance from the south of the country at almost any point he chooses. Even the breach of his defensive line will probably only oblige him to pull back a short distance to another one equally strong. Nevertheless, the country does have one overwhelming disadvantage for the defender. It is a peninsula, and is thus extremely vulnerable to outflanking moves behind the main line of defence. But such outflanking moves must of necessity be amphibious operations, and as such dependent on landing craft to bring the troops into action. In this item of hardware, however, the Allies were sadly deficient. Certainly, landing craft were being built in considerable quantities, for it had been clear from an early stage that the defeat of both Germany and Japan would revolve around sea-borne assaults.* It had been assumed, however, that the only significant European requirement in 1943 or 1944 would be for a cross-Channel attack, and though the Americans did allow landing

---

* Between 1940 and 1945 the British built 4,290 landing craft of all types and the Americans 37,720, a grand total of just over 42,000 craft.

craft to remain in the Mediterranean for the Sicily and Salerno landings, they were thereafter adamant that all landing craft would be required for the Normandy landings and that there was no surplus to permit major amphibious operations in the Adriatic or Tyrrhenian Seas. Indeed, at both the Trident and Quadrant Conferences, one of the most insistent American demands was that any concessions they might make must not affect the strict timetable for the return of landing craft from the Mediterranean to ports in the south of England.

American intransigence meant that Allied strategic options and hitting power for Italian operations were severely circumscribed. Even the Salerno landings were affected, and during the planning Alexander confided in a small group of British and American visitors: 'The operation, he told us, was a dangerous gamble, because such inadequate forces had been allocated to it. The Germans already had some 19 divisions in Italy . . . But Alexander said he would have only from 3–5 Anglo-American divisions for our initial landings, to a maximum build-up of 8 divisions over the following two weeks.'[43] After Salerno only one other major amphibious operation in Italy was attempted, at Anzio, in January 1944, as the Allies sought to unhinge the Germans' Gustav Line by landing troops behind it, within striking distance of Rome. Once again, however, even after the Americans had acceded to pleadings by Churchill that some extra landing craft be temporarily held back in the Mediterranean, only a fairly small operation could be mounted. Also again the commanders on the spot were less than convinced that the lift was adequate. The man in charge of the landing force for Operation Shingle, General John P. Lucas, noted in his diary less than two weeks before D-Day: 'I feel like a lamb being led to the slaughter . . . I have the bare minimum of ships and craft . . . The force that can be gotten ashore in a hurry is weak and I haven't sufficient artillery to hold me over.'[44]*

Clearly, then, the Italian campaign cannot be regarded as just another example of Allied reliance on overwhelming numerical or material superiority. With regard to numbers, moreover, one must also bear in mind that throughout the campaign there was a chronic

---

* There was, in fact, only one other attempt at an end-run, on 3 October 1943, when 3 Army and 40 Royal Marine Commandos, followed by 36 Infantry Brigade, landed at Termoli, behind German defences along the Biferno. This force was almost overrun by a German counter-attack before reinforcements managed to push across the Biferno and an extra infantry brigade to land at Termoli.

bleeding of formations to fight elsewhere.* The much narrower margin of superiority this gave to the Allies has already been recorded in table 13 above, but one must also be careful not to exaggerate the significance of a simple divisional tally. Respective strengths within these formations were in fact very different and invariably meant that an equal number of divisions gave the Allies a considerable superiority of fighting troops. Acute shortages of personnel in the German divisions were apparent from the moment the Allies first set foot on mainland Italy. To face the twin landings at Salerno and in Calabria and Apulia, General Heinrich von Vietinghoff's Tenth Army 'could dispose of six or seven divisions . . . but they were divisions in name only.'[45]† Two were being rebuilt after the Sicily evacuation, one of which, the Hermann Göring Division, could muster only one two-battalion regiment of infantry, a tank battalion of 20 tanks, a company of assault guns, 12 field howitzers and an engineer battalion. The other division rebuilding, 15 Panzer Grenadier, was also badly undermanned and could spare for the first Salerno counter-attacks only two infantry battalions and an engineer and a reconnaissance unit. The divisions that would face Montgomery's invasion in the south were just as badly off. 1 Parachute Division was very short of men at the best of times and had just had to give up yet more to assist in the defence of Rome. 29 Panzer Grenadier Division was moderately well equipped, though not with the assault guns that supposedly differentiated it from ordinary infantry divisions, and 26 Panzer Division was short of tanks proper, having but two companies, only one of which reached the battle. This latter division also lacked one of its infantry battalions and most of its artillery. All in all, excluding those formations tied in place on more or less static defence duties, 'the real strength of the "mass of manoeuvre" . . . [von Vietinghoff] could hope to bring against the invader consisted

---

* After the conquest of Sicily two British and two American infantry divisions, as well as one American armoured division, were brought back to England to take part in the cross-Channel invasion. In May 1944 a British and an American airborne division also left to take part in this assault, and in July three American and four French infantry divisions were withdrawn to take part in Operation Anvil (later Dragoon), landings in southern France to take place in early August. Other withdrawals included that of one British and one Indian infantry division sent to Greece between October 1944 and January 1945, three British infantry divisions sent to Palestine in April and June 1944 and January 1945, and two infantry divisions, one Canadian and one British, and a Canadian armoured division sent to North-West Europe in March 1945.

† Tenth Army had only been established on 22 August.

of only one and a half divisions, without heavy tanks or medium artillery and seriously below strength in light field artillery.'[46]

Even when more combat divisions became available over the following months, the increase in manpower was not very substantial. Most of the extra divisions were very weak when they arrived and the subsequent drain of casualties only elicited a mere trickle of replacements. By January 1944, according to von Senger und Etterlin, now commanding XIV Panzer Corps, in 'most German divisions at this time . . . [the] battalion commanders were young men who led their forces, amounting to no more than 100 men, in the forward front line as if they were mixed assault companies.'[47] Allied infantry battalions at this time contained between 700 and 800 men. On 20 May 1944, after the fourth and final Battle of Cassino had been under way for more than a week, German strength returns gave 94 Infantry Division a fighting strength of 740 men and 15 Panzer Grenadier Division one of 405 men. Allied battalions, in other words, were in most cases better off than some German divisions. By the beginning of June the situation in 362 Infantry Division, resisting the breakout from the Anzio beachhead and commanded by General Heinz Greiner, was so parlous that the following piece of doggerel went the rounds:

> *Die Division Greiner*
> *Wird immer kleiner.*
> *Zum Schluss bleibt einer*
> *Und das ist Greiner.* *

The next major Allied assault after the Cassino battles was against the Gothic Line, in September and October 1944. That the Germans could man this position at all was a tribute to their consummate skill in withdrawing the rump of all the divisions in Tenth and Fourteenth Armies beyond the reach of the pursuing Allies, and thus maintaining vital cadres around which to rebuild these formations. But they could not be rebuilt up to anything like their proper establishment, and at the beginning of the renewed offensive, on 10 September, 58 of the 81 infantry battalions contained less than 400 men and 35 of these had less than 300. But even fully up to strength these battalions would have been thinly stretched, as each division in the German line was holding a front of some ten miles. The fighting that followed brought

---

* An English equivalent might be: This Division of Greiner/Gets chopped ever finer/Till roll-call's a one-liner/Which simply reads Greiner.

heavy casualties, and yet again the German divisions found that far too few replacements were being sent forward. By 25 September, Tenth Army reported that only 10 of its 92 infantry battalions now had more than 400 men whilst fully 38 had less than 200 effectives.*

But the real measure of Allied preponderance was the mass of matériel deployed, and throughout the Italian campaign, despite complaints that it was not being accorded sufficient support by the planners and decision makers in Washington and London, Allied superiority in tanks, guns and aircraft was overwhelming. As regards medium tanks, Allied totals at various dates are given in table 14. These figures represent not just the number of tanks in the armoured divisions but also those with the British-style tank brigades and the American tank battalions attached to their infantry divisions.†

Table 14: *Number of Allied medium tanks in Italy*
September 1943 – April 1945

	Medium tanks in				
	British-type	US	British-type	US	
Date	Divisions	Divisions	Brigades	Battalions	Total
Sept. 1943	247	-	582	224	1,053
Nov. 1943	494	186	776	448	1,904
May 1944	988	186	1,358	504	3,036
Oct. 1944	988	186	1,552	336	3,062
April 1945	741	186	1,552	336	2,815

It should be borne in mind, of course, that these figures represent establishment strengths and that units in the field were rarely able to put their full complement of tanks into action. Nevertheless, even granting that as much as a quarter of Allied armour was undergoing repair at any one time, or had been destroyed and not yet replaced,

* It should be noted that the British were also having trouble finding sufficient infantry replacements. In late September a whole brigade was reduced to cadre strength and its men split among other battalions in the parent division, and a little later all British infantry battalions were reduced from four to three rifle companies. The fact remains, however, that this still gave each battalion a strength of 700 officers and men.

† Each Tank Brigade (of which the Allies deployed a maximum of 8 in Italy) had almost exactly the same tank component as an armoured division, with 194 medium tanks and 43 light. Each US Tank Battalion (a maximum of 9 in Italy) contained 56 mediums and 17 light. To the figures in table 14 should be added roughly one-fifth as many light tanks and between 150 and 180 tank-destroyers, a form of self-propelled anti-tank gun used by independent US Tank Destroyer Battalions.

this would still have given Fifth and Eighth Armies a tremendous
superiority over their opponents. As we have already seen, the
Germans were feeling the pinch from the very beginning. 16 Panzer
Division began the Salerno battle with the handsome figure of 100
tanks, but by the evening of 14 September, after six days of battle
in which no replacements were forthcoming, was down to only 22.
By mid-October, the whole of Tenth Army could only muster 149
serviceable tanks and 112 assault guns. Even by the end of November
these figures had only risen to 229 and 173 respectively, facing the
almost 2,000 medium tanks deployed by the Allies.

The landing at Anzio and the opening of the Cassino battles did
provoke the German High Command into providing some modest
reinforcement, and by the end of April 1944 there was a total of 403
tanks in Italy, though only 310 of them were serviceable. Unfortunately, this was still only 10 per cent of the Allied establishment at
that date. At the start of the Gothic Line offensive, when Eighth
Army alone could deploy 1,276 serviceable medium tanks and 278
light, German Tenth Army had a grand total of 83. By April of the
following year the German situation had improved hardly at all, and
Tenth and Fourteenth Armies between them could only muster 200
tanks against some 3,000 available to the Allies. Probably no more
than two-thirds of the German figure were serviceable, whilst Eighth
Army alone could field 1,750 medium tanks fit for action.

Artillery ratios did not achieve quite the same disproportionate
levels as those for the armour, but the margin of Allied superiority
was always considerable. Again, the Germans laboured under considerable difficulties from the very beginning of the campaign. On 1
October 1943, 29 Panzer Grenadier Division reported that it could
muster only 16 out of 42 assault guns, 13 out of 42 artillery pieces,
14 out of 31 anti-tank guns and 25 out of 58 mortars. By the time
of the fourth battle of Cassino, some seven months later, the Allies
could deploy almost 2,000 artillery pieces in that sector. During the
Canadian assault on the Hitler Line, for example, just prior to the fall
of Cassino monastery, the attacking formations deployed 786 guns
against the Germans' 150. On the Gothic Line, Eighth Army's 1,121
guns faced only 351 with Tenth Army, whilst the ratio of anti-tank
guns was 1,055 to 235. By April 1945 the ratios for the whole theatre
gave the allies a 2:1 superiority in medium guns and 5:1 in heavy.

It was not only the number of Allied guns that impressed the
Germans but also the prodigality of their ammunition expenditure.
Two examples from the Cassino battles sum up the overall situation.

A German soldier on the Cassino massif, in March 1944, wrote in his diary: 'What we are going through here is beyond description. I have never experienced anything like this in Russia, not even a second's peace, only the dreadful thunder of guns and mortars, there are planes over and above . . . Here we have nothing but terror and horror, death and damnation.' A comment from the other side of the hill, by the commander of the New Zealand Corps artillery, offers telling evidence of Allied reliance on sheer material superiority: 'Once while observing from the castle on Monte Trocchio I saw a single German emerge from a hole near the Gari . . . and walk quietly south. He was engaged by a holocaust of fire, including that of 8-inch howitzers.'[48]

But artillery was not the only component of Allied firepower. On the beaches at Salerno and Anzio recourse was had to naval fire support, which proved just as successful as it had during the first stages of Operation Husky. It played an especially prominent part in the breaking up of German counter-attacks at Salerno, so much so that von Vietinghoff was moved to write on 14 September: '. . . above all the advancing troops had to endure the most severe heavy fire that had hitherto been experienced; the naval gunfire from . . . ships . . . lying in the roadstead. With astonishing precision and freedom of manoeuvre, these ships shot at every recognised target with very overwhelming effect.'[49] The naval contribution at Anzio was not so clear-cut but it was nevertheless an important component of the total volume of fire that the Allies were able to mass against the German counter-attacks on 16 and 28 February 1944. During these attacks the Germans were subject to 'unceasing and overwhelming bombardment' and 'enemy prisoners recounted often that it was the continuous Allied artillery fire that "caused heavy casualties, shattered nerves, destroyed morale, and brought some units on the verge of panic." '[50]

The third vital component of Allied firepower, just as in North Africa, was the ever-burgeoning air arm. At the time of the Salerno landings, for example, the Allies had on hand 3,127 combat aircraft and on D-Day were able to deploy just under 1,000 against the beaches themselves, as opposed to only 108 German. These latter put in a most creditable effort, and for ten days those in close support maintained a high average of two sorties per serviceable aircraft per day. The peak effort was some 150 sorties flown on 13 September. Unfortunately, this effort paled into insignificance beside that made by the Allies. On 10/11 September, for example, they flew

2,700 sorties and between the 12th and the 15th managed a further 6,000, with the bombers and fighter-bombers dropping over 3,500 tons of explosives and incendiaries. According to von Vietinghoff, his decision to withdraw from Salerno, taken on 16 September, was largely attributable to the fact that his counter-attacks 'were unable to reach their objectives owing to the fire from naval guns and low-flying aircraft.'[51] By 1 October more than 20,000 sorties had been flown and about 19,000 tons of bombs dropped.

In the face of such an awesome display of strength the already feeble *Luftwaffe* in Italy was all but overwhelmed. By the beginning of October, according to one official historian, the German air force in this theatre had 'virtually ceased to operate.'[52] By the beginning of the following year, there were only 300 combat aircraft in the whole central and western Mediterranean, less than a tenth of the total Allied figure. At about this time Geobbels wrote in his diary: 'The English are waging war in Italy most effectively . . .Their most striking advantage is their superiority in the air. Every day they lay a curtain of bombs on us in numbers hitherto unknown in this war.'[53] The actual victims of such attacks were somewhat more bitter, and in January and February 1944 it was a common gibe in the German front line that the poor old *Luftwaffe* had gone into hibernation. Sadly, it also failed to wake up come spring, and German war diaries were full of complaints, some about German aircraft turning tail, some about the almost complete lack of aerial reconnaissance and thus of useful intelligence about the enemy. One diary sadly acknowledged that 'the Allied air forces enjoyed *Alleinherrschaft*; they were the sole rulers of the skies. In the Italian theatre the M.A.A.F. had achieved not just air superiority but air supremacy.'[54]

The tactical impact of this air supremacy was considerable. On the Anzio beachhead, for example, where the Allies consistently flew seven and eight times more sorties than the Germans, aircraft played a more important part than even ground or naval gunfire. According to one official history, during the major German counter-attacks, 'the navy and the air forces had begun to intervene and play a great, perhaps a decisive part, in preventing the achievement of Kesselring's desire.'[55] The air forces' contribution during the Cassino battles was just as important. Their absolute supremacy over the battlefield allowed even unarmed aircraft to roam around at will, with consequences tersely described in the war diary of XIV Panzer Corps:

Today the Corps' hard defensive battles were again characterised by the enemy's suffocating superiority . . . and our troops again incurred very heavy casualties from their exposure to ceaseless shelling in coverless terrain. With absolutely no opposition from our own fighters, spotter-planes cruised all day over the battlefield and directed the enemy's fire on to our gun-sites and infantry positions, thus taking a heavy toll of all daytime movements behind the front as well as of the units which were in action.[56]

But the planes were also well able to wreak havoc on their own account. By the time of the fourth battle, as the Allies tried to break into the Liri Valley and push through to Rome, fighter and fighter-bombers were operating in 'cab ranks', with aircraft stacked in the sky until they were called down upon a particular target by the ground forces. As the same official history points out: 'Only when the air forces of a country have very great resources on which to draw, and the virtual certainty that air opposition will be negligible and will remain so, can they afford the luxury of a "Cab Rank" system.'[57] All German reports testified to the havoc wreaked by the dreaded 'Jabos', *Jagdbombers* or fighter-bombers. According to one report emanating from Kesselring's headquarters, at the end of May:

> Enemy air activity . . . has reached unprecedented proportions. Attacks are particularly heavy against places where no alternative roads are available, for example, defiles, bridges, and other bottlenecks. Regroupings and the movement of reserves have been thereby subjected to delays as long as 2–3 days. It is impossible, in the face of such air superiority, for command to make any computation of the time element in movements. Necessary countermeasures have frequently been too late to accomplish anything.[58]

Kesselring's panzer divisions were especial targets and the commander of 26 Panzer, with Tenth Army, recalled the remorseless hammering it took from the air in the first days of June. At this time the division was in full retreat, attempting to avoid Allied encirclement, and General von Lüttwitz would never forget 'the extraordinary difficulties encountered . . . in crossing the mountains whilst being constantly threatened from the air.' The Hermann Göring Division went into action around the Anzio bridgehead, but the preparatory march down from Leghorn, between 23 and 27 May, was fraught with difficulty. According to its commander, General von Greffenberg, it had been 'subject to practically unceasing low-level attacks by day and night. The losses were considerable. The Division reached the intended concentration area . . . with only eleven [out of 60] tanks.'[59] A few more tanks did eventually struggle in late on the 27th, but even these only brought the total number of tanks to 18 and only 8 out of 10 of them were ever fit for action at any one time.

Allied air supremacy remained in force right up to the end of the Italian campaign. At the end of the Cassino battles the *Luftwaffe* in this theatre was reduced to only 20 or so *Staffeln*, and by the time of the last major Allied offensive, in April 1945, 'Luftwaffe operations were barely perceptible.'[60] By this time the Allies could deploy 285 squadrons of over 4,000 aircraft in Italy, and these continued to have a paralysing effect on German ground operations. General von Vietinghoff was particularly impressed by the Allied fighter-bombers. 'They hindered essential movement, tanks could not move, their very presence over the battlefield paralysed movement. The smashing of all communications was equally disastrous . . .'[61] During the April battles, along the River Po, the whole Allied heavy bomber force in Italy, usually involved in 'strategic' operations over Germany, was also put at the disposal of the ground forces. According to von Senger und Etterlin their contribution to the battle was vital and speeded up the German collapse and eventual surrender. 'It was the bombing of the Po crossings that finished us. We could have withdrawn successfully with normal rearguard action despite the heavy pressure, but owing to the destruction of the ferries and river crossings we lost all our equipment. North of the river we were no longer an Army.'[62] As one eminent authority has pointed out, the application of the whole of Allied air resources 'achieved the isolation of the battlefield and demonstrated, under the perhaps somewhat exceptional circumstances of complete air supremacy, the power of the air arm to turn a withdrawal into a rout.'[63]

Massive material preponderance, however, was not the only ingredient of the Allies' brute force approach, and again the term can be applied as much to their methods as to their means. Certainly the campaign did not get off to a particularly scintillating start. The plans for the Salerno landing were poorly conceived, with the boundary between the two corps involved resting on a river valley which neither was ordered to seize. It thus provided the Germans with an ideal axis for their own counter-attacks. These latter were also greatly facilitated by the excessively cautious instructions to the assault forces, only two of whose brigades or regimental combat teams were to attempt the actual breakout from the beachhead, both of them infantry formations.

But it was not just the tactical handling of the battle that was amiss. Just as the breakout at Salerno did not fully utilise the available forces, so too was the whole of Fifth Army's effort carried out in unnecessary isolation. For in the ensuing battle its commander, General Mark Clark, received no assistance from Montgomery's Eighth Army, which, having crossed the Messina Strait and landed in Calabria, with an ancillary landing at Taranto, was plodding sedately towards Potenza and Foggia. To some extent, of course, Montgomery was impeded by the difficult terrain and the German propensity for ceaseless demolitions, but one can still not help feeling that no other commander would have moved quite so deliberately or cautiously. He proved himself particularly ponderous on the River Sangro, in November 1943. Here, even though his massive artillery barrage had all but smashed the one understrength German infantry division standing in his way, offering an excellent opportunity for 'bouncing' the river, he made no attempt to exploit the situation and insisted on adhering to his original and remarkably leisurely timetable.

The most striking examples of Allied maladroitness in Italy occurred on the major German defensive positions, the Gustav Line, running through Monte Cassino, and the Gothic Line, in the Apennine Mountains. The attempt to breach the Gustav Line, and the ensuing four battles of Monte Cassino, constitute an especially depressing saga and one which reveals the Allied commanders as being quite unable to adapt their tactics to the terrain in which they were fighting. To Alexander, Clark and General Oliver Leese, who succeeded Montgomery in December 1943, the only way to win a battle, in this case to push through to Rome, was to rupture the enemy line and then send in the tanks. Now tanks there were and, as we have seen, in profusion. Unfortunately, these needed good roads to travel on, and the latter were in such short supply in Italy that the Germans could easily identify all likely axes of advance and take steps to bar them. This point had quickly been appreciated by General Alphonse Juin, commanding the French Expeditionary Corps, when he arrived in Italy in October 1943. One of his first trips had taken him along the Salerno–Naples road where:

along the whole length of the road . . . we ran into the 7th British Armoured Division in close column, incapable of leaving the road and deploying in a terrain completely given over to mountains. I immediately concluded . . . that the widespread mechanisation of the British and American forces constituted a serious obstacle to any swift progress up the Italian peninsula.[64]*

Juin's fears were to be amply confirmed in the Cassino battles, in each of which the Allies attempted to batter their way into the Liri Valley, a narrow entrance overlooked by strong German positions on either side, and 'unleash' the armour up Highway 6. In the first battle the main blow was delivered by 36 US Division in an assault across the Rapido River, flowing right across the entrance to the Liri Valley. The attack was badly reconnoitred and ill-prepared, whilst one single infantry division was quite inadequate to the task of forcing the Germans' Main Line of Resistance. The division was smashed, one regiment being almost completely wiped out, and throughout the battle the defenders remained unaware that a major offensive was supposedly under way. A subsidiary attack was also made on the Cassino massif, by 34 US Division, but here the terrain was so intractable, offering only a few very narrow axes of advance, that attack after attack broke down in the teeth of enemy mortars and machine-guns.

Not one senior commander went up to examine the terrain personally and so the American Division was simply replaced by an Indian, which was ordered to take up where the other had left off and storm its way into the Monastery. But the chaos of rocks, screen, dense brush and gullies and ravines made it impossible for the Indians to concentrate their attack, such that when it began the main effort of the whole division was made by just one *company* of the Royal Sussex Regiment. Not surprisingly, they made little impact on the well entrenched defenders. Ignorance of the terrain was also the cause of another misconceived attack during the second battle. Unaware of the difficulties of simply moving forward on the massif, senior commanders had become convinced that the main obstacle to success

---

* The British did have a specialist mountain division, the 52nd, but this first saw service in the most inappropriate terrain, the flooded Scheldt estuary, in October 1944. It is also to be borne in mind that even when mobile formations could find the necessary roads, the British were considerably hampered by the fact that all but a few of their trucks only had two-wheel drive.

was German troops in the Monastery itself. As a preliminary to the Indians' attack, therefore, they had it bombed, desperately hoping that firepower alone could resolve their problems. The Monastery was heavily damaged, but this discommoded the Germans not at all as none of them had been in it prior to or during the bombing and because after it they were presented with eminently defensible heaps of rubble.

The commander of the Indian division, General Tuker, was to write after the war: 'I could never understand why the US Fifth Army decided to batter its head again and again against this most powerful position, held by some of the finest troops in the German Army in heavily wired and mined and fixed entrenchments.'[65] For Clark and Alexander, however, Monte Cassino and the Liri Valley had now become something of an *idée fixe*, and in March 1944 a third attempt was made to capture the Monastery. This time, sensibly, the massif was ignored and the axis of advance was to be through Cassino town, at the foot of Monte Cassino. Two divisions, 4 Indian and 2 New Zealand, were to attack, with the former clambering up towards the Monastery from the outskirts of the town and the latter clearing Cassino itself and opening up the entrance to the Liri Valley.

Again the Allies placed great reliance on firepower alone and again the bombers were called in, this time to pulverise the town. But even heavy bombers cannot make buildings simply disappear, and all they succeeded in doing on this occasion was to tumble masonry into the narrow streets and make it virtually impossible for the New Zealand infantry and their supporting armour to get forward at all. The almost imperceptible New Zealand advance also slowed down the Indians, who were having to use the same road to get to their jumping-off points below the Monastery. By the time they did begin their attack, again limited to uncoordinated rushes by individual companies, the Germans had recovered from the first shock of the aerial bombardment and had once again manned their mortars and machine-guns. After ten days of agonising close-quarters combat the attack was abandoned with the Germans still in control of the Monastery and a good third of the town.

For the fourth battle of Cassino, in May 1944, the Allies did at least attempt to concentrate their main effort, and much of Eighth Army was brought across from the Adriatic coast to swell the ranks. The main focus of the attack, however, was still the Liri Valley and the Monastery, with II Polish Corps assigned to taking the latter and three armoured divisions held ready for exploitation to Rome and beyond. Yet again the commander relied largely on their material superiority slowly to grind the Germans down. In the American sector, according to one reporter,

> always and everywhere procedure and pattern were always the same. German guns betrayed their presence. We called our planes to bomb them, and then we concentrated our own artillery, too numerous to be opposed, and they shelled the German guns. Thereupon the infantry flowed slowly ahead. At each strongpoint or village there were . . . a few snipers to be blasted out . . . [Then] the news would go out to the world that the place was 'liberated'. This is the way it was, day after day, town after town.[66]

In Eighth Army's sector methods were cruder yet, a point perceived with particular clarity by the Canadian contingent. In their attack on the Hitler Line, a switch position behind the Gustav Line, on 23 May, they were supported by British tank units and witnessed terrible casualties as these were directed straight into enemy minefields and into enfilading fire from anti-tank guns. On 2 Canadian Brigade's front on this day, 41 of the 58 tanks engaged were knocked out. In an attack across the Melfa two days later, units of 5 Canadian Armoured Division were employed but the tactics differed little. 'For the leading troops the advance was little better than a *kamikaze* charge and they ran straight into well-prepared ambushes by enemy tanks and anti-tank guns.' A staff officer in the division wrote of this battle:

> As for the main obstacle of the German tanks . . . the only reason why it was possible to make headway against their qualitative superiority was by weight of numbers . . . General Leese [has been cited] as saying that in his offensive he was prepared to lose 1000 tanks. As he had 1900 at his disposal, the Panther stood a fair chance of becoming an extinct species among the fauna of S. Italy. On our side losses had to be taken and replacements thrown in.[67]

The same point was made even more forcefully by a German soldier, a lieutenant captured in Italy and under guard by a young American soldier. That latter according to his own account, was 'a young punk' and was 'riding' the German:

I said, 'Well if you're so tough, if you're all supermen, how come you're here captured and I'm guarding you?' And he looked at me and said, 'Well, it's like this. I was on this hill as a battery commander with six 88-millimeter antitank guns, and the Americans kept sending tanks down the road. We kept knocking them out. Every time they sent a tank we knocked it out. Finally we ran out of ammunition and the Americans didn't run out of tanks.' That's it in a nutshell.[68]

If the Allies had had to rely only on tactics like these to break into the Liri Valley they might well have suffered even greater casualties than they did. Happily, however, General Juin had not limited himself to mere carping about over-mechanisation, and when the plans for the fourth battle were being drawn up he had reserved a role for his own troops that took advantage both of their abilities and of the Italian terrain. The majority of the French Corps were North Africans, well used to mountain warfare, and Juin decided to launch his attack in the Aurunci Mountains, to the west of the Liri Valley, in an area regarded by the Germans, and by his own superiors, as being impenetrable.

To the tribesmen of the Kabyles, however, the word simply did not exist, and they were specifically trained to capitalise upon even a small penetration in the enemy line, pushing troops through all the time, driving forward and into the enemy rear, and keeping him continually off-balance. Whereas the British and Americans tended to move forward with the utmost caution, jumping off from one preset phase line to another in measured sequence, the French preferred the sort of speed and flexibility called for in the following instructions drawn up by General de Monsabert, one of Juin's divisional commanders. He demanded above all that his men

> feel out the front and respond to any weakening of enemy resistance, as soon as it is detected . . . In this period there must be no rigid timetable for anyone; everything will be decided in response to how the attack progresses . . . [We must] exploit as vigorously as possible . . . Each regiment should have strong forces . . . [for just such] exploitation which will act resolutely without bothering about communications with their neighbours.

The Germans became very aware of how much more effective these tactics were than the predictable 'production number' assaults launched by Juin's allies. In one report, written in May 1944, an officer on the staff of Army Group 'C' commented: 'American and British tactics, as in the past, have been methodical: local successes have rarely been exploited. The French, on the contrary, particularly the Moroccans, have fought furiously and exploited each local success by immediately concentrating all their available forces at the point where resistance is weakening.'[69]

Such tactics certainly served the French well during the fourth battle of Cassino. They soon made a decisive break deep into the German rear and the whole defensive position had to be given up. It was this penetration, in fact, that compelled the Germans to relinquish Monte Cassino and not the unsuccessful, albeit heroic attacks of the Polish Corps. Once the Germans began to pull back, the door was theoretically open to Alexander's *corps de chasse* to burst into the Liri Valley, but it soon became apparent that Eighth Army had yet again rather muffed the pursuit phase and assembled too much *corps* for an effective *chasse*. Shortly after the Germans began to fall back, Alexander threw in every available division after them and soon five divisions – three infantry and two armoured – were all jostling for position in the narrow confines of the valley. Such a concentration brought with it a staggering array of armoured fighting vehicles and motor transport. If each division had its full complement one is talking about 450 medium tanks, 240 other tanks, 50 self-propelled guns, 320 armoured cars, 200 cars, 2,000 half-tracks and 10,000 trucks and lorries; and the road net in the valley was simply not adequate to handle such a weight of traffic.*

The whole British and Canadian advance, therefore, was plagued by bottlenecks and traffic jams which prevented supplies getting through, made it extremely difficult to bring forward infantry quickly to outflank potential German blocking positions, and often prevented the armour from even keeping up with the infantry on foot.† Consequently, between 24 and 26 May the Allied advance degenerated into an almost endless series of traffic jams, and the situation was hardly improved on the 29th when Alexander decided to throw yet another armoured division into the fray. According to one participant congestion swiftly became chaos and soon 'traffic became impossible . . . The jam . . . had coagulated and become a fevered stasis.'[70]

---

* These figures do not include the vehicles used by Corps or Army troops.
† For armoured regiments the problem became a vicious circle. A tank moving in slow traffic uses up to four times as much petrol as normal, but the jams also meant that it was that much more difficult to bring forward extra fuel.

Hindsight has only served to reinforce the impression of an ineptly staged pursuit, and the official historian could only take to task a commander-in-chief who, 'in spite of natural obstacles . . . rammed his divisions two abreast into these narrow defiles [in the Liri Valley] because he wished to exploit in strength. He approved when his corps commanders placed their armoured divisions in the lead in terrain which was so unsuitable for them that they, and everything behind them, crawled.'[71]

Eighth Army's pursuit, therefore, never seriously threatened the Germans with complete defeat and they were able to fall back in a fairly disciplined fashion, moving from one temporary defence line to another and only having to pull out their rearguards at the very last moment. According to General Juin, Eighth Army was 'always advancing in a very measured fashion' and von Senger und Etterlin, who played a large part in organising Tenth Army's withdrawal, described how he was able 'to prevent annihilation of . . . [XIV Panzer Corps] by instructing the troops who were being driven back to engage in delaying action and to withdraw in a generally northward direction . . . In view of the fact that the British Corps attacking in that area were not exerting much pressure this was a relatively simple mission.'[72]

Von Senger, it will be noted, withdrew his Corps northwards, which meant that they were in fact pulling back across the front of the advancing British, a manoeuvre in which tactical flair comes close to impertinence. Von Senger favoured this route because it took his units away from the Allied build-up in the Anzio bridgehead, from where a breakout was to be expected that would place Allied troops right across the line of any German retreat up Highway 6, towards Rome. In the event, though the Anzio forces did stage a successful breakout, they did not pursue the north-easterly axis favoured by Alexander but, on Clark's orders, veered directly northwards to Rome, a purely prestige target but one which had come to obsess Clark.* It has often been suggested that this change of direction by

---

* If the latter term implies a less than perfect mental equilibrium, the following report of an interview with Clark, after the war, would tend to support such a diagnosis. During the interview Clark gave full vent to his long-standing Anglophobia and stated that he had been quite convinced that 'the British definitely wanted Eighth Army to take Rome or at least to take part in its capture. When Alexander told Clark he wanted Eighth Army to take part in its capture, Clark got pretty sore. He told Alexander if Alexander gave him . . . such an order he would refuse to obey it and if Eighth Army tried to advance on Rome, Clark said he would have his troops fire on the Eighth Army.' (Quoted in J. Ellis, *Cassino, the Hollow Victory: the Battle for Rome January–June 1944* (André Deutsch, 1984), p. 430.)

Clark robbed Alexander of a decisive victory in the Liri Valley by permitting the escape of Tenth Army. In fact, Alexander had already robbed himself of victory, moving so slowly with his unwieldy *corps de chasse* that the Germans had been allowed to pick their optimum line of retreat, one which took them well away from any potential drive out of the Anzio beachhead. Moreover, even after Clark had turned the Anzio divisions away from the Germans' line of retreat, there would still have been a possibility of using the French Expeditionary Corps, advancing south of the Liri, to cut off Tenth Army. For the French, though operating in much more difficult terrain, were consistently ahead of Eighth Army and would have been able to follow the Germans across their front without causing undue disruption. Alexander, however, for reasons which remain obscure, adamantly refused permission for any French change of axis or any adjustment of inter-army boundaries.

The Germans, therefore, succeeded in extricating both Tenth and Fourteenth Armies from the defence lines south of Rome. To be sure, they had lost very heavily in men and equipment, and many divisions were reduced to little more than skeleton formations. But for the Germans these were enough and as long as a sufficient cadre of experienced offices and NCOs remained they were able remarkably quickly to rebuild a division into a fully effective fighting formation. During the retreat through Florence (and Ancona on the Adriatic coast) this task was made all the easier by the Allies, who were never able to force the pace enough seriously to inconvenience their opponents. According to one American staff officer interviewed after the war: 'The "pursuit between Rome and the Arno" is misnamed . . . It was a rapid advance but "pursuit" implies getting in behind the Germans. The Germans in this action controlled our pursuit – our rate of advance . . . The operations between Rome and the Arno was [sic] far from a rout. It was a calculated withdrawal.'[73]

It was, moreover, a calculated withdrawal into yet another strong defensive position, the Gothic Line, against which the Allies could confidently be expected to batter their heads with the customary lack of finesse. The Germans were not to be disappointed. Alexander's original plan for storming this line does seem to have considerable merit, as he proposed concentrating both his armies on a central axis towards Bologna. Once a breakthrough had been achieved his *corps de chasse* would speed across the Po Valley to seize a bridgehead over that river north of Ferrara and cut off the German line of retreat. The interdiction of the latter was to be further facilitated by a bombing offensive against all the 19 bridges across the lower Po.

General Leese, however, objected to this plan as it involved Eighth Army fighting in mountainous terrain to which it was still ill-adapted. His point had some validity but his alternative suggestion was hardly much of an improvement. He proposed that Eighth Army alone should launch the main attack and that it should be along the Adriatic coast, where the mountains were less fearsome and where there seemed to be more opportunity for Eighth Army's familiar set-piece assaults. In fact, the terrain in this area was if anything even more unpropitious than that in the centre. The area between Ancona and Ravenna was sliced up by numerous rivers that would require a whole series of organised river crossings, the mounting of which must deny Eighth Army any chance of building up a decent head of steam to penetrate deep into the German positions or get around their flanks. This proposal went counter to Alexander's thinking as well as to that of his Chief of Staff, General Harding, but the former meekly accepted Leese's objections and gave his approval for a major offensive on the coast.

Eighth Army's attacks began on 25 August 1944 and it fared even worse than Harding had feared. As it fell further and further behind schedule during the seemingly endless series of river assaults, the weather began to worsen and turned what had seemed like favourable flat tank country into a hopeless morass. It is a matter for wonder, indeed, that the Allies had ever really expected to send a *corps de chasse* 'swanning around' on the Lombardy Plain and Po Valley, for the axis chosen by Leese would have taken him through the Romagna, in the south-east corner of the plain. This, by Alexander's own admission, was 'nothing but a reclaimed swamp – and not wholly reclaimed in some parts . . . Even in the best drained areas the soil remembers its marshy origin, and when rained on forms the richest mud known to the Italian theatre . . . Under autumn conditions we should have difficulty in making full use of our armoured superiority.'[74]

But the terrain was not the only handicap to the effective use of tanks, and even in much more favourable country it seems doubtful that the Allies could have engineered a genuine strategic breakthrough. As a recent commentator has pointed out: 'Exploiting initial success, gained by carefully managed set-piece attacks, was a problem the Allies seldom mastered in Italy. Although coming close on several occasion, they were unable to force major offensives to decisive conclusions.'[75] On three occasions during the battle on the Gothic Line the Allies showed that they had learned little from the lessons of Fondouk Pass, Bou Arad, the Hitler Line or the Melfa.

On the first occasion the victims were again the luckless Canadians when, on 30 August, the British Columbia Dragoons made an attack on Point 204, west of Pesaro, across open ground and with no infantry or artillery support. Fifty tanks left the Dragoons' start-line, but within a few hours there were only 18 still able to fight. The next two incidents both involved 1 British Armoured Division, a formation that had not seen action since April 1943, in Tunisia, and which was entirely ignorant of the more cautious tactics evolved by veteran mixed tank/infantry teams in Italy. But even had it been apprised of these tactics, 1 Armoured Division would still have had to contend with the ignorance of senior commanders, veteran or not, who seemed incapable of directing effective armoured operations. On 1 September excellent progress was made by the Canadian infantry, and for a short while a considerable gap appeared in the German line through which a well poised mobile force might have poured. But 1 Armoured, although specifically assigned to exploit any Canadian success, was held back over 50 miles in the rear. Two recent students of this battle have described as 'incomprehensible . . . the failure to bring 1st Armoured Division to a point close behind the front from which it could exploit the opportunity on September 1 for which Leese had been hoping.' They also dub as 'criminal inertia' his failure to 'improvise a mobile group to exploit . . . [the Canadian] success. A German or an American general would have galvanised his staff into immediate action. Any action would have been better than none. Leese did nothing.'[76]

In the event, the Canadians had to wait for 1 Armoured to move slowly forward, an utterly exhausting journey that was not complete until the evening of the 3rd. When the attack did go in, on the 4th, the three armoured regiments had already lost 15 per cent of their tanks to mechanical faults developed on the approach march. They also discovered that the Germans had had plenty of time to plug the gap. The attackers ran straight into a dense screen of anti-tank guns and the assault was a costly failure, with two regiments losing a total of 63 tanks. Moreover, not only had there been a complete absence of infantry support throughout the attack but afterwards such progress as was made had to be given up again because there were still no infantry near enough to take over the ground captured.

The next major operation by 1 Armoured Division was yet another fiasco, in many ways a carbon copy of the effort on 4 September. Again the tanks were well to the rear of the infantry whose success they were supposed to exploit and the approach march along narrow, congested roads played havoc with the tanks and their crews' nerves. Once arrived at the start-line, the leading regiment, the Bays, found that the high ground overlooking their axis of advance had been retaken by the Germans and that the ridge they were to attack was almost two miles away. The rolling open countryside offered no cover, hardly even a tree, and it was clear that any advance must soon turn into 'an armoured Balaclava'. But, on 9 September, the order was given and the Bays started off into their own valley of death: 'As the tanks sailed into view over the crest, the enemy anti-tank gunners must have rubbed their eyes with astonishment. Peering into the sights of their 88-mm. guns, they were roughly in the position of snipers with precision rifles firing at infantry trotting slowly forward in undeviating line across country where no cover was available. The range was known to within a metre or two.'[77] The anti-tank gunners were able to inflict just such punishment as snipers might, and in the attack the Bays lost 24 tanks and 64 men killed and wounded. Brigade headquarters then ordered that 9 Lancers should pass through the burning Shermans and resume the attack, and it was only after the most urgent representations from the commanders of both armoured regiments that Brigade was prevailed upon to cancel this second attack.

With the failure of these attempts to make a decisive rupture in the German line the weather worsened considerably and operations of any kind soon became virtually impossible. By the end of October the Allies had completely run out of steam and their offensive, in the words of General Clark, 'died out, slowly and painfully, and only one long stride from success, like a runner who collapses reaching for, but not quite touching, the tape at the finishing line.'[78] Eighth Army operations, in fact, continued until the end of December, but more with the aim of drawing level with Clark's Fifth Army, just short of Bologna, than of making any deep penetration into the German line. Once the Germans had been pushed back behind the Senio, however, both sides effectively went into winter quarters until the following year.

In April, Fifth and Eighth Armies drove forward once again, but by now the German situation on other fronts was so parlous, and the material superiority of the Allies so marked, that the final issue

PART FOUR

'ONE BRICK AT A TIME'
North-West Europe
June 1944 – May 1945

'To have the United States at our side was to me the greatest joy . . . Hitler's fate was sealed. Mussolini's fate was sealed. As for the Japanese they would be ground to powder. All the rest was merely the proper application of overwhelming force.'

Winston Churchill on US entry into the war in December 1941

'The OKW will henceforth often be no longer able to meet demands, however urgent and justifiable, for air, armour and artillery support, even when enemy superiority is overwhelming. Any shortage of weapons, therefore, must be made good by strengthening the morale of the troops.'

Oberkommando der Wehrmacht, August 1944

7

Lodgement and Breakout

6 June – 31 August 1944

This book has already had much to say about the chronic weakness of the German war economy. Inadequate production of tanks and motor vehicles as early as 1939 and 1940, growing shortages of aircraft and of fuel during the Combined Bomber Offensive, an abysmally low level of U-boat production, and totally inadequate supplies of aircraft, tanks, artillery and other munitions during the Russian and Mediterranean campaigns have all already been commented upon. In this latter regard the disparity between German and Russian production has received the most attention but one must always remember that the latter, mighty an achievement as it was, represented only one part of the total Allied effort. Prior to embarking upon a discussion of the last year of the war in North-West Europe, therefore, it would be appropriate to re-emphasise the contribution of the other Allied war economies, notably the American, as well as to highlight the sheer magnitude of their and the Russians' aggregate output.

The American contribution to this effort was, as will be seen, prodigious, but in the early stages of the war the Nazis (and, as we shall see, the Japanese) were remarkably dismissive of US capabilities, both industrial and military. Probably the most outrageous of the *Gröfaz*'s numerous tactical, strategical and geopolitical miscalculations was contained in a letter to Mussolini, written six months before Hitler's casual decision to follow Japan in declaring war on America. In this missive, dated 21 June 1941, he airily assured the *Duce*: 'Whether or not America enters the war is a matter of indifference, in as much as she is already helping our enemy with all the power she can muster.'[1] Another cuckoo on this cloud was Göring, who told his aircraft production chief, Ernst Udet, in August 1941 that the latter's fears about the potential of the US aircraft industry were groundless. 'It is a bluff,' he laughed. 'They can make cars and refrigerators, but not aircraft.'

By February of the following year the laughter had faded, though Göring still refused to believe a report by his own staff that US aircraft production could be expected to reach 40,000 planes per annum. To one of its authors he shouted: 'Everything you have written in this report is utter nonsense. You need a psychiatrist to examine your head.'[2] Only two months later Joseph Goebbels was sneering at American naval capacity, noting in his diary on 14 April: 'The Americans have launched a naval building programme in the columns of the neutral press which is nothing short of grotesque. But we know what to think of American statistics. The Americans are trying to impress world public opinion by fantastic figures.'[3]

But it was not long before the Nazi leadership was forced to reconsider their assessments of American industrial power and begin to face reality, a reality pithily summed up in one of the US Strategic Bombing Survey reports. By the end of 1942 it noted,

> the terms of warfare were ceasing to be those of Hitler, and were becoming those of his enemies. The outcome of the war no longer depended on skilful strategy and well-timed shock effects – the kind of war, in short, that Germany could hope to win. It was becoming, instead, a war in which military manpower and economic resources would be decisive.[4]

In moments of lucidity even the staunchest of Hitler's supporters were forced to recognise the impossibility of their situation. Less than a year after his dismissal of the American naval programme, Goebbels was beginning to temper his contempt with a certain nervousness about the growth of the American arsenal. On 9 May he wrote in his diary: 'The American soldiers, for the most part, have no idea why this war is being fought. If we could face them with numbers and weapons equal to theirs, we could indulge in a regular rabbit chase.' By September, he had admitted to himself the ultimate futility of such 'if only's' and stated quite simply: 'Sooner or later we shall have to face the question of inclining toward one enemy side or the other. Germany has never yet had luck with a two front war; it won't be able to stand this one in the long run either.'[5]

Certain of Hitler's generals also began to see the writing on the wall. Rommel had been the first to face American air power and their technology on the ground and he had been quickly impressed. Musing on his defeat in North Africa he stated flatly that 'from the moment the overwhelming industrial capacity of the United States made itself felt in any theatre of war, there was no longer any chance of ultimate victory in that theatre . . . Tactical skill could only postpone the collapse [in Africa], it could not avert the ultimate fate of this theatre.' At the very beginning of the Battle for Normandy he tried to make this clear to Hitler: 'I reported to the Führer yesterday. Rundstedt [OB West] is doing the same. It's time for politics to come into play . . . The long-husbanded strength of the two world powers is now coming into action. It will all be decided quickly.'[6]

Hitler, of course, could not afford to face such facts squarely and admit that defeat was, in the long run, inevitable. Nevertheless, even he had to give at least a passing nod at reality. His gloomy assessment of the situation in May 1944 has been mentioned in chapter 2, but he was equally frank in another address at about the same time, described by General Walter Warlimont, Jodl's deputy in the OKW Operations Branch. Referring to the impending Allied landings in France Hitler conceded: 'If we don't throw the invaders back, we can't win a static war in the long run because the matériel our enemies can bring in will exceed what we can send to that front. With no strategic reserves of any importance, it will be impossible to build up sufficient strength along such a line [inland, along e.g. a French river]. Therefore the enemy must be thrown back at the first attempt.'[7]

It is quite clear in hindsight, however, that if this was in fact a real chance for German forces in the West, it was most certainly their one and only chance, and one that even then could bring only temporary relief. For by that stage of the war, even though German production of most categories of munitions had increased in almost every year to 1944, it was nevertheless lagging increasingly behind Allied production, offering no real hope that superior German military technique could do anything like enough to offset the consequent disparity in armaments, both at the front and in reserve.

This basic fact is highlighted in tables 46–55 in the Statistical Appendix, where the burgeoning Allied productive effort and its increasing margin of superiority over the German is set out in detail. The essential points about overall Allied superiority are summed up in the figures below, which show that between 1942 and 1945, when both the USA and the USSR were fully involved in the war, and the absolute centrality of the battle of production was apparent to all, the following Allied:German production ratios were achieved. In raw materials:

Coal	2.6:1	Aluminium	3.5:1
Iron ore	3.7:1	Oil	47.0:1
Crude steel	5.1:1		

In munitions:

Tanks and SP guns	5.0:1	Machine-guns*	7.0:1
Artillery	5.6:1	Trucks and lorries	12.7:1
Mortars*	8.7:1	Military aircraft	5.4:1

* 1939–45.

In many ways the raw figures have still greater impact. Thus it might also be borne in mind that the figures for munitions production in the periods just specified involved an Allied surplus over the Germans of:

156,000 tanks and SP guns	4,070,000 machine-guns
644,000 artillery pieces	2,457,000 trucks and lorries
583,834 mortars	400,428 military aircraft
	(inc. 133,453 fighters)

At 1944 establishment, had the Germans actually been able to match Allied production and thus have this amount of extra equipment to allocate, they would have been able to equip or completely re-equip well over 700 panzer and panzer grenadier divisions and (if only the surplus of fighter aircraft is considered) over 1,000 fighter *Geschwader*. Obviously, such figures are not to be taken too seriously, as the essence of maintaining armed forces in the field is to set aside a large proportion of one's production to provide a continuous flow of replacements for existing formations, but they do nevertheless give at least some impression of the sheer scale of Allied material preponderance.

The data for munitions production, set out in more detail in tables 51–55, is also interesting in that it clearly shows that when it came to converting raw materials into finished munitions, the disparity between German and Allied performance became yet more pronounced. Production figures for these latter offer an interesting corrective to two myths about German economic performance which, despite scholarly rebuttal, still seem to enjoy popular consensus. These are that, on the one hand, German industry was particularly efficient and, on the other, that the maximum resources possible were devoted to military production, much more than in the 'democratic' economies. In fact, the figures show that the Allies were much better at converting raw materials into weapons, such that whilst

Germany managed to produce, for example, 50 per cent as much coal as the Allies or one-third as much steel, the figure for combat aircraft, tanks, artillery and trucks was only one-fifth, machine-guns one-seventh, and mortars barely more than a tenth. The precise figures are set down in table 15, which shows German output of certain items during the whole war as a percentage of that of the Allies, as well as showing this same relationship in the year 1944 alone. The latter year is chosen not simply because it is of particular relevance to the campaign being discussed in this part of the book, but also because it was one during which German production reached a peak. However, though many industries attained levels that would have seemed impossible at the beginning of the war, these were still completely inadequate when compared with those reached by the Allies.

Table **15**: *German production of raw materials and munitions 1939–45, and in the single year 1944, as a percentage of Allied production in the same periods*

	Coal	Iron ore	Crude steel	Aluminium	Crude oil
1939–45[*]	54.3	40.7	32.2	46.6	4.3
1944	48.6	26.3	23.3	38.8	2.4

a) Raw materials

[*]USA 1942–5; USSR 1941–5.

	Tanks & s.p guns	Artillery	Mortars	Machine-guns	Military trucks	Combat aircraft	Transport aircraft
1939–45	20.6	19.6	11.2	14.2	19.4	20.9	7.2
1944	37.2	?	?	21.4	9.6	28.1	2.7

b) Munitions

A particularly significant feature of the figures above is that it is in those items most fundamental to her military effort that Germany was most lacking. Having evolved in the early months of the war, albeit in a somewhat *ad hoc* fashion, a mode of warfare that depended largely upon the psychological dislocation created by fast-moving armoured formations, the Germans soon found themselves unable to equip anything like the number of armoured divisions that their opponents could put into the field. During the war as a whole they were able to produce only one-fifth of the tanks turned out by the Allies, and

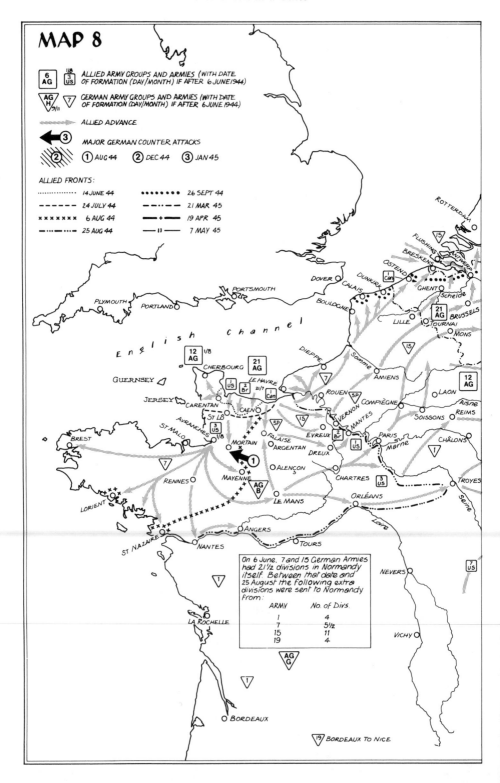

MAP 8

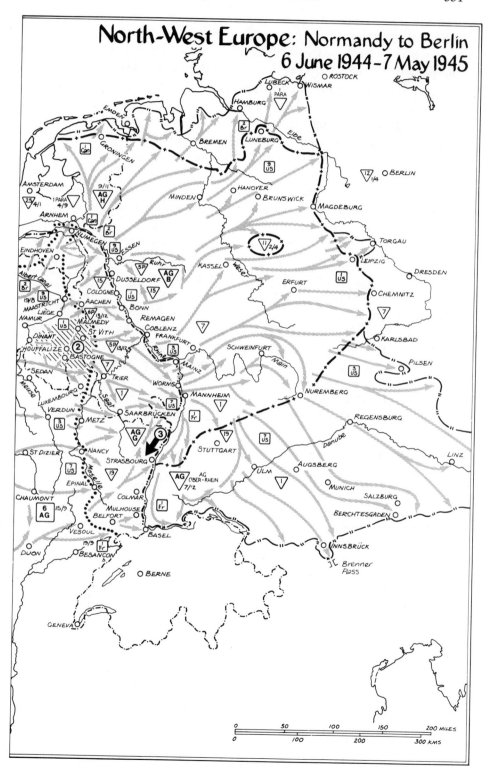

North-West Europe: Normandy to Berlin
6 June 1944–7 May 1945

even between 1943 and 1945, when both sides were producing the models that were to do the bulk of the actual fighting, the figure was still only one-quarter. Production ratios like that boded ill for the panzer regiments, the very cutting edge of *blitzkrieg*.

But even had tanks been available in the requisite numbers, it would still have been hardly possible for the Germans to re-enact the triumphs of September 1939 and June 1940 and 1941. For the other acute shortages highlighted in table 15, those of oil, trucks and transport aircraft, all meant that the Army *as a whole* could never attain the necessary level of mobility. In other words, even if a limited number of panzer divisions were properly equipped and motorised, as well as being allocated adequate amounts of fuel, these could never obtain more than short-term tactical successes. For there were not enough trucks or transport planes, nor fuel for even those that did exist, to properly supply panzer formations along long lines of communication, or to bring up and later supply the mass of infantry divisions that must eventually properly occupy the ground that the panzers had staked out. Even by 1942, as was evident on the Eastern Front, a proper war of movement already demanded much more than the intrepid exploits of a few gung-ho tank commanders, generating panic by their very appearance at the front. Ever since the rebuff before Moscow, élan at the front and *panjes* in the rear had been less than adequate to the demands of modern warfare.

By mid-1944, therefore, it was well established that the majority of an army's divisions, as well as of the rear echelon supply units, had to be mobile, capable of bringing up the maximum amount of firepower to the front, of keeping it supplied during a prolonged slogging match, and, if necessary, of switching it from one important sector to another. Without such mobility in depth, strategically significant offensive operations soon became impossible and an army so deprived could look forward to nothing but the slow haemorrhage of static defensive warfare. It could well be argued, indeed, that the most significant figures in the tables just cited are the 2,400,000 military trucks produced in the United States as against only 346,000 in Germany.* Göring's taunt about 'cars and refrigerators' becomes

---

* See Statistical Appendix, table 54. Especially as trucks were probably the most important item of Lend-Lease equipment sent to Russia during the war. Russian historians, echoing Stalin, might cavil at the value of certain Lend-Lease items, notably some of the tanks and aircraft, but they cannot gainsay the inestimable value of the 432,659 trucks they received, more than double their own production of civilian and military models combined.

yet more fatuous, completely underestimating as it does not only the phenomenal productive potential of the American economy but also the central role of the internal combustion engine in modern warfare. Many battlefields have been cited as being particularly significant in Germany's defeat in the Second World War. Not the least of them should be Detroit.

It was, therefore, with an already massive overall material preponderance that the Allies made ready for their next major offensives of mid-1944 – in Italy towards Rome, against Army Group Centre in Byelorussia, and across the English Channel to the Normandy beaches. The eventual outcome of this combined onslaught could never really be in doubt, for the *Wehrmacht*, quickly debilitated by ruthless attritional trade-offs of matériel, soon showed itself incapable of countering three such major operations, particularly when the Combined Bomber Offensive was also beginning to erode German productive capacity significantly. By mid-1944, it was becoming increasingly clear that the Thousand-Year *Reich* had not even that number of days still to run. Certainly there was much fighting still to come but, fierce as it must be, it was, in Churchill's telling phrase, simply 'the proper application of overwhelming force'.[8]

Nevertheless, it has to be conceded that in the Normandy offensive there were considerable *initial* difficulties in translating industrial superiority into actual military superiority on the ground. Indeed, Allied planners had at one stage been in danger of making the problems worse than they need be, limiting their original estimate of the D-Day assault force required to only three infantry divisions, three tank brigades and one airborne division. However, once Montgomery had been appointed as commander of all Allied ground forces during the first weeks of the invasion, he campaigned long and hard for this force to be increased, until it was finally agreed that the first waves should include five infantry divisions, three armoured brigades and three airborne divisions. But this was the limit, because there were not enough landing craft to bring any more men on to the beaches in the first assault. On paper, then, Montgomery's chances still did not look especially good. As against his eight divisions on D-Day, to be built up to 24 by the end of the first month and 30-plus by the end of July, Field Marshal von Rundstedt, now OB West, could call upon 56 divisions distributed as follows:

Within immediate range of the D-Day beaches	6 Inf. and 1 Pz.
Within 100 miles of the D-Day beaches a further	6 Inf. and 3 Pz.
Within 200 miles of the D-Day beaches a further	17 Inf. and 2 Pz.
Elsewhere in OB West a further	16 Inf. and 5 Pz.

It might well be assumed, therefore, that in the first week or so of the battle the Germans should be able to concentrate a markedly superior force against the 16 infantry and four armoured divisions that the Allies hoped to have ashore.

However, just as in the Italian campaign, the mere comparison of the number of divisions gives a very misleading impression of relative strengths. For one thing, it was extremely unlikely that the Germans would attempt to concentrate all their forces against any Allied lodgement. Some divisions, especially in the South of France, were in the process of being formed and in early June were not yet deemed fit for combat. More importantly, despite some strong suspicions, Hitler could not bring himself fully to accept that the Allies would make their main effort in Normandy and Normandy alone, and thus for some weeks after the invasion a considerable number of divisions were to remain outside the battlefield, guarding the coasts of the Pas de Calais, between the Seine and the Scheldt. That Hitler continued to be fearful about these northern French coasts for as long as he did was due largely to the Allied planners. For, whatever the shortcomings of their original assault plan, and many of these derived from other people's overly parsimonious assumptions about available resources, the provisions made for deceiving the German High Command as to Allied intentions were masterly, and dramatically reduced the number of divisions that the former regarded as freely disposable reserves. It is quite remarkable, in fact, how few German divisions were speedily committed. Even on 24 July, Fifteenth Army in the north-east and First and Nineteenth Armies in the south still retained command in their own sectors of just under 50 per cent of the total forces available to OB West.*

Of course, with regard to the armour, a much greater proportion *had* been committed to the battlefield proper, with only three panzer divisions holding their positions elsewhere and two extra ones, of the highest quality, being brought across from the Eastern Front. By 24 July, ten panzer divisions were at the front, as against only four

* In addition, two SS panzer divisions had been brought over from the Eastern Front and one infantry division from Denmark.

British and four American.* Such a cursory head-count, however, conceals much. For one thing, an Allied armoured division was a significantly more powerful beast than a German. In June 1944 the British version included 247 medium and 63 light tanks whilst the American weighed in with 186 medium and 77 light. It is impossible to generalise about German strengths except to say that few of their panzer divisions were at the authorised strength of 200 tanks. 21 Panzer, for example, went into battle with 127 tanks, 12 ss Panzer with 177; on 1 June, 1 ss and 2 ss Panzer reported tank strengths of 88 and 69 respectively; Panzer Lehr drove north on 7 June with 182 tanks and 2 Panzer left the Somme on the 8th with 161.† Some of the more far-flung divisions – 9 Panzer near Marseilles, 11 Panzer near Bordeaux and 19 Panzer Division in Holland – were at this stage of the war divisions in name only. On 9 June 19 Panzer reported that it still had not received any heavy weapons at all and remained so deprived for another fortnight. Even on 25 June 9 Panzer possessed only four tanks (Mark IVs) whilst 11 Panzer was so short of motor transport for its Panzer Grenadier regiments that the commander doubted it could function effectively as an armoured division.

A yet more serious problem for the Germans was their total inability to maintain the panzer divisions even at these reduced establishments. The Allies, from the very beginning of the North-West European campaign, had recourse to a substantial park of reserve tanks from which they could quickly replace any casualties.‡ Even after a particularly costly encounter with the enemy no Allied tank unit was much below its official establishment for long. The Germans, on the other hand, had almost no reserve at all, and their panzer units were slowly bled to death. Between 6 June and 17 July, for example, during which period it is estimated that the eight panzer divisions committed in Normandy lost at least 250 tanks destroyed, they were all supposed to make good their losses out of a grand total of 17 replacements.

The situation hardly improved in the following weeks. In July and August the German Army on all fronts lost approximately

* 4 Canadian Armoured Division did not actually enter the line until 31 July.
† The figure for 2 ss Panzer Division (from G. A. Harrison, *Cross-Channel Attack*, (The us Army in World War II), (Government Printing Office, Washington, 1951), p. 240) is wildly at variance with that given by Max Hastings (in his excellent *Das Reich* (Michael Joseph, 1981), pp. 1 and 25). I have preferred the former simply because a seemingly authoritative source is given whilst Mr Hastings gives none.
‡ In mid-July this reserve numbered about 500 tanks.

Table 16: *Tank strengths of panzer divisions in Normandy June–August 1944*

	21 Pz	12 SS Pz	Pz Lehr	2 Pz	2 SS Pz	1 SS Pz	9 SS Pz	10 SS Pz	116 Pz
June	(6)* 127	(6) 177	(6) 182	(6) 161	(1) 69	(1) 88			
	(7) 70	(7) 90	(25) 66						
July	(1) 40	(1) 51	(7) 30			(2) 80			
		(8) 85	(25) 45		(23) 57				
			(26) 14						(30) 62
August		(7) 54	(5) 13	(7) 45		(7) 60			(7) 60
		(8) 48	(6) 9						
		(10) 39		(13) 25		(13) 30			
		(15) 15		(19) 15			(21) 25		
	(23) 10	(23) 10		(23) 0	(23) 15	(23) 0	(23) 22	(23) 0	(23) 12

* Figure in brackets = date.

4,300 tanks and assault guns destroyed, perhaps 1,500 of them in Normandy. Yet in the same period only 2,378 replacements went out to the front, and only a very small proportion of these were sent west. Worse, the proportion that could actually be used was smaller still. The main reasons for this have been dealt with in earlier chapters, chapter 4 pointing out how many tanks were 'lost' between acceptance by the Army and actual arrival at the front, and chapter 2 showing how the insatiable demands at the front led to tanks being hurried forward before they had been properly tested or run in, which in turn led to an inordinate number of breakdowns. A typical example of this latter problem in Normandy was the experience of 2 ss Panzer Division, which on 10 June reported that 60 per cent of its tanks were unserviceable and that these, as well as the division's towing vehicles, would require at least another four days before they were ready to move, even though they were under orders to begin doing so immediately.

Two other sets of figures concern the much-vaunted Tiger tank, in theory at least the state of the art as regarded heavy tank design. How much impact these weapons had on the actual battlefield, however, remains open to doubt, for only a very small proportion seem to have been serviceable at any one time. On 15 June, for example, I ss Panzer Corps had no Tigers ready for combat, 30 in short-term repair and 8 in long-term. A fortnight later ss Panzer Abteilung 101, equipped with 28 Tigers, reported that 25 of them were in the repair shops. Clearly, then, the panzer divisions were

Table 17: *Allied armour committed in Normandy June–July* 1944

| | Tanks | | SP |
	Medium	Light	Guns
5 US armoured divisions	930	385	270
5 Brit./Can. armoured divisions	1,235	315	120
11 Brit./Can. armoured brigades	2,134	473	-
14 US tank battalions	784	238	-
22 US tank destroyer battalions	-	-	792
TOTAL	5,083	1,411	1,182

once again pretty much a doomed species, a fact corroborated by the figures in table 16, which show sample tank strengths at various dates in June, July and August.

Trying to assess relative tank strengths by simply counting divisions also fails to take into account the numerous sub-divisional formations that the Allies put into the field. In First Canadian and Second British Armies these were mainly armoured brigades, of which ten arrived in North-West Europe in June and July 1944.* These brigades, it will be recalled, contained almost exactly the same number of tanks as an armoured division, so that by the end of July the presence of these formations actually doubled the number of tanks available to the Allies, there being ten armoured divisions and eleven armoured brigades in the line. The Americans, too, had their own sub-divisional units, the tank and tank-destroyer battalions, of which 39 of the former and 54 of the latter served in this theatre, mainly attached to US infantry divisions.† At the end of July, 14 tank and 22 tank-destroyer battalions had actually arrived in Normandy, augmenting Allied armoured strength by a further 784 medium and 238 light tanks, and 792 self-propelled guns, the equivalent of the tank component of another four armoured divisions.

The overall figures for each side amply confirm the massive Allied superiority. In June and July, according to the OKW War Diary, the Germans committed 1,347 tanks and 337 assault guns to the

* Seven of these arrived as armoured brigades (with cruiser tanks) and three as army tank brigades (with Infantry tanks). One was Canadian, one Czech and the rest British. One was disbanded in August 1944 and another absorbed into 79 Armoured Division. However, a second Canadian armoured brigade arrived from Italy in March 1945, making ten independent brigades at the end of the war.
† 38 US infantry divisions served in North-West Europe.

Normandy battles. The Allied armoured commitment is shown in table 17.

In fact, even these figures still considerably understate Allied superiority for, unlike the German figures just cited, they do not include replacement tanks that entered the battle in this period. Given that US forces alone were losing around 500 medium tanks per month during the Normandy battle, and that there is no reason why British and Canadian figures should be significantly less, one might reasonably add another 2,000 tanks to the totals cited in table 17, giving a superiority over the Germans of more than 5:1 in medium and heavy tanks. Figures for individual battles offer further proof of the Allies' material preponderance. During an early attack towards Caen, Operation Epsom, on 26 June, 21 Army Group* employed some 600 tanks against less than 200 German. By the time of Operation Charnwood, a renewed assault on Caen on 7 July, the British and Canadians had attained a 4:1 superiority over the panzers in their sector, and their advantage in the attack zone proper was probably considerably more. On 18 July, during Operation Goodwood, yet another attempt to penetrate to the flat country south of Caen, 1,350 British and Canadian tanks faced perhaps 400 German. On 25 July, at the start of Operation Cobra, a major American effort to smash out of the western end of the beachhead, 12 US Army Group employed 750 tanks against little more than a hundred German.

But if the relative weakness of von Rundstedt's panzer divisions was a cause for concern, yet more acute was that of the

---

* The Allied order of battle in Normandy between June and August was as follows. In charge of Supreme Headquarters Allied Expeditionary Force (SHAEF) was General Eisenhower, though he did not actually take over command of ground operations until 1 September. Until then the overall ground commander was General Montgomery, coordinating the operations of his own 21 Army Group and 12 Army Group under General Bradley. The Army Groups were subdivided as follows:

12 US (From 1 August)		21	
1 US Army (Bradley) (Hodges from 1 August)	3 US Army (Patton) (from 1 August)	1 Canadian Army (Crerar) (from 21 July)	2 British Army (Dempsey)

It will be seen that 12 Army Group did not come into being until 1 August, but for convenience's sake I have so referred to the US forces throughout the Normandy fighting. Equally 21 Army Group only ever refers to the English and Canadian Armies (and attached allies).

infantry. On 6 June, OB West could call upon 45 infantry divisions,* but many of these, particularly the 26 'static' divisions, were less than lavishly equipped or impressively manned. By mid-1944 their best personnel had been taken away in mass drafts to the Eastern Front, and replaced with newly called up 18-year-olds, men over 35, men with third-degree frostbite, and members of the *Ostbataillone*, formed from Red Army prisoners-of-war. The Canadian official historian gave further details about the static divisions which were

> denied . . . the most modern equipment . . . Their 'little anti-tank guns and baby cannon' [as the commander of Fifteenth Army called them] were out of date; some of them had machine-guns of First World War type. Within the divisional artilleries of one Army there were ten different gun types, many of them captured pieces. Of the divisions under the Commander-in-Chief West, 17 had two regiments or the equivalent instead of the normal three; most had limited mobility, and there was much horse-drawn transport; six had less than two battalions of artillery . . .[9]†

According to the War Diary of Army Group 'B', in charge of German forces north of the Loire, at the end of January 1944 Seventh Army possessed over 30 different weapons with 252 different types of ammunition, almost 50 of which were no longer produced. The entire Army had only 170 75mm anti-tank guns and 68 88mm guns. It also had fewer assault guns than might have been expected because four of its divisions had been stripped of theirs and seen them sent to Romanian formations on the Eastern Front.

The infantry divisions were also bedevilled by a serious shortage of replacements. Between 6 June and 23 July, for example, the Germans in Normandy lost 117,000 men killed, missing and wounded, but only 10,000 replacements arrived from the infantry training depots plus another 10,000 paratroops and low-grade *Luftwaffe* ground-crew. Of

* This count omits three reserve divisions which were confined to occupation duties, even after the invasion. Also omitted are one infantry division occupying the Channel Islands and a security division in Paris. Three reserve divisions that did get embroiled in major combat *are* included.

† With regard to mobility it is significant that even élite units were desperately short of motor transport. 6 Parachute Regiment, for example, possessed only 70 trucks and these comprised *50* different models.

the situation in mid-July, Rommel* wrote: 'Due to the severity of the fighting . . . our casualties are so high that the fighting power of our divisions is rapidly diminishing. Replacements from home are few in number and, with the difficult transport situation, take weeks to get to the front . . . Material losses are also huge and have so far been replaced on a very small scale.'[10] A German return up to 6 August gave a detailed breakdown of casualties, showing that 3,219 officers (including 14 generals) were reported killed, missing or wounded, as well as 141,046 NCOs and men. But only 19,914 replacements had arrived, though another 16,500 were supposed to be on the way. Typical of the straits to which the German divisions were reduced was the situation of LXXXIV Corps, facing the Americans around Caumont. On 25 July, three of its four infantry divisions could muster only 2,500 rifles between them, the (rifle) equivalent of only five or six Allied battalions.

The Allies' superiority of numbers was evident in almost every other military sphere. The naval balance of forces was positively grotesque. Whatever hopes the more optimistic German land commanders might have had about containing the Allied beachhead or even throwing it back into the sea, the naval chiefs were aware from the very first that there was absolutely no possibility of being able to interfere with the invasion armada *en route*. The German Navy in the West at this time could muster only 100 obsolete submarines, 3 or 4 destroyers, 40 torpedo boats and about 500 minesweepers and patrol vessels of negligible fighting value. The invasion fleet, on the other hand, was protected by 5 battleships, 2 monitors, 23 cruisers, 79 destroyers, and 38 sloops, frigates and corvettes. There were also 1 battleship, 26 destroyers and 92 sloops, frigates and corvettes held in reserve.

The Germans were similarly outclassed in the air, with possibly even less chance of effecting an aerial interdiction of the invasion

---

* In October 1943, after Kesselring had taken charge of Italian operations, Rommel was given responsibility for inspecting the defences along the Atlantic coast and was allotted an unemployed Army Group Staff to help him. In December, Rommel and his staff, Army Group 'B', were given command of Seventh and Fifteenth Armies as well as of German troops in the Netherlands. Rommel nominally worked under von Rundstedt but could count on direct access to Hitler should he so wish. Also under von Rundstedt's command were Army Group 'G', controlling First and Nineteenth Armies, and Panzer Group West, set up in November 1943 to supervise the forming and training of all armoured formations in the west.

route. In May and early June 1944 the *Luftwaffe* presence around the English Channel, *Luftflotte* 3, had dwindled to 496 aircraft, only 319 of which were serviceable. There were even fewer actual operational aircraft, the figure for fighters on 6 June being 119. On this same day the whole of *Luftflotte* 3 managed to put up only 319 sorties.* The Allies, blessed with 12,837 aircraft (including 5,400 fighters) assigned to Eisenhower's Supreme Headquarters, attained 10,585 sorties. By the end of June the commander of *Luftflotte* 3 reported:

> Ground installations being systematically smashed, especially all fighter fields . . . Enemy carpet-bombing raids . . . especially against transport installations. Ratio of air strength: generally 1:20, during major operations about 1:40 . . . Own fighter operations now only conditionally possible. Effective fighter and reconnaissance operations entirely ruled out in the invasion area.[11]

It was with good reason that Eisenhower had categorically stated in a D-Day briefing to the troops: 'If you see fighter aircraft over you, they will be ours.' German troops had long been aware of this, a saying current in 1944 gloomily asserting: 'If you see a white plane it's an American, if you see a black plane it's the RAF. If you see no planes at all it's the *Luftwaffe*.'

But Allied naval and air power did not only serve to protect the invasion convoys. Combined with the enormous tank and artillery arsenals at the disposal of 12 and 21 Army Groups, it also provided decisive assistance in the land battles proper, utterly swamping the firepower available to OB West. All German sources, in fact, are unanimous that what defeated them in Normandy was not the enemy's strategic vision, tactical adroitness, or superior soldiery, but simple material might. Speaking of the June battles to his son, some weeks later, Rommel told of the devotion to duty of the German troops.

> 'But,' he added, 'all the courage didn't help. It was one terrible blood-letting. Sometimes we had as many casualties on one day as during the whole summer fighting in Africa in 1942 . . . And the worst of it is that it was all without sense or purpose. There is no longer anything we can do. Every shot

---

* Attempts to disrupt preparations at British ports, or even to find out what these were, were virtually non-existent. In the six weeks before D-Day the *Luftwaffe* managed to put only 129 sorties into British air space.

we fire now is harming ourselves, for it will be returned a hundredfold.'[12]

On 17 July General von Lüttwitz, the commander of 2 Panzer Division, passed on a series of written comments to the infantry division that was relieving him. Amongst his memoranda was the comment: 'The Allies are waging war regardless of expense . . . Our soldiers enter the battle in low spirits at the thought of the enemy's enormous material superiority.'[13] Only three days later, Army Group 'B' headquarters spoke in awe of 'the extraordinary vigour and the colossal material superiority of the enemy'.[14]

What impressed German soldiers at every level was the Allied artillery and their aircraft when employed in a ground support role. Rommel wrote on 10 June: 'The material equipment of the Americans, with numerous new weapons and war material, is far and away superior to that of our divisions . . . In evidence is their great superiority in artillery and outstandingly large supply of ammunition.'[15] Von Lüttwitz's report, just cited, stressed the demoralising effect of 'the incredibly heavy artillery and mortar fire of the enemy [which] is something new, both for the seasoned veterans of the Eastern Front and the new arrivals . . . The average rate of fire on the divisional sector is 4,000 artillery rounds and 5,000 mortar rounds per day. This is multiplied many times before an enemy attack, however small.'[16] An example of the latter was given by a gunnery officer who helped deliver several crushing barrages to soften up enemy defences. At this stage of the war the artillery often

> used such a concentration on such a small area that it is incredible to think of. I have seen Battleships, Cruisers, Destroyers, Superheavies, Mediums, Heavy A.A., Light A.A., and Field Guns, all pour shells as hard as they can into one field for five minutes . . . When synchronisation is perfect, first you have an ordinary field, maybe full of Jerry dug-outs and lined with Tigers; you look at your watch and for Time on Target [or T.O.T., the name given to such a synchronised bombardment]; a roar and the area boils for half a minute; after that, you can see nothing, and you proceed on your way knowing that that field at least will not molest you. You don't, of course, go across it, as all it consists of is several feet of loose earth . . . Definitely it is superiority of fire, not accuracy, that counts.[17]

The artillery also played a vital role in breaking up German counter-attacks, as for example on 7 June, when 21 and 12 SS Panzer drove against the fairly small British beachhead. According to one SS officer cadet: 'Our counter-attack . . . was brought to a standstill mainly by the artillery of the invasion fleet. Because of this concentrated fire, such as I had never seen before on any European battlefield, both officers and men became demoralised and were forced to dig in.'[18] The naval guns were equally decisive during the panzers' last fling around Mortain, on 7 August, when Hitler threw in the remnants of four armoured divisions to try and forestall the post-Cobra breakout. The commander of one of the divisions, 116 Panzer, told Allied interrogators after the war: 'The strong enemy artillery, whose effects in decisive phases of the battle could not be reduced by our planes, nipped in the bud any serious attempts at attack made by the [supporting] infantry. The infantry, therefore, was demoralised, and was unable to deploy in a superior aggressive spirit.'[19] Another counter-attack nipped in the bud was that during Operation Epsom, on 29 June, when the newly arrived 2 SS Panzer Corps threatened to make serious penetrations into the Allied line. By the 30th, however, von Rundstedt was reporting: 'After several hours of fluctuating fighting . . . the attack of 2 SS Panzer Corps broke down. The enemy air force and naval artillery – reported . . . to have reached a hitherto unprecedented strength – have inflicted particularly heavy damage on our assault formations.'[20] A staff officer in 9 SS Panzer Division, one of those involved, recollected that 'the heavy guns of the battleships . . . were devastating. When one of these shells dropped near a Panther, the 56-ton tank was blown over on its side, just from the blast. It was these broadsides from the warships, more than the defensive fighting of the enemy's troops, which halted our Division's Panzer Regiment.'[21]*

But naval gunfire was not simply being used as a weapon of last resort in a particularly desperate situation. No doubt with memories of the Salerno landings well to the fore, Allied planners had made full provision for the systematic use of naval ordnance at all stages of the

* The battleships in question were HMS *Warspite, Ramillies, Nelson* and *Rodney*, along with USS *Texas, Nevada* and *Arkansas*. These were variously equipped with 16-, 15-, 14- and 12-inch guns. Also present, along with dozens of cruisers and destroyers, were the monitors *Roberts* and *Erebus*, both equipped with 15-inch guns.

land battle.* From the very beginning it had a paralysing effect on German operations. Referring to the support given to British troops during the first few days, Rommel wrote that one of the main reasons that operations in Normandy were 'tremendously hampered, and in some places even rendered impossible' was the 'effect of the heavy naval guns. Up to 640 guns have been used. The effect is so immense that no operation of any kind is possible in the area commanded by this rapid-fire artillery, either by infantry or by tanks.'[22] This view was fully endorsed by von Rundstedt, on 11 June, when he categorically stated that the naval gunfire made 'any advance into this zone dominated by fire from the sea impossible'. After the war, he pointed out: 'Besides the interference of the Air Forces, the fire of your battleships was a main factor in hampering our counter-attacks. This was a big surprise, both in its range and effect.'[23] A German report of 16 June even ventured the thought: 'It may be that the part played by the fleet was more decisive than that of the air forces.'[24] Perhaps the most convincing testimony of all was provided by Hitler himself who, on 29 June, in response to numerous references to the Allies' devastating naval firepower, issued a directive in which 'the Führer made it clear that he regarded the destruction of the enemy's battleships as of outstanding importance.'[25] Not surprisingly, he neglected to specify just how it was to be done.

However, notwithstanding certain contrary opinions expressed above, it now seems clear that the most effective component of Allied firepower was their air arm. Rommel had warned of this in a report submitted to Hitler in December 1943, when he had been asked for his recommendations as to the best way to defend the French coastline. With his experiences in Africa still fresh in his mind, he came close to offering a mere counsel of despair:

> . . . our principal reserves . . . will . . . be under constant danger from the air. Bearing in mind the numerical and material superiority of the enemy striking forces, their high state of training and tremendous air superiority, victory in a major battle on the continent seems to me a matter of grave doubt. British and American superiority in the air alone has again and again been so effective that all movement of major formations has been rendered completely impossible, both at the front and behind it, by day and by night . . .[26]

---

* As long, of course, as they were still in range. Nevertheless, Caen, some 15 or 16 miles inland, was well within reach of the battleships.

Actual events were soon to confirm Rommel's gloomiest forebodings. On 10 June he wrote that a main cause of the virtual Allied stranglehold on German operations was 'the immensely powerful, at times overwhelming, superiority of the enemy air force . . . Even the movement of minor formations on the battlefield – artillery going into position, tanks forming up etc. – is instantly attacked from the air with devastating effect. During the day, fighting troops and headquarters alike are forced to seek cover in wooded and close country in order to escape the continual pounding from the air.'[27] Nothing was to change in the following weeks, and on 15 July Rommel wrote to von Kluge, who had taken over from von Rundstedt on the 1st of that month: 'The position in Normandy is . . . approaching a serious crisis. Owing to the exceptionally strong material supplies of the enemy . . . and the operation of their air force, which commands the battlefield unchecked, our own losses are so high that the fighting strength of the divisions is rapidly sinking.'[28]

But von Kluge was able to draw his own conclusions, none of which gave many grounds for hope. On 22 July he informed Hitler that 'discussion yesterday with the commanders in the Caen sector has afforded regrettable evidence that, in face of the enemy's complete command of the air, there is no possibility of finding a strategy which will counter-balance its truly annihilating effect, unless we give up the field of battle.'[29] Ten days later, his spirits had in no way improved and during a conversation with General Warlimont, speaking as Hitler's representative, he pointed out that 'the enemy air superiority is terrific, and smothers almost every one of our movements . . . Losses in men and equipment are extraordinary. The morale of the troops has suffered very heavily . . .'[30]

Two types of aircraft were particularly successful in ground support operations: rocket-firing fighter-bombers and, surprisingly perhaps, medium and heavy bombers. The latter were not especially useful in attacks on static defences – a saturation bombing of Caen prior to Operation Charnwood was as counter-productive as the flattening of Cassino monastery and town a few months earlier. Against armoured formations out in the open, however, even working within broad tolerances, the bombers often wreaked havoc. Reporting to Hitler after Operation Goodwood, which had been preceded by fierce air attacks, von Kluge wrote, on 22 July:

> Whole armoured formations, allotted to the counter-attack, were caught in bomb-carpets of the greatest intensity, so that

they could be extricated from the torn-up ground only by prolonged effort and in some cases only by dragging them out. The result was that they arrived too late. It is immaterial whether such a bomb carpet catches good troops or bad, they are more or less annihilated.[31]

Saturation bombing attacks also preceded Operation Cobra, and though the 'heavies' aroused the wrath of American troops by dropping many bombs in their own lines,* they provoked more serious indignation amongst the Germans, notably *Panzer Lehr* Division, which bore the full brunt of the air raid. According to the division's commander, General Fritz Bayerlein, 'the planes kept coming over, as if on a conveyor belt, and the bomb carpets unrolled in great rectangles . . . By noon nothing was visible but dust and smoke. My front lines looked like the face of the moon and at least 70 per cent of my troops were out of action – dead, wounded, crazed or numbed. All my forward tanks were knocked out, and the roads were practically impassable.'[32]

Equally effective were the Typhoon fighter-bombers, which performed various roles, one as an adjunct to naval gunfire in repelling German counter-attacks. As early as 8 June the war-diarist at OKW was recording that 'our own panzer counter-attacks are immediately strangled by enemy air attacks that destroy headquarters and all communication networks.'[33] They were hated by everyone in the German army. A Corps commander wrote of 'the dreaded fighter-bombers, which dominated the battlefields in the West . . . It was clear that American air power put our panzers at a hopeless disadvantage, and that the normal principles of armoured warfare did not apply in this theatre.'[34] An ordinary soldier had more subjective memories of these planes and recalled: 'Unless a man has been through these fighter-bomber attacks he cannot know what the invasion meant . . . Not until they've wiped out everything do they leave . . . Ten such attacks in succession are a real foretaste of hell.'[35]

The 'Jabos' were again in their element during the German counter-attack at Mortain. According to the staff of the Corps that handled the attack, within a few hours of jump-off 'the activities of the fighter-bombers are almost unbearable. The *Leibstandarte* [1 SS Panzer Division] reports that air attacks of such intensity have never before been experienced. Its attack has been stopped.'[36] According

---

* There were 558 casualties all told, including one American general.

to von Lüttwitz, his 2 Panzer Division made a swift advance of ten miles or so, suffering only minor losses. But then

> suddenly the Allied fighter-bombers swooped out of the sky. They came down in hundreds firing their rockets at the concentrated tanks and vehicles. We could do nothing against them, and we could make no further progress. The next day the planes came down again. We were forced to give up the ground we had gained and by 9 August the division was back where it had started from . . . having lost 30 tanks and 800 men.[37]

The commander of a third division involved, 116 Panzer, was adamant that 'the enemy air force paralysed every movement on the battlefield, especially those of the tanks . . . [It] also decisively impeded the command of the conflict on and behind the front by destruction or crippling of command means.'[38]

With all this in mind, it might seem surprising that there is still a body of historical opinion that would seek to minimise the effectiveness of Allied air power in Normandy. The role of the fighter-bombers is most usually called into question, particularly their effectiveness in actually destroying enemy vehicles. These doubts stem largely from certain reports by Operations Research teams, attached to SHAEF, who toured the battlefields shortly after the battles and tried to assess what damage had been done by what weapons. In several places these teams did establish that pilots' claims, made in the heat of battle, had been seriously exaggerated. Be that as it may, the German sources cited above make it abundantly clear that more than a few of their armoured casualties *were* attributable to air attack* and, more important still, that such attacks fatally disrupted command channels and made movement and concentration, the very bedrock of tactics, virtually impossible. A German historian of the Normandy fighting made a crucially important point about the nature of armoured combat in this theatre when he noted:

---

* Allied claims in the Mortain counter-attack, for example, had to be substantially downgraded. Nevertheless, it was still conceded that of the 78 armoured vehicles destroyed, 21 had definitely been destroyed by air action and 29 by ground units. 15 were destroyed by agents unknown, 9 were abandoned intact and 4 destroyed by their own crews. Allowing, therefore, that at least a quarter of the unknowns fell victim to aircraft and that most of the abandonments were precipitated by panic under aerial attack, it seems reasonable to suggest that getting on for half of the armoured casualties were a result of air operations.

In Normandy, the individual tank became the nucleus of infantry units. The infantry platoon, the company, the combat team – they were all based on the tank. Without tanks no position was taken. And without tanks no position could be held . . . The *Panzer Lehr* [for example] . . . found itself forced into an entirely new mode of fighting. The division had been created as an élite unit for offence; now it was being expended as a defensive unit. Its splendid fleet of 750 armoured and superbly armed infantry carriers had to be put in store. They were being kept at a depot sixty miles behind the fighting front . . . Armoured divisions engaged in static defence – it was . . . a depressing chapter in the history of the war.[39]

But here in a nutshell is the tremendous achievement of the Allied air forces. Because of the damage they did inflict, and the Germans' ever-present fears about what they *might* inflict, the once all-powerful panzer divisions were prevented from fighting in the open in mass formation, that is as united divisions and corps. As General Bayerlein himself later wrote: 'During the entire Invasion, there was only one real mass tank attack. It took place at Bayeux . . . On all other occasions, the tank was auxiliary to the infantry which surrounded it. In real tank tactics, the tanks should be the dominating factor.'[40] That this was largely attributable to the air forces was underlined by General Warlimont: 'All commanders,' he told Allied interrogators after the war, 'were discouraged by your overpowering airforce. They said that whatever they planned to execute was impossible to execute and control because your airforce spotted and attacked every movement.'[41]

And without the ability to stage large-scale, coordinated armoured attacks, the Germans lost whatever slim chance they might have had of throwing the invaders back into the sea. The defensive tactics to which they were obliged to resort did inflict considerable damage on their opponents and held up the latter's own armour for several weeks. But these delays could have no decisive effects. The only way to give the Allies serious pause for strategic thought, rather than mere regret over heavy casualties, was to effect a major encirclement, split the beachhead, or get amongst the rear areas in strength, and the only way to accomplish any of these was by large-scale mobile operations. Thanks largely to the RAF and the USAAF, such operations were just not feasible.

But the weight of Allied air power was also vitally important in hampering German ability to effect a proper *strategic* concentration of their armour, and bring together the various panzer divisions scattered hither and thither throughout France and the Low Countries. The essential point has been well put by the Canadian official historian, in his discussion

> of the enemy's employment of his mobile reserves. He brought them into action with rapidity and good local effect. At the same time it must be added that he threw them in piecemeal. So far was this the case that for a long period he seems never to have achieved a genuinely coordinated attack on even a divisional level . . . The armour was thrown in helter-skelter . . . and the enemy continued to use it in much the same manner throughout the bridgehead campaign . . . The result was a series of counter-attacks which, while extremely formidable in terms of a battalion or even a brigade locality, held out comparatively little hope of serious effect upon the Allied position as a whole.[42]

Again it was the fear of Allied aircraft that strangled German movements, obliging formations to move only at night or to split into small units taking widely dispersed routes, causing innumerable delays along blocked roads or severely damaged railway lines, and physically destroying vital maintenance equipment or fuel supplies. On 10 June Rommel complained that the Allies had 'total command of the air over the battle area up to a point some 60 miles behind the front. During the day, practically our entire traffic – on roads, tracks and in open country – is pinned down by powerful fighter-bomber and bomber formations, with the result that the movement of our troops on the battlefield is almost completely paralysed.' At the end of June, he emphasised the way in which Allied command of the air 'limits the possibilities of command and manoeuvre . . . [and attacks] cannot as a rule develop into anything more than operations with limited objective.'

On 3 July his main concern was the delays in getting forward the reserves: 'All the reserves that came up arrived too late to smash the enemy landing by counter-attacks. By the time they arrived the enemy had disembarked considerably stronger forces and himself gone over to the attack under cover of powerful air and artillery support.'[43] Von Rundstedt, when interviewed at the end of the war, was of just the same opinion, claiming that his forces had had no hope of driving the invaders back into the sea 'after the first few days. The Allied Air Forces paralysed all movement by day and made it very difficult even at night. They had smashed the bridges over the Loire as well as over the Seine, shutting off the whole area. These factors greatly delayed the concentration of reserves there – they took three or four times longer to reach the front than we had reckoned.'[44]*

This complete dislocation of the road and rail network also affected the bringing in of supplies to divisions that *had* got to the front. Of the whole period June to August, General Bayerlein remarked: 'In fact nothing arrived from the other side of the Seine and Loire. We were on a transportation island.'[45] On 15 July a report written at Rommel's headquarters by his Chief of Staff pointed out:

> Due to the destruction of the railway system and the threat of the enemy air force to roads and tracks up to 90 miles behind the front, supply conditions are so bad that only the barest essentials can be brought to the front. It is consequently now necessary to exercise the greatest economy in all fields, and especially in artillery and mortar ammunition.[46]

The experiences of a few sample German divisions clearly show the enormous difficulties under which they were labouring. 12 ss and *Panzer Lehr* Divisions, being fairly close to the front, 75 and 125 miles respectively, were able to get leading elements there on the morning and early afternoon of 7 June. Both were severely harassed from the air, however, and because 12 ss, when it arrived, had 'neither the time nor the space for a formation operation, its attack could not be driven home.' *Panzer Lehr*, being 'hindered in its advance by low-flying aircraft', found that 'the wheeled units became separated from the tracked. As a result their attack could no longer be put in.'[47]† 2 Panzer Division left its staging area near

---

* So serious was the disruption of rail traffic that, on 11 June, Seventh Army closed down the office it had set up on D-Day to organise train movements.
† During its approach, according to Bayerlein, *Panzer Lehr* lost 130 trucks (40 carrying petrol), 84 half-tracks and prime movers, and five tanks. 'These losses were serious for a division not yet in action.' (Quoted in C. Wilmot, *The Struggle for Europe* (Collins, 1952), p. 300.) The exact number of 12 ss Panzer's losses are not known, though one of its members recalled that after one attack 'the length of the road was strewn with anti-tank guns (the pride of our division), flaming mortars and charred implements of war. The march was called off and all vehicles that were left were hidden in the dense bushes or in barns.' (Quoted in J. R. G. Finlayson, 'The Soldier's Battle in an Uncertain Air Situation', in *Army Quarterly*, April 1950, p. 67.) When the commander of the division arrived at the front, in advance of his men, he told the infantry commander in whose sector he was to operate: 'I have been on my way to you for about eight hours. I lay a good four hours in roadside ditches because of air attacks.' (Quoted in C. P. Stacey, *The Victory Campaign* (Official History of the Canadian Army in the Second World War), (Queen's Printer, Ottawa, 1960), p. 129.)

Abbeville, on the Somme, on 8 June. The distance from the front was only 160 miles but six days later, on 13 June, only advanced infantry elements had arrived there. The surviving armour, 80 out of 120 tanks, did not begin arriving until the 18th. 17 ss Panzer Grenadier Division was ordered to move up from south of the Loire on D-Day. It did not intervene in the fighting in any numbers until 12 June, having taken six days to cover 200 miles. 2 ss Panzer Division began moving north from Montauban, 450 miles from the front, on 8 June. Its units trickled into the assembly areas between the 15th and the 30th, to be thrown into battle as they arrived. The division did not, in fact, fight as a unified formation until 10 July, by which time it had suffered severe tank and personnel losses. 1 ss Panzer was ordered to be ready to leave Belgium on 8 June but, thanks to the threat of a second Allied landing in the Pas de Calais, it was not actually sent to Normandy until the 15th. Their 400-mile journey took the fastest units ten days, and the division as a whole did not make any significant impact on the battle until the 29th. Even on the 30th, however, it had still not assembled all its surviving tanks in the battle area. 9 and 10 ss Panzer Divisions were ordered to transfer from the Eastern Front shortly after D-Day and on 12 June were entraining in Poland. Four days later they had reached Lorraine but had to quit their trains because lines further west were too badly damaged. The rest of the journey had to be made by road, and this last 400-mile stretch took them until the 25th. Even by the 28th only 9 ss was in a position to make any sort of concerted attack.

Infantry divisions were equally handicapped. Three that were ordered east on D-Day itself were 3 Parachute, 77 and 275 Infantry Divisions. All took between five and six days to reach the front though none were more than 150 miles away. The journey of 275 Division was particularly arduous. The trains they were travelling in took them reasonably close to the front but were then either destroyed by air attack or rendered useless through multiple breaks in the line ahead. On 9 June 'higher command therefore decided to disembark all passengers and equipment and send them forward by road. They had taken two nights and three days to cover less than thirty miles and had at least another three days before them on the road. First to arrive at the battlefront, on June 11th, were two infantry battalions which had covered the distance on bicycles.'[48]

In the days that followed the transport situation simply went from bad to worse. On 12 June 276 Division left Bayonne, on a journey of some 400 miles. The last elements had not arrived in Hottot until

4 July, over three weeks later. Part of 276 Infantry Division left Nice by train on the evening of 19 June. It followed a circuitous route via Montpellier–Narbonne–Toulouse–Bordeaux–Rochefort–La Rochelle to Thouars, south of the Loire. There it had to detrain because of a blocked tunnel and after another tortuous journey by bus and on foot it reached Evrécy on 8 July, 19 days after its departure from the Côte d'Azur. 344 Division, in the Pas de Calais, was not ordered south until 3 August and by then the front was only 75 miles away. Even so, according to the division's commander, 'the first of the twenty-eight trains carrying my division was derailed south of Amiens, and as a result the men were sent by a long circuitous route to Rouen. They were shunted around France for days on end and it took them no less than nine days to make this 120-kilometre journey by rail.'[49]

Clearly, then, the Germans were almost completely hamstrung by the Allies' huge superiority in air and ground firepower. With such restrictions on movement as those detailed above, the notion of *blitzkrieg* was little more than a joke, and even simple static defensive warfare was extremely difficult. One emphasises again that it was Allied firepower – bombers, 'Jabos', battleships and ground artillery – that had brought the Germans to this pass and that the superiority of fire was of such dimensions that nothing the Germans could do would have done much to offset it. Many accounts of the Normandy campaign have claimed that the fatal German mistake was to have their panzer divisions so scattered around France and the Low Countries, and that had they been concentrated nearer the coast, as Rommel wanted, they might have been able to throw the first Allied waves off the beaches. One is inclined to doubt whether it would, in fact, have made an appreciable difference. For had the divisions been concentrated the Allies, through Ultra, would have known of it and would have been able to make their preparations accordingly, reaping considerable advantage from having the tactical air effort and naval gunfire concentrated within a fairly circumscribed sector.* Such, indeed, was Rommel's own opinion and he wrote after the defeat in Normandy:

> The Allies had time and material enough . . . It is my belief that even if we had had . . . several Panzer divisions, an A.A. Corps, a Nebelwerfer Brigade, and Parachutists . . . at the scene

---

* Assuming, of course, that the Germans had concentrated in the right place. It is by no means certain that even if Hitler had accepted the principle of concentration, he would not have preferred to position most of the panzer divisions in the Pas de Calais.

of the landing, we would still have lost the battle, as our counter-attacks would have been smashed by the Allied naval guns and air force, and our artillery and Nebelwerfer positions would have been put out of action one after another by the fantastic Allied barrage . . . Ultimately . . . no compromise of any kind can make up for total enemy air and artillery superiority.[50]

Having established that the Allied commanders in Normandy went to war, as usual, with numbers on their side, it now behoves us once again to examine the way in which they deployed these numbers. On centre stage for most of the period covered in this chapter was General Montgomery, the temporary overall ground commander, and it was to his basic plan that operations in the first three months adhered. Exactly what this strategy was has been the subject of some considerable debate, not least because Montgomery was too experienced in the vagaries of high command ever to commit himself to a precisely defined timetable or particular course of action. Commenting on his statements about Operation Goodwood, in July, two British historians made a point that holds true for almost all of Montgomery's 'explanations' of intent: 'His directives and letters on the objects of the *Goodwood* offensive were ambiguous. Like the prophecies of the Delphic Oracle, his orders could be interpreted in several ways, depending on what the interested parties expected and hoped for.'[51]

Certain basic suppositions in Montgomery's planning can, however, be isolated. One was that the main British and Canadian mission, in the eastern half of the beachhead, was to prevent German reserves from moving against the Americans, in the west, as the latter pushed southwards towards St Lô and later into Brittany. General Sir Miles Dempsey, the commander of Second British Army, remembered vividly one conference spent crawling around maps spread out on the floor, at which

> Monty stressed the fact that after the immediate reserves had been drawn in all German reserves would arrive at the battle front from the East and Southeast, thus to get across to the American sector of the bridgehead, they would have to pass across the British front around Caen. It was my job to make sure they didn't move across, that they were kept fully occupied fighting us in the Caen sector.[52]

Also of interest is a planning document drawn up on 7 May which spoke of the 'aim . . . to contain the maximum enemy forces facing the Eastern flank of the bridgehead, and to thrust rapidly towards Rennes.'[53] It also seems to have been clearly accepted that major exploitation out of the original beachhead was to be by the Americans, not only into Brittany where they were to open up the ports of Brest, Lorient and St Nazaire, but also in a major movement *eastwards*, when they would 'pivot on the British position like a windlass in the direction of Paris'.[54]

Another vital ingredient of the plan, the one that Montgomery possibly stressed most of all, was that the invading forces were at all times to act with the utmost aggression, attempting always to close with the enemy or to draw him upon themselves. The front-line troops would have to be sent 'in to this party "seeing red" . . . Nothing must stop them.' From the word go, according to Montgomery's briefing of 15 May, 'we must blast our way ashore and get a good lodgement before the enemy can bring sufficient reserves up to turn us out. Armoured columns must penetrate deep inland, and quickly on D-Day . . . We must gain space rapidly and peg out claims well inland.'[55] The spirit of élan that Montgomery expected from his armoured commanders in the early days of the invasion is clearly shown in a letter sent to Bradley and Dempsey, on 14 April:

> . . . having seized the initiative by our initial landing, we must insure [sic] that we keep it. The best way to interfere with enemy concentrations and countermeasures will be to push forward fairly powerful armoured force thrusts on the afternoon of D-Day . . . The whole effect of such aggressive tactics would be to retain the initiative ourselves and to cause alarm in the minds of the enemy . . . Armoured units . . . must be concentrated quickly . . . Speed and boldness are then required, and the armoured thrusts must force their way inland . . . I am prepared to accept almost any risk in order to carry out these tactics.[56]

In other words, though 21 Army Group might have basically a holding role in their half of the beachhead, this was *not* to mean that they should go on to the defensive as soon as they came ashore. They were instead to attract the enemy forces to them by aggressive, mobile operations of their own, and keep them on their front by embroiling them in a whole series of armoured actions. Again and again Montgomery emphasised that though the major breakthroughs were likely to come on the American flank, this must not mean that the British and the Canadians were any less forceful in their own armoured thrusts. It was hoped, indeed, that their aggressiveness would confuse the Germans as to which side of the beachhead the main effort was being made. The planning document of 7 May, already alluded to, made several references to 'successful strong thrusts . . . kept up alternatively [sic] by us toward the Seine and Loire' and at one point stated that by such 'thrusts . . . we should be able to retain the initiative, reap the benefit of interior lines, and keep the enemy moving his reserves from one flank to the other.'[57]*

All this sounded very well, but subsequent events revealed it to be largely rhetoric rather than a realistic forecast of actual operations, blurb rather than blueprint. Indeed, the more one is able to look back on Montgomery's military career with some sort of detachment, the more surprising it seems that anyone really believed that he, the man who had waddled tortoise-like behind Rommel across North Africa, who had traversed Sicily, Calabria and Campania with if anything even more circumspection, should suddenly have become transformed into a dashing amalgam of Frederick the Great and J. E. B. Stuart. What Montgomery was proposing was authentic mobile warfare – what the Germans knew as *Bewegungskrieg*. Unfortunately he was probably the Allied general the least able properly to orchestrate this mode of warfare. The tactical recipe he put forward would have been meat and drink to the likes of Manstein, Heinrici, Hoth or von Senger und Etterlin, but was far too *haute cuisine* for Montgomery himself. A man who had been cowed by the prospect of a Rommel counterstroke when the latter was *known* to be unable to muster more than 37 German tanks, as in December 1942, was hardly likely to be boldly 'knocking about' with his own armour against a Rommel who could call upon upwards of nine panzer divisions.

Any lingering hopes that the worm had really turned were swiftly dispelled. British forces fell at the first hurdle. The basic prerequisite for Montgomery's armoured probing was the seizure of Caen and access to the plain beyond but, although Bradley has claimed that

* At one stage Montgomery went so far as to suggest that alternate thrusts toward the Seine and Loire gave 'our best chance of *one or the other* succeeding' (quoted in C. d'Este, *Decision in Normandy* (Pan Books, 1984), p. 101; my emphasis), but General Bradley has remained adamant that pre-D-Day planning never really envisaged anything but an American breakout. Montgomery 'did not ever envision a major "breakout" from his lodgement; the major breakout was to be conducted by my forces . . . Monty would absorb the main shock of the enemy counterattack, pin down as many of the enemy as possible (keeping them off my forces), providing the solid nub on which we could turn our wheel.' (O. Bradley and C. Blair, *A General's Life* (Sidgwick and Jackson, 1983), p. 234. See also pp. 264–5.)

the approaches to Caen were wide open on 6 June, 3 Infantry Division failed to seize the town. The only real attempt to rush the German defences hereabouts involved one single battalion from the division, supported by the self-propelled guns of a Royal Artillery field regiment and a few tanks. Conspicuous by its absence was 27 Armoured Brigade, one of the formations that were to take 'almost any risk' to seize their first objectives. The bulk of the brigade had simply not got forward at all, becoming snarled up in fighting on the beaches themselves or just inland. That they were so involved scotches any imputations about their zeal for battle, but it does little to excuse the planners or senior commanders who had not stated quite explicitly that the armoured formations must not get tied down in local firefights, and who had not ensured that these formations would be afforded speedy exit from the beaches. Second Alamein, where the British armour had become involved in horrendous traffic-jams in the narrow lanes through the minefields, should surely have taught Montgomery and his staff that the most meticulous planning and the most emphatic assignment of priorities was necessary to get armoured formations forward on time, *en masse*. As it was, in the words of one of the best historians of the Caen battles, what was supposed to have been 'the lightning punch at Caen had been reduced to a few hundred plodding riflemen'.[58]

Their inevitable failure to take the town allowed the Germans to move up their nearest divisions, 21 and 12 SS Panzer and *Panzer Lehr*, to form a shield around Caen which, reinforced by 2 and 116 Panzer as well as 1, 9 and 10 SS Panzer Divisions, held firm until the town was finally stormed on 9 July, during Operation Charnwood. But even then the Germans only gave up a limited amount of ground, and several more major operations, Goodwood, Bluecoat, Totalise and Tractable, were necessary before 21 Army Group broke through on 17 August to Falaise. The town had been named by Montgomery, in a letter to the War Office, as an *immediate* objective for Second Army as early as 8 June.

None of the operations just mentioned could really be described as the sort of mobile thrust that Montgomery seemed to have in mind prior to D-Day. As he himself wrote, on 7 May, these had been conceived above all to prevent the 'grave risk of operations stabilising on a line which gives the Germans advantages in defence. The greatest energy and initiative will be required . . . to ensure the enemy is not allowed to stabilise his defence.'[59] The feeble early attacks, however, had completely failed to do this, whilst later major operations in 21 Army Group's sector soon came to consist almost entirely of head-on assaults against just this kind of defensive line. Mobile warfare went out of the caravan window and Montgomery fell back on the kind of ponderous set-piece attack that had characterised his Mediterranean operations. 'Initiative', 'risk', 'deep penetration', 'speed', 'boldness', all these laudable concepts were abandoned and replaced by the key notion of 'writing down' the enemy armour, like 'crumbling' a new euphemism for attrition, for doggedly accepting enormous armoured casualties in the knowledge that the enemy's own losses, though smaller, would have a much greater impact on his ability to fight on. The term occurs in, for example, Montgomery's operation order to the divisions involved in Goodwood which defined as 'OBJECT . . . To engage the German armour in battle and "write it down" to such an extent that it is of no further value . . . Generally to destroy German equipment and personnel . . .'[60]

In one respect, of course, Montgomery's purpose did remain what it had always been, the pinning of the German panzers on his side of the Allied beachhead, but it seems clear that the way this pinning was now to be done had been modified considerably, with Allied tanks taking the part of the French knights at Crécy rather than that of a genuine *masse de manoeuvre*. To this extent at least, Montgomery's later claim that 'the outstanding point about the Battle of Normandy is that it was fought exactly as planned before the invasion' is simply not true.[61]* In the long run, it might be asked, does that really matter? Is not the important point that the large proportion of German armour was attracted to the British and Canadian front,† and that this in

* It is also worth while to note that the Germans did not cluster around 21 Army Group simply because they regarded the mighty Montgomery as the more formidable military opponent. Simple logistic considerations, of prime importance to the Germans as we have seen, also had a lot to do with it. As General Warlimont wrote: 'When we started to move divisions from the Fifteenth Army sector, it was often found *much easier* to commit them around our right flank near Caen . . . rather than moving them *additional distances* to reinforce our weakening flank opposite the American forces.' (W. Warlimont, 'From the Invasion to the Siegfried Line', Pamphlet ETHINT-1, p. 17, in D. S. Detweiler *et al.* (eds), *World War II Military Studies*, Garland, New York, 1979, vol. 2; my emphasis.)

† According to Montgomery, British and Canadian troops were tying down the following percentages of German armour up to the American breakout:

15 June	25 June	30 June	5 July	10 July	15 July	20 July	25 July
88	74	84	76	76	77	75	77

turn unquestionably enabled the Americans to break through the thinner defences along their own front? If historical interpretation were to be entirely devoid of personality, such a simple statement of the facts would be all that was required. But personality is very much in evidence in the history of this particular campaign, and notably Montgomery's ego, which tried so hard to shape our perception of events that it often succeeded in distorting them. It seems important, therefore, to draw some attention to his more questionable claims. When a commander obviously thinks of himself as a military genius, and will assiduously bruit that assessment abroad, there seems to be good reason for emphasising that his conduct of a campaign had very little to do with his original plans and that, moreover, the verve and deft footwork that figured so prominently in the latter were conspicuously absent in the operations themselves, operations which increasingly relied, like a latter-day Verdun, on brute force and sheer material preponderance.

Churchill's remark, already cited, that after the entry of the United States into the war 'all the rest was merely the proper application of overwhelming force', could well have been Montgomery's text throughout almost all the Normandy fighting. Its relevance as regards the numbers of tanks, guns and aircraft employed by the Allies has already been dealt with, though the sheer brutality of the concept is further highlighted by the scale of losses that British and Canadian commanders were prepared to tolerate. Before Operation Goodwood, in mid-July, General Dempsey realised that his attempt to crash through the German gun lines on Bourguebus Ridge 'would be costly, but he was, he said, "prepared to lose two or three hundred tanks" in the course of the battle. He had tanks enough and to spare . . .'[62] On 1 August, during a drive towards Aunay, during Operation Bluecoat, 7 Armoured Division received orders from XXX Corps which bluntly pointed out: 'You may lose every tank you have but you must capture Aunay by midnight.'[63]

In Goodwood, the armour almost lived up to Dempsey's worst expectations. On the first day, 18 July, two of the divisions involved, Guards Armoured and 11 Armoured, lost 60 and 126 tanks respectively. Forty of the latter figure had been destroyed completely. By the end of the battle, on the night of 20 July, though the attacking forces had fully cleared only the northern slopes of the vital Bourguebus Ridge, and completely failed to break through at any point,* they had lost possibly as many as 400 tanks, and certainly at least 300 had been written off completely. In the immediate aftermath of the battle, many units, like 3 Royal Tank Regiment, felt that they 'were through. They had started with 52 tanks, been given 11 replacements, making 63 tanks in all. With Bras now in our hands, they had 9 tanks left . . . "A" Squadron had lost 17 tanks in two days, seven being completely destroyed . . .'[64] In terms of personnel losses and the rending of the regiment's social fabric, 3 RTR and units like it had indeed been dealt a serious blow. In purely material terms, however, even such heavy tank losses were no more than a passing inconvenience. As one recent historian has properly reminded us, though 400 tank casualties would have represented perhaps 30 per cent of the British armoured strength then in France, 'so prodigious were Allied reserves of *matériel* that replacements reached almost every armoured division within 36 hours.'[65]

There were also high losses on 8 and 9 August during Operation Totalise, a Polish/Canadian effort to push strong forces down to Falaise, link up with the Americans and so trap most of German Seventh Army. In 48 hours, against weak German forces, the attackers contrived to lose 150 tanks, 47 of them in one single regiment. Yet still First Army had failed to break through, and commanders immediately began thinking in terms of another phalanx-like assault on the German positions. But all in due time. One historian's comments are particularly pertinent:

> It is an astounding reflection upon the relative weight of forces engaged north of Falaise that by the night of 10 August, the German tank strength was reduced to 35 (15 Mark IV, five Panther, 15 Tiger), while the Canadian II Corps, even after losses, mustered around 700. Yet on 10 August, with some German reinforcements moving on to the front, it was decided that nothing less than a new full-scale, set-piece attack with massed bomber preparation would break the Canadians through to Falaise [Operation Tractable].[66]

This, of course, was just the sort of thing one might expect from Montgomery *Africanus*, but it is still worth while emphasising what

* Whether Montgomery was hoping for a complete rupture of the enemy line and the debouching of his armour into the enemy rear, or whether his aims were more modest, has been and will continue to be the subject of keen historical debate. What *can* be asserted with some confidence is that he did not expect to be held up on the enemy's gun line, without having even completely subdued that.

an utterly different philosophy of action it indicates from that pro-
pounded with such zeal in April 1944. Not only were his forces not
prepared to take the boundless risks he had so airily recommended,
but they seemed to have developed little short of an acute inferiority
complex vis-à-vis the Germans. Certainly, only those privy to the
Ultra secret could know the exact sum of their twenty-to-one
superiority over the panzers, but surely those in the know, notably
Montgomery, could have conveyed a sufficient sense of urgency
and reassurance to keep Totalise going, rather than sitting back
and waiting for another set-piece offensive that did not get under
way until 14 August. But this was all along one of Montgomery's
major shortcomings in Normandy, and one that further encourages
a dismissal of the April exhortations as largely rhetoric. For he seems
to have made little effort to pick commanders and planners or instil
tactical doctrines that would encourage the kind of aggressive, mobile
operations he seemed to have taken to heart. Montgomery dominated
21 Army Group and formed it pretty much in his own image – but it
was an image that had been immutably shaped in North Africa, and
its most prominent features were caution, proper procedures and yet
more caution.

   A good insight into the British Liberation Army's limited potential
for mobile warfare is given in this comment on tactical methods by
two British writers who were actually there. The chief weakness,
they felt, was 'a ponderous approach to any problem . . . [The
British] always tended to organise their movements according to
the text-book and official manuals. A whole series of elaborate
conferences, often starting at the divisional headquarters and going
down through brigade to battalion level, tended to be organised
at every opportunity. This consumed valuable time and was much
too reminiscent of training schemes at home.'[67] The Germans offer
perhaps the best testimony on Montgomery and his soldiers, and their
overall judgement is hardly flattering. Of the great man himself, von
Rundstedt said: ' "Field-Marshal Montgomery was very systematic.
That is all right if you have sufficient forces and sufficient time."
. . . [His Chief of Staff] made a similar comment . . . "Field-Marshal
Montgomery was the one general who never suffered a reverse. He
moved like this." Blumentritt took a series of very deliberate and
short steps, putting his foot down heavily each time.'[68] Another
General wrote: 'In contrast to the Eastern theatre of operations, in
the West it was possible to still straighten out seemingly impossible
situations because the opposing Armies there . . . despite their

enormous material superiority, were limited by slow and methodical modes of combat.'[69]

Divisional commanders were similarly unimpressed. That of 346 Infantry Division commented on the lack of real Allied pressure, observing that even when his troops were in some danger of being encircled and he was obliged to fall back a little,

> we were never hurried in these movements because of the systematic . . . tactics of the Allies. When we had been thrown back during the day, we always knew that there would be a pause at night when the enemy would regroup for the next day's operations. It was these hours of darkness that enabled us to retire without suffering many casualties.[70]

The commander of *Panzer Lehr* was especially critical of the ordinary British soldier, and in a report written in June, addressed to General Guderian, he said: 'A successful break-in by the enemy is never exploited to pursuit . . . The fighting morale of the British infantry is not very high. They rely largely on artillery and air support . . . The enemy is extraordinarily nervous of close combat . . . He strives therefore to occupy ground, rather than to fight over it.'[71] Another report, originated by 21 ss Panzer Grenadier Regiment, part of 10 ss Panzer Division, was more scathing yet, doubting even the British and Canadian ability to *occupy* ground: 'The morale of the enemy infantry is not very high. It depends largely on artillery and air support. In case of a well-placed concentration of fire from our own artillery the infantry will often leave its position and retreat hastily. Whenever the enemy is engaged with force, he usually retreats or surrenders.'[72]

The actual progress, or lack of it, of the Normandy battles also makes it fairly clear that 21 Army Group was not a force geared up for integrated, quick-fire operations. The feeble armoured effort on 6 June has already been dealt with. On the 9th, in another attempt to rush Caen, the Canadian infantry demonstrated a marked lack of aggressiveness, concentrating mainly on holding the ground they had already taken. The attack towards Villers-Bocage, on the 13th, was a lamentable affair in which cooperation between armour and infantry was almost non-existent, neither being in a position to support the other's operations when most needed. The tanks' performance, indeed, from 7 Armoured Division of Desert renown, gave rise to the 'suspicion . . . which hardened rapidly in the following weeks that . . . [it] seriously lacked . . . spirit and determination . . . Many of its veterans . . . had become wary and cunning in the reduction of risk, and lacked the tight discipline which is even more critical on the battlefield than off it.'[73]

During Epsom, the British attack foundered on a rather curious combination of factors. The advancing infantry adopted extremely old-fashioned mass formations that virtually ignored modern thinking about infiltration or fire and movement, yet even deployed thus they failed to develop any sort of momentum to carry them through the extremely fragile German defences. The attacks began on the 25th and by the 28th reports from the front were mainly concerned with sniper fire. In fact, it was 'not snipers at all, not a thin screen out in front of the main German battle line; those scattered shots, with an occasional burst of machine-gun fire, *was* the main German position – all that was left of 12 ss Panzer Division on that front.'[74] But this line held, as did a detachment of 12 ss Panzer Division a week or so later. On 4 July, in Operation Windsor, the Canadians attacked Carpiquet airfield, near Caen, with ten battalions of infantry, a tank regiment plus other specialised armour, and support from 428 guns on the ground and several ships at sea. The Germans mustered 150 infantry, two or three tanks and a borrowed 88mm gun. The attack failed.

Later assaults, notably Goodwood and Totalise, revealed a similar marked lack of aggressiveness, as though the massive material resources that the Allies could deploy had robbed the troops themselves of any sense that they too must make a contribution, and take risks. During July, according to Rommel's Chief of Staff, the Germans were daily expecting that 'the enemy will succeed in breaking through our thin front, above all Seventh Army's, and thrusting deep into France . . . We dispose of no mobile reserves for defence against such a breakthrough.'[75] Yet even in August, after the American breakthrough, 21 Army Group found it extremely difficult to build up any sort of head of steam, the whole of First Canadian Army being held up on the approaches to Falaise, for almost a fortnight, by 'the ragged remains of two German divisions and a handful of tanks'.[76] The commander of 2 Canadian Division said frankly that at Caen and Falaise his men were 'no match' for the Germans and 'would not have been successful had it not been for our air and artillery support.'[77]

Clearly, then, the British and Canadian armies that went across to fight in Normandy were not finely tuned fighting machines and comparison with their opponents can only be invidious. Once again much of the responsibility for this must lie with Montgomery, for a great commander must not only know how to define his optimum objectives and how to shape his operations to achieve them, but must also make every effort to ensure that his forces are a suitable instrument for the task. Here Montgomery fell down badly. Though his own ideas on how a campaign *ought* to be fought did develop, revealing sound inferences from the enemy's methods and a laudable desire to improve on the Allies' many previous lack-lustre performances, he neglected to try to similarly develop the attitudes and methods of the rest of the army. The force he had inherited in August 1942 had exhibited the most notable characteristic of the British soldier, a bloody-minded capacity to endure when the chips were really down and when sheer grit was at a premium rather than flair and tactical suppleness in a fast-moving situation. At Alam Halfa this had been just what was required. In the months that followed, however, the increasing mechanisation and motorisation of the army demanded a rather different philosophy of war and new doctrines and procedures to put it into effect. However, having gone some way to taking the most important intellectual steps, at least by the spring of 1944, Montgomery failed to broadcast them sufficiently, to pick subordinates who fully understood them, or to ensure that training manuals and battle schools were hammering them home.* 21 Army Group landing in Normandy might be compared to a road-gang come to repair a stretch of highway. They had good maps and clear instructions, they had a foreman who knew what he wanted done, a nice soft stretch of road, a truckful of jack-hammers and generators galore. Unfortunately nobody knew much about electricity.

---

* This failure to match theory with practice is persistently evident in the inadequate staff-work that preceded almost every major armoured attack. That the problems caused by the Alamein minefields ought to have remained etched in Montgomery's memory has already been mentioned, as has the abject failure to actually show any evidence of this during the abortive 'thrust' to Caen on 6 June. Things did not improve. During Epsom, the main axes having been chosen without prior reconnaissance, one village became a tank bottleneck, but absolutely no attempt was made either to bulldoze a way through the rubble, or to clear paths through the surrounding minefields, which were not under fire. During Goodwood, just the same problems repeated themselves when the main advance, by three armoured divisions, each containing 3,500 vehicles, had to pass over only six narrow bridges and then through minefields in which only the narrowest lanes had been cleared. Not surprisingly, terrible traffic jams ensued, making it almost impossible to get the infantry forward to support those tanks that had penetrated beyond the bridges and were grappling unaided with the German anti-tank guns.

The discussion thus far has very much concentrated on Montgomery's role in Normandy and the efforts of First Canadian and Second British Armies. That Montgomery should be singled out for examination is appropriate, for he was the Allied ground commander during these first three months. It should not be thought, however, that his weaknesses and those of the divisions he commanded were unique to them. American formations, too, made less than impressive debuts, laying themselves open to just the sort of criticism that has already been levelled at 21 Army Group. They were, for example, equally prone to rely simply on material superiority to blast a way through the German positions. General Bradley's comments on his own employment of armour show that it closely matched British practice. Allied tanks, he noted, were never a match for Panthers and Tigers

> in a direct frontal attack. But . . . in dependability . . . the American tank clearly outclassed the German. This advantage, together with our u.s. superiority in numbers enabled us to surround the enemy in battle and knock his tanks out from their flanks. But this willingness to expend Shermans offered little comfort to the crews who were forced to expend themselves as well.[78]*

The Americans were yet more dependent on their tremendous artillery superiority, and all were agreed that the guns were the very bedrock of American tactical thinking. An anonymous captain with 12 us Infantry Division said simply: 'We let the artillery fight the war as much as possible.'[79] General William H. Simpson, who commanded us Ninth Army after its arrival in Brittany on 5 September, wrote that it was the rule in his army to 'never send an infantryman in to do a job that an artillery shell can do for him'.[80] The intention, of course, is sound, but the result tended to be just the sort of 'stickiness' – and hence loss of time and momentum – that has been noted among British and Canadian units. According to a German critic in 3 Parachute Division, American troops around St Lô, in June and the first half of July, were notably cautious:

---

* It is revealing to note that although the us Army had expected the rate of tank losses in Normandy to run at about 6 per cent of authorised establishment per month, raised to 9 per cent in June 1944 on the basis of experience in Italy, the actual percentages lost (complete write-offs) were: June 26.6 per cent; July 24.4 per cent; August 25.3 per cent.

At the smallest resistance the infantry stops and retires, and a new artillery bombardment takes place in order to stamp out the remaining opposition . . . In defence the enemy is a hard fighter only so long as he has good support from the artillery and mortar units . . . So far his tank crews have not shown much enthusiasm for fights between tanks.[81]

A more recent but very neat summary of American methods points out that in Normandy 'American infantry tended to transpose the doctrine of fire and manoeuvre into one of manoeuvre and fire; instead of using fire to fix the enemy and manoeuvre to trap and destroy him, troops manoeuvred to find the enemy and then called in aerial and artillery firepower to try to destroy him.'[82]

The author just quoted was making his point with particular reference to the dense hedgerows of Normandy, the *bocage*, which did most certainly limit the fighting troops' freedom of action. The fact remains, however, that even when they had escaped this constricting terrain, the Americans still failed to show any marked penchant for mobile operations that might pin and entrap significant enemy pockets. General Halder, speaking in broad terms about American operations throughout the war, told the authors of a new set of US Army regulations that American 'historical material superiority' had led them to 'display a marked tendency to underestimate the importance of surprise, manoeuvre and improvisation'.[83] Of the particular situation in late July and early August 1944, General Elfeldt, commanding one of the most vulnerable German corps in the aftermath of the Cobra breakout, told an interrogator: 'The American troops, of the 1st Army, on my front were not tactically at all clever. They failed to seize opportunities – in particular they missed several chances of cutting off the whole of my corps. The Allied air force was the most serious danger.'[84] An American general, John S. Wood, involved in this fighting was positively incensed. If he had been allowed to push straight on from Angers to Chartres, in early August, he felt he 'could have been in the German vitals in two days'. But Bradley and First Army headquarters 'could not react fast enough' and actually turned their troops right away from the main German presence to engage in sterile siege operations against Lorient and Brest. This surrender of the initiative remained 'one of the colossally stupid decisions of the war'.[85]

Eventually US armour was given its head and General Patton, commanding the newly arrived Third Army, was allowed to switch the majority of his formations eastwards. Patton's progress thereafter was most impressive, with Third Army spearheads jumping off on the 5th from Avranches, reaching the Seine on the 20th and the Meuse on 1 September, a total distance of 300 miles as the crow flies, covered in only 25 days. Such a justly celebrated achievement, it might be thought, gives the emphatic lie to my earlier comments about the Americans' limited penchant for mobile operations. But what should be remembered is that by the time Patton moved off, the Germans had already begun to withdraw and there was no longer any real chance of trapping large numbers of Germans or of actually getting in among the retreating units and provoking a complete administrative collapse. Throughout the whole pursuit, indeed, except for a few scattered outposts, the Germans remained just out of Patton's reach. And this must be accounted an American failure, for authentic mobile operations are a very different thing from a simple pursuit. The former subsume actual attacks against the original enemy line and an adroit sequence of blows that causes this line to break. The term also implies concerted attempts to pin at least a part of the broken enemy and to trap and destroy it. It also usually implies the necessity to fight enemy rearguards and decisions about whether such groups can be safely bypassed and how many troops should be left behind to contain them.

Almost none of this, however, figured in Patton's dash across northern France which, like his much overrated pursuit through Sicily a year earlier, was more of a triumphal procession than an actual military offensive. Logistically it was a tremendous feat. General Patton should always be remembered as one of the best traffic policemen in the history of warfare, but in no other way does his advance really stand up as a significant military achievement. There was neither much opposition at the beginning – First Army veterans remain adamant that 'he didn't break out; he walked out'[86] – nor was there ever one occasion on which a major rearguard had to be dislodged or an important body of German troops actually headed off by Third Army. General Bradley, in the second version of his autobiography, was less than complimentary to Patton, claiming at one point that the latter's jump-off from his Meuse bridgeheads, on 5 September, towards the Moselle, 'was the first time in his rush across France that Patton had met serious opposition.'[87]*

* A little earlier he had written: 'Without meaning to detract from his extraordinary achievements, Patton's great and dramatic gains, beginning in Sicily and continuing through Brittany and on across the Seine at Mantes, Melun and Troyes had been

It has to be admitted that in his later years Bradley was something of a cantankerous commentator on his past colleagues, but other less subjective commentators have come up with very similar conclusions. A distinguished American historian has recently stated: 'The speed of the Third Army's advance was accomplished in large part through the avoidance of fighting . . . When the Third Army could not bypass opposition, its record was not nearly so impressive as its performance travelling on the open road.'[88] The Germans made the same point during postwar interrogations, and in this respect can hardly be accused of buttering up their captors. Guderian, a man well qualified to pass comment on mobile operations, said that during late July 'there was a great shortage of troops which could not be made up; hence Patton, in his race across France, found no real resistance. He saw a good opportunity and made good use of it.'[89] Equally pertinent is the judgement of General Max Simon, the commander of XIII ss Infantry Corps. Asked about Third Army's tactics, Simon retorted that he found them 'very cautious and systematic', the Americans only advancing when they 'had secured control of the first ground taken'. Asked specifically about Patton's armoured tactics, he stated:

> Had we had the necessary counter-measures – anti-tank guns, airplanes and gasoline – many local penetrations would not have succeeded. The tactics of the Americans were based on the idea of breaking down a wall by taking out one brick at a time. They did this with tanks, against which we had nothing to employ. However, since your tanks were divided among several local attacks instead of being concentrated at one point, we, with adequate equipment, could have repelled these attacks and rejoined our broken line. Had you made such attacks (an attack of 5–20 tanks accompanying the infantry) on the Eastern Front, where our anti-tank guns were echeloned in depth, all your tanks would have been destroyed.[90]*

Here is the story of the Normandy campaign in a nutshell: acute German shortages of munitions on the one hand, and on the other

footnote continued

made against little or no opposition. Until now Patton had not really had a serious fight on his hands.' (Bradley and Blair, op. cit., p. 317.)

* It is possible, of course, that some of these attacks were made by the independent tank battalions with the infantry divisions, but as this is the only mode of operation that Simon mentions it can only be assumed that the armoured divisions acted in much the same manner.

8

Inching to Victory
September 1944 – May 1945

After the eruption of American armour into the German rear as it exploited Operation Cobra, and after Hitler's insistence upon keeping his own armour dangerously far forward, for the Mortain counter-attack, von Kluge's forces in the west faced the prospect of almost complete destruction. Both Seventh and Fifth Panzer Armies* were pinned down between Mortain and Falaise, with 12 Army Group threatening to sweep right round them and link up with Montgomery's armies around Falaise to form a well-stuffed pocket. Any hopes the Germans might have about bringing up extra forces from the south, from the divisions still allocated to Army Group G, were soon to be nullified by an Allied landing in southern France, Operation Dragoon. Moreover, if the Allies were able to follow up a coup at Falaise quickly enough, especially if the major part of Patton's Third Army were to forget about clearing Brittany and drive straight for the Seine and middle Meuse, there might well be a chance of bagging large parts of Fifteenth Army as well, pinning it against the coast between Le Havre and Breskens. During the second week of August, in other words, it was not unrealistic to think in terms of eliminating more than 30 divisions from the German order of battle. If one included the divisions trapped in Brittany the figure became nearer 40.

A victory on this scale must surely have ended the war, for the Germans would not have been able to transfer anything like enough divisions from other fronts across to the west, giving the SHAEF forces, hesitant and ponderous as they might be, virtually open access across the whole length of the German frontier. But it was

---

* Formed on 6 August from units that had belonged to Panzer Group West.

not to be. At Falaise, as has already been indicated in the previous chapter, neither the British nor the Americans displayed anything like the necessary determination to close the trap on the retreating Germans. Montgomery, for his part, completely failed to impart any proper sense of urgency to Canadian operations and permitted an extraordinary delay between Operations Totalise and Tractable. He compounded his dilatoriness by leaving this vitally important thrust completely in the hands of relatively inexperienced Canadian and Polish forces.

He also failed to provide any reinforcement from Second Army, even though support would have been readily available as British units were not heavily engaged at this time. Indeed, such attacks as they were making were only serving to drive the Germans eastwards towards the Seine, *away* from the American pincer moving up towards Argentan. Whilst it is unlikely that the arrival of additional British formations would have transformed tactical doctrine in First Canadian Army, the extra men, guns and tanks might well have provided the last straw to break the straining German back. But, at the very moment when simple brute force might have sufficed to get the job done, Montgomery provided nothing at all.

Bradley made a similarly unhelpful contribution to the battle. In his memoirs he spoke of being 'mystified' by Montgomery's tactics and related how 'a shocked Third Army looked on helplessly as its quarry fled, [and] Patton raged at Montgomery's blunder.'[1] In fact, Patton was silently seething over Bradley's own blunder, for on 13 August the latter had halted Patton's lead formation, XV Corps, south of Argentan and categorically forbidden it to move any nearer the Canadians. Bradley's given reason was that if American units crossed over into what was technically 21 Army Group's sector, there was a serious risk that they might be fired on by friendly troops. There seems little reason to believe that this would have been the case, and even had there been the chance of some casualties it seems hard to equate Bradley's decision with Montgomery's pre-D-Day exhortation 'to accept almost any risk'. A later Bradley claim, that 'nor was there any way in which my weakened forces could fight through to Falaise', would also seem rather dubious. The main opposition to XV Corps, Panzer Group Eberbach, could muster on the 13th no more than 70 tanks and a few shattered infantry formations, while XV Corps 'could muster over 300 Shermans and 22 battalions of artillery and two infantry divisions, all with sky-high morale, and under the experienced leadership of

. . . [commanders] all spoiling for a fight and, added to all these advantages, with complete command of the air.'[2] Patton himself was certainly confident enough and later wrote, without actually blaming Bradley by name: 'The XV Corps . . . could easily have entered Falaise and completely closed the gap, but we were ordered not to do this . . . This halt was a great mistake, as I was certain that we could have entered Falaise and I was not certain that the British would.'[3]

But no matter how one cares to allocate responsibility, the essential point is that the Falaise Gap was not properly closed until 18 August, and in these precious extra days the Germans managed to extricate thousands of men. An enormous amount of matériel *was* lost, let us be quite clear. Later tours of the pocket by Allied investigation teams found wrecked or abandoned 688 tanks and self-propelled guns and over 1,000 artillery pieces. In 21 Army Group's sector alone there were also 1,778 lorries and 669 cars. The prisoner-of-war cages began to bulge too, Army Group B estimating on 23 August that 50 to 60 per cent of the original troops were still trapped in the pocket. Exact computation will never be possible, though the fact that, between 18 and 23 August, 208 officers and 13,475 other ranks passed through the Canadian cages alone gives a fair idea of the magnitude of German losses.

Nevertheless, the victory was still nothing like as complete as it might have been. Twenty-six German divisions – nine panzer, two parachute and 15 infantry – were involved in the Falaise battles, but of these only one, 77 Infantry, was permanently eliminated from the German order of battle.* To be sure, many of the others were reduced to a shadow of their former selves. Three of the panzer divisions, one parachute and ten infantry divisions had to be pulled out of the line immediately after the Falaise battles and sent to rear areas to reform. But the rest, six panzer, one parachute and four infantry divisions, albeit no more than weak battlegroups, absorbed their replacements on the move and

---

* The divisions were 2 and 116 Panzer, *Panzer Lehr*, 1, 2, 9, 10 and 12 ss Panzer and 17 ss Panzer Grenadier; 3 and 5 Parachute; 77, 84, 85, 271, 272, 275, 276, 277, 326, 344, 346, 352, 353, 363, and 708 Infantry.
Other divisions were lost during the Normandy/Brittany fighting, but of these 709 Infantry was destroyed in Cherbourg and 243 Infantry was annihilated before the Falaise battle, whilst Hitler was responsible for the incarceration of 265 Infantry in Lorient, 266, 343 and 2 Parachute in Brest, and 91 Air Landing in Saint Malo.

where necessary fought stubborn rearguard actions all the way back to the Siegfried Line or into Holland.* More important still, almost all of the divisions that were withdrawn to the rear had important cadres of NCOs, junior officers and headquarters staff still intact. Thus, exactly as with Tenth and Fourteenth Armies in Italy only two months previously, they retained a nucleus of experience and expertise to provide real military stiffening to the mass of replacements they now had to absorb. These replacements, moreover, were absorbed remarkably quickly, and all of these divisions returned to the line, as more than adequate fighting formations, within a few months. Three divisions were back in action in September, four in November and the remaining three in December.†

But it was not just divisional cadres that escaped. The Chief of Staff of Army Group B recalled after the war that 'of the two army, four corps and thirteen divisional staffs which had been in the pocket, only one corps and two to three divisional were wholly destroyed. All the others were either ready for immediate commitment, or would be after a few days.' A recent historian presents slightly different figures‡ but forcefully draws the pertinent conclusions:

At least symbolically, the Falaise pocket fell short of being another Stalingrad because there was no general surrender. It was of more than symbolic importance that German higher headquarters for the most part escaped the envelopment, as the Allies were to learn when these headquarters demonstrated the remarkable rapidity with which they could reconstitute divisions and corps around themselves. Of fifteen divisional commanders in the pocket, only three did not get away. Only one of five corps commanders did not reach safety . . . The survival of cadres and

* These divisions were 116 Panzer, *Panzer Lehr*, 2, 9, 10, and 12 SS Panzer; 3 Parachute (withdrawn once in Belgium); 85, 275, 344 and 346 Infantry.
† The September divisions were 84, 363 and 353 Infantry Divisions. (The latter division's HQ was later removed to establish a new 353 Infantry Division in November. The September personnel were absorbed into 275 Infantry Division. 363 Division reappeared as a *Volksgrenadier* (VG) Division. These were infantry divisions on a somewhat reduced establishment of men and equipment. They were, however, perfectly competent fighting formations, not to be confused with the almost worthless *Volksturm*.) The November divisions were 271, 272, 352, and 708 VG. The December divisions were 276, 277 and 326 VG.
‡ The figure chosen depends on the date at which the count was made, and the definition of the Pocket proper.

headquarters influenced the whole German conception of the battle, with much benefit to German morale apart from their practical utility in repairing shattered organisations . . .[4]

These two crucial points, that German morale remained unbroken and that effective operational control was still possible at army, corps and divisional level, go a long way towards explaining German achievements in the following weeks, as they successfully withdrew their disparate battle groups and divisional rumps through northern France and the Low Countries, and eventually contrived to establish a new defence in the Siegfried Line.*

The Allied commanders must accept considerable responsibility for allowing the Germans such a respite. As we have seen, it was their shilly-shallying around Falaise and Argentan that allowed the Germans to maintain in the field a far more responsive military organism than should have been the case. But it was still a remarkably frail creature and one which the Allies, with their now almost indecent material preponderance, should have been able to see off with ease. It was beset with problems from every side. At times it looked as if those tanks which had escaped the Falaise Pocket might be finally halted by a lack of fuel. According to one panzer commander, as 2 ss Panzer Division approached Brussels, it ran into pursuing 'enemy columns, and had to blow up all of . . . [its] tanks because of the lack of sufficient fuel to resist.'[5] Army Group B explained that during the Falaise battle 'losses in material were very high because . . . enemy fighter-bombers had fired nearly all vehicles and fuel reserves.' Moreover, Seventh Army had also 'gradually . . . lost all of its radio stations and thus became unable to carry out its command functions.'[6] At times this latter point threatened to negate the fact that so many staffs had evaded capture. Field Marshal Jodl went as far as to refer to the whole withdrawal across France as 'an evacuation which degenerated into planless flight', though this seems to overstate what was only an intermittent breakdown of communications in particular sectors. Nevertheless, occurrences such as the following, described by the commander of 116 Panzer Division, can hardly have simplified matters. At one stage, 'the Division had received no orders from any higher headquarters. Corps, Army and Army Group radio stations no longer answered, and no higher command existed for the next few days. Apparently

* Also known as the West Wall.

these higher headquarters had also tried to escape the threatened encirclement.'[7]

The position regarding men and matériel was dire. Some panzer returns for 23 August were given in table 16, in the previous chapter, and there was little improvement over the next month. On 29 August, von Rundstedt was told that the only replacements allotted to his command in the immediate future would be 61 Panzer IVs and 34 assault guns. According to one of the First Army corps commanders, at the end of August the whole Army comprised nine battalions of infantry, two batteries and ten tanks. When *Panzer Lehr* was added, in early September, having been 'refitted' as an independent command (it had fought through Falaise as part of 2 ss Panzer Division), it comprised one panzer grenadier battalion, six 105mm howitzers, one engineer company, a reconnaissance platoon and five tanks.

Speaking of the army in the west as a whole, Field Marshal Model* told Jodl on 29 August that his panzer divisions had 'five to ten tanks each' and that his infantry divisions were the equivalent of only four full-sized ones. They 'have only a few heavy weapons and for the most part are equipped with nothing more than small arms . . . The supply of replacements in men and material is utterly inadequate . . . There is no reserve whatever of assault guns or other heavy anti-tank equipment.'[8] The next week saw no changes for the better. On 5 September, of the 48 infantry divisions available to ob West only 13 were deemed completely fit for offensive operations, another 9 were reorganising, 12 were partially fit, and 14 totally unfit. Of the 11 panzer divisions, only three were completely up to scratch whilst fully seven were completely unfit. All in all Model estimated that his divisions, now trying to hold a 400-mile front, had the fighting value of no more than 25 divisions. Von Rundstedt, taking the helm once again on 7 September, could not but agree. To Field Marshal Keitel he wrote:

> In the face of all this Allied strength, all German forces are committed. They are badly depleted, in some cases crushed. Artillery and anti-tank weapons are lacking. Reserves worth much do not exist. Army Group B has about 100 tanks in working order. Considering Allied armoured strength the implications are clear.[9]

* Model took over as ob West From 16 August to 4 September, before handing back command to von Rundstedt.

Considering Allied armoured strength the implications should have been a foregone conclusion. In August, one American, one French and one Polish armoured division had been added to their order of battle. One armoured brigade had been disbanded but seven independent tank battalions had arrived as well as 11 tank-destroyer battalions. SHAEF was therefore maintaining an establishment tank strength, to which the units were usually kept topped up, of 5,961 medium tanks and 1,690 light.

The Allies continued to maintain this sort of material superiority throughout September. On the 15th, OB West could muster only 271 serviceable tanks, with another 73 in repair and 321 in shipment.* The respective figures for assault guns were 122, 73 and 393. The situation in Army Group B was equally bad. In the Schnee Eifel, south of the Ardennes, for example, 2 Panzer Division was down to just three tanks. In that it was probably not unique. Referring to the Army Group as a whole, von Rundstedt told Jodl that along its whole 400-km. front Army Group B

> fights with the strength of about twelve divisions and, at the moment, 84 tanks, assault guns and light anti-tank guns on Mark IV chassis, against a fully mobile enemy with at least 20 divisions and roughly 1,700 tanks fit for commitment. The danger of new reverses . . . can be removed only by speeding up the despatch of the reinforcements that have repeatedly been requested.[10]

Von Rundstedt was probably not accurately apprised of the overall air situation in his theatre, which was for the best. At this time *Luftwaffe Kommando West*, the old *Luftflotte 3*, could deploy 573 serviceable planes. In the United Kingdom and France the Allies

---

* The figure for tanks in transit includes many of the 13 independent Panzer Brigades raised in this period of the war. Numbered 101 to 113, these went into the line in the west between 2 August and 25 September. Their establishment included a battalion of between 30 and 90 tanks, but very few of these had been properly run in, whilst their crews were extremely raw. Most of the Brigades were sent to Lorraine to face Third Army and were decisively worsted, many units quickly losing 80 to 90 per cent of their tanks through enemy action or breakdown. By November all the Brigades except one had been absorbed into existing panzer or panzer grenadier divisions, half of them on the Eastern Front.

With regard to the number of tanks under repair, the Tigers again figured prominently. On 27 August, for example, all but ten of I SS Panzer Corps' 43 Tigers were in the workshops.

were able to put up 5,059 US bombers, 3,728 US fighters and 5,104 RAF combat aircraft, a grand total of almost 14,000.

September continued to be a desperate month for the Germans. From the southern sector of the front one corps commander reported that those formations in the line that had been pulled back from France still

> could not be regarded as tactical units . . . The panzer divisions, except 11 Panzer Division, were also in very poor condition and the three panzer brigades subordinated to Army Group G during the last weeks were new untried units . . . In summation it must be said that the condition of the troops in [the] Army Group G area between the middle and the end of September 1944, was as bad as possible. They were in no fit state to resist a major enemy attack.[11]

Nor was there much improvement in Army Group B. On 27 September, it could field 239 tanks and assault guns and its total artillery complement numbered 821 light and medium guns. Yet despite this small number of artillery pieces the Germans were still continuously short of ammunition. Little could be done, moreover, to bolster the divisions decimated in the Normandy fighting. Between 1 and 25 September the troops of Army Group B sustained a further 75,000 casualties yet replacements amounted to only 6,500.

With the *Wehrmacht* in the west reduced to such straits, one cannot but wonder why the war was not won before the end of the year. The question is hardly a new one, though most attention still tends to focus on the possibility of lightning thrusts by Montgomery or Patton into the heart of Germany. The potential of such a strategy will be examined below, but it is important first to take note of the continued Allied failure to cut off any substantial bodies of German troops before they got back to the Siegfried Line.

The point is particularly pertinent in the north where Montgomery, with First US Army to his right, had an excellent opportunity to cut off Fifteenth Army and the remnants of the Seventh and pin them against the coast. A partial success was gained in the so-called Mons Pocket, by the Americans, in mid-September, but though some 25,000 prisoners were netted, once again the headquarters staffs in the area, notably LVIII Panzer and II SS Corps, were allowed to slip through. A substantial portion of the divisional staffs also escaped and the main divisions involved, including two crack paratroop divisions, later reappeared in the west, where they continued to give excellent account of themselves.

Except for this partial success, attempts to entrap the Germans either misfired or were simply non-existent. At one stage those who regretted the less than total success at Falaise comforted themselves with the prospect of a 'long envelopment' on the Seine, where Third Army's spearheads had established a bridgehead, at Mantes, on 21 August. Exploitation out of this bridgehead down the east bank of the river offered enormous opportunities and 'the Germans believed that they were so weak on the right bank that this manoeuvre might well have assured the entrapment of the remains of Army Group B in a worse débâcle than the Falaise Pocket. A wide and probably irreparable gap would then have opened between those parts of the Fifteenth Army in the Pas de Calais that had not yet been committed to battle and the First Army trying to organise the defense of the upper Seine.'[12]

The Allies, however, preferred to try and close the trap by wheeling down the west bank, relying on the speed of their advance and their firepower to close off any crossing points used by the Germans. However, mobility was not their strongest suit, whilst their track record in applying firepower, especially aerial, to the interdiction of ferry routes was not encouraging. This record did not improve during the Seine crossings. Whilst it is true that Allied aircraft were hampered by the persistent rain that fell in late August, their efforts to interfere with the German withdrawal still seem to have been remarkably ineffective. In the first five days of mass crossings, between 20 and 24 August, the Germans employed ferries (there were 60 between Elbeuf and the sea), pontoon bridges and improvised rafts, and swimming pure and simple, by which means 25,000 vehicles were ferried to the east bank. Further major crossings took place on the 26th and 27th, at the end of which over 300,000 men were also across. Once again almost all the higher headquarters escaped.

They continued to elude their pursuers all the way to the Siegfried Line. That they evaded Patton, in the south, was hardly his fault. His pursuit to the Meuse had been carried out with his usual panache and it did seem that this time, particularly when two bridges at Verdun and Commercy were captured before the Germans could blow them, he might succeed in getting among the German remnants and completely destroying their command structure. Patton himself was convinced that he could go on to 'bounce' the Rhine and on the 21st was writing in his diary:

We have at this time the greatest chance to win the war ever presented. If they will let me move on with three corps . . . we can be in Germany in ten days. There are plenty of roads and railways to support the operation. It can be done with three armoured and six infantry divisions . . . It is such a sure thing that I fear these blind moles don't see it.

On the 29th, having captured the Meuse bridges, he wrote: 'We should cross the Rhine in the vicinity of Worms, and the faster we do it, the less lives and munitions it will take. No-one realises the terrible value of the "unforgiving minute" except me.' On 1 September, he wrote to a friend:

I am impatient with my friends for not letting me go faster, as I am sure – although people do not agree with me – that the Boche has no power to resist . . . [Eisenhower] kept talking about the future great battle of Germany, while we assured him that the Germans have nothing left to fight with if we push on now. If we wait there *will* be a great battle of Germany.[13]

Patton was not quite right in claiming that people did not agree with him – the Germans most certainly did. After the war, General Siegfried Westphal, Rundstedt's Chief of Staff from 5 September, declared:

The overall situation in the West was serious in the extreme. A heavy defeat anywhere along the front, which was so full of gaps that it did not deserve this name, might lead to a catastrophe, if the enemy were to exploit his opportunity skilfully. A particular source of danger was that not a single bridge across the Rhine had been prepared for demolition, an omission which took weeks to repair . . . The West Wall . . . was no longer in a defensible state . . . [and] it was at least six weeks before even the essential preparations could be laboriously made. Until the middle of October the enemy could have broken through at any point he liked with ease, and would then have been able to cross the Rhine and thrust deep into Germany almost unhindered.[14]

But it was not to be, though the responsibility in this instance lay not with any field commander but with the D-Day planners. For they had seriously underestimated the number of trucks that would be needed to haul supplies up to the front lines. The US Transportation Corps, in fact, had advised that 240 truck companies would be required in Europe, but the SHAEF planners had called for only 100. Eventually both sides compromised at 160 companies, with the shortfall further accentuated by the fact that far fewer heavy trucks were provided for long hauls than the number suggested by the Transportation Corps.

One cannot entirely blame the planners, however. For not only were they extremely concerned to economise on ship cargo space, but they also had little reason to believe, on past evidence, that Allied operations would suddenly become extremely mobile, with lines of communication stretched to their limit almost overnight as the forward troops surged away from their supply bases. When this did happen during the great German withdrawal, petrol suddenly became the most important commodity in the whole European theatre, both to keep the Allied spearheads moving and to fuel the trucks that supplied them. But, just as was noted in North Africa, the petrol itself also has to be brought forward by road and there were simply not enough trucks to keep it flowing in the requisite amounts to all the Allied Armies.* And at the very time that Patton was clamouring for fuel to sustain his dash to the Rhine his rivals also included First Airborne Army, in England, whose voracious transport aircraft were scheduled to make a drop in front of 21 Army Group, at Tournai. It was quite impossible to find enough transport to supply everyone and on 29 August Eisenhower, who had already decided that operations in Belgium and Holland must have priority, halted Patton by cutting off his fuel supply.

He remained virtually static until 5 September, when the advance resumed thanks to petrol acquired from various sources. But the time for simply brushing aside disorganised remnants was now past. The Germans had become noticeably stronger in Patton's sector during the five-day delay and their First Army, commanded by Eastern Front veteran General Otto von Knobelsdorff, was immeasurably

---

* A certain amount of fuel was also transported by air, especially to Third Army. Most went by road, however, where the truck shortage was made even worse by two additional factors. First, the US Communications Zone, controlling theatre supply, had been allowed to establish a huge semi-permanent depot in the Cotentin peninsula and when the time came to move bases nearer the front, an inordinate number of trucks were involved in just shipping Com Z's Nissen huts etc. Bradley later wrote that 'no-one could compute the cost of that move in lost tonnage on the front.' (O. Bradley, *A Soldier's Story* (Eyre and Spottiswoode, 1951), p. 406.) Second, the truck shortage in the British sector was greatly exacerbated by the fact that 1,400 British three-ton lorries were found to have defective pistons, rendering them useless. All the replacement engines for this model had the same fault.

better organised, its seven divisions* having had time to begin
settling into their own sectors and to improve the defences there.
Nor did it take long to make the defences along the Moselle extremely
strong. The paucity of good roads, the terrain, the existence of
elaborate strongpoints dating from the First World War and before,
as well as the generally atrocious weather in Lorraine at this time
of year, all combined to give enormous advantage to the defender.
Thus Patton's advance stalled around the middle of the month, with
one prong becoming tied down around Metz, where the core and
ancillary defences dominated the ground for up to 10 miles south
of the city and 20 to the north, another hemmed into a bridgehead
across the Moselle at Nancy, and a third similarly placed at Lunéville.
This was the situation on 25 September when Patton was once again
told that 21 Army Group was to have priority for petrol and that he
was to suspend major operations.

Events at the northern end of the Allied line had similarly
disappointing results, though here major errors of judgement were
the basic cause rather than logistical or physical constraints. As
early as 18 August, Montgomery had been forcefully suggesting
to American commanders that the main Allied axis of advance
should be north of the Ardennes and, most important, should
be under his direction. On this date he had written to Brooke
proposing that 21 and 12 Army Groups should be kept together
as 'a solid mass of some forty divisions', with the former moving
towards the Pas de Calais and Antwerp and the latter advancing
north of the Ardennes along the axis Brussels–Aachen–Cologne.
Montgomery added that 'Bradley agrees entirely with the above
conception', which was simply not true. On 22 August this message
was substantially repeated to Eisenhower, just prior to his assuming
command of Allied ground forces, with the stipulation that 'the
force must operate as one whole . . . Single control is vital for
success. This is a *whole time* job for one man.'[15] Montgomery
could not believe that the one man would not be him. On the 23rd
he explicitly asked Eisenhower to halt Patton, to divert almost all his
supplies to 21 Army Group, and to give him control of the SHAEF
strategic reserve, First Airborne Army. He does, however, seem to
have realised that asking for the whole of 12 Army Group might

* In this period the Army was built up from the remnants described a little
earlier to an order of battle that included three panzer grenadier divisions and
4½ infantry. Two more infantry divisions were in transit and a Volksgrenadier
and a panzer division were refitting to the rear.

seem a little excessive, and now limited his request to Simpson's First Army.

Neither Eisenhower nor Bradley, and most certainly not Patton, favoured this approach, not simply because they themselves were reluctant to give so much of the limelight to a British commander, but also because they realised that American public opinion would never stand for it. Eisenhower in particular favoured an advance into Germany along a broad front, with First and Third Armies each being allocated important axes of their own, broadly towards Cologne and Frankfurt. On 22 August, Eisenhower reminded de Guingand, Montgomery's Chief of Staff, that the SHAEF planners had 'wanted "a broad front both north and south of the Ardennes" and [that he] Eisenhower backed them to the full.'[16] On the following day, Bradley told Montgomery face to face that he went even further than Eisenhower and favoured making the main advance *south* of the Ardennes, over the Moselle and the Saar towards the Rhine, at Frankfurt. But he was due to be disappointed. The deplorable fuel situation ruled out Eisenhower's favoured option and forced him to plump for one axis or another, and he eventually chose Montgomery's. This was not because of any particular admiration for his military abilities; rather it was because, first, considerable political pressure was building up to try and overrun the V-1 and V-2 rocket sites in western Holland, and, second, Montgomery was closest to the Channel ports and Antwerp, whose capture would substantially ease Allied supply problems. In his own mind Eisenhower was clear that this was a pragmatic decision, tailored to the immediate demands of the situation, and that it did *not* represent a permanent commitment to the primacy of the northern axis. A letter to Marshall on the 24th categorically stated: 'I have *temporarily* changed my basic plan of attacking both to the north and east in order to help Montgomery seize tremendously important objectives in the north-east.'[17]

Unfortunately, Eisenhower did not make the temporary nature of this reallocation of priorities sufficiently clear to Montgomery,* and the latter was tempted to regard the concessions made – authority over First US Army, flank protection from the whole of 12 Army Group, permission to use First Airborne Army, fuel priority – as

* Though Eisenhower's letter to Montgomery confirming these details did point out that 'Bradley's Army Group will be directed to thrust forward on its left, with its principal offensive mission, *for the moment*, to support the Army Group of the North.' (A. D. Chandler *et al.* (eds), *The Papers of D. D. Eisenhower* (5 vols, Johns Hopkins University Press, Baltimore, Md, 1970), vol. 4, p. 209.)

a whole-hearted commitment to making his northern axis the main route into Germany and himself the principal ground commander. Thus deceived, Montgomery rather lost sight of his immediate target, Antwerp, and began to indulge in renewed fantasies about hard-hitting mobile operations 'cracking about' hither and thither. His eyes became fixed on the Rhine, and by 4 September he had formulated a plan to seize bridges at Wesel and Arnhem with an airborne drop. But this was only a stepping-stone to greater things. As he explained to Eisenhower that same day: 'I consider we have now reached a stage where one really powerful and full-blooded thrust towards Berlin is likely to get there and thus end the German war . . . In my opinion the thrust likely to give the best and quickest results is the northern one via the Ruhr.'[18]

With the prospect of such heady conquests before him, Montgomery virtually forgot his actual mission, the opening up of Antwerp as a working port, and proceeded to make some of the most fateful decisions of his career. The first British troops had arrived in Antwerp on 4 September, but were then ordered by Montgomery to halt for three days to prepare themselves for a push to the Rhine to link up with First Airborne Army. But if Antwerp was to be taken over *as a working port* this could not be effected simply by liberating the city itself and then standing pat. Shipping could only arrive there if the banks of the Scheldt were also in Allied hands, a point that had been succinctly put to Montgomery by Admiral Sir Bertram Ramsay, the SHAEF naval commander-in-chief, on 3 September: 'Both Antwerp and Rotterdam are highly vulnerable to mining and blocking. If the enemy succeeds in these operations the time it will take to open ports cannot be estimated . . . It will be necessary for coastal batteries to be captured before approach channels to the river route can be established.'[19]

Thus British troops should have been pushed through Antwerp and over the intact bridges on the Albert Canal to clear the northern bank of the Scheldt. These troops would also have been in a position to block off the retreat, across the Scheldt, of Fifteenth Army units which were being shunted up the coast by First Canadian Army. By the time of the entry into Antwerp many of these units were trapped in the Breskens Pocket and their only possible escape route into Holland and Germany was via Beveland or Walcheren. On 4 September it would have been perfectly easy to get British troops across the Albert Canal. General Brian Horrocks, commanding XXX Corps, the formation actually in Antwerp, has since declared that the halt ordered by Montgomery:

was a tragedy because, as we now know, on . . . 4 September the only troops available to bar our passage northwards consisted of one German division, the 719th, composed entirely of elderly gentlemen who hitherto had been guarding the north coast of Holland and had never heard a shot fired in anger . . . This meagre force was strung out on a fifty-mile front along the [Albert] Canal.[20]

Once across, Horrocks' troops could have completely sealed off the Breskens Pocket, condemning Fifteenth Army to complete destruction.* The Scheldt could then have been quickly cleared for shipping and sufficient fuel landed to support operations all along the front.†

Montgomery's decision to halt XXX Corps from 4 to 6 September becomes even more unaccountable when one realises that Ultra had informed him on the 4th that the Germans intended to evacuate troops via South Beveland, and on the 5th that Hitler fully intended to hold on to both banks for as long as possible. Montgomery's own observations on future operations also stand in stark contrast, once again, to his actual tactical decisions. On 26 August, for example, he had told Horrocks that he must not relax his pressure, neither by day nor by night. ' "The Germans are very good soldiers," he said, "and will recover quickly if allowed to do so. All risks are justified – I intend to get a bridgehead over the Rhine before they have time to recover." '[21] But allowing Fifteenth Army to escape was not Montgomery's only blunder at this time. By halting he was also allowing the Germans to build up their forces along the Albert Canal, for which express purpose a special Army Headquarters, First Parachute Army, under General Kurt Student, was inserted into the German order of battle. By the middle of the month, 719 Infantry Division had been joined by another infantry and a parachute division as well as elements of four other infantry divisions. As we saw, pretty much the same thing had happened on Patton's front, but there the fault had been hardly his. It had been on Montgomery's insistence that Patton had been halted, and First Army given time to recover, yet Montgomery then completely failed to take any advantage of the extra resources allocated to him and allowed exactly the same kind of breathing space to First Parachute Army, along his own front.

* It should be noted that when Horrocks halted, his tanks still had 100 miles' worth of petrol in their tanks.
† The port of Antwerp was not opened to shipping until 28 November.

One of Montgomery's divisional commanders commented after the war that 'Monty's failure at Antwerp is evidence again that he was not a good general at seizing opportunities.'[22] One might legitimately ask whether a general who cannot seize opportunities is a good general at all. He certainly tends to make things rather difficult for himself, as Montgomery did by allowing Fifteenth Army to pull back across the Scheldt. Using all kinds of regular and makeshift ferries, and yet again operating with seeming impunity in the face of Allied air power, the Army, between 4 and 23 September, managed to extricate 86,100 men, 6,200 horses, 6,200 vehicles, 616 guns and much other equipment across the estuary. Most of these took up positions alongside Student's ever-burgeoning forces, well positioned to strike at the flank of Montgomery's much-vaunted drive to the Rhine bridges.

The latter project continued to dominate the new Field Marshal's thinking, and his relentless advocacy of it eventually began to impress Eisenhower. Having earlier backed a northern thrust only as a means of opening Antwerp to Allied shipping, he too now began to see a possibility of taking advantage of German disorganisation in Holland and pushing through quickly to the Rhine. On 10 September, therefore, he approved Montgomery's plan for airborne drops at the various bridges that spanned the rivers and canals between the Meuse–Escaut Canal* and Arnhem, drops that were to provide an airborne carpet for XXX Corps to motor through to the Rhine. Realising the need for getting such an operation under way as quickly as possible, Eisenhower was prepared to let Montgomery defer the clearance of the Scheldt and, at least according to his Chief of Staff, to halt Patton once more, to strip three US divisions of their transport, and to divert extra supplies to 21 Army Group. Talk like this was balm to Montgomery's ears and he began to give his strategic ideas freest rein, letting his eyes wander towards Germany itself and perhaps even Berlin. In his new instructions to XXX Corps he laid it down that 'after relieving 1st Airborne Division at Arnhem, they would push on to the Zuider Zee, and wait for the rest of Second Army to catch up with them before advancing to the North German Plains, thus outflanking the Siegfried Line.'[23]

This was not at all Eisenhower's intention, however. For him, as he later made clear in his memoirs, Operation Market Garden, as

---

* After fierce fighting in the sandy heaths that lay between the Albert and Meuse–Escaut Canals, which lasted from 6 to 11 September, a small bridgehead was eventually established over the latter waterway.

the plan was now known, was merely an *ad hoc* effort to take advantage of temporary German disorganisation, 'merely an incident and extension of our eastward rush to the line we needed for temporary security. On our northern flank that line was the lower Rhine itself.'[24] Eisenhower's overall strategy was still to advance on a broad front and eventually occupy 'the Ruhr, the Saar and the Frankfurt area.' After that, 'simply stated, it is my desire to move on Berlin by the most direct and expeditious route, with combined US–British forces supported by other available forces moving through key centres and occupying strategic areas on the flanks, all in one co-ordinated, concerted operation.' In other words, though Eisenhower clearly stated that he regarded Berlin 'as the main prize', he was not prepared to say by which axis it was to be approached, nor by which Army, until much nearer the time, when the whole of the Allied force had drawn up abreast well into Germany.[25]

By 26 September, the question of immediate exploitation towards Berlin, at least on the northern axis, had become rather academic, the drive to Arnhem having completely broken down. The tanks of XXX Corps had been unable to link up with 1 British Airborne Division in time and the latter had been smashed, losing 1,130 dead and 6,500 prisoners-of-war, and the survivors being pulled back over the Rhine. During the battle, however, Montgomery made light of the problems at Arnhem, emphasising to Eisenhower the extent of the territory already gained across the Maas and the Waal. Throughout the operation, and for some days after, he seems to have convinced SHAEF and the American generals that 21 Army Group was on the verge of seizing its Rhine bridgehead. Not surprisingly, this encouraged Eisenhower to think that he had found his proper axis of advance towards Berlin and on 22 September, even as 1 Airborne Division was preparing to evacuate, he met with de Guingand and, as the minutes of this conference put it,

approved the following:
a)   the envelopment of the Ruhr from the north by 21st Army Group supported by 1st [US] Army, is the main effort of the present phase of operations . . .
d) (i) 12th Army Group . . . will be prepared to seize any favourable opportunity of crossing the Rhine and attacking the Ruhr from the south in concert with 21st Army Group's attack . . .

(ii) The commander of 12th Army Group will take no more aggressive action than is permitted by the maintenance situation after the full requirements of the main effort have been met.[26]

As late as 8 October, Eisenhower still endorsed this concept of operations, declaring that the Allies 'must retain as first mission the gaining of the line north of Bonn as quickly as humanly possible.'[27]

At almost exactly the same moment, however, Eisenhower received a situation report from 21 Army Group that dispelled at a stroke any thoughts about their being on the verge of a decisive breakthrough on the Rhine. Not only was this not possible, admitted Montgomery, but his efforts to clear the Scheldt had also fallen behind schedule, because too many resources had been directed eastwards. And without the port of Antwerp, he had further to concede, no renewed drive towards the Rhine was possible. On reading this report Eisenhower became furious, feeling that Montgomery had pulled the wool over his eyes both about the real chances of success at Arnhem and about the scale of his effort on the Scheldt.* Just on its own the report seriously impaired Montgomery's chances of ever leading the major advance into Germany. But these chances were completely scuppered by his dogged inability to realise just how badly he had blotted his copy-book and by his insistent harping on the theme of a single commander for a concentrated thrust. On 10 October, he actually suggested that he should take command of 12 Army Group. On 30 November, he demanded that one man be given full operational control north of the Ardennes, strongly hinting that it should be himself. On 29 December, he raised the subject of 'a sound set-up for command . . . [which] implies one man directing and controlling the whole tactical battle on the northern thrust.'[28] Montgomery's own chief and greatest ally, Field Marshal Brooke, was himself less than happy with his protégé's obsession. On 9 November, he wrote in his diary: 'Monty goes on harping over the system of command in France which prolongs the war. He has got this on the brain as it affects his own personal position and he cannot put up with not being in sole personal command of land operations.'[29]

Certainly Eisenhower was not prepared just to sit back and be lectured to in this way. On two of the above occasions, indeed, he

---

* Though Eisenhower had temporarily allowed Montgomery to accord the clearance of the Scheldt a lower priority, the latter, from 13 September, had given the definite impression that it and the Arnhem operation were *both*, simultaneously, well within the compass of 21 Army Group.

came very close to having Montgomery dismissed. In October, he wrote to Montgomery pointing out: 'If you as Senior Commander in this theatre . . . feel that my conceptions and directives are such as to endanger the success of operations it is your duty to refer the matter to higher authority for any action they may choose to take however drastic.'[30] Montgomery swiftly backed down. However, his promise that 'you will hear no more from me on the question of command' was not kept and his intervention in late December once again almost brought about his dismissal.[31] This time Eisenhower did not bother suggesting that Montgomery seek the opinion of higher authority but himself drafted a telegram to the Combined Chiefs of Staff that in effect asked them to sack Montgomery. The Field Marshal only survived because de Guingand got wind of Eisenhower's high dudgeon, was able to delay the fateful cable, and then persuaded Montgomery to apologise fulsomely and promise to leave command arrangements entirely to the Supreme Commander.

With these serious incidents in mind, it comes as some surprise to find that throughout the first two months of 1945 Eisenhower was still talking in terms of making his major thrust into Germany from 21 Army Group's sector. A directive to Montgomery on 31 December ordered: 'Prepare for crossing the Rhine with the main effort north of the Ruhr . . . the front south of the Moselle to be strictly defensive for the time being . . .' On 10 January he wrote to Marshall and spoke of committing 'to the invasion of Germany the strongest possible forces with the main effort north of the Ruhr'. On 20 February a directive to Bradley stated categorically that 'the main effort is to be north of the Ruhr.'[32] With hindsight, however, such pronouncements have an increasingly rhetorical ring, for little of what Eisenhower actually did, as opposed to what he said he was going to do, reflected this strategy of a strong northern thrust. Part of him might well have wanted to adopt this option, might well have seen it as the quickest way to end the war, but such was his irritation with Montgomery that when it came to the crunch he could not bring himself to give the latter the starring role.

His get-out can be found in some of the same documents just cited. Thus, in his letter of 10 January he reminded Marshall that 'the thing that has guided us all the way through these operations [in N.W. Europe] has been the great hope of attaining defensive flanks that were strong enough and then to commit to the invasion of Germany the strongest possible forces . . .' The February directive to Bradley informed him that operations *south* of the Ruhr were 'to gain secure flanks so as to permit heavy concentration in . . . [the North], and eventually to provide secondary threats and thrusts that will assist the main effort.'[33] This notion of strong flanks, of a solid defensive line along the whole of the Allied front, dominated Eisenhower's thinking throughout the late autumn and winter, as for example on 15 January when he again told Marshall that strong defences enabled one 'to concentrate *safely* for counter-attack . . . *Unless we get a good natural line for the defensive portions of our long front, we will use up a lot of divisions in defence.* That line ought to be, substantially, the Rhine.'[34]

In other words, the desire to provide a strong flank in the south, and to ensure that the whole Allied line was anchored on the best positions, gave Eisenhower a perpetual excuse to permit large-scale operations by First and Third US Armies, and later by 6 Army Group,* that had no obvious connection with building up a strong thrust in the north. When Eisenhower bowed to the blandishments of Bradley or Patton for a greater commitment in their own sectors, he was to some extent at least letting his annoyance with Montgomery colour his decisions. But that is not to say that he was wilfully deceiving Montgomery, or anyone else to whom he had given assurance that northern operations had priority. For, in his own mind at least, there were perfectly sound reasons for major operations in the centre and the south, reasons moreover that made such operations entirely consistent with the avowed strategy of concentrating in the north.†

---

* Formed on 15 September from the Dragoon forces and incorporating Seventh US Army and First French. Seventh US Army had actually joined hands with 12 Army Group on 12 September.

† Though others might discern something of a contradiction. The ambiguities of Eisenhower's position are highlighted in a communication to the Combined Chiefs of Staff meeting on Malta, in January 1945. From Eisenhower's operations hitherto it seemed fairly clear that he intended to close up to the Rhine along its whole length before beginning his main thrust into Germany. In an appreciation of 20 January he wrote: 'Only when we . . . have closed [to] the Rhine shall we share with the enemy a strong defensive barrier giving us the ability to hold defensive sectors with security and economy of effort.' (Chandler *et al.*, op. cit., vol. 4, p. 2453.) This alarmed the British Chiefs of Staff, who demanded an assurance that Eisenhower was not intending to clear all territory west of the Rhine before launching the northern thrust. He replied: 'I will seize the Rhine crossings in the north immediately this is a feasible operation and without waiting to close to the Rhine throughout its length . . . I will advance across the Rhine in the north . . . as soon as the situation in the south allows me.' (ibid., vol. 4, p. 2463.) The insistence upon feasibility and a satisfactory situation in the south in fact meant that though Eisenhower might not draw up to the Rhine along its whole length, he most certainly would not be happy with less than 90 per cent.

These reasons, combined with his irritation with Montgomery, persistently obtruded into Eisenhower's thinking, such that from an early date he allowed more ambitious operations in Hodges' and Patton's sectors than might seem consistent with his supposed strategy.* In early September, even though he had agreed, albeit temporarily, that Montgomery should have priority in the north, he first gave Patton permission to cross the Moselle, on the 2nd, and a few days later actually diverted almost 2 million gallons of petrol to the Third Army. On the 4th, in a memorandum for his own record, Eisenhower wrote: 'I now deem it important, while supporting the advance eastward through Belgium, to get Patton moving once again so that we may be fully prepared to carry out the original conception for the final stages of the campaign.'[35] At a conference on 18 October, because Montgomery was at last fully occupied in clearing the Scheldt, Eisenhower gave 12 Army Group the main offensive tasks for November, namely to drive east and try to obtain a bridgehead over the Rhine south of Cologne. He told Montgomery that once Antwerp was functioning, 21 Army Group would again have priority, but it is hard to envisage Eisenhower not making a maximum effort to exploit an American bridgehead had one been secured.+

On 7 December, at a conference at Maastricht, Eisenhower reiterated that operations in the north had first priority but still insisted on making another thrust to the south, from Frankfurt. He even upbraided Montgomery at one point, to the effect that he 'must not put too much stress on the Ruhr; it is merely a geographical objective; our real objective was to kill Germans and it did not matter where we did it.'[36] On 13 December, in a letter to Marshall, Eisenhower once again envisaged a major role for 12 Army Group, along its own axis, stating that he still believed it was 'most vitally important when the time comes that . . . we should be on the Rhine at Frankfurt.'[37] In January of the following year he continued to dilute his commitment to the supposedly predominant northern axis and, despite the wheedlings of Churchill, Brooke and Montgomery, held out for the launching of a strong thrust in the south. In one letter to his own Chiefs of Staff he contrasted the two axes, north of the

* The actual operational consequences of the orders and plans detailed below can be most easily followed on map 8, which clearly demonstrates the 'broad front' nature of Eisenhower's advance.
+ In fact, the first bridge over the Rhine was not taken until 7 March 1945, at Remagen.

Ruhr and toward Frankfurt, and stated that 'it may be necessary to use either or both of these two avenues'. A little later on he revealed plans that would have filled the triumvirate just named with horror: 'The possibility of failure to secure bridgeheads in the north or in the south cannot be overlooked. I am therefore making logistical preparations to switch my main effort from the north to the south should this be forced upon me.'[38]

The real value Eisenhower accorded these preparations is attested to by his reaction to First US Army's unexpected seizure of the Ludendorff railway bridge at Remagen, on 7 March. The first person at SHAEF to hear of this coup was General H. R. Bull, Eisenhower's Assistant Chief of Staff for Operations. He was pleased that it was Americans who had scored this first but told Bradley, who happened to be with him: 'You're not going anywhere down there at Remagen; it just doesn't fit in with the plan.' This indeed seemed a proper reaction given Eisenhower's countless assurances to Montgomery, but when the former was informed by Bradley about the bridge he told him: 'Get across with whatever you need – but make certain you hold that bridgehead.'[39] Later orders from SHAEF restricted the number of divisions Bradley might employ to only four, but within a few days this order, too, had been rescinded and by 22 March the Allied 'hole card' in the south consisted of three corps.

On the 23rd Montgomery was allowed to go ahead with Operation Plunder, 21 Army Group's own set-piece crossing of the Rhine, but it seems clear that by this stage Eisenhower *was* wilfully deceiving him as to what was to be the main axis of advance into Germany. For on the 21st Eisenhower had instructed Patton to establish another American bridgehead, in the Frankfurt area, from which they were to link up with First Army coming from Remagen. Such a link-up, he pointedly informed Marshall, would give him a force south of the Ruhr at least equal in strength to 21 Army Group. As a recent and compelling analysis of the Montgomery/Eisenhower controversy has pointed out: 'That order sounded, irrevocably, the death-knell for Montgomery's ambition to lead the Allied armies in their triumphal march on Berlin.'[40]

The axe itself fell on 28 March, just five days after the start of Operation Plunder. As we have seen, Montgomery's constant harping on the question of command had long irritated Eisenhower and caused him again and again to draw back from fully committing his forces to a strong northern thrust. In March his irritation was allowed to bubble over, for he felt he had discovered a sufficient reason for explicitly abandoning the northern thrust, and making his main effort to the south. This justification derived from a sudden volte-face over the question of Berlin. In September, as has been noted above, Berlin was regarded as 'the main prize' and the fact that Montgomery's axis led there most directly obliged Eisenhower to bite the bullet somewhat. On 30 March, however, he sent a signal to Montgomery pointing out: 'You will see that in none of this do I mention Berlin. So far as I am concerned the place has become nothing but a geographical location. I have never been interested in these. My purpose is to destroy the enemy.'[41]

With Berlin off the agenda and with Eisenhower now only contemplating an advance as far as the Elbe, there was no reason why one of the American Armies south of the Ruhr should not undertake the major operations. The actual capture of Berlin could be left to the Russians, who had a positive passion for geographical locations. The new orders to Montgomery, within the parameters of military officialese, were downright insulting. The Field Marshal was told that Ninth US Army, which he had had under command since 20 December, was to be handed back to Bradley immediately. The latter 'will be responsible for mopping up and occupying the Ruhr and with minimum delay will deliver his main thrust on the axis Erfurt–Leipzig–Dresden to join up hands with the Russians . . . The mission of your army will be to protect Bradley's northern flank.' A follow-up signal was more precise about 21 Army Group's new role, though hardly less crushing. It was 'to cross the Elbe without delay, drive to the Baltic coast at Lübeck and seal off the Danish Peninsula.'[42] Thus was it Montgomery's destiny to save everybody's bacon, though not in quite the way he would have wished.

Such then, in broad outline, is the single thrust/broad front debate that dominated Allied strategic councils for much of the North-West European campaign. It has also, understandably, dominated much of the historiography of that campaign. Many of the books that take the debate as a major theme tend to assume that Eisenhower, as Supreme Commander, continued to have a real choice of opting for Montgomery's narrow axis or of moving all his armies in parallel and thus of necessity dispersing his maintenance resources. But this is to fall into the same trap as those historians of the Eastern Front who equally assume that Hitler had a real choice in 1941 as to whether he drove straight for Moscow or first cleaned up on his flanks. In fact, as was seen in chapter 1, Hitler had no real choice at all, for both of these tasks were equally urgent and, because he did not have armoured forces adequate to performing both simultaneously, whichever 'choice' he made was bound to be wrong.

Eisenhower was similarly stymied, though for somewhat different reasons. On the whole, the constraints upon him were not material, except for the period in August and early September when he was forced temporarily to back either Montgomery or Patton and halt the other. Under normal circumstances, however, Eisenhower was simply not at liberty to choose to concentrate the bulk of Allied resources behind 21 Army Group and so immobilise the large proportion of American divisions. For he was strait-jacketed by political consideration well summed up by Patton, who wrote in his diary in March 1945: 'It is essential to get First and Third Armies so deeply involved in their present plans that they cannot be moved north to play second fiddle to the British-instilled idea of attacking with 60 divisions in the Ruhr plain.'[43]

Now Patton was an Anglophobe pure and simple, and the overt duplicity suggested here was never Eisenhower's chosen *modus operandi*.* But this entry does highlight a core element of American policy in North-West Europe, namely that their armies could not be seen to be playing second fiddle and that a drive towards Berlin in the north would be regarded as a 'British-instilled' strategy. Eisenhower himself had made pretty much the same point to Montgomery in September 1944, when he gave his reactions to the latter's proposals for an absolute commitment to the northern thrust:

> Incidentally I do not yet have your calculations on the tonnage that will be necessary to support 21st Army Group on this move. There is one point, however, on which we do not agree, if I interpret your ideas correctly. As I read your letter you imply that all the divisions we have, except those of the 21st Army Group and approximately nine of the 12th Army Group, can stop in place *where they are* and that we can strip all these additional divisions from their transport and everything else to support one single knife-like thrust towards Berlin. This may not be exactly what you mean but it is certainly not possible.[44]

---

* Though he was quite capable of turning a blind eye to his subordinates' flouting his orders and getting their divisions too deeply committed either to call off an (illicit) operation or to permit the transfer of formations to the British front. Space does not permit any details on this point but the interested reader is referred to, e.g., C. Wilmot, *The Struggle for Europe* (Collins, 1952), which gives examples for September (pp. 493, 496), October (p. 563), November (pp. 563–4), December (p. 583) and March (p. 676).

And it was not possible simply because nearly all the stranded divisions would be American. Whether or not Montgomery's own strategy was militarily sound (a question we shall return to below) is in the last analysis beside the point. For it would have involved British pipers playing a British tune and, faced with such a programme, American paymasters became resolutely tone-deaf.*

Thus, despite many writers' depiction of Eisenhower's strategy as being plodding and unimaginative, it cannot really be written off as just another example of Allied 'brute force'. Certainly the chosen strategy may have seemed rather ponderous, with the constant emphasis upon alignment all along the front and the almost complete absence of major mobile thrusts at any one point, but this was largely a function of the political realities of coalition warfare rather than a measure of Eisenhower's strategic abilities. Indeed, it might well be argued that, even had Eisenhower had the freedom to put Montgomery in charge of the major Allied thrust, he did well not to do so. For at this point we must return to the questions raised in the last chapter about Montgomery's ability to match strategic posturing and tactical practice. Could he, in short, have put his money where his mouth was and led a compact and highly mobile force slicing a path to Berlin?

The available evidence suggests not. His performance around Caen and the Falaise Gap has already been mentioned. He himself seems to have thought that the dash into Belgium in late August had shown that 'when it came to mobile battles . . . [British forces] were just as good as the next man', and thus exonerated him of any charge of slowness or excessive caution in the previous weeks.[45] In fact, just as with Patton during the dash to the Meuse, the advance to Antwerp was simply a case of the British taking up the slack as the Germans withdrew. The hallmark of the good mobile commander would have been to catch the Germans rather than simply to plough along in their wake. And surely even a moderately competent commander would have put the lid on the Fifteenth Army *Kessel* around the Scheldt Estuary. But the case against Montgomery as a would-be leader of mobile thrusts does not end there. The later history of

---

* The reader is referred again to the production figures in tables 46–55, which show the respective American and British industrial contributions. It should also be borne in mind that by April 1945 there were 55 American divisions in Europe (and 9 American-equipped) as opposed to 13 British and Canadian (and one British-equipped).

the North-West European campaign only serves to confirm the impression that he was hardly the man to administer a swift *coup de grâce* to the German Army, no matter how bloodied the latter might be.

Much of this evidence is to be found in Montgomery's handling of the Arnhem operation. Almost every feature of Operation Market Garden, in fact, simply reaffirmed what had already become evident in North Africa, that Montgomery was generally incapable of conducting anything but stolid defences or attacks with generous lead times, massive material superiority and no urgent deadlines during the battle itself. One might even go so far as to say that Market Garden showed Montgomery and the army he had created in the worst possible light, revealing serious lapses in planning as well as severe shortcomings in operational and tactical command. There was, for example, little cooperation between the various staffs responsible. The success of the operation depended on a link-up, at various crossing points between the Meuse–Escaut Canal and the lower Rhine, between First Airborne Army and XXX Corps, yet once First Airborne began detailed planning of its drops no senior staff officer from 21 Army Group, Second Army or XXX Corps ever attended its meetings.* There was also a serious lack of cooperation with the air forces, one result of this being that no air reconnaissance pictures were taken of the route to be covered by XXX Corps. This was partly responsible for an early setback to the Corps' spearhead unit, the Irish Guards, on 17 September, which lost several tanks to guns that had not been pinpointed. Also lacking was any liaison between the Airborne Army and those units responsible for the cooperation of ground troops and tactical air power, the Air Support Signals Units and the Forward Air Controllers. The lack of tactical air support was sorely felt by 1 Airborne Division during its ordeal at Arnhem.

Neither was First Airborne Army's own planning particularly impressive, even with regard to matters in which one might have assumed a certain expertise. The fundamental flaw was the decision to drop its divisions, notably 1 Airborne around Arnhem and 82 US Airborne around Nijmegen, too far from the main objectives,

---

* Market Garden in fact remained two operations, Market being the airborne phase and Garden the ground operations. The airborne forces were to become part of Garden as they landed.

respectively the bridges over the lower Rhine and the Waal.* This meant that at the first of these a good part of 1 Airborne was written off just forcing its way through to the bridge, leaving only a small remnant actually to hold it against German counter-attacks. That 2 Battalion The Parachute Regiment held on for as long as it did is one of the epic tales of the Second World War. That it was required to do so is one of its sorriest blunders. A similar foul-up at Nijmegen only added to their problems. There 82 Airborne was also faced with long approach marches to its primary targets, and though it did succeed in capturing the bridge over the Waal, at Graves, it was held up short of the Nijmegen bridge for a whole day. When the leading elements of XXX Corps arrived, they had to join the American paratroopers in attacking the bridge instead of being able to dash straight across and on to Arnhem.

An even more remarkable planning lapse, considering the urgency of the whole operation, was the refusal to attempt more than one airborne lift on the first day. As a post-mortem analysis by an RAF staff officer put it:

> *The air plan was bad.* All experience and common sense pointed to landing all three Airborne Divisions in the minimum period of time, so that they could form up and collect themselves before the Germans reacted. All three Divisions could have been landed within the space of twelve hours or so, but F.A.A.A. [First Allied Airborne Army] insisted on a plan which resulted in the second lift (with half the heavy equipment) arriving more than 24 hours after the Germans had been alerted.[46]

Here was the dead hand of Montgomery-style warfare. Supposedly fired with objectives that were to be seized 'with thunderclap surprise' and a timetable that was 'ambitious to the point of recklessness', those responsible for actually turning these grandiose aims into detailed plans were incapable of perceiving that this might be an occasion on which the aircrews could be asked to work double shifts.[47†]

* The drop of 101 US Airborne around Eindhoven was tighter around the objectives, but a failure to drop troops *north* of the Zon bridge, over the Wihelmina Canal, meant the division was unable to prevent this bridge being blown up in their faces. The necessity to build another was an obvious source of further delay.

† The dead hand is also in evidence at one remove, in General F. A. M. Browning's (Deputy C.-in-C. First Airborne Army) crucial but sadly unadventurous decision not to allow a second attack on the Nijmegen bridge on the afternoon of the second day, even though 82 Airborne's second lift had now arrived. Far from

But complacent and inadequate planning procedures were not the only problem at Arnhem. Equally pernicious was the fact that Montgomery himself could do little to mitigate their unhappy effects. Because of the lack of cooperation between the various staffs, his own did not see the final plan until a mere 48 hours before the battle, by which time it was too late to make anything but the most trivial adjustments. Even had Montgomery wanted to impart a little more ginger he would not have had the time to do so without delaying the start of the operation, a self-defeating option. He had made himself largely redundant. Indeed, throughout the period of mobile operations, in August and September, Montgomery, the man whose main criticism of Eisenhower was his lack of 'grip', seems to have remained remarkably out of touch with day-to-day operations and singularly incapable of controlling events. During the race for Antwerp, according to the commander of 11 Armoured Division, 'none of Monty's liaison officers could possibly contact me. We were going too fast; Monty and Dempsey were many, many miles behind.' During Market Garden, he only once got as far as Nijmegen and even then did not actually cross the Waal. At no stage during the battle did he visit XXX Corps HQ (admittedly only possible during the first two days), and not until 23 September, when it was almost over, did he visit Dempsey at Second Army HQ. Montgomery's Chief of Staff recalled that he remained 'uncharacteristically remote from . . . [Market Garden's] actual execution'. There was ' "a lack of grip in Montgomery" and . . . the army group commander appeared to let things go their own way.'[48]

One doubts, however, whether any amount of grip could have done much to bring together Market and Garden into a working relationship. For XXX Corps had taken on an almost impossible task. When the idea of an advance towards Arnhem had first been mooted, Dempsey had injected a rare note of realism when he 'said that the unexpectedly tough resistance on the Albert Canal made him doubt whether he could advance north fast enough to link up with the drop at Arnhem.'[49] During the battle, Horrocks made it crystal clear why this might be the case, when he told General James Gavin, commanding 82 Airborne: 'Jim, never try to fight an entire corps off one road.'[50] For XXX Corps' axis in the drive to Arnhem was terribly constricted:

Footnote continued

seeing anything amiss here, Montgomery informed Brooke after the battle that he would like Browning as a corps commander at the first opportunity.

a narrow corridor through . . . swampy heath, all the way to Arnhem . . . a single two-lane highway, bounded immediately by small, open cultivated fields hedged in by poplar trees and surrounded by drainage ditches. Occasionally the road ran past thick pine forests. Up the road the Irish Guards would lead 30 Corps on a front two tanks wide.[51]

The Irish Guards were part of Guards Armoured Division, which formation was expected to cover a considerable stretch of such highway, 60 miles as the crow flies, in two days. A previous advance of around 12 miles, between Beeringen and the de Groote Barrier, along an exactly similar road, in the face of much lighter opposition, had taken the best part of three days.*

But the critical factor in the failure on the road to Arnhem was that poor local leadership dissipated whatever slight chance there might have been, if not of keeping up with the original timetable, then at least of locking hands with 1 Airborne Division before they were overwhelmed. Almost every unit involved showed the same lack of drive. When the Irish Guards drove into Graves, on the 17th, they discovered that the Zon bridge had been blown, upon which they promptly leaguered for the night rather than move forward at least to stake out the bridge site and perhaps undertake some preliminary work. Nor was any attempt made to send forward an infantry unit to flush out Germans in its vicinity. But the whole of Guards Armoured maintained a rather measured pace in its advance. When the bridge at Nijmegen was finally taken, on the 20th, the whole night was again allowed to elapse before any effort was made to send even a small force up to Arnhem, where 1 Airborne had already described their situation as 'critical'.

Fire in the belly was even more lacking among the division's rear echelons, whose lack of initiative summed up everything that was wrong with the British Liberation Army. On either side of the road to Nijmegen were grass verges, and beside the odd roadblock that the Germans had erected these verges were mined. By one roadblock was the wreckage of two British three-tonners which had gone off the road, and by them a sign erected by conscientious sappers admonishing drivers to 'KEEP ON THE ROADS. VERGES NOT CLEARED OF MINES'. Faced with this warning,

* At the village of Hechtel, on the road to Eindhoven, most of Guards Armoured Division, infantry and tanks, was held up for six days by just 850 paratroopers and three tanks.

British drivers, ever cautious, took due note of it. Over the next
five miles . . . the concrete road was only just wide enough for
two vehicles. There were ample grass verges, but whenever
convoys were halted to let more urgent columns through, the
drivers clung to the concrete, creating a succession of traffic
blocks which took hours to clear. The stretch of road between
the frontier and Valkenswaard became a bottleneck which governed and restricted the northward flow of convoys. Another
bottleneck soon developed in Eindhoven which was heavily
attacked by the Luftwaffe on the evening of the 19th.[52]

In fact, the verges were not mined, not surprisingly given that the
Germans had been using the road as a supply route of their own
only a few days previously. Traffic was being limited to only two
lanes when, because the verges on either side were level and firm
enough for motor transport, it could have been using four, or at
least taking advantage of two hard shoulders to keep the runners
moving. One is not, of course, suggesting that truck drivers should
have acted as their own mine detectors, for they were not to know
that the verges were not mined,* but one might have thought that
someone in authority would see fit to have them tested.

It was not just Guards Armoured Division that proved dilatory.
Following behind it, to mop up pockets of resistance and thus allow
the tanks to keep moving forward, was 43 Infantry Division. Despite
the mopping up role, a portion of the division was to keep pace with
Guards Armoured and provide assistance in staking out the Arnhem
bridgehead. In fact, though keeping pace with Guards Armoured
on this axis was surely no great challenge, 43 Division managed to
fall well behind. Part of the reason was that they were snarled up in
traffic jams; the truck-borne infantry took 72 hours to cover only 55
miles. But there were also some remarkably ponderous minor actions
fought, in which whole brigades were swallowed up in clearing out
non-existent German remnants or mounting set-piece attacks against
the tiniest of garrisons. A real desire to close up to Arnhem seems
to have been almost entirely absent.

One leading historian of the operation has rightly pointed out
that in the winter fighting in the Reichswald and beyond, this
same 'tough line division was again to show its formidable fighting
qualities.'[53] But this is just the point. The fighting in the Reichswald,

---

* Though at least one journalist, Chester Wilmot, impatient as only his tribe can
be, showed the way by driving his jeep all along one verge.

in February 1945, was a dour, yard-by-yard slogging match with very discrete battalion objectives, maximum preparation and maximum fire-support. That was what Montgomery's army was good at. At bridge-hopping, it was less adept. Even Horrocks, though generally rated to have been a first-class exponent of mobile operations, did not show himself to advantage during Market Garden. At no stage, faced as he was with the lamentably limp efforts of both his forward divisions, does he seem to have made much effort to spur on his subordinates and inject a sense of urgency commensurate with the desperate situation at Arnhem. It is difficult to disagree with the commander of 1 Airborne, General 'Roy' Urquhart, who felt 'that for once Horrocks' enthusiasm was not transmitted adequately to those who served under him and it may be that some of his more junior officers and NCOs did not fully comprehend the problem and the importance of great speed.'[54]

But it is also surely true that some of Horrocks' senior commanders were equally devoid of zest, just as it is a fact that the one man who could bear down uponHorrocks was absent from the battlefield throughout and did not even make any attempt to buck up the latter's ideas from a distance. A plan conceived in haste and thus riddled with flaws, an absentee commander with his finger noticeably off the pulse of the battle, an inability to cope with a constricted axis of advance, troops of all ranks almost congenitally unsuited to mobile operations of this kind – given all this, one increasingly wonders how anyone could ever have supposed that Montgomery and his army would suddenly change their spots and become the sort of force capable of conducting a fast, concentrated, fully mobile thrust into the heart of Germany. The Panzer Armies of 1940–2 had been able to bring off operations of this kind because they were led by generals able to think on their feet* and who would take risks when the potential rewards were great enough. Moreover, these generals commanded subordinates imbued with these same ideas, and who were quite

---

* One contrasts this again with Montgomery's poor planning for Market Garden, or rather his toleration of others' poor planning. One authority has pointed out in Montgomery's defence that 'time . . . seemed always to be the missing element: time for clear thought, time for consultation, discussion and argument, time for . . . detailed and involved planning . . .' (G. Powell, *The Devil's Birthday: the Bridges to Arnhem 1944* (Buchan and Enright, 1984), p. 243.) This is perfectly true, of course, but the crucial point in my argument is that in operations of the kind Montgomery was envisaging, deep into Germany, time would always be at a premium and if his lack of it perforce involved shoddy planning then those operations would hardly get off to an auspicious start.

prepared to act on their own initiative when necessary. The army Montgomery claimed he could lead to Berlin was quite different, because he had created it in his own ponderous and ever-cautious image. To change it would have been the work of years.

There are, then, two main reasons why the 'debate' over the narrow thrust versus broad front strategy has always been somewhat artificial. For one thing, the narrow thrust advocated by Montgomery was totally unacceptable to the Americans purely in terms of national prestige.* For the other, even if Montgomery had been given his cherished opportunity, it is extremely unlikely that he and his army could have properly seized it.† There was, therefore, no real alternative to Eisenhower's broad front advance and the North-West European campaign settled into a familiar rut, the slow but remorseless application of overwhelming material preponderance. As far as *Bewegungskrieg* was concerned, the shots were not even on the table – for either side. For the Allies because it was neither appropriate to the strategy adopted nor feasible in the light of tactical and operational capabilities; for the Germans because they had neither the material back-up nor the psychological dominance to outmanoeuvre their opponents as of old.

Nothing showed this better than Hitler's Ardennes counter-offensive of December 1944. The operation has attracted enormous attention from military historians, but it was really little more than a

---

* Of course, this still left the option of an American narrow thrust, probably by Patton. However, for much of the campaign Eisenhower remained too much in awe of Montgomery's reputation to administer this sort of slap in the face. Moreover, even though the Americans could have ridden out the ensuing political storm, the outrage that would have been provoked in Britain – from Churchill to the popular press – would have done little to further the war effort.

† It was not only Montgomery's military doctrine and operational practice that were at issue, though these alone ruled out any real chance of storming through to Berlin. Two modern authorities have done their logistic sums and have concluded that though he might have got a substantial force as far as the Ruhr in September 1944, a drive to Berlin would have had to be on such a limited scale as to invite destruction, even by the meagre forces then available to the Germans. (See M. van Creveld, *Supplying War: Logistics from Wallenstein to Patton* (CUP, 1977), pp. 227–30, and R. F. Weighley, *Eisenhower's Lieutenants: the Campaigns of France and Germany 1944–45* (Sidgwick and Jackson, 1981), p. 281.) One wonders also whether Montgomery's tanks could have stood up to more hard pounding. The history of 11 Armoured Division tells us that by 3 September, in the six days since it had crossed the Seine, the division had travelled 340 miles. From the Normandy beachhead the distance covered had been 580 miles, *none* of which had been aboard tank transporters.

hiccup in the relentless unfolding of the campaign. True, Hitler made enormous efforts to build up the kind of strike force that had served him so well in 1940 and 1941, and on the eve of the offensive, which opened on 16 December, he had amassed 2,567 tanks and assault guns in the west, 1,241 of which were posted with the eight panzer and two panzer grenadier divisions involved in the Ardennes attack and perhaps a further 600 with the various panzer and assault gun battalions and brigades also involved.* In terms of hitting power this was a considerably more powerful force than those that had invaded France and Russia – the panzer divisions included 294 Panthers and 45 Tigers, some 44 per cent of the total *tank* strength, whilst all the rest were Panzer IVs – yet it made no decisive penetration into the Allied line.

Not surprisingly, this force did make a preliminary breakthrough of sorts, but not one that got deep into the American rear or, most important of all, that induced any lasting sense of panic or bewilderment among front-line troops or commanders. The oft-quoted anecdote about the commander of the encircled garrison at Bastogne, General Anthony McAuliffe, whose response to a German offer of surrender terms was the one-word reply 'Nuts!', is pertinent in that it bespeaks a sense of self-confidence that was simply not present in France and Belgium in 1940 or in Russia in 1941. More important still, however, was the material might that lay at the root of this self-confidence. OB West might have accumulated over 2,500 tanks and assault guns, but the Allies now had an establishment strength of 7,079 medium tanks alone.† And Allied replacement rates were of a quite different order to those of the Germans. Whereas 21 Army Group, which was hardly involved in the battle, sent forward 351 new Shermans to its units, the three German armies were assigned only 340 replacement tanks and assault guns, of which only 125 actually got forward. There were, moreover, only limited possibilities for battlefield repair: the whole German force was assigned only six tank repair companies,

---

* The three armies involved – Seventh and Fifth and Sixth Panzer – contained many familiar formations: 1 ss, 2 ss, 9 ss, 12 ss Panzer and 3 Panzer Grenadier Divisions in Sixth Panzer Army and 2, 9, 116 Panzer and *Panzer Lehr* in Fifth Panzer. Seventh Army included 15 Panzer Grenadier Division.
† The German build-up, moreover, had terrible repercussions for the already critical situation on the Eastern Front. In November and December, 2,300 tanks and assault guns were delivered to the west and only 900 to the east. This was hardly a generous allocation for the 34 panzer and panzer grenadier divisions stationed on this front.

and there were hardly any low-loaders to move crippled tanks to the rear.

But if it was American grit and firepower on the ground that robbed the German spearheads of their early momentum,* it was Allied airpower that ensured they never even got beyond the Meuse and forced Hitler to abandon the whole enterprise after only 18 days. As one source has noted, once the weather cleared completely on 24 December, 'the initiative was wrested entirely from the Germans . . . Allied fighter-bombers and medium and heavy bombers were all thrown in, and Allied ascendancy was such that German troop movements by day became almost impossible. The bombing of roads and railways in the rear was so successful that the supply situation, already bad, became catastrophic.[55†]

The Germans had, in fact, made a desperate effort to make available the maximum air support for this operation. By mid-December 2,295 aircraft were available on the Western Front as against only 1,500 held back to defend the Reich against the Bomber Offensive. But in terms of combat effectiveness, this impressive-sounding force was but a pale shadow of, for example, the 2,700 aircraft assigned to the 1940 and 1941 campaigns. Serviceability rates were dreadful, whilst a high proportion of those aircraft that did get into the air were little better than death-traps, especially to the half-trained youngsters who were required to fly them. An order of Göring's

* The Americans also derived great benefit from the difficult terrain. Whilst the Germans had found it fairly easy to drive through the Ardennes in May 1940, when the lack of enemy resistance made the operation almost like an exercise, it was a very different proposition $4^{1}/_{2}$ years later when the enemy was prepared to stand and fight. Then the poor roads, difficult terrain and execrable weather made it virtually impossible to concentrate the available firepower at a decisive *Schwerpunkt*. The commander of Sixth Panzer Army, Sepp Dietrich, was positively scathing about his mission, at least after it had failed: 'All I had to do was to cross the River [Meuse], capture Brussels, and then go on to take the port of Antwerp. The snow was waist deep and there wasn't room to deploy four tanks abreast, let alone six armoured divisions. It didn't get light till eight and it was dark again at four, and my tanks can't fight at night. And all this at Christmas.' (Quoted in M. Cooper and J. Lucas, *Panzer: the Armoured Force of the Third Reich* (Macdonald and Jane's, 1976), pp. 78–9.)

† The attack on the rearward depots was the most telling. Speer later confided: 'Transport difficulties were decisive in causing the swift breakdown of the Ardennes offensive . . . the most advanced railheads of the Reichsbahn were withdrawn further and further back during the offensive owing to the continuous air attacks.' (Quoted in J. F. C. Fuller, *The Second World War 1939–45* (Eyre and Spottiswoode, 1948), p. 348. See also R. Bennett, *Ultra in the West: the Normandy Campaign of 1944–45* (Hutchinson, 1979), p. 202.)

at this time underlined the extent of the problem. 'No pilot,' he fumed, 'is to turn back except for damage to the undercarriage: flights are to be continued even with misfiring engines. Failures of auxiliary tanks will not be accepted as an excuse for turning back.'[56]

Further evidence of the twin problems of poor serviceability and training is offered by the 'mass' air attack of 1 January, which was supposed to cripple the Allied Tactical Air Forces in their airfields in Holland and Belgium. Only something like 800 aircraft could be assembled for the operation and only 620 put into the air. The 'motley armada' included a precious training unit (*Jagdgeschwader* 104) and comprised 'every type of aircraft save the heavy bomber and light communications Storch. Instructors and experienced pilots had been drawn from bases as far away as Vienna and Prague.'[57] The latter were needed as formation leaders because most of the pilots could not be guaranteed to find their way to the target. The mission enjoyed a moderate amount of success, knocking out 134 Allied aircraft. The Germans, however, lost around 220 planes and an almost equal number of pilots, some of them the irreplaceable instructors. The real cost to each side was even more disproportionate. Allied losses represented roughly 0.5 per cent of the total combat aircraft available to SHAEF; the German losses were getting on for 30 per cent of their carefully husbanded strike force, the last one they would ever have in the west.

For the remainder of the campaign in this theatre, protracted though it proved to be, the *Wehrmacht* was waging an entirely hopeless struggle against overwhelming odds. So overwhelming, indeed, that it seems remarkable that the Germans were able to hang on for as long as they did. Of course, they could still call upon some powerful natural allies. There was, for example, the weather, which was usually bad in the Low Countries, the Rhineland and Lorraine, and which in the winter of 1944–5 was utterly appalling. In one letter to Marshall, Eisenhower was driven to complain: 'I am getting exceedingly tired of the weather. Every day we have some report of the weather that has broken records existing anywhere for twenty to twenty-five years.'[58] A British regimental history was moved to rare eloquence in describing the conditions between the Maas and the Roer and the 'physical agony of the infantryman' fighting forward through continuous freezing rain that 'seemed to penetrate the very marrow of every bone in the body, so that the whole shook as with ague, and then after shaking would come a numbness of hand and leg and mind, and a feeling of surrender to forces of nature far greater than any enemy might impose.'[59]

Terrain, too, was a serious handicap during this winter. The Low Countries and the Franco-German marchlands were largely made up of swampy heathland, river lines, forests, high hills and mountains, offering only narrow corridors into Germany which could be easily defended to deny the Allies the chance to make the most of their material superiority or to trap the Germans by manoeuvre. Of the opening phase of Operation Veritable, in February 1945, General Horrocks was to write: 'There was no room for manoeuvre and no scope for cleverness. I had to blast my way through three defensive systems, the centre of which was the Siegfried Line . . . After the initial attacks this was a battle in which generalship played no part at all: it developed into a slogging match in the mud between regimental officers, NCOs and men.'[60]

Even so, important as were the constraints imposed by weather and terrain, one cannot avoid the impression that the Allies did not make the most of their material advantages. General Guderian was surely correct when he told Allied interrogators 'that in the last months of the war Allied generals had practically no opposition and it was very easy for you to win the rest of the war. For you it was a supply and communications problem only. After arranging your supplies, victory was easy.'[61]

The relevant figures certainly confirm this analysis. The German tank situation, for example, after the build-up for the Ardennes counter-offensive, quickly deteriorated. The Allies, by the end of March 1945, had 24 armoured divisions, 11 armoured brigades and 39 independent tank battalions in N.W. Europe, an establishment strength of just over 8,000 medium tanks. German delivery figures of tanks and assault guns to OB West, in the first three months of 1945, were

January	443
February	67
March	134
Total	644

This figure did not go very far when spread between 13 panzer and panzer grenadier divisions and a number of independent battalions, particularly given that losses in the Ardennes operation had been upwards of 600 tanks.*

In fact, the post-Ardennes panzer divisions were never more than a shadow of their former selves. In February 1945, for example, in the Schnee Eifel, the three panzer divisions available totalled no more than 70 tanks and assault guns, not much more than an American tank battalion. In the following month, General Bayerlein was assigned four panzer divisions for the high-priority task of crushing the Remagen bridgehead. His force totalled no more than 60 tanks and 5,000 men. At this stage one of these divisions, 11 Panzer, mustered four tanks only and another, *Panzer Lehr*, counted just four more as well as eleven tank destroyers. On 5 April, 11 Panzer had no tanks at all, though it had acquired four assault guns and ten tank destroyers. On 25 April this division had twelve tanks and ten self-propelled anti-tank guns yet was still regarded as 'by far the prime unit' in Seventh Army and had more armoured fighting vehicles than the rest of the Army put together. On 28 April Army Group Centre and Seventh Army, by now virtually back to back, conferred about a counter-attack the latter was planning. The Army Group gravely informed its western neighbour that it could spare seven tanks but these must be returned without fail on the following day.

Things were no better for those divisions facing 21 Army Group. The history of one British armoured division points out that throughout the closing months of the war, 'the resistance to our armour was coming increasingly from infantry [with bazookas] rather than from other tanks.' By early April it was still the case that 'not since Antwerp had any part of the division been attacked by enemy tanks. We had met tanks, it is true, usually in ones and twos . . . but these engagements had been fought by our own armoured units who were invariably the attacking side.'[62]

But it was not just in tanks that the German Army was deficient. The whole organisation, by the last year of the war, was on the verge of collapse, virtually incapable, one might have thought, of putting up a coherent defence. Of First Parachute Army, which barred Montgomery's way into Germany, one of its opponents wrote:

> . . . although General Student's forces nominally contained divisions, the combatant formation was almost invariably the

* Sixth Panzer Army was pulled out of the Ardennes salient on 8 January, well before other formations, and on 22 January moved over to the Eastern Front. On its arrival, the whole army, an élite formation, mustered only 128 tanks.

battle-group, an organisation designed to afford the maximum of flexibility. For the German manpower situation was now so chaotic, and their transport so disorganised that flexibility had become the first essential of their units. Such bodies must now be able to absorb stragglers and accept reinforcements of whatever kind, and they must fight on in their allotted positions, not relying upon the arrival of guns to support them or other troops to relieve them. In the current state of German communications they could not depend on knowing the situation elsewhere, not even on their immediate flanks, and even if a withdrawal were planned the order to implement it might never reach them.[63]

All units were in similarly parlous states. Hitler's obsession with building more and more new divisions (from September 1944 twenty-five *Volksgrenadier* divisions appeared on the Western Front) meant that existing formations were continually starved of replacements. By the end of 1944 the old divisions, even though their original aggregate establishment had been cut by 700,000 thanks to a reduction in the tables of organisation, were still 800,000 men short.

What this meant on the battlefield can be seen from the orders of battle for two of Montgomery's battles, in February and March. In Operation Veritable, First Canadian Army launched two armoured divisions, three armoured brigades and five infantry divisions against two German infantry divisions and a parachute regiment. The latter force possessed no armour and only 100 artillery pieces. 'Further, the many different calibres of guns made the ammunition problem almost insoluble. In any case there was an acute shortage at this time and some guns had only twenty rounds of ammunition available. A daily divisional artillery allotment was twenty-five rounds.'[64] The Canadian attack, on the other hand, was preceded by the heaviest barrage of the whole war. On hand were 122 heavy guns (240mm, 8-inch, 7.2-inch and 155mm), 280 4.5 and 5.5-inch, 72 3.7-inch anti-aircraft, and 576 25-pdrs.

Similar strength ratios applied during Operation Plunder, Montgomery's set-piece crossing of the Rhine on 2 March. The main British assault force was XII Corps, which had under command one armoured division, two armoured brigades, three infantry divisions and an infantry and a commando brigade. Opposing it were two German divisions, a parachute and an infantry. 7 Parachute Division's three regiments numbered less than one thousand troops all told, whilst 84 Division's three regiments amounted to only five hundred, almost all of whom were raw replacements. The paratroopers had 25 or so field guns, 20 mortars, four 7.5cm anti-tank guns and four 88mm. 84 Division had ten field guns and two 7.5cm anti-tank. There were perhaps another 30 field and medium guns from non-divisional sources. XII Corps, on the other hand, could call upon the following guns:

	25-pdr	Rocket launchers	3.7-in. mountain	3.7-in. A.A.	4.5-in.	5.5-in.	155 mm	7.2-in.	8-in.	240 mm
Divisional	312	12	24	16	16	32	-	-	-	-
Non-div.	24	-	-	80	-	128	52	16	2	4
TOTAL	336	12	24	96*	16	160	52	16	2	4

* 48 of these were used in a ground role.

This was a grand total of 670 guns used in a ground role, to which can be added a divisional complement of 1,500 mortars. But this kind of superiority was duplicated all down the Rhine. An American officer who took part in Ninth us Army's own crossing, Operation Flashpoint, spoke for the whole of 21 Army Group when he told an interviewer, 'There was no real fight. The artillery had done the job for us.'[65]

Such a material disparity was to vitiate all further German attempts to stem the Allied tide. In the air, the German presence became almost negligible. Throughout 1945, in North-West Europe, the Allies were putting up something like 4,000 sorties daily as against only 300 German and the *Luftwaffe* was losing aircraft in combat at the rate of 7 to 1. By April 1945 the Allies could deploy 28,000 combat aircraft in this theatre alone. Almost exactly half of these were American, including 6,000 fighters and 5,500 heavy bombers. The Germans, for their part, had 1,164 fighters on hand. But as this represented the total number of aircraft theoretically available to fly, it can be safely assumed that fuel and pilot shortages as well as mechanical faults reduced the figure by well over 50 per cent. The lack of training of most of the pilots who were available reduced the combat effectiveness of these *Luftwaffe* remnants even further.

The pathetic straits to which the *Wehrmacht* was reduced in the closing weeks of the war is best summed up in two vignettes. The first is provided by one of this campaign's more recent historians, who notes that 'by 27 March the Germans had been in many cases reduced to using oxen to draw their guns, and a captured artillery officer told his interrogators: "What is the use of having a battery if you have neither petrol nor ammunition?" while German staff officers argued whether farm carts should be used for barricades or for transport.'[66] Leaders of what had once been the world's most efficient mechanised army were now engaged in wranglings in which Wallenstein or Gustavus Adolphus would have felt at home. But even they might have been a little taken aback by the sheer viciousness of the following pronouncement by General Paul Hausser, commanding Army Group G in February 1945:

> The combination of depleted units, and the deployment of youthful and inadequate reinforcements, have had an untoward effect on morale. Moreover, the front is so wide that the influence of officers and Party officials is no longer as effective as it might be. Hence the danger of desertion has increased, and preventive measures are urgently needed. One of our Armies has accordingly asked that the measures regarding the arrest of family hostages be made known to the troops. It should, however, be remembered that the threat of arresting dependents has lost much of its force, particularly when the families concerned are in enemy-occupied territory.[67]

The vindictive plaintiveness of the final sentence is as good an example as any of the military imbecility of the German high command in this last stage of the war, as they refused to come to terms with the utter hopelessness of their situation.*

But it seems equally clear that the Allies failed to make the most of their enormous advantages. Although, as has been indicated earlier, it is unfair to overlook the powerful political pressures that obliged Eisenhower to adopt his ponderous broad front strategy, one still cannot avoid the impression that at times its execution lacked

---

* Those who took part in the March and April fighting might well object to such a cursory appraisal of its military significance. Certain regimental histories do show, in fact, that casualties rose appreciably in these months. Two British battalions in N.W. Europe recorded the following battle deaths:

	J	J	A	S	O	N	D	J	F	M	A	M
5 Coldstream	11	32	47	50	7	3	1	1	17	21	36	-
5 KOSLI	10	49	45	44	27	4	2	3	9	15	49	2

But the fact remains that the figures for these latter months only reveal local, tactical difficulties in the face of obdurate resistance from small groups of ss men and Hitler Youth fighting rearguard actions. They do not signify any meaningful strategic threat to the overall Allied advance.

imagination. Again one concedes the deleterious effects of weather and terrain, as well as the defences of the Siegfried Line, but it still comes as something of a disappointment to find 12 Army Group, on 12 December, summing up future operations in a manner reminiscent of Falkenhayn at Verdun:

> All of the enemy's major capabilities . . . depend on the balance between the rate of attrition imposed by the Allied offensives and the rate of infantry reinforcement. The balance at present is in favour of the Allies and with continuing Allied pressure in the south and in the north, the breaking point may develop suddenly and without warning.[68]

There is certainly considerable evidence that the Americans all too rarely attempted to hurry the breaking point by manoeuvre or operational subtlety of any kind. The central role of German fortresses such as Aachen and Metz in American operations is in itself an indication of their reluctance to think in terms of turning a position rather than tackling it head-on. In September 1944, for example, Bradley missed a definite opportunity to outflank the Siegfried Line south of Aachen, at a time when the defences between there and Trier were, according to Model, 'very thin and totally inadequate', held by 'only seven or eight battalions on a front of 120 kilometres.'[69]* Instead, Bradley had insisted on going through the Aachen Gap, a traditional route into Germany and therefore the most likely one to be well defended. His resolve to take this route did not falter even after the severity of the Aachen fighting. In November, with the city itself taken, he clung to this same axis in his drive to the Roer and the Rhine. Hereabouts, between the Hürtgen Forest and Geilenkirchen, German defences were known to be quite formidable but

> Bradley's plan did not provide for any preliminary diversion, nor even a holding attack, against the long and thinly-garrisoned front facing the Ardennes. He intended to rely on being able to crush the defences east of Aachen with an overwhelming bombardment by aircraft and artillery and to 'steam-roller' his way through in what General Marshall was to describe as 'a

---

* A German panzer commander was of the same opinion, telling Allied interrogators: 'If the American tanks had only continued their advance, having passed through the break in the West Wall south of Aachen, they could have occupied the town on the same day. No-one was there to resist them.' (G. von Schwerin, '116 Pz Div from the Seine to Aachen', Pamphlet ETHINT-18, p. 35, in D. S. Detweiler *et al.* (eds), *World War II German Military Studies*, Garland, New York, 1979, vol. 2.)

charging offensive' . . . The story of the attack which followed is summed up in one sentence from the history of Ninth Army: 'The enemy knowing how the attack must come, had only to block it head-on and inflict the maximum casualties.'[70]

Another city that seemed to mesmerise the Americans in September 1944 was Metz, and the entanglement of Patton's Third Army thereabouts has already been noted earlier in the chapter. There we saw that many of Patton's problems sprang from a shortage of fuel and supplies that had been diverted to Montgomery, but it is worth while emphasising here that, with or without these logistic difficulties, 12 Army Group was pursuing a singularly unimaginative strategy. Not because the Americans were advancing on a broad front, but because the *points d'appui* on that front were two widely separated fortresses instead of the thinly held hills between them, the Ardennes. It is not merely a yearning for poetic justice that suggests that far better use could have been made of this axis, but the real possibility that significant progress could have been made and would inevitably have forced the Germans to loosen their grip on one or other of the twin pillars of Aachen and Metz. As Professor Weighley has pointed out:

If the SHAEF planners had not ruled out the Ardennes as an invasion route [which planners' word Eisenhower seems to have taken as law], if the Schwerpunkt of Hodges' First Army had been aimed here instead of at the heavy fortifications in the Stolberg corridor, if the First Army had not been yoked to the British Second Army and the latter's weaknesses but had moved in tandem with the Third – these are probably more critical might-have-beens than the much debated ones of Field Marshal Montgomery's early autumn frustrations.[71]

Nor was this the only evidence of a rather heavy-handed predictability in American operations. To the south, in 6 Army Group's sector, tactics were often overly cautious and allowed the Germans a respite they never expected. During the pursuit into the northern Vosges, in mid-November, General von Mellenthin felt that the Americans were 'hesitant and cautious'. Even when they did show more aggression, flair remained conspicuously absent. Of attacks in this sector in March, Field Marshal Kesselring, who took over as OB West on the 10th, wrote: 'What clearly emerged was the rapid succession of operations . . . as well as the complacency of command

and the almost reckless engagement of armoured units in terrain that was quite unsuited to the use of heavy tanks.'[72]

Another fastness that the Americans would have done well to avoid was the Hürtgen Forest, just to the south of Aachen. The dense and dark terrain, worthy of the grimmest fairy-tale vision, formed a tactical quagmire for any attacking force. In September and October, however, the Americans insisted on plunging straight in, claiming that it represented a serious threat to their right flank. This was doubtful, as the Forest sheltered only one weak infantry division and was too dense to screen the assembly of a substantial force. By attacking into the Forest the Americans both multiplied the combat effectiveness of the incumbent division, fighting from strong prepared positions, and nullified the effects of their own aircraft, artillery and tanks. A German general was astounded when the Americans attacked: 'There was no use the Americans going through the Hürtgen Forest, as it was easy to see it would be hard to take and easy to defend. Had you gone around it on both sides, you would have had almost no opposition. We did not have enough troops in the area at the time. Also, had you bypassed the area, we could not have launched a big counter-attack there, not with the army of 1944.'[73]

Worse still, these battles continued into November and December, with American commanders seemingly resigned to mindless repetitions of Grant's Wilderness battle in 1864 and Pershing's Argonne offensive of 1918 and convinced that such wooded charnel houses were an inevitable feature of war. In fact, simple options were to hand, even in November and December. German positions on either side of the Hürtgen were not as flimsy then as they had been in autumn, but the southern flank, in particular, offered a much easier route to Schmidt and the Roer Dams.* General Gavin has pointed out that here ran a good approach road for tanks and one that bypassed the river valley that was proving such a killing ground for the American infantry. 'Why not stick to . . . [this] high ground, bypassing the Germans in the valley, and then go on to the Roer River? I raised this question with a Corps staff officer present,

---

* In the heady days of September the Hürtgen forest had been seen as part of the route to the Rhine. By November the immediate goal was the Roer Dams, which the Germans might burst to flood out the First Army's chosen axis. SHAEF planners as well as Eisenhower's and Bradley's staffs must be deemed remiss in not noting that this vulnerability, and the harsh necessity of capturing the Roer Dams to safeguard this axis, was another reason for looking long and hard towards the Ardennes. In the event the Roer Dams were blown on 9 February, which set back a major American offensive (Operation Grenade) for a further fortnight.

but he brushed it aside. I asked why in the world they had attacked through the Hürtgen Forest in the first place, but apparently that was a "no-no" question.'[74]

Any discussion of American generalship in the last months of the war must also take account of General Patton, if only because of his own assertion that 'compared to them [his fellow officers] I am a genius – I think I am.'[75] Unfortunately, Patton's actual record only serves to underline a point made in the last chapter, that though he was a masterly logistician who could do things on a limited road net that most formations would require a computer to work out, he was not a particularly successful combat commander. He himself would have pointed with pride to his handling of the Palatinate campaign in March 1945 or his eruption from his Rhine bridgeheads in April. But the same qualifications already applied to his advance to the Meuse are also pertinent in these two cases. Speaking of the Palatinate campaign, the advance from the Saar to the Rhine, one commentator noted that prior to it

> virtually all the German armour remaining on the Western Front had been drawn into the lower Rhineland . . . six of von Rundstedt's eight armoured divisions . . . [being] north of Cologne . . . Patton's sweep through the Palatinate was the counterpart of his 'end run' south of the bocage. Once again the German left flank was [already] broken and turned and, as in France, there were no reserves to restore the line.[76]

German resistance to Patton's drive out of his Rhine bridgeheads was, if anything, even less troublesome. There were some flickers of obduracy against the actual river assaults, on 25 March,* but *concerted* resistance thereafter was minimal: a handful of fanatics at a roadblock or a few snipers in a wood or village were the usual cause of delays and casualties. Once again I would emphasise that no slur is intended on those who had to undertake these last river crossings or deal with these last-ditch zealots. For them the problem of life and death loomed just as large as in a full-scale offensive against a coordinated defence line. Nevertheless, as far as divisional, corps and army commanders were concerned, the campaign of April 1945 was little more than an armed procession.

In such circumstances Patton was in his element; where the opposition was more spirited he was considerably less impressive.

* One bridgehead, at Oppenheim, had already been taken on the run, on 22 March.

In such situations, indeed, one begins to question his tactical acumen. The scathing criticisms of General Max Simon with regard to his handling of armour in set-piece attacks have already been cited, and the following nugget of Patton's own operational lore glisters less than gold. In a letter to his wife, in December 1944, he explained that he had attacked the Siegfried Line at what was, in his sector, its strongest part 'because a straight line is the shortest distance between points and also . . . [this part] is so strong that it is probably not too well defended.' Another revealing remark was that made in a letter to Stimson, in January 1945, when he wrote: 'The ability of American troops to manoeuvre when properly led is wonderful. Their ability to fight is not so good.'[77] The remark might make more sense if directed at Patton himself, for it pithily sums up both his good and bad sides. On the one hand there was his tremendous talent for probing into a disintegrating defence, selecting the optimum axes, and pouring his men through hell-for-leather. But on the other was a much less sure grasp of the attack proper, of the necessity to pin with fire whilst other units seek for relatively weak points, to be aware which points should be pinned and which probed, and to have an instinctive feel for the moment when probing should turn to barrage and bombardment and when to actual attack. In other words, Patton could manoeuvre wonderfully, but his ability to make his men fight effectively was not so good.

This was seen in November, for example, during the fighting towards the River Saar. Faced with cohesive, if weak, German positions on the 8th, Patton could think of nothing better than to attack all along his part of the line, turning the doctrine of fire and movement into one of 'everybody fire and everybody move'. His refusal to wait for an abatement in the weather, which was denying his troops any air cover, did little to enhance his chances of a breakthrough. 'With every division trying to make a breakthrough, the artillery support was dispersed and . . . [the attack] was able to gain only fifteen miles in eight days. The German line sagged, but did not break, for at no point was it subjected to an overpowering onslaught.'[78]

Perhaps the clearest example of the two very different facets of Patton's generalship was his role in the Battle of the Bulge. Soon after the German attack started he was ordered by Bradley to suspend all operations eastward and to send units north. Patton said three divisions could be turned around in 24 hours. These were already on their way when Eisenhower next asked him to bring the major portion of Third Army to bear on the southern flank of the salient, primarily around the important road junction at Bastogne. Patton's seemingly off-the-cuff estimate of how long it would take him to make a total realignment of his axis – only 72 hours – was greeted with disbelief by his fellow generals. But Patton attacked exactly on time, on the morning of 22 December, with two corps totalling seven divisions in all.

Thereafter, however, his progress was less good. Professor Weighley's summary of events again perfectly illustrates Patton's ungainliness when attacking fixed positions, even fairly weak ones:

> Patton forsook the advantages of a concentration . . . in favour of yet another broad-front effort to go forward everywhere. In the end, Patton accepted Eisenhower's adjurations to attack on a large scale that undermined all ideas of going like hell . . . He substituted breadth for depth . . . [and] so wide was the front that, far from advancing in column of regiments, the divisions were hard put to keep their regiments in touch with each other's flanks. The outcome was another slugging match in which the breadth of the front dissipated American strength enough to compensate considerably for German weakness.[79]

In fact, although Patton was facing an 'outnumbered, outgunned, outarmoured force holding a hopelessly overextended line', it took him 'five days to advance one armoured column, the westernmost, into Bastogne, another week to push the Germans away from the southern perimeter and a further two weeks to drive through to Houffalize.'[80] How long he might have taken without the benefit of massive superiority in ground and airborne firepower can only be guessed. But certainly rather too long for a genius.

Another commander who hardly enhanced his reputation in the last months of the war was Montgomery. His operations since the closing down of Market Garden had been decidedly lack-lustre, though the enormous difficulties of the ground and the climate did much to excuse the two months it took to clear the Peel Marshes, between October and December, and the long, bloody slogging match in Walcheren and Beveland, which were not finally cleared until 8 November. But one cannot pass quite so lightly over Montgomery's strange behaviour during the early drives to the Maas Bend and the Roer. A German pocket here, around Venlo, had been under attack for some days and by mid-October was on the point of being cleared. On the 17th, however, Montgomery suddenly deprived the Corps operating there of a reinforcement division and the attack ground to a halt. This gave the Germans time to strengthen their positions and renewed attacks later did not clear the pocket until 4 December. The division so rudely snatched away was destined to be used in the Scheldt operations, admittedly a matter of increasing urgency for SHAEF, but it does seem that Montgomery might have left it in place for the 48 hours that the local commanders felt was all that was required to draw up to the Maas.

Like Patton, Montgomery did not really shine during the Allied counter-offensive in the Ardennes. On 20 December, to simplify command arrangements, he was given *temporary* charge of all Allied forces on the northern (only) side of the salient. At a press conference on 7 January, however, he managed to give the impression that all counter-measures were entirely his idea and that but for him the Americans would have made a complete hash of things. In fact, Montgomery's part in the major operational decisions was minimal and, moreover, what part he did play was almost entirely negative.*

Two points stand out. The first is his remarkable timidity regarding the Allies' own counter-attack against the German 'Bulge'. The most obvious strategy would have been to attack at either side of its base and chop off all three German armies therein. This was considered, by the Americans at least, but they felt that the time consumed in shifting First and Third Armies eastwards to build up suitable strike forces might allow the Germans too many opportunities to develop their own attacks. They preferred, therefore, to attack the waist of the salient, converging from north and south on Houffalize. This was a somewhat conservative option, making it impossible to bag anything but a portion of the German force. But even half a *Kessel* is better than none, and Montgomery's own proposal, that the counter-attack be made at Celles, against the western tip of the German penetration, was breath-takingly inadequate. 'Montgomery's idea made no sense in terms of any large offensive . . . To attack at Celles was so modest a method that Montgomery's preference for it can scarcely be explained, except as an expression of no confidence in First Army's ability to accomplish anything more ambitious.'[81] In fact, though it is true that Montgomery had always rather mistrusted American capabilities, this extremely limited objective is perfectly

* For an excellent statement of just how limited Montgomery's contribution was see C. B. MacDonald, *A Time for Trumpets: the Untold Story of the Battle of the Bulge* (Morrow, New York, 1985), pp. 611–13.

consistent with his military career as a whole and his pathological fear of sustaining any sort of rebuff.

Eventually he was persuaded to accept Houffalize as the objective, presumably because American troops could carry the can if necessary. But he still refused to launch his northern thrust as quickly as Eisenhower and other American commanders wanted. The latter hoped to jump off on 1 January but Montgomery refused to budge until the 3rd, claiming that further strong German attacks were to be expected. Eisenhower persisted and eventually Montgomery did agree to attack on the 1st if these attacks did not materialise.* They did not, but unfortunately neither did Montgomery's, and when Patton duly attacked on the 1st the Germans were able to pull units out of the still quiescent northern front and blunt his momentum. Deaf to American anger at his duplicity – only de Guingand's personal intervention saved Montgomery from being ordered to get on or get out – the Field Marshal lumbered into action on the 3rd and fought a 'tidy battle, phase line by phase line, that would slowly close the door of the barn by pushing the Germans back on their supply bases and their frontier.'[82]

This latter point remains the major issue arising out of Montgomery's conduct during the Ardennes battle. From the very beginning – true to the track record he had established at Alamein, Falaise and Antwerp – he remained incapable of seeing the forces under his command as anything other than a croupier's rake, slowly pushing the enemy before them back to their start line. At no stage did he envision operations that might cut off enemy formations and envelop them, in short destroy them for good. Worse still, he remained completely unaware of how second-rate his chosen strategy was. It was this immense smugness in the face of his own mediocrity that made his performance at the 7 January press conference so distasteful. In it he spoke of throwing in formations 'with a bang' and of the enemy being 'written off' as a 'heavy toll . . . [was being] taken of his divisions by ground and air action.' A heavy toll, perhaps, but what was *not* happening, and what never did happen in a Montgomery battle, was that armies were written off. Once again substantial numbers of enemy troops escaped as well as the staffs and cadres who would provide some sort of homogeneity and leadership to the raw replacements. Montgomery, however, could not see it. The

* The assurance was verbal and thus Eisenhower's claims must remain unverifiable. For a lucid summary of this episode see S. E. Ambrose, *Eisenhower: the Soldier 1890–1952* (Allen and Unwin, 1984), pp. 374–5.

enemy thrust had failed and he was now being pushed back to his start line. That for Montgomery was total victory. His complacency has evoked a real anger in Professor Weighley, who states that amongst Montgomery's 'defects of character' was his

remarkable capacity to derive complete satisfaction from a victory so manifestly incomplete as the Ardennes . . . The enemy . . . was not being 'written off'. Montgomery betrayed no regrets about this less than satisfactory outcome . . . His generalship had nothing in it of the Clausewitzian conviction that war is 'an act of force to compel our opponent to fulfil our will,' and that if he is to be made to fulfil our will, the opponent must be disarmed completely, or at the least threatened with complete loss of his capacity to make war. Montgomery's aggressiveness was that of the energetic fencer, not that of the general who annihilates enemy armies, of Napoleon, of Grant, of Moltke.[83]

Nothing that Montgomery did in the remaining months of the war causes one to revise this judgement. Indeed, 'energetic fencer' rather overstates the case, for it was his ponderous unadventurousness that shone through to the very end. So it was as he approached the Rhine, preparatory to the great assault that was supposed to drive through to Berlin. Though German positions east of this river were, as has already been seen, very weak, Montgomery would not hear of any attempt to capitalise upon this. Thus, when Simpson's Ninth US Army, under Montgomery's command, expressed a desire to force a crossing on the run, between Düsseldorf and Duisburg, in the first week of March, the Field Marshal refused to permit it. Even Chester Wilmot, a staunch Montgomery supporter, was forced to admit that Allied operations were now being badly hobbled by his 'insistence on tight control and balance . . . his inflexible pursuit of his planned purpose'. This, Wilmot claims, had once

been a source of strength; now it was a weakness. The master of the set-piece assault and 'tidy battle', he did not appear to realise that American 'untidiness' and improvisation, however dangerous when the enemy was strong, could now yield great dividends. An improvised crossing of the Rhine, even in the 'wrong' place, might disturb his own plans, but it promised to disrupt and confound the enemy's.[84]

It also seems more than possible that this particular decision sprang not just from Montgomery's extreme caution and rigidity of mind but also from baser motives. Throughout March, he looked on his own Operation Plunder* as the centre-piece of Allied operations, and feared that any surprise bouncing of the river by Ninth Army, however militarily advantageous, would deny him the publicity attendant on a formal offensive. Worse, it would divert some of that publicity to General Simpson, an American commander. Unpalatable as such an accusation is, it is only thus that one can explain a parallel decision by Montgomery that his own crossing could be carried out without the assistance of Ninth Army. Or at least without the assistance of Simpson's headquarters, which was where rival claims to the limelight might originate. American blood was not to be spurned, and one corps from Ninth Army was taken under Second Army command. Moreover, 'with a marked lack of consistency, given his reluctance to use US Ninth Army, Montgomery also badgered Eisenhower for an additional ten American divisions in order to guarantee success.'[85] But Eisenhower, inadvertently or otherwise, rather exposed Montgomery when he suggested that the divisions might be made available as long as Bradley and his headquarters could command all American troops used in the crossing. Montgomery swiftly decided that he did not need the American divisions after all.†

A final point about Plunder was, once again, the inordinate lead time that Montgomery deemed necessary. Though Simpson had been ready to bounce the river on the 4th or 5th, Montgomery did not move until the 23rd. Chester Wilmot contented himself with saying that the Field Marshal 'might have attacked sooner than he did'.[86] But it was a German commander who properly exposed the consequences of Montgomery's delay:

> There was no doubt that Allied strategy was not on a high level at this period of the war; it was rigid, inflexible and tied to preconceived plans. The whole German defence on the lower Rhine was collapsing, but the Allied leaders would not allow their subordinates to exploit success. Everything had to wait until Montgomery had prepared an elaborate setpiece attack and was ready to cross the river according to plan. Thus Field Marshal Model's Army Group B was given a new lease

* There were also Operations Varsity and Turnscrew, respectively an airborne drop over the Rhine and a subsidiary attack to the left of Plunder by XXX Corps.
† Montgomery was eventually prevailed upon to let Ninth Army's Corps cross under its parent HQ. Certain British bridges were also allocated to Simpson so that he could hasten the American build-up.

of life and the long agony in the West was prolonged for a few weeks.[87]*

The final advance into Germany did little to encourage a reappraisal of Montgomery's laboured performance. That these operations were less than spectacular is hardly his fault, for his orders on the 28th had explicitly stated that his role thenceforward was to be a supporting one. Patton himself would have been hard put to present an advance to the Baltic, to safeguard Allied access to the Danish peninsula, against negligible opposition, as a war-winning manoeuvre. He might, nevertheless, have acted a little more promptly than Montgomery. On the 27th the latter made another of his ritualistic obeisances to *Bewegungskrieg* and issued orders that Second and Ninth Armies 'should advance with maximum speed and energy to the Elbe . . . Great emphasis was made on the need to "get the whips out" and lead the advance with fast moving armoured spearheads, capturing airfields on the way to ensure their subsequent use for close air support.'[88] Actual operations fell somewhat short of this laudable goal.† Bradley felt that he moved 'at a turtlelike pace', the advance 'from the Rhine to Lübeck . . . [being] one of the most cautious and uninspired of the war. It began with flamboyant overkill on the Rhine in a typical Monty set-piece and petered out to his usual desultory pursuit and reluctance to go for the jugular, to make the kill, to take risks.'[89]

Once Montgomery actually reached the Elbe, on 20 April, he dawdled for so long in his preparations for a crossing that Eisenhower actually wrote to Brooke expressing his fears that the Russians might well get to Lübeck and the neck of the Danish peninsula first, and appealing to him to urge Montgomery forward.‡ On

* The extent of Montgomery's over-cautiousness was underlined by the fact that the staking out of the bridgehead, for which he had allocated two weeks, was completed within only five days.
† It might be argued that these orders were issued when Montgomery still believed his was the vanguard role in a drive to Berlin. But it would surely be unpardonable for a commander suddenly to lower the tempo of his operations just because he no longer had a starring role. Particularly as Montgomery had assured Eisenhower, on 8 April, that he was quite happy with his new role: 'It is quite clear to me what you want. I will crack along on the northern flank one hundred per cent and will do all I can to draw the enemy forces away from the main effort being made by Bradley.' (Quoted in R. Lamb, *Montgomery in Europe 1943–45* (Buchan and Enright, 1983), p. 380.)
‡ On 27 April, after being rebuked by Eisenhower for his tardiness, Montgomery actually had the gall to say that delays in crossing the river were due to his not having Ninth Army under command.

27 April he prevailed upon the Field Marshal to accept General Matthew Ridgway's XVIII Airborne Corps, a formation which included an American armoured and infantry division. On the 30th, having been rushed forward from the Ruhr, the Corps crossed the Elbe and quickly showed how unnecessary had been Montgomery's elaborate preparations. Ridgway sped forward to Wismar, blocking the Russians, and *en route* accepted the surrender of 360,000 German troops. General Gavin wrote that Bradley later 'said there was much laughter in his 12 Army Group h.q. when they heard of . . . [this] accomplishment . . . Montgomery had been complaining that the opposition was too great for him to cross the Elbe River. When the 82nd [Airborne Division] crossed it, it advanced thirty-six miles the first day and captured 100,000 prisoners.'[90]

There was good reason for their derision, though they might have done well to reflect that progress such as Ridgway's had been uncommon in *any* Allied army for almost all of the North-West European campaign. Except in the most favourable circumstances, when the Germans were in headlong retreat or when the imminence of complete defeat became apparent to all, Americans, British, Canadians, Frenchmen, Poles had all inched forwards with extreme circumspection, only making such progress as they did by resort to an overwhelming superiority of fire. Nazi Germany was bludgeoned to death, and such operations as Ridgway's advance beyond the Elbe, or Patton's barn-storming joy-ride at the other end of the Allied flank, from the Main to Nuremberg, were simply mortician's flourishes.

PART FIVE

'ONE HELL OF A WAY TO RUN A WAR'

The Pacific, December 1941 – August 1945

'If we can make a plan for unified command [in the Pacific] now it will solve nine-tenths of our problems.'

Admiral Ernest King USN, 24 December 1941

'Our fighters were nothing but so many eggs thrown at the stone wall of the indomitable enemy formation.'

Vice-Admiral Shigeru Fukudome,
Formosa, 12 October 1944

9

Collapse and Containment

December 1941 – February 1943

In September 1940 Admiral Isoruku Yamamoto, the Commander-in-Chief of the Imperial Japanese Navy (IJN), discussed with Prince Konoye, a leading proponent of Japanese expansion in Asia, the likely outcome of a war with the United States. He was less than encouraging, stating bluntly: 'If I am told to fight regardless of the consequences I shall run wild considerably for the first six months or the first year, but I have absolutely no confidence for the second and third years.'[1] The following July another admiral, Osami Nagano, the Chief of the Naval General Staff, expressed similar reservations. At one Cabinet meeting he stated:

> As for war with the United States, although there is now a chance of achieving victory, the chances will diminish as time goes on. By the latter half of next year it will already be difficult for us to cope with the United States; after that the situation will become increasingly worse . . . If we conclude that conflict cannot ultimately be avoided, then I would like you to understand that as time goes by we will be in a disadvantageous position.

In September he told a meeting of service chiefs and ministers that, although he agreed that a surprise attack on Pearl Harbor gave Japan 'a chance to win the war', he nevertheless felt that the Japanese empire was even then

> getting weaker. By contrast the enemy is getting stronger. With the passage of time, we will get increasingly weaker, and we won't be able to survive . . . Regarding war, the navy thinks both in terms of a short war and a long one. I think it will probably be a long war. We hope that the enemy will come

out for a quick showdown . . . But I do not believe that the
war would end with that. It would be a long war . . . [But] if
. . . we get into a long war without a decisive battle, we will be
in difficulty especially since our supply of resources will become
depleted. If we cannot obtain these resources, it will not be
possible to carry on a long war.[2]

Even before the war began, therefore, two of the most senior
officers in the Japanese Navy were sharply aware that their chances
of victory in a Pacific war were far from good. Above all they
perceived that if such a war were to become a protracted struggle
then the vastly superior economic capacity of the United States must
make her eventual victory inevitable. For war over such vast expanses
of ocean was not simply a matter of men, no matter how skilful or
dedicated to nation and Emperor, but also of matériel. What would
count in the long run were the merchant ships to carry reinforcements
and supplies, the naval vessels to keep the sea-lanes clear, and the
aircraft, carrier-borne and land-based, to provide an aerial umbrella
for these tasks. And if the war were to be a matter of years rather
than months, then there was no hope that the Japanese could keep
up with American production of such hardware. Even if they quickly
succeeded in achieving their major war aim, the seizure of the Dutch
East Indies and their precious raw materials, even if they managed
to protect these conquests by fortifying a defensive cordon all the way
from Sumatra to Wake, and even though the United States would
be obliged to concentrate vastly superior forces to crack any portion
of such a well-garrisoned line, even then American industrial might,
given sufficient resolution, would surely prevail in the end.

But here was the crucial point – the enemy's resolution. At first
sight – and Yamamoto and Nagano were far from being lone voices
crying in the wilderness* – one might wonder why Japan ever risked
war in the first place, knowing that a protracted struggle must
eventually turn against her. The answer is simply that her leaders
never envisaged that a war with the United States would last more
than a few months. Just like Hitler in Europe, they were convinced
that the Western democracies were utterly degenerate and that a few

* Several officers were less than cheered by the outcome of a large-scale Navy map
exercise in spring 1940. This showed that a protracted war with the United States
would be one in which Japanese 'chances of winning would be nil'. (R. Spector,
Eagle Against the Sun (Free Press, New York, 1985), p. 144.) Unfortunately,
neither the Naval Minister nor the Naval Chief of Staff felt it necessary to report
these conclusions either to the rest of the government or even to the Army.

early military reverses would precipitate political collapse. After the war, the members of the United States Strategic Bombing Survey, having conducted exhaustive interviews with Japanese commanders and politicians, uncovered the fundamental precept behind their decision to resort to arms:

> A genuine war of attrition, in which the United States would turn the tables and stage an all-out offensive against Japan proper, was considered unlikely. The international situation, the 'degeneracy' of American democracy and the demoralisation of the United States which would follow disastrous defeats and vain attempts at a come-back, were expected to prevent Washington from continuing, very long, a hopeless struggle.[3]

Thus the Japanese confidently expected the war to be a short one in which ruthless surprise attacks, simultaneously delivered all along a huge arc of the southern and central Pacific, would soon bring about the enemy's complete demoralisation. Not that they ever expected to be able to demand American surrender or to gain any rights whatsoever in mainland America. All the Japanese ever expected was the right to do whatever they wanted within their own Pacific sphere of influence – a Japanese equivalent of the Monroe Doctrine which they expected to be able to wring out of the Americans once their military presence in that ocean had been smashed. As the USSBS points out: 'There is no evidence in the Japanese plans of an intention to defeat the United States. Japan planned to fight a war of limited objectives and, having gained what it wanted, expected to negotiate for a favourable peace.'[4]

At first glance, the word 'limited' might not seem entirely appropriate to the defensive perimeter envisaged by the Japanese planners in 1941 (see map 9). For they were, in fact, contemplating the rapid conquest of Hong Kong, Thailand, Malaya, the Philippines, the Dutch East Indies, Guam, Wake, the Bismarck Archipelago, the north-east littoral of Papua/New Guinea, the northern Solomon Islands and the northern Gilbert Islands, as well as dealing a death-blow to the US Fleet at Pearl Harbor. Two things should be borne in mind, however. First, the Japanese had already acquired a substantial empire in the central Pacific, embracing the island groups of the Bonins, the Marianas (except Guam), the Carolines and the Marshalls; and these were to provide invaluable staging posts for the initial thrusts eastwards and southwards.* Second, and more important, the strategic concept behind these plans was essentially defensive. Granted, of course, that the sequestration of the precious oil and other raw material resources of the East Indies was an almost unprecedented act of international piracy, all other conquests, as well as the attempted destruction of the US Fleet in the Pacific, were not seen as part of a remorseless advance towards mainland America, but as the establishment of a *ne plus ultra* line that would deny potential air and naval bases to the enemy.† When the Japanese commanders sanctioned their amphibious *blitzkrieg* it was on the clear understanding that the initial conquests were to be the only conquests, and that there was to be no thought of fighting a protracted war to the death with the Western powers in the Pacific. To use a modern analogy, they wished to force their enemy to negotiate by establishing impregnable 'no-go' areas rather than by attacking the 'imperialist' homeland itself.

By the spring of 1942 even the Japanese could scarcely credit the overwhelming victories they had achieved. Every single bastion of their proposed defensive line was now in their hands and their enemies' counter-strike capabilities grievously weakened. American resistance on land had flickered and died on Guam, Wake Island and Corregidor, demolishing their vital strategic corridor from Hawaii

---

* Other Pacific islands were owned or mandated as follows:

Solomon Is.	British.	Hawaii	US.
Santa Cruz Is.	British.	Wake	US.
Gilbert Is.	British.	Philippines	US.
Borneo	British.	Guam	US mandate.
Nauru	Br. Emp. mandate.	E. Samoa	US mandate.
New Hebrides	Anglo-French mandate.	Papua	Austr.
New Caledonia	French.	New Guinea	Austr. mandate.
East Indies	Dutch.	Bismarck Arch.	Austr. mandate.
Timor	Portuguese.	W. Samoa	NZ mandate.

† What is rather curious, however, though it does emphasise the fact that Japan was not thinking in terms of a protracted war, is that this line was not primarily intended to defend the East Indies and the sea-lanes through which their vital booty must pass, but as a guarantee of the immunity of Japan proper. According to one Japanese authority: 'When Japanese ships and aircraft swept over more than six thousand miles of the Pacific and Indian oceans to launch the Pacific War, the government had specific plans for the defence of the homeland. We would capture every enemy air-base outpost within bombing range of Japan to deny the Americans or the British the installations from which to mount air attacks; further [at Pearl Harbor] we would destroy the majority of enemy aircraft-carriers so that their smaller planes would not be able to bomb our cities.' (M. Okumiya and J. Horikoshi, *Zero: the Story of the Japanese Navy Air Force 1937–45*, (Corgi Books, 1958), p. 341.)

to the Philippines. The Dutch had been brushed aside in the East Indies, the British in the Solomons and Gilberts and the Australians in the Bismarck Archipelago and northern Papua. The 'impenetrable' jungle of Malaya had proved no obstacle at all to the hardy Japanese infantry who had sneaked up behind the Singapore garrison, tapped it on the shoulder and watched it die of shock.

Naval victories were equally overwhelming. In the surprise attack on Pearl Harbor, on 7 December 1941, the US Navy lost four battleships sunk, one beached and the remaining three badly damaged. Three cruisers and three destroyers were also virtually written off. In the next months the balance was tilted yet more decisively in Japan's favour as the naval presence of the other Pacific allies was virtually destroyed. Two British battleships were sunk by Japanese torpedo-bombers off the coast of Malaya on 10 December 1941. On 27 February 1942, at the Battle of the Java Sea, an Allied fleet met a force of Japanese warships escorting troop transports to Java and was thoroughly trounced. In early April the Japanese carrier fleet sallied into the Indian Ocean where the British had concentrated their fleet after the defeats in the East Indies. Within one week the naval bases at Colombo and Trincomalee had been severely damaged and the British Eastern Fleet had lost an aircraft-carrier, two heavy cruisers and a destroyer. Table 18 shows the overall naval losses inflicted by the end of April 1942.

Table 18: *Allied and Japanese naval vessels sunk in the Pacific December 1941 – April 1942*

	Ships Sunk	
	Allies	Japanese
Battleships	4 US	0
	2 GB	
Aircraft-carriers	1 GB	0
Heavy cruisers	2 US	0
	2 GB	
Light cruisers	1 US	0
	2 GB	
	1 Austr.	
	2 Dutch	
Destroyers	15 Allied	5

No wonder, then, that American commanders wondered how they were to hold on to such Allied territory as still remained in the Pacific. Admiral Ernest King, the Commander-in-Chief of the US

MAP 9

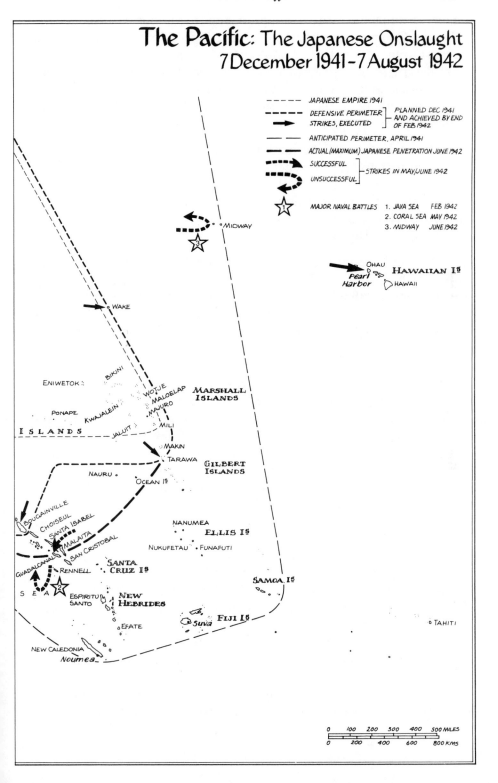

The Pacific: The Japanese Onslaught 7 December 1941 – 7 August 1942

JAPANESE EMPIRE 1941

DEFENSIVE PERIMETER — PLANNED DEC 1941 AND ACHIEVED BY END OF FEB 1942
STRIKES, EXECUTED

ANTICIPATED PERIMETER, APRIL 1941

ACTUAL (MAXIMUM) JAPANESE PENETRATION JUNE 1942

SUCCESSFUL — STRIKES IN MAY/JUNE 1942
UNSUCCESSFUL

MAJOR NAVAL BATTLES
1. JAVA SEA — FEB 1942
2. CORAL SEA — MAY 1942
3. MIDWAY — JUNE 1942

MIDWAY

OHAU
Pearl Harbor — HAWAIIAN IS
HAWAII

WAKE

ENIWETOK
BIKINI
WOTJE
PONAPE — KWAJALEIN — MALOELAP — MAJURO — MARSHALL ISLANDS
ISLANDS — JALUIT — MILI

MAKIN
TARAWA — GILBERT ISLANDS
NAURU — OCEAN IS

BOUGAINVILLE
CHOISEUL
SANTA ISABEL
MALAITA — NANUMEA — ELLIS IS
SAN CRISTOBAL — NUKUFETAU — FUNAFUTI
GUADALCANAL — RENNELL — SANTA CRUZ IS
SAMOA IS
SEA — ESPIRITU SANTO — NEW HEBRIDES
EFATE — SUVA — FIJI IS — TAHITI

NEW CALEDONIA
Noumea

0 100 200 300 400 500 MILES
0 200 400 600 800 KMS

Fleet (Cominch), expressed his anxieties to various correspondents. To one Congressman he wrote: 'I feel I can admit to you that 1942 seems to me to be the critical year for our cause.' To a rear-admiral he described the problems of even contemplating simultaneous operations in the Pacific and the Atlantic, when all one could do was 'rob poor Paul to pay impoverished Peter.' To another rear-admiral he wrote:

> The plain facts of the matter are that we do not have 'tools' wherewith to meet the enemy at all the points he is threatening. Hawaii must be held [and] we must do what we can to maintain the lines of communications with Australia – you know how little there is left over for . . . [other operations]. All in all we have to do the best we can with what we've got.[5]

The virtual eclipse of American power was equally apparent to the Japanese. Even in January 1942, therefore, they were beginning to wonder whether they had not set their sights too low when they delineated their original defence perimeter. So in the middle of this month, Yamamoto ordered his Combined Fleet Headquarters to examine the possibility of further operations. His Chief of Staff, Rear-Admiral Matome Ugaki, came up with several suggestions. An early one favoured an invasion of Hawaii, via Midway and the Palmyra Islands, but this had to be reluctantly abandoned as it was felt that Japanese carrier strength was not sufficient to guarantee clear-cut air supremacy so far from home. Ugaki then proposed an invasion of Ceylon and India. But the army claimed they did not have troops to spare, whilst the Navy's own Special Naval Landing Forces were far too few for such an ambitious undertaking. Then Nagano's Naval General Staff got in on the act and suggested an invasion of northern Australia. Again the Army pleaded a shortage of troops. In the end the Navy had to content itself with a plan simply to isolate Australia, the most likely base for any American attempt at a counter-offensive, from the United States.

To this end it was proposed to seize Port Moresby, on the southern coast of Papua, the rest of the Solomons, the New Hebrides, New Caledonia, the Fiji Islands and Samoa. But the strike eastwards to Hawaii was not completely abandoned. Now, however, Yamamoto would content himself with seizing Midway, with a possible invasion of the Palmyra Islands to be launched some time later. Possession of Midway would deny this important staging-post to the Americans and would do much to blunt their sorties from Pearl Harbor.

Most important of all, the mere threat to Midway should force the remainder of the US Fleet in the Pacific to give battle, the 'Decisive Battle' that was so dear to the hearts of naval strategists. Final orders for this dual thrust were issued in April 1942. The preliminary southern move, to Port Moresby, was dubbed Operation Mo and that towards Midway (with a diversionary attack on the Aleutians) Operation Mi.* The former was to begin in the first week of May with a diversionary attack on Tulagi, the latter in late May.

Even on the eve of the Midway operation, despite their phenomenal successes to date, the Japanese would have done well to consider whether things were going entirely their way. Since the war, indeed, many Japanese historians have pointed to a lack of strategic realism in the plans for a second round of conquests and have diagnosed the onset of the so-called 'Victory Disease', characterised by a blind faith in the superiority of Japanese arms. There were, in fact, several considerations that should have prompted some sense of caution. For one thing the Japanese had lost the advantage of complete surprise. Certainly they still held the initiative, but never again could they reasonably expect to find an enemy so utterly enfeebled by the paraplegia of peacetime routine. Secondly, their forces were spread somewhat thin. Though the Army's reluctance to provide troops for amphibious operations in Ceylon and Australia owed something to bitter Army–Navy rivalries, it also reflected the fact that Japan had entered the war with only 51 infantry divisions, and with these they were supposed to garrison dozens of Pacific islands, hold Malaya, Thailand and Indo-China, complete the conquest of China begun in 1935,† and be ready to take the offensive against Russia should Stalin become involved in a war on his western front.

Most serious of all, the Japanese had failed fatally to undermine America's capacity to make war. In terms of US material resources the Japanese had been plain unlucky, in that the Pearl Harbor strike force had not found the aircraft carriers then in the Pacific, *Saratoga*, *Enterprise* and *Lexington*, in harbour.‡ Others, moreover, were

* The Midway attack alone was known as Operation AF.

† This chapter can provide little space for a discussion of the Sino-Japanese War (see instead D. Wilson, *When Tigers Fight*, Penguin, 1983), but it should be continually borne in mind that the Japanese always maintained a very large army in China. In December 1941, for example, they had 27 divisions in China and Manchuria and in August 1943 there were 41.

‡ *Saratoga* was operating out of San Diego.

quickly dispatched thither – *Yorktown* in January 1942, *Hornet* in April and *Wasp* in June – and though all were rarely in service at any one time,* the Americans did at least have a nucleus of capital ships with which to contemplate a tolerable level of naval activity. Nor was the damage inflicted on the ships caught napping at Pearl Harbor as decisive as Yamamoto might have hoped. Though five battleships and three destroyers were out of action for a year or more, three battleships and three cruisers were available for service again within three to six months. By March 1942, in fact, by dint of herculean labours in the dockyards and the redeployment of other ships to the Pacific, the US Navy had increased the size of their fleet there to include 7 battleships, 5 carriers, 25 cruisers, 92 destroyers and 61 submarines. Though still appreciably outnumbered by the Japanese,[†] the Americans were in a far from hopeless position and knew, moreover, that if they could but hang on they could expect by the end of the year to reap the benefits of a crash ship-building programme. In the Pacific alone this was to yield 3 new battleships, 10 aircraft-carriers, 6 cruisers, 44 destroyers and 13 submarines.

But it was not only America's material reserves that posed a threat to Japanese plans. Perhaps the latter's greatest blunder was in gravely underestimating their opponent's psychological resilience. Appalled as commanders, politicians and public opinion were by the extent of American reverses, there was never any suggestion that they should do anything but soldier on regardless. In the darkest days of early 1942 there was hardly anyone who was not already looking forward to an American counter-offensive in the Pacific. Surrender or negotiated peace were simply not on the agenda, and even a strategy of mere containment was regarded as very much a temporary concession to military realities. Within days of the Pearl Harbor attack, Admiral Husband Kimmel, who as the man responsible for the safety of that anchorage might have been expected to be somewhat chastened, was writing: 'The losses of battleships commit us to the strategic defensive until our forces can again be built up. However, a very powerful striking force of carriers, cruisers and destroyers survives. These forces must be operated boldly and vigorously on the tactical offensive in order to retrieve our initial disaster.'[6] Kimmel was relieved of his command shortly afterwards

---

* *Saratoga* and *Enterprise* were out of action twice in 1942 (Jan.–July/Aug.–Sept. and Aug.–Sept./Oct.–Nov. respectively) and *Yorktown* for one week in May.
† See the Japanese columns for December 1941 in table 57. (Their fleet saw hardly any significant additions between January and March.)

but his defiant spirit was reflected throughout the Navy. In February 1942, Admiral King told the Secretary of the Navy that in 1942 the Americans could only contemplate a defensive posture. Nevertheless, even this was to be regarded as a 'defensive-offensive' which 'may be paraphrased as "hold what you've got and hit them where you can"', the hitting to be done not only by seizing opportunities but by making them. By 1943, moreover, 'as soon as the accumulation of necessary means rolls out', the Americans would be ready to embark on a strategic offensive of their own.[7]

The aggressive nature of even the American defensive phase was soon apparent. Maximum use was made of the carriers. On 1 February 1942, naval task forces under Admirals William Halsey and Frank Fletcher attacked air-bases in the Marshalls and the Gilberts. On 4 March, Marcus Island was attacked and on 18 April bombers from the carrier *Hornet*, under Colonel James Doolittle, had the temerity to mount an air raid on Tokyo and other towns on Honshu Island. But these were only pin-prick attacks, and a more concerted effort could not be made until American commanders had at least some idea of what the Japanese planned next. They did not have long to wait. The Doolittle raid and the subsequent outcry in Japan forced Yamamoto to hurry along his preparations for Operations Mo and Mi, and on 30 April the task force for the former, with orders to seize first Tulagi, in the Solomon Islands, and then Port Moresby (Papua), set sail from Truk and Rabaul.

But the Japanese had now lost the advantage of surprise. For the Americans had broken their naval code and tireless cryptanalysts had both pin-pointed the prime targets and established, within a day or so, when the enemy force was due to sail. Obviously they would have to traverse the Coral Sea, and so Admiral Chester Nimitz, Kimmel's replacement as Commander of the Pacific Fleet (Cincpac), positioned his own forces, including the carriers *Yorktown* and *Lexington*, on the flank of the likely Japanese route. His movements were too late to permit him to interfere with the Tulagi landing, which was completed on 3 May, but he was well in range by 7 May, when the remainder of the Japanese task force arrived. In the somewhat confused battle that ensued, losses were about even. On the 7th, a small Japanese carrier, *Shoho*, was sunk by carrier planes as it was escorting the Port Moresby troop transports. On the 8th, the main carrier forces (*Zuikaku* and *Shokaku* with the Japanese) both made aerial sightings and in simultaneous attacks *Shokaku* was heavily damaged and *Lexington* mortally crippled.

But the significance of the battle does not lie in the respective loss rates. More important was the fact that for the first time a Japanese offensive had been halted, the loss of the *Shoho* having persuaded the Japanese commander to withdraw the Port Moresby invasion force. At the time this was regarded as a purely temporary rebuff, but in fact the IJN never again penetrated this far south. For already they were finding their ambitions outstripping their means. It had only been possible to mount Operation Mo at all by pulling out the ships that had rampaged across the Indian Ocean. Moreover, whilst five carriers had been thus withdrawn, in the event only two of them were able to join Operation Mo. This was because their losses at the hands of the British, although meagre on paper (perhaps 90 planes as against several hundred), were still sufficient to denude three carriers of aircrews, there being neither new planes nor trained pilots immediately to hand.

Equally worrying was the fact that material shortages seemed to be matched by serious shortcomings in military proficiency. By demonstrating the potential of aircraft-carriers in the Pearl Harbor raid, and by leaving the Americans with only their carrier force intact, the Japanese had helped to usher in a new era of naval warfare, in which major engagements were to be fought by forces separated by dozens of miles of empty ocean. But in the Coral Sea the Japanese had shown that they were not very adept in this kind of fighting. To be sure, their carriers themselves were state of the art and their naval aircraft, notably the Mitsubishi Zero,* were far superior to anything the Americans possessed at the beginning of the war.[†] But the tactical direction of the massed Zeros and the dive- and torpedo-bombers they were supposed to escort had been poor. Above all the admirals on the spot had failed to be sufficiently aggressive. *Yorktown* had been damaged in the first Japanese attack on the 8th but little attempt had been made thereafter to track it down and finish it off, and whilst *Lexington* did sink, this was not due to a

---

* The Mitsubishi A6M, whose actual Allied codename was 'Zeke'. The Japanese type-number, however, was oo and the resultant nickname took on semi-official status.
† A Grumman Wildcat pilot reported after the Battle of the Coral Sea that 'a pilot alone was a dead duck' against a Zero, whilst another naval flyer complained: 'The F2A-3 [Brewster Buffalo] is *not* a combat airplane. The Japanese Zero can run circles round [it] . . . It is my belief that any commander that orders pilots out for combat in an F2A-3 should consider the pilot lost before leaving the ground.' (J. H. and W. M. Belote, *Titans of the Seas*, (Harper and Row, New York, 1975), pp. 82, 92–3. Emphasis in original.)

Japanese *coup de grâce* but followed the explosion of accumulated petrol vapour as she was limping away. Such inexperience is not altogether surprising. As the historians of the Japanese Naval Air Force have pointed out:

> A post-battle study of the Coral Sea engagement brought out the fact that neither Vice-Admiral Inoue [chief planner of Operation Mo] nor Vice-Admiral Takagi [commander of the carrier group] had on their immediate staffs a single air officer with combat experience in carrier-based or land-based air operations. It was incredible to realise also that both admirals likewise lacked any experience in this type of combat![8]

The admirals were hardly exceptional in this regard, for neither the Japanese nor the Americans had more than a handful of officers with carrier experience. Both navies had shown little real interest in these types of operations and had built carriers simply because the other side had them. In common with most navies the world over, both had gone to war fully expecting the battleships and heavy cruisers of the classic First World War line of battle to dominate the oceans. Throughout the Thirties the Japanese were only interested in maintaining parity with the Americans in carriers. In the view of their Naval Staff 'the carrier might or might not be an all-important weapon. Probably it would not, and unless war experience proved otherwise, the battleship must remain the supreme weapon of naval warfare.' The US Navy's General Board was similarly lukewarm about the potential of carriers and in 1939 envisaged only four more being built for the whole of the 1940s, two of these merely to replace the ageing *Saratoga* and *Lexington*. On the whole 'the Board was satisfied if the number of US flat-tops should roughly equal Japan's in tonnage . . . [and] was much more interested in battleships, which it still regarded as the backbone of the fleet.'[9] But, quite unforeseen, both sides had been obliged to rely on carriers – the Americans because they had little else, the Japanese to provide an aerial umbrella for their long-distance amphibious operations – and thus both were now forced to learn new rules and techniques from scratch. The seeming invincibility of the conquerors of Singapore and Manila could no longer be taken for granted.

Lessons were soon to recommence. Operation Mo, it will be recalled, was but one prong of the renewed offensive in the Pacific. The other was towards Midway, where the Japanese hoped to fight the decisive naval battle that would break US sea power for good.

The operation at least began well, for a large naval battle certainly did ensue. In two important respects it was very similar to that fought in the Coral Sea. First, the Americans, thanks to their cryptanalysts, again knew when the Japanese were coming and where they were aiming for. Second, the battle hinged upon carrier actions. It was not that either side had a positive preference for a carrier battle, but that both were constrained by circumstance. Nimitz had simply no choice at all as *Enterprise, Yorktown* and *Hornet* were the only really battleworthy capital ships to hand. Yamamoto, now in personal command of the fleet at sea, *was* able to indulge more traditional preferences, at least in the composition of his mighty task force, and in his eyes its backbone were the *eleven* battleships that he had with him. However, because the Americans had carriers, because the assault landing required air cover, and because this was to be *the* decisive naval battle, the task force also contained five fleet carriers and three light. Because of the threat they posed to the American carriers, and because they usually took up a vanguard station, it was these ships that were likely to be the Americans' main targets.

Yamamoto had divided the carriers amongst four separate groups. Two light carriers, *Ryujo* and *Junyo*, were attached to an Aleutians invasion force, essentially a diversion to draw Nimitz away from Midway. One of the fleet carriers, *Zuiho*, was with the Midway assault force to provide air cover against the land-based US planes there. The third light carrier, *Hosho*, was with Yamamoto, whilst the remaining four fleet carriers and the main force of battleships were under Vice-Admiral Nagumo's command in an autonomous carrier group. Yamamoto has been severely criticised for dispersing his carriers in this way. Admiral Nimitz himself has categorically stated:

> had the Japanese fleet been properly concentrated . . . it is inconceivable . . . even with the most complete warning . . . that the three US carriers could by any combination of luck and skill still have defeated and turned back the seven [sic] carriers, eleven battleships, and the immense number of supporting vessels which the Japanese committed to this action . . .[10]

But what should be borne in mind is that Yamamoto did not expect to fight a purely carrier battle, and regarded his own merely as useful subsidiary vessels. They had specific tasks to perform in the actual invasion and might also prove useful in pinning down the Americans until the main force of battleships arrived, but it was these latter, commanded by Yamamoto himself, that would deliver the decisive blow and actually destroy the US Fleet. As two Japanese historians of the battle have reminded us, Yamamoto's whole plan 'rested on the obsolete concept . . . that battleships rather than carriers constituted the main strength of the fleet.'[11]

What Yamamoto had completely failed to realise was how expensive his preliminary pinning move might be. Even after Coral Sea he still seemed unaware of how much damage carriers could do to each other and how quickly it might be done. Thus, whereas he seems to have expected that the opposing carriers would merely spar with one another for the best part of a full day, whilst his battleships closed in, the crucial damage was in fact done between breakfast and lunch, on 4 June 1942. Contact was established around 9 am, upon which the Americans immediately sent off most of their aircraft. Japanese planes, however, were already aloft and fully occupied in the bombardment of Midway. They were recalled but were still being refuelled and rearmed when the first wave of American torpedo-bombers struck. These were engaged by Japanese fighters that had remained in the air to protect the bombers and torpedo-planes returning from Midway, and suffered terrible casualties, one squadron being completely wiped out. Not for nothing had Nimitz told his subordinates before the battle that his aim was 'to inflict maximum damage on the enemy by employing strong attrition attacks.'[12]

A few minutes later, however, just as the fighters were engaged at low altitudes with the torpedo-planes, the American dive-bombers arrived overhead and immediately scored vital hits on three of the fleet carriers, *Kaga*, *Soryu* and *Akagi*, all of which sank within the next 24 hours. Nagumo's fourth fleet carrier, *Hiryu*, escaped detection for the time being and dispatched a bomb and torpedo attack of its own against *Yorktown*, which was hit several times and began to lose way.* At 5 pm, however, *Hiryu* was in turn attacked by aircraft from the other American carriers and was quickly reduced to a blazing wreck and sank the next morning. Stunned by the loss of four of his major carriers, Yamamoto, still far to the west with the battleship group, broke off the operation. In the ensuing pursuit he lost one cruiser sunk and another cruiser and two destroyers severely damaged.

The Battle of Midway occupies a somewhat anomalous position in the history of the Pacific War. There are, to be sure, certain similarities with the Coral Sea action, notably Japanese unfamiliarity

---

* Great efforts were made to save her, but she was detected by a Japanese submarine and sent to the bottom on 7 June.

with carrier operations and capabilities, and the tremendous advantage bestowed upon the Americans by their access to the most privy communications of the enemy.* Yet one of the major themes of the Pacific conflict, the material weakness of the Japanese that had already had a baleful effect in the Coral Sea and was to hamstring their operations more and more as the war progressed, was noticeably absent. At Midway, Yamamoto had succeeded in deploying the bulk of the Imperial Japanese Navy, a vast armada that should have completely overwhelmed Nimitz's puny force. Even discounting the Aleutians group, Yamamoto had six carriers against three, 11 battleships against none, 16 cruisers against 8, 46 destroyers against 16. And even forgetting the fact that he might have had eight carriers within mutually supporting distance of each other, the four he did have so arrayed might reasonably have been expected to put up a far better show than they did.

But in the last analysis the Battle of Midway, more than almost any other on an equivalent scale, shows the importance of blind luck. In other words, almost all of the key variables were outside American control and in no sense can their commanders be said to have manipulated *tactical* circumstances to their advantage. When their planes took off they did not know that most of the Japanese ones were engaged in the Midway assault. It was not intention that made their dive-bombers take a somewhat circuitous route and thus arrive after the torpedo planes. It was not a deliberate ploy to let the latter attack first so that the enemy fighters would be pulled down almost to sea level. Things just happened that way, and for a few precious minutes three squadrons of Dauntless dive-bombers had before them the openest goal in the history of naval warfare. Not for nothing did the leading historian of US Naval operations in the Second World War give due credit to 'luck – the constant and baffling major factor in naval warfare', or Japanese historians ruefully note: 'Despite exhaustive planning and preparation prior to any battle, only the gods know what course the battle will take. It appears that in any conflict . . . some force beyond that exercised by man is responsible for the final decision.'[13]

Be that as it may, the net result was devastating for the Japanese.

* In this latter regard, one American authority has bluntly stated: 'Without that knowledge [of Japanese plans] it is difficult to see how the United States could have met the Japanese successfully at either Coral Sea or Midway.' (C. W. Nimitz and E. B. Potter (eds), *The United States and World Sea Power* (Prentice-Hall, Englewood Cliffs, NJ, 1955), p. 674.)

Now both of their major drives to establish an extended perimeter had been repulsed. Worse, in the second defeat, having been shown conclusively that carriers were the new queens of the seas, they had just lost four of their most powerful ones. All that their renewed drive could show on the credit side was the seizure of Tulagi, whence a small party of troops and construction workers had been sent to begin establishing an airstrip on Guadalcanal, towards the southern end of the Solomons chain. Nevertheless, the Japanese High Command had still not given up hope of further conquests. In July they resolved to attack Port Moresby once again, this time landing at Buna, via the more secure Bismarck Sea, and thence pushing through the Owen Stanley Mountains for a land assault on Moresby. The new airstrip at Guadalcanal would provide cover for this operation.

However, the Americans were acutely aware that the successes at Coral Sea and Midway must speedily be followed up, and they had formulated offensive plans of their own. On 2 July the US Joint Chiefs of Staff (JCS) issued a directive envisaging the conquest of Tulagi, Guadalcanal and the Santa Cruz Islands (Operation Watchtower), to be followed by the seizure of the rest of the Solomons, key positions in Papua and, eventually, Rabaul and New Ireland. Command of these operation was given to General Douglas MacArthur, previously in charge of US forces in the Philippines, and Vice-Admiral R. L. Ghormley. The former was responsible for the culminating assault on Rabaul, as well as operations in Papua/New Guinea, whilst the latter was in charge of clearing the Solomons. Naturally, the two were expected to work closely together, but a potential source of friction was that MacArthur was ultimately responsible to General George Marshall, the US Army Chief of Staff, and Ghormley to his superiors in the Navy hierarchy, Nimitz, as Cincpac, and above him Admiral King, the Navy Chief of Staff.*

* This arrangement stemmed from a reorganisation of the Pacific command authorised on 31 March 1942. The Pacific was divided into two basic sectors, the South-West Pacific Ocean Area and the Pacific Ocean Area. MacArthur was given command of the first, as Comsowespac, and Nimitz of the latter, as Cincpoa. Nimitz's command, however, was further subdivided into North, South and Central Pacific Ocean Areas. The South was given to Ghormley (Comsopac), whilst North and Central were directly commanded by Nimitz. He thus wore three hats at three different levels of command. As Cincpac he commanded all naval units in the Pacific, including any that might be assigned to MacArthur. As Cincpoa he was responsible for all planning outside the South-West Pacific, and as commander of the Central Ocean Area (Comcenpac) he was directly in charge of operations in by far the largest of these Areas. The reasons for such a byzantine command structure will be dealt with at more length in the next chapter.

The JCS directive became a matter of some urgency almost as soon as it was issued. In the first week of July, MacArthur was warned by radio intelligence that the Japanese landing at Buna was imminent, and on 14 July first reports came through of the airfield works on Guadalcanal. The response of the Area commanders was hardly inspiring. When urged to assault Guadalcanal on 1 August, Ghormley demurred, and was fully supported by MacArthur, who claimed that adequate means did not exist for a speedy assault and rapid build-up. MacArthur was yet more dilatory about New Guinea. Despite the warnings he had received, and despite the reserves of American and Australian troops available on the Australian mainland, he was remarkably slow actually to transfer them across the dividing strait. Only a single battalion was moved up to Kokoda, on the vital trail across the Owen Stanley Mountains, and a counter-landing at Buna was timed for mid-August, by which date the Japanese would certainly have already acted. Even after the Japanese had landed, little effort was made to set up an effective air-supply system to this dreadfully inhospitable region and it was not until mid-August, when the Japanese were nearing the summit of the Owen Stanleys, that a corps commander and staff were sent over and the movement of a realistic number of reinforcements began. As one historian has observed: 'During these months the conventional picture of MacArthur as a far-sighted, omnicompetent generalissimo collapses in the face of the facts. What is particularly disturbing is the cavalier attitude displayed towards sound intelligence sources . . . The message was there, available – but the messengers were cold-shouldered.'[14]

Happily, both operations were ultimately successful, though each absorbed the remaining months of 1942. In Papua the American and Australians slowly forced the Japanese back over the dreadful Kokoda Trail. An attempted Japanese landing at Milne Bay was repulsed and by January 1943 their last-ditch positions at Buna and Gona had been taken after a bloody siege. In Tokyo it was now accepted that the invasion of Papua had been stemmed and that Port Moresby was no longer an attainable objective. Nevertheless, as fine a testimony as these operations were to the courage and stamina of the Allied troops, they hardly constituted much of a vindication for MacArthur's reputation. The American official history has passed brusque sentence: 'The only result, strategically speaking, was that after six months of bitter fighting and some 8,500 casualties, including 3,000 dead, the South West Pacific area was exactly where it would have been the previous July had it been able to secure the beachhead before the Japanese ever got there.'[15]

Despite eventual American success, the same point could well be made with regard to Guadalcanal and the South Pacific. The dilatory response to the news of the Japanese landing on Guadalcanal has already been noted. Even before this, however, as early as 28 May, Nimitz had suggested to Ghormley and MacArthur that a Marine Raider Battalion, then on Samoa, should swoop on Tulagi and Guadalcanal. Both objected, saying that they had insufficient strength to hold the islands once taken, but, according to one well-informed source, 'many in the Navy believed that we missed a golden opportunity to slip into [these islands] . . . when the enemy's back was turned, for at that time almost the entire Japanese Navy was converging on the Aleutians and Midway.'[16] Though the Japanese would almost certainly have responded it is likely that a counter-invasion, as at Milne Bay, could have been repulsed and the Americans spared many of the 6,100 casualties they were to suffer on Guadalcanal.

It has to be admitted, however, that if it had not been Guadalcanal, then one or other of the Solomon Islands would have had to become a killing ground. For there is no question that the Japanese now saw them as an absolutely vital buttress to their imperial defences. Thus, though their original garrison was scattered by the American invaders, who had finally landed on 7 August, they immediately resolved to give up as little ground as possible. Ceaseless air attacks were launched, reinforcements moved up, and on 31 August the island was marked down as a prime Army objective. New Guinea operations were now being accorded only second priority, and everything was to be concentrated on Guadalcanal. On 18 September Operation Ka got under way, all three services straining themselves to the utmost to dislodge the Americans. Reinforcements were filtered in whilst vicious air battles went hand-in-hand with fearful naval slugging matches as the Japanese made repeated attempts to destroy the invasion fleet and build up their own forces. The naval battles of Savo Island (8/9 August), the Eastern Solomons (23/25 August) and Cape Esperance, off northern Guadalcanal (11/13), were all fought to these ends whilst the Battle of the Santa Cruz Islands (26/27 October) was an American attempt to break up the large Japanese naval presence that had built up in the area. There is no space here to go into any detail about these battles, but Samuel Eliot Morison summed them up graphically at the end of his own detailed account: 'So reader, if this tale has seemed repetitious with shock and gore, exploding magazines, burning and sinking ships and plummeting planes – that is simply how it was.'[17]

In November Japanese Army and Navy planners agreed on yet more far-reaching measures. Piecemeal infiltration tactics were to be abandoned and an entire field army to be immediately established for a decisive drive from staging areas in the north of the island. To this end, the Japanese intended to move in 30,000 extra men, 300 guns and 30,000 tons of supplies by mid-December. The first lift included 13,000 troops and was accompanied by a sizeable naval force. But this blundered into an American escort group and during the First Naval Battle of Guadalcanal (12/13 November), though the Americans lost heavily, the troop transports were forced to turn back. They again tried to make land the next day but were remorselessly harried by the Americans, who allowed only 4,000 soldiers to get ashore. An attempt to sneak in supplies was likewise thwarted at the Battle of Tassafaronga (30 November) and thereafter effective control of the Solomon seas passed to the US Navy. This sealed the fate of the Japanese troops left on Guadalcanal. During December and early January the Americans were able methodically to build up their own forces and slowly drive north. By the beginning of 1943 the jungle that had been intended as the launching-pad of a great offensive became a last bolt-hole for the starving, diseased survivors.

The campaign had posed tremendous problems for both sides. The Americans had made serious mistakes at the beginning, revealing their almost total lack of experience in this type of operation. Logistical support had been particularly shaky at first, provoking one commander to paint a vivid picture for General Marshall: 'Army, Navy and Marines all mixed in the jungle, mountains of supplies all piling up on the beach, and a road-stead full of ships, bombs and fuel drums scattered through the coffee and cocoa was a fine picture of war *as she is* but not as it should be.'[18] Nor do the American planners seem to have realised the vital importance of air power in island warfare and the necessity to give top priority to establishing their own aerial cover. This may seem strange when one considers that the whole rationale of the Guadalcanal operation was to deny the enemy an airstrip, but the fact remains that hardly any provision had been made for bringing in the necessary engineering equipment or personnel. In a letter to General Arnold, the same commander cited above wondered 'if the Navy really and fully appreciated this necessity in the beginning. They seemed to as we talked to them, but the positive action was not taken . . . The point is that it is not the consuming thought in every naval commander's mind and the plan did not have as its first and immediate objective the seizure and development of Cactus [codename for Guadalcanal] *as an Air Base*.'[19] The Navy's use of its own aircraft also showed how little they appreciated the fundamental importance of air cover. A carrier force under Admiral Frank Jack Fletcher had been assigned to protect the initial landing, but on the afternoon of D-Day itself, Fletcher, having lost only 20 of his 100 fighters, decided to turn tail, leaving the remaining transports almost completely unprotected. He did not deign to seek sanction for his unilateral withdrawal until he had been running south for 12 hours. As one authority notes: 'Fletcher had entered battle determined to accept no risks; he left it with the same determination.'[20]

Furthermore, despite undoubted improvements in logistical and tactical techniques, the Americans cannot be said to have finished the campaign on a particularly high note, muffing as they did the endgame in a manner strikingly reminiscent of later Allied failures in Sicily, the approaches to Rome and Normandy. Having pushed the Japanese survivors into one corner of the island, they inexplicably failed to finish them off. Completely inadequate patrolling, by land, sea and air, allowed these remnants to withdraw methodically back to the beaches where 19 destroyers, signal lamps flashing, came within 750 yards of the coast and took aboard over 5,000 men, who made the passage in previously concealed landing barges. This was on 1 February. On the 4th and 7th exactly the same thing happened, and altogether over 13,000 men were rescued, without a single ship being attacked during the return voyages to Shortland Island.

But American shortcomings paled into insignificance when compared with the problems of the Japanese. For they were already beginning to discover that they had bitten off substantially more than they could chew. No matter how well they fought, they found themselves increasingly hamstrung by the lack of adequate resources. At sea they performed superbly. Their night-fighting techniques, as at Savo Island, Cape Esperance and Naval Guadalcanal, were without peer, and in the Guadalcanal battles as a whole they inflicted serious losses on the Americans, sinking two aircraft-carriers, nine cruisers and ten destroyers for the loss of one escort carrier, two battleships, three cruisers and thirteen destroyers. But it was becoming apparent to the more perceptive Japanese commanders that this sort of attrition ran very much in the Americans' favour, simply because the latter could replace their losses almost immediately. As Admiral Nagano had told one of his subordinates even before the first battle, at Savo Island: 'The Japanese Navy is different from the American Navy. If you lose one ship it will take years to replace.'[21]

Exactly the same point applied to their aircraft, and the more than 800 planes lost over Guadalcanal made serious inroads into their total strength. Naval aircraft, the *sine qua non* of oceanic warfare, were particularly badly hit, and this at a time when the production of the Zero was pitifully low. The average monthly output between April 1942 and June 1943 was only 221 aircraft. Of this period two Japanese have remarked: 'Replacement of Zekes . . . was becoming more and more difficult, and never achieved the numbers requested by the combat leaders. Japan lacked other fighters in sufficient numbers to replace the Zeke, and our strength was steadily whittled down, even as enemy air power gained monstrous proportions.'[22] Equally serious was the terrible loss of pilots, as the Japanese, expecting to fight a naval *blitzkrieg*, had made little effort to provide an adequate supply of replacements. By the end of the carrier engagement at Santa Cruz almost all of the 400 or so élite pilots assigned to the original carrier force had been lost. Land-based flyers had been hit just as hard. Saburo Sakai, the most famous Japanese ace, noted that by January 1943, of the original 150 pilots in his Tainan Fighter Wing, less than 20 were still alive.

Most seriously of all, it had been brought home to the Japanese that they were incapable of adequately supplying the outlying garrisons of their far-flung empire. To do this properly required a large merchant fleet, but here too the problem of heavy losses and a limited capacity to provide replacements was proving insurmountable. Japanese planners had hardly expected this fleet to get off scot-free, and had anticipated a loss of about 800,000 tons during the first year of the war. In the event, by the end of 1942 they had lost over one million tons and this discrepancy, slight though it might seem, proved fatal to their ambitions. During the high-level hand-wringing that took place in Tokyo early in 1943, it was the inability to find an extra 300,000 tons or so of merchant shipping, to service further action in the Solomons, that forced the decision to evacuate Guadalcanal.

In the interim, the subsequent shortages affected all arms. Engineering back-up was very feeble and air operations were sorely hampered by a failure to start building air-bases between Rabaul and Guadalcanal/Tulagi until September 1942. The air force also suffered serious fuel shortages – so serious, in fact, that Hideki

Tojo, the Japanese prime minister, instructed his technical experts 'to devise some way to fly planes without gas, suggesting that they use "something like air". They laughed aloud until they realised he was serious, then unanimously pledged themselves to a program for peace.'[23] The Army fared even worse, and senior officers later painted

> a vivid picture of the intolerable position in which inability to achieve air control placed them. General Miyazaki testified that only 20 per cent of the supplies dispatched from Rabaul to Guadalcanal ever reached there. As a result the . . . troops . . . lacked heavy equipment, adequate ammunition and even food . . . Approximately . . . 10,000 *men starved to death*.[24]

The whole thing was put in a nutshell by Admiral Nagano, during a postwar interrogation: 'I look upon the Guadalcanal and Tulagi operation as the turning point from offence to defence, and the cause of our set-back there was our inability to increase our forces at the same speed as you did.'[25] At the time Yamamoto, too, clearly saw that the writing was on the wall. To the commander of Japan's submarine forces, Admiral Mitsumi Shimizu, he wrote: 'Guadalcanal was a very fierce battle. I do not know what to do next . . . At this moment I would like to borrow some knowledge from a wise man.'[26]

10

The Counter-Offensive

March 1943 – August 1945

In one report to Tokyo, a local commander on Guadalcanal included the observation: 'It must be said that success or failure in recapturing Guadalcanal, and the results of the final naval battle relating to it, is the fork in the road that leads to victory for them or for us.'[1] By the beginning of 1943 this fork had been reached, and the Japanese had taken the wrong turning. From then on they were almost completely on the defensive, forced first to surrender the initiative to the Americans and then gradually to pull back from one defensive line to another, each one bringing American military might ever closer to the homeland and the vital sea-lanes through which it was succoured.

From very early in the war, in fact, there were those in Japan who perceived that ultimate defeat was inevitable and that the pinch they had been feeling in 1942 must soon become a bear-hug. In May 1943 Vice-Admiral Takijiro Onishi told a friend that overweening ambition was leading more and more to a dangerous dispersal of their forces. Most of the island garrisons were becoming terribly vulnerable, and he cited the example of Attu, in the Aleutians, which had just been nipped out by the Americans. The Japanese, he stated, should never have been there in the first place. 'But we took a foolish liking to the place and poured in too much matériel and unnecessary personnel, making it impossible to leave. There are also many islands like that in the south.'[2] In the following September a Japanese diplomat in Lisbon sent an astonishingly frank signal to Tokyo: 'It is generally considered here that the eventual outcome of the war is settled, and that it is now only a question of time. This verdict, of course, includes the war in the Pacific.'[3] In June 1944 the Army General Staff's Conduct of War Section produced a report on the overall strategic situation. Its conclusion was succinct, stating flatly that there was 'now no hope for Japan to reverse the unfavourable war situation . . . It is time for us to end the war.'[4] The Navy agreed. In May, Rear-Admiral Takagi of the Navy's General Staff completed a study of military trends in the previous nine months. 'Based on analysis of air, fleet and merchant shipping losses, Japan's inability to import essential materials for production, and the potentiality of air attacks on the home islands, Takagi concluded that Japan could not win and should seek a compromise peace.'[5] In July Admiral Toyoda, Commander-in-Chief of the Combined Fleet, called on the new Navy Minister, Admiral Yonai. In Toyoda's words: ' "Can we hold out to the end of the year?" Yonai asked. I replied simply, "It will probably be extremely difficult to do so." '[6]

Most noteworthy of the above comments are those by Rear-Admiral Takagi, who confronted the essential *economic* reasons for Japan's complete inability to take on the Americans in any sort of protracted struggle. And the most fundamental of these reasons was the lack of adequate supplies of raw materials. Seizure of these had, of course, been one of the main reasons for Japan going to war at all but, because of acute shipping shortages that will be examined in detail a little later, she always remained incapable of transferring enough of this booty to the factories back home. The effects of such shortages even in 1942 have already been touched upon, but it is now necessary to look more closely at the fatal long-term effects of the grave weaknesses in Japan's economic infrastructure. For, whilst she may have been an industrial prodigy in terms of non-Western development, she was still lamentably ill equipped to take on maturer rivals in anything but a very limited conflict.

Almost every key industry was affected. Steel production, in particular, was seriously hampered by the declining imports of coal, iron ore and pig-iron. Thus, even though domestic production actually increased every year until 1944, this production was well short of that demanded by the armaments industry, and such stockpiles as had been accumulated before the outbreak of war were inexorably eaten up. Nor did it help that domestic production was not to be the only source of finished iron and steel. Mills in Manchuria, Korea and China also had an important part to play, but from these too exports ineluctably declined. Other strategically vital items became in equally short supply, notably bauxite, lead, tin, zinc, phosphorite, phosphate, dolomite and magnesite. Table 56 in the Statistical Appendix gives the basic details and shows that imports of, for example, coal, iron ore, bauxite and finished iron and steel declined steadily during the war and by 1945 were only 8.6, 7.2, 4.9 and 17.1 per cent respectively of their 1942 levels.

Perhaps the most vital raw material of all was oil, and supply of this, too, depended largely on imports. The Japanese did have a synthetic oil industry but it was far too small to make a significant contribution to the overall oil economy. The effective functioning of the latter, therefore, was to depend on the substantial stockpile of oil that had been built up prior to Pearl Harbor – some 43 million barrels – and the ability to ship in extra oil to replace any undue inroads into these reserves. At first sight one might assume that the Japanese kept ahead of the game, for imports during the first years of the war substantially increased. In 1941 they had imported 8.37 million barrels. In the following year 10.52 million barrels were appropriated and in 1943 the figure rose to 14.50 million. Unfortunately, even increases of this magnitude were not enough to keep up with the insatiable demands of trying both to boost industrial production and to fuel far-ranging military operations. The Midway operation, for example, had consumed vast amounts of oil, and Admiral Toyoda admitted after the war that this alone had severely limited naval options for the remainder of the war. Day-to-day activities placed equally heavy demands on fuel stocks, above all the incessant movement of shipping to bring supplies and reinforcements to the numerous scattered garrisons, as well as the maintenance of continued air cover over these outposts and over the sea-lanes that connected them.

It was soon apparent that there was simply not enough fuel to go round. In spite of the most stringent efforts to economise, inventories of crude oil were on the decline throughout the war, fuel oil from the beginning of 1943, and motor fuel from June 1944. During the autumn of 1944, though the tempo of US attacks was increasing almost daily, diesel consumption had to be cut by half from its wartime peak, fuel oil by 40 per cent and aviation fuel by 25 per cent. But such cuts could not halt the erosion of the prewar stockpile, and when attacks on Japanese shipping were stepped up in 1944 and 1945, reducing yet further the amount imported, the situation became all but hopeless, as can be seen in table 19. A further indication of the extent of the oil problem is that Japanese planners had, on the one hand, expected oil imports to reach at least 28.5 million barrels annually by 1943 whilst, on the other, they had estimated that the minimum consumption for effective military operations would be 85 million barrels annually. In fact, between 1943 and 1945, aggregate imports amounted to only

Table 19: *Japanese oil imports, domestic production and consumption 1941–5 (in millions of* US *barrels)*

		Production					
	Imported	Home Crude	Home Synthetic	Total	Used in Year	Deficit	Stocks on 1 April
1941	8.37	1.94	1.22	11.53	22.58	-11.5	48.90
1942	10.52	1.69	1.50	13.71	25.80	-12.09	37.85
1943	14.50	1.79	1.05	17.34	27.80	-10.46	25.76
1944	5.00	1.58	1.23	7.81	19.40	-11.59	15.30
1945	-	0.81	0.18	0.99	4.60	-3.61	3.71
							0.10 (1 Sept. 1945)

22.8 per cent of this forecast, which in turn permitted an aggregate consumption that was only 20.3 per cent of the supposedly minimum requirements.

This critical shortfall in imports was made even worse by the fact that the Japanese had entered the war with a totally inadequate tanker fleet, too small to absorb even the most perfunctory interdiction effort by the Americans. In December 1941, because the Japanese had even at this late date allowed the bulk of their oil imports to be carried in foreign bottoms, the tanker fleet totalled only 575,000 tons. The tanker building programme was greatly accelerated in 1942 and 1943,* such that construction did for a while outstrip losses, and by December 1943 total tonnage had risen to 873,070. But the losses that were sustained were nevertheless critical, for fully three-quarters of the remaining fleet was tied up in bringing the crude oil back to Japan, leaving a wholly inadequate number to re-ship refined oil to the theatres of war where it was most needed.

In 1944 and 1945 the situation worsened, as American aircraft and submarines undertook a more concentrated offensive against oil traffic. In 1944 tanker losses quadrupled, outstripping production. In March of that year, for example, the Japanese Army's Far Eastern Summary included a recent signal from Manila: 'While returning to Japan, a convoy of six tankers was attacked by enemy submarines in the waters NW of the Philippines and five tankers were sunk . . . *The present situation is such that the majority of tankers returning to Japan are being lost.*'[7] In fact, the proportion

* Though it still accounted for only 27 per cent of total merchant tonnage built.

of oil produced in the southern fields that actually reached Japan fell from 40 per cent in 1942 to 29 per cent in 1943, 13.5 per cent in 1944 and zero in 1945. The deterioration of the tanker situation as a whole is outlined in table 20. Speaking of the last months of the war a Japanese naval captain testified: 'Toward the end the situation was reached that we were fairly certain a tanker would be sunk shortly after departing from port. There wasn't much doubt in our minds that a tanker would not get to Japan.'[8]

Table 20: *The decline of the Japanese tanker fleet* 1941–5

	Tonnage built	Tonnage sunk	Tonnage available at end of year
1941			575,000
1942	20,316	9,538	686,498
1943	254,927	169,491	873,070
1944	624,290	754,889	860,971
1945	85,651	351,028	266,948

The fate of the Japanese tanker fleet is a perfect microcosm of the story of their merchant marine as a whole. Thus at the beginning of the war imports of every kind were far too dependent on foreign bottoms. In 1938, for example, of the 18,490 ships that entered Japanese ports only 11,456 were flying the Japanese flag, the respective tonnages being 62.2 and 36.6 million. Indeed, it is only by emphasising once again that Japanese leaders expected a *short* Pacific war that one can make any sense at all of their woeful neglect of this most vital of their logistical sinews. Though even then, given that they were waging war specifically to seize remote deposits of raw materials, it is difficult to comprehend how they could so consistently underrate the necessity for a strong merchant fleet.

For not only was the existing fleet far too small, but plans for expansion had hardly been considered. The total inadequacy of the provisions for new construction soon became apparent. Whilst losses in the early *blitzkrieg*, to May 1942, were small – some 67 vessels totalling 314,805 tons – these were still in excess of the number of new ships built. The USSBS has rightly remarked:

In this period it is astonishing that the Japanese should have prepared so inadequately for an ocean war that, in spite of the windfall of captured ships, an [American] attack as weak and sporadic as that directed against them during the first nine months of the war should have been able to accomplish the signal success of starting Japanese net merchant tonnage on the downward trend as early as April 1942.[9]

American attacks were to be better orchestrated in the years that followed. In January 1943, at the Casablanca Conference, authorisation was given for an all-out submarine offensive against Japanese shipping. By the end of 1944 the Americans had 200 such craft operating in the Pacific, mostly in the same kind of wolf packs that had proved so successful for the Germans in the Atlantic. The campaign did not really get into top gear until spring 1944, partly because of the new tactics, but more importantly because of long-overdue improvements in the standard American torpedo. American aircraft also participated in this campaign and they and the submarines respectively accounted for 2,298,000 and 4,889,000 tons of merchant shipping sunk. They shared the credit for a further 114,300 tons, which meant that between them they accounted for 84.7 per cent of the 8,617,000 tons lost in the war. The annual rate of construction and loss detailed in table 21 clearly demonstrates into what a blind alley the Japanese planners had blundered:

Table 21: *The decline of the Japanese merchant fleet 1941–5*

	Tonnage captured and built	Tonnage sunk	Tonnage afloat at end of year
1941			5,996,657
1942	945,374	1,123,156	5,818,875
1943	878,113	1,820,919	4,876,169
1944	1,734,847	3,891,019	2,719,897
1945	565,443	1,782,140	1,503,200

Such figures made a mockery of prewar projections. In terms of new building these had in fact erred on the cautious side, one predicting that only 1,400,000 tons would be launched between 1941 and 1943, as opposed to the 3,500,000 tons actually completed. The key blunder, however, was in the estimate of likely shipping losses. This was put at 2,400,000 tons for this same period, whereas the actual figure was 6,800,000 tons, almost three times as much. Thus, even though the Japanese made sterling efforts to compensate for this grotesque underestimation – to increase planned output by over 250 per cent in such a short period was no mean feat – they simply did not possess the means even to reduce the net monthly loss of tonnage, yet alone to reverse the trend.

Nor had the Japanese military done much to help matters when, just prior to the outbreak of war, they peremptorily requisitioned a large chunk of the merchant fleet to ferry their troops and supplies all over the Pacific. Whilst this was clearly one of its important functions, it was surely overdoing things to leave only 37 per cent of the existing fleet for the equally vital work of shipping in raw materials. But neither can one give much credit to a High Command that took account of its shipping requirements only on the very eve of a premeditated declaration of war. For not only did this give the relevant authorities very little time to respond to the services' immediate demands, but it also denied them the opportunity to make plans for providing sufficient merchant shipping for future military needs – needs, moreover, which became ever more insistent. During the Guadalcanal campaign the military pressed for the allocation of a further 620,000 tons, but were this time informed that these simply could not be spared. As Tojo remarked: 'Even if we wanted, we could not give the General Staff all the ships they demand. If we did, our steel-production quota would be cut by half and we would be unable to continue the war.'[10] By March 1943 the situation was so bad that the Navy was unable to requisition merchantmen at all, and had to use its own destroyers and submarines as transports, thus making them unavailable for fleet and convoy protection as well as for commerce raiding on their own account.

The authorities at home did try to respond to the crisis. In March 1943 an ambitious building programme was initiated and the tonnage launched increased appreciably over the year. Production was stepped up yet further at the beginning of 1944. By now five-sixths of all shipping steel was allocated to the merchant marine and building was eventually running at six times the level for 1941. But it was all too late, if indeed the Japanese could *ever* have produced a merchant fleet large enough to be proof against American naval might. Even the substantially increased building programme was nowhere near enough to balance losses. In 1943 it replaced only 45 per cent of them, whilst in December 1944 a state-of-the-nation report noted gloomily: 'Shipping lost and damaged amounts to two and a half times newly constructed shipping, and forms the chief cause of the constant impoverishment of national strength.'[11]* Once again, Japanese projections of likely losses had proved to be wildly optimistic. The Japanese Planning Board had estimated that by the end of 1944, if the war lasted that long, Japan would require 5,050,000 gross tons and would have on hand, after balancing losses against replacements, 5,250,000 gross tons of shipping. 'Actually, after the third year of the war Japan was down to 2,100,000 tons of shipping, only half of which was serviceable, and seven months later, at the end of the war, total *serviceable* shipping available to the Japanese was only some 700,000 gross tons. Never in modern times was an island nation so thoroughly cut off.'[12]

But the Japanese plight was not simply a question of the ever-decreasing tonnage available. Equally disastrous was their consistent failure to make optimum use of the ships they did have. An early, almost incomprehensible blunder was the lack of any attempt to sail their merchant ships in convoy. In 1941 the Navy boasted only 30 escort vessels, all of them unarmed, with no new ones to be laid down until early 1943. Moreover, at the outbreak of war, all shipping protection was the responsibility of one single officer, with the derogatory title of 'Staff Officer for Training', and he seems to have made no attempt to dissuade ship-masters from sailing alone. The First Convoy Escort Fleet was set up in June 1942, but it was allocated a mere eight destroyers. The Second Fleet did not appear until March 1943, and even then total resources amounted to only 16 destroyers, five coast defence frigates and five torpedo boats. September saw the creation of the Grand Escort Command, with an admiral in charge, but whatever prestige he might have brought to the job was hardly enhanced by the additional tools put at his disposal: five escort carriers, all in need of extensive repair. Eventually, in March 1944, a proper convoy system was instituted, though even then each convoy contained an average of only 20 merchant ships as opposed to the 70 or so in

---

* It is also to be noted that the new shipping built was hardly of a high standard. The USSBS observes that, in 1943 and 1944, 'the quality of vessels produced suffered very considerably from the haste and hysteria which characterised the program. Harbor officials and ship captains tell monotonously similar stories of incessant breakdown of machinery at sea and cargo gear in port. Furthermore, in the interests of simplicity and speed of construction, every possible feature that could be dispensed with was abandoned. Bulkheads were minimised, double bottoms were eliminated. The net result made the product even more vulnerable to submarine, air and mine attack. The likelihood of a hit resulting in a ship sinking was greatly increased.' (USSBS (Transport Division), *The War Against Japanese Transportation* (GPO, Washington, May 1947), p. 56.)

Allied Atlantic convoys. Regular merchant shipping routes were established to Saipan, Manila, Saigon, North Borneo and Formosa, and the number of escort vessels was increased to roughly 150.

But the effectiveness of this belated effort was low. The escort carriers had an inglorious career: four were sunk between December 1943 and November 1944, none actually joined a convoy until June 1944, and none escorted more than two convoys. One was used entirely for training pilots to work on convoy protection, though the latter's effectiveness was always limited because many of their planes were not fitted with radar, as was also the case with the escort vessels until late 1944. Communications between merchantmen, escorts and aircraft were rudimentary. Few pilots even had the necessary equipment, whilst specialist ratings on the ships tended to be conscripted into the Army as soon as they had gained any experience. Experience was also at a premium in the Navy, and no sooner had the pilots assigned to convoy protection attained a reasonable degree of proficiency than the whole of their Naval Air Group was thrown away as a reconnaissance group in the savage air battle off Formosa in October 1944.

This inefficient use of resources was not entirely the fault of the Japanese, however. Convoying itself was something of a double-edged sword in that individual ships made many fewer journeys than they would have done under the old autonomous system. This was both because they had to spend longer in harbour waiting for a convoy to be assembled or for one of the paltry number of escorts to become available,* and because they could only follow certain prescribed routes which, as the American offensive mounted, became more and more tortuous, hugging the coastline wherever possible. In the early days of the war the journey between Singapore and Japan took ten days; by late 1944 it required well over three weeks. According to the USSBS: 'Convoying and rerouting decreased the freight moved per ship by a factor amounting to 43 per cent in the closing months of the war.'[13]

But the Japanese also created a rod for their own backs by their abject failure properly to coordinate the convoy system at the highest level. In March 1942 all civilian ships had been seized under the terms of the Wartime Shipping Control Ordinance. The prime role

---

* On one occasion, according to an officer with First Convoy Fleet, 'thirty-two ships in Palau harbour waited ninety-five days for lack of one escort ship to travel back to . . . [Japan] with them.' (Quoted in J. Winton, *Convoy* (Michael Joseph, 1983), p. 313.)

of these 'C' ships was to import raw materials and food into the home islands, and thus most of them went out to the South-East Asian and Indies ports in ballast. Military convoys proper, to take supplies out to the Pacific and Asian garrisons, were controlled by the Army and Navy, each of which had completely separate shipping departments. On their return from such great military ports as Truk and Rabaul these ships usually travelled empty in their great hurry to take on more troops or supplies. 'Thus developed the paradox of a maritime nation, desperately short of ships, waging a far-flung war across the seas, but still permitting a condition to exist where empty ships might frequently pass each other going in opposite directions.'[14]

All this, as we have seen, had grave implications for the Japanese war economy, which found the flow of vital raw materials reduced to a trickle. As one authority has emphasised, the resulting shortage was the fundamental weakness of the Japanese economy, the one that was eventually to render futile all attempts to increase the size of her industrial base:

> The basic irony – and for the Japanese, tragedy – of their industrial war effort was that by the time they belatedly recognised the need for raising the level of industrial output, and took energetic and, for their economy, enormous strides in increasing capacity and output, it was too late. The declining flow of raw materials would not support the new higher level of output. Capacity increased but output fell . . . By the middle of fiscal 1944 the Allied attack on shipping had so reduced the importation of raw materials that not only was a further rise of total output impossible, but the foundations of the basic economy crumbled. The Japanese war economy disintegrated at its base . . . [and] by the beginning of 1945 most of the oil refineries were out of oil, the alumina plants out of bauxite, the steel mills lacking in ore and coke, and the munitions plants low in steel and aluminium.[15]*

The absolute dependence of Japan on her merchant marine is

---

* The fatal decline in production that began in 1944 is highlighted by the following figures for Japanese steel and aluminium production during the whole war. Figures represent 1,000 metric tons.

	Steel	Aluminium
1941	5,120	72
1942	5,166	103
1943	5,609	141
1944	4,320	110
1945	803	7

nowhere better illustrated than in this exchange between the head of Mitsubishi Heavy Industries Ltd and American interrogators, shortly after the war:

Q. Do you feel that the Japanese fighting forces suffered shortages of military supplies? And, if so, what specific supplies were most lacking?

A. Aircraft.

Q. What were the limiting factors in aircraft production?

A. Especially skilled workmen, light metals and special steel.

Q. Which specific light metals?

A. Duraluminium.

Q. What was the trouble with aluminium?

A. Lack of bauxite.

Q. Was it through lack of bauxite in the Empire or lack of shipping facilities?

A. Lack of shipping facilities.[16]

In the last analysis, however, it seems clear that Japanese economic weakness was more than just a matter of their feeble merchant fleet. In fact, even if their supply of raw materials had been *absolutely secure* for *whatever* length of time they might have been at war with the United States, they still could not have hoped even remotely to match the massive industrial output of the enemy. Once it became clear that the Americans were not to be bounced out of the ring or psychologically cowed at the first enemy onrush, the Pacific War became a no-contest. Though the Japanese achieved some remarkable increases in production, particularly with regard to munitions, they were merely spitting in the wind. During the first three years of the war, for example, the Japanese increased the share of gross national product devoted to the manufacture of munitions from 23 to 52 per cent. But the Americans equalled this and more, and *their* 50 per cent was beyond the wildest dreams of their opponents. It is a historical commonplace that the Battle of Midway was the turning-point of the Pacific campaign, but this was not so much because one tiny atoll was secured, or even that four carriers were sunk, but because 'henceforth the US . . . would conduct the Pacific War with mass-production methods.'[17]

The Japanese tried valiantly to follow suit, and from the winter of 1942–3 enacted a whole series of draconian measures designed to maximise war production. But it was a fruitless exercise. With regard to the naval war, an American source has concluded: 'Still better

Japanese resistance would not have mattered in the long run, because in no way could Japan have matched America's massive output of pilots, planes and flattops. As the North submerged the South in the American Civil War, so did the United States submerge Japan under a tidal wave of carrier power.'[18] The Japanese have drawn similar conclusions, bemoaning the fact that their 'leaders woefully lacked a true understanding of the United States; they did not . . . appreciate the overwhelming military strength American industry could bring to bear against any enemy.'[19] Table 22 gives some comparative figures for the production of certain strategic items. Even granted that the United States had to split its resources in a war on two fronts, its margin of superiority over Japan is so marked that the figures require little elaboration.

Table 22: us *and Japanese output of selected strategic items 1942–5*

	Unit of measurement	USA	Japan	Ratio
Bituminous coal	000,000 metric tons	2,154	189.8	11.3:1
Crude oil	000,000 us barrels	6,661	29.6	222.0:1
Pig-iron	000,000 metric tons	215	14.1	15.3:1
Finished steel	000,000 metric tons	231	17.1	13.6:1
Aluminium	000 metric tons	2,487	361.0	6.9:1
Merchant shipping	000,000 gross tons	54	3.3	16.4:1
Artillery* (not AA)	units	257,390	7,000	36.7:1

* The following figures, giving Japanese munitions production as a percentage of American, cast further light on the total imbalance between the two economies. The figures relate to production in 1944.

Mortars	4.0%	Aerial bombs	0.6%
Small arms ammunition	6.5%	Tanks	4.7%
AA ammunition	8.0%		

Inherent economic weaknesses and acute shortages such as those described above obviously had a grievous effect on Japanese front-line capabilities, not least upon their most important component, the Navy. Full details can be found in tables 57 to 60 in the Statistical Appendix, which chart the decline of the ijn by type of ship as well as its increasing weakness vis-à-vis the us Navy. Table 57 shows that even in December 1941 Japan's naval superiority rested more upon the quality of her ships than upon their quantity. Indeed, she only exceeded the United States in one category of vessel, aircraft-carriers, and in others, notably destroyers and submarines, was markedly inferior. Pearl Harbor and Java Sea did much to tilt the scales back, but this advantage was transitory, and once American yards got into top gear the ratio of strengths became completely disproportionate, the Americans building five times as many battleships as their opponents, ten times as many aircraft-carriers, six times as many cruisers, and six times as many destroyers. In simple numbers this meant that they built eight more battleships than the Japanese and 124 more carriers.* Armed with a margin for error of these dimensions it is hard to see how the Americans, even with a markedly less competent leadership than they had in the Pacific, could ever have lost the war in that theatre.

Carrier production offers a particularly revealing example of the total supremacy of the American economy. As we have seen, both navies had been slow to appreciate the future importance of carriers and both therefore had to institute crash building programmes early in the war. In the next four years the Americans launched 17 fleet carriers, nine light and over one hundred escort. The Japanese delayed giving a high priority to carrier construction until after the Battle of Midway. Then, however, all battleship projects were cancelled and orders given for *Hiryu*-class fleet carriers and five *Taiho*-class super carriers. Actually building them was quite a different matter, and even though the Navy soon halted construction on all other vessels larger than light cruisers, only four of the planned fleet carriers left the slipways and none of the super carriers. A few conversions were also made, turning two seaplane tenders into light carriers, four liners into escort carriers, and a battleship and cruiser into fleet carriers,† but total production during the war still only amounted to ten fleet carriers, five light and five escort.

Similar ratios applied right across the board, as American shipyards went from strength to strength and the Japanese slowly stagnated. As each month passed, American naval superiority increased (see tables 58 and 60) and with it their ability to concentrate an overwhelming force against any chosen portion of the Japanese perimeter. This meant in turn that the loss ratio also increasingly turned against the Japanese (see tables 59 and 60), so that by the

---

* Over 90 per cent of carriers built fought in the Pacific. It is true of course that the figure for total US carrier production is a little misleading in that a large proportion of them were escort carriers. These, however, were far from negligible ships, carrying approximately 35 planes each, and it must be emphasised that American construction of fleet carriers alone was almost double that of the Japanese. Table 59 gives details on carrier construction by type.

† The battleship conversion, *Shinano*, never even saw action. She was sunk by an American submarine as soon as she put to sea.

end of the war they had lost many more ships than the Americans in every category. Table 59 gives the relevant figures and shows amongst other things that the Japanese lost 20 aircraft-carriers to 11 American, 11 battleships to 2, and 38 cruisers to 10. It further shows that as a proportion of their available fleet Japanese losses were more serious than even the bald figures suggest. The 135 destroyers they lost, for example, were not only double the American figure but represented 80 per cent of the total built as against an equivalent figure of only 15 per cent for the Americans.

It was Japanese awareness of this growing disparity in naval strengths that largely explains the paucity of fleet actions in the Pacific between 1943 and 1945. Whilst it is true that for six months after the evacuation of Guadalcanal *neither* side felt strong enough to try to force the issue – with the Japanese waiting for replacements for the Midway losses and the Americans for the arrival of the new *Essex*-class fleet carriers – for the rest of the war all such constraints only affected the Japanese, who realised that just one unsuccessful fleet engagement could break the back of their naval power once and for all. For their ships, as Admiral Nagano had already pointed out, were virtually irreplaceable.

It is rather ironic that a service that had for years shaped its strategic thinking around the Nelsonian concept of the Decisive Naval Battle should end up being afraid of that very eventuality. But there is no way in which any belligerent can win a war by constantly refusing to face the enemy's main forces and the Japanese realised that they would have to risk all at some stage. Though their fleet was constantly on the retreat right through to mid-1944, moving first out of Rabaul, then Truk, then Davao (Mindanao) until it finally took station in Tawi Tawi (north-east Borneo) and the Lingga Roads (off Singapore), it was realised that some *ne plus ultra* line had to be nominated, some point beyond which US amphibious forces must not pass. By spring 1944, Biak, off the northern coast of New Guinea, was regarded as the most likely target for the next major naval offensive and plans were drawn up for Operation A, to engage the US fleet in a decisive action thereabouts.

In fact, the Americans plumped for Saipan, in the Marianas, instead and so the Japanese now dispatched their fleet into the Philippine Sea to take final issue with Nimitz. Battle was joined on 15 June 1944, the Americans deploying 15 carriers against the Japanese 9 and 890 naval aircraft against 430. The combats with the poorly trained Japanese aircrew* were so one-sided that the first stage of the battle soon became known as the Great Marianas Turkey Shoot, the Japanese losing 400 planes to the Americans' 130.[†] The former limped back to port, with their naval aircrews decimated once again and minus three of their precious fleet carriers, two of which had been lost to submarines snapping at the heels of the retreating fleet. Responsible naval planners estimated that the surviving fleet would not be in anything like trim again, especially with regard to carrier aircraft, until March 1945.

Unfortunately, there was no hope that they would be given such a respite, and the American steamroller drove remorselessly forwards. Once more the Japanese had to put up or shut up, either risk their fleet for possibly the last time or slink back to the home islands. Leyte, in the Philippines, was nominated as the new sticking point. As Admiral Soemu Toyoda wrote:

> Since without the participation of our Combined Fleet there was little possibility of our land forces in the Philippines having any chance against MacArthur, it was decided to send the whole fleet, taking the gamble . . . There was a chance we could lose the entire fleet, but I felt the chance had to be taken. Should we lose in the Philippines operations, even though the Fleet should be left, the shipping to the south would be completely cut off so that the Fleet, if it should come back to Japanese waters, could not obtain its fuel supply. If it should remain in southern waters, it could not receive supplies of ammunition and arms. There would be no sense in saving the Fleet at the expense of . . . the Philippines.[20‡]

The fleet set sail once more in October 1944, to engage the vast American armada that had assembled to cover the Leyte landings. The balance of forces most definitely favoured the Americans, as

---

* See below for details on the deteriorating standards amongst Japanese naval flyers.

† Many of the latter were not lost in combat but had to ditch into the sea operating beyond their fuel capacity. Yet others smashed up in perilous deck landings at night.

‡ Here one notes the direct operational effects of Japan's oil shortage. Lingga Roads and Tawi Tawi had become major naval bases at this stage of the war simply because it was impossible to provide adequate fuel for ships stationed in Japan. But taking oil almost directly from source had its drawbacks. For it was not refined and was thus highly volatile. If a ship thus fuelled were to be hit, and many were, the chances of explosion were greatly increased.

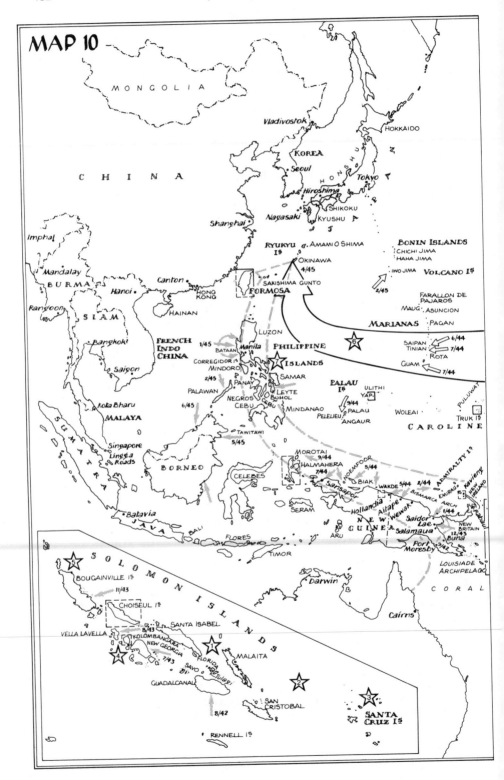

MAP 10

MONGOLIA

Vladivostok
HOKKAIDO

KOREA
Seoul
Tokyo
HONSHU
Hiroshima
SHIKOKU
Nagasaki   KYUSHU
Shanghai

CHINA

Imphal
Mandalay
Hanoi   Canton
BURMA
HONG KONG
Rangoon
SIAM   HAINAN
Bangkok
Saigon
FRENCH INDO CHINA

RYUKYU Is   AMAMI O SHIMA
OKINAWA 4/45
SAKISHIMA GUNTO
FORMOSA

BONIN ISLANDS
CHICHI JIMA
HAHA JIMA
IWO JIMA   VOLCANO Is
2/45
FARALLON DE PAJAROS
MAUG ASUNCION
MARIANAS   PAGAN

LUZON
1/45   Manila   PHILIPPINE
BATAAN
CORREGIDOR Is   ISLANDS
MINDORO
2/45   PANAY   SAMAR
PALAWAN   LEYTE
NEGROS BOHOL
6/45   CEBU
CEBU   MINDANAO
PALAU Is   ULITHI
YAP
9/44
PALAU
PELELIEU
ANGAUR
WOLEAI
PULUWAT
TRUK Is
CAROLINE

SAIPAN   6/44
TINIAN   7/44
ROTA
GUAM   7/44

Kota Bharu
MALAYA
TAWITAWI
5/45

Singapore
Lingga Roads
BORNEO
CELEBES
MOROTAI 9/44
HALMAHERA 7/44
Sansapor   NOEMFOOR 5/44
BIAK   WAKDE 5/44 2/44
SERAM   Hollandia   Aitape
Wewak
NEW   Saidor
GUINEA   Lae
ARU   Salamaua
Port Moresby
ADMIRALTY Is
BISMARCK ARCH   Kavieng
EMIRAU   NEW IRELAND
NEW BRITAIN
Buna
12/43
9/42
LOUISIADE ARCHIPELAGO

Batavia
JAVA
BALI
FLORES
TIMOR
Darwin
Cairns
CORAL

SOLOMON ISLANDS
BOUGAINVILLE Is
11/43
CHOISEUL Is
VELLA LAVELLA   8/43   SANTA ISABEL
KOLOMBANGARA
NEW GEORGIA
1/43   FLORIDA
GUADALCANAL   SAVO
8/42
SAN CRISTOBAL
MALAITA
RENNELL Is
SANTA CRUZ Is

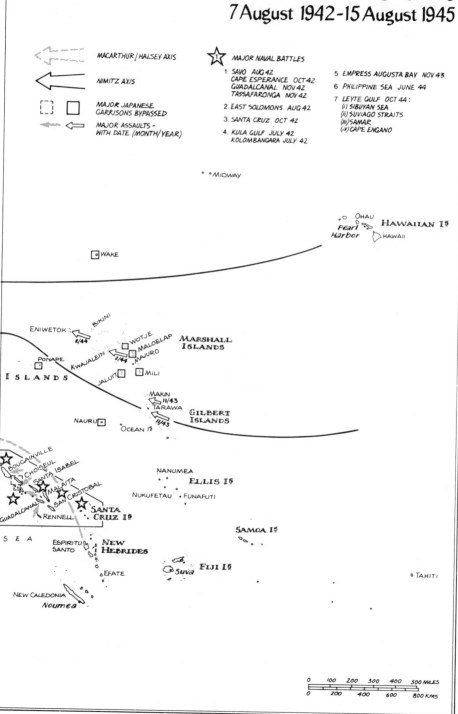

The Pacific: The American Counter-Offensive 7 August 1942-15 August 1945

MACARTHUR / HALSEY AXIS

NIMITZ AXIS

MAJOR JAPANESE GARRISONS BYPASSED

MAJOR ASSAULTS – WITH DATE (MONTH/YEAR)

MAJOR NAVAL BATTLES

1. SAVO AUG 42
   CAPE ESPERANCE OCT 42
   GUADALCANAL NOV 42
   TASSAFARONGA NOV 42
2. EAST SOLOMONS AUG 42
3. SANTA CRUZ OCT 42
4. KULA GULF JULY 42
   KOLOMBANGARA JULY 42

5. EMPRESS AUGUSTA BAY NOV 43
6. PHILIPPINE SEA JUNE 44
7. LEYTE GULF OCT 44:
   (i) SIBUYAN SEA
   (ii) SUVIAGO STRAITS
   (iii) SAMAR
   (iv) CAPE ENGANO

MIDWAY

OHAU
Pearl Harbor
HAWAIIAN IS
HAWAII

WAKE

ENIWETOK
BIKINI
2/44
WOTJE
KWAJALEIN
MALOELAP
2/44
MAJURO
MARSHALL ISLANDS
PONAPE
JALUIT
MILI
ISLANDS

MAKIN
11/43
TARAWA
GILBERT ISLANDS
NAURU
OCEAN IS
11/43

BOUGAINVILLE
CHOISEUL
SANTA ISABEL
MALAITA
SAN CRISTOBAL
GUADALCANAL
RENNELL
SANTA CRUZ IS

NANUMEA
ELLIS IS
NUKUFETAU FUNAFUTI

SAMOA IS

SEA

ESPIRITU SANTO
NEW HEBRIDES
EFATE
Suva
FIJI IS
TAHITI

NEW CALEDONIA
Noumea

0   100   200   300   400   500 MILES
0   200   400   600   800 KMS

can be seen from the figures in the table below. Equally one-sided was the disparity in losses. For the Americans they were one light carrier, two escort carriers and three destroyers. The Japanese, on the other hand, lost all their four carriers, three battleships, ten cruisers and nine destroyers, not to mention almost all of their remaining naval aircrew.

	Fleet/ light carriers	Escort carriers	Battle- ships	Cruis.	Dest.	Aircraft Naval	Land
USA	8	26	12	24	111	1,400	-
Japan	1	3	9	19	35	116	300

There were no more fleet actions for the rest of the war, and almost all subsequent Japanese naval losses were to aircraft or submarines, suffered either as they tried to get reinforcements through to the remaining Pacific garrisons on Luzon, Iwo Jima and Okinawa or, as in the case of the battleship *Yamato* and its escort group, in futile naval variants of *hara kiri*. To June 1945 three battleships were lost on such missions, along with two carriers and six cruisers. Thereafter the remnants of the fleet did not even venture out of port and the Americans pulverised them where they lay. Many were holed up at Kure, 'the port where Jap warships went to die'. The US carriers struck in late July. By the evening of the 25th

> the Japanese Navy had ceased to exist. Photographs showed the battleship *Ise* down by the bow and resting on the bottom; her sister ship, the *Hyuga* was awash amidships; the *Haruna* was beached and burning, with a large hole in her stern. The *Katsaguri*'s flight deck was torn and buckled; the *Amagi*'s could have been used as a ski-slide. The heavy cruisers *Tone* and *Aobe* were beached . . . [Admiral Toyoda] could reach the cabin of his flagship, the light cruiser *Oyodo*, only in a diving suit.

It was Pearl Harbor all over again, and it was meant to be. Admiral Halsey, who ordered these carrier strikes, admitted in his memoirs that 'appropriate retaliation' was a prime motive, 'for the sake of national morale'.[21] There was certainly no other reason, for Halsey must have been aware that all these ships had already been decommissioned and were either in mothballs or being used as anti-aircraft platforms of dubious efficacy. A few more ships were dotted around the home islands or skulking in Singapore. But it was a pathetic tally. Only two heavy cruisers were still afloat, both damaged. Two light cruisers were extant and 44 destroyers, but of these latter only five were fully operational.

Along with the navies, the other major component of warfare in the Pacific was the opposing air forces, and the course of their struggle differed little, in broad outline, from that of the war at sea. The Japanese actually began the war with a margin of aerial superiority, their numerical advantage considerably enhanced by greater combat experience, gained in China in the late 1930s, and technically more advanced aircraft. As the war progressed, however, American production completely outstripped their own, despite considerable increases in the early years, and by late 1943 the Americans had the virtual run of the skies. The bare figures tell their own story. Thus, in December 1941, the Americans, British and Dutch had 1,290 aircraft in this theatre, mostly obsolete, as opposed to 1,650 front-line Japanese planes. By the end of the war, however, when the Japanese had managed to turn out a further 64,800 planes, the Americans had produced just under 300,000.

Little wonder that Admiral Nagano told American interrogators in 1946: 'If I were to give you one factor as the leading one that led to your victory, I would give you the air force.'[22] Or more precisely, he might have added, the lack of a Japanese one. For, although their factories accomplished remarkable feats in overcoming the shortage of basic materials and inadequate tooling up before the war,[*] they simply could not keep pace with the Americans. In 1944, for example, the latter's factories turned out 96,318 machines, 50 per cent more than the Japanese produced in the whole war. The figures for aircraft engines were even more dramatic – 256,912 American in 1944 as against 104,446 Japanese during the whole war. Moreover, the boost in Japanese production was not only inadequate, it could only be temporary. The extra demand for raw materials, when added to the clamour of the shipyards for more of the same, was more than supplies could meet. As the USSBS remarked:

> Altogether, the Japanese aircraft industry was in far worse shape by the fall of 1944 than we realised . . . The pro-duction peak achieved . . . was gained only at the expense

[*] Production rose from 12,151 aircraft in 1941 to 46,526 in 1944.

of exhausting stock piles. We did not fully appreciate how far the national economy had thus been undermined by . . . the demands of a prolonged war against all basic commodities.[23]

The inadequacy of production levels is further highlighted by the impossible demands of the armed forces. In September 1943 the Army and Navy let it be known that they would require a minimum of 55,000 planes during the next year. Only 28,000 were produced. Towards the end of 1944 they demanded 5,000 new planes per month for the foreseeable future. Average monthly production until the end of the war was a mere 1,200. American industry, on the other hand, produced everything that was asked of it, and table 23 shows just what a devastating aerial supremacy they established.

Table 23: US *and Japanese front-line aircraft strengths in the Pacific January 1943 – July 1945*

	Front-line Strength		
	USA	Japan	Ratio
Jan. 1943	3,537	3,200	1.1:1
Jan. 1944	11,442	4,050	2.8:1
Jan. 1945	17,976	4,600	3.9:1
July 1945	21,908	4,100	5.3:1

Local shortages were often yet more acute. Even in late 1943, both spearheads of the dual MacArthur–Nimitz offensive were amply supplied. In the Solomons and Bismarcks the Japanese could muster only 292 aircraft to meet MacArthur and Halsey's 631, whilst in the Gilberts, Nimitz's first major assault, the respective figures were 46 and 340. Early the next year the ratios were yet worse, and at Rabaul one Japanese air officer found on his arrival 'an astonishing conviction that the war could not possibly be won, that all we were doing was postponing the inevitable'.[24] That conviction grew. After a particularly fierce carrier raid on Truk, in April 1944, a Japanese naval commander came close to despair: 'The seasons do not change. I try to look like a proud rear-admiral, but it is hard with a potato hook in my hands. It rains every day, the flowers bloom every day, the enemy bombs us every day – so why remember?'[25] As Nimitz blasted the Marianas, in June 1944, the Japanese commander on Saipan wrote to Tojo: 'There is no hope of victory in places where we do not have control of the air.'[26] A little later, with both prongs of the US offensive converging on the Philippines, a senior Japanese commander maintained that his aircraft would easily repulse any amphibious assault. A local commander, more in touch with military realities, took bitter exception. The idea was fine in theory, he agreed, but one could not 'fight with concept alone. Words will not sink American ships and that becomes clear when you compare their aircraft with ours.'[27]

Clearly, such overwhelming local superiorities gave the Americans a tremendous advantage in actual aerial combat. The carrier planes were particularly well blessed, making the most of their ability to swoop on one Japanese base or another, unleash the payload of half-a-dozen fleet carriers or more, and quickly withdraw. In 1944 and 1945 this was just as important a role for Nimitz's fleet* as was the physical assault on the various islands, and it wreaked enormous carnage. Some comparative loss rates, including certain operations by MacArthur's land-based Fifth Air Force, are given in table 24.

So well were Nimitz's carrier operations orchestrated that the Japanese were as often as not caught completely napping and only managed to get a fraction of their planes airborne. In this regard it is interesting to note that fully 40 per cent of the Japanese planes destroyed by US Navy squadrons were still on the ground. Other figures speak just as eloquently of the total US superiority. Japanese pilot losses, averaging 500 per month in early 1942, had by late 1944 climbed to four times that figure. Total plane losses are perhaps the most revealing of all. According to the best estimates, the Americans lost some 8,700 planes in the Pacific whilst the Japanese lost 38,000, over four times as many. The utterly desperate straits

---

* Nimitz's actual weapon, in his capacity as Cincpoa, was the US Fifth Fleet (as distinct from MacArthur's Seventh Fleet and Halsey's Third). The carriers were its cutting edge and in late 1943 were grouped together, along with considerable ancillary shipping, as Task Force 50. In January 1944 this was renamed TF58 and divided into four autonomous Task Groups. At the same time, command of the Fifth Fleet was given to Admiral Raymond Spruance (though Nimitz was still Cincpoa) and that of TF58 to Admiral Marc Mitscher. In June 1944 Admiral Halsey left the South Pacific Area, but it was deemed impossible not to keep him on as a fleet commander. His ships, therefore, were merged with Spruance's and from September he and Spruance took alternate command of Fifth Fleet, though under Halsey it was known as Third Fleet. Mitscher always kept control of the carriers, though when Halsey was his superior his Task Force was known as TF38.

Table 24: US *and Japanese aircraft losses in selected engagements 1943–5*

		Losses	
Date	Place	US	Japanese
16 June 1943	Guadalcanal	6	107
Nov. 1943 – Jan. 1944	Rabaul	136	359
17 Feb. 1944	Truk	13	270
23 Feb. 1944	Marianas	6	168
29–30 April 1944	Truk	35	91
15–16 June 1944	Bonins	22	300
28 Aug. 1944	Yap, Palaus, Mindanao	8	200
7–24 Sept. 1944	Philippines	72	1,200
10–15 Oct. 1944	Formosa	90	600
14–16 Dec. 1944	Luzon	65	270
1 April – 15 June 1944	Okinawa	763	7,830

to which Japanese aviation was reduced are encapsulated in this poignant diary entry by Vice-Admiral Fukudome. Referring to his pilots' efforts to repulse enemy carrier attacks on Formosa, in October 1944, he wrote: 'Our fighters were nothing but so many eggs thrown at the stone wall of the indomitable enemy formation.'[28]

But Japanese weakness in the air was not simply the result of the lack of planes. Pilot losses have already been touched upon, and the problem here, just as in Germany, was compounded by the acute shortage of adequately trained replacements. Once again, the Japanese conviction that the war would be a short one was at the root of the problem, as they had assumed that the aerial élite that existed in December 1941 would more than suffice to drive the Americans out of the skies for good. Thus they made little provision for the training of new pilots, and by the time the need for them had become fully apparent they had neither the fuel nor the spare aircraft, particularly of the newer types that were actually used in combat, to give new recruits the proper amount or the proper type of flying time. By late 1944, when every American pilot had undergone a rigorous two-year training programme, clocking up over 300 hours of flying time, no Japanese pilot had had more than six months and many, especially carrier pilots, had had only two or three. The regulation 100 hours of flying instruction was cut to 40 in 1944 'and navigational training was cut altogether, pilots being instructed to follow their leaders into action. Naturally many failed to return to base, even if they survived the air battle.'[29] Of his experiences as an instructor in 1944, one Japanese pilot has written:

Everything was urgent. We were told to rush the men through, to forget the fine points, just to teach them how to fly and shoot. One after the other, singly, in twos and threes, the training planes smashed into the ground, skidded wildly through the air. For long and tedious months, I tried to build fighter pilots . . . at Omura. It was a hopeless task. Our facilities were too meagre, the demand too great.[30]*

These same shortages of fuel and planes also meant that not enough pilots could be trained, even to the most rudimentary level. By August 1945 total Japanese flying personnel numbered 35,000. Even by the end of the previous year, however, the Americans had graduated 226,000 pilots alone, so many, in fact, that, as we saw in an earlier chapter, the pilot training programme was *cut* by two-thirds.

The low calibre of the Japanese fliers that *were* turned out made them an extremely dubious military asset. This was already apparent in early 1944, when the Japanese tried to expand their land-based fighter units in the Marianas, the Carolines and the Palaus for a concerted air assault against the American spearheads. Pressure from MacArthur and Nimitz was too heavy, however, and the pilots were obliged to hop endlessly from one air base to another to avoid increasingly heavy air strikes. It has been estimated that the 1,600 Japanese planes assembled in this area suffered up to 80 per cent losses, well over half of them from 'operational' causes, that is crashing on landing or take-off or having to ditch into the sea.†
The raw replacements performed just as badly in actual combat, as was evidenced during the Great Marianas Turkey Shoot. US pilots were unanimous in their opinion. One wrote that 'the enemy planes seemed to have no formulated defence tactics. The [dive-]bombers did not appear to cover them, but went into individual . . . manoeuvres . . . to escape the Hellcats.' According to a post-combat analysis, 'it was the opinion of all the fighter pilots . . . that the Japanese attack was not a good one. Many of the fighter pilots were content to stay out of the action entirely. The dive-bombers and torpedo planes were

---

* It should also be noted that this pilot only had a training function because he had been injured. It was not standard Japanese practice to rotate veteran pilots into the training command, and this inevitably led to poor practical instruction as well as to a higher wastage of the best pilots.
† Of the total number of pilot losses throughout the war, 60 per cent were estimated to have been operational.

loathe to keep their defensive formations, and separated, thus losing all chance of co-ordinated attack.'[31]* A Hellcat pilot passed terser comment, stating that enemy fighter pilots 'couldn't hit an elephant if it was tied down for them.'[32]

It has also been variously noted that the whole tactical direction of this battle was remarkably crude, the air commanders relying on a straight thrust, with little or no evasion, simply to punch a hole through the American defences and pounce on the vulnerable carriers with whatever aircraft remained. Such tactics were simply not adequate now that all American ships were fitted with serviceable radar, and could thus locate and interdict an attacking force up to 60 miles away, forcing it to run the gauntlet for a full 15 minutes. It is important to realise, however, that the feeble standard of Japanese training simply did not allow them any alternative, as anything more sophisticated would have been beyond the capabilities of their hapless mobs of fledgling pilots desperately hanging on to the tails of the handful of veterans. The Japanese After Action (Air) Report pointed out that whatever ploys and gambits might have seemed attractive to the planners, the players themselves were simply not up to it:

> It reads in Chapter 49 of the Combat Sutra that 'tactics is like sandals. Those who are strong should wear them. A cripple should not dare to wear them.' The plan in [this] . . . operation is minutely worked and the strategy of the operational unit has been checked in great detail. But the training for combat duty in each detachment is not complete. Therefore, it looks, as said in the Combat Sutra, as if well-made sandals were allowed to be worn by a cripple.[33]

Similar considerations also go a long way towards explaining the Japanese resort to *kamikaze* tactics.† Given the poor standard of airmanship, the acute shortage of fuel, and the desperate need to improve the 'productivity' of the dwindling air fleets, such a tactic seemed to many hard-headed commanders to be the only feasible option. The *samurai* ethic did have its part to

---

* Not that the bombers would have done much even if they had kept formation. A Japanese source notes that, in late 1942, nine such planes attacking a target ship taking evasive action at 16 knots could reasonably expect to score nine direct hits. By late 1944 such practice runs rarely scored any hits at all.
† The Japanese referred to the suicide pilots as *shimpu* units.

play, of course, but the primary consideration was simply to make each single aircraft as potent a weapon as possible. Indeed, Allied commanders at the time, who had much to say about the 'barbarism' and 'lunacy' of such tactics, might have done well to ponder whether there was much difference between the life expectancy of a Japanese suicide pilot and an aircrew in the Strategic Bombing Offensive.

But it was not simply the lack of planes and pilots that so hampered the Japanese air effort. For the same logistical shortages and inherent productive constraints that limited aircraft manufacture and pilot training also had deleterious effects on every aspect of performance and maintenance. Shortages of fuel meant that aircraft were flown as little as possible. By 1944 first-line planes were flown on average once every three weeks, so that their engines were seldom turned over and thus in poor condition. This same shortage, coupled with the lack of merchant shipping,* also meant that it was difficult to get adequate numbers of maintenance personnel out to the scattered air-bases, and even harder to keep them supplied with spare parts and tools. As the USSBS commented, the Japanese could never provide 'adequate maintenance, logistic support, communications and control, and airfields and bases adequately prepared to handle large numbers of planes. As a result they were unable to concentrate a large percentage of their air strength at any one time or place.'[34] And just as they never got enough maintenance personnel† and equipment into conquered islands, so did they find it difficult to get them out again when it became time to evacuate. Japanese sources complained: '. . . the mechanics and engineers who kept planes in operation were left on islands. As islands fell, pilots came home; but maintenance men did not, and gradually skilled mechanics ran short . . . Men whose skills represented the experience of many years were deserted . . . Thus we lost for ever their ability to contribute to subsequent air operations.'[35] The Americans had no such problems. A 1944 sample of Army, Navy and Marine Corps planes in the Pacific revealed that a remarkable 80 per cent of them were operational at any one time.

---

*And of transport aircraft. Throughout the war, the average number built was less than 400 annually.

† Lack of personnel training was also a problem. The US Army Air Force, on the other hand, had alone graduated 997,000 mechanics and fitters by the end of 1944.

Acute logistic difficulties also affected the quality of new planes manufactured. According to the Japanese:

> . . . those aircraft that we did manage to produce . . . were less effective than usual, for the inferior materials employed in their manufacture reduced flight performance and increased the time spent in maintenance and overhaul. Vital equipment failed all too often, and our pilots cursed the planes which failed them just as they attacked the great enemy air fleets.[36]

Air-frame quality plummeted, mainly because of the poor quality of jigs and fixtures and the consequent lack of interchangeability. But defects in the air-frames often went unnoticed because test-flight times were reduced more and more. At the beginning of the war two to three hours, with five take-offs and landings, was the norm, but later, due to demand at the front and shortage of fuel, an aircraft often received its only test-flight whilst en route to the depot where it was to be delivered. And if it actually reached the depot most defects that showed up were simply overlooked. But many never got there at all. 'An outstanding case of faulty material and poor maintenance was shown in a Japanese diary covering the delivery of 80 Ki-84 (Franks) from Japan to Lingayen Bay, 4 November 1944, where only 14 planes reached their destination. Trouble with engines, fuel systems, hydraulics, and failure of landing gears were the principal causes of trouble.'[37]

Engines became increasingly unreliable. Friction test runs became more and more infrequent – every engine at the beginning of the war, one in ten towards the end – whilst running-in times were cut by a third. Yet these cuts were made at the very time when testing was most needed, for much greater tolerances had been allowed on small parts, to maximise production, whilst the quality of the alloys used had deteriorated badly. Towards the end of the war, because of their virtual unavailability, the percentages of nickel and molybdenum in the steel for crankshafts had dropped from 4 to zero and 0.5 to zero respectively.* The effects of all this were summarised by the US Army's Air Technical Intelligence Group shortly after the war:

---

* It was not only the quality of the resulting alloy that deteriorated. As the supply of various raw materials dried up, alloy specifications were constantly changed – 20 times by May 1944 – and this made it impossible to keep up a regular flow of the metals affected.

As an indication of the deteriorating quality of workmanship and materials, particularly in engine and power plant accessories, it was stated that at the beginning of the war the Japanese Navy was able to maintain operational availability of 80 per cent. The percentage progressively became 50 and in some cases 20. These losses were due to a combination of poor factory workmanship, inferior materials and poor maintenance. In many cases only one out of three airplanes ever reached the front lines due to engine failure.[38]

A final instance of the baleful influence of the various constraints on production concerns the fate of the downed aircrew. Until mid-1943 the problem was admittedly somewhat academic, as they were not provided with parachutes. Later, however, at the very time when the shortage of experienced pilots was becoming acute, the Japanese still refused to rescue any that splashed down because of the shortage of flying boats. The flyers themselves were less than impressed with this argument and the 'attitude . . . that [we] could not tolerate the *possible* loss of a large flying boat merely to effect the *certain* rescue of one aircrew.'[39]

For all these reasons, then, it is scarcely to be wondered at that, by 1944, the Americans were able to roam the skies with virtual impunity. The operations of Japanese and American carrier aircraft mirror the situation perfectly. In 1943 and 1944 the former, because of the growing lack of land-based planes, were forced to press their carrier pilots into tours of duty on the island strips. Three times they were transferred from the flat-tops to beef up strengths for supposedly decisive land-based strikes against the advancing Americans. In April 1943 they took part in Operation I against New Guinea and the Solomons, when 160 carrier planes were used. Their efforts were largely ineffective and numerous planes were lost. In November of the same year another 173 such aircraft participated in Operation Ro. Brought down from Truk to Rabaul, they were intended to help break up MacArthur and Halsey's drive towards Bougainville. The operation was directed by Yamamoto personally, and when he called it off on 12 November he claimed complete success. Those on the spot knew better. American losses had in fact been light, whilst it was only a sad remnant of planes and pilots that returned to the carriers at Truk. Until October 1944 the Japanese were busy trying to scrape together replacements for these losses, not to mention the 400 planes and pilots downed over the Philippine Sea in June, but then they were yet again dissipated in land-based operations from Formosa. By the time of Leyte Gulf only 100 or so carrier aircraft remained, whose pilots were not even trained in deck-landing, being expected to make for the nearest *terra firma* if they survived combat. They did not.

The Americans, on the other hand, possessed a veritable floating cornucopia. The tremendous loss rates inflicted on Japanese aircraft have already been noted, but it is worth while to stress here how ineffective this rendered Japanese resistance. Even at the beginning of Nimitz's offensive, during the assaults on the Gilbert and Marshall Islands,

> our carrier forces had in excess of nine hundred aircraft, more than five times the number possessed by the enemy in the entire . . . area. Due to the enemy dispersion of this limited number . . . it was highly improbable that our carrier forces would encounter as much as one to twenty in air opposition . . . Events . . . fully substantiated this estimate, for enemy air efforts were *less than one to our one hundred* in terms of sorties encountered.[40]

Such ratios were more or less the norm. During the war as a whole US Navy fighters made 500,000 sorties, yet only 12,000 of these (2.5 per cent) resulted in aerial combat. During 1944 and 1945 their dive- and torpedo-bombers made 102,000 sorties of which only 740 (0.7) per cent) resulted in combat. In that same period those bombers lost only 18 planes, and even when the 1943 total is added, losses were still a mere 43. In other words, dozens of pilots must never even have seen a Japanese plane throughout their tour in the Pacific, whilst literally hundreds were never actually involved in combat.

Equally revealing of the US aerial superiority was the tactic they most favoured towards the end of the war. This was known as the Big Blue Blanket,* in which an umbrella of fighters was kept over enemy airfields day and night so that their planes could not take off to interfere with amphibious operations. At certain moments, when squadrons were being relieved, bombers would be sent in to destroy the grounded planes. As one senior carrier commander, Admiral McCain, wrote, the aim was to 'blanket the threatening enemy air opposition day and night with the most air power available . . . [Under that] blanket the enemy's air is . . . held thoroughly helpless

---

* US Navy planes were painted blue.

while it is being systematically destroyed.'[41]

The number of carriers, planes and pilots needed for these aerial swarms was prodigious, and yet the Americans found them without much difficulty. The Japanese, in contrast, were reduced to turning their surviving aircraft into flying bombs, hoping against hope that the suicidal devotion of individuals could somehow offset the total material supremacy of their enemy. *Kamikaze*, 'Divine Wind', was a reference to the fortuitous storm that had turned back a Mongol invasion fleet in 1570. But war was now more than a matter of mere chance. Gross national product, raw materials reserves, productivity, industrial manpower – these were the new determinants of victory, and against the mighty American economy the *kamikazes* were just more eggs against the wall. Ironically, the American fleet off Luzon *was* struck by a great typhoon, on 17 December 1944, and a considerable ordeal it was for all involved. Three destroyers were swamped, 790 men lost, and 28 lesser craft had to return to port for repairs. Unfortunately this still left the Americans with some 1,500 naval vessels in the Pacific. Divine Winds were not what they used to be.

It seems fairly clear, then, from all the details given above, that the American victory in the Pacific relied heavily on industrial predominance and the enormous margins of superiority in military hardware that flowed from it. The details of the actual island fighting substantiate this point, showing that along both MacArthur's and Nimitz's axes of advance the attackers relied very heavily upon simply saturating their opponents with massed firepower. The logistical problems solved in these advances by Third, Fifth and Seventh Fleet planners represent a prodigious achievement, but it is difficult to avoid the impression that, rather as with Patton in Europe, when it came to actually deploying men at the sharp end, commanders lacked subtlety.

Both Japanese and American accounts of 'island hopping' make the point about material superiority very clearly. On Iwo Jima the local naval commander, Admiral Ichimaru, wrote a letter to President Roosevelt in which he complained that 'only brute force rules the world'. At about the same time, the Japanese authorities produced a propaganda leaflet on 'The Psychology of the Individual American'. They were, it claimed, 'expert liars. They are taken in by flattery and propaganda. They go into battle with no spiritual incentive, and rely on material superiority.'[42]

The effects of the latter were apparent at all levels. Most obvious on the Pacific islands themselves was the massive firepower that the Americans could bring to bear on even the least significant strongpoint. Their basic doctrine was expounded by a us divisional historian: 'The Yank style of fighting was to wait for the artillery to come up and let the big guns blast the enemy positions as barren of all life as possible. It saved many American lives and got better results, although it took longer.'[43] It was also rather expensive. On Pelelieu, in the Palaus, it was estimated that it took an average of 1,589 rounds of heavy and light ammunition to kill each Japanese soldier. But the effects on the Japanese were devastating. On New Georgia, in August 1943, 'the Americans inundated the hills with mortar and 37mm fire until they literally made the top of Biblio [Hill] bounce. Japanese soldiers' guns and pill-boxes flew as much as fifteen feet into the air, while other unfortunates blown out of their holes "ran around in little circles like stunned chickens", to be mown down by machine guns.'[44]

On Kwajalein, in January 1944, the defenders 'were convinced the Americans had a secret weapon, a device that could detect men in the dark; every time someone left his hiding place he was killed. Word spread to take off helmets and ground bayonets after dusk. They still were killed; the "secret weapon" was concentrated and steady fire power.'[45] On Saipan, in June 1944, the commander, General Igeta, radioed his superior that his position was fast becoming hopeless:

> . . . we are menaced by brazenly low-flying planes, and the enemy blasts at us from all sides with fierce naval and artillery cross fire. As a result, even if we remove units from the front lines and send them to the rear, their fighting strength is cut down every day. Also, the enemy attacks with fierce concentration of bombs and artillery. Step by step he comes toward us and concentrates his fire on us as we withdraw, so that wherever we go we are quickly surrounded by fire.[46]

In the following month, on Noemfoor, off New Guinea, supporting naval gunfire was so intense that it 'pounded the defenders into that desirable state known to pugilists as "punch drunk". Japanese encountered . . . were so stunned from the effects of the bombardment that all fight was taken out of them; even those in nearby caves were dazed and . . . milled about aimlessly, showed neither fight nor desire to surrender, and were mowed down by rifle fire and machine guns.'[47] On Guam, in the same month, a Japanese soldier wrote in his diary: 'We had been thinking that we might win through a night counter-attack; but when the star shells came over one after another, we could only use our men as human bullets . . . I was horrified by the number of deaths on our side due to naval gunfire, which continued daily.'[48] The last message from General Ushijima on Okinawa, in April 1945, read: 'Our strategy, tactics and techniques were all used to the utmost and we fought valiantly. But it was as nothing before the material strength of the enemy.'[49] Towards the end of this battle, according to one Japanese account, 'individual fighting of a desperate nature continued for a while with rifles, grenades and swords but, against enemy superiority . . . human beings were helpless.'[50] All that remained was the last futile *samurai* gesture, as described here by a Marine lieutenant: 'We cornered fifty or so . . . on the end of the island, where they attempted a banzai charge, but we cut them down like overripe wheat, and they lay like tired children with their faces in the sand.'[51]

In fairness to American commanders along both axes, there was probably little alternative to this heavy-handed response in the tactical situation. When one examines certain of the decisions made at the operational level, however, one can discern a definite ham-fistedness in direction that, in MacArthur's case at least, is considerably at odds with the version of events produced by his own publicity machine and put forward in his *Reminiscences*. These latter constitute a fulsome tribute to his own strategic genius, picking out for particular praise his reputed eagerness not to waste lives and where possible to bypass Japanese garrisons, cut their supply lines and leave them to rot on the vine. According to MacArthur himself the key principle was

> . . . 'to hit 'em where they ain't' . . . [This] called for the careful selection of key points as objectives and the choosing of the most opportune moment to strike. I accordingly applied my major efforts to the seizure of areas which . . . were only lightly defended by the enemy. Thus, by daring forward strikes, by neutralising and by-passing enemy centers of strength, and by the judicious use of my air forces to cover each movement, I intended to destroy Japanese power in New Guinea and adjacent islands, and to clear the way for a drive to the Philippines.[52]

On occasion this was done, particularly in New Guinea in 1944, where a series of amphibious assaults on neighbouring islands such as Wakde, Biak and Noemfoor, as well as selected landings on the mainland at Hollandia and Sansapor, did succeed in cutting off some 180,000 Japanese troops to the east of Hollandia. Yet it seems excessive to claim that such operations were 'miraculous' or that through them ran 'a red thread of design, an operative leitmotif'.[53] As to miracles, more sober comment on 1944 operations comes from an Australian historian who has pointed out: 'The bald facts were that [by] now MacArthur possessed command of the sea and air [and] he could land troops where he chose, whereas the opposing armies . . . could respond only by laborious movement along primitive roads or perilous coastwise advances in small craft.'[54]

The existence of the 'leitmotif' must also remain somewhat implausible when one takes full account of MacArthur's operations elsewhere. In many cases the important bypasses that were made were nothing to do with MacArthur and were sometimes actually opposed by him. This was the case with Rabaul, which some observers realised could be effectively isolated without the necessity for a frontal assault. It could be done with landings in the Admiralties, on eastern New Britain and at Hollandia, in all of which signals intelligence had shown Japanese forces to be relatively weak. MacArthur, however, 'wanted to smash his way into Rabaul, blind to the fact that it was now irrelevant. He argued his case vehemently, before the Chiefs of Staff [at the Quadrant Conference*] decided to let Rabaul wither in isolation and instructed MacArthur to leave the great base alone; and he continued to argue even after these clear instructions had arrived.'[55] Another base easy to isolate was Kavieng, on New Ireland, whose position 'begged for another bypass'. The keys were Green Island, Emirau and Manus, all three of which, according to Halsey's intelligence, 'were push-overs'.[56] But MacArthur was determined to storm Kavieng, and he was only dissuaded by Halsey after three long and stormy personal meetings. Similarly, the decision to bypass Mindanao, which with Rabaul were 'the two dramatic bypasses of the Pacific War',[57] had little to do with MacArthur. The idea was Halsey's, who had been struck by the increasing ineffectiveness of Japanese air power in the southern Philippines, and it was vigorously seconded by first Nimitz and then, in late September 1944, by the JCS. Indeed, MacArthur himself enthusiastically came round to their point of view, but one is nevertheless entitled to wonder why a commander whose whole attention was supposedly concentrated on seeking out such opportunities had never himself even hinted at the possibility.

* This was held in Quebec, 14–24 August 1943, when Pacific operations began to assume much more importance after the British gave notice of their inability to mount an effective offensive in Burma until well into 1944.

MacArthur's operations in the last year of the war do equally little to justify his reputation. Their leitmotif, indeed, is the very opposite of that discerned by his admirers. For throughout the South-West Pacific Area he seems to have developed a definite obsession with mopping up islands and garrisons that could just as well have been left to wither. In New Guinea, the Solomons and New Britain this tedious, and costly, task was handed over to the Australians. From October 1944 twelve full brigades were employed on Bougainville, New Georgia, New Britain and New Guinea, and rarely was the fighting easy. By the end of the war neither Bougainville nor New Britain had been fully cleared, and nor had Borneo, where yet more Australians had been sent in July 1945. One writer has been scathing about this needless squandering of life. When MacArthur handed over responsibility for these islands he signalled Marshall that their bypassed garrisons' '"capability for organised offensive activity had passed. The various processes of attrition will eventually account for their final disposition." What he meant was that having swept forward 1,000 miles with his American troops, he was marching on to glory while the Australians cleaned up the pigsty.'[58]* The remark is a trifle unfair, but only because MacArthur was equally hard on his American troops. In the Philippines, in fact, he displayed an almost obsessive eagerness to clean up the Archipelago. Hardly any garrison was to be left to atrophy of its own accord, and instead General Robert L. Eichelberger's Eighth us Army had to undertake 14 major and 24 minor landings within a space of 44 days. As a logistical exercise it was an impressive performance, but one is entitled to doubt its real military value. The Joint Chiefs certainly did, and had explicitly stated that once Leyte and Luzon were taken further military operations in the Philippines would not be necessary. As Morison darkly remarks: 'It is still something of a mystery how and whence, in view of these wishes of the JCS, General of the Army Douglas MacArthur derived his authority to use United States forces to liberate one Philippine island after another.'[59] More direct is a recent historian who has dismissed the whole exercise as being 'militarily pointless'.[60]

---

* And the Australians knew it. On Bougainville, a brigadier spoke of 'a tendency among all ranks, including officers, to question vigorously the purpose and soundness of operations in the Solomons . . . [It became necessary] to bring to the notice of commanders the dangers of permitting unchallenged discussion on such a contentious subject.' (Quoted in J. Vader, *Anzac* (New English Library, 1970), p. 104.)

There are many more criticisms that could be directed at MacArthur's generalship.* But to dwell for too long on his tactical shortcomings, considerable though they were, risks losing sight of one fundamental area of operational policy – nothing less than the overall strategic orientation of the campaign in the Pacific – about which I shall argue that MacArthur was absolutely correct. Sadly, however, in this one area where he *was* right, he was not given his head and the whole conduct of the war in the Pacific was sadly flawed because of it.

The point at issue was the dual nature of the American advance in the Pacific, which has already been touched upon in the previous chapter and whose twin axes are clearly discernible in map 10. There it can be seen that one axis, commanded by MacArthur and using Australia as its first logistical base, pushed north-westwards through New Guinea and the Philippines, aiming above all to cut Japanese communications with the East Indies and thus deny them the raw materials vital to the sustenance of their war machine. The other main effort was orchestrated by Nimitz and pushed westwards, utilising Hawaii as its first staging post. This drive had two main objectives: the Marianas, held to be the linchpin of the Japanese supply network in the central Pacific, and Formosa and the Chinese coast, from where it was hoped to launch a bombing offensive against the Japanese mainland. Both of these objectives would also necessitate the seizure of intermediate staging posts along the way, to provide docking facilities and airfields for land-based planes.

Before going on to discuss MacArthur's own views on the desirability of the advance from Hawaii – to which he was vehemently opposed – it is necessary to understand just how the Americans ever got saddled with it in the first place. The most important reason was simply that they, or at least their Army and Navy planners in the interwar years, had prepared to fight the wrong

---

* On his cavalier attitude to intelligence, particularly if it did not suit him, see R. Lewin, *The American Magic* (Penguin Books, Harmondsworth, 1983), pp. 180–1, 268. On his tendency greatly to exaggerate operational possibilities see G. Long, *MacArthur as Military Commander* (Batsford, 1969), pp. 100–1 and S. E. Morison, *The History of United States Naval Operations in World War II* (15 vols, OUP, 1948–62), vol. 4, p. 262, and vol. 13, pp. 7–9, 18. On his inadequate preparations for air support and logistical support in the Philippines see ibid., vol. 12, pp. 60–1, and vol. 13, p. 185. For further evidence of his propensity to conjure up grand plans and 'motifs' only in hindsight see Long, op. cit., pp. 94–5 and L. H. Morten, *Strategy and Command: the First Two Years* (US Army in World War II: War in the Pacific), (GPO, Washington, 1962), p. 251.

war. Not unreasonably, they had assumed that when hostilities in the Pacific began they would still be in possession of at least part of the vital Hawaii–Wake–Guam–Philippines line of communication, as well as most of the Pacific fleet. Operations, therefore, would centre upon the recapture by the Navy of the rest of that line and the re-establishment of contact with the Philippines. The methods of doing this were laid down in the so-called Orange plans, Orange being the colour code for Japan in the list of potential aggressors. These various colour plans were first drawn up in 1904 and were leisurely updated in the years that followed.

At the centre of all variants of the Orange plan were the Philippines, the basic assumption being that the Army garrison there would be able to hold out until the Navy, like the US Cavalry of old, steamed in to rescue them. However, the various plans put forward such different projections of how long such resistance was supposed to last that it is difficult to believe that they were based on a hard-headed analysis of the Navy's real capabilities. The 1913 Plan asked the garrison to hold out for two to three months; that of 1924 spoke of three months *at least*; in 1936 two to three *years* was mentioned (though now the Army was only to cling on to the naval installations in Manila Bay); the 1938 Plan rather gave up the ghost and suggested no time-scale at all. In the light of later events it was a pity that the 1922 Plan was not studied more closely. For this had stated bluntly that the role of the Philippine garrison could only be sacrificial and it would inevitably be overrun before relief arrived. It was only this and other 1920s plans, indeed, that gave anything but the most cursory attention to how the trans-Pacific rescue was to be effected, that of 1926 cautioning that existing US possessions there were probably too far apart, and that it might be necessary first to conquer at least some intermediate islands in the Marshalls, the Carolines and the Marianas.*

What none of the plans had foreseen, however, was that initial reverses would be so disastrous that not one of the stepping stones to the Philippines would remain, nor even a viable Pacific fleet. If the 1923 Plan had predicted that 'the recapture of the Philippine islands would be a long and costly undertaking',[61] how much more difficult must it now be with almost every department of the Navy's

---

* The 1923 Plan also recommended that a joint services commander be appointed for any such amphibious trek. The Joint Board, however, refused to allow the Joint Planning Committee even to introduce the idea into concrete discussions. Such jealous concern for service autonomy was to be a constant stumbling-block over the next 20 years.

effort having to start from scratch. Surely, in fact, there was good reason after Pearl Harbor to discard the Orange plan entirely, to forget preconceived strategic notions and think hard about the new situation. For with the final collapse of MacArthur's last stand in the Philippines, in March 1942,* the centre of gravity of Pacific operations had moved away from the Hawaii–Philippines axis to Australia and southern Papua, now the only reasonably secure staging posts for continued operations. MacArthur himself, on his arrival in Australia, was adamant that making full use of Australia's potential as a war base should be at the very heart of American strategy.

At first it seemed that this revised strategy was to find a consensus. When Admiral King became Cominch, on 30 December 1941, he told Nimitz that his main task, other than holding on to Midway and Hawaii, was that of 'maintaining communications between the west coast and Australia, chiefly by covering, securing and holding the Hawaii–Samoa line, which should be extended to include Fiji at the earliest possible date.'[62] It was not long after this that the Americans began to consider taking the offensive themselves, and the Navy did seem to have abandoned the Orange axis in favour of one that struck out from Australia. In March 1942, as King was urging that offensive operations get under way, he suggested to Marshall establishing a number of island strong-points for a step-by-step advance through the New Hebrides, the Solomons and the Bismarck Archipelago. On 2 July, his promptings bore fruit and the JCS issued a directive to seize, in sequence

    a)   the Santa Cruz Islands and Tulagi;
    b)   Lae, Salamaua and northern New Guinea;
    c)   Rabaul and the adjacent New Guinea/New Ireland area.

In other words, the MacArthur axis, as shown on map 10, was the only one envisaged at this stage of the war.

Or more accurately, it was the only one envisaged by the Joint Planners, who saw in it not only the most effective use of the Australian base but also the surest way to strike at Japan by, eventually, pushing forward from Rabaul to slice through the vital Japanese communications between the home islands and the raw material reserves in the East Indies. An Allied plan for measures to be taken against potential Japanese aggression, the ABC-1 Agreement of 27 March 1941, had even then stressed that the US would 'employ

---

* Though American and Filipino remnants, under General J. M. Wainwright, did not surrender on Corregidor until 6 May.

the . . . Pacific Fleet offensively in the manner best calculated to weaken Japanese *economic* power . . .'[63] A draft US naval plan drawn up in April 1942 also seemed to re-emphasise this economic rationale, nominating the Dutch East Indies as the ultimate target.

But all Navy plans drawn up around this time contained some curious qualifications to their apparent endorsement of a concerted drive along a single southern axis. The Navy's version of the ABC plan, for example, saw little scope for full Army involvement. The following extract from King's memorandum is almost contemptuous about the Army's role in future operations:

> When the advance to the northwest begins, it is expected to use amphibious troops (chiefly from the Amphibious Corps, Pacific Fleet [i.e. the US Marine Corps]) to seize and occupy 'strong points' under the cover of appropriate naval and air forces. The amphibious troops should be relieved by garrison troops as soon as practicable in order that the advance may be continued . . . [These] garrison troops the Army would have to furnish.[64]

The July 1942 directive from the JCS went some way to smoothing ruffled Army feathers, but it attempted to solve the problem not by subordinating Army and Navy to one unified command but by splitting the Australia–Rabaul axis into two, giving the Army, under MacArthur, responsibility for New Guinea, and the Navy, under Ghormley then Halsey, that for the Santa Cruz Islands and the Solomons. And even though Army and Navy were supposed to work closely together, MacArthur could not deploy any naval units without Nimitz's express approval. Another important qualification to the Navy's apparent acceptance of the southern axis was also to be found in the April draft plan, where it was anticipated that once secure positions had been established in New Guinea and the Solomons, the Navy might consider launching a completely new Central Pacific drive, sending in amphibious forces to seize key points in the Marshalls and Carolines after first subjecting them to intensive aerial attack.

Two crucial points emerge here. The first is that relations between the Army and Navy were less than harmonious, neither being prepared to work under an overall commander from the other service. According to a senior British observer: 'The violence of inter-service rivalry in the United States in these days had to be seen to be believed and was an appreciable handicap to their war effort.'[65] The second is that the Navy had never in fact given up on the

Orange plan. The two are of course interrelated in that the particular appeal of this plan had little to do with its strategic pertinence, now notably lacking, but everything to do with its promise of operational autonomy in a separate theatre of operations. As one historian has observed, referring to the activities of the naval planners in early 1942: '. . . in their view all amphibious operations – any operation in the Pacific would be amphibious – should be under naval command . . . The major offensive when it came, the Navy believed, would be across the Central Pacific along the route marked out in the prewar Orange Plan.'[66] That jealousy between the services was the main reason for this harping on the Central Pacific route is all too apparent. Throughout 1942 Henry Stimson, Roosevelt's Secretary of War, was most disappointed by the Navy's constant sniping at the Army and its commanders. 'The admirals,' he found 'were uncontrolled either by their Secretary or the President . . . General MacArthur was a constant bone of contention. Stimson was bound to admit that the extraordinary brilliance of that officer was not always matched by his tact, but the Navy's astonishing bitterness against him seemed childish.'[67]

But the Army, too, evinced considerable bitterness about the Navy's behaviour, though in certain regards with more justification. Of the plans to use the Army as a garrison force only, one planner wrote, in February 1942: 'The Navy wants to take all the islands in the Pacific – have them held by Army troops, to become bases for Army pursuit planes and bombers. Then the Navy will have a safe place to sail its vessels.'[68] For carving out their own theatre does seem to have been a major preoccupation with both King and Nimitz. By the end of March 1942, as we saw earlier, they had prevailed upon the President to authorise the setting up of separate South-West Pacific and Pacific Ocean Areas, one for each of the services. Regarding the machinations that led up to this decision, one historian has regretfully pointed out:

> Though there was no urgency in the Pacific Ocean Area, the naval planners wished to establish both areas simultaneously. Failure to do this . . . [it was] thought, might open the way for an Army effort to enlarge the South West Pacific . . . The naval planners feared also that the Army might raise objections, if the opportunity arose, to placing its forces under naval control.[69]

Once the decision had been taken to divide the Pacific into Army and Navy zones of control it was but a short step to each adopting its own separate axis of advance, MacArthur pursuing the original southern axis and the Navy, although heading like him towards the Philippines and the East Indies, island-hopping through the Marshalls and the Carolines. On 8 May 1943 the principle of the dual thrust was accepted by the JCS. Their original instructions to Nimitz called for his first attack to be delivered against the Marshalls, but on 20 July the Gilberts were added as a preliminary objective. The dual thrust was approved by the Combined Chiefs of Staff in August, at the Quadrant Conference, where Nimitz was also given a series of additional suggested objectives. Now, after the Carolines had been secured, it was mooted that he either move further westwards to the Palaus or north-westwards to the Marianas. The actual choice was made at the Sextant Conference, in Cairo in December, when the CCS issued a document entitled 'Specific Operations for the Defeat of Japan, 1944'. The dual thrust was now part and parcel of strategic orthodoxy and the new directive stipulated: 'The advance along the New Guinea–Philippines axis will proceed concurrently with operations for the capture of the Mandated Islands.'* What was new was that the Marianas also were now included as a Navy objective,† though for the benefit of another service. The operations blueprint went on: 'A strategic bombing force [USAAF] will be established in Guam, Tinian and Saipan for strategic bombing of Japan proper.'[70]

Thus in nine months of often bitter wrangling, from March to December 1943, Admiral King had succeeded in completely changing the Navy's role in the Pacific. In March he had told Roosevelt that his aim was to 'drive northwards from the New Hebrides into the Solomons and the Bismarck Archipelago after the same fashion of step by step advances that the Japanese used in the South China Sea.'[71] By the end of the year the involvement along MacArthur's axis was seen as something of a chore, from which it would be best to disentangle Halsey at the earliest opportunity. For the Navy now had a vast expanse of ocean all of their own and it was here that they wished to concentrate their forces and burnish their reputations.

The net result, unfortunately, was that the American effort in the Pacific was hamstrung. A nation that was to display consummate professionalism in organising armaments production and its logistical links with the front found itself not only with one part of its arsenal so

---

* i.e. the Central Pacific Islands. See footnote on p. 446.
† Although they were regarded as an alternative to the Palaus at the Quadrant and Sextant Conferences, a later JCS directive, of 12 March 1944, stipulated that both could and should be taken.

far apart from the other that mutual support was impossible, but also incapable of nominating an acceptable supreme theatre commander who might have rectified this situation.

It was not as if the Americans were not constantly alerted to the dangers of what was happening. General Marshall himself, in December 1941, had stressed the importance of unity of command in the Pacific: 'I am convinced that there must be one man in command of the entire theatre – air, ground and ships. We cannot manage by cooperation. Human frailties are such that there would be emphatic unwillingness to place portions of troops under another service. If we can make a plan for unified command now it will solve nine tenths of our problems.'[72] He reiterated his demand for a single commander to Roosevelt in October 1942, stating that 'the present complication of the employment of air in the Pacific [Navy carrier-borne and Army land-based] emphasises the necessity.'[73]* There were plenty of others who agreed. In March 1942, Roosevelt told Churchill that he wished to appoint a supreme commander in the Pacific. General Arnold, in October, expressed the Air Force's bemusement at Army–Navy obduracy and called for the speedy selection of a single theatre supremo. The British too were somewhat nonplussed, though their objections centred upon what they saw as an unnecessary waste of resources in maintaining two separate axes of advance. At the Quadrant Conference, 'Sir Alan Brooke inquired whether it was essential, in order to retain the initiative, that *both* the advance into the Mandated Islands and that from New Guinea should be pressed forward with vigor . . .'[74]

Not surprisingly, some of the most vociferous objections came from General MacArthur. The basis of his argument was that the old Orange concept was now out of date because it

> had in mind the relief of the Philippines *before* these islands fell to the Japanese in the event of attack. This necessitated securing the lines of communication and supply between the Philippines and the United States which were threatened so long as Japan continued to hold and occupy the flanking Central Pacific Islands mandated to her . . . [But a] belated Central Pacific drive . . . could at best produce [only] local tactical successes

---

* Admittedly Marshall here was referring only to the South-West and South Pacific Areas, but it will be recalled that at this time the Central Area had little operational significance.

without bringing to bear any decisive influence upon the course of the war.[75]

However, his own axis – through New Guinea to Mindanao, Leyte and Luzon – could, he felt, exert that decisive influence. As he told Roosevelt, in July 1944:

> . . . I felt that if I could secure the Philippines, it would enable us to clamp an air and naval blockade on the flow of all supplies from the south to Japan, and thus, paralysing her industries, force her to early capitulation. I argued against the naval concept of a frontal assault against the strongly held island positions . . . [in the Central Pacific] . . . I stressed that our losses would be far too heavy to justify the benefits gained by seizing these outposts . . . and by cutting them off from supplies . . . their effectiveness [could be] completely neutralised with negligible loss to ourselves.

The economic basis of MacArthur's argument was also stressed in his plans for Operation Reno, the final version of which, in June 1944, dealt with the assault upon the Philippines themselves. The plan

> was based on the premise that the Philippine Archipelago, lying directly in the main sea routes from Japan to the source of her vital raw materials and oil in the Netherlands, East Indies, Malaya, and Indo-China, was the most important strategic objective in the Southwest Pacific Area. Whoever controlled air and naval bases in the Philippine islands logically controlled the main arteries of supply to Japan's factories. If this artery was severed, Japan's resources would soon disappear, and her ability to maintain her war potential against the advancing Allies would deteriorate to the point where her main bases would become vulnerable to capture.[76]

Of course, MacArthur's thesis was not an entirely disinterested one. For not only would concentration on one axis, his own, make it almost inevitable that a supreme commander would be appointed, but it would also pretty much ensure that he would be it. His ambitions were clearly revealed in a private letter to Stimson, in early 1944:

> These frontal attacks by the Navy . . . are tragic and unnecessary massacres of American lives . . . The Navy fails to understand the strategy of the Pacific . . . Give me central direction of the war in the Pacific, and I will be in the Philippines in ten

months . . . Don't let the Navy's pride of position and ignorance continue this great tragedy to our country.[77]

It seems clear, then, that the dual axis was not regarded by either side as a satisfactory compromise. Indeed, though the official record is almost mute on the subject, there is little doubt that feelings ran high about it throughout the war. In June 1942, at the height of a row over the Navy's role in the forthcoming South-West and South Pacific offensive, Admiral King actually threatened to ignore the Army entirely. During one planning meeting, 'he chopped off further debate by saying that if necessary he would open the offensive without the "support of Army forces in the South Pacific". Then, to leave no doubt that he meant what he said, he ordered Nimitz to make his plans on the assumption that he must depend solely on the Navy and the Marines in the forthcoming attack.'[78] According to General Kenney, the commander of MacArthur's Fifth Air Force, there was much acrimony at a conference in March 1943, to discuss future operations in the Carolines and the Bismarck Archipelago. 'Though the official record contains no mention of command problems during the Pacific Conference, General Kenney states that there were heated discussions about it with the delegates.'[79] By November of that year, according to MacArthur, General Marshall was becoming increasingly critical of what he felt was the Navy's disregard for the common good. Marshall felt that King

claimed the Pacific as the rightful domain of the Navy; he seemed to regard operations there as almost his own private war; he apparently felt that the only way to remove the blot . . . [of] the Navy disaster at Pearl Harbor was to have the Navy command a great victory over Japan . . . He resented the prominent part . . . [MacArthur] had in the Pacific War; he was vehement in his personal criticism . . . and encouraged Navy propaganda to that end.[80]

Even General Arnold was driven to take sides, and his memoirs included a blistering attack on Navy conduct. Throughout the war, he felt it had

followed its approved policy with regard to the Pacific. Accordingly, we had to accept Navy control, command and administration . . . of the islands. Another thing – the War Department . . . seemed to have the attitude that we shouldn't try to obtain unification of command in the Pacific. We must not bring the facts out squarely. We must not get the Navy mad at us right now. We must accept things as they were, even though we thought a change might be for the best; and we must not criticise the Navy . . . Fortunately, the war came to an end much sooner than any of us expected, so these problems never reached a point where they caused an open break between the Army and Navy.[81]

But General Arnold goes a little far in ascribing Army reticence about forcing the issue of unified command solely to their respect for Navy sensibilities. For the Army, too, had much to gain from not forcing the issue. Unsatisfactory though it might be, the original command carve-up in early 1942 had at least given them an Area of their own, one whose future they were most reluctant to jeopardise. Discussion about unified command might do just this. In other words, the longer the war went on the less likely it became that *either* service would risk giving up its own theatre of operations and its freedom of action therein. Positions on both sides became entrenched and the respective commanders preferred to make do with an unsatisfactory *status quo* rather than risk any erosion of their autonomy in a radical rearrangement of command structures. Marshall revealed this quite clearly at the Quadrant Conference when Brooke presumed to question the wisdom of the dual advance. Despite his earlier strictures about the absolute necessity for unified action, Marshall actually took sides with Admiral King and 'pointed out that, as the troops to be employed . . . were either there or in transit, no saving would be made by omitting one of the lines of advance.'[82] Such reasoning does seem a little specious, as surely it was not beyond the wit of man to reroute troopships or to organise transfers. Moreover, even assuming that it was impossible to abort one particular operation along one axis or the other, this did not preclude a decision to run that axis down in the future. It is interesting to observe that Marshall's earlier pronouncements on the importance of unity of command were made in the context of an Allied Pacific campaign, before the disappearance of the British and Dutch fleets. Then unity of command implied an American commander. By the time of Quadrant it might mean the subordination of the Army to the Navy, which was it seems a different matter entirely.

The Navy, too, was loathe to risk its autonomy in the name of operational ideals, and by early 1943 the issue of a supreme commander was to all intents and purposes a dead duck. A tacit truce was declared at the highest levels, with Roosevelt actually agreeing to omit all mention of it at the Sextant Conference lest it give the British another chance to ask awkward questions. Commenting on the Navy's point of view, an anonymous staff officer wrote in March 1943:

> I have come to the conclusion that Admiral King considers his relations with General Marshall on such a successful plane . . . that there are some matters in which he will not proceed to their logical accomplishment believing that even if he succeeded he would damage the relationship beyond repair. One of these items is the unification of command in Cincpac, including the efforts of General MacArthur up the New Guinea Coast.[83]

And if he *didn't* succeed, who knew what the consequences might be!

This truce lasted throughout the war, with neither King nor Marshall willing to rock the boat. Even in late 1944, when MacArthur had liberated the Philippines and thus reached the terminus of his own axis, there was no suggestion of a supreme commander to manage what would be a joint Army–Navy assault on Okinawa and the home islands. As Professor Morten has pointed out: 'The most logical solution, of course, was to name a single commander for the entire Pacific with separate air, ground and naval commands. The service interests and personality problems that had ruled out such an arrangement in the spring of 1942, however, were even stronger in the fall of 1944. No-one, therefore, seriously pressed for a supreme commander at this time.'[84] Perhaps most revealing of all is the fact that at no stage *throughout* the war did the JCS formally even discuss the appointment of a supreme commander for the Pacific.

The mere existence of inter-service rivalries and wrangling, as detailed above, is not in itself particularly noteworthy, as such tensions seem almost endemic to the world's armed forces even today. However, those that bedevilled the relations between the US Army and Navy during the Pacific War are very relevant to our theme because of the effect they had on the conduct of the war, leading to a wasteful allocation of resources, a dispersion of effort and a consistent failure to pursue the most effective and economical strategy against the Japanese. General Arnold was quite clear on the matter, and wrote in his memoirs that throughout the war 'we continued operating in our inefficient way, with first three, then two commands . . . both working towards the same end – the defeat of Japan, with overlapping lines of communication, overlapping air operations, overlapping sea operations, and, finally, overlapping land Army operations. In my opinion that was one hell of a way to run a war.'[85]

It is here that we return to General MacArthur's basic strategy for defeating Japan, outlined above, and find eminent vindication of his plea for a single axis and his assertion that the surest way to defeat Japan was to advance by the shortest route, in the maximum force, across her sea links with the East Indies. This route had to be along the New Guinea–Philippines axis for several reasons. First, Australia, which had become the first practicable advanced base in the Pacific, was the obvious springboard for this axis. Second, it was quicker to reach the Philippines via the Solomons and New Guinea than via the vast sprawl of the Mandated Islands. Third, the denser land masses along the former route offered many more opportunities for establishing air-bases and thus supporting the advance with land-based aircraft.

This was, indeed, the direction MacArthur took, but how much more effective his thrust could have been if supported by Marine divisions, a full quota of landing craft, the superb naval Construction Battalions and, above all, by the burgeoning might of Nimitz's fast carrier force. Army and Navy could have meshed perfectly, with the latter employing its concentrated resources to support one series of amphibious assaults; keeping its capital ships on the alert to protect the Army's right flank against incursions by the Japanese fleet; dispatching its submarines virtually to isolate the islands along a single axis; and using naval air to protect the Army when the latter's land-based planes were temporarily left behind awaiting the construction of new bases. It might be objected that all this is a counsel of perfection, that the fierce rivalry between the services already described rendered this degree of cooperation impossible. Perhaps, but the fact remains that if Army–Navy antagonisms were so potent as to nullify the authority of the JCS and the President, who in theory only had to *order* these services to get on with it, then it is a sad reflection on the ability and resolve of the United States at this time to wage war most effectively.

For there is no question that the 'compromise' strategy represented a grotesque dispersion of resources. The Navy planted itself at Hawaii, as far away from the cockpit of the war as it was possible to imagine, and there proceeded slowly and deliberately to build up amphibious task forces on its own. These were to offer little assistance to MacArthur's axis, yet were themselves not adequate to start out along their own axis until almost the end of 1943. How much better, surely, if these ships and Marine divisions had been sent piecemeal, as soon as they became available, to assist operations in the one area of the Pacific that was already fully active. For there they would have been hitting Japan where it really hurt, along the axis that soonest threatened her *economic* capacity to continue the war.

Concentration on MacArthur's axis offered the speedy seizure of the Philippines and thus the slamming of the door on any viable level of supply between Japan and her Empire. Certainly, the Navy too was island-hopping – gradually – towards the Philippines. But what was the point of its having its own, slower axis? What was the point of the Navy laboriously capturing its own quota of islands, each one more economically useless than the last, when it could have been used to speed up dramatically the advance from New Guinea? Moreover, with only one set of amphibious operations to be supported, a much greater proportion of the Fleet would have been regularly available, even before the Philippines were taken, for strikes against Japanese merchant shipping taking raw materials to the home islands. As the USSBS pointed out: 'Japan's merchant shipping fleet was not only a key link in the logistical support of her armed forces in the field, but also a vital link in her economic structure. It was the sole element of this basic structure which was vulnerable to direct attack *throughout a major portion of the war*.'[86]

But the Navy does not seem ever to have fully grasped the importance of the economic dimension. To be sure, it did eventually launch damaging forays into the South China Sea, in 1945, but by then Japan's industrial base was already tottering, and two years had already been wasted in building up for and carrying out the Central Pacific advance. Looking at the Pacific War as a whole, one cannot but be struck by the small proportion of the Navy's total effort devoted to attacking Japan's supremely vulnerable economic capacity to wage war.* The point was not lost on the writers of the USSBS,

---

* Equally, it is difficult to avoid the impression that the concentration of such a large proportion of the Navy's resources along the Central Pacific axis, where the Japanese presence was hardly massive, tied up valuable shipping, aircraft and troops that could have been used to better effect elsewhere. Admiral Towers, a naval air commander with the Fifth Fleet, remarked prior to the invasion of the Gilberts that the sheer size of the armada being assembled indicated that 'Spruance wants a sledgehammer to drive a tack'. (Quoted in E. B. Potter, *Nimitz* (Naval Institute Press, Annapolis, Md, 1976), p. 255.)

and they pinpointed serious deficiencies right across the spectrum of naval activity. The submarine campaign, they felt, could have been much more effective 'had we constructed more submarines . . . and more fully coordinated long-range air-search and attack missions with submarine operations.'[87] Worse still was the failure to select the most appropriate targets, notably Japan's tanker fleet.

> Not until 1944 were submarines specifically directed to seek out tankers for destruction. Had submarines concentrated more effectively in the areas where tankers were predominant in use after mid-1942, oil imports probably could have been reduced sooner and the collapse of the fleet, the air arm, merchant shipping and all other activities dependent on oil fuel hastened. With the time lag required to shift the emphasis of shipbuilding to tankers, Japan could never have caught up even temporarily with the rate of sinkings that might have been produced by such preference. And fuel shortage might have been acute at the end of 1943 rather than a year later.[88]

Carrier aircraft, too, were not used as efficiently as they might have been, despite the fact that against large concentrations of merchant shipping carrier attacks 'were by far the most devastating attacks of all'.

> They were . . . sporadic and not part of a continuing program to neutralise enemy shipping lanes . . . However . . . since shipping was the most important single key to the logistic basis of the Japanese military . . . machine . . . [a concerted] policy would have been immensely profitable. For example, had carrier task forces been able to cruise south of Java or Sumatra [i.e. on the South-West Pacific axis] in the latter part of 1943, carrier aircraft could have caused devastation to Jap shipping in the Java Sea and Singapore areas where large tonnages, particularly of tankers, were concentrated.[89]

Indeed, the Navy's own figures show both how effective their planes could be against merchant shipping and at the same time how infrequently they were so used. Thus, though it was found to require an average of only nine naval planes and four tons of bombs/torpedoes to sink each thousand tons of such shipping, the us Navy, throughout the war, devoted only 4 per cent of its total combat sorties to this type of target. Yet this tiny fraction of the total effort accounted for over 16 per cent of the total merchant tonnage sunk. Clearly, even a fairly modest increase in the attack effort targeted on the sea-lanes would have reaped rich dividends.

The USSBS also had reservations about the underlying rationale of such attacks as were made.

> It should be emphasised . . . that the controlling motive in the attention . . . to Japanese merchant shipping was the tactical objective of interfering with the enemy's military logistics rather than the strategic objective of reducing his war-making potential at home . . . It is perhaps debatable whether a sharper realisation of the importance of reducing merchant tonnage [in general] would not have suggested a more intense and specialised employment of air against it.[90]*

Here is the whole point. The Navy *was* fighting a 'tactical' war in the sense that they only deemed as important those targets that could take a shot at them. Despite the fact that one part of their fleet was engaged in a life-and-death struggle in the Atlantic that wholly revolved around the maintenance of maritime supply routes, senior commanders completely failed to perceive that their enemy's were yet more important to them. Instead, the fierce rivalry between the Army and Navy usually forced each party to try and emulate the other, and they became obsessed with capturing bits of coral. One of the most telling comments on the origins of the Central Pacific drive was made by a lowly Army staff officer. Having participated in the planning for the invasion of the Gilbert Islands, he wrote somewhat bemusedly: 'There seems to have grown up in our Navy the fixation that any action by the Fleet must acquire territory.'[91] It should not be surprising, therefore, that the most enduring icon of the US Navy's Pacific campaigns should be a small group of Marines raising the flag over Iwo Jima.

We are left, then, with a rather odd variation on our central theme of brute force. At first sight, the story is as elsewhere, with the Americans bringing to bear in the Pacific such an overwhelming material superiority that the ultimate issue of the contest was never really in doubt. However, whilst there was certainly no doubt as to

---

* And it is worth noting that even this tactical interdiction would have been much more effective along a single axis. In 1943 only 17 per cent of Japanese Army supplies sent to the island garrisons were lost. In late 1944 and 1945, when the two axes had converged, these percentages were dramatically higher. Around Leyte, where they finally met, almost 80 per cent of all Japanese vessels dispatched were sunk.

the inevitability of America's eventual *strategic* victory, it does seem that they went a long way towards minimising their preponderance in *tactical* situations, considerable though this still was, by insisting on advancing in force along two quite separate axes. The economic rationale for a single axis has already been elaborated, but there were also important operational considerations, notably that the balance of military power would have been even more in the Americans' favour. For American power concentrated on a single axis could not have been opposed by anything like a *pro rata* increase in Japanese resistance. The latter had decided to scatter their forces all over the Pacific almost from the very outset – it was in the nature of the amount of territory they set out to absorb – and would have been hard pushed to find the necessary shipping for a massive transfer of forces into one particular sector. Not that they would have been likely to consider such a transfer in the first place, because their very imperfect intelligence as to American intentions always left them unsure whether they could risk stripping garrisons in one sector for transfer to another. In other words, had the Americans placed only a diversionary force in the Central Pacific, adorned with the appropriate fake signal traffic and the like, and concentrated the mass of their resources along MacArthur's axis, the Japanese would still have felt obliged to leave *in situ* most of their considerable forces in the Central Pacific. Thus the battles along the single South-West Pacific axis would have been that much easier, at first simply because of the greater forces available and soon afterwards because increasing interdiction of the vital sea-lanes would hamstring both the production of weapons at home and their shipment to the front.

Yet the Navy, in particular, seems never even to have realised that the shot was on the table. Forces rivalry and a very imperfect appreciation of Japan's economic vulnerability led to the pursuance of two simultaneous offensives along quite separate axes. In the Pacific, in fact, we have the exact opposite of what happened during the Strategic Bombing Offensive in Europe. In the latter the weapon was neither powerful enough nor precise enough by itself to make the decisive strategic contribution to the war effort that the bomber barons hoped for. Naked attrition did eventually break the back of the *Luftwaffe*, but *not* of the German economy, which had too much latent capacity to be knocked out in this way. The strategic concept was good, but it was tactically impossible because of the inherent defects of the weapon to hand. The Japanese economy, on the other hand, with its total reliance on the movement of raw materials by sea, *was* vulnerable to strategic interdiction, and the Americans had just the triphibious arsenal best equipped to apply it. The tactical tools and means were to hand and so too, indeed, was the strategic concept that envisaged their proper deployment. But the vision was MacArthur's and as such was automatically perceived as a threat by the Navy. At the first suggestion that the correct use of their vast resources might involve working too closely with the Army, even – God forbid! – under an Army commander, they promptly packed their bags and raised anchor for their own backyard.

Unfortunately, strategic vision seems also to have deserted MacArthur towards the end of the war and in the last months it became increasingly unrealistic to characterise the Navy as the sole villain of the piece. Indeed, once the latter had emphatically asserted its independent status and clocked up its own string of island victories, roles became somewhat reversed, with Nimitz and King decrying the necessity for securing yet more real estate and proposing reliance on a complete blockade. By June 1944, according to Roosevelt's Chief of Staff, Admiral William Leahy, 'combined Navy surface and air force action even by this time had forced Japan into a position that made her early surrender inevitable . . . [It was the Navy's opinion], and I urged it strongly at the Joint Chiefs, that no major land invasion of the Japanese mainland was necessary to win the war.' Moreover, when MacArthur and Nimitz actually met together, in July 1944, both reached 'agreement that . . . Japan could be forced to accept our terms of surrender by the use of sea and air powers without an invasion of the Japanese homeland.'[92]

This remained the Navy's position until the end of the war. They agreed to work with the Army in preparing plans for the invasion of the home islands, but 'King and Leahy did not like the idea . . . [However] as unanimous decisions were necessary in the Joint Chiefs meetings they reluctantly acquiesced, [despite their] feeling that in the end sea power would accomplish the defeat of Japan . . .' The Navy maintained that they agreed only because of 'Marshall's insistence, which also reflected MacArthur's views . . . that the use of ground troops would be necessary.'[93] MacArthur's own memoirs make no attempt to gainsay this, and he cheerfully admits to being a member of that 'school of thought . . . [which] believed in driving straight into Japan as soon as the forces can be mounted . . . [On April 20 1945 I wrote] strongly recommending a direct attack on the Japanese mainland at Kyushu for the purpose of securing airfields to cover the main assault on Honshu.'[94]

There seems little doubt as to why MacArthur suddenly forgot all about his earlier insistence on directing the war effort against Japan's economy rather than trying to seize territory for its own sake. When he had first mooted his original strategy, it had seemed more than likely that its acceptance would lead to his being charged with its coordination, for it was to be mounted along his axis and would be just as much an Army as a Navy operation. By late 1944, however, a specifically economic strategy would no longer require many Army units at all. The Navy could quite feasibly undertake such an offensive almost by themselves, with a commensurate eclipse of MacArthur's prestige. This was quite unacceptable to him, and so the perceptive strategist who had once lambasted 'frontal attacks by the Navy' as 'tragic and unnecessary massacres of American lives' was now whole-heartedly advocating just such operations. The boot was now truly on the other foot, and it is hard to disagree with Admiral King's assessment, albeit terribly belated, of the proper strategic option in 1945. An invasion, he felt, was simply not necessary, nor indeed the A-bomb attacks which replaced it, for

> had we been willing to wait, the effective naval blockade would, in the course of time, have starved the Japanese into submission through lack of oil, rice, medicines and other essential materials. The army, however, with its underestimation of sea-power, had insisted upon a direct invasion and an occupational conquest of Japan proper. King still believes this was wrong.[95]

It is only a pity that King had not recognised that this same sea-power could have been brought to bear yet more effectively, along a different axis, much earlier in the war. Instead, he had allowed the Army and the Navy to fight the same war twice, and at Tarawa and Makin, Kwajalein and Eniwetok, Saipan, Tinian and Guam, Pelelieu and Iwo Jima, paid a quite unnecessary butcher's bill as the latter beat its separate, redundant path across the Central Pacific.

Appendix:
The war in South-East Asia 1941–1945

The men of the 'forgotten Army', the Fourteenth in Burma, will no doubt regard it as one further slight on their achievements that they should be relegated to a short appendix. In fact, derogation is not my intention at all and I have in an earlier book, about the ordinary soldiers' life at the 'sharp end', attempted to draw proper attention to the extremes of climate and terrain and the consequent appalling hardships endured by all those who fought in South-East Asia. The sufferings of the Chindits, for example, almost beggar belief, as do the achievements of the ordinary line battalions that held out during the epic sieges of 'Administration Box', of Kohima and of Imphal. The fact remains, however, that British operations in this theatre were hardly a decisive contribution to the overall defeat of Japan.* Churchill himself was uncomfortably but frankly aware of this fact. In April 1943 he told the Cabinet that 'it could not be said that the conquest of Burma was an essential step in the defeat of Japan.' A year later, he told the assembled Commonwealth Prime Ministers: 'We must regard ourselves as junior partners in the war against Japan.'[96] Certain figures about the Japanese war effort amply support such an assessment. Thus, though the British were

---

* The term 'British' has been retained throughout this Appendix but, as in North Africa, it can be very misleading. Thus, whilst British generals did plan and direct the operations in this theatre, they relied heavily on the Empire for the men who actually did the marching and the dying at the front, as well as the more routine graft in the rear. In February 1943, for example, during the Japanese Operation Ha in Arakan, 57 battalions were brought into action against the Japanese, 32 of which were Indian or Gurkha and seven West African. In January 1945, the 'British' portion of the Allied Land Forces in South-East Asia (ALFSEA) contained 970,000 men of whom only 127,000 (13 per cent) were British. The rest were made up of 581,000 Indians and Gurkhas (60 per cent), 60,000 West Africans (6 per cent), 45,000 East Africans (5 per cent), and 158,000 civilian labourers (16 per cent).

obviously contributing something to the allied effort just by tying down enemy troops, this contribution was not really a major drain on Japanese manpower. Table 25 gives details on the distribution of Japanese divisions at various dates in the war and clearly shows that the Supreme Command in Tokyo never regarded Burma, or even South-East Asia as a whole, as anything but a secondary theatre. At the four dates selected, in fact, the British were never facing more than 15 per cent of Japanese land forces and never more than 20 per cent of the Army air. This latter figure, indeed, was more usually well under 10 per cent, whilst the percentage of naval air power engaged varied between minimal and non-existent.*

The question of naval air power brings us to the central point about British participation in the air war against Japan, the fact that their operations had little bearing on the real war-winning offensive against the Japanese economy. Burma did have a part to play in the Japanese war economy as it provided significant exports of oil and rice, but the oil and paddy fields were in the south of the country and were thus not overrun by the British until very late in the war.† And it was only by physically occupying these fields that the British could themselves interdict the flow of exports, as the Royal Navy and the Fleet Air Arm were unable to do much about blockading the sea-lanes through which they passed on their way to Japan. This was hardly their fault, and for many months after the hammering received in the Indian Ocean the British

Table 25: *Deployment of Japanese Army and Army Air Force divisions August 1943 – June 1945*

Number of divisions in:

	Japan and N.E. Islands		Korea		China and Manchuria		Indo-China, Malaya and Siam		Pacific		Burma	
	Army	Army Air Force	A	AAF	A	AAF	A	AAF	A	AAF	A	AAF
August 1943	7	-	2	-	41	3	3	-	10	2	6	1
August 1944	15	4	1	-	36	1	2	-	37	8	10	1
January 1945	15	4	-	-	34	1	4	-	40	9	10	1
June 1945	60	4	7	-	43	1	6	1	34	4	9	-

* A more gruesome but equally pertinent statistic is that the 185,000 Japanese troops who died in Burma were only 8 per cent of total Japanese casualties in the war.
† Rangoon was not evacuated by the Japanese until May 1945.

were unable significantly to rebuild their naval presence in the east because of the enormous demands of amphibious operations in the Mediterranean and the Channel, as well as of the Battle of the Atlantic. Nevertheless, it has to be recognised that even when these demands eased in 1945, the British contribution to the naval war against Japan, the real war, offered only invidious comparison with the American. In February 1945, when the British sailed their newly assembled Pacific Fleet into Australian waters, and thence to the Admiralties, it comprised 4 fleet carriers, 2 battleships, 3 cruisers and 10 destroyers. The US Navy in the Pacific at this time included 14 fleet carriers, 65 escort carriers, 23 battleships, 45 cruisers and 296 destroyers. American victory against Japan may have been obtained in a wasteful and needlessly profligate fashion, but there is absolutely no question but that it was an *American* victory.*

However, relatively unimportant as British operations in Burma were, they are of some interest in this book in that they do tend to lend support to one or two of its assertions about the role of brute force in the Second World War. Whilst the later operations

---

* There is no implication here that the British shirked their responsibilities, as some Americans felt at the time, but simply that they did not have the resources, even with the considerable manpower reserves of the Empire, to field large forces in two completely separate continents. Early in the war, and it was this that most provoked American resentment, military operations in Burma were almost imperceptible, with the British declaring at the Casablanca Conference in January 1943 that they would be unable to mount any sort of significant offensive until the end of 1944. The Americans took this news so badly that Churchill did propose a limited attack into Burma, Operation Anakim, in the autumn. But the idea was quietly dropped at the Trident Conference in Washington, in May, and at Sextant, in November, Churchill also prevailed upon Roosevelt to absolve the British from another rash commitment to an amphibious landing in the Andaman Islands in the Bay of Bengal, Operation Buccaneer. British support for operations in northern Burma or Arakan, Operations Tarzan and Pigstick respectively, was also decidedly lukewarm. Early in the following year, however, Churchill began to realise that military impotence must bring with it a corresponding slump in British political prestige in Asia, with serious repercussions for the Empire, and he suddenly began to press for much more ambitious military operations, notably Operation Culverin, an amphibious landing in Sumatra with a view to later landings on the Malayan coast and in Singapore. But his Chiefs of Staff remained more realistic and relations between them and the Prime Minister became extremely strained. Eventually, however, he saw sense. Having been forced for lack of resources to postpone Operation Dracula, an amphibious landing west of Rangoon, and cancel an attack on the Kra isthmus, he contented himself, in September 1944, with offering the Americans the services of a small British Pacific Fleet as their major contribution to the actual defeat of Japan.

in this campaign were undoubtedly very well led and organised, notably General (later Field Marshal) William Slim's advance from the Chindwin to Rangoon between February and May 1945, it is also the case that this and other offensives, even those that failed, were able to call upon an enormous superiority in men and matériel. In October 1942, 14 Indian Division invaded Arakan, where its 12 battalions were faced by only two Japanese. Only limited progress was made, however, and in January 1943 Japanese reinforcements began to arrive. By April these had still only redressed the balance to the extent that eight Japanese battalions now faced 19 British, but the former proved more than adequate to push the latter back to their start line. In November the British invaded Arakan once again, but by the following February, though $6^1/_2$ divisions were deployed against only one Japanese, only limited progress had been made. Shortly thereafter the Japanese launched two linked attacks of their own. The first was Operation Ha, a diversionary attack into Arakan intended to draw British troops away from the main axis of advance, Operation U towards Imphal and the frontier with India. Three Japanese divisions were involved in U Go, a total of 26 battalions, but by the end of June the British, thanks largely to their considerable armada of transport aircraft, were able to deploy a corps of 49 battalions and 120 tanks in the Imphal–Kohima area as well as a reserve corps of a further 34 battalions between there and the frontier. Transport aircraft were not the only significant component of Allied air power. Whilst Japanese operations were supported by at most 50 to 60 operational aircraft in 5 Air Division, which put up some 1,750 sorties between 10 March and 30 July, the British and American fighters of the Third Tactical Air Force flew just under 30,000 sorties.

Allied superiority for the final march on Rangoon was more overwhelming yet. The brunt of the offensive was borne by the Japanese Fifteenth Army whose four divisions could muster only just over 20,000 emaciated and lamentably equipped men.* Against this force, Slim's Fourteenth Army 'of six divisions, two independent brigades, plus the lines of communication troops east of the Chindwin and two tank brigades, totalled a ration strength of 260,000 men. With this overwhelming superiority, tactics were not so important for victory as the logistics of manoeuvring such a force into position

* As early as August 1944 Japanese forces in S.E. Asia had been told to expect no further reinforcements or extra equipment.

when so far away from reliable bases.'[97] Allied strength in the air was still more overwhelming. They could field 48 front-line fighter and bomber squadrons comprising over 4,600 aircraft. Against these the Japanese could muster just 66 planes, and only 50 of these were serviceable by the end of March. Slim's forces might have been the 'Forgotten Army', at least in terms of public attention, but those of the Japanese in Burma were utterly forsaken, in every respect.

CONCLUSION

'From the moment that the overwhelming industrial capacity of the United States could make itself felt in any theatre of war, there was no longer any chance of ultimate victory in that theatre . . . Tactical skill could only postpone the collapse, it could not avert the ultimate fate of . . . [that] theatre.'

Field Marshal Erwin Rommel

'The American Army does not solve its problems – it overwhelms them.'

US General to Wynford Vaughan-Thomas, 1944

No conflict has been so much written about as the Second World War, and yet probably no other corpus of writing has done so much to distort popular conceptions of what actually happened. In an earlier book of my own, I was emboldened to try and give some impression of what life was like on the various fronts for the ordinary soldier, simply because after almost 40 years still no historian had seen fit to make it clear just how grim this life could be and how similar to that of the Poor Bloody Infantry of the First World War.* But it is not just day-to-day life at the 'sharp end' that has been consistently misrepresented in the vast bibliography of the Second World War. The fundamental reality of the tactical, operational and strategic

* See J. Ellis, *The Sharp End Of War* (David and Charles, Newton Abbot, 1980). Of course several soldiers had already given accounts of their individual experiences and some of these were extremely successful. (Exceptional British books include S. Bagnold, *The Attack*; P. Davis, *A Child At Arms*; P. Elstob, *Warriors for the Working Day*; J. Foley, *Mailed Fist*; M. Lindsay, *So Few Got Through*; F. Majdalany, *Patrol* and *The Monastery*; N. McCallum, *Journey With A Pistol*; W. Robson, *Letters From A Soldier*; P. Towry, *Trial By Battle*; A. Wilson, *Flamethrower*.) But none of these books have ever attracted the same sort of attention or reputation as the literature of the First World War, by Owen, Sassoon, Blunden, Graves and the like. Thus whilst the latter authors' (perfectly fair) picture of the hellish quality of life on the Western Front is now part of popular consciousness, there seems to be no equivalent appreciation of how grim things could be in the slit-trenches and fox-holes of Europe, Africa and Asia during the Second World War.

conduct of the war has also been distorted or obscured, notably by the enormous number of books and magazines that seem to concentrate almost exclusively on the hardware deployed in the war. Illustrations and specifications of tanks, aircraft, warships, submarines and all manner of electronic devices are presented in loving detail, the accretion of which has now laid on a technological gloss so thick that the reader inevitably loses sight of the essential character of military operations.*

The character of the fighting by air, sea and on land has been misrepresented in this way. The Bombing Offensive, for example, has been bedaubed with layers of detail about wingspans, maximum speeds, ceilings, rates of climb, bomb-loads and the like and bejewelled with a dazzling array of contemporary electronic aids. Yet the undoubted ingenuity of the latter, and the complexity of the story of measure and counter-measure, tends to obscure the fact that they rarely achieved much more than to allow pilots to blunder about in the dark with a little more confidence. Still less does their story help to focus attention on the essential brutality of the Bomber Offensive and the stark reality of 'area bombing', incendiary raids and the basic reliance upon a favourable rate of aircrew attrition. Bomber Command, in the last analysis, pinned its hopes for victory on being able to fry enough German civilians. The US Strategic Air Forces adopted an identical strategy in Japan, whilst in Europe the laudable restraint they envisioned in 'precision' bombing was belied by the increasing use of the bombers as decoys to draw up the *Luftwaffe* fighters, American commanders being confident that lost planes and crews were easily replaceable. As David Divine cautioned, in a study of British air power written over 20 years ago: 'To accept that this was a war of sophisticated weaponry has become a convention in the West, but it was in reality a war of desperate attrition, and victory in the end hinged upon human death.'[1]

The truth of this was evident on both sides of the bombsight. It was certainly abundantly clear on the ground, where 570,000 German

* This is *not* to disparage these books themselves. Publishers like Arms and Armour Press, Ian Allen, Macdonald and Jane's and Patrick Stephens have done sterling work in producing well researched monographs on all aspects of the hardware of the Second World War, and such books have provided invaluable background material for my own researches. My reservation is that the sheer number of such works, and their tendency to say very little about the real tactical and operational world in which such equipment was operated, has tended to encourage a kind of military fetishism that has increasingly lost sight of the actual dynamic military context.

civilians died as a result of the Combined Bombing Offensive and between 500,000 and 900,000 Japanese perished in the fire-raids and in the A-bomb attacks on Hiroshima and Nagasaki.* In Germany and Japan, moreover, something like 10 million and 8.5 million people respectively were made homeless. But the consequences of a crude attritional strategy were equally apparent to Allied aircrew, who endured some of the worst casualty rates of any branch of the services. In Bomber Command, as has been noted in an earlier chapter, losses of aircrew at one stage actually exceeded the number of adult male German civilians killed, whilst throughout the period 1941 to late 1944 Bomber Command casualties were something like 65 per cent of the total number of aircrew that served in those years. In the face of figures like these, indeed, one is entitled to wonder why Allied observers were quite so amazed and outraged at the Japanese resort to *kamikaze* tactics. Granting, of course, that very few Allied bomber crew actually wanted to die, and that equally few of their commanders wished this upon them, the fact still remains that the more realistic fliers and the more honest commanders *knew* that few men would complete their tours of duty. It is interesting to note, moreover, that in the 2,314 *kamikaze* sorties flown only 1,228 Japanese planes were expended, a loss rate of 53 per cent.†

It is the sheer scale of the loss of human life outlined above that must always be borne in mind when reading accounts of bomber operations that seem unable to see beyond the plotting table, the instrument panel or the headset. And in this regard one draws attention once again to the saddest irony of the Bombing Offensive over Germany: that it had begun as a radical technological solution to the deadlock of trench warfare but itself ended up being governed by the same logical vicious circle that had determined the course of operations on the Western Front. As a modern scholar has pointed out, speaking of Bomber Command's role in the war, its commander's reputation has suffered almost as much as that of Field Marshal Sir Douglas Haig, and for analogous reasons: the decisive breakthrough in the air for which Harris worked always seemed, like Haig's, to be just around the corner, would be attained with further massive injections

---

* Also killed in Allied air raids were 64,000 Italians and 58,000 Frenchmen. The latter figure is almost exactly equivalent to the number of British civilians killed in air raids.

† Of course, had the *kamikaze* campaign been more sustained the pilots involved would eventually have clocked up a 100 per cent casualty rate.

of precious manpower and material, and other major war operations should be relegated behind the primary objective of achieving victory on this new Western Front. Harris' aggressive self-defence, in the book he wrote shortly after the war, was also similar to that of Haig's Final Report, that success in the air ultimately depended not on well-defined moments of breakthrough, but rather on the back- and heart-breaking attritional slog of men going out night after night, developing a continuity of attack under the accumulating weight of which Germany finally cracked.[2]

As far as technology and the war at sea are concerned, one finds that accounts of the Battle of the Atlantic, in particular, have concentrated so much on the R&D work involved with producing torpedoes, sonar and radar that they have lost sight of some fundamental points. It tends to be overlooked, for example, that even with all the technical aids available by the end of the war, the killing of a submarine, usually with depth-charges, was like nothing so much as catching fish by throwing stones at them. In this respect, it is important to remember that during one of the most crucial periods of the Battle of the Atlantic, in the second half of 1941, by far the most effective Allied tactic was to route their convoys where the U-boats were not. The gathering of the necessary intelligence to do this, of course, owed much to the very technically advanced Ultra operation, yet the fact remains that a convoy's surest tactic during this period was that of the venerable Quintus Fabius Maximus, of avoiding the enemy. Two years later, when the Air Gap was finally covered, this was admittedly no longer the favoured method and the new, fully evolved air and sea escort/hunting techniques relied heavily on strong technological and scientific inputs.

Having said that, however, it is still important to appreciate that it was not these techniques that were the ultimate arbiters of the battle. In the last analysis, victory in the Atlantic depended on German industrial weakness, on the simple fact that the Allies could build merchant ships faster than the Germans could sink them. Or more accurately, faster than the Germans could build the U-boats to sink them, for it was the lack of anything like an adequate submarine arm from the very outbreak of the war that condemned Hitler and Dönitz to defeat in the war of commerce. Exceptionally amongst all the major theatres, Germany could have won the Battle of the Atlantic, and they could have won it before the Americans became fully involved, but only if the requisite number of U-boats had been made available by 1940 at the latest. Thereafter, the demands of continental warfare, in the air as well as on the ground, would always make it impossible to allocate to the submarine yards resources that were even remotely commensurate with those lavished on Allied shipyards. Hitler's mistakes during the Second World War have filled whole books, but surely the greatest of them was to go to war against a country that depended for its survival upon maritime imports with so feeble a submarine fleet and building programme that for the first 15 months it could only average 20 boats at sea in the Atlantic at any one time.

Our perception of land operations in the Second World War has also been distorted by an excessive emphasis upon the hardware employed. The main focus of attention has been the tank and the formations that employed it, most notably the panzer divisions. Despite the fact that only 40 of the 520 German divisions that saw combat were panzer divisions (there were also an extra 24 motorised/panzer grenadier divisions), the history of German operations has consistently been written largely in terms of *blitzkrieg* and has concentrated almost exclusively upon the exploits of the mechanised formations.* Even more misleadingly, this presentation of ground combat as a largely armoured confrontation has been extended to cover Allied operations, so that in the popular imagination the exploits of the British and Commonwealth Armies, with only 11 armoured divisions out of 73, and of the Americans in Europe, with only 16 out of 59, are typified by tanks sweeping around the Western Desert or trying to keep up with Patton in the race through Sicily and across northern France.† Of course, these armoured forces did play a somewhat more important role in operations than the simple proportions might indicate, but it still has to be stressed that they in no way dominated the battlefield or precipitated the evolution of completely new modes of warfare.

Even the history of panzer operations fails to justify the tank pioneers' claim that 'a new Excalibur' had been born. Thus, whilst the crushing victories in Poland and France were certainly a vindication of *mobile* operations, they did not necessarily prove that the tank was their *sine qua non*. The aggressive use of artillery and aerial firepower, including guns brought up by the infantry divisions, was equally important, whilst it now seems fairly clear that *any* reasonably cohesive force of fast-moving vehicles impervious to small-arms fire

---

* Of these 520 divisions, 49 were 'retreads', divisions that had been destroyed/disbanded and later reformed under their original title or as *Volksgrenadiers*.
† Only Allied divisions that saw combat are included in these figures.

– which was all that many of the German 'tanks' were – would have sufficed to disrupt the terribly ponderous Allied communications system and unhinge a chain of command that was about as responsive as a dinosaur under ether.

In Russia, the Germans put a somewhat more authentic panzer force to the test and fought according to a more specific and systematised armoured doctrine. Yet after the successes of the first three months – and even these were only partial, as none of the *Kessels*, even in aggregate, became the *Vernichtungsschlacht* that would decide the campaign – panzer operations in Russia singularly failed to achieve very much. Leningrad was not taken in late July 1941; the drives on Moscow begun in October and November both failed; in December 1 Panzer Group proved incapable of holding on to Rostov. In spring 1942 a major offensive was launched towards the Don and into the Caucasus, but though armoured forces penetrated eastwards as far as Stalingrad and southwards almost to the Black Sea, these advances brought the panzers, rather than the Russians, to the end of their tether. The former had covered the ground and had pushed the enemy back but they had *not* destroyed his cohesion, the ultimate rationale of armoured operations. In the winter of 1942–3 the panzers were operating on a drastically reduced scale. The drive to relieve Stalingrad was a miserable failure, and whilst von Manstein's counter-attack to Kharkov was a virtuoso performance it did little to alter the picture of overall German failure. Thereafter, German armoured operations had little positive strategic contribution to make to the war effort, even the major offensive at Kursk in July 1943, which made no ground at all and succeeded only in squandering the Germans' precious panzer reserves. Such successes as there were, like von Manstein's brilliant counter-attack at Krivoi Rog, in October 1943, were only of very local significance and even there could only delay the inevitable.

In the last 12 months of the war, armoured operations in both the east and the west only rarely enjoyed any success. In Normandy, in June and July, the steady build-up of panzer divisions did succeed in holding British forces for a while around Caen, but the armour signally failed to reduce the Allied bridgehead. A little later, when attention was switched to the American sector, around Mortain, the panzers made equally negligible headway as their counter-attack broke down almost as soon as it was launched. In Russia, in August, a temporary respite was gained along the northern Baltic coast, when the Riga corridor was reopened, but yet again this was only delaying the inevitable, and in October Army Group North was brusquely bundled into the Courland Pocket. A month later, in the west, the careful hoarding of armoured reserves permitted an attack against Patton's spearheads in Lorraine. However, though this was to be OB West's major effort along the whole front, the attack mustered in its armoured component only one badly understrength panzer division, a panzer grenadier division in similar shape, and three of the raw, poorly trained panzer brigades. The two main attacks were held without too much difficulty and whilst the momentum of Patton's advance was undoubtedly disturbed, subsequent delays were more attributable to the petrol crisis and the appalling weather. December 1944 saw one of the biggest German armoured offensives of the latter half of the war, in the Ardennes, but all of Hitler's careful build-up and preparation went for nothing when, despite gaining almost complete surprise, the two Panzer Armies were brought to a halt within only eight days.

The following month saw another major German armoured counter-attack, this time into Alsace, but this too, despite early penetrations, did not achieve any lasting success and after a few days began to fall back in front of the remorseless American and French counter-offensive. For the rest of the war, except for some fruitless attacks against the Remagen bridgehead in March 1945, the major German attacks, such as they were, were on the Eastern Front. Prominent amongst them were an attack in Pomerania, in February, against Stargard, which completely failed to live up to Hitler's extravagant promises, and an attempt in February and March to drive Sixth SS Panzer Army through to relieve the besieged garrison in Budapest. The preliminary attacks did succeed in driving back Russian bridgeheads north of the Danube, but the main effort around Lake Balaton made only the most limited headway and was called off on 15 March.

If we recall also that Panzer Army Africa, despite often seeming to be on the verge of spectacular victories, never had the proper logistic base to translate its dazzling advances into lasting military advantage and was eventually completely destroyed in the Tunis pocket, and that the terrain of Sicily and Italy, coupled with chronic shortages of equipment, kept panzer operations in that theatre at a minimal level, then it becomes clear that the overall contribution of the panzer arm in the Second World War was hardly commensurate with the astonishing amount of attention lavished upon it ever since. Indeed, such temporary victories as the German Army did win were as often as not infantry victories in which a combination of fixed defences, a masterly deployment of artillery and assault guns, and a positive genius for the well-timed *local* counter-attack time and again prevented the enemy from completely shattering or rolling up the German front until they were at the very gates of Berlin itself. In the long run, the achievement was futile, and in so far as it perpetuated Nazi rule wicked, but the fact remains that it *was* a considerable military achievement, and one largely attributable to the infantry and the artillery. It was these arms as much as the panzer units that Field Marshal Alexander had in mind when he wrote:

> . . . the enemy is quicker than we are: quicker at regrouping his forces, quicker at thinning out on a defensive front to provide troops to close gaps at decisive points, quicker in effecting reliefs, quicker at mounting attacks and counter-attacks, and above all quicker at reaching decisions on the battlefield. By comparison, our methods are often slow and cumbersome, and this applies to all our troops, both British and American.[3]*

This latter point about Allied tactical inferiority vis-à-vis the Germans brings us back to my earlier point about the actual utility of armour during the Second World War. In other words, although it seems clear that the successes of the panzer arm have been greatly exaggerated, this does not necessarily mean that their relative failure was a result of superior Allied technique. Indeed, over the war as a whole the Allies seem to have accomplished even less with their tanks than the Germans, a point that holds true in most theatres. In the Pacific and the Far East the relatively limited role played by the armour was simply a consequence of the inimical terrain and the impossibility of deploying tanks except in penny packets. In Tunisia

* Another remarkable German quality was their adaptability. On the one hand was their ability to draw shattered divisions out of the line and within a few weeks flesh out the cadres with new replacements so that the division was once again a competent fighting formation. On the other hand was the astonishing flexibility of the chain of command which permitted the instantaneous welding together of the most heterogeneous units, from all arms, into effective battle groups. Air Marshal Slessor commented after the war on 'that tactical flexibility which has always been such an admirable quality in German defensive fighting, his ability to pick up a battalion here, the contents of a leave train there, a machine gun *abteilung* from one division and a couple of batteries from another, and fling them in . . . to save a local situation.' (J. Slessor, *The Central Blue* (Cassell, 1956), p. 584.) At Velletri, in Italy, in May 1944, it was found that the 377 prisoners taken there came from 50 different companies from a whole variety of different battalions, regiments and divisions.

and Italy the terrain *should* have been just as forceful a constraint but instead the Allies insisted on clogging up the fragile road nets with their armoured regiments and their ancillary transport. Their actual contribution to the fighting was small, however, and they either slowed the advance of the whole Army in a massive snarl-up of traffic or were thrown away in futile assaults down rocky defiles overlooked on either side by enfiladed and well dug-in anti-tank guns.

But even where the terrain was much more propitious for armoured operations, as in Libya and Egypt, the Allies conspired to make the worst possible use of such units. Again enemy anti-tank guns were the main problem, though this time the Allies did not even have the excuse that these guns were almost impossible to get at because of the terrain. Usually, in fact, the PAKs would have been extremely vulnerable to artillery fire if only such weapons had been kept well forward with the tanks and the latter not allowed to charge off 'into the blue', unsupported by any other arms.

But if the tactical handling of the armour in Africa was bad, its operational control was execrable, especially during Montgomery's ponderous advance from Alamein to Wadi Akarit. Though Montgomery was working on a perfectly valid theory, holding back an armoured *corps de chasse* which could be used to drive deep into the enemy rear once the initial infantry breakthrough had been made, he remained consistently incapable of translating theory into practice. At Alamein, the first armoured breakthrough was attempted too early and got snarled up in the infantry's lines of communication or fell victim to anti-tank guns that the infantry and artillery had not yet been able to deal with. Thereafter, the armour got increasingly involved, in a piecemeal fashion, in the infantry slogging match and less and less thought was given to keeping in being the *corps de chasse* to exploit Rommel's inevitable decision to fall back. When this decision was made, therefore, it proved impossible, on three separate occasions, to administer a proper *coup de grâce*, and this despite the fact that Montgomery was well apprised of Rommel's intentions through Ultra, which source also informed him that he enjoyed a 15:1 superiority in tanks. This proved to be the pattern of events for the rest of Eighth Army's trek along the African coast, with Montgomery either refusing even to attempt to cut off the retreating Panzer Army, as at Sollum or across the Cyrenaican bulge, or botching such an attempt, as at Benghazi, El Agheila, Buerat and Mareth.

On the two major fronts of the war against Germany, in the east and in North-West Europe, there were some notable armoured advances. On the Eastern Front there were the great Russian breakthrough battles from the Don to the Donets, in the Ukraine, in Romania, the Destruction of Army Group Centre, and in the drives to the Oder–Neisse line and to the Elbe, whilst in the west, Second British Army pulled off the great dash from the Seine to the Scheldt and Third us Army thrice effected substantial and rapid advances, in Brittany, from Le Mans to Lorraine, and from Nuremberg to Berchtesgaden. Yet two important qualifications should be borne in mind. On the one hand, in the British and American theatre such advances were in no way typical armoured operations and a much more common role for the tanks was to work hand-in-hand with the infantry, at their pace, slowly helping to winkle out German machine-gun and mortar posts, pill-boxes and bunkers. The idea of the sabre-like slash or the rapier-like thrust, exemplified in the instances just cited, greatly appealed to both commanders and journalists, but in fact the usual tankers' role was the more prosaic one of the thingummyjig that extracts stones from horses' hoofs.

The second qualification applies also to operations in the east, and is simply that when a big breakthrough and swift advance was made it was almost always because the attackers had built up a massive material superiority (the reader is referred again to tables 16, 17 and 34) which no defender could hope to withstand. In the west, indeed, in the twin drives to the Scheldt and into Lorraine, these defenders had already decided to pull back, so that all Montgomery and Patton were doing was taking up the slack. Both advances represented notable administrative feats – Patton's ability to switch axes and make the best use of a road net was almost unrivalled on either side – but they had little significance as a vindication of the Allies' handling of armour or of their tactical competence vis-à-vis the Germans. Indeed, when it was necessary for the Allied armour to advance against sterner resistance, as against Caen or Bastogne, along the Arnhem road, or even in the drive to Lübeck, such operations revealed an almost complete lack of flair. Worse still, even when all that was required was a modicum of speed and determination, to finish off a distinctly groggy opponent, as in the closing stages of the Battle of the Falaise Gap, on the Seine and in Antwerp, the Allies showed themselves just as incapable as Montgomery in North Africa or Alexander in Sicily and before Rome, and completely muffed what should have been the endgame of the campaign in the west.

But perhaps the major objection to attempts to portray the Second World War in Europe as an essentially armoured conflict, with a supposed emphasis upon speed and mobility that sets it apart completely from the Great War, is that Allied commanders in particular made only sporadic attempts actually to wage *Bewegungskrieg*, let alone anything that might be construed as *Blitzkrieg*. Even in North Africa Montgomery's plans for his *corps de chasse* and for his armoured hooks and end-runs have a curiously half-hearted feel about them, and one constantly has the impression that it was in the frontal infantry assault, with lots of artillery and a generous lead time, that Montgomery felt most at ease. Whilst I do not suggest that Montgomery was careless of the lives of his men, the fact remains that his style of generalship was more appropriate to the Western Front in 1914–18. This impression is not dispelled by Montgomery's record in Europe, where Operations Charnwood, Goodwood and Totalise smack of naked attrition, where the failures at the Breskens Pocket and Arnhem suggest a complete inability to conduct mobile operations, and where the deliberation with which the Rhine Crossings and the subsequent advance to Lübeck were planned and conducted seem to indicate a quite debilitating lack of verve or even self-confidence.

But all Allied generals relied in the last analysis on firepower and sheer material superiority to win their battles rather than on any concept of unbalancing the enemy or forcing him to give up ground by threatened moves into his flanks and rear. Time and again the favoured method was simply to shell and bomb him into submission. This point was tersely made by no less a commentator than Patton, who said after the war: 'I do not have to tell you who won the war. You know our artillery did.'[4] General Marshall was a little more circumspect but made it equally clear that the artillery was the Americans' favoured weapon: 'We believe that our use of massed heavy artillery fire was far more effective than the German techniques and clearly outclassed the Japanese. Though our heavy artillery from the 105mm up was generally matched by the Germans, our method of employment of these weapons has been one of the decisive factors of our ground campaigns throughout the world.'[5]

The point was also made by a panzer commander who at the same time made clear the Allies' reluctance to use their armour as a tool for precipitating true mobile operations. According to his experience in Normandy: 'At the smallest resistance the enemy stops and retires, and a new artillery bombardment takes place in order to stamp out the remaining opposition . . . In defence the enemy is a hard fighter only so long as he has good support from the artillery and mortar units . . . So far his tank crews have not shown much enthusiasm for fights between tanks.'[6] One returns here to a Rommel remark cited in an earlier chapter, that 'in static warfare, victory goes to the side which can fire the most ammunition.'* For much of the fighting in North-West Europe and elsewhere *was* static fighting, both because the Germans had little option but to pin their own hopes on the maintenance of fixed defensive lines and because the Allies had little notion of how to tackle such defences except by throwing in every shell, bomb and bullet they could possibly employ. In general, the Allies were only ever mobile when the Germans had been finally blasted out of one defensive line and were falling back to the next.

Artillery, therefore, was a dominant weapon in the Second World War and one comparison, though a little rough and ready, does seem to indicate that it was employed on much the same scale as during the First World War. Thus, whereas the British Armies in France and Belgium, between September 1914 and November 1918, expended 187 million shells, the US Armies in North-West Europe, in one single year, expended 48 million, almost exactly one-quarter as many in one-quarter of the time. But Allied firepower in the Second World War was also supplemented by a weapon hardly available in the First, tactical and 'strategic' air power, and its influence on ground operations is still greatly underestimated. It had its prominent failures, of course, notably during the German evacuations from Sicily and over the Seine, but the mass of enemy testimony paraded in previous chapters has demonstrated that aircraft nevertheless had an enormous impact on German operations, grievously impeding the flow of supplies and reinforcements in every major theatre. The importance of the Allied air forces was certainly apparent to a one-time *Luftwaffe* Chief of Staff, General Karl Koller, who told Allied interrogators in 1945: 'Everything depends on air supremacy, everything else must take second place.'[7]

Firepower was also the dominant weapon in the Pacific. The theatre's most eminent historian wrote: 'The Army, in World War II, preferred to take an objective slowly and methodically, using mechanised equipment and artillery barrages to the fullest extent, and advancing only after everything visible in front had been pounded down.' But, because of the superb Japanese defences and their refusal to yield a position until almost every defender had been killed, one cannot see that the Americans had much alternative. Be that as it

*See p. 275.

may, the campaign in the Pacific remains as a particularly grim example of the role of brute force in the Second World War. The historian just cited speaks a little later of the clearing of Eniwetok, which had to be conducted by small demolition teams and flame-thrower parties, accompanied by tanks, who had to blast or burn out each Japanese fox-hole or bunker. According to one Marine: 'Finally we killed them all. There was not much jubilation. We just sat and stared at the sand, and most of us thought of those who were gone – those whom I shall remember as always young, smiling and graceful, and I shall try to forget how they looked at the end, beyond all recognition.'[8]

But, having granted the considerable tactical constraints on the Americans in the Pacific, operations there were in many respects still as badly flawed as those of the Allies in Africa and Europe. Though there was no alternative to brute force on each individual island, it does seem that the strategic conduct of the overall campaign led to quite unnecessary losses of life. For it was conducted along two separate axes, and along each of them there were numerous fearsome Japanese strongholds to be battered down. Had just one single axis been followed – preferably MacArthur's, which led most easily and directly across the absolutely vital lines of communication joining Japan and her newly conquered raw material deposits in South-East Asia and the East Indies – then a whole sequence of bloody island-hopping could have been avoided and the us Navy would have been free to devote much more attention to the essential task of destroying Japanese merchant shipping. In many respects the performance of the us Pacific Fleet was exemplary, with the organisation and sustenance of the great carrier Task Forces taking pride of place, but it is at least arguable that too little of their actual combat effort was directed towards the speediest and most cost-effective way of defeating Japan, by strangling her economically.*

---

* It is in this regard that the question of the use of A-bombs against Japanese cities comes to the fore. Horrific as these weapons were, it is not necessarily the case that their use constituted an example of brute force, for on the operational level at least there was considerable justification for trying to avoid an amphibious assault on the main Japanese islands that must have involved enormous casualties. Nevertheless, on a broad strategic level the Americans can surely be criticised for having forced such options upon themselves by not consistently attempting to bring Japan to its knees through a concerted economic offensive. Hiroshima and Nagasaki were rational alternatives to invasion, but this choice would never have been necessary if economic blockade had been the consistent watchword of the American forces.

Yet in the broadest sense, in the Pacific as elsewhere, it *was* economic might and productive capacity that determined the outcome of the Second World War. In the final analysis, once America and Russia had been drawn into the war and once each had blocked its opponent's first mad rush, then there was absolutely no chance that the Axis powers could salvage even a negotiated peace. The relevant statistics have been presented at some length throughout this book and there is no need to repeat them here, except simply to re-emphasise that a *Reich* that would wage *Blitzkrieg* with only 47,000 tanks against its enemy's 227,000, 116,000 guns against 915,000 and 350,000 trucks against 3,000,000, or a would-be maritime empire that aims to maintain its grasp by producing only 13 aircraft-carriers against its opponent's 137, has not much real chance of imposing its will. As usual, the United States Strategic Bombing Survey was very clear about the real nature of total war, at least in the pre-nuclear era, when it pointed out that from 1943 'the terms of warfare were ceasing to be those of Hitler, and were becoming those of his enemies. The outcome of the war no longer depended on skilful strategy and well-timed shock effects . . . [but] was becoming, instead, a war in which military manpower and economic resources would be decisive.'[9] In short, Russian blood and American steel.*

It may be felt by some readers that this book has rather harped on the point about Allied economic superiority and made far too much of their generals' reliance on matériel and brute force rather than on

---

*The point about Russian blood is not merely rhetorical. Because of the division of military labours early in the war, the British and Americans both found themselves short of actual fighting troops, a situation that would have proved much more serious had not the Russians always had available an enormous pool of manpower that they were prepared to expend ruthlessly, and so tie down a large proportion of the German Army. The question of Russian manpower was quite crucial in the early phase, when it was her ability to fall back before the Barbarossa forces in considerable disarray whilst still managing to throw more and more reserves into the battle that staved off complete defeat. It is still not fully recognised, moreover, that this represented a considerable administrative achievement and that the ability to maintain a flow of reinforcements, albeit poorly trained and equipped, was largely beyond the Poles and the French, who caved in almost as soon as their brittle front line was ruptured.

† It would not do to exaggerate the number of lives actually saved. For the ordinary riflemen in the infantry divisions life expectancy at the front was no better than that of the Tommies and Doughboys of the First World War. The following table gives the percentage casualties amongst the riflemen of certain US infantry divisions that fought for nine months or more in North-West Europe. 1, 3, 9, 36 and 45 Infantry Divisions are not included because I have been unable to find casualty figures that refer only to their period of service in that particular theatre.

manoeuvre and adroit tactics. What does the elegance of a battle or campaign matter, it might be asked, as long as it is won and, moreover, lives are saved in the process?[2†] Why should not General Simpson prefer doing the job with an artillery shell rather than an infantryman, and what is wrong with a member of Montgomery's staff admitting: 'We were always very aware of the doctrine "Let metal do it rather than flesh". The morale of our troops depended on this. We always said – "Waste all the ammunition you like, but not lives."'?[10]

There is, in fact, a twofold objection to such a mode of warfare, one concerning our perceptions of the actual historical events and the other having serious implications for our defence posture in the years to come. With regard to the campaigns themselves, I have already had much to say about the way in which generals like Montgomery and Patton, and their chorus of apologists, have seriously distorted our view of the Second World War, greatly overestimating the role of manoeuvre and mobility in their battles, as they actually fought them, and playing down their constant resort to overwhelming firepower and head-on assault. The essential point here is not merely that such generals have excessively glamorised their own roles, and still less that their actual tactics were imaginatively or 'aesthetically' lacking: what matters is that the very assertion that the massive effusion of ammunition saved lives is not necessarily true. On the contrary, any armed forces that embrace such a dictum are likely to waste more lives than they save, by failing to look at a whole range of tactical situations as anything but problems to be battered remorselessly into submission. Thus notions such as maximum mobility, outmanoeuvring, exploitation, indirect approach, surprise attack, local initiative – all these are stifled,

footnote continued:

Div.	Battle Casualties			Percentage	
	Months	Dead	Wounded	Dead	Wounded
4	11	4,834	17,371	18.1	65.1
29	11	3,786	15,541	15.9	56.3
30	11	3,516	13,376	16.5	62.7
79	11	2,943	10,971	16.1	59.8
83	11	3,620	11,807	19.2	62.5
90	11	3,930	14,386	17.3	63.2
5	10	2,656	9,549	15.9	60.3
8	10	2,820	10,057	16.3	45.3
35	10	2,947	11,526	15.6	61.0
28	9	2,683	9,609	16.1	57.7
80	9	3,480	12,484	17.0	61.1

and commanders, together with the forces they build in their own image, become incapable of perceiving and seizing those fleeting opportunities that may considerably shorten a campaign or war, and thus save thousands of lives.

This certainly seems to have been the case during the Second World War. Alexander during the pursuit after Cassino; Montgomery desperately reaching out to Arnhem; Zhukov and Konev painstakingly amassing their vast forces behind the Oder and the Neisse; MacArthur assiduously mopping up whatever could be mopped; and Harris refusing to acknowledge any valid target but urban acreage pure and simple, are all examples of commanders and forces that had made firepower their totem. Consequently, they had almost completely lost the ability to know when the enemy was reeling and to follow up with the requisite speed and dash, and the gift of realising just which trees in the strategic wood were vital to the enemy and which could be left to stand and rot. In the final analysis the defect was not crucial, for the firepower at their disposal assured these commanders of victory in the end, but their lack of tactical and strategic touch meant that the end was a long time coming, and many soldiers, sailors, airmen and civilians a long time dead.

But the point about Allied reliance upon their overwhelming material superiority is also pertinent to modern defence policy. Here we return to the theme of a false and long-established perception of just how victory was achieved in the Second World War. For by ignoring the vital question of material preponderance we do not only inflate the reputations of 'great' commanders, but we are also in danger of encouraging absurd assessments of innate national military ability at the expense of a sober admission that the odds were stacked heavily in the Allies' favour. From there it is a short step to believing that the Falklands or Grenada incidents were significant military victories, confirming the prowess of the victors. Worse still, governments may be tempted by this false perspective to accept a level of *conventional* armaments and logistic capability that bears little relation to the actual ratios of superiority required. Unless our histories take full cognisance of just how big a margin was required in the Second World War, we shall leave ourselves without adequate conventional capacity in any future war. In Britain, we have already gone a long way down this road, most notably in the sphere of logistics, and our two essential indigenous buttresses in the Second World War, our merchant fleet and our heavy industrial and engineering base, have already been seriously eroded. With them has gone our ability most usefully to support NATO (the North *Atlantic* Treaty Organisation, one emphasises) in a protracted conventional war. But that in turn has considerably increased the likelihood that that Organisation would be forced to be the first to resort to nuclear weapons. And that would be brute force . . . and ignorance for ever.

Statistical Appendix
Tables 26 – 63

Table 26: *British and German single-engined fighter production*
June 1940 – April 1941

	Britain	*Germany*
1940		
June	446	164
July	496	220
Aug.	476	173
Sept.	467	218
Oct.	469	144
Nov.	458	?
Dec.	413	?
1941		
Jan.	313	136
Feb.	535	255
March	609	424
April	534	446

Table 27: *Total losses, production and availability of serviceable single-engined fighters and Fighter Command reserves July – October 1940*

					Single-engined aircraft in storage units	
Week of month ending	*S-E aircraft destroyed in month*	*S-E aircraft built in month*	*Serviceable S-E aircraft*	*Fighter Command pilots*	*Immediately available*	*Other*
July 6			644	1,259	373	181
13			686	1,341	355	161
20			658	1,365	333	213
27	81	496	651	1,377	312	217
Aug. 3			708	1,434	336	261
10			749	1,396	372	292
17			704	1,379	289	258
24			758	1,377	249	259
31	293	476	764	1,422	191	291
Sept. 7			742	1,381	194	196
14			725	1,492	208	152
21			715	1,509	192	197
28	476	467	732	1,581	225	244
Oct. 5			734	1,703	236	188
12			735	1,752	248	227
19			734	1,737	309	189
26	176	469	747	1,735	305	220

Table 28: *German and Allied bombing effort September 1940 – February 1941 and June–November 1944*

1940–1	Sorties	Luftwaffe Tons dropped	Tons per sortie	1944	Sorties	RAF and USAAF Tons dropped	Tons per sortie
Sept.	7,260	7,044	0.9	June	36,305	111,471	3.1
Oct.	9,911	9,113	0.9	July	30,364	98,399	3.2
Nov.	c. 6,000	6,510	c.0.9	Aug.	28,977	109,975	3.8
Dec.	3,844	4,323	1.1	Sept.	22,045	88,919	4.0
Jan.	2,465	2,424	0.9	Oct.	27,251	100,165	3.7
Feb.	1,401	1,127	0.8	Nov.	24,834	89,113	3.6
TOTAL	30,881	30,541	0.9		169,776	598,042	3.6

Table 29: *German and Russian combat strengths, 14 November 1943*

Formations German A Gp	Russian Front	Combat Infantry* German	Russian	Armour German†	Russian	Artillery German	Russian
A	N. Cauc. 4 Ukr.	54,400(17)	283,500 (75)	105	960	808	2,900
South	1 Ukr. 2 Ukr. 3 Ukr.	140,800 (44)	616,140 (163)	271	3,290	2,263	6,380
Centre	Byelorussia West 1 Balt.	147,200 (46)	650,160 (172)	216	3,060	2,577	6,720
North	N.West Volkhov Leningrad	140,800 (44)	355,320 (94)	108	650	2,389	3,680
TOTALS		483,200 (151)	1,905,120 (504)	700	7,960	8,037	19,680

*Assuming that 40 per cent of the paper combat strength of the German divisions and 60 per cent of the Russian were actually availabl
(Paper strengths taken from J. F. Dunnigan (ed.), *The Russian Front*, (Arms and Armour Press, 1978), pp. 98 and 121.) The figures i
brackets indicate the number of infantry divisions. Infantry attached to armoured and motorised formations are not included.
† Operational.

Table 30: *German and Russian AFV production (with 75mm guns and above) 1943–5*

		German	Russian	Ratio
Tanks	1943	5,570	16,044	
	1944	8,337	16,525	
	1945	998	20,030	
	TOTAL	14,905	52,599	1:3.5
Assault guns	1943	3,245	–	
	1944	7,328	–	
	1945	2,200	–	
	TOTAL	12,773		
Tank destroyers	1943	76	1,489	
	1944	2,040	4,310	
	1945	650	2,705	
	TOTAL	2,766	8,504	1:3.1
Self-propelled artillery	1943	2,458	2,558	
	1944	871	7,648	
	1945	87	3,562	
	TOTAL	3,416	13,768	1:4.0
	GRAND TOTAL	33,860	74,871	1:2.2

Table 31: *German and Russian military aircraft production 1943–5*

		German	Russian	Ratio
Fighters	1943	10,898	14,590	
	1944	25,285	17,913	
	1945	4,936	8,849	
	TOTAL	41,119	41,352	1:1
Ground attack	1943	3,266	11,177	
	1944	5,496	11,100	
	1945	1,104	5,484	
	TOTAL	9,866	27,761	1:2.8
Bombers	1943	4,649	4,074	
	1944	2,287	4,186	
	1945	–	2,085	
	TOTAL	6,936	10,345	1:1.5
Jet	1943	–	–	
	1944	1,041	–	
	1945	947	–	
	TOTAL	1,988		
	TOTAL COMBAT	59,909	79,458	1:1.3
Transport	1943	1,028	3,744	
	1944	443	5,508	
	1945	–	2,885	
	TOTAL	1,471	12,137	1:8.2
	GRAND TOTAL	61,380	91,595	1:1.5

Table 32: *German and Russian artillery production (75mm and above) 1943–5*

	German	Russian	Ratio
1943	27,000	48,400	
1944	41,000	56,100	
1945	10,000	28,600	
TOTAL	78,000	133,100	1:1.7

Table 33: *German and Russian military aircraft strengths on the Eastern Front 1943–5*

	German	Russian	Ratio
Feb. 1943	1,800	3,250	1:1.8
June 1943	2,500	8,300	1:3.3
Sept. 1943	1,750	8,000	1:4.6
Jan. 1944	1,800	8,300	1:4.6
June 1944	2,100	11,800	1:5.7
Jan. 1945	1,900	14,500	1:7.7
April 1945	1,500*	16,000	1:10.7

* All types.

Table 34: *German and Russian forces at the beginning of certain major offensives 1944–5*

Date	Sector	Formations German	Formations Russian	Combat Infantry German	Combat Infantry Russian	Ratio	Tanks and self-propelled guns German	Tanks and self-propelled guns Russian	Ratio	Artillery German	Artillery Russian	Ratio
14 Jan. 1944	Leningrad	18 Army	Leningrad Fr. Volkov Front	49,500	290,000	1:5.9	200	1,200	1:6	?	?	1:3
30 Jan. 1944	Krivoi Rog/ Nikopol	6 Army	3 Ukr. Front 4 Ukr. Front	46,800	257,000	1:5.5	250	1,400	1:5.6	?	?	?
4 March 1944	River Pripet/ Nikolaev	4 Pz Ay 1 Pz Ay 8 Army 6 Army	1 Ukr. Front 2 Ukr. Front 3 Ukr Front	107,200	890,000	1:8.3	1,300	6,400	1:4.9	?	?	?
5 March 1944	Uman/ Kirovograd	8 Army	2 Ukr. Front	13,700	287,000	1:21	310	2,400	1:7.7	?	?	?
8 April 1944	Crimea	17 Army	4 Ukr. Front Independent Coastal Army	35,700	136,000	1:3.8	70	900	1:13	?	?	?
22 June 1944	Vitebsk/ River Pripet	A Gp. Centre	1 Baltic Front 1 Byelo. Front 2 Byelo Front 3 Byelo. Front	110,000	595,000	1:5.4	800	4,100	1:5.1	?	24,000	?
12 July 1944	Kovel/ Tarnopol	A Gp. North Ukraine	1 Ukr. Front	101,800	403,000	1:3.9	700	2,040	1:2.9	6,000	14,000	1:2.3
18 July 1944	Chelm/ Rava Russkaya	4 Pz Ay	3 Guards Army 13 Army 1 Guards Tank Army	33,000	171,000	1:5.2	174	550	1:3.2	?	?	?
19 July 1944	Marianpol/ Daugavpils	3 Pz Ay	1 Baltic Front 3 Byelo.Front (parts)	11,000	91,000	1:8.3	95	1,100	1:11.4	?	?	?
20 Aug. 1944	Bendory/ Chernovitsy	A Gp. South Ukraine	2 Ukr. Front 3 Ukr. Front	121,000 (60% Romanian)	464,000	1:3.8	400	1,880	1:4.7	?	19,000	?
14 Sept. 1944	Narva	A Gp. North	Leningrad Fr. 1 Baltic Front 2 Baltic Front 3 Baltic Front	79,800	539,000	1:6.7	400	3,000	1:7.5	?	?	?
6 Oct. 1944	Hungary	A Gp. South	2 Ukr. Front	71,500 (55% Hungarian)	259,000	1:3.6	?	750	?	?	?	?
12 Jan. 1945	Warsaw/ Tarnow	A Gp.A	1 Byelo. Front 1 Ukr. Front	66,000	660,000	1:10	770	6,460	1:8.4	4,100	32,100	1:7.8
13 Jan. 1945	E. Prussia	A Gp. Centre	2 Byelo Front 3 Byelo. Front	93,500	405,000	1:43	750	3,300	1:4.4	?	28,400	?
1 March 1945	Pomerania	3 Pz Ay	1 Byelo. Front (part)	22,000	130,000	1:5.9	70	1,600	1:23	240	?	?
16 April 1945	Oder/Neisse confluence to Stettin	A Gp. Vistula	1 Byelo. Front 2 Byelo. Front	55,000	445,000	1:8.1	750	4,100	1:5.5	1,500 (75%A.A.)	23,600	1:15.7
16 April 1945	Neisse	4 Pz Ay	1 Ukr. Front	33,000	176,000	1:5.3	200	2,150	1:10.7	?	?	?

Note: Most of the above figures (i.e. all those for combat infantry and all tank figures in italics) are my own estimates from the number of divisions present in each offensive. These estimates assume that German divisions were at 40 per cent of establishment strength and Russian at 80 per cent (on the dates specified the Russian Fronts had been specially reinforced for major operations). These establishment strengths were as follows:

	Combat Infantry	Tanks and SP guns
German		
Infantry division	5,560	14
Motorised division		110
Panzer division (44)	not	250
Panzer division (45)	included	200
Russian		
Infantry division	6,300	not inc.
Mechanised corps		250
Tank corps	not	280
Tank brigade	included	65

Estimated German figures also include a 10% increment of non-divisional AFVs.

Table 35: *Distribution of German combat divisions by theatre June 1941–March 1945*

	East	West	Norway/Finland	Denmark	Balkans	Italy	Africa
27 June 1941	134(32)*	38(0)	13(0)	1(6)	7(0)	–	2(2)
Sept. 1941	144(32)		14(0)	1(0)	7(0)	–	3(3)
Dec. 1941	146(32)	32(2)	15(0)	1(0)	8(0)	–	3(3)
March 1942	164(34)		16½(½)	7(0)	–	–	3(3)
June 1942	171(34)	27(3)	16½(½)	1(0)	8(1)	–	3(3)
Sept. 1942	171(33)		15½(½)	1(0)	9(1)	–	4(3)
Dec. 1942	178(33)	36(5)	15½(½)	2(0)	10(1)	–	6(4)
March 1943	175(29)		16½(½)	1(0)	15(1)	–	7½(4½)
June 1943	179(28)	42(8)	16½(½)	2(0)	17(1)	–	–
Sept. 1943	181(26)		18(0)	2½(½)	19(1)	7(6)	–
Dec. 1943	175(34)	37(6)	17(0)	5½(½)	24(2)	14(6)	–
March 1944	169(36)		16(0)	4½(½)	21(5)	19(6)	–
6 June 1944	157(30)	56(11)	16(0)	3½(1½)	20(4)	22(6)	–
Sept. 1944	127(33)	55(14)	15(0)	2½(½)	17(3)	21(4)	–
Dec. 1944	132(44)	71(15)	14(0)	2½(½)	16(3)	22(4)	–
March 1945	166(43)	63(9)	9½(0)	5½(½)	–	19(3)	–

* Number in brackets = panzer and motorised divisions.

Table 36: *Number of German combat divisions engaged by the Russians and by the Western Allies June 1941 – March 1945*

Date	Number of German divisions engaged by Russians	W. Allies	Percentage engaged by Russians	W. Allies
27 June 1941	147 (32)*	2 (2)	98 (97)	2 (3)
Dec. 1941	161 (32)	3 (3)	98 (91)	2 (9)
June 1942	187 (34)	3 (3)	98 (92)	2 (8)
Dec. 1942	183 (33)	6 (4)	97 (89)	3 (11)
June 1943	195 (28)	–	100 (100)	–
Dec. 1943	192 (34)	14 (6)	93 (85)	7 (15)
6 June 1944	173 (30)	78 (17)	70 (70)	30 (30)
Dec. 1944	162 (47)	93 (19)	64 (71)	36 (29)
March 1945	166 (43)	82 (12)	67 (78)	33 (22)

* Number in brackets = panzer and motorised divisions. The figure for the total number of divisions faced by the Russians is very slightly inflated as it also includes the number of German divisions in Norway.

Table 37: *Numbers of U-boats sunk, at sea in the Atlantic, and built, per quarter 1939–45*

Legend:
- U-boats sunk
- Avge No. U-boats at sea
- U-boats built

Y-axis: Number of U-boats

Year	Quarter	U-boats sunk	Avge No. U-boats at sea	U-boats built
1939	O/D	9	14	7
1940	J/M	8	13	6
1940	A/J	6	20	6
1940	J/S	5	12	18
1940	O/D	3	11	18
1941	J/M	5	11	39
1941	A/J	6	25	39
1941	J/S	6	33	60
1941	O/D	17	33	60
1942	J/M	11	47	57
1942	A/J	10	56	65
1942	J/S	31	55	85
1942	O/D	34	66	99
1943	J/M	40	60	108
1943	A/J	73	70	105
1943	J/S	71	68	68
1943	O/D	53	77	79
1944	J/M	60	63	68
1944	A/J	68	49	55
1944	J/S	81	51	50
1944	O/D	52	46	69
1945	J/M	68	47	79

Table 38: *Allied merchant tonnage sunk by U-boats in the Atlantic January 1943 – May 1945*

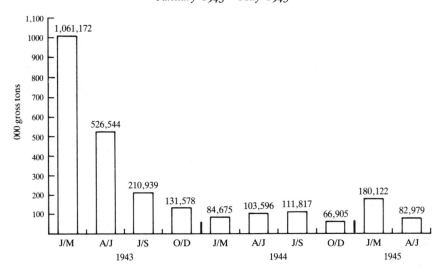

Table 39: *U-boat efficiency: quarterly merchant shipping tonnage sunk in the Atlantic per U-boat at sea 1939–45*

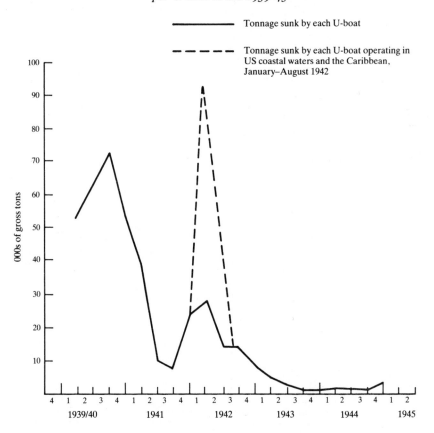

Table 40: *Primary targets assigned to Bomber Command and Eighth US Air Force 1939–45*

● Bomber Command abandons daylight operations

● First attack on mainland Europe (Stavanger)

● First attack on mainland Germany

● First raid on Berlin

● Attacks on occupied countries sanctioned

● 1,000-bomber raid on Cologne

		PRIMARY SHORT-TERM TARGET						PRIMARY LONG-TERM TARGET

German fleet in port — mining — leafleting

a/c industry | ports | aircraft industry

submarine yards | transportation system | sub. yards

various precision targets

OIL

AREA TARGETS AND GERMAN MORALE

1939 — Oct. Nov. Dec. Jan. Feb. March April May June July Aug. Sept. Oct. Nov. Dec. 1940 — Jan. Feb. March April May June July 1941 — Aug. Sept. Oct. Nov. Dec. Jan. Feb. March April May June 1942

● First bombing mission by 8US Air Force (Rouen)

● Combined Bomber Offensive sanctioned

● Start of the Battle of the Ruhr

● First Bomber Command attack on Berlin

● Combined Bomber offensive begins

● Start of the Battle of Berlin

● SHAEF takes command of strategic air forces

● SHAEF relinquishes control of strategic air forces

PRIMARY SHORT-TERM TARGET

various precision targets

submarine bases and yards | fighters and fighter industry | air-frames and ball-bearings | tanks and radar | aircraft and aircraft industry | tanks and motor transport | jets

PRIMARY LONG-TERM TARGET

AREA TARGETS AND GERMAN MORALE

GERMAN INDUSTRY

OIL AND TRANSPORTATION

OIL

July Aug. Sept. Oct. Nov. Dec. 1942 — Jan. Feb. March April May June July Aug. Sept. Oct. Nov. Dec. 1943 — Jan. Feb. March April May June July Aug. Sept. Oct. Nov. Dec. 1944 — Jan. Feb. March April 1945

Table 41: *Axis and Allied aircraft production 1939–45*

	Germany		Italy		USA		USSR		UK		Total Axis		Total Allied	
	Total Combat	Total A/c	Total Combat	Total A/c	Total Combat	Total A/c	Total Combat	Total A/c	Total Combat	Total A/c	Total Combat	Total A/c	Total Combat	Total A/c
1939	1,476	2,372	–	–	–	–	–	–	3,161	7,431	–	–	–	–
1940	6,201	9,430	1,795	2,943	1,785	3,806	8,145	10,385	7,771	14,573	7,996	12,373	17,701	28,764
1941	7,624	10,930	2,093	3,260	8,531	19,163	12,377	15,735	11,732	18,862	9,717	14,190	32,640	53,760
1942	11,266	13,994	2,054	2,739	23,396	44,479	21,480	25,235	16,102	22,590	13,320	16,733	60,978	92,304
1943	18,953	23,372	631	948	53,343	81,028	29,841	34,845	18,455	24,543	19,584	24,320	101,639	140,416
1944	33,804	39,626	–	–	73,876	91,546	33,209	40,245	18,633	22,642	33,804	39,626	125,718	154,433
1945	6,987	7,521	–	–	36,829	43,208	16,408	c.20,000	7,257	9,235	6,987	7,521	60,494	72,443
TOTAL	86,311	107,245	6,573	9,890	197,760	283,230	121,460	146,445	83,111	119,876	91,408	114,763	399,170	542,120

Table 42: *German and Allied front-line combat aircraft
at selected dates September 1939 – April 1945*

	Germany	USA*	USSR	UK	Total Allied
Sept. 1939	2,916	–	–	1,660	1,660
Aug. 1940	3,015	–	–	2,913	2,913
Dec. 1940	2,885	–	–	1,064[†]	1,064
June 1941	3,451	–	8,105	3,106	11,211
Dec. 1941	2,561	4,000[‡] / 957	2,495	4,287	6,782**
June 1942	3,573	? / 1,902	3,160	4,500§	9,562
Dec. 1942	3,440	10,885 / 4,695	3,088	5,257	13,040
June 1943	5,003	? / 6,586	8,290	6,026	22,902
Dec. 1943	4,667	23,807 / 11,917	8,500	6,646	27,063
June 1944	4,637	? / 19,342	11,800	8,339	39,481
Dec. 1944	5,041	33,179 / 19,892	14,500	8,395	42,787
April 1945	2,175[†]	31,235 / 21,572	17,000	8,000§	46,752

* US Army Air Force only.
† Fighters only.
‡ In the US column the top figure is total aircraft available, the bottom total aircraft overseas.
§ Estimate.
** Does not include US.

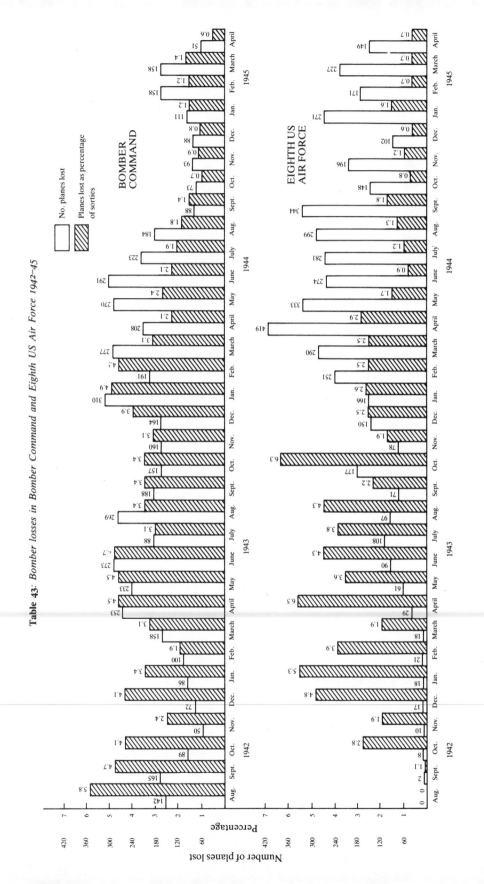

Table 43: *Bomber losses in Bomber Command and Eighth US Air Force 1942–45*

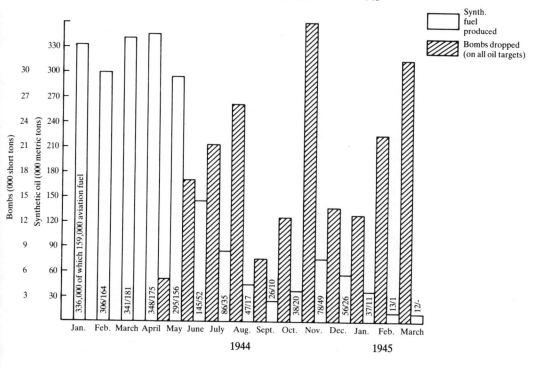

Table 44: *German synthetic and aviation fuel production and tonnage of Allied bombs dropped on oil targets January 1944 – March 1945*

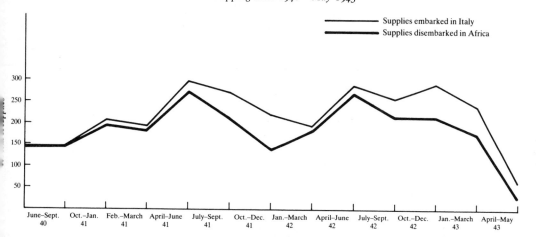

Table 45: *Embarkation and disembarkation of supplies to North Africa by Axis merchant shipping June 1940 – May 1943*

Table 46: *Axis and Allied coal production 1939–45 (million metric tons)*

Axis Total = 2,624.9

Allied Total = 4,283.6

	Germany	Italy	Japan*		US	UK	USSR	Canada
1939	332.8	3.2	–	1939	–	231.3	–	13.3
1940	364.8	4.4	–	1940	–	224.3	–	14.9
1941	402.8	4.4	–	1941	–	206.3	151.4	15.3
1942	407.8	4.8	61.3	1942	528.5	204.9	75.5	15.9
1943	429.0	3.3	60.5	1943	535.3	198.9	93.1	14.7
1944	432.8	–	51.7	1944	562.0	192.7	121.5	14.2
1945	50.3	–	11.0	1945	523.9	182.8	149.3	13.6
TOTAL	2,420.3	20.1	184.5	TOTAL	2,149.7	1,441.2	590.8	101.9

* inc. imports.

Table 47: *Axis and Allied iron ore production 1939–45 (million metric tons)*

Axis Total = 266.1

Allied Total = 591.1

	Germany*	Italy	Japan*		US	UK	USSR	Canada
1939	18.5	–	–	1939	–	14.5	–	0.1
1940	29.5	1.2	–	1940	–	17.7	–	0.4
1941	53.3	1.3	–	1941	–	19.0	24.7	0.5
1942	50.6	1.1	7.4	1942	107.6	19.9	9.7	0.5
1943	56.2	0.8	6.7	1943	103.1	18.5	9.3	0.6
1944	32.6	–	6.0	1944	96.0	15.5	11.7	0.5
1945	?	–	0.9	1945	90.2	14.2	15.9	1.0
TOTAL	240.7	4.4	21.0	TOTAL	396.9	119.3	71.3	3.6

* inc. imports.

Table 48: *Axis and Allied crude steel production 1939–45 (million metric tons)*

Allied Total = 497.1

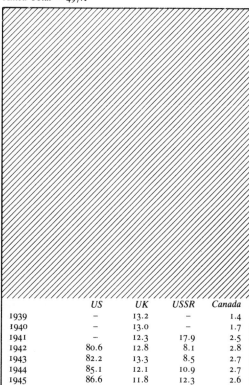

Axis Total = 191.8

	Germany	Italy	Japan
1939	23.7	–	–
1940	21.5	2.1	–
1941	28.2	2.1	–
1942	28.7	1.9	8.0
1943	30.6	1.7	8.8
1944	25.8	–	6.5
1945	1.4	–	0.8
TOTAL	159.9	7.8	24.1

	US	UK	USSR	Canada
1939	–	13.2	–	1.4
1940	–	13.0	–	1.7
1941	–	12.3	17.9	2.5
1942	80.6	12.8	8.1	2.8
1943	82.2	13.3	8.5	2.7
1944	85.1	12.1	10.9	2.7
1945	86.6	11.8	12.3	2.6
TOTAL	334.5	88.5	57.7	16.4

Table 49: *Axis and Allied aluminium production 1939–45 (000 metric tons)*

Allied Total = 4,642.7

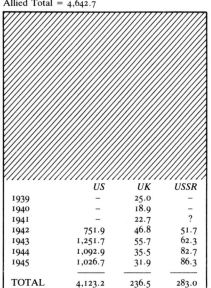

Axis Total = 2,503.3

	Germany	Japan
1939	239.4	–
1940	265.3	–
1941	315.6	–
1942	420.0	103.0
1943	432.0	141.0
1944	470.0	110.0
1945	?	7.0
TOTAL	2,142.3	361.0

	US	UK	USSR
1939	–	25.0	–
1940	–	18.9	–
1941	–	22.7	?
1942	751.9	46.8	51.7
1943	1,251.7	55.7	62.3
1944	1,092.9	35.5	82.7
1945	1,026.7	31.9	86.3
TOTAL	4,123.2	236.5	283.0

Table 50: *Axis and Allied crude oil production 1939–45 (million metric tons)*

Allied Total = 1,043.0

Axis Total = 50.45

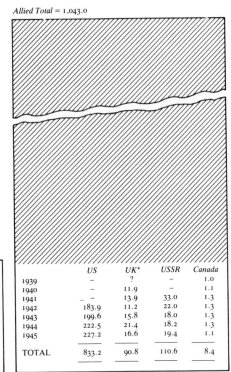

	Germany*	Italy	Japan*
1939	8.0	–	–
1940	6.7	0.01	–
1941	7.3	0.12	–
1942	7.7	0.03	1.82
1943	8.9	0.01	2.29
1944	6.4	–	1.04
1945	?	–	0.13
TOTAL	45.0	0.17	5.28

	US	UK*	USSR	Canada
1939	–	?	–	1.0
1940	–	11.9	–	1.1
1941	–	13.9	33.0	1.3
1942	183.9	11.2	22.0	1.3
1943	199.6	15.8	18.0	1.3
1944	222.5	21.4	18.2	1.3
1945	227.2	16.6	19.4	1.1
TOTAL	833.2	90.8	110.6	8.4

* inc. imports.

Table 51: *Axis and Allied production of tanks and self-propelled guns 1939–45 (units)*

Allied Total = 227,235

Axis Total = 51,845

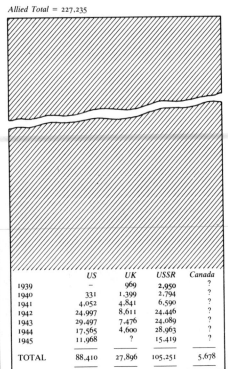

	Germany	Italy*	Japan*
1939	247	40	–
1940	1,643	250	315
1941	3,790	595	595
1942	6,180	1,252	557
1943	12,063	336	558
1944	19,002	–	353
1945	3,932	–	137
TOTAL	46,857	2,473	2,515

	US	UK	USSR	Canada
1939	–	969	2,950	?
1940	331	1,399	2,794	?
1941	4,052	4,841	6,590	?
1942	24,997	8,611	24,446	?
1943	29,497	7,476	24,089	?
1944	17,565	4,600	28,963	?
1945	11,968	?	15,419	?
TOTAL	88,410	27,896	105,251	5,678

* excludes light tanks and tankettes.

Table 52: *Axis and Allied artillery production (inc. A/Tk and A/A) 1939–45 (units)*

Allied Total = 914,682

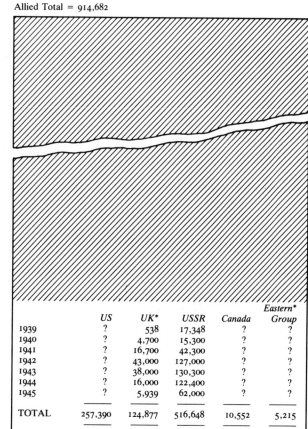

Axis Total = 179,694

	Germany	Italy	Japan*
1939	1,214	?	?
1940	6,730	?	?
1941	11,200	?	2,250
1942	23,200	?	2,550
1943	46,100	?	3,600
1944	70,700	–	3,300
1945	?	–	1,650
TOTAL	159,144	7,200	13,350

	US	UK*	USSR	Canada	Eastern* Group
1939	?	538	17,348	?	?
1940	?	4,700	15,300	?	?
1941	?	16,700	42,300	?	?
1942	?	43,000	127,000	?	?
1943	?	38,000	130,300	?	?
1944	?	16,000	122,400	?	?
1945	?	5,939	62,000	?	?
TOTAL	257,390	124,877	516,648	10,552	5,215

* Inf. guns only.

* Australia, NZ, India and S. Africa.

Table 53: *German and Allied production of mortars and machine-guns 1939–45 (units)*

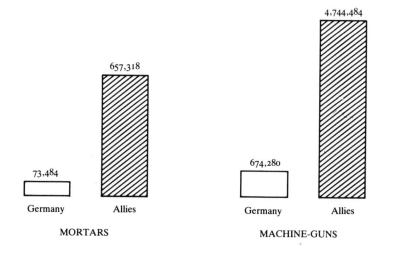

Table 54: *Axis and Allied production of military trucks and lorries 1939–45 (units)*

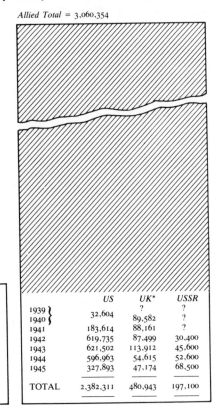

Allied Total = 3,060,354

Axis Total = 594,859

	Germany	Italy	Japan
1939	32,558	?	?
1940	53,348	?	38,056
1941	51,085	?	46,389
1942	58,049	?	35,386
1943	74,181	?	24,000
1944	67,375	?	20,356
1945	9,318	?	1,758
TOTAL	345,914	83,000	165,945

	US	UK*	USSR
1939 }	32,604	?	?
1940 }		89,582	?
1941	183,614	88,161	?
1942	619,735	87,499	30,400
1943	621,502	113,912	45,600
1944	596,963	54,615	52,600
1945	327,893	47,174	68,500
TOTAL	2,382,311	480,943	197,100

Table 55: *Axis and Allied production of military aircraft 1939–45 (units)*

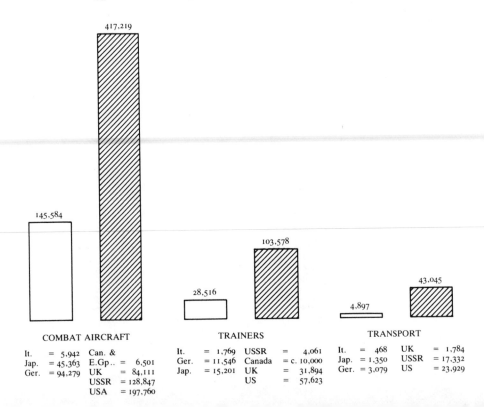

COMBAT AIRCRAFT	TRAINERS	TRANSPORT
417,219	103,578	43,045
145,584	28,516	4,897

COMBAT AIRCRAFT
It.   = 5,942   Can. &
Jap. = 45,363   E.Gp.. = 6,501
Ger. = 94,279   UK   = 84,111
                USSR   = 128,847
                USA   = 197,760

TRAINERS
It. = 1,769   USSR   = 4,061
Ger. = 11,546   Canada = c. 10,000
Jap. = 15,201   UK   = 31,894
                US   = 57,623

TRANSPORT
It. = 468   UK   = 1,784
Jap. = 1,350   USSR = 17,332
Ger. = 3,079   US   = 23,929

Table 56: *Japanese imports of selected raw materials 1942–5 (000s of metric tons)*

	1942	1943	1944	1945
Coal	6,388	5,181	2,615	548
Coking coal	4,025	2,939	1,435	116
Iron ore	4,700	4,298	2,153	341
Pig-iron	878	1,134	942	51
Finished iron and steel	993	977	1,097	170
Bauxite	305	909	376	15
Lead	11	25	17	4
Tin	4	27	23	4
Zinc	8	10	6	2
Phosphorite and phosphate	342	237	90	23
Dolomite and magnesite	469	437	287	66

Table 57: *US and Japanese fleets December 1941 and total US and Japanese naval ships built 1942–45*

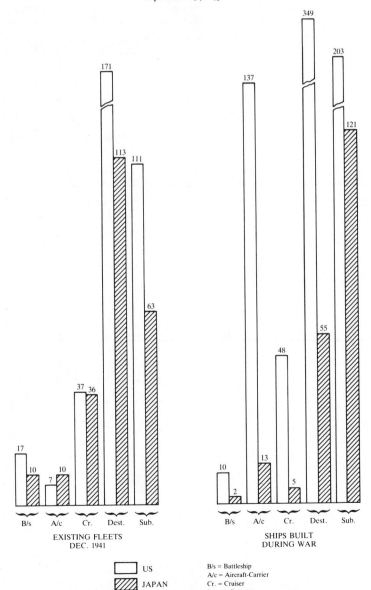

EXISTING FLEETS
DEC. 1941

SHIPS BUILT
DURING WAR

US

JAPAN

B/s = Battleship
A/c = Aircraft-Carrier
Cr. = Cruiser
Dest. = Destroyer
Sub. = Submarine

Table 58: *US and Japanese naval strengths in the Pacific 1942–45*

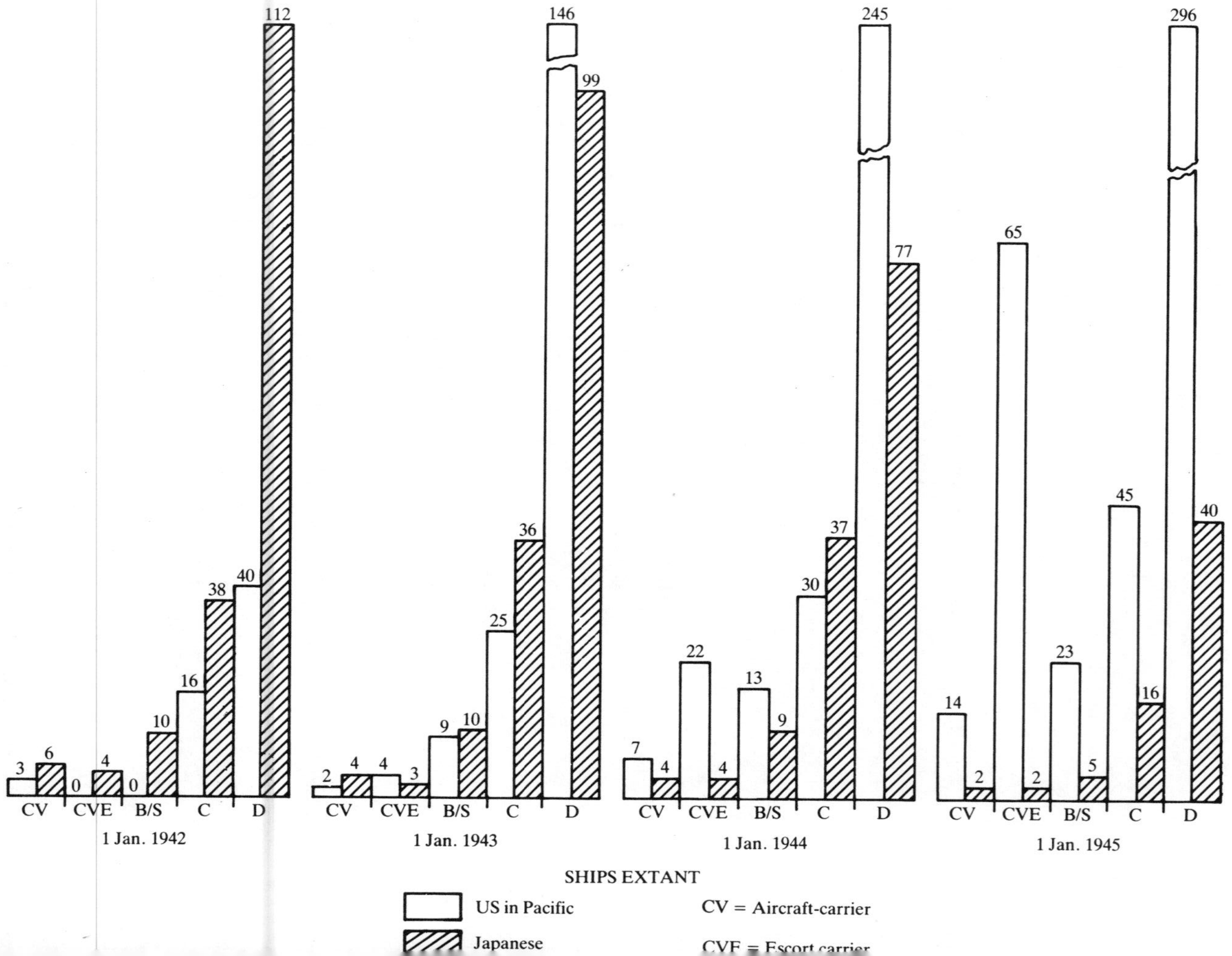

1 Jan. 1942

CV: 3, 6 | CVE: 0, 4 | B/S: 0, 10 | C: 16, 38 | D: 40, 112

1 Jan. 1943

CV: 2, 4 | CVE: 3, 4 | B/S: 9, 10 | C: 25, 36 | D: 146, 99

1 Jan. 1944

CV: 7, 4 | CVE: 22, 4 | B/S: 13, 9 | C: 30, 37 | D: 245, 77

1 Jan. 1945

CV: 14, 2 | CVE: 65, 2 | B/S: 23, 5 | C: 45, 16 | D: 296, 40

SHIPS EXTANT

US in Pacific
Japanese

CV = Aircraft-carrier
CVE = Escort carrier

Table 59: *US and Japanese naval losses in the Pacific 1941–5*

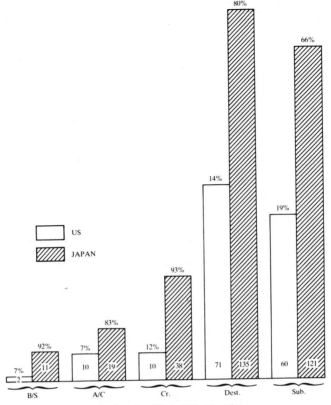

x% = Total ships sunk as % age total ships Dec. 1941 plus total built in wartime.

Table 60: *US and Japanese carrier strengths and losses in the Pacific 1941–5*

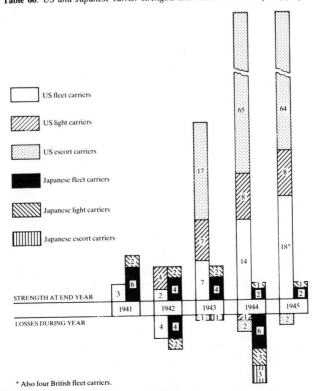

* Also four British fleet carriers.

Table 61: *Armament and armour of principal Allied and Axis tanks 1939–45*

Country	Tank	Date* in Service	Gun	Thickness of Armour (mm)		
				Hull Side	Hull Front	Turret (max.)
USA	M3 Grant Mk I	1941	75mm +37mm	38	51	57
	M4A1 Sherman	1942	75mm	51	51	76
	M4A1(76mm) Sherman	1944	76mm†	51	51	76
USSR	KV1 Model 42	PW / 1942	76.2mm	90–130	110	120
	T34 Model 42	1940 / 1942	76.2mm	47	47	65
	T34/85	1944	85mm	60	47	90
	JS2	1944	122 mm	120	95	160
UK	Matilda II	1939	2pdr	65	78	75
	Crusader I	1941	2pdr	27	40	39
	Crusader II	1941	2pdr	27	51	51
	Valentine II	1941	2pdr	60	60	65
	Churchill VII	1942 / 1944	75mm	76	152	89
France	Renault FT	PW	37mm	max. 15mm		
	Renault D1	PW	47mm	?	30	40
	Renault D2	PW	47mm	?	30	40
	FCM 21	PW	75mm	max. 25mm		
	Renault B1 *bis*	PW	75mm +47mm	60	60	56
	Somua 35S	PW	47mm	40	35	56
Germany	Pz I	PW	m.g.	13	13	13
	Pz II	PW	20mm	20	35	30
	Pz IIIG	PW / 1940	50mm short	30	30	30
	Pz IIIJ (Special)	1941	50mm long	30	50	30
	Pz IVD	PW / 1939	75mm short	14.5	14.5	30
	Pz IVF² (Special)	1942	75mm long	40	50	50
	Pz VG	1943 / 1944	75mm	50	80	100
	Pz VI Tiger I	1942	88mm	80	100	100
Italy	L3	PW	m.g.	8.5	13.5	–
	M11/39	1940	37/40mm	14.5	30	30
	M13/40	1940	47/32mm	25	30	40

* PW = pre-war. Entries with two dates separated by a diagonal indicate the date the type of tank entered service (on the left) and the date the particular model did so.
† In 1944 both the American M4A1 (76mm) and the British Sherman IIC (Firefly) were fitted with a 76mm gun.

Table 62: *Armour-piercing capabilities of major Allied and Axis tank and anti-tank guns 1939–45*

Country	Gun	Thickness of armour penetrated at x yards (mm)*					
		250	500	750	1,000	1,500	2,000
US	Boys 2/tank rifle	21mm at 300 yards					
and	2 pdr (shot)	58	52	46	40		
UK	2 pdr (high velocity shot)	64	57	51	45		
	37mm	58	53	48	47		
	6 pdr		79	72	65	52	
	17 pdr			120	113	96	82
	75mm M2 14AP M72		61	?	53	46	38
	firing: M61		66	?	61	56	51
	75mm M3 firing: M61		66	?	61	56	51
	76mm				98	?	?
	25pdr (towed) firing:						
	20AP shot		63	58	54	?	?
USSR	37mm	38mm at 400 yards					
	45mm		80	?	50		
	57mm		140	?	?	?	
	76mm F.34 firing DS a.p.		92	?	60	?	?
	85mm		138	?	100	?	?
	100mm D-10 firing He a.p.		195	?	185	?	?
	122mm firing HE a.p.		145	145	145	?	?
Germany†	37mm (L/45)	32(40)	28(28)				
	50mm short (L/42)	56(83)	53(60)	46(42)	40	28	22
	50mm long (L/60 & 38)	67(109)	61(77)	56(46)	50	38	29
	75mm short (L/24)		46(75)	42(75)	41(75)	33	30
	75mm long (L/43 & PAK43)		92(108)	?	82(87)	72(69)	63
	75mm long (L/48 & PAK39)		96(120)	?	85(97)	74(77)	64
	88mm (L/36 & PAK36)		110(156)	?	100(138)	91(123)	84(110)
Italy	20mm (towed)	29	24				
	37/40mm	32mm at 1,000 yards					
	47/32mm	?	48	38	32		
		(at 400 yd)					

* Empty boxes at beginning of line signify gun could penetrate almost any thickness at this range. Empty boxes at end of line signify gun almost useless at this range.
† Figures in brackets are capabilities using Pz Gr 40 ammunition.

Table 63: *The uses of raw materials in the munitions industry 1939-45*

RAW MATERIAL	DERIVATIVE	USES
COAL		Fuel for power stations
	Coke	Fuel for iron and steel furnaces
	Coal tar (partic. benzene)	Synthetic rubber; DDT; motor fuel additive; sufa drugs; aspirin; explosives (RDX)
	Coal gas	Dyes; explosives, fertilisers
	Methane	Methyl alcohol/methanol (industrial solvent)
	Light oils	Explosives (toluol/toluene for TNT)
	Artificial fuel	When combined with hydrogen (partic. Germany)
PETROLEUM	Gasoline	Auto and aviation fuel
	Fuel oil	Marine furnaces
	Kerosene	Lamps and heating
	Lubricating oil	
	Paraffins	Wax (sealing and waterproofing)
	Ethene/Ethylene	Industrial solvent
IRON ORE	Pig-iron	Ore with oxygen removed
	Cast iron	Pig-iron with impurities removed and then moulded
	Steel	Iron ore minus carbon. Also alloyed. (a) Cast steel: moulded (b) Forged/rolled steel: cast steel re-rolled into blooms/billets (c) Hot or cold finished into end product.
ASBESTOS		Brake shoes and clutch linings
BAUXITE (also Cryolite)	Aluminium	Electric cables; aircraft parts; moving parts in engines; explosives

COPPER		Electric wires and cables; boiler and condenser parts; armatures and electro-magnets in dynamos, motors and magnetos
	Brass	Alloyed with zinc. Cartridge and shell cases.
GLYCERINE	Nitroglycerine	Treated with nitric and sulphuric acid. Explosives.
	Cordite	Nitroglycerine plus nitrocellulose (paper and wood shavings treated with nitric and sulphuric acid). Propellant.
GRAPHITE		Electrodes; electric motor brushes
LEAD		Batteries to store electricity. Alloyed with bronze for bearings.
	Lead azide	Explosives
	Lead oxide	Anti-rusting paint
	Lead tetraethyl	Anti-knock agent in gasoline
MAGNESITE		Brick for furnaces
	Magnesium	Light steel alloys
MANGANESE		Steel alloys: vital if short of quality iron ore
MOLYB-DENUM		Steel alloys
NICKEL		Steel alloys. Gears; shafts; engine parts.
NITROGEN	Nitric Acid	Explosives; fertilisers
POTASSIUM	Potash/Potassium Carbonate	Fertilisers
RUBBER		(useless unless vulcanised with heat and sulphur) Tyres; sealing rings
SODIUM*	Carbonate	Manufacturing glass and paper
	Chloride	Explosives; chemicals; oil refining
	Hydroxide	Chemicals; aluminium; oil refining

*Sodium is never found in a pure form.

Sources for Tables

Table 1 Royal Navy Pink Lists, June and September 1940; S. W. Roskill, *The War at Sea* (History of the Second World War: United Kingdom Military Series), (3 vols, HMSO, 1954–61), vol. 1, p. 440.

Table 2 M. Cooper, *The German Army 1933–45: Its Political and Military Failure* (Macdonald & Jane's, 1978), pp. 270, 276, 280; J. Lucas, *War on the Eastern Front* (Jane's, 1979), p. 47; J. Erickson, *The Road to Stalingrad* (Weidenfeld & Nicolson, 1975), p. 98; R. J. Overy, *The Air War 1939–45* (Europa, 1980), p. 49; E. Bauer, *The History of World War II* (Orbis, 1979), p. 375.

Table 3 A. Milward, *War, Economy and Society 1939–45* (Allen Lane, 1977), p. 45.

Table 4 Based on tables 30–2.

Table 5 B. Mueller-Hillebrand, *Das Heer 1933–5* (E. S. Mittler und Sohn, Darmstadt/Frankfurt, 1954–9), *passim*: S. W. Mitcham, *Hitler's Legions: the German Army Order of Battle, World War II* (Leo Cooper/Secker & Warburg, 1985), *passim*.

Table 6 *United States Statistical Abstract* (1947); J. Costello & T. Hughes, *The Battle of the Atlantic* (Fontana, 1980), pp. 329–31.

Table 7 *United States Statistical Abstract* (1947); C. B. A. Behrens, *Merchant Shipping and the Demands of War* (History of the Second World War: United Kingdom Civil Series), (HMSO, 1958), p. 69; D. J. Payton-Smith, *Oil: a Study of Wartime Policy and Administration* (History of the Second World War: United Kingdom Civil Series), (HMSO, 1971), pp. 245, 488.

Table 8 Costello & Hughes, op. cit., pp. 330–1; S. E. Morison, *History of United States Naval Operations in World War II* (15 vols, OUP, 1948–62), vol. 1, p. 412, and vol. 10, p. 365; J. Rohwer, 'The U-Boat War against the Allied Supply Lines', in H.-A. Jacobsen & J. Rohwer, *Decisive Battles of World War II: the German View* (Deutsch, 1965), pp. 264–6; Board of Trade, *Shipping Movement at United Kingdom Ports . . . 1938–45* (HMSO, 1946), pp. 2, 7.

Table 9 Sir C. Webster & N. Frankland, *The Strategic Air Offensive Against Germany* (History of the Second World War: United Kingdom Military Series), (4 vols, HMSO, 1961), vol. 4, pp. 454–7; R. Freeman,

The U.S. Strategic Bomber (Macdonald & Jane's, 1975), p. 155.

Table 10   USSBS (Military Analysis Division), *Air Force Rate of Operation* (GPO, Washington, January 1947), pp. 26, 58–69; Freeman, loc. cit.

Table 11   F. H. Hinsley, *British Intelligence in the Second World War* (3 vols, HMSO, 1979–88), vol. 2, p. 297; Mitcham, op. cit., p. 145; I. S. O. Playfair (ed.), *The Mediterranean and the Middle East* (History of the Second World War: United Kingdom Military Series), vol. 3 (HMSO, 1960), pp. 220, 383, and vol. 4 (HMSO, 1966), p. 9; B. H. L. Hart, *The Tanks* (2 vols, Cassell, 1959), vol. 2, pp. 154–5; C. Messenger, *The Unknown Alamein* (Ian Allen, Shepperton, 1982), pp. 58–9; M. Carver, *El Alamein* (Batsford, 1962), p. 73; S. Westphal, *The German Army in the West* (Cassell, 1951), p. 108.

Table 12   Great Britain (Cabinet Office), *Principal War Telegrams and Memoranda 1940–43* (K.T.O. Press, Liechtenstein, n.d.), vol. 3 (Hist. (B) (Crusader)5), *passim*; Hart, op. cit., vol. 2, p. 236; Cooper, op. cit., p. 390; W. Schumann *et al.*, *Deutschland im Zweiten Weltkrieg* (Pahl-Rugenstein, Cologne, 1979), p. 123; Hinsley, op. cit., vol. 2, p. 460.

Table 13   Derived from author's own database, based mainly on Mueller-Hillebrand, op. cit., vol. 3 (1969), pp. 285–314; Mitcham, op. cit., *passim*; H. F. Joslen, *Orders of Battle 1939–45* (History of the Second World War: United Kingdom Military Series), (HMSO, 1960), vols 1 & 2, *passim*.

Table 14   Inferred from known establishment totals.

Table 15   Inferred from data in tables 46–55.

Table 16   Inferred from known establishment totals.

Table 17   Mainly R. Bennett, *Ultra in the West: the Normandy Campaign of 1944–45* (Hutchinson, 1979), *passim*; G. A. Harrison, *Cross-Channel Attack* (United States Army in World War II), (GPO, Washington, 1951), p. 240; C. P. Stacey, *The Victory Campaign* (Official History of the Canadian Army in the Second World War), (Queen's Printers, Ottawa, 1960), *passim*; C. Wilmot, *The Struggle for Europe* (Collins, 1952), *passim*.

Table 18   H. Pemsel, *Atlas of Naval Warfare* (Arms & Armour Press, 1977), pp. 125–8; M. Okumiya & J. Horikoshi, *Zero: the Story of the Japanese Navy Air Force 1937–45* (Corgi, 1958), pp. 144–6.

Table 19   S. W. Kirby, *The War Against Japan* (HMSO, 1958–69), vol. 5, p. 468.

Table 20   ibid, p. 475; USSBS (Transport Division), *The War Against Japanese Transportation* (GPO, Washington, May 1947), p. 54; USSBS, *The Effects of Strategic Bombing on Japan's War Economy* (GPO, Washington, December 1946), p. 183.

Table 21   Kirby, op. cit., vol. 5, p. 475.

Table 22   Milward, op. cit., p. 69; J. B. Cohen, *Japan's Economy in War and Reconstruction* (University of Minnesota Press, Minneapolis, 1949), pp. 128–60 *passim*; Kirby, op. cit., vol. 5, p. 475; USSBS, *Japanese*

Transportation, op. cit., p. 29; USSBS, *Effects Strategic Bombing*, op. cit., pp. 111, 220; *US Statistical Abstract* (1946), pp. 728, 744, and (1948), p. 879; V. R. Sill, *American Miracle* (Odyssey Press, New York, 1949), p. 160; H. C. Thomson & L. Mayo, *The Ordnance Department: Procurement and Supply* (US Army in World War II), (GPO, Washington, 1960), p. 101.

Table 23 Overy, op. cit., p. 94.

Table 24 Derived from numerous sources, mainly Morison, op. cit., *passim*.

Table 25 S. W. Kirby *et al.*, *The War Against Japan* (History of the Second World War: United Kingdom Military Series), (HMSO, 1958–69) vol. 3, pp. 472–3, vol. 4, pp. 448–51, vol. 5, pp. 461–4.

(Statistical Appendix)

Table 26 C. Bekker, *The Luftwaffe War Diaries* (Macdonald, 1966), p. 164; Webster & Frankland, op. cit., vol. 4, p. 494.

Table 27 ibid., p. 494; Bekker, op. cit., p. 164; D. Wood & D. Dempster, *The Narrow Margin: the Battle of Britain and the Rise of Air Power 1930–1940* (Arrow, 1967), pp. 84, 477–8.

Table 28 Webster & Frankland, op. cit., vol. 4, pp. 433, 456; Freeman, op. cit., p. 155; Bekker, op. cit., p. 181.

Table 29 H.-A. Jacobsen & H. Dollinger, *Der Zweite Weltkrieg* (Verlag Kurt Disch, Munich, 1963), vol. 2, p. 390.

Table 30 USSBS, *The Effects of Strategic Bombing on the German Economy* (GPO, Washington, 1945), p. 163; F. von Senger und Etterlin, *German Tanks of World War II* (Galahad Books, New York), pp. 211–12; S. J. Zaloga & J. Grandsen, *Soviet Tanks and Combat Vehicles of World War Two* (Arms & Armour Press, 1984), p. 225.

Table 31 Bekker, op. cit., p. 377; M. Harrison, *Soviet Planning in Peace and War 1938–45* (CUP, 1985), pp. 250–1; O. Groehler, *Geschichte des Luftkriegs 1910–80* (Militärverlag der DDR, Berlin, 1981), p. 345.

Table 32 H.-A. Jacobsen, *Der Zweite Weltkrieg* (Fischer Bücherei, Frankfurt-am-Main, 1965), p. 195; Harrison, loc. cit.

Table 33 J. F. Dunnigan (ed.), *The Russian Front* (Arms & Armour Press, 1978), p. 155; E. F. Ziemke, *Stalingrad to Berlin: the German Defeat in the East* (GPO, Washington 1968), p. 418; Anon, *The Rise and Fall of the German Air Force* (reprint, WE Inc., Old Greenwich, Conn., 1969), p. 392; A. Boyd, *The Soviet Air Force since 1918* (Macdonald & Jane's, 1977), p. 180; Harrison, op. cit., p. 264; Groehler, op. cit., p. 502.

Table 34 E. von Manstein, *Lost Victories* (Arms & Armour Press, 1982), pp. 457, 528; P. Carell, *Hitler's War on Russia*, vol. 2, *Scorched Earth*

(Harrap, 1970), pp. 377–8, 437; Ziemke, op. cit., pp. 177–8, 241, 251, 293, 319, 332–3, 471–2; Bauer, op. cit., pp. 389, 545, 577–8; J. Erickson, *The Road to Berlin* (Weidenfeld & Nicolson, 1983), pp. 171, 214, 231–2, 347, 351, 449; E. Lederrey, *Germany's Defeat in the East* (War Office, 1959), p. 156; M. Mackintosh, *Juggernaut: a History of the Soviet Armed Forces* (Secker & Warburg, 1967), p. 218; A. Seaton, *The Russo-German War 1941–45* (Arthur Barker, 1971), pp. 446, 494, 523, 531; Cooper, op. cit., p. 477; E. Raus, 'The Pomeranian Battle and the Command in the East 1945', Pamphlet D-189, p. 36, in D. S. Detweiler *et al.* (eds), *World War II Military Studies* (Garland, New York, 1979), vol. 16.

Tables 35–6 Derived from Mueller-Hillebrand, op. cit., vol. 3, pp. 284–315, and Mitcham, op. cit., *passim*.

Table 37 H. Busch, *U-Boats at War* (Ballantine, New York, 1962), p. 176; Morison, op. cit, vol. 1, p. 410, vol. 10, p. 366.

Table 38 ibid., vol. 1, p. 410, vol. 10, p. 365.

Table 39 Busch, loc. cit.; Rohwer, loc. cit., pp. 265–6; Costello & Hughes, op. cit., pp. 330–1.

Table 40 Webster & Frankland, op. cit., vol. 4, pp. 109–83.

Table 41 W. Baumbach, *The Broken Swastika* (Robert Hale, 1960), pp. 213–14; G. Santoro, *L'Aeronautica Italiana nella Seconda Guerra Mondiale* (Edizione Milano Roma, Rome, 1957), vol. 2, pp. 480–1; W. F. Craven & J. L. Cate, *The Army Air Forces in World War II* (7 vols, Chicago University Press, Chicago, 1948–78), vol. 6, p. 352; Harrison, op. cit., pp. 250–1; M. M. Postan, *British War Production* (History of the Second World War: United Kingdom Civil Series), (HMSO, 1958), pp. 484–5.

Table 42 Webster & Frankland, op. cit., vol. 4, pp. 501–3; Craven & Cate, op. cit., vol. 6, p. 423; Harrison, op. cit., p. 264.

Table 43 Webster & Frankland, op. cit., vol. 4, pp. 432–3; Freeman, op. cit., pp. 156–7.

Table 44 USSBS, *Effects . . . German Economy*, op. cit., pp. 78–80.

Table 45 M. A. Bragadin, *The Italian Navy in World War II* (US Naval Institute Press, Annapolis, Md, 1957), pp. 68, 82, 190, 192, 198, 222–3, 247.

Tables 46–50 Cohen, op. cit., pp. 116, 128, 160; Harrison, op. cit., p. 124; G. Janssen, *Das Ministerium Speer* (Verlag Ullstein, Frankfurt, 1968), p. 326; Milward, op. cit., pp. 69, 91; Payton-Smith, op. cit., pp. 482–3; United Nations, *Statistical Bulletin* (July 1950); UNRRA, *Survey of Italy's Economy* (Rome, June 1947), p. 103; USSBS, *Effects . . . German Economy*, op. cit., pp. 98, 247, 257; US Bureau of Census, *US Historical Statistics to 1957* (GPO, Washington, 1959); Webster & Frankland, op. cit., vol. 4, pp. 508–10.

Tables 51–5 Baumbach, op. cit., pp. 212–14; Central Statistical Office, *Statistical Digest of the War* (HMSO, 1947); Cohen, op. cit., pp. 211, 237;

Craven & Cate, op. cit., vol. 6, p. 352; H. D. Hall, *North American Supply* (History of the Second World War: United Kingdom Civil Series), (HMSO, 1955), p. 25; H. D. Hall *et al.*, *Studies in Overseas Supply* (History of the Second World War: United Kingdom Civil Series), (HMSO, 1956), p. 477; Harrison, op. cit., pp. 250–1; Janssen, op. cit., p. 337; F. Minnitti, 'Il Problema degli Armamenti nella Preparazione Militari Italiana dal 1935 al 1943', *Storia Contemporania* 9, 1/1978, pp. 26–8, 39; Postan, op. cit., p. 109; Santoro, loc. cit.; Thomson & Mayo, op. cit., pp. 101, 181, 263, 296; USSBS, *Effects . . . German Economy*, op. cit., pp. 278–9, 281; USSBS, *Effects . . . Japan's War Economy*, op. cit., p. 220; USSBS, *The Japanese Aircraft Industry* (GPO, Washington, May 1947), pp. 155, 166; E. Zaleski, *Stalinist Planning for Economic Growth* (Macmillan, 1980), p. 604; Webster & Frankland, op. cit., pp. 469–70.

Table 56 USSBS, *Effects . . . Japan's War Economy*, op. cit., pp. 111, 189–93; USSBS, *Japanese Transportation*, op. cit., p. 109.

Tables 57–60 Derived from numerous sources, mainly: J. H. Belote & W. M. Belote, *Titans of the Seas* (Harper & Row, New York, 1975), pp. 323–4; M. Ito, *The End of the Imperial Japanese Navy* (Weidenfeld & Nicolson, 1963), pp. 215–21; H. Silverstone, *U.S. Warships of World War II* (Ian Allen, Shepperton, 1965), *passim*; *United States Statistical Abstract* (1946), p. 234; L. H. Morten, *Strategy and Command: the First Two Years* (US Army in World War II: War in the Pacific), (GPO, Washington, 1962), p. 539; E. J. King & W. M. Whitehill, *Fleet Admiral King: a Naval Record* (Eyre & Spottiswoode, 1953), p. 418; Roskill, op. cit., vol. 2, p. 476; Pemsel, op. cit., pp. 125–31, and 137–50 *passim*.

Tables 61–2 Aberdeen Proving Ground, *Tank Data* (WE Inc., Old Greenwich, Conn., n.d.), *passim*; P. Chamberlain & C. Ellis, *British and American Tanks of World War II* (Arms & Armour Press, 1969), *passim*: P. Chamberlain & T. J. Gander, *Anti-Tank Weapons* (Macdonald & Jane's, 1974), *passim*: T. J. Gander, *German Anti-Tank Guns* (Almark, New Malden, 1973), *passim*; J. Milsom, *Russian Tanks 1900–70* (Arms & Armour Press, 1970), *passim*; Playfair (ed.), op. cit., vol. 3, pp. 442–4, vol. 4, pp. 505–6; R. Riccio, *Italian Tanks and Fighting Vehicles of World War 2* (Picque Publications, Henley, 1975), *passim*; F. M. von Senger und Etterlin, *German Tanks of World War II* (Arms & Armour Press, 1969), pp. 194–210; P. Touzin, *Les Engins blindés français 1920–45* (Sera, Paris, 1976), vol. 1, *passim*; Zaloga & Grandsen, op. cit., *passim*.

Notes

Prologue: The Last European War

1   S. Zaloga & V. Madej, *The Polish Campaign 1939* (Hippocrene Books, New York, 1985), pp. 70–1.
2   ibid., pp. 137–8.
3   W. S. Churchill, *The Second World War* (6 vols, Cassell, 1948–54), vol. 2, p. 42.
4   M. Cooper, *The German Army 1933–45: Its Political and Military Failure* (Macdonald & Jane's, 1978), p. 229.
5   Quoted in J. Benoist-Méchin, *Sixty Days That Shook the West: the Fall of France 1940* (Jonathan Cape, 1963), p. 72.
6   B. H. L. Hart, *The Defence of the West* (Faber, 1950), p. 10.
7   B. A. Lee, 'Strategy, Arms and the Collapse of France 1939–40', in R. Langhorne (ed.), *Diplomacy and Intelligence During the Second World War: Essays in Honour of F. H. Hinsley* (CUP, 1985), p. 49.
8   S. Bidwell & D. Graham, *Fire-Power: British Army Weapons and Theories of War 1904–45* (Allen & Unwin, 1982), pp. 209–10.
9   Anon, *The Diary of a Staff Officer* (Methuen, 1941), pp. 12, 17, 23, 26–7.
10   A. de Saint-Exupéry, *Flight to Arras* (Pan Books, 1975), pp. 59–60.
11   B. H. L. Hart (ed.), *The Rommel Papers* (Collins, 1953), p. 7.
12   Anon, op. cit., p. 24.
13   ibid., p. 18.
14   Quoted in Benoist-Méchin, op. cit., p. 121.
15   ibid., p. 92.
16   Quoted in J. Costello & T. Hughes, *The Battle of the Atlantic* (Fontana, 1980), p. 73.
17   A. Bryant (ed.), *The Alanbrooke War Diaries* (2 vols, Fontana, 1965), vol. 1, pp. 155, 177–8.
18   W. Murray, *Luftwaffe: Strategy for Defeat 1933–45* (Allen & Unwin, 1985), p. 46.
19   W. Murray, 'The Luftwaffe Before the Second World War: A Mission, A Strategy', *Journal of Strategic Studies* 4, September 1981, p. 262.
20   A. Galland, *The First and the Last: the German Fighter Force in World War II* (Methuen, 1955), p. 60.
21   Quoted in H. Faber (ed.), *Luftwaffe: an Analysis by Former Luftwaffe Generals* (Sidgwick & Jackson, 1979), pp. 171–2. (A distillation of a 12-

vol. study written after the war by various *Luftwaffe* commanders, notably Generals Andreas Nielsen, Klaus Uebe, Paul Deichmann, Hermann Plochner, Karl Drum and Fritz Morzik.)

22 B. H. Klein, *Germany's Economic Preparations for War* (Havard University Press, Cambridge, Mass., 1959), p. 188.

23 Air Ministry, *The Rise and Fall of the German Air Force 1933–45* [1948], (WE Inc., Old Greenwich, Conn., 1969), p. 205.

24 R. J. Overy, 'From "Uralbomber" to "Amerikabomber": the Luftwaffe and Strategic Bombing', *Journal of Strategic Studies* 1, September 1978, p. 5; and E. L. Homze, *Arming the Luftwaffe: the Reich Air Ministry and the German Aircraft Industry 1919–39* (University of Nebraska Press, Lincoln, Neb., 1976), pp. 246, 265.

25 Quoted in F. K. Mason, *Battle Over Britain* (McWhirter Twins, 1969), p. 115.

26 Galland, op. cit., p. 57.

27 ibid.

28 ibid., p. 84.

29 Quoted in D. Irving, *The Rise and Fall of the Luftwaffe: the Life of Field Marshal Erhard Milch* (Futura, 1976), p. 178.

30 Quoted in Mason, op. cit., p. 613.

31 R. J. Overy, *The Air War 1939–45* (Europa, 1980), p. 32.

32 Murray, *Luftwaffe*, op. cit., p. 48.

33 B. Collier, *The Defence of the United Kingdom* (United Kingdom Military Series), (HMSO, 1957), p. 258.

34 ibid., p. xvii.

35 Overy, *Air War*, op. cit., p. 33.

Chapter 1: Blitzkrieg Founders: June 1941 – June 1943

1 Quoted in B. A. Leach, *German Strategy Against Russian 1939–41* (Clarendon Press, Oxford, 1973), pp. 251–2.

2 Quoted in ibid., pp. 263–4.

3 Quoted in A. Turney, *Disaster at Moscow* (Cassell, 1971), p. 29.

4 Quoted in A. Milward, *The German Economy at War* (Athlone Press, 1965), pp. 39–40.

5 M. Mackintosh, *Juggernaut: a History of the Soviet Armed Forces* (Secker & Warburg, 1967), p. 136.

6 R. J. Overy, *The Air War 1939–45* (Europa, 1980), p. 49.

7 P. H. Vigor, *Soviet Blitzkrieg Theory* (Macmillan, 1984), p. 123.

8 Field Marshal Kesselring, *Memoirs* (William Kimber, 1964), p. 99.

9 ibid., p. 89.

10 Vigor, op. cit., p. 60.

11 B. H. Klein, *Germany's Economic Preparations for War* (Harvard University Press, Cambridge, Mass., 1959), p. 188.

12   M. van Creveld, *Supplying War: Logistics from Wallenstein to Patton* (CUP, 1977), p. 154.
13   ibid., p. 152.
14   ibid., p. 151.
15   A. Seaton, *The Russo-German War 1941–45* (Arthur Barker, 1971), p. 114.
16   Quoted in D. Orgill, *T-34* (Macdonald, 1970), p. 54.
17   Turney, op. cit., p. 95.
18   A. Seaton, *The Battle for Moscow 1941–42* (Hart-Davis, 1971), p. 95.
19   Orgill, op. cit., pp. 45–6.
20   Quoted in B. H. L. Hart, *The Other Side of the Hill* (Cassell, 1948), p. 188.
21   Quoted in Turney, op. cit., p. 107.
22   M. Cooper, *The German Army 1933–45* (Macdonald & Jane's, 1978), p. 298.
23   Quoted in Seaton, *Russo-German*, op. cit., p. 175.
24   Quoted in R. Garthoff, *How Russia Makes War* (Allen & Unwin, 1954), pp. 431–2.
25   Quoted in Cooper, op. cit., p. 334 (my emphasis).
26   Quoted in P. Carell, *Hitler's War on Russia* (Corgi, 1967), p. 204.
27   Quoted in Turney, op. cit., pp. 137–8.
28   Quoted in Carell, op. cit., p. 91.
29   Quoted in A. Seaton, *The German Army 1933–45* (Sphere, 1983), pp. 178–9.
30   Quoted in Carell, op. cit., p. 91.
31   Van Creveld, op. cit., p. 162. (This section relies heavily on chapter 5 of van Creveld's pioneering work.)
32   ibid., p. 166.
33   Leach, op. cit., p. 210.
34   Van Creveld, op. cit., pp. 172–3.
35   H. von Greiffenberg, 'The Battle of Moscow', Pamphlet T-28, p. 26, in D. S. Detweiler *et al.* (eds), *World War II Military Studies* (Garland, New York, 1979), vol. 16. (This Garland series binds together several facsimile pamphlets in each volume. There is no overall pagination, so the pages cited refer to the individual pamphlet rather than to the entire volume.)
36   Seaton, *Moscow*, op. cit., p. 141.
37   Quoted in Turney, op. cit., pp. 153–4.
38   Quoted in E. Lederrey, *Germany's Defeat in the East* (War Office, 1959), p. 46. (The general is not named.)
39   Quoted in Turney, op. cit., p. 146.
40   Quoted in ibid., pp. 148–9.
41   Carell, op. cit., pp. 170–1.
42   Van Creveld, op. cit., p. 174.

43 Quoted in S. Bialer, *Stalin and His Generals* (Souvenir, 1969), p. 587.
44 Quoted in Garthoff, op. cit., p. 428, and Leach, op. cit., p. 201.
45 Quoted in Cooper, op. cit., p. 299.
46 Greiffenberg, op. cit., pp. 256–7.
47 Quoted in Lederrey, op. cit., p. 30.
48 Quoted in ibid., p. 29.
49 Quoted in Cooper, op. cit., p. 320 (my emphasis).
50 A. Seaton, *Stalin as Warlord* (Batsford, 1976), pp. 124–5.
51 M. Simon, 'Experience Gained in Combat with Russian Infantry', Pamphlet C-058, p. 3, in Detweiler *et al.* (eds), op. cit., vol. 19.
52 Greiffenberg, op. cit., p. 223.
53 Quoted in Turney, op. cit., p. 154.
54 Quoted in E. Bauer, *The History of World War II* (Orbis, 1979), p. 185.
55 Overy, op. cit., pp. 59–60.
56 Quoted in Turney, op. cit., p. 131.
57 Quoted in Garthoff, op. cit., p. 433.
58 Quoted in Seaton, *Russo-German*, op. cit., p. 256.
59 Greiffenberg, op. cit., p. 118.
60 S. J. Lewis, *Forgotten Legions: German Army Infantry Policy 1914–41* (Praeger, New York, 1985), p. 163.
61 L. P. Lochner (ed.), *The Goebbels Diaries* (Hamish Hamilton, 1948), p. 124.
62 Carell, op. cit., p. 334.
63 Quoted in Cooper, op. cit., p. 410.
64 Quoted in Hart, op. cit., p. 204.
65 H. R. Trevor-Roper (ed.), *Hitler's War Directives 1939–45* (Pan, 1973), p. 182.
66 Quoted in E. F. Ziemke, *Stalingrad to Berlin: the German Defeat in the East* (GPO, Washington, 1968), p. 44.
67 ibid., p. 33.
68 Seaton, *Russo-German*, op. cit., p. 211.
69 Quoted in Hart, op. cit., p. 211.
70 W. Goerlitz, *Paulus and Stalingrad* (Methuen, 1963), p. 59.
71 Quoted in Hart, op. cit., p. 214.
72 Quoted in Goerlitz, op. cit., p. 189.
73 Lederrey, op. cit., p. 78.
74 Quoted in Ziemke, op. cit., p. 19.
75 Carell, op. cit., p. 610.
76 E. von Manstein, *Lost Victories* (Arms & Armour Press, 1982), p. 292.
77 Seaton, *Russo-German*, op. cit., p. 324 (my emphasis).
78 Von Manstein, op. cit., p. 319.
79 ibid., p. 312.

80 Seaton, *Russo-German*, op. cit., pp. 348–9.

Chapter 2: The Long Retreat: July 1943 – May 1945

1 A. Seaton, *The Russo-German War 1941–45* (Arthur Barker, 1971), p. 350.
2 H. Guderian, *Panzer Leader* (Futura, 1974), p. 312.
3 T. von Busse, 'Operation Citadel', Pamphlet T-26, p. 8, in D. S. Detweiler *et al.* (eds), *World War II Military Studies* (Garland, New York, 1979), vol. 16.
4 E. von Manstein, *Lost Victories* (Arms & Armour Press, 1982), p. 443.
5 Quoted in B. H. L. Hart, *The Other Side of the Hill* (Cassell, 1948), p. 221.
6 M. Cooper & J. Lucas, *Panzer: the Armoured Force of the Third Reich* (Macdonald & Jane's, 1976), p. 59.
7 Quoted in E. F. Ziemke, *Stalingrad to Berlin: the German Defeat in the East* (GPO, Washington, 1968), p. 44.
8 Quoted in von Busse, op. cit., p. 26.
9 Quoted in D. Orgill, *T-34* (Macdonald, 1970), p. 111.
10 Guderian, op. cit., p. 312.
11 L. P. Lochner (ed.), *The Goebbels Diaries* (Hamish Hamilton, 1948), pp. 313, 321.
12 ibid., p. 198.
13 ibid., p. 339.
14 Quoted in P. Carell, *Hitler's War on Russia*, vol. 2, *Scorched Earth* (Harrap, 1970), p. 314.
15 Lochner (ed.), op. cit., p. 405.
16 Quoted in Ziemke, op. cit., p. 200.
17 Von Manstein, op. cit., p. 473.
18 Quoted in Carell, op. cit., pp. 520–1.
19 Quoted in S. J. Lewis, *Forgotten Legions: German Army Infantry Policy 1914–41* (Praeger, New York, 1985), p. 166.
20 Quoted in C. V. von Lüttichau, *The Ardennes Offensive: Germany's Situation in the Fall of 1944: Part Three, The Military Situation*, Pamphlet R-19 (OCMH Research Section, Washington, May 1953), p. 80.
21 J. Erickson, *The Road to Berlin* (Weidenfeld & Nicolson, 1983), p. 135.
22 Seaton, op. cit., pp. 389–90.
23 Lochner (ed.), op. cit., p. 399.
24 Quoted in von Manstein, op. cit., p. 522.
25 Quoted in Hart, op. cit., p. 51.
26 Quoted in Ziemke, op. cit., p. 226.
27 F. von Senger und Etterlin quoted in J. Ellis, *Cassino: the Hollow*

Victory: the Battle for Rome January–June 1944 (Deutsch, 1984), p. 278.

28 E. Bauer, *The History of World War II* (Orbis, 1979), p. 546.

29 Ziemke, op. cit., p. 321.

30 P. von der Gröben, 'The Collapse of Army Group Centre 1944', Pamphlet T-31, p. 8, in Detweiler *et al.* (eds), op. cit., vol. 16.

31 Quoted in A. Clark, *Barbarossa* (Penguin Books, Harmondsworth, 1966), p. 443.

32 Guderian, op. cit., p. 411.

33 P. H. Vigor, *Soviet Blitzkrieg Theory* (Macmillan, 1984), pp. 88–9.

34 Anon, 'Small Unit Actions during the German Campaign in Russia', Pamphlet 20–269, p. 4, in Detweiler *et al.* (eds), op. cit., vol. 18.

35 Anon, 'Russian Combat Methods in World War II', Pamphlet 20–230, p. 73, in ibid., vol. 18.

36 Quoted in R. Garthoff, *How Russia Makes War* (Allen & Unwin, 1954), p. 125.

37 F. W. von Mellenthin, *Panzer Battles 1939–45* (Cassell, 1955), p. 289.

38 Quoted in Hart, op. cit., p. 232, and Garthoff, op. cit., p. 301.

39 M. Simon, 'Experience Gained in Combat with Russian Infantry', Pamphlet C-058, p. 18, in Detweiler *et al.* (eds), op. cit., vol. 19.

40 Quoted in Garthoff, op. cit., p. 301.

41 Quoted in E. Lederrey, *Germany's Defeat in the East* (War Office, 1959), p. 30 (fn.).

42 Quoted in J. Lucas, *War on the Eastern Front* (Jane's, 1979), p. 193.

43 Seaton, op. cit., p. 194.

44 Ziemke, op. cit., p. 148.

45 Quoted in Carell, *Hitler's War on Russia*, vol. 1 (Corgi, 1967), p. 396.

46 A. Werth, *Russia at War 1941–45* (Corgi, 1965), p. 571.

47 Von Mellenthin, op. cit., p. 159.

48 Quoted in Lucas, op. cit., p. 36.

49 Von Mellenthin, op. cit., p. 242.

50 Ziemke, op. cit., p. 189.

51 Quoted in B. H. L. Hart, *The Defence of the West* (Faber, 1950), p. 34.

52 Quoted in Orgill, op. cit., p. 85.

53 Anon, 'Russian Combat Methods', op. cit., p. 52.

54 L. Rendulic, 'The Fighting Qualities of the Russian Soldier', Pamphlet D-036, p. 12, and 'The Russian Command in World War II', Pamphlet P-079, p. 2, in Detweiler *et al.* (eds), vol. 19 (emphasis in original).

Chapter 3: The Battle of the Atlantic: September 1939 – May 1945

1 Quoted in J. Costello & T. Hughes, *The Battle of the Atlantic* (Fontana, 1980), p. 39.
2 K. Doenitz, *Memoirs* (Weidenfeld & Nicolson, 1959), p. 125.
3 ibid.
4 J. Rohwer, 'The U-Boat War Against the Allied Supply Lines', in H.-A. Jacobsen & J. Rohwer (eds), *Decisive Battles of World War II: the German View* (Deutsch, 1965), p. 263.
5 P. Joubert de la Ferté, *Birds and Fishes: the Story of Coastal Command* (Hutchinson, 1960), pp. 131, 134.
6 Quoted in Costello & Hughes, op. cit., p. 102.
7 Sir J. Slessor, *The Central Blue* (Cassell, 1956), p. 481, and W. S. Churchill, *The Second World War* (6 vols, Cassell, 1948–54), vol. 4, p. 107.
8 H. R. Trevor-Roper (ed.), *Hitler's War Directives 1939–45* (Pan, 1973), pp. 102–3.
9 Churchill, op. cit., vol. 3, p. 107.
10 Quoted in Costello & Hughes, op. cit., p. 117.
11 ibid., p. 179.
12 J. Rohwer, 'Radio Intelligence in the Battle of the Atlantic', in C. Andrew & D. Dilks (eds), *The Missing Dimension* (Macmillan, 1984), p. 165.
13 ibid. (my emphasis).
14 Doenitz, op. cit., p. 153.
15 ibid., p. 160.
16 ibid., pp. 200–1.
17 Costello & Hughes, op. cit., p. 189.
18 Doenitz, op. cit., p. 197.
19 Quoted in Costello & Hughes, op. cit., p. 195.
20 J. Rohwer, 'The Operational Use of ULTRA in the Battle of the Atlantic', in C. Andrew & J. Noakes (eds), *Intelligence and International Relations 1900–45* (University of Exeter Press, 1987), pp. 284–5.
21 Quoted in Slessor, op. cit., p. 522.
22 Quoted in S. W. Roskill, *The War At Sea 1939–45* (History of the Second World War: United Kingdom Military Series), (3 vols, HMSO, 1954–61), vol. 2, p. 210.
23 Quoted in Costello & Hughes, op. cit., p. 266.
24 Roskill, op. cit., vol. 2, pp. 367–8.
25 Quoted in P. Kemp, *Decision at Sea: the Convoy Escorts* (Elsevier-Dutton, New York, 1978), p. 152.
26 Rohwer, 'U-Boat War', in Jacobsen & Rohwer (eds), op. cit., pp. 301–2, and Doenitz, op. cit., p. 306.
27 Quoted in Rohwer, 'U-Boat War', loc. cit.

28 Quoted in Sir C. Webster & N. Frankland, *The Strategic Air Offensive Against Germany* (History of the Second World War: United Kingdom Military Series), (4 vols, HMSO, 1961), vol. 4, p. 243, and vol. 1, p. 340.

29 A. Bryant (ed.), *The Alanbrooke War Diaries* (2 vols, Fontana, 1965), vol. 1, p. 323.

30 Joubert de la Ferté, op. cit., p. 151.

31 P. M. S. Blackett, *Studies of War* (Oliver & Boyd, 1962), p. 230.

32 Roskill, op. cit., vol. 2, p. 371.

Chapter 4: The Bomber Offensive: June 1940 – May 1945

1 Quoted in A. Boyle, *Trenchard: Man of Vision* (Collins, 1962), p. 470.

2 Quoted in M. Hastings, *Bomber Command* (Pan, 1981), p. 54.

3 Quoted in N. Longmate, *The Bombers: the RAF Offensive Against Germany 1939–45* (Hutchinson, 1983), p. 67.

4 Quoted in Sir C. Webster & N. Frankland, *The Strategic Air Offensive Against Germany* (4 vols, HMSO, 1961), vol. 4, pp. 110, 121.

5 Quoted in Longmate, op. cit., p. 87.

6 Quoted in Webster & Frankland, op. cit., vol. 4, pp. 119–20.

7 Quoted in Longmate, op. cit., p. 92.

8 Quoted in A. Price, *Battle Over the Reich* (Ian Allen, Shepperton, 1973), p. 12.

9 Quoted in R. Jackson, *Before the Storm: the Story of Bomber Command 1939–42* (Arthur Barker, 1972), p. 82.

10 Quoted in Longmate, op. cit., p. 95.

11 Quoted in A. Price, *Instruments of Darkness: the History of Electronic Warfare* (Granada, 1979), p. 109.

12 Quoted in Webster & Frankland, op. cit., vol. 4, p. 205.

13 Quoted in Longmate, op. cit., p. 121.

14 P. M. S. Blackett, *Studies of War* (Oliver & Boyd, 1962), pp. 224–5 (emphasis in original).

15 Quoted in Webster & Frankland, op. cit., vol. 4, pp. 143–4.

16 Price, *Reich*, op. cit., p. 97.

17 Quoted in J. Terraine, *The Right of the Line: the Royal Air Force in the European War 1939–45* (Hodder & Stoughton, 1985), p. 293.

18 Quoted in Hastings, op. cit., p. 131.

19 J. Kennedy, *The Business of War* (Hutchinson, 1957), p. 247.

20 Quoted in Hastings, op. cit., p. 132.

21 Quoted in ibid., p. 133.

22 Quoted in ibid., p. 152.

23 W. S. Churchill, *The Second World War* (6 vols, Cassell, 1948–54), vol. 2, pp. 567, 405–6.

24 Hastings, op. cit., p. 137.
25 Quoted in R. Beaumont, 'The Bomber Offensive as a Second Front', *Journal of Contemporary History* 22, January 1987, p. 6.
26 Quoted in B. Richards, *Portal of Hungerford* (Heinemann, 1977), p. 191.
27 Quoted in Sir J. Slessor, *The Central Blue* (Cassell, 1956), p. 345.
28 Quoted in Beaumont, op. cit., p. 5.
29 Quoted in Webster & Frankland, op. cit., vol. 4, pp. 144, 148.
30 F. L. Loewenhein *et al.* (eds), *Roosevelt and Churchill: their Secret Wartime Correspondence* (Barrie & Jenkins, 1975), p. 235.
31 Beaumont, op. cit., p. 12.
32 Quoted in Richards, op. cit., p. 314.
33 Quoted in A. McKee, *Dresden 1945*: the Devil's Tinderbox (Dutton, New York, 1984), p. 58; Hastings, op. cit., p. 113.
34 Quoted in Webster & Frankland, op. cit., vol. 4, pp. 128–9 (my emphasis).
35 Quoted in ibid., pp. 135–6, 138, 141.
36 Quoted in Beaumont, op. cit., p. 225.
37 Richards, op. cit., p. 225.
38 Quoted in Webster & Frankland, op. cit., vol. 4, p. 153.
39 Quoted in M. Hastings, *Overlord: D-Day and the Battle for Normandy 1944* (Michael Joseph, 1984), p. 40.
40 Quoted in Webster & Frankland, op. cit., vol. 2, pp. 190–207, 265.
41 Air Ministry, *The Origins and Development of Operational Research in the R.A.F.* (Air Publication 3368), (HMSO, 1963), p. 57.
42 S. Zuckerman, *From Apes to Warlords 1904–46* (Hamish Hamilton, 1978), p. 243.
43 Quoted in R. C. Cooke & R. C. Nesbit, *Target: Hitler's Oil* (Kimber, 1985), p. 199.
44 Quoted in ibid., p. 168.
45 ibid., p. 180.
46 Quoted in Longmate, op. cit., p. 346.
47 Quoted in Webster & Frankland, op. cit., vol. 4, p. 161.
48 Quoted in ibid., p. 171.
49 Quoted in Cooke & Nesbit, op. cit., p. 160.
50 Quoted in Webster & Frankland, op. cit., vol. 4, p. 299.
51 Quoted in Richards, op. cit., pp. 319–22.
52 Quoted in A. Price, *Luftwaffe* (Macdonald, 1969), p. 126.
53 R. J. Overy, 'From "Uralbomber" to "Amerikabomber": the Luftwaffe and Strategic Bombing', *Journal of Strategic Studies* 1, September 1978, p. 11.
54 A. Galland, 'Defeat of the Luftwaffe', in E. M. Emme (ed.), *The Impact of Air Power* (Van Nostrand, New York, 1959), pp. 256–7.
55 Air Ministry, *The Rise and Fall of the German Air Force 1933–45* (WE Inc., Old Greenwich, Conn., 1969), p. 220.

56 G. Aders, *History of the German Night-Fighter Force 1917–45* (Arms & Armour Press, 1979), p. 61.

57 A. Galland, *The First and the Last: the German Fighter Force in World War II* (Methuen, 1955), p. 264.

58 W. Murray, *Luftwaffe: Strategy for Defeat 1933–45* (Allen & Unwin, 1985), pp. 123, 159.

59 L. P. Lochner (ed.), *The Goebbels Diaries* (Hamish Hamilton, 1948), p. 395.

60 H. H. Arnold, *Global Mission* (Hutchinson, 1950), p. 125.

61 Quoted in United States Strategic Bombing Survey (USSBS) (Military Analysis Division), *The Defeat of the German Air Force* (GPO, Washington, January 1947), p. 15.

62 Quoted in ibid., p. 14, and Air Ministry, *German Air Force*, op. cit., p. 296.

63 H. Faber (ed.), *Luftwaffe: an Analysis by Former Luftwaffe Generals* (Sidgwick & Jackson, 1979), p. 100.

64 ibid., p. 143.

65 ibid.

66 ibid., pp. 141–2.

67 Murray, op. cit., p. 90.

68 Faber, op. cit., p. 245.

69 ibid., p. 145.

70 ibid., p. 239.

71 Air Ministry, *German Air Force*, op. cit., p. 204.

72 USSBS, *Overall Report (European War)* (GPO, Washington, September 1945), p. 22.

73 Murray, op. cit., p. 184 (n. 192).

74 Faber, op. cit., p. 248.

75 T. Wood & B. Gunston, *Hitler's Luftwaffe* (Salamander, 1977), p. 112.

76 A. Price, *Luftwaffe Handbook 1939–45* (Ian Allen, Shepperton, 1977), p. 64.

77 Faber, op. cit., p. 147.

78 Quoted in ibid., p. 148.

79 USSBS, *Overall (Europe)*, op. cit., p. 25.

80 Price, *Reich*, op. cit., p. 173.

81 Galland, 'Luftwaffe', in Emme (ed.), op. cit., pp. 259–60.

82 Air Ministry, *German Air Force*, op. cit., p. 380, and Faber, op. cit., p. 249.

83 Aders, op. cit., p. 167.

84 USSBS, *German Air Force*, op. cit., p. 14.

85 Lord Zuckerman, 'Strategic Bombing and the Defeat of Germany', *RUSI Journal* 130, June 1985, p. 69.

86 USSBS, *Summary Report (Europe)* (GPO, Washington, September 1945), p. 12.

87 Quoted in Webster & Frankland, op. cit., vol. 4, pp. 349, 352–4, 357.

88 Quoted in A. Kesselring, 'General Questions', Pamphlet ETHINT-72, p. 3, in D. S. Detweiler *et al.* (eds), *World War II Military Studies* (Garland, New York, 1979), vol. 3.

89 USSBS, *Overall (Europe)*, op. cit., p. 64.

90 ibid., p. 61.

91 ibid., p. 64.

92 R. F. Weighley, *Eisenhower's Lieutenants: the Campaigns of France and Germany 1944–45* (Sidgwick & Jackson, 1981), p. 379.

93 Galland, 'Luftwaffe', in Emme (ed.), op. cit., p. 258.

94 Zuckerman, 'Strategic Bombing', op. cit., p. 69.

95 USSBS (Overall Economic Effects Division), *The Effects of Strategic Bombing on the German Economy* (GPO, Washington, October 1945), p. 162.

96 USSBS, *Overall (Europe)*, op. cit., p. 45.

97 ibid.

98 Quoted in USSBS, *Effects*, op. cit., p. 126.

99 Hastings, op. cit., p. 156.

100 Webster & Frankland, op. cit., vol. 4, pp. 383, 375.

101 Cooke & Nesbit, op. cit., p. 157.

102 Quoted in Longmate, op. cit., pp. 352–3.

103 Quoted in M. Smith, *British Air Strategy Between the Wars* (Clarendon Press, Oxford, 1984), p. 64.

Chapter 5: The North African See-Saw: June 1940 – January 1943

1 Quoted in M. Knox, *Mussolini Unleashed* (CUP, 1982), p. 32.

2 Quoted in K. Macksey, *Beda Fomm* (Pan/Ballantine, 1972), p. 25.

3 Knox, op. cit., p. 21.

4 D. Mack Smith, *Mussolini's Roman Empire* (Longman, 1976), p. 179.

5 Macksey, op. cit., p. 15.

6 I. V. Hogg, *Armour in Conflict* (Jane's, 1980), p. 103 (emphasis in original).

7 Quoted in C. Barnett, *The Desert Generals* (Pan, 1960), p. 111.

8 F. de Guingand, *Operation Victory* (Hodder & Stoughton, 1947), p. 88.

9 K. Macksey, 'Operation Battleaxe', in *History of the Second World War* (Purnells, 1966), vol. 2, p. 638.

10 J. A. I. Agar-Hamilton & L. C. F. Turner, *The Sidi Rezeg Battles 1941* (OUP, 1957), pp. 15, 16.

11 Quoted in ibid., p. 39.

12 R. Lewin, *Rommel as Military Commander* (Batsford, 1968), p. 53.

13 Agar-Hamilton & Turner, op. cit., p. 39.

14 B. H. L. Hart (ed.), *The Rommel Papers* (Collins, 1953), p. 159. (In

this book Rommel's own narrative is linked by comments from Bayerlein and Hart.)

15 S. Bidwell, *Gunners at War* (Arrow, 1972), p. 175.

16 F. W. von Mellenthin, *Panzer Battles 1939–45* (Cassell, 1955), pp. 52–3 (emphasis in original).

17 General Bernard Freyberg quoted in Agar-Hamilton & Turner, op. cit., p. 146.

18 ibid., p. 159.

19 J. Wardrop, *Tanks Across the Desert* (Kimber, 1981), p. 61.

20 Quoted in Agar-Hamilton & Turner, op. cit., p. 558.

21 Hart (ed.), op. cit., p. 173.

22 ibid., p. 189.

23 Quoted in S. W. Mitcham, *Triumphant Fox* (Stein & Day, New York, 1984), p. 187.

24 W. Heckmann, *Rommel's War in Africa* (Granada, 1981), p. 220.

25 Quoted in B. H. L. Hart, *The Other Side of the Hill* (Cassell, 1948), pp. 173, 163.

26 Hart (ed.), op. cit., p. 328.

27 ibid., p. 141.

28 Quoted in E. Bergot, *The Afrika Korps* (Wingate, 1976), p. 130.

29 Quoted in D. Downing, *The Devil's Virtuosos: German Generals at War 1940–45* (New English Library, 1978), p. 101.

30 Field Marshal Kesselring, *Memoirs* (Kimber, 1964), p. 123.

31 J. A. I. Agar-Hamilton & L. C. F. Turner, *Crisis in the Desert May–July 1942* (OUP, 1952), p. 292.

32 Quoted in ibid., pp. 313, 314.

33 Quoted in M. A. Bragadin, *The Italian Navy in World War II* (US Naval Institute Press, Annapolis, Md, 1957), p. 201.

34 Hart (ed.), op. cit., p. 261.

35 Quoted in J. Hetherington, *Air War Against Germany and Italy 1939–43* (Australia in the War of 1939–45. Series III (Air)), (Australian War Memorial, Canberra, 1954), vol. 3. p. 257.

36 Hart (ed.), op. cit., p. 283.

37 Von Mellenthin, op. cit., pp. 139–40.

38 Quoted in M. Shulman, *Defeat in the West* (rev. ed., Coronet, 1973), p. 115.

39 Quoted in Hetherington, op. cit., p. 368.

40 F. H. Hinsley, *British Intelligence in the Second World War* (3 vols, HMSO, 1979–88), vol. 2, p. 427.

41 L. P. Lochner (ed.), *The Goebbels Diaries* (Hamish Hamilton, 1948), pp. 190–1.

42 S. Westphal, *The German Army in the West* (Cassell, 1951), p. 120.

43 M. van Creveld, *Supplying War: Logistics from Wallenstein to Patton* (CUP, 1977), p. 192.

44 ibid., p. 190.

45 W. Heckmann, *Rommel's War in Africa* (Granada, 1981), pp. 155–6.
46 Quoted in Hetherington, op. cit., p. 236.
47 Quoted in Agar-Hamilton & Turner, *Crisis*, op. cit., p. 314.
48 Quoted in Hetherington, op. cit., p. 246.
49 Hart (ed.), op. cit., p. 285.
50 W. Nehring, *Die deutsche Panzerwaffe, 1916–45* (Propyläen, Berlin, 1969), p. 213.
51 Quoted in Bragadin, op. cit., p. 198.
52 Hart (ed.), op. cit., p. 297.
53 ibid., p. 279.
54 ibid., p. 306.
55 Quoted in D. Richards & H. St. G. Saunders, *Royal Air Force 1939–45*, vol. 2 (HMSO, 1954), p. 197.
56 ibid., p. 162.
57 ibid., p. 188.
58 Von Mellenthin, op. cit., p. 75.
59 Quoted in Richards & Saunders, op. cit., p. 213.
60 Quoted in ibid., pp. 218, 219.
61 Quoted in Hetherington, op. cit., p. 261.
62 Quoted in D. Young, *Rommel* (Collins, 1950), p. 170.
63 Hart (ed.), op. cit., p. 283.
64 ibid., pp. 334, 285.
65 W. Murray, *Luftwaffe: Strategy for Defeat 1933–45* (Allen & Unwin, 1985), p. 113; S. Bidwell & D. Graham, *Fire-Power: British Army Weapons and Theories of War 1904–45* (Allen & Unwin, 1982), p. 227.
66 Hart (ed.), op. cit., p. 208.
67 K. Macksey, *Tank Warfare* (Panther, 1976), p. 201.
68 Von Mellenthin, op. cit., pp. 96–7.
69 Quoted in J. F. C. Fuller, *The Second World War* (Eyre & Spottiswoode, 1948), p. 174.
70 Von Mellenthin, op. cit., p. 105.
71 Heckmann, op. cit., pp. 260–1.
72 Agar-Hamilton & Turner, *Crisis*, op. cit., p. 124.
73 Quoted in C. Barnett, *The Desert Generals* (rev. ed., William Kimber, 1981), p. 246.
74 Hart (ed.), op. cit., p. 254
75 Barnett, op. cit., p. 210.
76 J. L. Scoullar, *Battle for Egypt* (Official History of New Zealand in the Second World War 1939–45), (OUP, 1955), p. 337.
77 G. P. B. Roberts in various, 'The Battle of Alam Halfa', *History of the Second World War* (Purnells, 1966), vol. 3, p. 1152.
78 Von Mellenthin, op. cit., p. 140.
79 Quoted in N. Hamilton, *Monty: the Making of a General 1887–1942* (Hamlyn, 1982), p. 732.
80 Quoted in ibid., pp. 720–1.

81 Quoted in Barnett, op. cit., p. 274.
82 M. Carver, *El Alamein* (Batsford, 1962), p. 123.
83 Lewin, op. cit., p. 181.
84 Quoted in Bragadin, op. cit., p. 223.
85 Quoted in Hinsley, op. cit., vol. 2, p. 448.
86 Quoted in D. Jewell (ed.), *Alamein and the Desert War* (Sphere, 1967), p. 81.
87 Lewin, op. cit., p. 170.
88 Hart (ed.), op. cit., p. 521.
89 F. I. S. Tuker, *Approach to Battle* (Cassell, 1963), p. 203.
90 Barnett, op. cit., p. 293.
91 Carver, op. cit., p. 184.
92 Lewin, op. cit., p. 188.
93 ibid., p. 187.
94 Quoted in Hetherington, op. cit., p. 366.
95 Hinsley, op. cit., vol. 2, p. 454.
96 ibid.
97 Hart (ed.), op. cit., p. 360.
98 ibid., p. 372.
99 Barnett, op. cit., p. 300.
100 Quoted in Hinsley, op. cit., vol. 2, p. 460.

Chapter 6: Tunisia and Italy: November 1942 – May 1945

1 G. A. Shepperd, *The Italian Campaign 1943–45* (Arthur Barker, 1968), pp. 11, 15.
2 A. Bryant (ed.), *The Alanbrooke War Diaries* (2 vols, Fontana, 1965), vol. 1, p. 508.
3 General the Lord Ismay, *Memoirs* (Heinemann, 1960), p. 298.
4 Montgomery of Alamein, *Memoirs* (Collins, 1958), p. 201.
5 Great Britain (Cabinet Office), *Principal War Telegrams and Memoranda 1940–43* (K.T.O. Press, Liechtenstein, n.d.), vol. 3 (Hist. (B) (Crusader) 5), p. 57.
6 Quoted in G. Blaxland, *The Plain Cook and the Great Showman* (Kimber, 1977), p. 106.
7 K. Macksey, *Crucible of Power: the Fight for Tunisia 1942–3* (Hutchinson, 1969), p. 124.
8 F. Howe, *Seizing the Initiative in the West* (US Army in World War II), (OCMH, Washington, 1957), p. 521.
9 Quoted in O. Bradley & C. Blair, *A General's Life* (Sidgwick & Jackson, 1983), p. 165.
10 Blaxland, op. cit., p. 195.
11 Macksey, op. cit., p. 227.
12 ibid., p. 229.

13 ibid., pp. 240–1.

14 S. Bidwell, *Gunners at War* (Arrow, 1972), pp. 204–5, 206 (my emphasis).

15 Macksey, op. cit., p. 255.

16 ibid., pp. 252–3.

17 Bradley & Blair, op. cit., p. 152.

18 Quoted in I. S. O. Playfair (ed.), *The Mediterranean and the Middle East* (History of the Second World War: United Kingdom Military Series), vol. 4 (HMSO, 1966), p. 359.

19 Quoted in J. Lucas, *Panzer Army Africa* (Macdonald & Jane's, 1977), p. 183.

20 Quoted in C. Messenger, *The Tunisian Campaign* (Ian Allen, Shepperton, 1982), p. 111.

21 Bidwell, op. cit., p. 207.

22 Blaxland, op. cit., p. 248.

23 Field Marshal Kesselring, *Memoirs* (Kimber, 1964), p. 158.

24 F. von Senger und Etterlin, *Neither Fear Nor Hope* (Macdonald, 1963), p. 128.

25 Quoted in D. Richards & H. St. G. Saunders, *Royal Air Force 1939–45*, vol. 2 (HMSO, 1954), p. 306.

26 Quoted in S. E. Morison, *History of United States Naval Operations in World War II* (15 vols, OUP, 1948–62), vol. 9, p. 117.

27 Quoted in ibid., p. 118.

28 Bradley & Blair, op. cit., p. 186, and M. Clark, *Calculated Risk* (Harrap, 1951), p. 163.

29 Quoted in Morison, op. cit., vol. 9, p. 206.

30 Quoted in Bradley & Blair, op. cit., p. 690.

31 ibid., p. 188.

32 M. Blumenson, *Sicily: Whose Victory:* (Macdonald, 1968), p. 84.

33 C. J. C. Molony (ed.), *The Mediterranean and the Middle East* (History of the Second World War: United Kingdom Military Series), vol. 5 (HMSO, 1973), p. 41.

34 Bradley & Blair, op. cit., p. 193.

35 Quoted in Molony (ed.), op. cit., vol. 5, p. 122.

36 Morison, op. cit., vol. 9, pp. 179–80.

37 ibid., p. 201.

38 Quoted in F. H. Hinsley, *British Intelligence in the Second World War* (3 vols, HMSO, 1979–88), vol. 3, p. 99.

39 S. Roskill, *The War at Sea* (History of the Second World War: United Kingdom Military Series), (3 vols, HMSO, 1954–61), vol. 3 (part I), p. 145.

40 Quoted in W. S. Churchill, *The Second World War* (6 vols, Cassell, 1948–54), vol. 5, p. 113.

41 Quoted in J. Kennedy, *The Business of War* (Hutchinson, 1957), p. 295.

42 A. Moorehead, *Eclipse* (Hamish Hamilton, 1945), p. 60.

43 E. Murphy, *Diplomat Amongst Warriors* (Doubleday, New York, 1964), pp. 236–7.

44 Quoted in C. Hibbert, *Anzio: the Bid for Rome* (Macdonald, 1970), p. 28.

45 D. Graham & S. Bidwell, *Tug of War: the Battle for Italy 1943–45* (Hodder & Stoughton, 1986), p. 47.

46 ibid., p. 49.

47 Von Senger und Etterlin, op. cit., p. 195.

48 Quoted in J. Ellis, *Cassino, the Hollow Victory: the Battle for Rome January–June 1944* (Deutsch, 1984), pp. 285, 216.

49 Quoted in Morison, op. cit., vol. 9, p. 292.

50 Graham & Bidwell, op. cit., p. 153, and W. L. Allen, *Anzio: Edge of Disaster* (Elsevier-Dutton, New York, 1978), p. 115.

51 Quoted in Richards & Saunders, op. cit., p. 339.

52 Air Ministry, *The Rise and Fall of the German Air Force 1933–45* (WE Inc., Old Greenwich, Conn., 1969), p. 360.

53 L. P. Lochner (ed.) *The Goebbels Diaries* (Hamish Hamilton, 1948), p. 447.

54 F. M. Sallager, *Operation Strangle* (Rand Corporation, Santa Monica, Cal., 1972), p. 12.

55 Richards & Saunders, op. cit., p. 356.

56 Quoted in Molony (ed.), op. cit., vol. 6, part I (HMSO, 1984), p. 142.

57 Richards & Saunders, op. cit., p. 352.

58 Quoted in Ellis, op. cit., p. 435.

59 Quoted in ibid., pp. 460, 423.

60 Air Ministry, op. cit., p. 385.

61 Quoted in Richards & Saunders, op. cit., vol. 3 (HMSO, 1954), p. 232.

62 ibid.

63 Shepperd, op. cit., p. 384.

64 A. Juin *Mémoires*, vol. 1 (Fayard, Paris, 1959), pp. 231–2.

65 Quoted in R. Trevelyan, *Rome '44* (Secker & Warburg, 1981), p. 132.

66 E. Sevareid, *Not So Wild a Dream* (Knopf, New York, 1946), p. 389.

67 Ellis, op. cit., pp. 399, 405.

68 Quoted in S. H. Loory, *Defeated: Inside America's Military Machine* (Random House, New York, 1973), p. 39.

69 Quoted in Ellis, op. cit., pp. 52, 369.

70 E. Linklater, *The Campaign in Italy* (HMSO, 1951), p. 267.

71 Molony (ed.), op. cit., vol. 6, part I, p. 291.

72 Quoted in Ellis, op. cit., pp. 447, 446.

73 Quoted in ibid., p. 466.

74 Quoted in ibid., pp. 184–5.

75 W. J. McAndrew, 'Eighth Army at the Gothic Line: Commanders and Plans', *RUSI Journal* 131, March 1986, p. 50.
76 Graham & Bidwell, op. cit., pp. 359, 357–8.
77 D. Orgill, *The Gothic Line: the Autumn Campaign in Italy, 1944* (Pan, 1969), pp. 176, 178.
78 Clark, op. cit., p. 378.
79 Kesselring, op. cit., p. 223.

Chapter 7: Lodgement and Breakout: 6 June – 31 August 1944

1 Quoted in R. de Belot, *The Struggle for the Mediterranean 1939–45* (Princeton University Press, Princeton, NJ, 1951), p. 132.
2 Quoted in A. Lee, *Goering: Air Leader* (Duckworth, 1972), pp. 149, 150.
3 L. P. Lochner (ed.), *The Goebbels Diaries* (Hamish Hamilton, 1948), p. 121.
4 USSBS, *The Effects of Strategic Bombing on the German Economy* (GPO, Washington, October 1945), p. 19.
5 Lochner (ed.), op. cit., p. 348.
6 B. H. L. Hart (ed.), *The Rommel Papers* (Collins, 1953), p. 491.
7 Quoted in W. Warlimont, 'From the Invasion to the Siegfried Line', Pamphlet ETHINT-1, p. 9, in D. S. Detweiler *et al.* (eds), *World War II Military Studies* (Garland, New York, 1979), vol. 2.
8 W. S. Churchill, *The Second World War* (6 vols, Cassell, 1948–54), vol. 3, p. 511.
9 C. P. Stacey, *The Victory Campaign* (Official History of the Canadian Army in the Second World War), (Queen's Printers, Ottawa, 1960), p. 52.
10 Hart (ed.), op. cit., p. 486.
11 Quoted in P. Carell, *Invasion – They're Coming!* (Transworld, 1963), p. 187.
12 Quoted in Hart (ed.), op. cit., p. 496.
13 Quoted in M. Shulman, *Defeat in the West* (rev. ed., Coronet, 1973), p. 159.
14 Quoted in Stacey, op. cit., p. 179.
15 Quoted in Hart (ed.), op. cit., p. 477.
16 Quoted in Shulman, op. cit., p. 159.
17 Quoted in A. McKee, *Caen, Anvil of Victory* (Souvenir, 1964), p. 329.
18 Quoted in ibid., pp. 78–9.
19 G. von Schwerin, '116 Panzer Division in Normandy', Pamphlet ETHINT-17, pp. 20–1, in Detweiler *et al.* (eds), op. cit., vol. 2.
20 Quoted in Stacey, op. cit., p. 149.
21 Quoted in McKee, op. cit., p. 179.

22 Hart (ed.), op. cit., pp. 476–7.
23 Quoted in E. Belfield & H. Essame, *The Battle for Normandy* (Batsford, 1965), p. 85, and S. E. Morison, *History of United States Naval Operations in World War II* (15 vols, OUP, 1948–62), vol. 11, p. 169.
24 Quoted in Morison, ibid.
25 Conference notes by Rommel's ADC quoted in Hart (ed.), op. cit., p. 480.
26 ibid., pp. 454–5.
27 ibid., pp. 476–7. Other sources date this report 12 June, when it seems it was actually sent to OKW.
28 Quoted in W. Murray, *Luftwaffe: Strategy for Defeat 1933–45* (Allen & Unwin, 1985), p. 257.
29 Quoted in C. Wilmot, *The Struggle for Europe* (Collins, 1952), p. 364.
30 Quoted in Shulman, op. cit., p. 192.
31 Quoted in Wilmot, op. cit., p. 364.
32 Quoted in ibid., p. 391.
33 Quoted in A. Seaton, *The Fall of Fortress Europe 1943–45* (Batsford, 1981), p. 115.
34 F. W. von Mellenthin, *Panzer Battles 1939–45* (Cassell, 1955), p. 309.
35 Quoted in Belfield & Essame, op. cit., p. 75.
36 Quoted in Wilmot, op. cit., p. 402.
37 Quoted in Shulman, op. cit., p. 197.
38 Von Schwerin, op. cit., pp. 20–1.
39 Carell, op. cit., pp. 162–3.
40 F. Bayerlein, 'Panzer Lehr Division January to 28 July 1944', Pamphlet ETHINT-66, p. 34, in Detweiler *et al.* (eds), op. cit., vol. 3.
41 Warlimont, op. cit., p. 29.
42 C. P. Stacey, *Canada's Battle in Normandy* (King's Printers, Ottawa, 1946), pp. 68–9.
43 Hart (ed.), op. cit., pp. 476–7, 485, 484.
44 Quoted in B. H. L. Hart, *The Other Side of the Hill* (Cassell, 1948), p. 253.
45 Bayerlein, op. cit., p. 22.
46 Quoted in Hart (ed.), op. cit., p. 487.
47 ibid., p. 483.
48 J. Keegan, *Six Armies in Normandy* (Jonathan Cape, 1982), p. 157.
49 Quoted in Shulman, op. cit., p. 216.
50 Hart (ed.), op. cit., pp. 510–11.
51 Belfield & Essame, op. cit. p. 151.
52 Quoted in C. d'Este, *Decision in Normandy* (Pan, 1984), p. 74.
53 Quoted in Stacey, *Campaign*, op. cit., p. 83.
54 Joint Outline . . . Plan, 8 February 1944, quoted in ibid., p. 84.
55 Quoted in d'Este, op. cit., p. 86.
56 Quoted in ibid., pp. 80–1.

57 Quoted in ibid., pp. 101, 103. D'Este gives the date of this document as 8 May.

58 McKee, op. cit., p. 61.

59 Quoted in Stacey, *Campaign*, op. cit., p. 84.

60 Quoted in Keegan, op. cit., p. 192.

61 Montgomery of Alamein, *Normandy to the Baltic* (1947), (Transworld, 1974), p. 383.

62 Quoted in Wilmot, op. cit., p. 356.

63 Quoted in R. Lamb, *Montgomery in Europe 1943–45: Success or Failure?* (Buchan & Enright, 1983), p. 161.

64 Quoted in E. Bauer, *The History of World War II* (Orbis, 1979), p. 488.

65 M. Hastings, *Overlord: D-Day and the Battle for Normandy 1944* (Michael Joseph, 1984), p. 236.

66 ibid., p. 299.

67 Belfield & Essame, op. cit., p. 116.

68 Hart, op. cit., p. 267.

69 B. Mueller-Hillebrand, *Das Heer 1933–45* (E. S. Mittler und Sohn, Darmstadt/Frankfurt, 1954–69), vol. 3, p. 170.

70 Quoted in Shulman, op. cit., pp. 214–15.

71 Quoted in Wilmot, op. cit., p. 428.

72 Quoted in J. A. English, *A Perspective on Infantry* (Praeger, New York, 1981), p. 185.

73 Hastings, op. cit., p. 135.

74 McKee, op. cit., p. 167.

75 Hart (ed.), op. cit., p. 487.

76 Hastings, op. cit., p. 305.

77 Quoted in Stacey, *Campaign*, op. cit., p. 276.

78 O. Bradley, *A Soldier's Story of the Allied Campaigns from Tunis to the Elbe* (Eyre & Spottiswoode, 1951), p. 41.

79 Quoted in R. F. Weighley, *Eisenhower's Lieutenants: the Campaigns of France and Germany 1944–45* (Sidgwick & Jackson, 1981), p. 28.

80 Quoted in N. Moseley, *Marshall: Organiser of Victory* (Methuen, 1982), p. 326.

81 Quoted in Wilmot, op. cit., p. 428.

82 ibid., p. 127.

83 Summarised in M. van Creveld, *Fighting Power: German and US Army Performance 1939–45* (Arms & Armour Press, 1983), p. 40.

84 Quoted in Hart, op. cit., p. 264.

85 Quoted in J. Wheldon, *Machine-Age Armies* (Abelard Schuman, 1968), p. 135.

86 Quoted in Hastings, op. cit., p. 281.

87 O. Bradley & C. Blair, *A General's Life* (Sidgwick & Jackson, 1983), p. 325.

88 Weighley, op. cit., p. 244.

89 H. Guderian, 'Panzer Employment: Western Front', Pamphlet ETHINT-39, p. 5, in Detweiler *et al.* (eds), op. cit., vol. 3.

90 M. Simon, 'XIII SS Infantry Corps in the Lorraine Campaign', Pamphlet ETHINT-33, pp. 2–3, in ibid., vol. 2.

Chapter 8: Inching to Victory: September 1944 – May 1945

1 O. Bradley, *A Soldier's Story of the Allied Campaigns from Tunis to the Elbe* (Eyre & Spottiswoode, 1951), p. 377.

2 H. Essame, *Patton: the Commander* (Batsford, 1974), p. 167.

3 G. S. Patton, *War As I Knew It* (W. H. Allen, n.d.), p. 105.

4 R. von Gersdorff, 'Reactions to Patton and the Third Army', Pamphlet ETHINT-59, p. 6, in D. S. Detweiler *et al.* (eds), *World War II Military Studies* (Garland, New York, 1979), vol. 3.

5 G. von Schwerin, '116 Panzer Division from the Seine to Aachen', Pamphlet ETHINT-18, p. 22, in ibid., vol. 2.

6 Quoted in C. P. Stacey, *The Victory Campaign* (Queen's Printers, Ottawa, 1960), p. 262.

7 Von Schwerin, op. cit., p. 21.

8 Quoted in C. Wilmot, *The Struggle for Europe* (Collins, 1952), p. 434.

9 Quoted in Stacey, op. cit., p. 320.

10 Quoted in ibid.

11 F. W. von Mellenthin, 'Comments on Patton and the Third Army', Pamphlet ETHINT-65, p. 3, in Detweiler *et al.* (eds), op. cit., vol. 3.

12 R. F. Weighley, *Eisenhower's Lieutenants: the Campaigns of France and Germany 1944–45* (Sidgwick & Jackson, 1981), p. 426.

13 M. Blumenson (ed.), *The Patton Papers*, vol. 2 (Houghton Mifflin, Boston, 1974), pp. 523, 531, 537.

14 S. Westphal, *The German Army in the West* (Cassell, 1951), pp. 172, 174.

15 Quoted in R. Lamb, *Montgomery in Europe 1943–45: Success or Failure* (Buchan & Enright, 1983), pp. 184, 185 (emphasis in original).

16 ibid., p. 186.

17 Quoted in L. F. Ellis, *Victory in the West 1944–45* (The Second World War: United Kingdom Military Series), vol. 1 (HMSO, 1962), p. 185.

18 Quoted in Weighley, op. cit., pp. 277–8.

19 Quoted in Ellis, op. cit., vol. 2, p. 5.

20 B. Horrocks, *A Full Life* (Collins, 1960), p. 205.

21 Quoted in B. Horrocks, *Corps Commander* (Sidgwick & Jackson, 1977), p. 69.

22 General P. Roberts, quoted in Lamb, op. cit., p. 201.

23 ibid., pp. 229–30.

24 D. D. Eisenhower, *Crusade in Europe* (Heinemann, 1948), p. 336.

25 A. D. Chandler *et al.* (eds), *The Papers of Dwight David Eisenhower: the War Years* (5 vols, Johns Hopkins University Press, Baltimore, Md, 1970), vol. 4, pp. 2149, 2148.

26 Quoted in Lamb, op. cit., p. 275 (my emphasis).

27 Chandler *et al.* (eds), op. cit., vol. 4, p. 2212.

28 Field Marshal Viscount Montgomery, *Memoirs* (Fontana, 1960), pp. 328–9.

29 Quoted in D. Fraser, *Alanbrooke* (Collins, 1982), p. 457.

30 Chandler *et al.* (eds), op. cit., vol. 4, p. 2222.

31 ibid., p. 2225.

32 ibid., pp. 2388, 2418, 2489.

33 ibid., p. 2489.

34 ibid., p. 2431 (emphasis in original).

35 ibid., p. 2122.

36 Montgomery, op. cit., p. 314.

37 Chandler *et al.* (eds), op. cit., pp. 2341–2.

38 ibid., pp. 2451, 2454.

39 Quoted in Wilmot, op. cit., p. 675.

40 Lamb, op. cit., p. 354.

41 Chandler *et al.* (eds), op. cit., p. 2568.

42 ibid., pp. 2552, 2568.

43 Blumenson (ed.), op. cit., p. 653.

44 Quoted in Montgomery, op. cit., pp. 289–90 (emphasis in original).

45 ibid., p. 279.

46 Quoted in G. Powell, *The Devil's Birthday: the Bridges to Arnhem 1944* (Buchan & Enright, 1984), pp. 235–6.

47 General Brereton, C.in-C. First Airborne Army, quoted in ibid., p. 29, and Lamb, op. cit., p. 228.

48 Powell, op. cit., p. 239.

49 Lamb, op. cit., p. 215.

50 J. Gavin, *On to Berlin* (Leo Cooper, n.d.), p. 170.

51 Weighley, op. cit., p. 295.

52 Wilmot, op. cit., p. 516.

53 Powell, op. cit., p. 240.

54 R. E. Urquhart, *Arnhem* (Pan, 1960), p. 207.

55 Air Ministry, *The Rise and Fall of the German Air Force 1933–45* (WE Inc., Old Greenwich, Conn., 1969), pp. 378–9.

56 ibid.

57 D. Richards and H. St G. Saunders, *Royal Air Force 1939–45*, vol. 3 (HMSO, 1954), p. 208.

58 Chandler *et al.* (eds), op. cit., p. 2296.

59 E. G. Godfrey, *History of the Duke of Cornwall's Light Infantry 1939–45* (pvte pub., Aldershot, 1966), p. 340.

60 S. Bidwell & D. Graham, *Fire-Power: British Army Weapons and*

Theories of War 1904–45 (Allen & Unwin, 1982), p. 289, and Introduction to P. Elstob, *Battle of the Reichswald* (Macdonald, 1970), p. 7.

61 H. Guderian, 'Panzer Employment: Western Front', Pamphlet ETHINT-39, p. 10, in Detweiler *et al.* (eds), op. cit., vol. 3.

62 E.W.I.P., *Taurus Pursuant: a History of 11 Armoured Division* (BAOR, 1945), pp. 87, 100.

63 ibid., p. 67.

64 BAOR, *Battlefield Tour: Operation Veritable* (Spectator's Copy), (BAOR, 1947), p. 8.

65 Quoted in C. Whiting, *Battle of the Ruhr Pocket* (Pan/Ballantine, 1970), p. 17.

66 Lamb, op. cit., p. 386.

67 Quoted in H. Dollinger & H.-A. Jacobsen, *The Decline and Fall of Nazi Germany and Imperial Japan* (Odhams, 1968), p. 63.

68 Quoted in Weighley, op. cit., p. 441.

69 Quoted in Wilmot, op. cit., p. 496.

70 ibid., p. 568.

71 Weighley, op. cit., p. 326.

72 Quoted in E. Bauer, *The History of World War II* (Orbis, 1979), p. 598.

73 R. von Gersdorff, 'Defence of the Siegfried Line', Pamphlet ETHINT-53, p. 7, in Detweiler *et al.* (eds), op. cit., vol. 2.

74 Gavin, op. cit., p. 265.

75 Patton's diary, 3 November 1942, in Blumenson (ed.), op. cit., p. 98.

76 Wilmot, op. cit., p. 681.

77 Blumenson (ed.), op. cit., pp. 585, 622.

78 Wilmot, op. cit., p. 565.

79 Weighley, op. cit., p. 521.

80 P. Elstob, *Hitler's Last Offensive* (Transworld, 1972), p. 468.

81 Weighley, op. cit., p. 546.

82 Gavin, op. cit., p. 258.

83 Weighley, op. cit., pp. 565–6.

84 Wilmot, op. cit., p. 677.

85 Lamb, op. cit., p. 359.

86 Wilmot, op. cit., p. 681.

87 Von Mellenthin, op. cit., p. 336.

88 J. Strawson, *The Battle for Berlin* (Batsford, 1974), p. 105.

89 O. Bradley & C. Blair, *A General's Life* (Sidgwick & Jackson, 1983), p. 434.

90 Gavin, op. cit., p. 288 fn.

Chapter 9: Collapse and Containment: December 1941 – February 1943

1 Quoted in D. MacIntyre, *The Battle for the Pacific* (Batsford, 1966), p. 211.
2 Quoted in E. P. Hoyt, *Japan's War: the Great Pacific Conflict* (Hutchinson, 1986), pp. 205–6, 211–12.
3 United States Strategic Bombing Survey (USSBS), *The Effects of Strategic Bombing on Japan's War Economy* (GPO, Washington, December 1946), p. 11.
4 USSBS, *Summary Report (Pacific War)* (GPO, Washington, July 1946), p. 27, and L. H. Morten, *Strategy and Command: the First Two Years* (US Army in World War II: War in the Pacific), (GPO, Washington, 1962), p. 108.
5 E. J. King & W. M. Whitehill, *Fleet Admiral King: a Naval Record* (Eyre & Spottiswoode, 1953), p. 164.
6 Quoted in W. D. Dickson, *The Battle of the Philippine Sea* (Ian Allen, Shepperton, 1975), p. 21.
7 King & Whitehill, op. cit., p. 164.
8 M. Okumiya & J. Horikoshi, *Zero: the Story of the Japanese Navy Air Force 1937–45* (Corgi, 1958), p. 142.
9 J. H. Belote & W. M. Belote, *Titans of the Seas* (Harper & Row, New York, 1975), pp. 23–4.
10 C. W. Nimitz & E. B. Potter (eds), *The United States and World Sea Power* (Prentice-Hall, Englewood Cliffs, NJ, 1955), p. 685.
11 M. Fuchida & M. Okumiya, *Midway: the Battle That Doomed Japan* (Hutchinson, 1957), p. 93.
12 Quoted in J. Toland, *The Rising Sun: the Decline and Fall of the Japanese Empire 1933–45* (Random House, New York, 1970), p. 374.
13 S. E. Morison, *History of United States Naval Operations in World War II* (15 vols, OUP, 1948–62), vol. 5, p. 63, and Okumiya & Horikoshi, op. cit., p. 146.
14 R. Lewin, *The American Magic: Codes, Ciphers and the Defeat of Japan* (Penguin, Harmondsworth, 1983), p. 184.
15 S. Milner, *Victory in Papua* (US Army in World War II: War in the Pacific), (GPO, Washington, 1957), p. 378.
16 Morison, op. cit., vol. 4, p. 254.
17 ibid., vol. 5, p. 315.
18 Quoted in L. H. Morten, *Strategy and Command: the First Two Years* (US Army in World War II: War in the Pacific), (GPO, Washington, 1962), p. 346.
19 Quoted in ibid., p. 353 (emphasis in original).
20 Belote & Belote, op. cit., p. 118.
21 ibid., p. 116.

22 Quoted in Toland, op. cit., p. 413.
23 Okumiya & Horikoshi, op. cit., p. 202.
24 Toland, op. cit., p. 541.
25 USSBS, *Summary*, op. cit., p. 5 (my emphasis).
26 Quoted in J. L. Zimmerman, *The Guadalcanal Campaign* (HQ US Marine Corps, Historical Division, Washington, 1949), p. 166.
27 Quoted in Belote & Belote, op. cit., p. 158.

Chapter 10: The Counter-Offensive: March 1943 – August 1945

1 Quoted in R. Lewin, *The American Magic: Codes, Ciphers and the Defeat of Japan* (Penguin, Harmondsworth, 1983), p. 155.
2 Quoted in J. Toland, *The Rising Sun: the Decline and Fall of the Japanese Empire 1933–45* (Random House, New York, 1970), p. 504.
3 Quoted in Lewin, op. cit., pp. 192–3.
4 Quoted in Toland, op. cit., p. 576.
5 USSBS, *Summary Report (Pacific War)* (GPO, Washington, July 1946), p. 25.
6 Quoted in S. E. Morison, *History of United States Naval Operations in World War II* (15 vols, OUP, 1948–62), vol. 12, p. 66.
7 Quoted in Lewin, op. cit., pp. 227–8 (emphasis in original).
8 Quoted in J. B. Cohen, *Japan's Economy in War and Reconstruction* (University of Minnesota Press, Minneapolis, 1949), p. 142.
9 USSBS (Transport Division), *The War Against Japanese Transportation* (GPO, Washington, May 1947), p. 45.
10 Quoted in Toland, op. cit., p. 481.
11 Quoted in USSBS, *Japanese Transportation*, op. cit., p. 48.
12 Cohen, op. cit., p. 104.
13 USSBS, *Summary*, op. cit., p. 12.
14 USSBS, *Japanese Transportation*, op. cit., p. 33.
15 Cohen, op. cit., pp. 106–7.
16 Quoted in ibid., p. 193.
17 Morison, op. cit., vol. 6, p. 253.
18 J. H. Belote & W. M. Belote, *Titans of the Seas* (Harper & Row, New York, 1975), p. 301.
19 M. Okumiya & J. Horikoshi, *Zero: the Story of the Japanese Navy Air Force 1937–45* (Corgi, 1958), p. 223.
20 Quoted in D. MacArthur, *Reminiscences* (Heinemann, 1964), p. 222.
21 W. F. Halsey, *Admiral Halsey's Story* (Curtis, New York, 1957), pp. 264, 265.
22 Quoted in E. M. Emme (ed.), *The Impact of Air Power* (Van Nostrand, New York, 1959), p. 209.
23 USSBS (Aircraft Division), *The Japanese Aircraft Industry* (GPO, Washington, May 1947), p. 5.
24 Okumiya & Horikoshi, op. cit., p. 289.

25 Quoted in E. Bauer, *The History of World War II* (Orbis, 1979), p. 438.

26 Quoted in Morison, op. cit., vol. 8, p. 334.

27 Quoted in Toland, op. cit., p. 602.

28 Quoted in Morison, op. cit., vol. 12, p. 93.

29 S. W. Kirby, *The War Against Japan* (5 vols, HMSO, 1958–69), vol. 5, p. 470.

30 S. Sakai, *Samurai* (Four Square, 1974), p. 126.

31 Quoted in Morison, op. cit., vol. 8, p. 267.

32 B. Tillman, *Hellcat* (Patrick Stevens, Cambridge, 1979), p. 58.

33 Quoted in W. D. Dickson, *The Battle of the Philippine Sea* (Ian Allen, Shepperton, 1975), p. 94.

34 USSBS, *Summary Report*, op. cit., p. 10.

35 Morison, op. cit., vol. 12, p. 108, and Okumiya & Horikoshi, op. cit., p. 203.

36 Okumiya & Horikoshi, op. cit., p. 335. See also pp. 338–41.

37 USSBS, *Aircraft Industry*, op. cit., p. 99.

38 Quoted in Cohen, op. cit., p. 230.

39 Okumiya & Horikoshi, op. cit., p. 295 (emphasis in original).

40 O. A. Anderson, 'Air War in the Pacific', in Emme (ed.), op. cit., p. 293 (my emphasis).

41 Quoted in Morison, op. cit., vol. 13, p. 58.

42 Quoted in Toland, op. cit., pp. 754, 735.

43 Quoted in G. Long, *MacArthur as Military Commander* (Batsford, 1969), p. 157.

44 Morison, op. cit., vol. 6, p. 206.

45 Toland, op. cit., p. 534.

46 ibid., p. 575.

47 Morison, op. cit., vol. 8, p. 138.

48 Quoted in ibid., pp. 392–3.

49 Quoted in Bauer, op. cit., p. 645.

50 Quoted in Kirby, op. cit., vol. 5, p. 122.

51 Quoted in Morison, op. cit., vol. 7, p. 299.

52 MacArthur, op. cit., pp. 166, 169.

53 C. Willoughby & M. Chamberlain, *MacArthur 1941–51: Victory in the Pacific* (Heinemann, 1956), p. 140.

54 Long, op. cit., pp. 135–6.

55 Lewin, op. cit., p. 249.

56 Halsey, op. cit., p. 188.

57 Lewin, loc. cit.

58 ibid., p. 253.

59 Morison, op. cit., vol. 13, p. 214.

60 R. H. Spector, *Eagle Against the Sun: the American War with Japan* (Free Press, New York, 1985), p. 526.

61 L. H. Morten, *Strategy and Command: the First Two Years* (US Army

in World War II: War in the Pacific), (GPO, Washington, 1962), p. 29.

62 E. J. King & W. M. Whitehill, *Fleet Admiral King: a Naval Record* (Eyre & Spottiswoode, 1953), pp. 144–5.

63 ibid., p. 121 (my emphasis).

64 ibid., p. 174.

65 Sir J. Slessor, *The Central Blue* (Cassell, 1956), p. 494.

66 Morten, op. cit., p. 251.

67 H. Stimson & M. Bundy, *On Active Service in Peace and War* (Hutchinson, 1949), pp. 280–1.

68 Morten, op. cit., p. 218.

69 ibid., p. 248.

70 Quoted in Morison, op. cit., vol. 8, p. 8.

71 Quoted in Morten, op. cit., p. 221.

72 Quoted in F. C. Pogue, *George C. Marshall: Ordeal and Hope 1939–42* (Viking, New York, 1966), p. 276.

73 ibid., p. 391.

74 King & Whitehill, op. cit., p. 276.

75 Quoted in Morten, op. cit., pp. 438–9 (my emphasis).

76 MacArthur, op. cit., pp. 197, 211.

77 Quoted in E. B. Potter, *Nimitz* (Naval Institute Press, Annapolis, Md, 1976), p. 280.

78 Pogue, op. cit., p. 380.

79 Morten, op. cit., p. 397.

80 MacArthur, op. cit., p. 183.

81 H. H. Arnold, *Global Mission* (Hutchinson, 1951), p. 249.

82 King & Whitehill, op. cit., p. 276.

83 Quoted in Morten, op. cit., p. 399.

84 L. H. Morten, *Pacific Command: a Study in Interservice Relations* (US Air Force Military Academy, Colorado Springs, 1961), p. 26.

85 Arnold, op. cit., p. 249.

86 USSBS, *Summary Report*, op. cit., p. 11 (my emphasis).

87 ibid., p. 12.

88 USSBS, *Japanese Transportation*, op. cit., p. 7.

89 ibid.

90 ibid., p. 34.

91 Quoted in Morten, *Strategy*, op. cit., p. 464.

92 W. Leahy, *I Was There* (Gollancz, 1950), pp. 289, 296.

93 King & Whitehill, op. cit., p. 389.

94 MacArthur, op. cit., pp. 260–1.

95 King & Whitehill, op. cit., p. 412.

96 Quoted in C. Thorne, *Allies of a Kind: the United States, Britain and the War Against Japan 1941–45* (OUP, 1978), pp. 294, 408.

97 M. Calvert, 'Victory in Burma', in E. Bauer, *The History of World War II* (Orbis, 1979), p. 631.

Conclusion

1   D. Divine, *The Broken Wing: A Study in the British Exercise of Air Power* (Hutchinson, 1966), p. 263.

2   M. Smith, '"Bomber" Harris in Perspective: Harris' Offensive in Historical Perspective', *RUSI Journal* 130, June 1985, p. 62.

3   Quoted in N. Nicholson, *Alex* (Weidenfeld & Nicolson, 1973), p. 273.

4   Quoted in R. F. Weighley, *History of the United States Army* (Macmillan, New York, 1967), p. 474.

5   Quoted in ibid.

6   General Bayerlein quoted in C. Wilmot, *The Struggle for Europe* (Collins, 1952), p. 428.

7   Quoted in E. M. Emme (ed.), *The Impact of Air Power* (Van Nostrand, New York, 1959), p. 209.

8   S. E. Morison, *The History of United States Naval Operations in World War II* (15 vols, OUP, 1948–62), vol. 7, pp. 298, 303.

9   USSBS, *The Effects of Strategic Bombing on the German Economy* (GPO, Washington, October 1945), p. 19.

10 Brigadier E. T. Williams quoted in M. Hastings, *Overlord: D-Day and the Battle for Normandy 1944* (Michael Joseph, 1984), p. 151.

Select Bibliography

Almost all of the works that I have found particularly useful in the preparation of this study are fully referenced in the Notes. The following list therefore contains only those titles (in English) that I regard as being of prime importance to any proper understanding of the course of military operations in the Second World War. Appended to the Bibliography is a short list of important titles that I was only able to read after completing the relevant section or chapter. Otherwise, they would almost certainly have appeared in the Notes, and in the main section of this Select Bibliography. Editions cited in brackets and preceded by an asterisk indicate those used in the Notes, and in the Sources for Tables, where these differ from the main entry.

G. ADERS, *History of the German Night-Fighter Force 1917–45*, Arms & Armour Press, 1979

J. A. I. AGAR-HAMILTON & L. C. F. TURNER, *Crisis in the Desert May–July 1942*, OUP, 1952

The Sidi Rezeg Battles 1941, OUP, 1957

AIR MINISTRY, *The Rise and Fall of the German Air Force 1933–45* (written in 1948), WE Inc., Old Greenwich, Conn., 1969

L. ALLEN, *Burma: the Longest War 1941–45*, Dent, 1984

S. E. AMBROSE, *The Supreme Commander: the War Years of General Dwight D. Eisenhower*, Cassell, 1971

C. BARNETT, *The Desert Generals*, Pan Books, 1960 (* rev. ed., William Kimber, 1981)

C. BABINGTON-SMITH, *Evidence in Camera: the Story of Photographic Intelligence in World War II*, David & Charles, Newton Abbot, 1974

E. BAUER, *The History of World War II*, Orbis, 1979

P. BEESLY, *Very Special Intelligence: the Story of the Admiralty's Operational Intelligence Centre 1939–45*, Hamish Hamilton, 1977

E. BELFIELD & H. ESSAME, *The Battle for Normandy*, Batsford, 1965

R. de BELOT, *The Struggle for the Mediterranean 1939–45*, Princeton University Press, Princeton, NJ, 1951

R. BENNETT, *Ultra in the West: the Normandy Campaign of 1944–45*, Hutchinson, 1979

S. BIDWELL, *Gunners at War*, Arms & Armour Press, 1970 (*Arrow Books, 1972)

S. BIDWELL & D. GRAHAM, *Fire-Power: British Army Weapons and Theories of War 1904–45*, Allen & Unwin, 1982

M. BLUMENSON (ed.), *The Patton Papers*, vol. 2, Houghton Mifflin, Boston, Mass., 1974

O. BRADLEY & C. BLAIR, *A General's Life*, Sidgwick & Jackson, 1983

M. A. BRAGADIN, *The Italian Navy in World War II*, US Naval Institute Press, Annapolis, Md, 1957

A. BRYANT (ed), *The Alanbrooke War Diaries*, 2 vols, Collins, 1957–9 (*Fontana, 1965)

P. CALVOCORESSI & G. WINT, *Total War: Causes and Courses of the Second World War*, Allen Lane, 1972

P. CARELL, *Hitler's War on Russia*, 2 vols (vol. 1 as cited, vol. 2, *Scorched Earth*), Harrap, 1964–70 (*vol. 1, Corgi Books, 1967)

A. D. CHANDLER *et al.* (eds), *The Papers of Dwight David Eisenhower: The War Years*, 5 vols, Johns Hopkins University Press, Baltimore, Md, 1970

G. CHAPMAN, *Why France Collapsed*, Cassell, 1968

A. CLAYTON, *The Enemy Is Listening: the Story of the Y Service*, Hutchinson, 1980

J. B. COHEN, *Japan's Economy in War and Reconstruction*, University of Minnesota Press, Minneapolis, 1949

R. C. COOKE & R. C. NESBIT, *Target: Hitler's Oil*, William Kimber, 1985

M. COOPER, *The German Army 1933–45: Its Political and Military Failure*, Macdonald & Jane's, 1978

J. COSTELLO & T. HUGHES, *The Battle of the Atlantic*, Collins, 1977 (* Fontana, 1980)

W. F. CRAVEN & J. L. CATE, *The Army Air Forces in World War II*, 7 vols, Chicago University Press, Chicago, 1948–78

M. van CREVELD, *Supplying War: Logistics from Wallenstein to Patton*, CUP, 1977
Fighting Power: German and US Army Performance 1939–45, Arms & Armour Press, 1983

W. DEIST, *The Wehrmacht and German Rearmament*, Macmillan, 1981

K. DOENITZ, *Memoirs*, Weidenfeld & Nicolson, 1959

F. DYSON, *Disturbing the Universe*, Harper & Row, New York, 1979

D. D. EISENHOWER, *Crusade in Europe*, Heinemann, 1948

J. ERICKSON, *Stalin's War with Germany*, 2 vols, Weidenfeld & Nicolson, 1975–83

H. ESSAME, *Patton: the Commander*, Batsford, 1974

C. d'ESTE, *Decision in Normandy: the Unwritten Story of Montgomery and*

the Allied Campaign, Collins, 1983 (*Pan Books, 1984)
D. C. EVANS (ed.), *The Japanese Navy in World War II*, Naval Institute Press, Annapolis, Md, 1986 (2nd ed.)

R. FREEMAN, *The U.S. Strategic Bomber*, Macdonald & Jane's, 1975
J. F. C. FULLER, *The Second World War 1939–45*, Eyre & Spottiswoode, 1948

M. GILBERT, *Winston S. Churchill 1874–1965*, vols 6 & 7, Heinemann, 1983 & 1986
D. GRAHAM & S. BIDWELL, *Tug of War: the Battle for Italy 1943–45*, Hodder & Stoughton, 1986
K. R. GREENFIELD, *American Strategy in World War Two: a Reconsideration*, Johns Hopkins University Press, Baltimore, Md, 1963
H. GUDERIAN, *Panzer Leader*, Michael Joseph, 1952 (*Futura Books, 1974)

W. HACKMANN, *Seek and Strike: Sonar, Anti-submarine Warfare and the Royal Navy 1914–54*, HMSO, 1984
M. HARRISON, *Soviet Planning in Peace and War 1938–45*, CUP, 1985
B. H. L. HART, *History of the Second World War*, Cassell, 1970
The Other Side of the Hill, Cassell, 1948
(ed.), *The Rommel Papers*, Collins, 1953
M. HASHIMOTO, *Sunk: the Story of the Japanese Submarine Fleet*, Cassell, 1954
M. HASTINGS, *Bomber Command*, Michael Joseph, 1979 (*Pan Books, 1981)
W. HECKMANN, *Rommel's War in Africa*, Granada, 1981
A. HEZLET, *Aircraft and Sea Power*, Peter Davies, 1970
The Electron and Sea Power, Peter Davies, 1975
The Submarine and Sea Power, Peter Davies, 1967
F. H. HINSLEY, *British Intelligence in the Second World War*, 3 vols, HMSO, 1979–88
A. HORNE, *To Lose a Battle: France 1940*, Macmillan, 1969
D. M. HORNER, *High Command: Australia and Allied Strategy 1939–45*, Allen & Unwin, 1982
Intelligence and National Security, quarterly since January 1986

W. G. F. JACKSON, *The Battle for Rome*, Batsford, 1969
The North African Campaign 1940–43, Batsford, 1975
H.-A. JACOBSEN & J. ROHWER, *Decisive Battles of World War II: the German View*, André Deutsch, 1965

J. KEEGAN, *Six Armies in Normandy: from D-Day to the Liberation of Paris*, Jonathan Cape, 1982

E. J. KING & W. M. WHITEHILL, *Fleet Admiral King: a Naval Record*, Eyre & Spottiswoode, 1953

B. H. KLEIN, *Germany's Economic Preparations for War*, Harvard University Press, Cambridge, Mass., 1959

R. LAMB, *Montgomery in Europe 1943–45: Success or Failure?*, Buchan & Enright, 1983

B. A. LEACH, *German Strategy Against Russia 1939–41*, Clarendon Press, Oxford, 1973

R. M. LEIGHTON & R. W. COAKLEY, *Global Logistics and Strategy 1940–45* (US Army in World War II: War Department), 2 vols, GPO, Washington, 1955–68

R. LEWIN, *The American Magic: Codes, Ciphers and the Defeat of Japan*, Hutchinson, 1982 (*Penguin Books, Harmondsworth, 1983)
Montgomery as Military Commander, Batsford, 1971

G. LONG, *MacArthur as Military Commander*, Batsford, 1969

N. LONGMATE, *The Bombers: the RAF Offensive Against Germany 1939–45*, Hutchinson, 1983

K. MACKSEY, *Crucible of Power: the Fight for Tunisia 1942–43*, Hutchinson, 1969
Tank Warfare, Hart-Davis, 1971 (*Panther Books, 1976)

E. von MANSTEIN, *Lost Victories*, Arms & Armour Press, 1982

F. K. MASON, *Battle Over Britain*, McWhirter Twins, 1969

M. MATLOFF & E. SNELL, *Strategic Planning for Coalition Warfare* (US Army in World War II: War Department), 2 vols, GPO, Washington, 1953–9

D. McISAAC (ed.), *The United States Strategic Bombing Survey*, 10 vols, Garland, New York, 1976 (a selection from the original Survey reports published between 1946 and 1947)

A. McKEE, *Caen: Anvil of Victory*, Souvenir Press, 1964

F. W. von MELLENTHIN, *Panzer Battles 1939–45*, Cassell, 1955

H. MICHEL, *The Second World War*, André Deutsch, 1975

A. MILWARD, *War, Economy and Society 1939–45*, Allen Lane, 1977

S. E. MORISON, *History of United States Naval Operations in World War II*, 15 vols, OUP, 1948–62

H. L. MORTEN, *Strategy and Command: the First Two Years* (US Army in World War II: War in the Pacific), GPO, Washington, 1962

W. MURRAY, *Luftwaffe: Strategy for Defeat 1933–45*, Allen & Unwin, 1985

M. OKUMIYA & J. HORIKOSHI, *Zero: the Story of the Japanese Navy Air Force 1937–45*, Cassell, 1957 (*Corgi Books, 1958)

D. ORGILL, *The Gothic Line: the Autumn Campaign in Italy, 1944*, Heinemann, 1967 (*Pan Books, 1969)

R. J. OVERY, *The Air War 1939–45*, Europa, 1980

Goering: the 'Iron Man', RKP, 1984

. PITT, *The Crucible of War*, 2 vols, Jonathan Cape, 1980–2
E. B. POTTER & C. W. NIMITZ, *The Great Sea War: the Story of Naval Action in World War II*, Prentice-Hall, Englewood Cliffs, NJ, 1960
A. PRICE, *Aircraft versus Submarine*, Jane's, 1980
Battle Over the Reich, Ian Allen, Shepperton, 1973

J. ROBERTSON, *Australia at War 1939–45* Heinemann, Melbourne, 1981 3 vols, HMSO, 1954–61
S. W. ROSKILL, *The War at Sea 1939–45* (History of the Second World War: United Kingdom Military Series) 3 vols, HMSO, 1954–61
R. RUPPENTHAL, *Logistical Suppport of the Armies* (US Army in World War II: European Theater of Operations), 2 vols, GPO, Washington, 1953–9

A. SEATON, *The German Army 1933–45*, Weidenfeld & Nicolson, 1982
The Russo-German War 1941–45, Arthur Barker, 1971
B. B. SCHOFIELD, *Operation Neptune*, Ian Allen, Shepperton, 1974
F. M. von SENGER und ETTERLIN, *Neither Fear Nor Hope*, Macdonald, 1963
G. A. SHEPPERD, *The Italian Campaign 1943–45*, Arthur Barker, 1968
M. SHULMAN, *Defeat in the West*, rev. ed., Coronet Books, 1973
R . H. SPECTOR, *Eagle Against the Sun: the American War with Japan*, Free Press, New York, 1985
A. SPEER, *Inside the Third Reich*, Macmillan, 1970
C. P. STACEY, *The Victory Campaign* (Official History of the Canadian Army in the Second World War), Queen's Printers, Ottawa, 1960
J. STRAWSON, *Hitler As Military Commander*, Batsford, 1971
T. TAYLOR, *The March of Conquest: German Victories in Western Europe in 1940*, Hulton, 1959
The Breaking Wave: the German Defeat in the Summer of 1940, Weidenfeld & Nicolson, 1967
J. TERRAINE, *The Right of the Line: the Royal Air Force in the European War 1939–45*, Hodder & Stoughton, 1985
C. THORNE, *Allies of a Kind: the United States, Britain and the War Against Japan 1941–45*, OUP, 1978
J. TOLAND, *The Rising Sun: the Decline and Fall of the Japanese Empire 1933–45*, Random House, New York, 1970
H. R. TREVOR-ROPER (ed.), *Hitler's War Directives 1939–45*, Sidgwick & Jackson, 1964 (*Pan Books, 1973)
B. TUCHMAN, *Sand Against the Wind: Stilwell and the American Experience in China 1911–45*, Macmillan, 1971

UNITED STATES STRATEGIC BOMBING SURVEY (USSBS), see McISAAC

A. VERRIER, *The Bomber Offensive*, Batsford, 1968

A. WATTS, *The U-Boat Hunters*, Macdonald & Jane's, 1976

R. F. WEIGHLEY, *Eisenhower's Lieutenants: the Campaigns of France and Germany 1944–45*, Sidgwick & Jackson, 1981

B. WHALEY, *Codeword Barbarossa*, MIT Press, Cambridge, Mass., 1973

J. WHELDON, *Machine-Age Armies*, Abelard-Schuman, 1968

C. WILMOT, *The Struggle for Europe*, Collins, 1952

D. WILSON, *When Tigers Fight: the Story of the Sino-Japanese War 1937–45*, Penguin Books, Harmondsworth, 1983

S. ZALOGA & V. MADEJ, *The Polish Campaign 1939*, Hippocrene Books, New York, 1985

E. F. ZIEMKE, *Stalingrad to Berlin: the German Defeat in the East*, GPO, Washington, 1968

S. ZUCKERMAN, *From Apes to Warlords 1904–46*, Hamish Hamilton, 1978

Recent books not consulted

R. BENNETT, *Ultra in the Mediterranean*, Hamish Hamilton, 1989

C. d'ESTE, *Bitter Victory: the Battle for Sicily 1943*, Collins, 1988

E. LARRABEE, *Commander in Chief: Franklin Delano Roosevelt, His Lieutenants and Their War*, André Deutsch, 1988

R. SCHAFFER, *Wings of Judgement: American Bombing in World War II*, OUP, 1985

J. SLADER, *The Red Duster at War: a History of the Merchant Navy During the Second World War*, William Kimber, 1988

D. van der VAT, *The Atlantic Campaign: the Great Struggle at Sea 1939–45*, Hodder & Stoughton, 1988

J. WILLIAMS, *The Long Left Flank: the Hard-Fought Way to the Reich 1944–45*, Leo Cooper, 1988

J. WINTON, *Ultra at Sea*, Leo Cooper, 1988

E. F. ZIEMKE & M. E. BAUER, *Moscow to Stalingrad*, GPO, Washington, 1988

Index

Index

609